EPUBLICS, 1958

BERING SEA

Anadyr

NOVO-SIBIRSK IS.

SEVERNAYA IS.

Verkoyansk

KAMCHATKA

Khatanga

Petropavlovsk

Okhotsk

SEA OF OKHOTSK

LENA

Yakutsk

SOCIALIST

REPUBLIC

SAKHALIN

LENA

Ust-Kut

KURILE ISLANDS (USSR)

R.R. UNDER

Komsomolsk

CONSTRUCTION

seisk

Kirensk

Khabarovsk

LAKE BAIKAL

AMUR

Chita

Harbin

Irkutsk

MANCHURIA

Vladivostok

40°N

talinsk

SEA OF JAPAN

Ulan Bator

Mukden

NORTH KOREA

JAPAN

MONGOLIA

SOUTH KOREA

rumchi

Peiping

Dairen

YELLOW SEA

CHINA

Shanghai

EAST CHINA SEA

1000 MILES

130°E

TRM

THE COURSE OF
RUSSIAN HISTORY

THE MACMILLAN COMPANY
NEW YORK · CHICAGO
DALLAS · ATLANTA · SAN FRANCISCO
LONDON · MANILA

IN CANADA
BRETT-MACMILLAN LTD.
GALT, ONTARIO

The Course of
Russian History

MELVIN C. WREN

Professor of History
Montana State University

THE MACMILLAN COMPANY · NEW YORK

Printed in the United States of America

Second Printing 1959

Library of Congress catalog card number: 58-5213

To Nancy and David

Preface

In November, 1917, Lenin and his comrades embarked upon a profoundly radical experiment aimed at steering Russian history along a new course. For a generation before and for years after the revolution the leading theorists in the Communist Party—unlike other revolutionary parties, the Mensheviks and the Socialist Revolutionaries for example—found little if anything to admire in the nation's past. They wanted to believe and they convinced themselves that the light of the revolutionary morning would clear away all the darkness in which the Russian people had been chained for centuries. The new Russia would be free, not only of the exploitation of one man by another in a political or economic or social sense. The new Russia would be free of its past. The old Russia would die and be interred at the birth time of the new. Individuals and classes as well as institutions which had their roots in the old regime must be destroyed. Even those symbols of the past which might survive—the churches, the palaces of the tsars, the town houses of the aristocrats—should be held up to scorn or made to serve the new society in some utilitarian way.

Many Westerners came to the conclusion that the new Russia was indeed as new as its leaders claimed it to be. Some of these Westerners admired the boldness, the fearlessness, the imagination with which the Bolsheviks had swept Russia clean of the evils which these sympathizers saw or imagined in their own societies. They went on pilgrimage to this new Land of Canaan, but many of them came away disillusioned and disappointed, and sometimes embittered, with all they saw. Other Westerners, less naive, were equally sure that the new Russia had cut completely adrift from its past. They were shocked at the revolution's disrespect for the stabilizing values of the old society, knowing little of the values and less of their stabilizing effect but assuming that they were the values which held all respectable societies together. They trembled at the thought of what the revolution, should it spread beyond Russia's borders, might do to their own cultures.

Russia's leaders were frankly admitting, before the Bolshevik Revolution was a generation old, that there was much in the nation's past that was worth retaining or reviving. Many old values were restored and promoted to blend with the modern ways of doing things in the new "Soviet society." The very words "Soviet society" and "Soviet culture" and "Soviet civilization" came to mean a strange fusion of revolutionary and pre-revolutionary features.

Many Westerners, particularly many Americans, cling to the view that the Soviet Union is something entirely new and that it can be understood by examining its present character and its development since 1917. This view is extremely unrealistic. No serious student can satisfy himself that he understands the Soviet Union unless he knows the Russia of the nineteenth and early twentieth centuries, the Russia of Peter and Catherine, the Russia of Ivan the Terrible and the Time of Troubles, the Russia of Mongol and of Kievan times. Modern Russia can no more wash away the imprint of her past than can any other nation. The reasons "why they behave like Russians" are not to be found only in the last chapter of their long history.

The suggested readings at the end of each chapter are designed to whet rather than to sate an appetite for Russian history. The lists are by no means exhaustive, although I have tried to include some of the most recent works along with those which have weathered the years. The limitation of the reading lists to works in English is deliberate. A short list, I am convinced, is more likely to be noticed than a long one. And those who read Russian, Polish, Czech, French, German, Italian, Swedish, Finnish, Dutch or Japanese will find works aplenty listed in the standard bibliographies or in references to be found in the monographs on various aspects of Russian history. Perhaps more important to the beginning student than works in other languages are the pertinent articles to be found in the *Slavonic and East European Review,* the *American Slavic and East European Review,* the *Journal of Modern History,* the *American Historical Review* and other scholarly journals.

I have said little of Russian literature in telling the story of Russia's past and that, too, has been deliberate. Simply to name Russian authors with the dates of their births and deaths and a listing of their works is of little value. Nor is a sentence or two outlining the plot of each creation much more satisfying. There is no substitute for reading many novels, short stories, essays and plays. Of no land's history can it be said that literature is more important to understanding. There is no surer way of catching the feel of the Russian land and the Russian people, of experiencing Russia's glories and her sufferings, than to read Krylov, Lermontov, Pushkin, Gogol, Belinsky, Griboyedov, Goncharov, Turgenev, Dostoyevsky, Tolstoy, Chekhov, Gorky and Sholokhov. The chief works of all of them have been translated into every Western language.

Until 1918 Orthodox Russia followed the Julian calendar, refusing to accept the time schedule that had been worked out by Pope Gregory. By the Julian calendar the Bolshevik Revolution took place on October 25, 1917— November 7 by the Gregorian calendar—and is still referred to as the "October Revolution." In the third month of the new era, however, the government put the nation on the modern calendar and Russia got in step with the rest of the world, at least in reckoning her time.

I am grateful to E. P. Dutton and Company and to J. M. Dent and Sons for permission to quote extensively from V. O. Kliuchevsky's *A History of Russia,* and also to the trustees of the Harvard University Press for permission to quote at length from S. H. Cross's translation of *The Russian Primary Chronicle.* Also I thank Brown Brothers, Sovfoto, and Wide World Photos for the halftone illustrations.

The debt I owe so many cannot be repaid by simple acknowledgments. A few, however, have contributed most especially to the work. Dr. Joseph Kramer, Professor of Botany at Montana State University, gave me my first lessons in the Russian language. His knowledge of the old Russia and his appreciation of Russian literature gave me a feeling for Russia's past that I could have acquired from few others. The late Robert J. Kerner, for many years Professor of Russian History at the University of California, was an inspiring mentor and a stern task-master. Professors Oleg Maslennikov and Liudmilla Patrick and the late George Patrick, all of the Department of Slavic Languages at the University of California, were the finest of teachers and the warmest of friends. I am profoundly grateful to Professor Charles A. Morley of Ohio State University for reading the entire manuscript and offering many helpful suggestions. Dr. J. Earll Miller, sometime Chairman of the Department of History at Montana State University, has done his best to get me to see the past steadily and see it whole. Upon none of these good friends, however, can I shift the responsibility for the errors which the work may still contain. That responsibility I must accept with a plea for the reader's indulgence. Mr. and Mrs. Ronald E. Brown of Battersea, London, and my friends on the Romney Marsh gave me many relaxing week-ends after long hours in the British Museum, the Public Records Office and the library of the London School of Slavonic Studies. My wife, Gwendolyn Schlunz Wren, has patiently borne all the irritations that life with a restless worker has brought her. Without her steadying hand I could never have completed the work.

M. C. Wren

Missoula, Montana,
January 3, 1958

Contents

Maps

by Theodore R. Miller

1

The Land of Russia

GEOGRAPHICAL FACTORS ARE ALWAYS important in influencing the development of nations. Frequently they are of cardinal importance. The proximity of the sea, and the familiarity which it bred, prompted the Phoenicians, the Athenians, the Romans, the Portuguese and Spaniards, the Dutch, the English, and the Japanese to exploit it as a bulwark of defense, as an avenue of communication, and as a source of food. Continentality may turn a nation away from the sea, as it has done in the case of the peoples of India and of China. Rivers have served as boundaries, as the Rhine and the Danube served the Roman Empire, or as highways, as the Ohio and the Mississippi have served the United States, or as means of irrigation, as the Nile and the Yangtze served the Egyptians and the Chinese. Climate may be stimulating, as it has been in northern Europe, or it may be enervating, as it has been in the tropics.

Geography has had a vital and determining influence upon the historical development of the Russian people. Russia is geographically isolated, for, except in the west, her borders rest on closed seas, deserts, and mountains. But if one aspect of the land of Russia may be said to be more impressive than any other, that aspect must be the enormous area covered by the modern Russian state. To foreigners travelling in Russia the effect of its overwhelming size has always been breath-taking. The boundaries of the Union of Soviet Socialist Republics in 1957 encompassed 8,708,070 square miles, or about one-sixth of the earth's land surface. Approximately 38,000 miles of land frontier, nine times that of the United States, bring many neighbors close up against her homeland. Nearly three times the size of continental United States and larger than all North America, Russia stretches nearly halfway around the globe. The traveller must reset his watch ten

1

times in journeying the nearly 6,000 miles between the Gulf of Finland and the shores of the Bering Strait. If he travels the country from south to north, he will cross forty-five degrees of latitude between the Indian border and Severnaya Zemlya in the Arctic Ocean. Even today the fastest Russian trains need ten days to cover the distance between Leningrad and Vladivostok. The shorter north-south distance from Murmansk to the Black Sea port of Odessa, about 2,500 miles, can be crossed in three and a half days. Russia's tremendous distances may be of defense value in time of war. In peacetime they are an obvious handicap.

The vast expanse of Russia seems greater because of the paucity of her transportation facilities. River travel, important ever since the East Slavs first settled in the area, is necessarily slow. Because of the scarcity of road-building materials, roads are seldom surfaced and often become impassable in inclement weather. While European Russia has a respectable railway grid, the entire country at the outbreak of World War II possessed only about 55,000 miles of railroad way, less than one-fourth as much as did the United States.

The great plain that stretches across the northern and western half of the Eurasian continent begins at the Pyrenees, sweeps over western and northern France and the Low Countries, and comes to its narrowest point in north Germany. Then it fans out to left and right, following the line of the Scandinavian Mountains on the north and, curving to the southeast along the Carpathians, continues on to the shores of the Black Sea. Except in the northern half of the Urals, no elevation on the Russian section of this sweeping plain exceeds 1,500 feet above sea level. From the Barents to the Black and Caspian Seas and from the Arctic to the Altai-Sayan range in southern Siberia, the topography is monotonously uniform.

The vast Russian plain is guarded on every border except at the Polish frontier by natural barriers, either seas or mountains. Its southern and eastern limits are formed by the Crimean or Yaila, Caucasian, Pamir, Tien Shan, and Altai ranges, and by the central Siberian plateau which rises 3,500 feet in elevation just east of the Yenissei river. The highest elevation in the Caucasus is over 18,000 feet, in the Altais 15,000 feet, and in the Tien Shan 24,000 feet. Mt. Stalin in the Tien Shan and Mt. Lenin in the Pamirs rise to heights of 24,000 and 23,000 feet respectively. East of the Yenissei river are the Sayan, Yablonoi, and Stanovoi mountains, forming a southern boundary to eastern Siberia; the Verkhoyansk range east of the Lena river; the Anadyr mountains in the northeast tip of Siberia; and the Kamchatkas, which include a score of active volcanoes, in the Kamchatka peninsula. One range of mountains in eastern Siberia, the Cherski, was only discovered as recently as 1926. Mountains cover about one-fifth of the land of Russia.

Inside this mountain- and sea-enclosed wall the monotony of the plain is broken along the sixtieth meridian by the Ural mountains, running for

1,500 miles from north to south, which form a traditional boundary between European and Asiatic Russia but which are too low and worn down to constitute a barrier. Indeed, the same climate, vegetation, and social culture are found on both slopes of the Urals. From north to south their elevation decreases from a height of 6,000 feet. South of Magnitogorsk they dwindle to modest hills, and even north of it there are many low passes. The Urals look more impressive on the map than they do on the ground. However, European Russia—that is, Russia west of the Urals—was the heart and strength of the empire until after 1917. The tsars of the nineteenth century, with the exception of the last, considered Siberia primarily as a huge prison to which undesirables might be sent in exile. Until recently, when its material potential was discovered and put to use, the land east of the Urals seemed more a source of weakness than of strength, requiring heavy financial outlay for a host of officials and troops and outposts to protect it.

Other hills line the west banks of the rivers that flow through South Russia. But the Volga hills, whose highest point is only a thousand feet above sea level, the Don, Donets, Dnieper, and Bug hills, are prominent only in the relief they afford to the flat country across the river in each case. For example, the city of Kiev, four hundred feet above the Dnieper, looks out upon a flood plain which stretches for twelve miles beyond the opposite shore. Across western Russia, from the Arctic Ocean to the Black Sea, extends a band of hills averaging about a thousand feet in elevation. North of the White Sea are the Kola hills, and south of it the Karelian. In the Valdai hills centering in the Novgorod-Smolensk-Moscow triangle, at no point more than one thousand feet above sea level, rise such important rivers as the Volga, the Dnieper, the Lovat, and the Western Dvina. South of the Valdais are the Kursk hills, which merge with those of the Don and the Donets bordering on the Black Sea.

The existence and extent of the plain, unchecked by the modest hills which dot it, have had important political implications for Russia. The absence of any serious interruption of the plain permitted an easy flow of population over the entire area, and in very early times invited colonization by the Russians. Furthermore, the whole expanse was easily brought under the rule of a single power. Lacking natural barriers, no state controlling only part of the area could hope long to maintain its independence against the power which dominated the rest of the plain. The protection afforded the plain by its natural frontiers gave reasonable assurance against invasion.* The Polish gap in those natural frontiers has complicated the problem of defending the homeland ever since the thirteenth century.

The Russian coastline is the longest of any nation, but is of limited utility because the country is ice-locked, and so in effect landlocked, through

---

* The nomadic hordes which swept into European Russia from 700 B.C. to A.D. 1250 came from inside the plain, beginning their drive from its eastern limits in central Asia.

much of the year. Most of Russia, and particularly its heart, is far from the sea, for it may be noted that for every mile of coast there are forty square miles of land. The Arctic Ocean, with its branches, the Barents, White, Kara, Laptev, East Siberian, and Chukotsk Seas, stretches along the entire north coast of Russia. With the exception of the port of Murmansk, which is warmed by the tip of the Gulf Stream, these northern seas are frozen from September to July. In recent years Soviet icebreakers have opened up the route from Murmansk to the Bering Strait, and the dream of the sixteenth-century explorers, Hudson and Jenkinson and Chancellor and Willoughby, of finding the northeast passage has been realized. The Pacific coast of Russia is washed by the Bering Sea, the Sea of Okhotsk which is closed by the island chain of the Kuriles, and the Sea of Japan whose outlets are guarded by the Japanese islands. On the west the port of Leningrad, Peter the Great's window on Europe, is frozen through the winter months; it looks out upon the Baltic, from which egress may easily be blocked by a hostile power in control of the approaches to the North Sea. The Black Sea is ice-free for the most part, but its outlet through the Dardanelles has never been controlled by Russia. Into the salty Caspian, which is eighty-five feet below sea level, runs Europe's mightiest river, the Volga, but the Caspian is landlocked. The Aral Sea, Lake Balkhash, and Lake Baikal, the deepest lake known to man, similarly are of value only for internal communications. Inability to control the outlets of the border seas, particularly in the case of the Black and Baltic Seas, has often compromised Russia's strategic position. The "urge to the sea" (Kerner)—the desire to obtain a warm-water outlet and the hope to reduce Russia's vulnerability by controlling the easy path into the Russian homeland—has been the most persistent aim of national policy.

The nineteenth-century Russian historians, Solovev and Kliuchevsky, pointed out the importance of rivers in the nation's history. Russia's rivers, wandering and slow-moving, provide the heart of the country with easy, if leisurely, access to the sea. They serve as highways, for boat and barge in summer and for sled and ski in winter, over which it is possible by short, easy portages or canals to travel from the Baltic to the Pacific and from the Arctic to the Black and Caspian Seas. Leningrad serves as an entrepôt for goods coming from the middle and lower Volga and even from east of the Urals, and Moscow is a port of five seas.

Of the Russian rivers, whose length totals 180,000 miles, only the most important may be noted here, but the names of many of them will appear again and again in the course of Russian history. The tiny Neva, less than forty miles in length, connects Lake Ladoga, the largest body of fresh water in Europe, to the Gulf of Finland. At its mouth stands the nation's second largest city, Leningrad, and on its left bank rests the fine equestrian statue of the city's founder, Peter the Great. Rising in the Valdais and flowing into Lake Ilmen is the river Lovat. Lake Ilmen is drained by the Volkhov river, which flows north into Lake Ladoga. The Lovat, Lake Ilmen, and the Volkhov form an important link in the western "water road," the highway over which in medieval times the raw materials of northern Europe moved to Byzantium. The Western Dvina also rises in the Valdai Hills, as does the Dnieper, whose 1,400 mile course to the Black Sea makes it the second longest river in European Russia. On the high western bank of the Dnieper is Kiev, the "mother" of Russian cities, and at the cataracts two hundred miles from its mouth is Dneprostroi, the great hydroelectric plant which produces the power for much of the industry of Ukraine. West of the Dnieper and forming at one time the western boundary of Russia flows the Dniester, near whose mouth lies the great Black Sea port of Odessa, the site of a Greek colony in ancient times and later named to commemorate the mythical hero Odysseus. East of the Dnieper and running into the Sea of Azov is the Don, along whose course, as along that of every river in South Russia, once settled a band of Cossacks. Near its mouth the Don is joined by the Donets, whose basin is one of the rich coal-producing areas of Russia. Just north of the Caucasus, and flowing into the Black and Caspian Seas respectively, are the Kuban and the Terek, whose valleys also invited early Cossack settlement. Into the Caspian, too, runs the longest river in Europe, the Volga—"mother Volga" the Russians call it. It was in the basin of the upper Volga that the East Slavs came finally to rest and to lay the basis for the modern state. Rising in the Valdai Hills, it wanders eastward across central European Russia, picking up the important tributaries of the Oka and the Kama, and then turns south to drain its several mouths into the Caspian below Astrakhan. The Caspian yields tons of sturgeon, and from Astrakhan comes the world's finest caviar. From its source northwest of Moscow the mighty Volga winds leisurely through a basin that encompasses half a million square miles, falling to the sea at the rate of only one foot in two and a half miles. Half the river-borne traffic of present-day Russia moves over the Volga system, for the river is navigable over two thousand of its 2,300 miles. The Ural and the Emba rivers also enter the Caspian from the north. Finally, flowing north into the Arctic Ocean are the Northern Dvina, at whose mouth lies the port of Arkhangelsk, and the Pechora, which drains a still rich fur-producing area.

Where the greatest rivers of European Russia flow south into the Black and Caspian Seas, most of the great rivers of Siberia flow northward into the Arctic. Next east of the Urals is the Ob, with its tributaries the Irtysh and the Tobol. Swamp land covers much of the valleys of the Ob and its tributaries, for this west Siberian lowland, extending 1,200 miles from east to west and 1,600 miles from north to south, is the lowest in elevation of any area in the Russian plain. The Trans-Siberian Railway crosses it in nearly a straight line. Farther east is the Yenissei, which gathers up the

Lower Tunguska, the Stony Tunguska, and the Angara or Upper Tunguska on its way to the Arctic. Still farther east is the Lena, which is fed by the Aldan and the Vilyui. The Ob, the Yenissei, and the Lena, each of which drains approximately a million square miles, are each longer than the Volga, as is the Amur, which runs into the Pacific carrying with it the waters of the Argun, the Sungari, and the Ussuri. The Amur is navigable over a third of its 2,700 miles, and the city of Nikolaevsk at its mouth is an important port. Other Siberian rivers, such as the Syr Darya and the Amu Darya, which flow into the Aral Sea, and the Ili, which enters Lake Balkhash, are becoming increasingly important in view of the plans to irrigate the deserts of southern Siberia.

While four-fifths of the nation lies in the temperate zone, and only 16 per cent in the Arctic, Russia lies farther north than any other great power. Leningrad is in the same latitude as the Shetland Islands, Stockholm, Sweden, and Anchorage, Alaska. Moscow is in the latitude of Edinburgh, Scotland and of Sitka, Alaska. Kiev in South Russia is as far north as Calgary, and the Crimean resort town of Yalta as far north as Minneapolis, Minnesota and Bangor, Maine.

Russian climate is distinguished by its continentality, with its extremes of heat and cold. Because of the nation's distance from the Atlantic, and because the warm air of the Gulf Stream is deflected northeastward by the Scandinavian mountains, temperatures are generally lower and winters longer in Russia than is the case elsewhere in the same latitudes. No protective mountains rise to keep back the cold air mass from the Arctic, and the icy blasts sweep out of the north unchecked over the Russian plain. The result is that while there is considerable difference in temperature between west and east, there is remarkably little between north and south. Violent storms which stir the Black Sea to fury in wintertime are raised by winds from the Arctic Ocean. The mean January temperature at Arkhangelsk near the Arctic Circle is 8° Fahrenheit, but it is the same at Kazan, five hundred miles to the south. At the same time the mean at Moscow is 12°. At Leningrad, three hundred miles farther north than Moscow, the January mean is 16°, while at Astrakhan on the Caspian it is only 19°. For comparison it may be noted that the January mean in London is 30°, in New York 31°, in Washington, D.C. 34°, in Minneapolis 14°, in St. Louis 32°, and in Denver 31°. In coldest winter the temperature may drop to −35° in Leningrad, to −44° in Moscow, to −60° in Tomsk, to −84° in Yakutsk, and to −90° in the Verkhoyansk-Oimekon area. Odessa is as cold in winter as Oslo, Norway, nine hundred miles to the north. The effect of such temperatures upon shipping is crippling. The port of Arkhangelsk is frozen for six months of the year, Leningrad for three months, the Black Sea ports for two, Astrakhan for four, Vladivostok for four and a half months. The rivers of Central Asia are frozen over from four to six months, and the north

Siberian rivers for from six to eight months each year. In mid-summer temperatures go to the other extreme. The July mean at Arkhangelsk is 62°, at Sverdlovsk 63°, at Leningrad 64°, at Moscow, Tomsk, and Yakutsk 66°, at Astrakhan 68°, at Kazan 69°, and at Odessa 73°. But July extremes may reach 97° in Leningrad, 99° in Moscow, 95° in Tomsk, 102° in Yakutsk, 109° in Tashkent, 93° in Verkhoyansk, well over 100° anywhere in the steppe, and as high as 158° in the Central Asian desert.

The growing season is short in nearly all of Russia. Less than two months of the year are free of frost in northern Siberia, about a hundred days in the north half of European Russia, and between four and six months in South Russia. The short summer forces the Russian farmer to work prodigiously if he is to beat the autumn frost. Little work can be done outside in the low temperatures and the few hours of daylight that come when winter closes in. Livestock left unsheltered will not survive the first blizzard. Travel is dangerous, and only the most urgent journeys are made during the bitterly cold months when wind whips the snow into impassable drifts. Leo Tolstoy, in his *Master and Man* and *The Snowstorm,* has written unforgettable stories of the perils of travellers caught in a blinding, swirling snowstorm on the steppe.

Spring comes with a rush in mid-April in most of European Russia. People gather at the river bank to watch the ice break up, the dramatic harbinger of long, warm days ahead when the farmer once more may live close to the land. With the spring come the green grass and the bright flowers, which flourish even in the desolate tundra. Iris, crocus, tulip, and hyacinth blanket the fields in South Russia. Autumn brings its own brilliant colors, as maple and birch and oak brighten with the early frost. Vivid pictures of the color to be seen in the Russian countryside have been drawn by Ivan Turgenev in *A Sportsman's Sketches,* by Gogol in *Taras Bulba,* by Chekhov in *The Steppe,* and more recently by Sholokhov in *The Quiet Don.*

For various reasons—of climate, of topography, or of soil—only 11 or 12 per cent of the Russian land can be profitably tilled. Most of this lies inside an elongated triangle whose base rests at Leningrad and the mouth of the Danube and whose apex reaches just east of the Ob river in the direction of Lake Baikal. About 375,000,000 acres of land were being farmed in 1940, an average of 2.2 acres for each of the then 170,000,000 inhabitants.

Great expanses cannot be brought under cultivation because of inadequate rainfall. In much of European Russia the annual precipitation is less than twenty inches. South and east of a line drawn from Odessa to Perm, except for local variations on the Black Sea, a normal year's rainfall amounts to between ten and sixteen inches. North and west of that line it varies between sixteen and twenty-two inches. The arid region north and east of the Caspian receives less than ten inches, in places as little as three. So delicate is the balance between sufficient moisture and aridity that famine may result from a delay of spring rains in the lower valleys of the Dnieper, Don, and Volga. Rainfall, often with violent electrical storms, is greatest in early summer. A sudden downpour may in an hour's time ruin a field on which many days of spring labor have been expended, and may even force a permanent retirement of the field from cultivation. Erosion is a serious problem in the porous black soil of the steppe, and a hard spring rain may cut deep gashes in the fields. Mid-July and August may be very dry, with some of the great rivers threatening to dry up near their mouths. Dredging to remove the silt brought down by spring floods is necessary to keep open the mouths of the rivers that flow into the Black Sea. Passengers on the flat-bottomed river steamers that ply the Don may see the captain forced to slow down "to avoid running down a man on horseback who was attempting to cross his bows in the middle of the stream." It has sometimes happened that "a Cossack passenger wished to be set down at a place where there was no pier, and on being informed that there was no means of landing him, coolly jumped overboard and walked ashore" (Wallace). The soil of the steppe soaks up the water at such a rate that the Volga empties less water into the Caspian than it receives from only one of its tributaries, the Kama.

While precipitation is greatest in spring and early summer, heavy snows in October and November lay a blanket which covers the ground for from four to six months. Additional snowfall during the winter months piles the snow deeply, and, particularly in Ukraine, strong winds heap it into drifts that cover the mile-posts along the roads. But spring brings warm weather so quickly in South Russia that most of the winter's precipitation is lost in runoff, and the farmer must have rain in the planting season if he is to reap a crop.

East of the Urals the amount of annual precipitation falls, being nowhere over twenty inches except in the Kamchatka peninsula and in the Maritime Province along the Sea of Japan. Huge areas in Russian Central Asia, in the Arctic, in the valley of the Lena, and in northeast Siberia receive less than ten inches of rainfall, with as little as three or four inches in the Arctic and in the deserts of the southwest. In the great basin of the Ob the precipitation varies from fourteen inches in the Arctic to eighteen in the upper valley, and only near its headwaters and those of its tributaries, the Irtysh and the Ishim, are crops raised in significant quantity.

In this huge country, which includes within its limits latitudes varying from subtropical to Arctic, there is a variety of vegetation found nowhere else in Eurasia. Distinct types of vegetation, which both reflect and influence climatic conditions and which have tended, also, to shape cultural patterns, run in east-west bands across the face of Russia from the Arctic to the southern seas and mountains.

Along the northern third of the Kola peninsula and in a widening span along the northern coast of Russia from the White Sea to the Bering Strait is the desolate waste known as the tundra. Nearly 15 per cent of present-day Russia is tundra, and most of it is uninhabitable. Much of it is covered by swamp, frozen most of the year and mosquito-infested during the two or three months of summer when only the surface thaws. Only moss and lichens grow in the northern tundra. Farther south the tundra is covered with a scrawny scrub, heather, blackberry, cranberry, and, during the short summer, with a profusion of brightly colored wild flowers. Over much of this land the subsoil remains frozen the year round, and trees with their long roots cannot grow in it. South of the shrub zone trees begin to appear, but the birch and fir and willow are stunted by the low rainfall and the Arctic cold. Still farther south the trees rise in height as the tundra merges with the next vegetation zone, the taiga.

Twenty per cent of the world's forests lie inside present-day Russia. The taiga, the zone of the coniferous forest of spruce and pine and cedar and fir, stretches from Arkhangelsk and the Gulf of Finland in a band that widens to include the Central Urals and Lake Baikal and continues on across Siberia nearly to the Sea of Okhotsk. While the forest of the taiga is predominantly coniferous, mountain ash, poplar, birch, and aspen frequently appear, sometimes in groves. Much of this zone is marshy, particularly east and north of Leningrad and in the river valleys immediately east of the Urals.

South of the taiga is the zone of the mixed forest, where coniferous and deciduous trees are found interspersed. Forests of oak alternate with those of fir; elm, maple, ash, linden, lime, birch, and hornbeam splash brilliant color in the autumn. Much of the mixed forest zone west of the Urals has been cleared and brought under cultivation, for one-third of the land of Russia now under the plough is in this zone. The present government has increased the cultivated area by nearly 50 per cent, and much of the increase has been brought about by drainage of swamps in this area. The gray, acid, podsol soil of the region provides sufficient nourishment for rye, the grain from which the Russian black bread is made, and for flax. Spring wheat has become popular in recent years, but the yield per acre remains low by American, and particularly by English, standards. Sunflowers are raised for their seeds, which Russians eat as Americans eat peanuts.

The forest, which, including the taiga and the mixed forest zone, still covers over half of all Russia, thins out south of a line connecting Kiev, Ryazan, and Kazan. A very thin band, widening toward the Urals, is called the wooded steppe, where grove and grassy meadow alternate.

Beyond the interval of the wooded steppe and running to the shores of the Black Sea is the true steppe. It continues east in an unbroken band to the Altai Mountains, narrowing as it passes north of the Caspian but

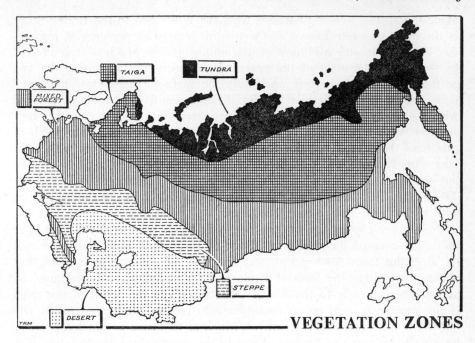

VEGETATION ZONES

fanning out again east of the Urals. This was the highway used by the nomads in their trek out of Asia into Europe. Over it ran the great Eurasian trade route linking China with the Danube. The steppe is treeless, except in the river bottoms and in the shelter belts which Russian governments have been maintaining since long before the 1917 Revolution. The rich black loess called *chernozem,* blown into the area by winds off the glaciers which once reached to the edge of the forest zone, makes the steppe, and particularly its western segment in Ukraine, one of the finest agricultural areas in the world. The soil crumbles into fine powder when dry and rapidly absorbs water. Rain turns it into a thick black paste. This is a natural grassland, and until the nineteenth century the grass grew tall enough to conceal a man on horseback. In the summer, however, the grass quickly parches, forcing early nomads to move their herds constantly in search of palatable pasturage. Now the steppe is nearly all under the plough, for two-thirds of the cultivated land of Russia is found in this zone. Winter wheat has long been the chief crop, and Ukraine has earned its reputation as the breadbasket of Europe, the envy for centuries of German expansionists. From Odessa on the Black Sea Russian wheat has been shipped all over the world. Sugar beets are now an important crop, as are soybeans, potatoes, sunflowers, hay and, locally, cotton and rice.

So vital to the national economy is the steppe and particularly Ukraine, where 20 per cent of the inhabitants of present-day Russia live in 2 per

cent of the national territory, that prolonged interference with the flow of
its products may paralyze or seriously cripple the rest of the nation. Drought
in the steppe may produce famine in South Russia and great hardship elsewhere in the nation which leans so heavily upon this area for its food
supply. Recent improvement in the transportation system may bring better
distribution of the available supply at such times, but there is no escaping
the fact that the elimination in any year of two-thirds of the arable land
must have serious consequences. During World War II the loss to the enemy
of Ukraine, which produces half the nation's coal and two-thirds of its iron,
and where heavy industry was so closely concentrated, meant that the
Russians were hard put to it to maintain the level of industrial output
necessary to national survival.

Northwest, north and east of the Caspian Sea, and extending past the
Aral Sea and Lake Balkhash to the foothills of the Pamir Mountains, is a
vast expanse of desert and semi-desert covering between a fifth and a sixth
of the area of the U.S.S.R. In the northern half of this region lies the semi-
desert, a zone of transition from the steppe north of it to the true desert
south of it. The clay soil of the semi-desert nourishes patches of coarse grass
and shrub, and may be profitably turned to agriculture if irrigated. Astrakhan
sheep thrive on the desert grass west of Lake Balkhash. The great sand
deserts of Kara Kum and Kizil Kum, lying east and west respectively of the
Amu Darya, receive very little precipitation. The rivers run intermittently
during the year, flowing from their source in the mountains to disappear
in the parched sands of the desert. Recently cotton fields have appeared in
the deserts of Tadjikistan and Uzbekistan, irrigated by the Ferghana canal
which brings water from the Syr Darya, and the rubber-producing kok-
saghyz is raised in growing quantity.

The Black Sea littoral from the south slope of the Caucasus to the
Turkish border, and the west shore of the Caspian south of Baku, enjoy
a very humid subtropical climate, where the annual rainfall may exceed
eighty inches and the average annual temperature approaches 60°. Oranges,
lemons, tea, olives, bamboo, and grapes that make the finest wines, grow
here. The Crimea and the north slope of the Pamirs have a similar climate
but much less precipitation. The valleys of Turkmenia and southern Tadjikistan, where the climate is referred to as "dry" subtropical, receive very
little rainfall but have recently been developed under irrigation schemes.
Olives, figs, almonds, apricots, oranges, lemons, and sugar cane thrive where
water is made available.

The mountains along the southern rim of Russia and Siberia show wooded
slopes up to varying altitudes, above which are alpine meadows whose rich
grasses offer splendid pasture for herds of sheep and goats. For centuries
nomads living in the upper reaches of the Central Asian mountains have
ignored international boundaries, and shepherds on both sides of the border

have driven their flocks back and forth over the frontier in search of grass and shelter from shifting winds.

In natural resources Russia is one of the most richly-endowed nations in the world, but only very late in her history was that potential realized or even suspected, and not until still more recently has its exploitation been seriously undertaken. One-fifth of the world's known coal deposits lie inside Russia, which ranks second only to the United States in the size of its reserves. One field alone, that at Kuznetsk in western Siberia, contains two and a half times as much coal as that still available in all the coal deposits of England. There are rich reserves in Ukraine, where the Donets field is the nation's leading producer, in the northern Urals, and in Kazakhstan. Smaller but still important deposits are found in every corner of Russia. Over half the world's known peat deposits are also available to the Russian people.

Fifty-five per cent of the world's oil reserves lie within the borders of the U.S.S.R. The chief oil-producing region centers around Maikop, Grozny, and Baku in the Caucasus, but important deposits have been discovered in the Urals, in the Emba and Volga valleys, in Central Asia, in Kamchatka, and on the island of Sakhalin. A pipeline connects the chief oil field at Baku on the Caspian with the port of Batum on the Black Sea, whence it may be shipped to railheads in Ukraine or exported through the Bosporus. There are also immense deposits of iron in Ukraine, the Crimea, the Urals and eastern Siberia, and south of Moscow; of copper in the Urals, in Kazakhstan, in Central Asia, and south of the Caucasus; of nickel and bauxite in the Urals; of zinc and lead in western Siberia, Central Asia, the Caucasus, and Kazakhstan; of gold in Siberia and the Urals; and of manganese in Ukraine, the Urals, and the Caucasus. Russia leads the world in possession of platinum deposits, which center in the Urals. Of tin, mercury, antimony, radium, molybdenum, graphite, boron, and many other elements important to modern industry, Russia possesses a rich supply.

Russia's mineral potential cannot yet be measured with accuracy, since only half the national territory has been carefully examined. Geological expeditions are constantly being sent out and are constantly returning with reports of newly-discovered wealth. It is only within the last generation that the nation has seriously undertaken to discover its natural resources, and the discovery of these geological frontiers has given modern Russia the character and the spirit of a pioneering nation.

This is the land of Russia—a land of extremes of cold and of heat, of rich black soil and sandy desert, of lofty mountains and monotonous plains, of limitless forest and treeless steppe. The peoples who inhabit the land have always had to give careful consideration to its limitations. Only recently have they awakened to its possibilities.

SUGGESTED READING

Balzak, S. S., *Economic Geography of the U.S.S.R.* (New York, Macmillan, 1949).

Cressy, George B., *Asia's Lands and Peoples*, 2d ed. (New York, McGraw-Hill, 1951).

———, *The Basis of Soviet Strength* (New York, McGraw-Hill, 1945).

Gregory, James S. and D. W. Shave, *The U.S.S.R., a Geographical Survey* (New York, Wiley, 1944).

Haviland, M. D., *Forest, Steppe and Tundra* (New York, Cambridge University Press, 1926).

Kerner, Robert J., *The Urge to the Sea* (Berkeley, University of California Press, 1946).

Mikhailov, Nicholas, *Land of the Soviets* (New York, Lee Furman, 1939).

———, *Soviet Russia: The Land and Its People* (New York, Sheridan House, 1948).

Mirov, N. T., *Geography of Russia* (New York, Wiley, 1951).

Simmons, Ernest J., *U.S.S.R.: A Concise Handbook* (Ithaca, Cornell University Press, 1947).

Stembridge, Jasper H., *An Atlas of the U.S.S.R.* (New York, Oxford University Press, 1942).

Wallace, D. M., *Russia* (New York, Cassell, 1912).

2

The People of Russia

Too MUCH HAS BEEN MADE OF THE fact that within the borders of the U.S.S.R. today there live nearly two hundred different nationalities speaking well over a hundred different languages and dialects and practicing some forty different religions. The fact is not to be denied, but to emphasize it is to leave a mistaken impression of the ethnological character of the nation. Three-fourths of the inhabitants are East Slavs, and the three constituent republics which they occupy cover four-fifths of the state territory. Furthermore, Great Russians, composing the most numerous branch of the East Slavs, have long been found in varying numbers in every one of the republics. Of most importance is the fact that intermarriage is breaking down, as it has been for centuries, the remaining purity of all ethnic groups.

The population of present-day Russia is just over two hundred million. The most numerous ethnic group is the Great Russian, or *Veliko-Russ*, of whom there are over a hundred million. The Great Russians are most heavily concentrated in the north central two-thirds of European Russia, in the area centering on Moscow. But another four million of them are found in the Ukraine, the southwestern border republic, and they are settled all over the U.S.S.R., particularly along the rivers and the railways. The Great Russians have always been overwhelmingly predominant in the population of every Russian state, and it is they who moved out to colonize Siberia, where millions of them live today.

The typical Great Russian is a mixture of East Slav and Finn, the result of the East Slav migration in the early Christian centuries from the steppe to the forest zone to the north and east, a territory then already inhabited by Finns. The squat nose, the prominent cheekbones, the ruddy complexion, the square-set shoulders, the dark hair are Finnish features which stand out in the East Slav-Finnish blend which many Great Russians are. Where the East Slav stock is purer and the Finnish element less apparent, the Great Russian is blond, blue-eyed, fair-haired, taller and not so stocky, with a finer nose. A characteristic of all Slavs is the round head, as distinguished from the long head which typifies the Nordic.

The White Russian, or *Belo-Russ,* is found chiefly in the area between the Pripyat marshes and the Western Dvina. Although now mixed with Lithuanian and Pole, the Belo-Russian retains consistently more of the features of the East Slav than does his cousin, the Great Russian. One of the three branches of the East Slav people, the Belo-Russians number about ten million today.

The third group among the East Slavs and second in numerical importance is the little Russian, or *Malo-Russ,* now most frequently called the Ukrainian. There are nearly forty million of them today, concentrated in the southwest corner of European Russia in the valleys of the Dniester, Bug, Dnieper, and Donets rivers. The East Slav blood of the Little Russian has been subject to more dilution than has that of the Great Russian or the Belo-Russian. The steppe which is his homeland has been a battleground through the centuries and a highway over which nomads from Asia moved to attack Europe. Germans, Poles, Iranians, Mongols, and Turks have added their blood to the East Slav base to form the modern Ukrainian. His language is distinct from, though allied to, the Great Russian which has always been the official language of the Russian state. If there can be said to be a typical Ukrainian, his complexion is more swarthy and his eyes and hair darker than either the Great Russian or the Belo-Russian, and there are often faint traces of Mongoloid features about him.

The many non-Slav nationalities living in Russia are, for the most part, to be found on the fringes of the state territory. So there are Finns in the north and northwest; Turco-Tatars in the Crimea, the Caucasus, the lower Volga, and Central Asia; Mongols all over Siberia but liberally interspersed with Great Russian islands; Balts in the Baltic provinces; and Jews in White Russia and Ukraine. To name only a few of the more important nationalities in these larger groupings is to encounter strange names of peoples long forgotten or seldom heard of until recent years. In the Turco-Tatar group are found such nations and tribes as the Kirghiz, Uzbek, Kazak, Oirot, Tatar, Chuvash, and Bashkir peoples. The Finno-Ugrian group includes the Finns, Mari, Mordvians, Udmurski, Karelians, and Estonians. The Buriats, Yakuts, Kalmucks, Evenki, Nentsi, Samoyeds, and Lapps are Mongoloid, while the Ossetes and Tadjiks are Iranian. Bulgars, Greeks, Arabs, Assyrians, Chinese, and Koreans are found in small numbers. A million and a half Germans were scattered through Ukraine and in the lower Volga before World War II. And Russia's greatest poet, Pushkin, boasted of his Negro blood.

After it has been noticed that there are nearly two hundred different ethnic groups in Russia, it is well to return to the fact that the Russian state has always been an East Slav, and predominantly a Great Russian, state. The story of the absorption of the minorities is the story of the colonizing activity of the Great Russian people, and that activity has gone on from the very beginning of Russian history.

Climate, topography, vegetation, geographical position, and socio-political factors have combined to produce certain characteristics and personality traits which seem to distinguish the Great Russian from other European peoples. While it is hazardous to attribute peculiar mannerisms and attitudes to the people of a particular nation, and while there necessarily must be many who do not conform to the general pattern, still there are characteristics which seem to typify some nationalities more than others. The insularity of the British mind has often been noted. The plodding thoroughness of the German is proverbial, as is the imperturbability of the Chinese, the temperamentality of Mediterranean peoples, and the ostentation of the American. The Welshman loves his song, the Chinese his pantomime, the Italian his opera.

One of the keenest analysts of the Russian character as it was molded by geographic factors was the nineteenth-century Russian historian Kliuchevsky. His description of the effect of life in the forest upon the character of his people has become classic:

Everywhere the swamps and forests of Great Russia confronted the settler with a thousand unforeseen risks, difficulties and hardships. Consequently he learned to watch nature very closely, "to keep an eye open on both sides of him" as the saying is, to scan and probe the ground on which he walked, and never to attempt the passage of a strange river where there was not a ford. All this bred in him resourcefulness in the face of minor perils and difficulties, and inured him to patient wrestling with hardship and misfortune. No people in Europe is so unspoiled, so handy, so taught not to wait upon nature or fortune, so long-suffering under adversity, as the Great Russian. The peculiar features of the country caused its every nook and cranny to beset the settler with some new and difficult problem to solve.

The forest and swamp, then, have made the Russian distrustful, but they also have made him resourceful and self-reliant. "God is too high and the Tsar is too far away" expressed perfectly the Russian's awareness that he must get himself out of difficulties, either alone or with the help of his fellows.

While the Russian must be cautious and careful in the forest, he has learned to use it and even to love it. At hunting, trapping, and beekeeping he is without a peer. He finds pleasure and profit in searching for the mushrooms which abound in the damp glades of the forest. He is literally an artist with his axe. And the typical animal of the forest, the bear—as a symbol of joviality and good temper, yet of caution and shrewdness—is the central figure in many a joke and folk tale. Finally, the Russian has learned to use the forest with awful effectiveness in defense against invasion. Enormous toll of lives was exacted from the armies of Napoleon and Hitler by the partisan bands who struck in the shadows of the forest and disappeared among the trees.

The plain, too, has exerted strong influence on the national character. The relative flatness of the Russian countryside, where for hundreds after hundreds of miles there is no barrier, has made the East Slav a natural colonizer and pioneer. Even today the colonizing goes on. Siberia has often been compared to the American West in the invitation it offered to settlement. Indeed, the movement over the plain and beyond has been made easy, from the Baltic to the Pacific, by the network of slow-flowing rivers. Very early in their history the Slavs were fashioning boats of hollowed logs and were moving out over the river system, stirred at times by simple curiosity, at others by hope of finding refuge from oppression, at still other times by the desire to improve their lot. The same culture pattern spread easily over the plain, and the absence of barriers within that wide expanse prevented the persistence of local peculiarities. Wherever the settler moved he found things pretty much as he had left them in his earlier home locality. Even the very setting and topography he left may be encountered many times in a land so much of which is characterized by monotonous regularity.

Once he has put forth his every effort, the Russian is inclined to be philosophical about what may come. "Man does what he can, God what he wills." He has grown used to disappointment and patiently accepts with fatalistic resignation the favors and frustrations that come to him. When asked whether something will come to pass, he is more apt to answer cynically, "Perhaps," than to express a hope that later may be dashed. Patience is a typical Russian virtue. Disappointment he accepts with a shrug of the shoulders and the expression *"Nichevo,"* which may be translated as "It doesn't matter," or "Never mind," or "It is nothing," or "Let it pass."

The short growing season makes the Russian sure of one thing, that if he is to bring in a crop he must work unceasingly through the summer months. No other is so capable of sustained, prodigious toil as is the Russian. There will be time enough to rest through the winter. But when the farmer has worked feverishly from before dawn until after dusk, night after night and week after week, when he sees his fields rippling with grain that will bring good living through the coming year, and then when he wakens some August morning to find the crop destroyed by an early frost, what is there to say? "Fortune and misfortune are next door neighbors," runs the Russian proverb. One of Russia's greatest historians, Solovev, has observed caustically that "nature has been a step-mother to Russia."

Through the long bitter cold of winter, when work outside is impossible, the Russian stays indoors and spends long hours by the fire, thinking over the problems of his existence and pondering the vagaries of nature. He is a natural philosopher. The time he has given to thinking through life's problems has made his language richer than any other in proverb and fable. Krylov, the Russian Aesop, left a collection of fables which Sir Bernard Pares has made accessible to English-speaking students in an excellent translation.

The Russian is of a speculative disposition, but he is also intensely realistic. In the Slav there is none of the intellectual escapism which so often crops out in the German. The peasant of the nineteenth century, one of the finest Russian types, was notoriously cynical. "If it were not for the thunder, the *muzhik* [peasant] would never remember to cross himself." The land may be bountiful if well cared for, but vagaries of climate may take away its rich promise. Only by feverish work may the soil be made to give up its fruit. There is no time during the work season for idle dreaming. There is no escape from the need to press on without interruption until the task is done.

From this realism, perhaps, comes a forgiving attitude toward his neighbor. The Russian is quick to admit his own faults and does not blame another for revealing the same weaknesses he finds in himself. He realizes that adversity may strike anyone, and that misfortune is to be pitied and shared rather than condemned. When his crops fail, he expects to be carried over to the next harvest by a loan from his neighbor or friend, and he is equally ready to come to the assistance of others in time of need. If successive crop failures strike over a large area, all will be faced with famine.

Severity of climate has forced upon the Russian a sense of the need for cooperation with others. Walking along the street of any Russian city in cold weather, one may be hailed by a total stranger and told to put snow to one's cheek. Wind and cold may turn the face white with frostbite, which may not be felt and which may cause serious injury if one's attention is not called to it and action quickly taken. Russians are no more immune to cold than are any other people, but they take precautions to protect themselves against it. They dress in heavy clothing and furs when they go abroad in winter, and their houses, with double-paned windows, are built to keep out the cold. The huge stove in the peasant's hut might occupy a quarter of the space, being large enough to permit two or three people to sleep upon it. This favored bed often is reserved for a sick one, or for the *babushka* or grandmother whose age makes her most vulnerable to the cold.

Whenever Russians gather, in a home on a winter evening or in the fields at harvest time, over a dish of tea or a bottle, as soldiers on the march or even prisoners working on the roads, they enjoy singing. Like the Welsh, they all sing in harmony, and their voices are inferior to none. The Ukrainian is reputed to be the best singer among the Slavs, and perhaps his repertoire of folk song is richer. Nearly every important Russian composer has found inspiration in the folk songs of his people, and Glinka made a particular effort to record as many of them as possible. These songs may go on endlessly, with a leader singing the verse, improvising a tale as he sings, and the group joining in the chorus. While some of his songs, like some of his stories, are full of sadness and fatalism, the Russian sings most often out of gaiety and lightheartedness. Whatever the diplomat or the civil servant may seem when on official business, the typical Russian in everyday life is a smiling, jovial, friendly fellow, and his love of song is expressive of his warmheartedness. Appreciation for the opera and the ballet has never been limited to the upper classes.

The Russian, like the Chinese, has a profound love of the land which gives him sustenance, but, unlike the Chinese, his attachment is not to a particular plot of ground, but to the land. He is a natural farmer and likes to live close to the soil. Isolated individual farms, except for a few years at the opening of the twentieth century, have never been typical of the rural scene in Russia. Farming has always been a communal enterprise, as certain farm tasks still are in the American Midwest. This attachment to the land is associated with a strong love of homeland and a zeal in guarding it against invasion. "Mother Russia," as the people call the national territory, has often been invaded, but the Russians have always ultimately put aside their differences and united to hurl back the aggressor. Any Russian government, no matter what its weaknesses, which places in the hands of the people the weapons with which to turn back the invader, has received universal support, and governments which have not been able to do so have been quickly overturned.

The communal spirit has long run stronger among the Russians than among any other people. Working on the open steppe in full sight of one's neighbor has made for easy cooperation. The dangers of the forest were best met by the group. Colonizing of the Russian land has been necessarily a collective enterprise. Group rather than individual effort has seemed most profitable under the limitations that short season and insufficient rainfall and dust storm and flood have imposed. Man risks his life to brave the blizzard alone. Individual selfishness might invite national disaster when the yield of the national economy is small. Group consciousness has had the effect of minimizing the importance of the individual. What has always mattered in this land which demands the communal approach to the problems it imposes is society, the nation, the village, or the family, and not the individual. It was no accident that the teachings of Karl Marx should first be tried out in Russia. Societal authority has impinged heavily upon the individual for centuries.

The typical Russian has often been accused of showing lack of restraint and moderation. When he takes to liquor he drinks himself into insensibility, and marriage feasts may continue for days. When he turns to cards he may play for days on end and literally gamble away the shirt he wears. The Russian may harbor a grudge long after others have forgotten what caused the disagreement. Pushkin's *The Shot* tells of a man who devoted his life to getting revenge for a fancied grievance and who then forgave his rival when the opportunity came to settle accounts. While he tends to nurse a grievance overlong, he will as soon cast off his moroseness and smilingly dismiss and forget it. Leroy Beaulieu attributes such quick shifts in mood to the influence of the Russian climate, which may change from one extreme to the other in a very short time. The utter abandon with which many Russian intellectuals in the nineteenth century cast aside all ties of friend and family to devote their lives to preaching reform and revolution, at the risk of exile and poverty or imprisonment and death, was evidence of typical Russian immoderation.

Finally, the Russian has about him an attitude of frankness often misunderstood in the West. It is difficult to be secretive and dissembling in a plain that stretches away to the horizon. The late Professor Miliukov observed that the Russian people lacked the "cement of hypocrisy." The Russian drinks in the street rather than behind doors, a fact which led foreign observers in the nineteenth century to suppose that the per capita consumption of liquor must be far higher in Russia than elsewhere, a presumption not warranted by the facts. In Leo Tolstoy's great novel *Anna Karenina,* Karenin seeks to keep his faithless wife with him, but she prefers to live out of wedlock with her beloved Vronsky. Russia, unshaken by the Protestant Revolt, never developed the Puritan sense of virtue which settled over the West.

Exceptions will be found. There are Russians who contradict these generalizations about the national character, just as some Englishmen are not typically English and some Germans are unlike most Germans. Differences in wealth, in social status, in heredity, in childhood training, will produce differences in personality and disposition. Changes in social organization may bring forth new attitudes and new characteristics. But the geographical factors which set the Russian land apart from the rest of Eurasia have helped produce a national character as distinctive as the land in which it grew.

SUGGESTED READING

Afanasev, I., *Russian Folk-Tales* (New York, Dutton, 1916).
Baring, M., *The Mainsprings of Russia* (New York, Nelson, 1914).
———, *The Russian People* (London, Methuen, 1911).
Crankshaw, E., *Russia and the Russians* (New York, Viking, 1948).

Pares, B., *Russia* (Baltimore, Penguin, 1941).

Vinogradoff, Paul, *Russia: The Psychology of a Nation* (New York, Oxford University Press, 1914).

Wallace, D. M., *Russia* (New York, Cassell, 1912).

Wiener, L., *An Interpretation of the Russian People* (New York, McBride, 1915).

Williams, H. W., *Russia of the Russians* (New York, Scribner's, 1914).

3

Ancient Russia

IT IS OFTEN FORGOTTEN THAT THE north coast of the Black Sea and the steppe hinterland beyond it were significant in Greek and Roman times as an important source of food and raw materials and as a market for the manufacturing centers to the south and west. Archaeological research among the burial mounds and cemeteries and ruined towns of South Russia has been going on for two centuries and has added much to the knowledge of Mediterranean and Near East cultures.

The Russian steppe, merging with the Central Asian plain on the east and with the Danube valley and the Polish plain on the west, attracted nomads from Asia in search of rich pasture for their herds. But its rich soil, too, prompted its inhabitants from earliest times to cultivate the land. The nomad came as conqueror and, finding on the steppe a wealthy, settled, agricultural civilization, stayed to feed his herds and flocks and to exact tribute from the natives he brought under submission. He merged the Oriental culture he brought with him with the indigenous civilization he found. He taxed and then stepped forward to take part in the trade which the steppe peoples had developed with peoples of the other shores of the Black Sea and the Aegean. Strands of western civilizations were woven into the fabric of his own, and South Russia came to be a fusion point of many cultures. Then the nomad conqueror found himself overwhelmed by new invaders from Asia, and the process repeated itself. Oriental tribesmen, pushed out of Asia or following their flocks to the rich grassland of South Russia, moved into the steppe land, conquered it, and settled down, later to be inundated by fresh waves out of the east. The Cimmerians, the first invaders of whom there is evidence, subdued the Copper age peoples whom they found tilling the soil of South Russia. The Cimmerians were over-

22

whelmed by the Scythians, who in their turn were conquered by the Sarmatians. Goths from the north and Huns and Avars from the east in turn passed over the steppe and moved on into central Europe.

THE MAEOTIANS

Two types of culture were found in Russia three thousand years and more before the Christian era, the one based upon the use of stone implements and centered in the valleys of the Dnieper, the Bug, the Dniester, and the upper Volga, the other employing copper and based in the valley of the Kuban east of the Black Sea. These cultures existed at the same time, but the neolithic peoples of the Dnieper-Dniester area were prevented from rising above the use of stone by the fact that tin and copper were not found in the river valleys where they settled.

The neolithic peoples of the Russian steppe progressed beyond the hunting stage to a settled life of agriculture; to the products of the soil they added the meat and milk of their own domesticated herds of goats, cattle, and horses to bring variety to their diet. They arranged their half-cave, half-hut dwellings in clan villages, which they fortified against marauders. The art of weaving was known to them. Religious ceremonies grew to such importance that temples were built to house them, and thousands of graves, sometimes grouped in cemeteries, attest neolithic man's care of his dead. The painted spiral pottery typical of the Neolithic period has been found as far north as Kiev and even inside the forest zone; it is of the same type found in central and southern Europe. Copper implements occasionally found suggest that some trade was carried on between the neolithic peoples of the Dnieper and the areas of the Carpathians, the Urals, or the Caucasus. But the use of iron waited upon the arrival of Asiatic peoples who had learned the techniques of applying it.

The peoples of the Kuban valley on the north slope of the Caucasus, while contemporary with those of the valley of the Dnieper, had passed beyond the use of stone and enjoyed a richer metal-based culture. Their burial mounds, or kurgans, have yielded rings, necklaces, earrings, bracelets, and vessels of copper, silver, and gold. Stone implements are mingled with others made of copper. Later, perhaps ten centuries before Christ, the Kuban peoples learned to fuse copper with tin, and so moved on to replace implements of copper with those of bronze. Ornaments in the shape of bulls, lions, antelopes, boars, panthers, and birds reveal a high degree of artistic interest and technical skill.

The peoples in the Don-Kuban area were known to the Greeks as Maeotians, from Maeotis, the Greek name for the Sea of Azov. Those in the Don delta were called Sauromatians, and those found on both sides of the Strait of Kerch, or the Cimmerian Bosporus, were called Sindians. These were only the most noted, and perhaps the most numerous, of the tribes among the Don-Kuban peoples whom the Greeks termed, generally, Maeotians. Their civilization antedates that of ancient Troy. Herodotus notes that Sauromatian society was matriarchal, that women ruled as sovereigns and fought as warriors among them. A goddess served by warrior priestesses, the Amazons, was their chief deity.

THE CIMMERIANS (1000 B.C.–700 B.C.)

Early in the tenth century B.C. there appeared in South Russia the Cimmerians, an Indo-European people of Thracian origin. Little is known of them, although Herodotus refers to a Cimmerian kingdom of considerable dimensions on the north shore of the Black Sea, with its center astride the Strait of Kerch. Indeed, the Strait was known to the Greeks as the Cimmerian Bosporus. The Cimmerian kingdom grew to such power that it expanded south across the Caucasus and into Armenia, and this overreaching ambition so weakened the center of the state that it fell easy prey to the Scythians from Central Asia. The Cimmerians were not numerous; they constituted only a thin crust of artistocracy over the mass of Maeotians whom they ruled.

During the Cimmerian period iron implements and weapons came into use, although their popularity seems to have been limited. The forging of iron developed first in the north Caucasus area, from which axes, hoes, swords, and plowshares were gradually introduced into South Russia.

The Cimmerian state was split in two by the Scythian invasion, one part continuing to live on in Cappadocia south of the Caucasus, and the other losing its identity among other subject tribes who came under Scythian domination. Those Cimmerians who had moved on from the Strait of Kerch to settle in the lower Dnieper were pushed out by the advancing Scythians; they fled down the west coast of the Black Sea and across the Dardanelles to join their people in Cappadocia. Another Cimmerian remnant found safety in the swamps of the Taman peninsula and vigorously maintained its independence in the delta of the Kuban. There Greek colonists later joined with them to build an autonomous state called the Kingdom of the Bosporus.

THE SCYTHIANS (700 B.C.–200 B.C.)

The period of the Cimmerian domination of the steppe was short, lasting for about three centuries after 1000 B.C. Late in the seventh century B.C.

there advanced out of Asia an array of tribes of Scythians, an Indo-European people related to the Medes and Persians, accompanied by numbers of Mongolians who served as foot soldiers in the Scythian army. There may have been earlier migrations from Asia into the Russian steppe, but this in the seventh century is the first of which there is any record. The Scythians and the Mongoloid peoples who came with them had been pushed off the grasslands of their home in Central Asia by Chinese expansion.

The host from the east seems to have divided to pass north and south of the Caspian. One group settled in Armenia and Asia Minor, but the great body moved into the Russian steppe. The army, led by Scythians and composed of Scythian cavalry and Mongolian infantry, met with stern resistance from the Cimmerian-Maeotian peoples, and the Scythian conquest was not completed until the end of the seventh century b.c. Islands of local resistance may have continued in the mountains of Crimea and in the swamps of the Don and Kuban deltas long after the main wave had passed on to the west.

By the beginning of the sixth century the Scythian power was well secured. The new state, centering between the Dnieper and the Don, covered the entire steppe area of South Russia, reaching into the Kuban valley and probably to the Caucasus on the east and the Carpathians on the west. In succeeding centuries the Scythian kingdom may have expanded into the Hungarian plain and into what is now Romania and Bulgaria.

As had been true of the Cimmerian power which preceded it, the Scythian ascendancy was marked by the domination of a Scythian minority over the Mongolian allies who had accompanied them and over the Cimmerians, Maeotians, and others who were subdued. Greek writers referred to the entire conglomerate of steppe dwellers as Scythians, but in fact only the ruling aristocracy was composed of them. The invaders imposed a military-feudal rule over the steppe, as did the various powers which succeeded them. The king was the military leader, his court the camp, and his retainers the army which he had led to victory and which he kept in readiness to put down revolt. For some time after their arrival on the steppe they continued the nomad's life of moving their tents and families to and fro over the rich grassland as they followed their herds to new pasture. Later, the Scythian king seems to have allotted a portion of the grassy steppe to each subdivision of the tribe to assure all the necessary pasturage. Slaves tended the flocks and herds, and with the produce of their own animals the Scythians combined the agricultural and other products gathered as tribute from the subject population. Areas like the valleys of the Dnieper, Bug, and Kuban, where the land was tilled by the conquered, were administered by princes or lieutenants, each with his own armed detachments, who gathered revenue for the king and rendered military service when there was need for it.

The military nature of Scythian rule is apparent from the artifacts recov-

ered from burial mounds, many of which have been carefully examined in
the past century. Herodotus has left a detailed account of the burial of a
Scythian king, and archaeological research has confirmed the general features of his account. The body of a Scythian king buried in the sixth century B.C. was surrounded by many servants and slaves and sometimes by
hundreds of horses, indicative of the military nomadic life of the Scythians.
Rich ornaments and utensils of gold and silver, many of them of Greek and
Persian manufacture imported from Asia Minor, have been recovered in
the graves, as well as scaled armor, Greek helmets, spears, arrows, and the
famed Scythian bows. When the funeral rites, "essentially a nomadic ceremonial, cruel, bloody, and luxurious" (Rostovtzeff), were over, the grave was
closed and a high mound of earth heaped over it. Many of these burial
mounds, or kurgans, have been scientifically analyzed, and many still may
be seen in South Russia.

Scythian military tactics are worth noting, for they were to be applied
many times in later centuries by the Russians. The cavalry, whose mobility
was enhanced by the use of the saddle, was equipped with deadly effective
short bow and arrows. Small detachments dashed at the enemy, released their
volleys of arrows at short range, and quickly withdrew. When the enemy
pursued, he was allowed to penetrate deep into Scythian territory, where he
could be surrounded and dispatched. When Darius moved against the
Scythians in 512 B.C., the Scythians arranged their defending forces in three
divisions, the better to harass the invader, and fell back, avoiding pitched
battle. The livestock were driven to safety, the steppe grass burned, and the
wells destroyed. The Persians penetrated deep into Scythian territory, but
when the withdrawal began the Scythians moved to the attack, and Darius
suffered heavily. A modification of these tactics, known as the "Scythian
Plan," was used against Napoleon when he invaded Russia in 1812, and the
Russians followed a similar "scorched earth" policy against the Germans
in 1941.

For four centuries the Scythian power was uncontested in the South Russian steppe. But the military organization of society encouraged constant
expansion, and the conquering army pressed on to the Danube and beyond
into Thrace and across the Caucasus to absorb the Scythian band which
had turned south of the Caspian when the tribes first wandered into western
Eurasia in the seventh century. But Scythian rule in eastern Asia Minor
and in Thrace threatened the flank of Darius, who dreamed of conquering
the Greek world, and Persian power soon put an end to the expansion of the
Scythian state, forcing it back to the Danube and the Caucasus. Later
Scythian pressure south of the Danube was fought off by Philip of Macedon
and his son Alexander the Great, although an independent Scythian state
in the Dobrudja continued to Roman times, even after the fall of the main
Scythian kingdom in South Russia.

In the latter part of the fourth and the early part of the third centuries
B.C. the Scythians were forced, by Macedonian attacks, by movement of
the Celts from the northwest into the Black Sea littoral between the Danube
and the Dnieper, and by the appearance of the Sarmatians, another Iranian
people, out of the east, to pull in their outposts and to concentrate between
the Don and the Dnieper. Pressure against them in the steppe forced the
Scythians north into the edge of the forest zone, and Kiev and Voronezh
became new centers of Scythian influence. An escape corridor was kept open
to the Crimean peninsula, however, where a last stand against the enemy
might be made. From the upper Dnieper, middle Volga, and Kama regions,
the Scythians continued, until their power was swept away, to draw the
furs and honey and wax and slaves which they sold in the Greek markets on
the shores of the Black Sea.

Toward the end of the second century the Sarmatians from the east
crossed the Don and moved firmly against the Scythians. Pressed on the
north by Celts and Germans and on the east by the new Iranian power, the
Scythians were overwhelmed or withdrew to the Crimean peninsula. The
great Scythian kingdom disappeared, although it is not unlikely that some
Scythian princes were allowed to retain local authority as vassals to the
Sarmatians. Scythian identity was not completely lost as long as Roman
supremacy on the Black Sea continued, but with the coming of the Goths
they disappeared.

From the beginning of the sixth to the end of the fourth centuries, the
Scythians brought peace to the steppe. The rich farm land was tilled by
subject peoples free from internal disturbance or outside pressure. Trade
flourished in the area, as Greek middlemen exchanged the produce of the
steppe and the forest for the manufactures of the Aegean area. Greek merchants did not move far inland, but the products of the interior were brought
to the Greek markets by Scythian agents and taxgatherers.

During the period of Scythian ascendancy two cultural streams merged
on the Russian steppe. The first of the two influences, the Oriental, the
Scythians had brought with them. The manufacture and use of iron weapons
and tools, for example, had been practised by these people in Asia. They
maintained the Oriental contact, perhaps with Mesopotamia by way of the
Caucasus and the Greek colonies in northern Asia Minor. The second cultural stimulus came from the west, from the Greeks on the shores of the
Aegean. During the early centuries of Scythian rule the Oriental influence
was predominant and almost exclusive. Scythian art was only a style of
Iranian, as Persian was another. By the fifth century Greek influence was
noticeable in Scythian art; it became complete when the Scythians turned
to Greek craftsmen for their ornaments and utensils. With the rise of Hel-
lenic and then of Hellenistic power, Scythian civilization received a strong
western orientation.

THE SARMATIANS (200 B.C.–A.D. 200)

In the second half of the fourth century B.C. a new flood of Iranian peoples began to pour out of the east. They were related to the Scythians but of purer blood, for the Scythians had mixed with the Mongoloids whom they led into Russia. This Sarmatian tide apparently moved into western Eurasia in waves, as successive tribes were driven from their homeland in Central Asia and Turkestan by Mongolians turned from their attack upon China by the newly-constructed Great Wall. The drift westward was slow, perhaps because these nomads let themselves be led by their flocks in search of grass. They crossed the Volga and settled east of the Don some time after the middle of the fourth century and did not appear in the area between the Don and Dnieper until a century later.

At about the same time the Celts moved into southeastern Europe from the north. Shortly after 300 B.C. they moved into the Balkan peninsula, and Celtic detachments pressed into western Ukraine. These Celts, or Gauls, left their name in Galicia, but they made no serious effort to settle permanently in the Russian steppe.

By early in the second century B.C. the Sarmatians had supplanted the Scythians in the Don-Dnieper territory, and by the end of the same century they were pressing on toward the Danube. Each tribe of the Sarmatian nation staked out a portion of the steppe—the Iazygians between the Danube and the Dnieper; the Roxalans, or White Alans, between the Dnieper and the Don; the Aorsians east of the Don; and the Siracians at the mouth of the Don and in the Kuban valley. East of the Volga were the Alans,* the largest of the tribes, who later came to dominate the eastern steppe. Their descendants, the Ossetians of the Caucasus, still retain their own nationality and language. By the middle of the first century A.D. the Roxalans had moved west of the Dnieper, and the Sarmatian advance guard, the Iazygians, had pushed into the Hungarian plain between the Theiss and the Danube, where they posed a threat to the power of Rome.

The Sarmatian and Germanic tribes joined forces to break over the Danube frontier, and had to be hurled back across the river in A.D. 63 by Nero's general Plautius Silvanus. Later the province of Dacia was organized to hold back the German-Sarmatian tide, but the relief was only temporary. While the Sarmatians alone never mustered the power to break through the Roman defenses, allied with the Goths, Suevi, Vandals, and others they finally surged over the Empire and overran Italy, France, Spain, and North Africa. That there were strong Sarmatian contingents in the bar-

* The Alans were known to the Greeks as As or Asii, whence the name of the continent of Asia.

barian armies that brought the downfall of Rome is well known. Whether they were forced to join the westward movement or chose to do so as allies of the Germans is not clear. The Sarmatian tribe of Alans was also drawn into the conquering armies of Huns which drove against Rome under the leadership of Attila. At the same time some of the Alans served as mercenaries in the Roman armies, whole corps, particularly of cavalry, being composed of them in the third and fourth centuries.

From the second century B.C. to the third century A.D. the Sarmatians, and particularly the Alans, were the controlling force in the eastern steppe. Like the Scythians before them, they dealt softly with the Greek colonies and left them to continue the trade with the Greek world. But the Sarmatians settled in Greek towns in much greater number than had the Scythians. After A.D. 200 they were overshadowed by the Goths, although their influence was important in the governing class and in the armies of the Gothic bands. Whether the Sarmatian power was ever united into a single state, as was that of the Scythians, or whether each Sarmatian tribe ruled over its own territory and went its own independent way, is not known. Probably the better organization of the Germanic tribes was a factor in preventing Sarmatian unity.

The Sarmatians, like their kinsmen the Scythians, brought to the Russian steppe the Iranian culture they had known in Central Asia. The clothing and armor of the two peoples were similar. Like the nomads who had preceded and would follow them, they were excellent horsemen. The weapons and fighting tactics of the Sarmatians differed from those of the Scythians, however; the former used the heavy lance and the long sword and the shock power of their armored horses, while the Scythians preferred the bow and arrow, and the dagger for close-in fighting. The Sarmatians seem to have been more restless than their predecessors, but this may have been due to the disturbed conditions in the steppe brought about by the appearance of Celts, Germans, and Huns during the Sarmatian period.

Like the Scythians before them, they seemed willing to deal with the Greek cities on the north coast of the Black Sea rather than to destroy them, and attacked the Greek colonies seriously only later when the Goths led the way. For a short period after their arrival from east of the Caspian the Sarmatians were able to maintain peace in the steppe. They collected taxes in grain from the subject peoples on the land and encouraged the towns to continue the trade which had made them prosperous. By the beginning of the Christian era trade routes stretched so far into the east and north from the Black Sea ports that silk from China, furs from Siberia, and iron goods from the Baltic and Germany came into the Greek markets in South Russia. Before their departure from Asia some of the Sarmatians had grown wealthy from participation in the trade of goods exported from China to the northwest. "The transcontinental commercial highway from China to Turkestan

was the backbone of the commercial imperialism of the steppe leaders. By
moving to the Pontic [South Russian] steppes the Sarmatian chieftains were
now able to connect the transcontinental trade route with the maritime commerce of the Black Sea region" (Vernadsky). Over the trade route connecting China with the Russian steppe there was a continuous flow, in Sarmatian
times, of the goods and the culture of the East.

THE GREEKS (600 B.C.–A.D. 600)

Even before the coming of the Scythians to South Russia in the seventh
century B.C. it is likely that Ionian Greeks had ventured into the Black Sea
in search of iron and gold, and that colonies at Sinope and Trebizond on the
south shore were established as concentration points for exporting metals
to the Greek homeland. Finding the Black Sea teeming with fish, the
Ionians sailed east and north along the coast until they came to the best fishing grounds, the Cimmerian Bosporus. At this strait and at the mouths of the
Russian rivers which flow into the Black Sea the Greeks founded other
colonies. Phanagoria and Hermonassa were built on the Taman peninsula
in the delta of the Kuban, Panticapaeum and Nymphaeum across the straits
near the present site of Kerch, and Tanais at the mouth of the Don. Other
Greeks drifted up the west coast of the Black Sea, and colonies which began
as fishing villages were founded at the mouths of the Danube, the Dniester,
the Bug, and the Dnieper. Near the southern tip of the Crimea the Greeks
found an excellent harbor and built the seaport of Chersonese not far from
the modern city of Sevastopol.

Among the Greek colonies in the western Euxine by far the most important was Olbia, located on the west bank of the bay into which flow the
Bug and the Dnieper, near the site of modern Nikolaev. The mouths of the
rivers were excellent fishing grounds, and the hinterland was a rich agricultural district. Of most importance to the growth of Olbia was the fact that
the Dnieper river was potentially a great avenue of commerce down which
the furs and slaves and products of the forest to the north could move. At
the height of her eminence Olbia was trading with areas as far away as the
Kama and the middle Volga. The assurance of peace in the steppe, as Cimmerian and, later, Scythian power was firmly established, permitted the
Greek colonies to prosper as they could never have done in the absence of
political stability. The Scythians seem to have feared the sea and to have
been content to leave to Greek merchants the profitable commerce on the
Black Sea. Their policy was to encourage, not to cripple or hamper, the trade
which provided an exchange of the raw materials of the Russian hinterland
under their rule for the finished goods of the Greek world. Scythian princes
married Greek women, some built palaces in Olbia, and some of the bar-

barians went to Athens for an education. Olbia sent its own colonists to settle in native villages upriver and to promote an interest in Greek products. The rich treasure found in Olbian tombs indicates that the city grew extremely wealthy from the trade which the Scythian peace promoted.

In the eastern Euxine there were a number of Greek towns, particularly on either side of the Strait of Kerch. In eastern Crimea Panticapaeum, the chief city in the area, had been a Cimmerian capital before the Scythians took it over. Other Greek colonies were established on the Kerch peninsula, apparently with the encouragement of the Scythians, who appreciated the revenues they received from the Greek markets. Across the Strait, on the Taman peninsula, were several towns never conquered by the Scythians, where Cimmerians fleeing the Scythian invasion settled among the Greek colonists and carried on their own profitable trade in local manufactures and fish from the neighboring seas.

When Darius forced Scythian military concentration in the western part of the steppe, the Greek colonies banded together in a confederacy led by Panticapaeum. For some years the confederacy was dominated by Athens. When her plan to dominate Egypt did not materialize, and as her relations with Italy became strained, Athens turned to the Black Sea area for fish and grain to feed her people and for metals and other raw materials to feed her industries. In the fifth and fourth centuries the Bosporan area was Greece's chief source of grain. Athenian troops were poured into the Cimmerian Bosporus to stiffen the colonists against Scythian pressure, and Athenian merchants were given complete control of all goods exported from the area. So important to the Athenian economy were the grain and other products of these colonies that Pericles himself visited the Cimmerian Bosporus to inspect the defenses and the markets.

Shortly after Pericles' tour of inspection a revolution in Panticapaeum raised a tyrant over the city, and his successors as "Kings of the Bosporus" brought the Greek colonies of the Crimean and Taman peninsulas and of the shores of the Sea of Azov under one rule. The Athenian monopoly of trade was broken, although Athens continued to be the chief market for the products of the Bosporan kingdom. The Scythians accepted the independence of the new state, perhaps out of respect for its sizeable army and its commercial importance.

From the middle of the third century B.C. the political and economic power of the Bosporan state declined. Celts advancing into the steppe from the northwest and Sarmatians edging westward from the Volga precipitated the collapse of the Scythian empire. The Scythian market and source of raw materials dried up, while the need to draft more and more of the citizens of Bosporan towns into an army to resist the new Iranian horde deprived industry of craftsmen and impoverished the state.

During the period of its prosperity the Bosporan kingdom was a significant force in the life of the steppe. "It succeeded in spreading Greek civilization among its Scythian neighbours, and in saturating its non-Greek subjects with that civilization. For centuries it guaranteed the Greek world a cheap and abundant supply of provisions. It transformed wide tracts of steppe into cultivated fields. In a word, the [Cimmerian] Bosporus of the classical Greek period played an important part in the life of the ancient world" (Rostovtzeff).

Mounting pressure from Sarmatians, and from Scythians seeking refuge in the Crimean peninsula from the new invaders of the steppes, forced the kingdom of the Bosporus to seek an ally. It obtained assistance from Pontus, but only at a terrible price. The Pontic king Mithridates established garrisons in all the Greek cities of the Black Sea area as far west as Olbia, laid them under tribute, and sought to unite the Scythians and Sarmatians for an attack upon Rome which would be financed, in part at least, by the Greek towns. But the Greeks preferred the distant power of Rome to the heavy oppression of the Pontic king, and Mithridates lost his life in a rebellion of his own Greek subjects.

After the Mithridatic War Rome took the Greek towns of the Black Sea under her protection, and the Emperor Augustus later recognized the Bosporan kingdom as a vassal state. To assure a continuing flow of food to Greece and to obtain provisions for the Roman legions stationed in Asia Minor, the kingdom of the Bosporus was strengthened in its hegemony over all Greek towns on the Black Sea and was provided with Roman garrisons, forts, and sea patrols. For nearly two centuries the vassal state lived on, shored up by Roman power. But internal decay and barbarian pressure forced Rome to shorten her defense lines, and in the third century A.D. the legions were pulled out of South Russia. The kingdom on the Bosporus surrendered to an allied army of Sarmatians and Goths, and its capital, Panticapaeum, quickly lost its Graeco-Roman character. The Romans stayed on at the fine port of Chersonese, and Greek civilization there continued through the Byzantine period. But Olbia gave up its brilliant wealth and became a small fishing village, as did most of the other Greek towns in South Russia. When Roman power shifted to Byzantium the eastern empire revitalized Chersonese and Panticapaeum, and these towns recovered a mite of their former importance in serving as advance posts of Byzantine civilization.

Bosporan society showed a curious fusion of Greek and Oriental characteristics. The blood and customs of several peoples had intermingled since the first appearance of Greek colonies around the Sea of Azov. The land was owned by the religious temples and by a Cimmerian aristocracy; the fields were tilled by Maeotian serfs or slaves. Greek merchants operated industrial and commercial enterprises in the cities. Sarmatians later entered the cities and fused with the ruling class already there. In Roman times the kingdom of the Bosporus became a "Hellenized Oriental autocracy," whose ruling family was Iranian. The king was attended by courtiers with pompous titles, drawn from an aristocracy which filled all government posts and monopolized ownership of land and business ventures. Greek members of the upper class were content to hold down financial appointments in the government and to dominate trade interests. There was only one other class, that of the serfs and slaves who labored in urban industry, manned the docks and warehouses, and tilled the soil.

The grain, sown and reaped by armies of serfs who received a dole of the crop, was sold by the king and temple priests and other landowners to Greek shipowners, who exported it to the south shore of the Black Sea or to the Mediterranean. Pottery and glass, gold and silver ornaments, leather goods, and implements produced in Bosporan and particularly in Panticapaean factories were traded to Scythians and others for the wheat, hides, furs, honey, and slaves brought in from areas beyond Bosporan control. Products of local or Mediterranean' manufacture were exchanged for the spices and other luxury goods brought out of Central Asia by caravans, for the Scythians and particularly the Sarmatians kept their contacts with their original homeland. Tombs of Bosporans, of which thousands have been opened, yield ornaments, garments, weapons, and coins of Panticapaean, Aegean, and Asiatic make in such rich profusion as to suggest that many Bosporans were extremely wealthy.

The Kingdom on the Bosporus down to the Age of Pericles was a powerful Hellenizing force in the Russian steppe. With the decline of the Scythian state and the surge of barbarian power that succeeded that decline, there was a waning of Greek influence. Rome restored the Bosporan kingdom and for two more centuries Greek civilization was again influential in the steppe. But with Rome's withdrawal Greek culture was submerged in the flood of Iranian influence. The outgrowth was a fusion of Greek and Iranian, particularly Sarmatian, cultural strands—a fusion that still provided the steppe with a high degree of civilization to pass on to succeeding waves of barbarian invasion. For twelve centuries, from 600 B.C. to A.D. 600, the Bosporan kingdom was a significant force in South Russia.

THE GOTHS (200–370)

Population pressure in Scandinavia in the first century A.D. forced the Germanic people known as the Goths to emigrate to the valley of the Vistula. Toward the end of the second century these Goths moved southeast into the region of the lower Dnieper, perhaps in search of more land to accommodate their growing numbers. Some of them crossed the Dnieper in the vicinity of Kiev and moved south into both the Crimea and the Kuban valley. Those who remained on the right bank of the Dnieper continued down the river to its mouth and on down the seacoast to the Danube. The name of Visigoths, or West Goths, came to be attached to those tribes which settled between the Dniester and the Danube. The Ostrogoths, or East Goths, settled farther east along the north shore of the Black Sea.

By the year 250 the north coast of the Black Sea was under Gothic control. The Roxolans were conquered or pushed eastward, although the Sarmatian tribe of Alans, settled in the Dnieper-Volga area, seems to have been undisturbed and to have maintained friendly relations with the Goths. The former Greek colonies of Olbia and Panticapaeum were not destroyed, but apparently were used as bases for Gothic attacks against Roman power in the Balkans and in the Aegean. Being preeminently a seafaring people, the Goths took full advantage of the Russian rivers and the Black Sea to plunder Roman settlements in the area. Their relations with Rome were frequently peaceful and commercial, however. The trade which had long focused in South Russia continued under the new masters of the steppe. By the beginning of the fourth century, furthermore, the Goths accepted the religion of the Romans and became Christians.

The various Gothic tribes, and particularly those in the eastern steppe, seem to have maintained their local independence until the middle of the fourth century. Then Ermenrich, or Hermanric, was chosen king of all the Ostrogoths and set out, after firmly uniting his own people, to conquer the surrounding territory. In a generation's time he built an empire which stretched from the Kuban to the Dniester and north to the Baltic. Ostrogothic power waned as quickly as it grew, however, for it was swept away about 370 by another surge of nomad immigration from Central Asia.

THE HUNS (370–558)

The grassy steppeland of South Russia extends from the Carpathians eastward nearly to the Altai-Sayan mountains, narrowing in a wedge as it passes beyond the Urals into Asia. This grassland was an inviting highway to nomadic herdsmen, and the Scythians and the Sarmatians in turn had followed it into the Black Sea area. Looking out over this sea of grass in A.D. 360, guards posted on the heights along the west bank of the Volga might have watched the approach of another horde of nomads. First to appear would have been scouting parties, feeling out the way, preventing surprise, and searching for river crossings; then the main body of horsemen; far back, and moving less resolutely, herds of cattle and horses; in the rear, the wagons carrying the women and children. These were the Huns, who crossed the Volga in 360 and attacked the Alans, the Sarmatian tribe living west of the river. The Huns were Turkic peoples, but they had conquered various Mongol and Ugrian tribes in their progress westward and forced the vanquished to join the migration.

The Alans were defeated. Some of them were absorbed into the conquering group while others escaped, some to the Kuban valley to the south, others to the west and north into the forest zone. Those Alans who were drafted into the service of the Hunnic khan were forced to serve as the advance guard of the westward-moving Huns. The whole force pushed on against the Ostrogoths, a small band of whom sought refuge in the Crimean peninsula and accepted Hunnic rule, while most of them fled west to the Dniester. The Ostrogoths in turn pressed against their kinsmen the Visigoths, who obtained from the Roman emperor permission to cross the Danube and find sanctuary inside the empire. So began the period of "the great migrations" of the German tribes, a movement provoked by fear of the Hunnic invaders from Asia.

The Huns settled down in the Russian steppe and for two generations quietly enjoyed its bounty. Shortly after the turn of the fifth century, however, they were again on the move and drove into the Danube valley and the Hungarian plain. Under the great leader Attila, Hunnic power was consolidated from the Caucasus to the middle Danube. Constantinople paid him heavy tribute, the Roman emperor in the west sought his favor, and the khan even considered marrying the emperor's sister.

In 451 Attila moved to attack Roman power in France, counting as vassals and allies in his army Alans, Visigoths, Vandals, and Franks. Indeed, Russia was "swept clean of her German, Iranian and Mongolian inhabitants" to swell his conquering host. Near Troyes, southeast of Paris, he was defeated by a Roman force, strongly supported by Germans, and withdrew to the middle Danube whence he had come. The following year he invaded Italy, but was prevailed upon by the pope and delegates from the emperor to return to the Danube. With the death of Attila in 453 the Hunnic empire dissolved. Some of the Huns settled in the Balkans, accepting service in the Roman army, while others withdrew east of the Carpathians to surge briefly to power again under the name of Bulgars. During the rest of the fifth century and the first half of the sixth, they appear alternately, from their headquarters between the Don and the Dnieper, as harriers of the eastern empire and as allies of the Roman emperor in his efforts to suppress uprisings among his German subjects.

In 558 a formidable force of Bulgars attacked Constantinople by land and by sea, and so likely seemed the prospect of the capital's fall that the emperor was forced to buy off the invaders. Then the Bulgars hurried back to their home on the north coast of the Black Sea. Word had come that a new horde of nomads was pouring out of the east.

THE AVARS (558–650)

The Avar horde which moved into the Russian steppe in 558 was made up of Turkic and Mongolian tribes. Its fighting force may have numbered no more than twenty thousand, but the use of stirrups made the Avar more difficult to unseat and consequently gave him an advantage over European horsemen. It was the Avar who introduced the stirrup into Europe.

The new force moved sternly against the Bulgars in the steppe; indeed, it was paid by the eastern emperor for doing so. In three years' time the Avars had brought the Bulgars under their rule, and had pushed on to the Dniester and then to the Danube. They established their headquarters in the area of the middle Danube, and from there they ruled over the entire area between the Volga and the Hungarian plain. During the last quarter of the sixth century and the first quarter of the seventh, the Avars constituted the most serious threat to the security of Constantinople. Avar raids south of the Danube constantly threatened the emperor's hold on the Balkans.

The height of Avar power was reached in 626, when they laid siege to Constantinople. An epidemic which decimated the attacking host forced its retirement, and the Avars returned to their camp on the Danube. The peoples whom they had subjugated recovered their independence, and the Avar state was swept away. There is a Russian saying, "they perished like the Avars," which refers to the complete vanishing of a sometime conqueror.

THE KHAZARS (650–737)

There was a momentary resurgence of Bulgar power in the Russian steppe after the withdrawal of the Avars, but with the death of the leader, Kurt by name, who had reunited the various tribes, the Bulgars again separated into independent communities and scattered. One group drifted into the middle Danube and there joined the remnant of the Avars. Another settled in northern Italy. A third moved to the lower Danube. Still another remained in the lower Don valley and accepted the overlordship of the new masters of the eastern steppe, the Khazars. From the standpoint of the history of Russia, the most important segment migrated to the middle Volga and settled around the mouth of the Kama. There they gathered under their authority the loosely organized Finnish tribes of the area and gained control of western Siberia as well.

In the area between the Kuban valley and the lower Volga there appeared in the seventh century a new political power, that of the Khazars.

The Khazars were a Turkic people, with a heavy admixture of Sarmatian, Ugrian, and Hunno-Bulgar blood. They had once been part of the main Turkish nation centering in Turkestan, but seceded and set up an independent state known as the Khazar kaganate or khanate on the north slope of the Caucasus and around the head of the Caspian. These nomads, like the many who had gone before, kept to the grassland where their herds could find pasturage but, by bringing firm rule and peace to all the area under their control, they set the conditions in which trade could prosper.

With the founding of the Mohammedan religion and the erection of the Arabian Empire, the Khazar state was hard pressed to defend itself against the crusading zeal of the Moslems. However, the rapid expansion of the Arab caliphate may have been of indirect service to the peoples on the north shore of the Black Sea. The eastern empire was trimmed to a modest size and limited to Asia Minor and the Balkans south of the Danube. In seeking to defend itself by fostering war among the various peoples of the steppe, the eastern or Byzantine Empire had promoted perennial unrest in South Russia.

The Khazar state between the Caucasus and the Volga was in an admirable position to profit from the trade routes which crossed its territory. Arab merchants brought to the markets in Khazaria the riches of Persia and of China, and exchanged them for the food, horses, and forest products —wax, honey, and fur, particularly marten and sable—which came down the Volga from the Volga Bulgars. The trade along the Volga extended over its upper reaches even to the Baltic, from which the Vikings from Scandinavia had been exploring the Russian river system as early as the sixth century. The peace which the Khazar power brought to the lower Volga did much to encourage agriculture in the region, but the primary concern of the khan was to foster the trade which moved back and forth over the land and water routes threading his territory and from the taxing of which he profited so richly.

While the center of Khazar power rested between the Caucasus and lower Volga, a loose hegemony extended over European Russia far to the north and west. Local autonomy was enjoyed by the various tribes in the western steppe and by the disorganized bands of Finns in the Oka and the upper Volga, but these areas recognized the suzerainty of the Khazar state upon which they depended for goods and markets. Khazar rule seems to have been particularly mild. While the Khazars themselves embraced Judaism, they never sought to impose their religion upon subject peoples. Christian churches and Moslem mosques, as well as Jewish synagogues, were to be found in their cities. In the capital, Itil, near modern Astrakhan, judges tried cases by Moslem, Jewish, Christian, or pagan law or practice, according to the nationality of the offender or the offended. Cordial relations were maintained with neighboring states—with the Byzantines at

Constantinople, the Turks in Turkestan, and the Volga Bulgars at the mouth of the Kama. Peace encouraged a free flow of goods, and trade brought the khan rich income from customs.

In the late seventh and early eighth centuries the Khazars were involved in war with the Arabs, who were seeking to cross the Caucasus into the Russian steppe at the same time that they were pushing across the Pyrenees into France. In the ninth century the Khazar state was threatened by the rise of a new power in the steppe, that of the Slavs.

THE SLAVS (500 B.C.–A.D. 737)

Until recently the idea, given wide currency by Pan-Slav enthusiasts, was popular that all Slavic peoples once spoke a common, parent language and originated in a common homeland, supposed to have been between the Carpathians, the Vistula, and the Dnieper. From this ancestral homeland the Slavs were supposed to have moved west into central and east central Europe, south into the Balkans, and east into Russia, and so to have given rise to the East Slav, West Slav, and South Slav branches of the Slavic nation. The work of modern scholars, Russian and American chiefly, has overthrown this misconception and has laid a scientific basis for an understanding of the history of the early Slav, and particularly the East Slav, or Russian, peoples. The earliest evidence shows that the ancestors of the Slavs were settled in ancient times in distinct areas and probably even then were speaking separate dialects.

At the beginning of the Christian era the Slavic peoples were settled roughly in three large linguistic and cultural groups: the West Slavs, residing along the middle and upper Vistula in what is now central Poland; the Middle Slavs, who were settled between the east slope of the Carpathians and the middle Dnieper; and the East Slavs, grouped in the Don valley and in the triangle between modern Kursk, Kharkov, and Voronezh. The evidence suggests that these three branches of Slavs had been located in those areas for at least five centuries before the birth of Christ. Through the millenium between 500 B.C. and A.D. 500 the population increased rapidly, and the Slavs moved out to the north, east, and west. By the latter date they were to be found in every corner of what is now European Russia, with perhaps the exception of the tundra zone in the north. Much of central Russia into which they migrated, particularly the Oka and middle and upper Volga valleys, was also inhabited by scattered tribes of Finns.

The successive waves of political control which passed over South Russia affected the lives of the native population only slightly. The people kept to their customs and worked the soil, contacting the ruling foreigner perhaps only when the taxgatherer or the merchant came round. Occasionally

Slavs were drafted into the armies of the ruler, particularly in Hunnic times. But by and large the lives of the native inhabitants went on quite apart from those of the nomads who fought for the pasture, for control of the trade routes, and for the power to levy tribute upon the peaceful agriculturists. There was, of course, some intermarriage, and each new wave of conquerors added its mite to the main blood strain of the Slavs.

The Middle and East Slavs, then, are the ancestors of the Russians. At first these Slavic tribes lived chiefly along the northern edge of the steppe, with some small groups edging south into the grassland and others drifting north into the forest zone. Culturally, they were in the Iron Age, for at the turn of the Christian era the Slavs were mining their own ore and smelting their own iron. Those who lived on rich soil were tilling the land; those in the forest hunted and gathered honey and mushrooms and planted small patches in the clearings; those on the grassy steppe were herdsmen; all fished, for the Slavs settled along the rivers and traveled over them in canoes. From the beginning the Russians have been a "river-folk" (Kerner), in contrast to the nomads who ruled the steppe, who kept to the high ground and the watersheds and who were satisfied simply to control the rivers over which trade moved.

During the Cimmerian and Scythian periods the basic population of the steppe and the southern forest zones was Slav. Slav farmers tilled the soil and raised the produce, especially the wheat, which in Scythian times was exported to Greece in such volume. Taxes in kind were levied upon the farming population by the Scythian taxgatherers, and the grain found its way into the markets of the Greek colonies along the north shore of the Black Sea, whence it was shipped to Athens.

The chief tribe among the Sarmatians, who controlled the steppe between 200 B.C. and A.D. 200, was that of the Alans. Some of the clans in this tribe were called the *Rukhs-As,* or Light *As.* At the time of Alanic supremacy the most important group among the East Slavs, who were subjects of the Alans, were the Antes. Some of the Antes took from their conquerors the name of *Rukhs-As,* which later was corrupted into *Rus,* hence Russian. By the beginning of the third century the Antes tribe of the East Slavs had become so numerous that it stretched over the steppe from the Donets to the mouth of the Danube. The appearance of the Goths in the Dnieper valley at that time split the Antes into an eastern and a western branch. It was the eastern branch that took the name of the Alanic clans which ruled it, the *Rukhs-As* or *Rus.*

The Goths brought the East Slavs of the steppe under their rule and forced them to take part in some of their forays. Maritime raids against the Roman power in the Balkans and in the Aegean frequently were carried out in boats built by the Slavs at Gothic command. For two centuries the East Slavs were ruled by various Gothic bands, culminating in the union of most of them in the Gothic Empire, reaching from the Black Sea to the Baltic, welded together after the year 350 by Ermenrich.

The Hunnic invasion in 360, which struck terror into the hearts of the Alans and the Goths who then controlled the steppe, had the curious effect of liberating the East Slavs. The overpowering by the Huns of the rulers of South Russia freed the Slavs from the possibility of being Germanized by the Goths or Iranized by the Alans. Both Goths and Alans fled westward or were drafted into Hunnic service. Slavs, too, were forced into the armies of the Huns, and in that service acquired military knowledge of which they thus far had been ignorant.

With the collapse of Hunnic power following upon the death of Attila in 453, Antic or East Slav power surged to the fore. Slavs attacked the Roman Empire along the Danube, and detachments of them broke through and drove to the Aegean and the Adriatic. An independent west Antic state— the first Slav state—was established between the Dnieper and the Danube. At times when relations with the Byzantine Empire were friendly, Antic soldiers served as mercenaries in and Antic generals even led imperial armies. At other times the Slavs raided deep into the Balkans and on several occasions attacked Constantinople itself.

The presence of a powerful force on his borders was not to the emperor's liking, and when the Avars appeared out of the east in 558 they were hired to attack the Antic power in the western steppe as well as the Bulgar power in the eastern steppe. The Avars swept away the west Antic state which had prospered since the Hunnic collapse. The Slavs were badly beaten, and the western branch of the Antes, at least, was forced to accept Avar rule. As vassals of their new overlord, Slav armies continued their attacks on the eastern empire, while Slav farmers were forced to raise food for the Avars. The eastern branch of the Antes, living east of the Dnieper, managed to remain independent of Avar rule, but occasionally joined the Avars as allies in attacks upon Constantinople.

By the beginning of the Khazar period, the East Slavs or Russians, as they may now be called, were settled thickly over the South Russian steppe, and considerable numbers of them were to be found in the forest zone as well. Mingling there with the Lithuanian and Finnish peoples native to central and northern Russia, the Slavs who settled in the forest zone acquired some of the physical features of the peoples, particularly of the Finns, with whom their stock was blended. In settling in the forest zone, too, the Slavs adapted themselves to the economic opportunities which the region afforded. They used the vast river system of central Russia to exploit the resources of the forest for the purpose of trade with the Volga Bulgars and with the Arab merchants who travelled the lower Volga. The peace in the Volga basin which the Khazar hegemony assured encouraged the Slavs, both of the steppe and of the forest, to take full advantage of the opportunity to trade. The reputation of the Russian as a trader, which continued into the twentieth century, may have had its origin in the Khazar period.

Early in the eighth century Khazar power was seriously curbed by attacks from north and from south. In 737 the Arabs invaded from the south, overran the Kuban and lower Don valleys, and carried twenty thousand Slavs into captivity. Even earlier the Vikings had begun to inch their way into what is now Russia, and by 737 they had reached the headwaters of the Donets. Their appearance in the land heralded a new epoch in Russian history. With the arrival of the Vikings the history of ancient Russia came to an end.

SUGGESTED READING

McGovern, W. M., *The Early Empires of Central Asia* (Chapel Hill, University of North Carolina Press, 1939).

Minns, E. H., *Scythians and Greeks* (New York, Macmillan, 1913).

Rostovtzeff, M., *Iranians and Greeks in South Russia* (Oxford, Clarendon, 1922).

Runciman, S., *A History of the First Bulgarian Empire* (London, Bell, 1930).

Vasiliev, A. A., *The Byzantine Empire* (Madison, University of Wisconsin Press, 1929).

———, *The Goths in the Crimea* (Medieval Academy of America, 1936).

Vernadsky, G., *Ancient Russia* (New Haven, Yale University Press, 1943).

4

Kievan Russia[*]

THE EAST SLAVS WERE WIDELY AND thickly settled in the forest and wooded steppe zones of what is now Russia by the beginning of the eighth century. As heirs to the Iranian, Greek, German, and Turkic civilizations that had centered in South Russia since 1000 B.C., they received a rich heritage of political and economic experience. Naturally a river folk themselves, the Slavs had had long acquaintance with the importance of waterways in commerce. They took over and maintained the urban trade centers along the Dnieper, Don, upper Volga, and Volkhov, and goods continued to move over the rivers of North and South Russia and over the great highway link with Central Asia and China. The towns in Russia continued to flourish and to enjoy the rich cultural advantages which commerce made possible. The Slavs who lived in rural areas followed a more primitive pattern of existence. Agriculture, apiculture, hunting, and fishing meant ceaseless toil and little reward, particularly as the profit from exchanging their products went chiefly to the city merchants and the tribute-gatherers.

Russia in the eighth century was a confederation of city-states, each city controlling a surrounding area whose trade it dominated and from whose rural inhabitants it wrung taxes in kind. Each town was governed by an assembly of its citizens, through a council of elders and elected administrative officials, the power probably resting in an oligarchy of its wealthier merchants. The organization of the countryside followed a loose, primitive tribal pattern and stood in sharp contrast to the political order which town life and trade promoted. To protect its commerce from encroachment by

[*] The chapters on Kievan Russia owe much to the many works of Professor George Vernadsky, and especially to his *Ancient Russia* and *Kievan Russia*.

42

other cities, from Viking raids from the Baltic, from pressure by steppe nomads, and from uprising by the rural subject population, the towns in the ninth century invited, or hired, bands of Scandinavian warriors led by their own prince to take over the tasks of defense and sometimes of administration, thus leaving the citizens free to pursue their primary interest, trade. The leader of one of these bands brought all the Russian cities under a single rule, and so established a new state with its capital on the Dnieper river at Kiev.

Imposition of foreign military rule over the commercial and agricultural populations in the Russian land was not new. The nomads had similarly organized South Russia for centuries. A military minority of Cimmerians, Scythians, Sarmatians, Goths, Huns, and Khazars had served successively as organizers of the land, and each in turn had maintained the peace which made possible the cultivation of the soil and the trade which flowed into and through the area over the natural highways with which it was so well endowed. The subject peoples in each case had worked the land and had paid their masters a tithe of the food raised, of the wax and honey gathered, and of the skins and hides produced. Some had fought in the ruler's army; others had been sold as slaves in the markets of Constantinople. The wealth which came to the nomad conquerors was never the product of their own toil. As producers they never had contributed more than the meat and milk of their own herds. The luxury they enjoyed was the fruit of the toil of subject peoples and of the trade which brought into their markets the goods of the Baltic, the Russian hinterland, China, Persia, and the Aegean and Mediterranean worlds. The trade raised cities to house it, and so it is not surprising that when the Slavs succeeded to the political control of the Russian land they acquired a ready-made urban civilization.

The land was politically organized, then, more or less successfully by the Cimmerians, by the Scythians, and by the Sarmatians. Anarchy followed the appearance of the Goths, but Ermenrich made a serious effort to organize European Russia when he united the Black Sea and Caspian lands with the Baltic in the middle of the fourth century. Shortly after his death the Huns organized the area, and finally the Khazars brought the land under their control in the period just preceding the rise of East Slav power. The Slavs inherited, as had their predecessors, the cities and the commerce which had been thriving for centuries. The culture to which they succeeded was that of the Greeks and Iranians who had laid its foundations, modified by the geo-social environment peculiar to the area and by the continuing cultural stimulation from the Orient and the Mediterranean to which the area had been subjected.

The Scandinavians, or Varangians as the Russians called them, soon showed themselves much better organizers than the Slavs. The state they built was strong and vigorous. Under its protection the Russian merchants returned to Constantinople, one terminus of their water-road "from the Varangians to the Greeks." Trade with the Orient and the Arabs through the Khazar state, with the Baltic through Varangian contacts, and with the Finno-Slav interior through the hegemony that was soon established over the area, assured Kievan Russia a sound and rich economic basis. The Varangians soon were drowned in the Slavic sea, and in a century's time Scandinavian names disappear among the rulers of Russia.

The Kievan period is one of transition from ancient to modern history of the Russian land, and one of transition from Mediterranean to Russian or Muscovite focus. Kievan Russia is the last of the commercial empires which had flourished since 1000 B.C., and at the same time it is the progenitor of the East Slav state on the upper Volga which was to develop into modern Russia.

THE RUSSIAN KAGANATE

By the middle of the eighth century population pressure crowded some of the Germanic peoples out of their homeland in the Scandinavian peninsula. Those who attacked western Europe were known as Vikings, a name that came to be synonomous with scourge and depredation. Those who moved east the Russians called Varangians or *Variags*.

The south and east coast of the Baltic had been scouted by the Varangians for two centuries. Before 600 a colony of them was established at the mouth of the Western Dvina, and by 700 Livonia and Estonia were incorporated into the kingdom of South Sweden. From this bridgehead on the eastern shore of the Baltic the Varangians moved up the Dvina and even portaged into the Volga and Oka. Circling the strong and well-defended Slavic city of Novgorod, they found little opposition farther east and southeast and soon were trading with the unorganized Finns scattered thinly over the area. But the way was blocked in the middle Volga by the powerful Volga Bulgars, and the Slav tribes in the neighborhood of Smolensk discouraged any attempt to enter the Dnieper. An alternative was to enter the Oka, on which Varangian trading posts were set up shortly after 700. From the Oka and its tributaries the way lay open to the Don and the Donets.

A band of Scandinavians drifted down the Donets and the Don to the Sea of Azov, which they reached in 739, and a detachment moved into the Kuban valley. They were in search of a highway to the Orient, from which the flow of goods into Europe had temporarily been cut off by Arab expansion. The small trading state which the Varangians organized in the lower Don and on the Sea of Azov came to be known as Great Sweden, or Tmutorokan, after the name of its capital. The peoples they subjugated were the *Rukhs-As,* or *Rus;* in time the Scandinavians took the name of their vassals and called themselves *Rus*, or Russians, and their state the Russian kaganate.

With the founding of Great Sweden on the lower Don and its expansion into the North Caucasus, the trade link between the Baltic and the Orient was re-established. An Arab writer of the ninth century tells of "Russian" traders who gathered together the products of every corner of their land and brought them down the Don, thence to the Caspian, and by camel caravan even into the markets of Bagdad, where the chronicler himself had seen them. Many a Norse merchant grew wealthy from the Oriental trade. Many of them chose to live and die in the steppe, but others, after making a fortune, retired to Scandinavia to spread tales of the wealth to be gained from the traffic that moved over the Russian river system. *Variag,* the name by which the Vikings were known in Russia, means trader or peddler.

Scandinavians or "Russians" from Tmutorokan were in touch with Constantinople before 840, and others joined with Prince Oleg of Kiev in forcing a treaty from the Byzantine emperor in 911. Occasionally the state was on good terms with Byzantium, and there is evidence of "Russian" ships and men serving in the imperial navy.

The Russian kaganate, or Great Sweden, or Tmutorokan, as it is variously called, continued to prosper and expand. Its population increased as new bands of emigrants from the Scandinavian peninsula came to seek a share in the trade which dealt in the luxury goods of the East and in the furs of the Russian hinterland. By 800 this state on the Sea of Azov, with its control over the waters all the way to the Baltic, may have been comparable in wealth and strength to the states of the Volga Bulgars and the Khazars. Contacts between the Swedes on the Sea of Azov and the Slav tribes settled along the water route between the Baltic and the lower Don must have been frequent, mutually advantageous, and usually cordial. Arab writers, however, remark that the *Rus* often attacked the Slavs and seized prisoners whom they sold to the Khazars.

With the subsidence of Arab pressure in the eighth century, the Khazar state recovered its freedom of action and sought to bring back under its control the Russian kaganate which had declared its independence. Khazars and Byzantines joined to exert pressure upon Great Sweden, and the Scandinavian *Rus* were hemmed into a small pocket around their capital Tmutorokan, on the Taman peninsula. The Khazars recovered control of the steppe as far west as Kiev and regained commercial hegemony over the forest zone of the upper Volga and the eastern Baltic. Envoys sent from Tmutorokan to seek an alliance with the Byzantine emperor against the Khazars were received coolly in Constantinople, and the Russian kaganate took its vengeance by a raid upon Byzantine territory in 840. A generation later another expedition carried the attack to the very walls of Constantinople. On this occasion the forces of the Russian kaganate were joined by another Russo-Scandinavian band, which in the meantime had appeared in the valley of the Dnieper.

THE EAST SLAVS AND THEIR NEIGHBORS IN THE NINTH CENTURY

Early in the ninth century the East Slav peoples were scattered over the forest and steppe between the Baltic, the lower Volga, and the Black Sea. They were grouped in tribes, each of which governed itself free from any higher Slav authority, although most of them lived in some degree of subjection, political or economic, to Khazar, *Rus,* or other non-Slav power.

Perhaps the most numerous of the East Slav tribes in South Russia was that of the Poliane, a name meaning "people of the steppe." In the ninth century they were living in the lower Dnieper between Kiev and the cataracts. Earlier they had controlled the mouth of the river, but the Magyars, a Hunnic remnant, held the Dnieper below the rapids for a century between 800 and 900, when they were driven west by the appearance in the steppe of a new horde of nomads, the Pechenegs, from Central Asia. The Poliane were noted for their ability to work iron tools and weapons; they were particularly famous for their double-edged swords. The author of the *Primary Chronicle,* one of the earliest Russian historical sources, reports that when the Khazars came to exact tribute from the Poliane, the latter offered to pay in swords. The Khazar khan was warned against the levy, his advisers reminding him, "[Some day] these men shall impose tribute upon us."

West of the Poliane, in the valleys of the Bug and Dniester, were the Ulichi and the Tivertsi. To their west, in the valley of the lower Danube, lay the khanate of Bulgaria, whose southern neighbor was Byzantium and whose western neighbor was the empire of the Franks, which Charlemagne had pushed to the vicinity of modern Belgrade.

Northwest of Kiev and south of the Pripyat river lived the Drevliane, or "forest people," and to their north, across the Pripyat, were the Dregovichi. These tribes residing in the marshes of the area seem to have been poor in comparison to the Poliane, who lived in the fertile steppe, and indeed the people of that area have always been among the poorest and most backward of the East Slavs.

Just inside the forest zone, in the valley of the Desna northeast of Kiev, lived the Radimichi. The valley of the Donets was occupied by the Severiane. With the coming of the Pechenegs, the Severiane were pushed out of the steppe into the forest to the northwest, and the Radimichi were forced to move into the upper Dnieper south of Smolensk. The upper Don was the land of the Viatichi. The mouth of that river, as of the Kuban, was con-

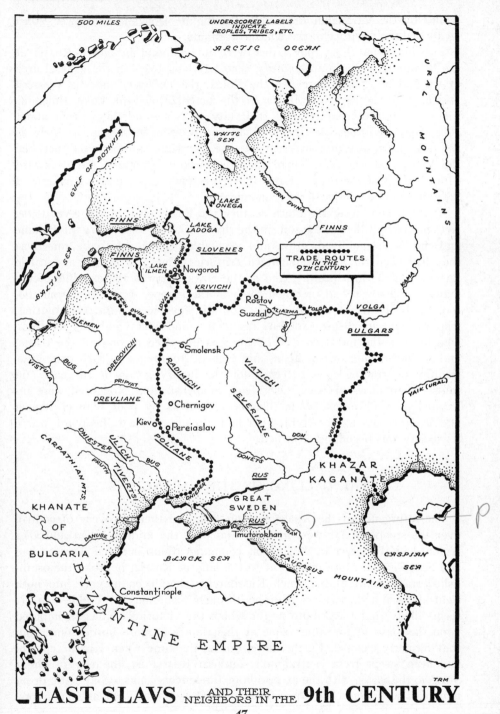

EAST SLAVS AND THEIR NEIGHBORS IN THE **9th CENTURY**

trolled by the Varangian *Rus,* while the middle Don and the lower Volga comprised the territory of the Khazar kaganate.

Two important East Slav tribes were to be found in North Russia at the beginning of the ninth century. The Krivichi dwelt in the general area of the Valdai Hills, where rise the Volga, the Dnieper, and the Western Dvina. The Slovene were living in the neighborhood of Lake Ilmen as early as the fifth century, and their city of Novgorod dates from about 600. From these localities the Krivichi and the Slovene began, as early as the seventh century, to move east into the "Russian Mesopotamia" between the Volga and the Oka. There they displaced or subdued the backward Finnish clans of the region. Later they themselves came under Khazar and Scandinavian control, at least economically.

At the beginning of the ninth century the East Slavs, of whatever tribe, were primarily tillers of the soil. In the rich black-soil zone where the Poliane and the Severiane lived, grain and vegetables continued to be raised as they had been for at least eighteen centuries. Herds of horses and cattle fattened on the lush pasture land as the Slavs followed the example of the many peoples who had preceded them in the steppe. Agriculture went on, too, in the clearings of the forest, for all Slavs were farmers. Hunting, trapping, and apiculture added meat and furs and honey and wax for those who lived in the forest zone. Weaving was practised among all the tribes, and all forged their own weapons and tools of iron. Some in each tribe grew wealthy by trading raw materials for the luxury goods of the east and south. Their cities of Kiev, Chernigov, Smolensk, and Novgorod were inhabited by well-to-do Slav merchants as well as by poor Slav craftsmen and laborers. East Slav civilization had already reached the point where its society was becoming stratified.

THE CALLING OF THE VARANGIANS

The resurgence of the Khazars about 840, and their recovery of control over the steppe as far west as Kiev and over the middle Volga and Oka region, had the effect of cutting off communications between Tmutorokan and Scandinavia. More important to the land of Russia, it broke the established trade relations by which Russian furs had been moving into both Central Asia and northern Europe through Scandinavian middlemen. It seems likely that the tribute in fur which the victorious Khazars imposed upon the Slavs of the forest zone at this time was more burdensome than that formerly exacted. Furthermore, during the time when Khazar control had been swept from central and southern Russia by the rise of Great Sweden, the Slavs, with the exception of the Slovene, had to pay little or no tribute. The Vikings had come into the land as traders, not as conquerors.

The Slovenian capital Novgorod, situated in an area which the Vikings managed to retain, suffered through the severance by the Khazars of its connection with the Oka region, from which it drew much of its food supply.

The slow strangulation of Novgorod made imperative a campaign to reopen its supply route to the Oka and its trade route to the south and southeast. The most promising solution was to invite a force of Vikings, who had their own grievance against the Khazars in the restraint imposed upon the Scandinavian state on the Sea of Azov, to lead the attack against the khan of Khazaria. This, then, was the situation leading to the "calling of the Varangians."

The invitation sent to the Varangians by the Slav tribes of the Slovene and the Krivichi, and by the *Rus* or Varangian settlers and traders in the Lake Ilmen area, urged: "Our land is great and abundant but there is no order in it; come to rule and reign over us." The disorder may refer to unrest or even uprisings among the inhabitants of Novgorod because of the shortage of food and the stagnation of trade. Implicit in the invitation to "rule and reign over us" was the request to assume all the responsibilities connected with it, particularly to break the Khazar hold upon the land.

The man who accepted the call to assume the leadership of North Russia was Rurik, a Danish chieftain from Jutland who had had long and successful experience in leading raids against the coasts of England, France, and western Germany. In 856 Rurik led a band of Danes into North Russia. He stopped first at Ladoga at the mouth of the Volkhov river, edging his way cautiously into the country and watching anxiously his way of retreat. From Ladoga he moved on to Novgorod and soon brought the surrounding area under his rule. Like all the Scandinavians then in Russia, whether in the Novgorod area or on the Sea of Azov, Rurik and his followers became known as *Rus*, the name by which the Slavs had long been known but which came to apply as well to those who ruled over them.

Placing sub-chiefs in control of the neighboring towns and building castles at strategic points to fix his hold upon the land, Rurik settled down to enjoy his new acquisition. But he showed no disposition to undertake the campaign against the Khazars, which was the real reason he had been called to military and political leadership of North Russia. Impatient to restore the trade and supply routes, Askold and Dir, two leaders of the Swedish settlers in North Russia who had been living in the region long before Rurik's coming, sought and obtained Rurik's consent in 858 to lead an expedition to the south. Their intention was to restore communications with the Scandinavian state on the Sea of Azov. The established route by way of the Donets or the Don was blocked by the Khazars, and Askold and Dir were forced to search out a new path. They moved down the Dnieper and seized Kiev, only to find that its environs must be cleared of wild Pecheneg tribesmen from the east before the river could be followed to its mouth. Askold slew great numbers of the nomads upon his arrival in Kiev and managed to effect a reopening of the lower Dnieper.

Soon after their entry into Kiev, Askold and Dir sent word of their arrival to the "Russian" ruler in Great Sweden, and arrangements were made for a joint expedition against Constantinople. The attack was made in 860. A fleet from the Sea of Azov joined another from Kiev at the mouth of the Dnieper; the force slipped down the west coast of the Black Sea and landed near the walls of Constantinople before it was discovered. Their tarrying to pillage in the outskirts of the capital gave the emperor time to marshal his defenses, and the Russians were driven to their boats. A storm and the "Greek fire" employed by ships of the imperial navy took a heavy toll, and the attackers withdrew to Russia. The raid had two notable results, however. Contact had been established between the Scandinavian powers in western and southeastern Russia. And more important, the Vikings of the Dnieper water-road had enjoyed a taste of the wealth to be acquired by trade or plunder from Constantinople.

THE COMMERCIAL EMPIRE ON THE DNIEPER

Almost from the very moment of the coming of the Varangians, the line of development of the new state became clear. While efforts later were made to draw Tmutorokan into the Kievan orbit, the attention of the state on the Dnieper was primarily and almost exclusively focused upon Constantinople. This interest in the capital of the eastern empire was due to two factors. Firstly, Constantinople was geographically the obvious terminus of the water route that led from the Baltic to the Black Sea, "from the Varangians to the Greeks," as the chroniclers put it. Secondly, from the end of the fifth century to the beginning of the thirteenth, Constantinople, or Byzantium, was far and away the most important city in the European world. Commercially, it was without a peer until the rise of the cities of North Italy during the time of the Crusades. Culturally, it was the transmitter of the heritage of Greece and Rome. Religiously, the leadership of the eastern Mediterranean was hardly challenged until the eleventh century. Politically, the Byzantine Empire was the most important state in Europe until the sack of Constantinople by the Fourth Crusade. Constantinople's position as entrepôt of world trade, as warehouse for the silks of China and the spices of India, and as market where the raw materials of Russia found ready sale; Constantinople's position as spiritual leader of millions whose chief shrine was the Church of St. Sophia; Constantinople's position as tutor to those whose only contacts with the wisdom of the ancients had to come through Byzantium or from the Arabs; her position as capital of the state which mattered most in international affairs and whose diplomatic envoys commanded universal respect because of the power they represented—these things fascinated the rulers of Kievan Russia, who sought to turn Kiev and Novgorod into "little Constantinoples."

The newly organized state on the Dnieper enjoyed indirect contact with the other great civilizing power of the period, the Arab, through Byzantium and through the Volga Bulgars, who were Moslem.

OLEG, THE FOUNDER OF THE KIEVAN STATE

In 873 Rurik led his Danes back to Denmark to press his hereditary claim to a fief there, and he died two years later without returning to Novgorod. His interest in Russia had always been transitory. He never revealed any intention of attempting to drive back the Khazars, although he had tacitly committed himself to do so when he accepted the invitation to rule over the land.

Shortly after Rurik's departure for the west a new band of Varangians, this time Norwegians, swept into northwest Russia. Their leader, Oleg, established himself in Novgorod and was accepted as successor to Rurik as ruler of all the tribes in North Russia. It took him no more than five years to win the recognition of the Slavs and Scandinavians who inhabited the area. Then he set off at the head of a mixed band of his own followers and natives to re-establish contact with Kiev. Working his way deliberately down the Dnieper, he left detachments at Smolensk and other strategic points to establish his control and protect his rear. Arriving before Kiev, his boats were drawn up under the bank above the city, and Oleg sent word to its rulers that merchants from Smolensk wanted to trade. Askold and Dir came to the river bank unguarded to investigate, and were promptly killed by Oleg's followers. Oleg then took over the city and, as the *Primary Chronicle* relates, "set himself up as prince in Kiev." By that act the Kievan state was born.

Kiev immediately became the administrative center and the base from which Oleg set forth to unite forest and steppe, to bring the native tribes under his control, to restore contact with Tmutorokan, and to complete the conquest of the water road. Continuing the policy initiated by Rurik in North Russia, Oleg placed a trusted follower in control of each city, built forts and settled garrisons at strategic points, and pushed the conquest of those Slav tribes who did not voluntarily submit.

In the very year of his arrival in Kiev, Oleg subdued the Drevliane dwelling in the Pripyat marshes northwest of the new capital and forced them to agree to an annual tribute of furs. The Poliane accepted his rule from the moment of his disposal of Askold and Dir, whose authority they had earlier recognized. To open the way to the Scandinavian state on the

Sea of Azov, Oleg advanced against the Slav tribes east of the Dnieper, who at that time were under Khazar control. First in the way were the Severiane, who were defeated after what was probably a halfhearted show of resistance. Tribute was imposed upon them and they agreed to have no more to do with Khazaria. The Radimichi, dwelling northeast of Kiev, voluntarily deserted their Khazar overlords and transferred their tax payments to Oleg. Then the prince turned to the southwest against the Ulichi and the Tivertsi. These Slav tribes were supported by the Magyars, who were in control of the mouth of the Dnieper. When the Ulichi and Tivertsi were subdued is not known, although they took part in Oleg's attack upon Constantinople in 907. By the end of the century the Magyars had been driven out of South Russia and had moved into the area of modern Hungary. Their removal from the lower Dnieper completed the clearing of the water-road from the Baltic to the Black Sea.

By the end of the ninth century Oleg had made notable progress toward fulfilling the tasks which lay before him when he assumed the leadership of Russia. Many of the Slav tribes—the Krivichi, Slovene, Poliane, Drevliane, Severiane, Radimichi, and perhaps the Ulichi and Tivertsi—had been brought under his rule. Much of the forest and steppe had been united. Tenuous contact with Tmutorokan was now possible. The Dnieper lay open all the way to its mouth. There remained the task which probably had been foremost in Oleg's mind when he set out from Novgorod, namely the completion of the conquest of the water-road. This involved an expedition against Constantinople, not necessarily with the idea of capturing it or of putting it to sack, but of forcing the eastern empire to open its markets to Russian merchants.

Shortly after his arrival in Kiev Oleg made contact with the Russian kaganate on the Sea of Azov. Envoys from Kiev went to Tmutorokan to plan common action in the Black Sea area, and a small force sent by Oleg took part in an unsuccessful attack which the Russian kagan mounted against the Khazars. Naval detachments from Tmutorokan may later have accompanied Oleg in his raid upon Constantinople. It must be borne in mind that through the early Kievan period, down to the end of the tenth century, Tmutorokan was at least as powerful, commercially and politically, as was Kiev. It is for this reason that Oleg and his successors strove so persistently to maintain contact with the Russian kaganate on the Sea of Azov.

By 907 Oleg had consolidated his position at Kiev sufficiently to be ready for his most ambitious undertaking—an attack against the Byzantine Empire. A flotilla of two thousand boats moved from the Dnieper down the west coast of the Black Sea, while a cavalry force crossed the Danube and drove toward Constantinople. The Byzantines stretched chains across the Golden Horn and so kept the Russian boats out of the harbor. But Oleg countered by setting his boats on wheels and moving his force overland to a position under the city walls. Outmaneuvered and threatened with a serious defeat, the emperor agreed to a treaty of peace on Russian terms.

By the treaty of 907 the Byzantine emperor agreed to pay a sizeable indemnity and to set aside funds to provide hospitality for Russian traders coming to Constantinople. Each Russian city—Kiev, Pereiaslav, Liubech, and Smolensk on the Dnieper, Chernigov on the Desna, Polotsk on the Western Dvina, Rostov in the upper Volga, "and others,"—was assigned its own fund from which its merchants were to be cared for. Russian traders were to be allowed access to Byzantine markets without payment of customs and were to be fed and provided for during their stay in the capital. They agreed to remain in a suburb of Constantinople during their stay, from which they were to be escorted, fifty at a time and unarmed, inside the walls during trading hours. Their boats were to be stocked and provisioned for the voyage home at the emperor's expense. The seriousness of the Russian threat to Constantinople in the attack of 907 is evidenced by the favorable terms which Oleg received. Four years later a second treaty provided for punishment for crimes committed by citizens of each state against those of the other, regulated disposition of runaway slaves, and provided sanctuary for shipwrecked traders of both signatories.

Oleg's brilliant career set the Kievan state upon firm foundations. By the time of his death in 913, the water-road from the Baltic to Constantinople had been cleared, and the state he had founded was provided with a trade axis which would assure its future prosperity. A long step had been taken toward uniting the Slavs of the forest and steppe under a well-organized government whose early leaders had the vision to forsee the needs of the future.

IGOR CONTINUES THE WORK OF OLEG

Igor, who became Grand Prince of Kiev in 913, was Rurik's grandson. His youth was spent at Oleg's court, and Oleg arranged his marriage with a Slav girl bearing the Scandinavian name of Olga. Their son was given the Slavic name of Sviatoslav, and with his assumption of the princedom upon the death of Igor Scandinavian names disappear from the roster of those who ruled in Kiev.

In the first year of his reign Igor led an army to Tmutorokan to join the Russians there in an expedition down the west coast of the Caspian. The campaign seems to have been planned by Oleg, who was prevented by death from carrying it out. Before the combined operation could be launched, however, Igor received word that the Drevliane tribe had risen against him. With a small following he returned to Kiev, leaving the bulk of his army to carry on with the projected campaign. The Russian forces, made up of

Igor's troops and those of the kagan at Tmutorokan, plundered along the west coast of the Caspian and started home laden with booty. On the way they were attacked by the Khazars, and all but a few of Igor's men were wiped out.

The uprising of the Drevliane was put down by Igor, and tribute which Oleg had levied upon them was increased. Igor then had to face an attack by the Pechenegs. The main body of this new nomad horde from Central Asia had not yet crossed the Volga, but an advance party had driven through Khazar territory to the lower Dnieper region even in Oleg's time. Their attacks at the cataracts upon the merchant convoys which yearly floated down the Dnieper were becoming increasingly irritating, and Igor was forced to move against them. The Pechenegs agreed to a truce and moved on west to raid Bulgaria.

For a generation after his war with the Pechenegs, Igor spent his time perfecting his control over the subject tribes and marshalling his strength for further expansion. Little is known of the period, but apparently toward its close the Byzantine emperor abrogated the treaty of 907. To restore the commercial link with Constantinople was imperative to the survival of the Kievan state. Accordingly, in 941 Igor set out to punish the empire, and in cooperation with a force from Tmutorokan he raided the Byzantine provinces along the south coast of the Black Sea. The Russians were driven off by the imperial navy. They withdrew to Tmutorokan and from there moved to attack the Moslems on the southwest coast of the Caspian. Their purpose may have been to drive through to the west and so take the Byzantines in the rear. Whatever their intent, the expedition ended in failure as the Russians were surrounded and killed.

Igor now gathered a huge force for a campaign against Constantinople itself. A band of Pechenegs was persuaded to join him as allies. Contingents from the Slav tribes of the Krivichi, the Slovene, and the Tivertsi were gathered into his army. And a mercenary force from Scandinavia was brought to Kiev to take part in the project. At the head of this formidable array Igor set out for a land attack upon the eastern capital. On the banks of the Danube Igor was met by a delegation from the emperor with gifts and an offer of peace. Igor accepted both, and a new treaty was drawn up between Kiev and the Empire. By its terms trade was restored on the basis of the agreement of 907, except that Russian merchants now had to pay the customs exacted of all foreign traders in the capital. The treaty also recognized Kievan and Byzantine spheres of interest in the Crimean peninsula. Igor promised to respect and to protect the Byzantine colonies along the south shore of the peninsula, and the emperor agreed to assist him in subduing the tribes in the peninsula who were still under Khazar rule. The eastern tip of Crimea at this time was governed by the Russian kagan at Tmutorokan, who was Igor's ally.

Igor was slain by the Drevliane while on a tribute-gathering mission. During his reign Russian warriors had won respect in campaigns from the Caspian to the Danube. Of their appearance and conduct an Arab chronicler observed: "They are a mighty nation [people] with vast frames and great courage. They know not defeat, nor does any of them turn his back till he slay or be slain." Igor had established firm contact with the Russian state on the Sea of Azov, as Oleg had foreseen must be done. Trade relations with Constantinople had been restored after an interruption which had threatened to undo the work of Oleg. Revolt among the subject tribes had been put down, and Slavs had marched and sailed in common cause with Varangians.

OLGA UNDERTAKES REFORM

Because Igor's son Sviatoslav was only a child at the time of his father's death, the widow Olga succeeded to the throne of Kiev. Her reign is remarkable on two counts—for the administrative reforms she initiated and for her acceptance of Christian baptism.

Hoping to prevent the recurrence of such an incident as had cost her husband's life, Olga set about to reform the financial administration of the state. She ended the practice of gathering tribute from semi-autonomous local tribes. Heretofore the grand prince had journeyed annually to the land of each subject tribe and had seized the tribute imposed upon the tribe at the time of its subjugation. Some tribes had been placed under the administration of a lieutenant of the grand prince, but their identity had not been destroyed. Now the grand principality was divided into districts for financial administration, in each of which an agent from Kiev or a local board was assigned the responsibility of gathering taxes. Tribute, for which a whole tribe was responsible, gave way to rates levied upon individuals regardless of tribe. This move undermined the identity of the tribe, for tax purposes at least, and through the tax agents sent out from Kiev all districts were bound more firmly to the capital. In addition to increasing the efficiency of revenue collection, the effect of the reform was to reduce opposition to the overlordship of Kiev by weakening tribal consciousness.

By the middle of the tenth century many Russians, Varangians as well as Slavs, had probably been baptized. The intimate trade contact with Constantinople, by which scores of merchants annually visited the Byzantine capital and marveled at the splendor of its churches, was responsible for many conversions. Indeed, this trade contact paved the way for the eventual acceptance of Christianity by Kiev. The Byzantine colonies in the Crimea brought Russians in contact with Christianity, and there had been a Christian bishop at Tmutorokan for nearly a century before Olga's conversion. The

Slavs of Moravia and of Galicia, with whom Kiev maintained trade contacts, had long been Christian, and the Bulgars had been won over by 864. Missionaries both from Moravia and from Constantinople had appeared in Kiev even before its seizure by Oleg.

Olga was baptized in Kiev by missionaries from Constantinople in 955. It may only be surmised that she accepted Christianity as a matter of state policy. She may have hoped that more cordial economic and political relations with the eastern empire would grow out of her baptism. The nation, however, did not follow her, nor did her son Sviatoslav, in spite of her earnest attempt to persuade him.

Whether Oleg and Igor ever considered accepting Christianity is not known. There was good reason why they should not accept it, if they ever did give it serious thought. That reason lay in the fact that converts to the church headed by the patriarch of Constantinople must accept the authority of the patriarch in religious matters, and at the same time the eastern emperor demanded that his authority over the new converts be recognized in political matters. Whenever a pagan nation in the East accepted the new faith, there arose this question of religious and political subjection to Constantinople, the two going hand in hand. The only possibility of retaining political independence was through the patriarch's consent that the new converts might have their own autonomous church under an archbishop or a metropolitan bishop. The consent was never lightly given, and had to be wrung from the patriarch in each case. For example, the Bulgars for a time transferred their allegiance to the pope at Rome because the patriarch at Constantinople would not accede to their demands for an autonomous church. The patriarch was brought round and the Bulgars were given their own metropolitan bishop, whereupon they returned to the Eastern orbit.

This same problem of obtaining religious autonomy for Russia faced Olga after her conversion. She journeyed to Constantinople after her baptism to seek the appointment of a metropolitan bishop in Kiev, but her plea was turned down. She then resorted to the tactics the Bulgars had applied nearly a century earlier and asked the Holy Roman emperor, Otto I, to send priests and a metropolitan bishop to Kiev. Otto sent an ordinary bishop, with the implication that the Russian church in accepting him should accept a position subordinate to the German clergy. This Olga would not accept, and the status of the Russian church was left to be settled later. Olga's toying with the idea of accepting a religious tie with the West must have been only a ruse. Cordial economic relations with Constantinople were too vital to the Kievan state to permit their being endangered by a religious alliance with the West.

Olga's efforts to work out a satisfactory religious settlement with Constantinople met with failure at the time. However, her own conversion must have given considerable impetus to the trend away from paganism, and the stubbornness with which she held out for her own terms must have impressed upon Constantinople the need to compromise when the question of religious administration came up again.

SVIATOSLAV AND THE DREAM OF EMPIRE

His mother's failure to obtain concessions from Constantinople brought into popularity Sviatoslav and the pagan party which opposed the acceptance of Christianity. Olga stepped aside and Sviatoslav, now grown to manhood, became grand prince of Kiev in 962. Olga had carefully husbanded the resources of the state and had saved its manpower through nearly a generation of peace. For the next decade those reserves were to be put to use by her son in a succession of brilliant campaigns.

Sviatoslav first moved to incorporate Tmutorokan into the Kievan state, then to bring the lower Volga under his control, and finally to open the way to the Caspian and so to the trade of the Orient. First he advanced against the Khazars, driving them back from the lower Don and seizing their forts on that river. Then he swung south and brought the Kuban valley under his rule. Entering Tmutorokan he was hailed as the new ruler of the Russian kaganate on the Sea of Azov. To destroy Khazaria he must control the Volga, and to do that he must first subdue the Volga Bulgars. Proceeding deliberately and systematically, Sviatoslav first conquered the Slavic tribe of Viatichi, who dwelt in the valley of the upper Don. Then he pressed on against the Volga Bulgars and sacked their capital. While Sviatoslav was reorganizing for the expedition down the Volga to strike at the heart of Khazaria, an envoy from Constantinople came into camp to ask his help in curbing the Danubian Bulgars who were threatening the eastern empire. In return Sviatoslav was apparently offered a free hand in the Balkans, at least in the territory of the Bulgar khan, whose lands extended on both sides of the Danube. At the head of forty thousand men the grand prince of Kiev drove across the Danube and overran northern Bulgaria. The Bulgars appealed to the Pechenegs, the main host of which was still camped east of the Volga, for assistance against Sviatoslav. At about the same time the Khazars, fearful of the invincible Kievan prince, let down their defenses and invited the Pechenegs to move into the Russian steppe. The Pechenegs poured into Russia but, instead of proceeding against Sviatoslav, struck for Kiev and laid siege to his capital. Sviatoslav left part of his army in Bulgaria; with the rest he hurried back to Kiev and drove off its attackers.

To punish the Khazars for setting the Pechenegs upon him, Sviatoslav sent a powerful army to complete the destruction of Khazaria. The Russians proceeded first to the middle Volga and once more plundered the capital of the Volga Bulgars. Then moving downriver they attacked the Khazars, sacking their chief cities and thoroughly routing the forces sent against them. The Khazar state was swept away, leaving the Volga frontier unguarded against later invasions from Central Asia.

Back in Kiev Sviatoslav waited for news of the expedition against the Khazars. Once that campaign had been brought to a successful conclusion, Sviatoslav hoped to return to the Danube. So enamored of the Danube basin had the prince become that he made up his mind to shift his capital from Kiev to the lower Danube and to leave Russia to be governed by his sons. Announcing his intention to his mother Olga, he said, "I do not care to remain in Kiev, but should prefer to live in Pereiaslavets on the Danube, since that is the center of my realm, where all riches are concentrated: gold, silks, wine, and various fruits from Greece, silver and horses from Hungary and Bohemia, and from Russia furs, wax, honey, and slaves." His mother died a few days later, and Sviatoslav set out for the Danube after dividing the land of Russia among his sons, expecting never to return to Kiev.

Sviatoslav returned to Bulgaria and took up once more his successful raiding over the land south of the Danube. Now the Byzantines, seeing that the most serious threat to Constantinople was posed not by the Bulgars but by Sviatoslav, came to terms with the Bulgars and the two combined their forces against the Russians. Sviatoslav, outnumbered, lost several engagements and finally agreed to withdraw from Bulgaria and to surrender the entire Crimean peninsula to the emperor.

With the bitter loss of the land which he preferred to his own, Sviatoslav set out for Kiev. The Bulgars hurried word to the Pechenegs that the Russians were returning to the Dnieper, and the Pechenegs lay in wait at the cataracts. In the battle that ensued most of the Russians escaped through to Kiev, but Sviatoslav lost his life. His skull was fashioned into a drinking cup for use by the Pecheneg chieftain.

The ten years of Sviatoslav's short reign were packed with adventure. The state territory had been enormously increased. The trade possibilities of the area were seen perhaps more clearly by Sviatoslav than by any of the Kievan princes. The entire Russian steppe, from the Volga and the Kuban to the Danube, had been united. The Kama region and the valley of the lower Volga had been added to the principality, and the states which had shared with Kiev the control of the Russian land—Tmutorokan, the Volga Bulgars, and Khazaria—had been absorbed or swept away. Sviatoslav's successes were only temporary, however, and began to melt away even before his death. The Danubian lands were quickly won and as quickly lost. And the destruction of Khazaria later brought only grief, since its reduction left nothing to stem the flood of nomad invasion from the east.

VLADIMIR AND THE RUSSIAN CONVERSION

When Sviatoslav left Kiev to return to Bulgaria in 969, thinking to establish his capital permanently upon the Danube, he turned over the administration of certain districts in Russia to his three sons. Since he was killed on his way back to Kiev, his death left the land divided among his children. The eldest, Iaropolk, was ruling in Kiev; Oleg administered the lands of the Drevliane; the youngest, Vladimir, had been given Novgorod.

For the next five years the brothers warred over the succession. Oleg was killed in a war with Iaropolk, and Vladimir fled to Scandinavia to gather troops for an attack upon his oldest brother. Iaropolk was advised to call in the Pechenegs to back him, but he hesitated too long. Vladimir returned to Novgorod with a strong band of Varangians, enlisted parties of Slovene and Krivichi in North Russia, seized Polotsk and Smolensk, and advanced down the Dnieper to Kiev. Iaropolk came out to negotiate with his brother and was struck down by some of Vladimir's followers. The question of the succession was settled in a fratricidal war prophetic of times a century later.

Iaropolk, whose wife had been a nun, seriously considered accepting Christianity. This put him at some disadvantage during the war with Vladimir, whose enthusiastic paganism brought him wide support among the people of Russia. Indeed, the religious issue seems to have provoked more interest among those who watched the war between the brothers than did the question of the succession.

For over a decade after becoming grand prince, Vladimir followed in the fighting footsteps of his father. While he showed no disposition to pursue his father's interest in the Danube, he did attempt to push Kievan influence west of the capital in the interest of improving trade relations with the Czechs in Central Europe. He advanced against the Poles, capturing a number of their cities in what is now western Ukraine. Then he moved into north Poland, and brought under his rule the Slavic tribes of the upper Niemen region. His concern here was to improve Russia's access to the Baltic. The way from Kiev into the Baltic by way of the Dnieper and the Niemen was considerably shorter than the other routes in use at the time over the Western Dvina or by way of the Lovat, Lake Ilmen, the Volkhov, Lake Ladoga, and the Neva.

The campaigns in the west, if vigorously pursued and decisively concluded, might have brought some gain to the Kievan state by improving its trade position. However, Vladimir's most persistent and aggressive moves were toward the east, with the purpose of restoring control over the middle Volga and the Don. Revolts in the area after Sviatoslav's death had once more severed connections between Kiev and Tmutorokan, and Vladimir determined to recover his father's gains. The Slavic tribe of Radimichi, southeast of Smolensk, had never been completely brought to heel, and now Vladimir conquered them. Farther east, the Viatichi, who had risen in revolt after Sviatoslav's death, were subdued. Then Vladimir advanced against the Volga Bulgars, as his father had done twice before him. The victory over them was not as clear-cut as Sviatoslav had managed, and the Russians had to be satisfied with a negotiated peace. Vladimir did not recover control of the Volga, down which he had intended to proceed in order to restore the tie with Tmutorokan. He returned to Kiev after spending nearly a decade in winning only partial successes east and west of the Dnieper.

Vladimir had won the title of Grand Prince of Kiev in the role of champion of paganism against the rising tide of Christianity which had been washing over the area from Constantinople, from Moravia and Central Europe, and from the Russian state on the Sea of Azov with its bishopric at Tmutorokan. Missionaries from the west and south had been at work in Kiev in the time of Askold and Dir. Some of Igor's *druzhina,* or bodyguard, had been baptized, and Olga had accepted the new faith. Many Russian merchants, Varangian and Slav, who constituted the dominant class in a commercial state, had been won over. And there were few of Kiev's neighbors who had not forsaken their pagan gods. The Khazars were Jewish and the Volga Bulgars Moslem. Poland, Hungary, and Bulgaria had become Christian. Even the Varangians in their Scandinavian homeland were welcoming Christianity. The kings of Denmark and Norway were converted shortly after Vladimir assumed power in Kiev. The pressures upon Vladimir, then, were strong and mounting to accept the new faith and the new civilization that went with it.

After Vladimir's accession there had been a brief, violent reaction in favor of continuing pagan worship in Kiev. On the hills of the city the new grand prince set up idols to the pagan gods of the Slavs and offered human sacrifices of Christian martyrs to them—to Perun, god of thunder and lightning; to Veles, protector of flocks and herds; to Svarog, the god of the heavens; and to his children, Dazhbog, giver of warmth and fertility, Stribog, who controlled the atmosphere and brought the wind and rain, and Khors, the god of sunlight. Contemptuous of the virtues which the Christian missionaries proclaimed, Vladimir took seven wives, one of them the beautiful widow of his murdered brother Iaropolk, and in addition, says the chronicler, kept hundreds of concubines.

After the brief orgy of paganism which opened the new reign, Vladimir went off on campaign. Everywhere he went, to west or to east, the grand prince came up against the fact that only Kiev was behind the times in still clinging to her old gods. During the negotiations to end his indecisive war with the Volga Bulgars his recent antagonists urged him to accept Islam. Returning from that campaign, Vladimir decided to examine the various religions with which pagan Kiev was surrounded. Elders of the capital and members of the Prince's bodyguard, or *druzhina,* were brought together to discuss the merits of the various faiths, and it is not unlikely that the meetings were harangued by missionaries from east, west, and south. Those who spoke for affiliation with Constantinople could make the best case. They could remind the prince that his grandmother Olga had chosen the faith that emanated from the eastern capital. They could plead the advantages that must come from association with the greatest city of the Western world, the city upon whose markets Kievan prosperity in large measure depended.

While the question of accepting one of the new religions was under discussion, envoys came to Kiev from the emperor in Constantinople to beg Vladimir's help in putting down a revolt in Asia Minor which threatened to take over the capital. The envoys offered as an inducement that Vladimir might marry the emperor's sister, a signal honor from the head of so powerful a state. Vladimir, in turn, had to accept Christianity before the marriage could be consummated. He must have been flattered. The Christians in his entourage must have urged him to accept. But behind all the pressures of the moment, Vladimir must fully have realized that Russia's religious isolation had to end sooner or later, and he must have understood as well that the logic of Russia's geographical, economic, and political situation was overwhelmingly on the side of accepting the faith of Constantinople in preference to any other.

Vladimir was baptized early in 988. During the negotiations with the emperor's envoys, the grand prince must have been promised that Kiev should have her own metropolitan bishop and that the Russian church should be given autonomy. Remembering his grandmother's failure to settle the question of church government, and having before him the example of the Bulgarians in their struggle with the patriarch, it is inconceivable that Vladimir should have accepted the new faith without a full understanding that the Russian church should be autocephalous. But after the emperor had put down the revolt against him, which he managed with the aid of a Russian band of six thousand warriors, he seemed reluctant to follow through in his promises to Vladimir. His sister was not sent to Russia for the marriage, and the metropolitan bishop for Kiev was not named.

Having taken the step of accepting Christianity, from which there could hardly be any turning back, Vladimir determined to force a settlement of church government compatible with the independence of the Kievan state. He launched a campaign in the Crimean peninsula designed to restore the Kievan hegemony which his father had surrendered to the Empire at the end of his Bulgarian disaster. Vladimir's chief concern, however, was to capture the imperial cities in the peninsula, some of which were episcopal centers, and particularly to reaffirm control over Tmutorokan, which was the seat of a metropolitan bishop, the autocephalous head of the Christian church in the Russian kaganate. When Vladimir captured the episcopal city of Korsun, the ancient Chersonese, the emperor gave in, at least partially, and sent his sister to become Vladimir's bride. After the marriage Vladimir returned the city to the emperor as a gift.

Before his marriage was arranged Vladimir sent for envoys from the pope at Rome to discuss the possibility of Russia's affiliating with the church of the West. Presumably, the terms they offered did not satisfy Vladimir's demand for Russian religious autonomy. This act must have been a ruse to bring the emperor and the patriarch of Constantinople to terms, for all of Russia's interests centered in the East. The authorities at Constantinople must not have been convinced of the sincerity of Vladimir's dealings with Rome, for they did not agree to send a metropolitan to Kiev. The prince stayed in the Crimea a year waiting for a favorable settlement. Not obtaining it, he determined to build his own church, and set off for Kiev with a number of priests and a supply of relics and icons in his baggage.

Upon his arrival in Kiev Vladimir set to work with a vengeance to establish the faith which he had espoused. The pagan idols in the city were hurled down and cast into the Dnieper. The entire population of the city was marched to the river to be baptized by the priests who had come from the Crimea. Couriers were sent off to the other cities of the realm to order similar measures. That very summer construction was begun on the first of a number of stone cathedrals, and a tithe of the princely revenue was assigned to its maintenance. Bishoprics were established in the chief Kievan cities, at Novgorod, Chernigov, Polotsk, and Rostov. The metropolitan at Tmutorokan seems to have served as head of the Kievan church for many years. The patriarch of Constantinople apparently was ignored by Vladimir, and there was no direct contact between the Russian church and Constantinople until 1037. In that year the first metropolitan bishop of Kiev was appointed by the patriarch and assumed the headship of the Russian church. The bishop of Tmutorokan was then reduced to the level of the other Russian bishops.

Christian churches were built all over Kievan Russia at Vladimir's command, the prince insisting that they should be built on the sites where pagan idols earlier had stood. Monasteries were founded, not only in Kiev but in the recesses of the forest. Schools were established to which members of the upper classes were ordered to send their children. The schools, as a matter of course, were church schools whose chief purpose was to train recruits for the clergy. A regular system of charity for the unfortunates of society was inaugurated under governmental auspices.

After his conversion Vladimir never again went to war with his Christian neighbors. The increasing severity of Pecheneg raids into his territory, however, brought energetic measures of defense. Along the northern and eastern banks of the rivers of South Russia Vladimir erected lines of forts to keep back the nomads; settlers from among the Slovene, Krivichi, and Viatichi were brought to the south to strengthen the defenses.

Toward the close of his reign Vladimir divided the land of Kiev into districts, over each of which he placed a son as lieutenant. Iaroslav, who ruled in Novgorod, threatened revolt against his father rather than pay the taxes imposed upon him, although it is certain that he was forced to it by the Novgorodians. Just as Vladimir was gathering a force to move against his son, the old prince died in 1015, leaving the succession in question as his father had done before him.

The reign of Vladimir is pre-eminently important in the history of Kievan Russia. By his decision to embrace Christianity, although it could not for long have been forestalled and the choice of a religion was never really seriously in doubt, he brought a new civilization to Russia. A new code of morals, a sense of social justice, a corps of literate clerics capable of keeping court records and of committing to writing the historical experience of the nation, a sense of the need for education, a school of art and architecture, an alphabet and a language, and a changed international position—all these came to Russia with the new faith. But Vladimir accepted the new religion without sacrificing his independence. The Russian church from its very founding was an intensely national church. Religiously Russia was not lost in the anonymity which characterized western Europe in medieval times. Indeed, there would be many times in later centuries when the most nationally conscious agency in the nation was the Russian church which Vladimir had founded and whose chauvinistic direction he had done so much to inspire.

IAROSLAV THE WISE

Vladimir's death precipitated a civil war among his sons to decide the succession. An older son, Sviatopolk, seized Kiev and murdered three of his brothers who might have contested his action. The eldest son, Iaroslav, whom his father before his death had named to rule in Novgorod, brought in mercenaries from Scandinavia and drove Sviatopolk from Kiev, although the latter had enlisted the support of Pechenegs and Poles. The two remaining brothers, Iaroslav and Mstislav of Tmutorokan, divided the Russian land between them; the older was to have the lands west of the Dnieper including Kiev, the younger to rule over the east. Mstislav moved his capital from Tmutorokan to Chernigov, and Iaroslav preferred Novgorod to Kiev. This shift of political focus away from Kiev also reduced the commercial importance of the former capital. Goods moving south from Novgorod were diverted, perhaps at Smolensk, away from the old channel and southeast

through Mstislav's lands, over the rivers and portages east of the Dnieper,
to Tmutorokan. From there, as in ancient times, distribution to the Caspian
and the east or to Constantinople and the west was easy. It seems likely,
too, that the lower Dnieper at this time was blocked by the Pechenegs, so
that the shift in the trade route from Novgorod south was a matter of
necessity. Possibly Mstislav was fired with the ambition to revive the old
Russian kaganate, which earlier had been brought under Kievan domination.

Mstislav's death without heirs in 1036 left Iaroslav in undisputed possession of the Russian land. His first act was to move his capital back to Kiev.
To settle any question about the disposition of Tmutorokan, he also assumed the title of Russian kagan.

Shortly after his removal to Kiev Iaroslav settled the question of Russia's relationship to the mother church at Constantinople. The patriarch
ordained and sent to Kiev a metropolitan bishop, thus making the Russian
church autocephalous under the patriarch of Constantinople. Now Kiev
was the religious as well as the political capital of the state. Iaroslav celebrated the settlement by building the beautiful cathedral of St. Sophia,
and other churches modeled after those in Constantinople were built in the
capital by architects brought from Byzantium. Scribes were set the task of
translating the holy books from Greek into Slavic, and the books and
chronicles deposited then and subsequently in St. Sophia in time raised the
church to the position of a national library.

Iaroslav added territory to the Kievan state, as had each of his predecessors before him. He pushed the boundary far to the west by attacking
Lithuania and incorporating nearly the entire valley of the Western Bug, a
tributary of the Vistula. He gave the Novgorodians a firmer hold on the
Gulf of Finland by driving back the Finnish peoples on its northern shore.
Earlier, while ruling jointly with his brother Mstislav, he had conquered
the Estonians on the southern shore of the Gulf of Finland and had built
the city of Iuriev, which the Germans later renamed Dorpat.

Contact between Kiev and Constantinople had been severed by Mstislav's
rerouting of Russian trade from Novgorod through Tmutorokan and by
Pecheneg seizure of the lower Dnieper. Now Iaroslav set out to restore it.
The need to do so became urgent when a number of Russian merchants were
murdered in Constantinople, and there seemed some danger that trade with
the eastern empire might be completely halted. The Pechenegs were driven
back from the Dnieper, and a flotilla of boats set off down the river to attack
Constantinople. The ensuing fight with the Greek navy ended in a Russian
victory, but the Russian army that attacked by land was overwhelmed. This
indecisive campaign is notable as the last made by a prince of Kiev against
Constantinople.

Iaroslav's war with the Pechenegs was decisive. Never again did they
threaten the water-road, nor were they ever again able to attack Kiev. The

state won only temporary relief from the steppe raiders, however. The place of the Pechenegs was soon taken by a fresh nomad people out of Asia, the Polovtsy, or Cumans.

Iaroslav married his sister to the king of Poland and three of his daughters to the kings of Norway, Hungary, and France. Kiev had long been a state of sufficient size and importance to merit international attention, but such recognition in the form of marriage alliances with her ruling house would have been unthinkable before the Russian conversion.

During the reign of Iaroslav a beginning was made on a collection of Russian laws, known as *Russkaia Pravda.* Although the code had been in process of development and refinement for a century and a half, its inception must be attributed to Iaroslav. A combination of Varangian and Slavonic practice, softened by the Christian aversion to vengeance, the code shows the effects of the Russian conversion, particularly in the field of criminal procedure. Iaroslav also delineated the powers and jurisdiction of church courts, in which all clergy were tried and which passed judgment upon laymen guilty of violating moral law.

In the two centuries after Rurik's coming, the Kievan princes had established a firm political organization in the Russian land. Their first concern had been to reopen the trade routes, and in this task they enjoyed the wholehearted support of the Slav merchants whose welfare had long depended upon the free movement of goods in and through the area. "Originally their only function was to organise the predatory exploitation of the east Slavonic hinterland by the armed merchants of Kiev and of the other cities associated with it" (Mirsky). One after another the grand princes had seen the vital need to keep open the water-road and its tributaries, to marshal the full economic potential of the forest and steppe, and to bring the full political and commercial weight of the state to bear upon Constantinople in order to insure Kiev's prosperity and continued growth. It is significant that when military pressure—under Askold, Oleg, Igor, and Sviatoslav—failed to establish or to maintain intimate relations with Constantinople, the Kievan rulers—Olga, Vladimir, and Iaroslav—accepted religious and cultural ties with the eastern capital in the hope of establishing once and for all the firm contact without which Kiev could not live. The deliberate contemplation, by Vladimir and his *druzhina* and the leading citizens of Kiev, of the various religions seeking to win Russia's conversion in the tenth century indicates clearly that the choice was a matter of high state policy. Even the account of the conversion in the *Primary Chronicle,* which was written by monks in the eleventh century, shows Vladimir's decision to embrace the faith of Constantinople to have been based upon cold calculation. "The trade of Russia gave direction to the foreign policies of the princes of Kiev" (Platonov), and Russia's religion had become an aspect of foreign policy.

The strengthening of the tie with the Byzantine capital and the assurance of its full and continued support were not enough to keep open the water-road and maintain the trade contact with Constantinople. From the time of the first Kievan prince new hordes of nomads were coming into the steppe from east of the Volga. From Oleg's time on through the eleventh century it was the Pechenegs, later followed by the Polovtsy and finally by the Mongol-Tatars. As the pressure mounted there was growing need for strong government and unity in Kiev to keep the trade routes open. The early princes with amazing energy had maintained that strong government and unity. After Iaroslav's death that strength and unity disappeared. Civil war over the succession, "the senseless brawlings of the princes" (Karamzin), left Russia divided and weak and unable to beat back the nomads who threatened—and finally accomplished—the destruction of the Kievan state.

SUGGESTED READING

See *Suggested Reading* at end of Chapter 6.

5

The Decline of Kiev and the
Tatar Invasion

Iaroslav's death brings to an end
the early period of Kievan history and introduces another, in which the
power of the state declines as precipitately as it had mounted during the
early period. The reasons for the change were the confusion over the succession that set in very shortly after the end of the reign, and the desolation
of the land wrought by a new horde of steppe-raiders who appeared from
out of the east in the very year of Iaroslav's passing.

THE SUCCESSION

The old prince had seen the possibility of dispute over the succession, and
he warned against it in his dying charge to his sons. The eldest, who might
have succeeded to an undivided patrimony, had preceded his father in
death. Since Iaroslav felt no confidence that any of the others could manage
the entire realm, he willed that the rule of the Kievan state should descend
to all his five sons as a group, the oldest son standing as leader and protector
of the rest. The younger brothers were delegated to govern as lieutenants
over the towns and districts of the realm. The *Primary Chronicle* reports
Iaroslav's deathbed disposition of the succession:

"My sons [said Iaroslav], I am about to quit this world. Love one another,
since ye are brothers by one father and mother. If ye dwell in amity with one
another, God will dwell among you, and will subject your enemies to you, and

67

ye will live at peace. But if ye dwell in envy and dissension, quarreling with one another, then ye will perish yourselves and bring to ruin the land of your ancestors, which they won at the price of great effort. Wherefore remain rather at peace, brother heeding brother. The throne of Kiev I bequeath to my eldest son, your brother Izyaslav. Heed him as ye have heeded me, that he may take my place among you. To Svyatoslav I give Chernigov, to Vsevolod Pereyaslav, to Igor the city of Vladimir, and to Vyacheslav Smolensk." Thus he divided the cities among them, commanding them not to violate one another's boundaries, not to despoil one another. He laid upon Izyaslav the injunction to aid the party wronged, in case one brother should attack another. Thus he admonished his sons to dwell in amity.

The warning against fratricidal war was prophetic of the next century and a half of Kievan history; and at the same time it was reminiscent of Iaroslav's own struggle with his brothers, the sons of Vladimir.

The sons received not only the chief towns named in the testamentary admonition. The whole land was apportioned among them. So Iziaslav was awarded Kiev and Novgorod, which gave him both ends of the water-road; Sviatoslav was assigned the districts of Murom and Riazan in the northeast and the Tmutorokan region in the southeast in addition to the province of Chernigov; Vsevolod received Suzdal, in the upper Volga, as well as Pereiaslav; and so on. It would seem that the old prince was not willing to trust his oldest son to provide for his younger brothers, and so assigned to each of his sons a sufficient portion of the state territory to provide them the income to which they were entitled. Indeed, "the productive values of the various provinces corresponded precisely to the relative degrees of seniority of their inheritors. That is to say, the older the prince, the better and richer was his allotted share" (Kliuchevsky). Thus Chernigov, the next richest of the towns after Kiev and Novgorod, which both went to the oldest son, was awarded to the second oldest son; Pereiaslav, the third richest town, went to the third son; and so on.

Beyond the distribution of land to provide an income for each son, Iaroslav had in mind a definite order of succession. His thought was not that the princedom of Kiev should descend according to the rule of primogeniture, but that each of his own sons should ascend the throne in order of seniority upon the death of the next oldest. If the grand prince of Kiev, the oldest of the brothers, should die, the second oldest was to move up from Chernigov to take over Kiev, and the rest of the brothers were each to move up one notch in the scale: the third brother to the second city, Chernigov; the fourth brother to the third city, Pereiaslav; and the fifth brother to the fourth city, Smolensk. If anyone in the scale should die, each of the rest was to move up one step. The death of any prince would leave the rule over the fifth city, Vladimir, vacant, and it was to be assigned to the oldest son of Iaroslav's oldest son. If this latter had brothers, the presumption was that he should apportion his inheritance among them, as the nation was divided among the sons of Iaroslav. But he and his dependents must move on to the next city when a death among those senior to him brought about his promotion. This complicated system of succession is known as the rota system. The underlying principle was that the power to rule over Kiev resided in the princely family of Iaroslav, and not in the line of any one of his descendants.

Whatever intentions and hopes for the land of Russia the dead prince may have had, his wishes were forgotten from the moment of his death. The oldest son, Iziaslav, was not allowed to rule alone in Kiev, and the realm was managed by a triumvirate of the three oldest brothers. After putting down a rebellion raised by a nephew and a cousin, disgruntled at being left unprovided for, the triumvirate broke down when two of the brothers joined to drive the oldest from the throne. As the brothers went to war over the succession, they solicited foreign aid. The Poles were enlisted in the struggle at one time, the pagan Polovtsy at another. Iziaslav appealed to Emperor Henry IV of Germany and later to Pope Gregory VII, promising to bring Russia into the western church in return for substantial assistance. The disgusting spectacle came to an end only when all but one of the brothers had died, leaving the throne to be occupied by the weakest of the lot, Vsevolod. But his reign saw no peace, for the second generation continued the civil war against the last of the first.

THE ROTA SYSTEM IN OPERATION

Among the more responsible of the descendants of Iaroslav there was deep respect for the system which the old prince had founded. For example, Vladimir Monomakh was urged to take over the throne upon his father's death in 1093. But his cousin Sviatopolk was senior to him, being the son of Iaroslav's oldest son. Monomakh refused to challenge the rota system, saying, "If I should seat myself upon the throne, then will there arise a feud between myself and Sviatopolk, seeing that his father sat thereon before my father." Even in the fourth generation, at the end of the twelfth century, the system still commanded respect. The prince of Smolensk said to the grand prince of Kiev, "We have agreed not to seek Kiev to thy despite, and by that agreement will we abide. Yet, shouldst thou bid us renounce Kiev forever, [bear in mind that] we are but grandsons of one grandfather with thyself. Wherefore, so long as thou livest, we will not seek Kiev; but when thou art gone, then let Kiev fall unto him unto whom God may grant it [that is, unto him who has the right to it]."

While the principle was generally accepted that the Kievan throne should be occupied by the oldest member of the generation nearest to Iaroslav, there was no such agreement over the disposition of the other districts into which Iaroslav had divided the realm. There were two reasons for this disagreement. In the first place, the descendants became so numerous that it soon became impossible to determine precisely who was senior to whom. "The custom of the early princes to marry early and die late often caused a nephew to be older than an uncle" (Kliuchevsky). Vladimir Monomakh had eight sons, the last three by a remarriage late in life. His fifth son once said to his sixth, "When thou wert born, I was already bearded." Under such circumstances the question often arose whether a man of a junior generation should precede a child of a senior generation, whether a bearded nephew should precede a toddling uncle. Every death in the princely family raised anew the question of succession. Occasionally the question was settled amicably in a conference of all the princes. More often it was settled in civil war.

The strict order of succession to the town and districts of the realm was complicated, in the second place, by the fact that the perennial shifting of the princes from one province to another as they graduated up the scale permitted the towns to acquire more and more control over their own affairs at the expense of princely power in the town. This growth of local power reached the point where towns frequently insisted upon raising a prince to rule over them regardless of whether or not he was entitled to the position under the rota system. Novgorod, particularly, time and again ignored the strict order of seniority and reached down for a junior prince to rule over the city. On one occasion, Novgorod took a younger son of a younger son, and raised and trained him from childhood for the task of governing the city. When the father of the legitimate claimant stepped forward to demand the principality of Novgorod for his own son, the citizens answered, "We desire neither thee nor thy son. Send thy son unto us only if he hath two heads. Already have we Mstislav, given unto us by Vsevolod his grandfather, and reared by us to rule Novgorod."

The effect of the operation of the rota system was to divide the Kievan state dynastically and territorially. There continued to the end of the period the myth of supreme authority of the grand prince and, until it was sacked by the Tatars, a degree of respect for Kiev as the political, as well as the religious, capital. But for the land of Russia, for its unity, for its people, for its welfare, the princes showed no concern. Now and again a minor prince broke away from the rota system and managed to keep for himself and his line the province to which he had succeeded. This had the effect of dividing the land into semi-autonomous and sometimes isolated units. Particularly was this tendency observable in small parts of districts lying a considerable distance from Kiev, far enough away to enjoy immunity from interference by the grand prince. From such a beginning the princes of Moscow after 1300 laid the basis for a new Russia.

THE POLOVTSY DEVASTATE THE STEPPE

In 1093 the last of Iaroslav's sons died and the oldest son of his oldest son became grand prince of Kiev as Sviatopolk II. Throughout the twenty years of his reign he was closely supported by his first cousin, Vladimir Monomakh, but not all the cousins saw the need as Monomakh did to rally behind the central authority.

The two tragedies which plagued the Kievan state after the death of Iaroslav were the princely feuds which sapped the nation's strength and the perennial attacks of the wild steppe nomads. Kiev had been subject to raids from the steppe from the very moment of the state's birth, but in the latter half of the eleventh century they became more frequent and more severe. The Pechenegs had been driven off by Iaroslav, but their place was taken by the Polovtsy, the cruelest of all the nomads. They first attacked Russia in earnest in 1061, although they had had to be bought off seven years earlier, and for the next fifty years their raids were an annual catastrophe. Each raid left its trail of burned villages, sacked cities, desecrated churches, and ruined farms. At one conference among the princes, called to plan a defense for the coming year, Vladimir Monomakh warned: "As soon as the peasant begins his plowing, the Polovtsy will come, shoot him down with his bolt, seize his horse, ride on into his village, and carry off his wife, his children, and all his property." The chronicler complained: "All our cities are desolate, our villages are laid waste. We traverse the fields where horses, sheep, and cattle once grazed in herds, and behold them desolate. The meadows are grown wild, and have become the lairs of wild beasts." Whole provinces were denuded as the land's inhabitants were massacred or were herded off in long columns to the Crimea, where they were sold for the slave markets of Asia. The *Primary Chronicle* recounts the misfortune of those who were led away to be sold into slavery:

A multitude of Christian people were thus reduced to dire distress: sorrowing, tormented, weak with cold, their faces ravaged with hunger, thirst, and misfortune, their bodies black with blows, as they made their painful way, naked and barefoot, upon feet torn with thorns, toward an unknown land and barbarous races. In tears they made answer one to another, saying, "I was of this city," and others, "I came from that village." Thus they tearfully questioned one another, and spoke of their families, as they sighed and lifted up their eyes to the Most High, who knoweth all secrets.

Sviatopolk fought relentlessly against the nomads of the steppe, joined on every occasion by his cousin Vladimir Monomakh, who was prince of Chernigov. But not all the princes were willing to risk life and fortune in

the common defense, and some chose to remain neutral, perhaps hoping
that deaths among the princes who led their men to battle might improve
their own position in the rota. And while the war against the invader went
on incessantly, the civil war among the princes flared up now and again, for
the struggle for position in the chain of succession never came to an end. At
the suggestion of Monomakh, a number of princely conferences were held in
an effort to reduce dissension in the family and to promote the unity so
necessary to national survival. The first conference closed with a grand
resolution to live in peace: "Why do we ruin the land of Rus by our continued strife against one another? The Polovtsy harass our country in divers
fashions, and rejoice that war is waged among us. Let us rather hereafter be
united in spirit and watch over the land of Rus, and let each of us guard
his own domain."

But the conference had hardly risen before the cousins were at it again.
The metropolitan of Kiev, head of the Orthodox church in Russia, made a
strong appeal for unity against the pagan nomads, saying to the grand
prince and his cousins: "We beseech you, oh Prince, and your brethren not
to ruin the land of Rus. For if you begin hostilities among yourselves, the
pagans will rejoice and seize our country which was won by your sires and
grandsires who, by waging war with great courage throughout the land of
Rus, added other territories to it. But you are in a fair way to destroy the
whole country." But the disastrous feuding went on.

The last decade of Sviatopolk's reign was comparatively free of fighting
among the princes. Not all of them joined in the effort to rid the land of the
nomads, whose hold over the steppe was strangling the nation economically,
but at least those who took no part in the crusade did nothing to hamper it.
Several of the princes joined Sviatopolk and Vladimir Monomakh to carry
the attack to the enemy's camps, and the Kievan forces won several impressive victories. The last attack carried as deep into Polovets territory as
the Don river, and such a crippling blow was dealt the nomads that for a
number of years the land was delivered from all but minor raids.

Since it was at the plea of Monomakh that the princes had agreed to a
truce among themselves, and since it was at his insistence that the war with
the Polovtsy had been carried to the enemy, and particularly since Vladimir
had led the forces of Kiev against the nomads, he became and has remained
a popular hero, a symbol of national unity and of grim determination to
hurl back the invader. While Grand Prince Sviatopolk cooperated in the
attacks against the Polovtsy, the initiative seems to have come from Vladimir. Sviatopolk's attention seems to have been devoted to trying to restore
the trade contacts of Kiev which had been severed by the steppe raiders. He
sought improved relations with Poland and with Hungary in an effort to
substitute a trade with the west for that with Constantinople, which was not
possible as long as the steppe was not secure.

Before their suppression by Vladimir Monomakh the Polovtsy had caused such havoc in South Russia that the nation was threatened with economic collapse. Thousands had been carried off into slavery, other thousands had been slain, and still others had fled to the forests. Many of those who stayed on were ruined financially, as their crops were seized year after year or their buildings burned. Some managed to hang on by borrowing at high interest rates from Kievan moneylenders, and others mortgaged themselves into economic slavery to a few great landowners. The grand prince of Kiev maintained a monopoly on the sale of salt, and the exorbitant prices Sviatopolk charged for it caused grumbling. There was a widespread demand to check the greed by which a few profited from the misery of the many, and the people looked to Monomakh, who had saved them from the Polovtsy, to bring relief from social and economic distress.

VLADIMIR MONOMAKH AND REFORM

The day after Sviatopolk's death in 1113, the *vieche,* or assembly of the citizens, of Kiev met in clamorous convocation and demanded the accession of Vladimir Monomakh, the prince of Chernigov. The prince refused to accept. He was not senior in the rota system, and only a conference of the princes could set aside the regular succession. Vladimir, who had always worked for peace among the princes, could hardly go back now on his principles and invite a reopening of the civil war. He may have hesitated, also, to accept an invitation that came only from the democratic elements of the city, for to do so might be to incur the opposition of the church and of the upper classes and financial interests, against whom he would be expected to move.

When Vladimir's refusal was announced in Kiev, riots broke out and the mob plundered the palaces and attacked the moneylenders. As the violence grew more desperate, the upper classes and the clergy began to fear for their own safety and frantically appealed to Vladimir to save the nation. This plea from the upper classes apparently decided Monomakh. He entered the capital and was welcomed by the metropolitan, the other bishops, and "all the inhabitants." With the appearance of the leader who had saved the state from annihilation by enemies from without, the riots came to an end. His acceptance of office "was approved by the people, who admired him, and by the princes, who feared and respected him" (Platonov).

Vladimir took steps to relieve the conditions which had brought suffering to the people and which had produced the riots. He replaced Sviatopolk's appointees with officials whom he could trust not to misuse their power. A reasonable limit was placed on interest rates, and a strict law against usury was incorporated into the *Russkaia Pravda*. Landowners who made loans to their tenants were forbidden to enslave those who could not pay, and the right of the bankrupt and the pauper to sell themselves into slavery was hedged about with restrictions which reduced the possibility of fraud.

His concern for the unfortunates of his time seems to have been sincere, for Christianity was to Vladimir a code of social justice. The testament which he wrote down for his sons is rich with sound advice. "According to the word of the Gospel," urged Monomakh, "learn to govern your eyes, to curb your tongue, to moderate your temper, to subdue your body, to restrain your wrath; and to cherish pure thoughts, exerting yourself in good works for the Lord's sake. Destroy sin, render justice to the orphan, protect the widow." Again, in the same vein, he exhorts his sons: "Give to the orphan, protect the widow, and permit the mighty to destroy no man. Take not the life of the just or the unjust, nor permit him to be killed. Destroy no Christian soul even though he be guilty of murder." Charity was to him the highest virtue. "Give alms generously, for such liberality is the root of all good." Humility he considered necessary, even in a prince. "Above all things, admit no pride in your hearts and minds. Honor the ancient as your father, and the youth as your brother." He asked his sons to be hospitable to strangers. "Wherever you go, as often as you halt, give the beggar to eat and to drink. Furthermore, honor the stranger, if not with a gift, at least with food and drink, whencesoever he comes to you, be he simple, or noble, or an emissary. For travelers give a man a universal reputation as generous or niggardly." Here, as in other bits of advice, there seems to be an ulterior motive for right conduct, as in his admonition to acquire knowledge. "Forget not what useful knowledge you possess, and acquire that with which you are not acquainted, even as my father, though he remained at home in his own country, still understood five languages. For by this means honor is acquired in other lands." Hard work and early rising he recommended as virtues to be cultivated. "Let not the rising sun find you in your bed. . . . Without fear of death, of war, or of wild beasts, do a man's work, my sons, as God sets it before you." Certainly this is sound advice, but if his sons remembered it, their sons forgot it. Soon the princes relapsed into their former way of ignoring the welfare of the land and the people of Russia.

THE SONS OF MONOMAKH

Vladimir's election as grand prince of Kiev violated the rota system, since he was not the senior, by generation or by age, among the descendants of Iaroslav. The succession after him further violated the principle of seniority, which frequently was the only thread of loyalty which kept the princely family together. After Monomakh's death the throne was occupied, not by his brothers, but by first one and then another of his sons. This destroyed all semblance of unity among the princes, although the succession of the

Monomashichi, or descendants of Vladimir Monomakh, was not immediately contested.

Mstislav I, the capable eldest son of Monamakh, succeeded his father in 1125, welcomed by the citizens of Kiev and not opposed by the princes. He had served as prince of Novgorod during his father's lifetime, and with the consent of the Novgorodians left his son there to rule after him. Mstislav's second wife was the daughter of the Novgorodian mayor, and the grand prince seems never to have forsaken his concern for the city's well-being.

During his seven-year reign there was relative harmony among the princes, and Mstislav did particularly well at keeping peace among his brothers, a problem not so ably handled by later *Monomashichi.* He enjoyed the close cooperation of his brother Iaropolk, and together they determined to reopen the trade route between the Baltic and the Sea of Azov. The grand prince devoted his attention to the north and west, while his younger brother exercised his brilliant military talents in trying to clear the Polovtsy from the lower Don. In this reign and in his own subsequent reign Iaropolk vigorously attacked the nomads and dealt them severe defeats, but he failed to regain control of the old Russian territory of Tmutorokan. The Polovtsy host was constantly being replenished from Central Asia, and the task of eliminating them once and for all was impossible to accomplish.

Mstislav directed his own efforts first against the princes of Polotsk, who had never been given a position in the rota system and who consequently were perennially at war with the ruling family at Kiev. Now they were driven from the territory and exiled to Constantinople, and their possessions were added to that of the grand prince. Pushing on west of Polotsk, Mstislav drove back the Lithuanians, while his son in Novgorod conquered the Finnish peoples living on the shores of Lake Peipus. Mstislav's concern was to improve Novgorod's access to the Baltic, as Iaroslav had attempted to do a century earlier.

When Mstislav died his brother was chosen to succeed him as Iaropolk II. This second son of Monomakh managed to hold the throne until his death seven years later, but to do so he had to fight constantly against other princes senior to him under the rota system. Even his own brothers rose against him and drove their attacking armies dangerously near the capital. Again the warring princes sought help from the Polovtsy, and once more the steppe-raiders spread terror over the land. By the time of Iaropolk's passing in 1139 the strength and the unity of the Kievan state had all but disappeared.

PRINCELY RIVALRY FOR KIEV

After the death of Iaropolk II the Kievan state rapidly disintegrated. The princes warred constantly among themselves, each trying to win the capital

and with it the titular headship of the nation, but none had sufficient resources or managed to enlist enough allies to manage it. Sometimes the
princes were aligned into two hostile groups fighting each other; occasionally
most of the princes came together to fight the Polovtsy; at other times the
Polovtsy fought as allies of one or more of the princes. Kievan Russia split
up into a number of principalities, in each of which the prince was supreme
and practically free of outside control or of responsibility to a central government. Almost the only unifying force was the church, and almost the
only prestige which still attached to Kiev grew out of the fact that the city
was the seat of the metropolitan and therefore the religious capital, if no
longer the effective political capital, of the nation. And, paradoxical as it
may seem, the princely family never lost sight of the fact that the state belonged to the family as a group. While there was constant disagreement over
who in the family should head the nation and its divisions, there was never
any thought that any outsider—Pole, Hungarian, Bulgar, or Byzantine—
should rule in Kiev.

It must not be supposed that the civil war that wracked Kievan Russia
after 1139 was entirely a matter of princely pettiness or greed. For a prince
to put an army into the field he must have the support of the warrior class
in his province, and more particularly he must have the financial backing
of the merchant class in the towns of his bailiwick. Once the commercial axis
around which early Kievan Russia revolved was broken by the Polovtsy's
seizure of the steppes and the lower Dnieper, a struggle developed among
the towns of Russia to reroute trade to their own advantage. Novgorod
and Rostov sought to restore the trade with the Orient which was cut off
when Tmutorokan was submerged by the Polovtsy. Smolensk hoped to force
through its own markets the commerce that passed between the Baltic and
the Volga. Chernigov, Pereiaslav, and Kiev tried to develop trade between
Galicia and central Europe on the one hand and the forest zone of Russia
on the other.

As the Polovtsy control tightened over the lower Dnieper, Constantinople
lost interest in the use of that waterway and in the trade with Kiev which
earlier had been so profitable. In 1082 the eastern empire arranged a treaty
with Venice by which the Venetians agreed to serve as carriers and whole-
salers of Byzantine trade. Finally, in 1204, the Fourth Crusade seized and
sacked Constantinople, and the city fell under Venetian, and then Genoese,
domination. Between 1082 and 1204 the trade that had flowed north from
Constantinople was rerouted through the Aegean and Mediterranean into
northern Italy and through the Alpine passes into central Europe.

For thirty years after the end of the reign of Iaropolk, Kiev was pulled
one way and then another in the wars among the princes. The citizens of
the capital preferred to be ruled by a descendant of Monomakh, and often
managed to keep one on the throne in defiance of his junior position in the

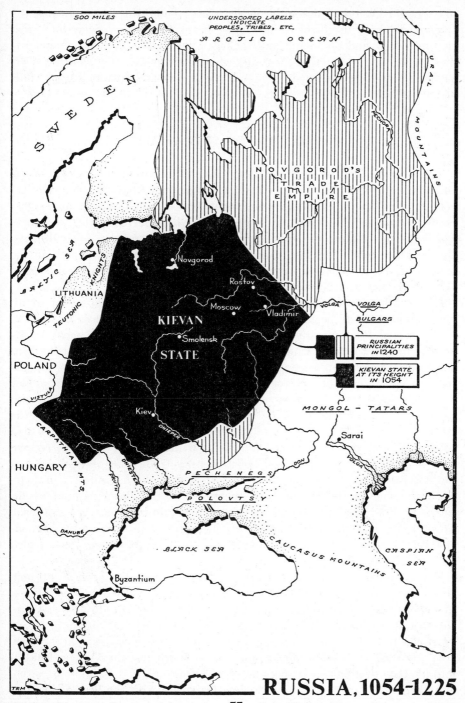

RUSSIA, 1054-1225

rota system. At other times the genealogical senior was able to seize the city and to drive the favorite into exile. In 1169 Prince Andrew of Suzdal captured Kiev and plundered and sacked it without mercy. What was left was of so little value that Andrew, whose conquest made him the chief among the princes, disdained to make it his capital, and returned to his lands in the northeast.

THE RISE OF SUZDALIA

The city of Suzdal, situated on a branch of the Kliazma, a tributary of the Oka, had grown to be one of the chief cities of the "Russian Mesopotamia" between the Oka and the Volga because of its favorable site for trade. It became a depot for the products of the forest which surrounded it, products which later moved into the Volga and so to the markets of the Volga Bulgars. On the other hand it became a distributing point for Oriental goods in the valleys of the Kliazma and upper Volga. The western outlet of the trade through Suzdal was Novgorod.

Andrew, the prince of Suzdalia, a descendant of the youngest son of Vladimir Monomakh, had been appointed while still a child to rule in the newly-built town of Vladimir, and so was literally raised a ruler of men. In his principality of Suzdalia, which by 1169 straddled the upper Volga, he beat down opposition to his authority by treating his boyars, or nobles, as personal servants and allied princes as his vassals. To free himself of popular control through the town *vieche,* or citizen assembly, he moved his capital from Suzdal to Vladimir, which had no *vieche.* After his sack of Kiev he removed many holy icons and relics from the capital to his own city of Vladimir, founded by and named for Vladimir Monomakh, where he erected several beautiful stone churches. His Uspensky Cathedral, or Cathedral of the Assumption, was the finest in the region. In it he deposited a miracle-working image of the Virgin Mary supposed to have been painted by St. Luke. In time Vladimir became the religious center of northeast Russia. Toward the end of his life Andrew sought a more quiet life away from his new capital and built a palace in the village of Bogoliubovo, from which he is called Andrew Bogoliubsky.

The despotism he practiced seems to have been of the benevolent sort. He always posed as the protector of the poor, and it was in their interest as well as his own that he reduced the power of his haughty boyars and banished many of them. He maintained peace in his principality and offered sanctuary to Russians fleeing the Polovtsy raids and the civil war in the Kiev area. He even welcomed Poles, Hungarians, Germans, and Volga Bulgars into his territory, and so its population swelled.

Andrew was a great warrior, wielding his sword with the best of his men and charging unhelmeted against the most stoutly held defenses. But he had no love for war as such, and was disgusted with the suicidal conflict among the princes which left "the heathens free to ravish Russia." Once he was established as grand prince, he forced them to stop their "senseless brawlings." He determined to prevent any such family strife in his own principality, and drove his brothers and nephews from Suzdalia rather than see his land devastated and the power which he had built up drained away in civil war. Contemporaries accused him of ambition to make himself "autocrat over all the land of Suzdal." He had a sentimental attachment to his capital of Vladimir, which he did so much to beautify, and hoped to make of it a second Kiev.

A prince so sympathetic to strong monarchy would have little patience with the citizens of Kiev, and so it is not surprising that Andrew turned the capital over to subordinate princes whom he dealt with as mere agents. Nor had he any more interest in settling in Novgorod, where the *vieche* had controlled the prince for many years. Andrew was anxious, however, to control Novgorod because of its importance to the economic welfare of his own principality. The year after his sack of Kiev this prince of Suzdalia attacked Novgorod unsuccessfully; but Andrew finally brought the city to heel by surrounding it and cutting off the area to the south and east, on which it was dependent for trade and food. His expeditions against Kiev and Novgorod laid him open to the charge of "seeking to throw the net of his ambitious schemes over the whole of Russian territory" (Kliuchevsky). If so, Bogoliubsky saw the need of a united land more clearly than did any of his contemporaries.

After forcing Novgorod to sue for peace and to accept a prince of his choice, Andrew turned east of Suzdal and launched an attack down the Volga against the center of Bulgar power at the mouth of the Kama. He may have broken through Bulgar defenses for trade expeditions down the Volga, but was unable to bring the area completely under his control. Many Russian merchants later settled in the lower Volga, in such numbers, in fact, that a Russian bishopric was established in Sarai.

For five years Bogoliubsky was grand prince in Kievan Russia, but he remained the grand prince of Vladimir, not of Kiev. The former capital on the Dnieper had surrendered its position as chief among Russian cities. When Andrew was assassinated in 1174, his brother Vsevolod "Big Nest," so-called because of his many children, succeeded as grand prince of Vladimir and ruler of the Russian nation.

When Vsevolod was crowned in Vladimir, which he continued as capital of the principality, and so in effect of the state, the citizens swore allegiance to him and to his sons after him. The other princes complained that the rota system was being set aside, but their complaint was ignored. During his reign, which lasted for over thirty-five years, Vsevolod treated the other princes as mere underlings and forced them to remain at peace. Like his predecessor, he ruled with firmness and would brook no opposition. He imposed upon Novgorod princes of his own choosing and ordered them to punish the guilty without resort to trial. He continued Bogoliubsky's policy of encouraging immigration, and promoted trade by maintaining close commercial relations with the Volga Bulgars. But he showed no concern for the fate of South Russia and ignored pleas that he help to drive back the Polovtsy, whose raids against Kiev and the surrounding territory became more ferocious than ever.

 When Vsevolod died in 1212 his sons and nephews fought over the succession and, since none was strong enough to win full control, the province of Suzdalia was split up into a number of nearly independent districts, each ruled by a descendant. The story of Kiev was repeated all over again, but there were two important differences. Most of the cities of the principality of Suzdalia had no *vieche* to check the growth of princely authority, or if they had assemblies they had been stripped of power. The prince in each small region and town, then, ruled his territory as though it were his personal estate or appanage. And the rota system which had contributed so much to the decline of the south was not applied in Suzdalia. After Vsevolod the principality was divided into districts, each to be held in perpetuity by its ruler. Upon the latter's death his district was further subdivided, and soon the northeast had splintered into a number of infinitesimal hereditary lots. So North Russia invented her own weakness in trying to escape the weakness of the rota system which had sapped the strength of South Russia.

During the period of Suzdalian ascendancy, South Russia was reduced to impotence by the devastating raids of the Polovtsy. While they showed no interest in organizing the steppe politically or economically, the Polovtsy annually scourged it, burning and plundering and seizing prisoners whom they sold to slave dealers from the Orient and from Venice, which had taken over the trade of Constantinople. The human and economic potential of South Russia was destroyed by the combined efforts of the princes, in their wars among themselves, and of the Polovtsy, whose attacks the princes were unable or unwilling to check.

There was some indication by the end of the twelfth century that relations between the Russian princes and the Polovtsy might become peaceful. At times the nomads fought shoulder to shoulder with Russians, as allies of one prince against another. Not infrequently Russian princes married Polovets maidens. It is not unlikely that the Russians and the nomads might have worked out a modus vivendi by which the Polovtsy would have been free to run their herds over the steppe while leaving the trade routes open for use by Kievan merchants. Such an eventuality was prevented, however, by a fresh invasion from Central Asia.

THE TATAR INVASION

During the eleventh century the Mongols, who are generally called Tatars by Russian writers, were living under Chinese hegemony in the area west and south of Lake Baikal. Shortly after 1200 they moved north to escape oppression, and in their new home the various tribes were united under the leadership of Chingis Khan. The first move in the expansion that followed upon the unification of the Tatar tribes was against China, and Peking fell before their assault in 1215. Then they turned to the west, and Turkestan was incorporated into the expanding empire. After absorbing Turkestan Chingis Khan sent a strong, highly mobile army to explore the Caspian region. Circling the Caspian this force came up against the Polovtsy, drove them back, and penetrated into the Crimea.

The Polovets khans hurried messengers to the Russian princes to seek an alliance against the danger that threatened them all. "Our land they have taken away today; and yours will be taken tomorrow," the Polovtsy pleaded. The chieftain even embraced Christianity to impress upon the Russians his good faith and the seriousness of the threat to which he and they were exposed. The princes of Novgorod, Kiev, Chernigov, and Volynia on the Polish border agreed to march against the Tatars, but the prince of Suzdalia and others held back.

Tatar envoys met the Russian force and offered an alliance against the Polovtsy, but the offer was spurned and the envoys slain. An advance guard of the Tatars was encountered by the Russians on the lower Dnieper and routed—a minor success which turned the heads of the Russian leaders. They decided to push on into the steppe to meet the enemy, and with their Polovets allies they came up against the main body of the Tatars on the river Kalka, which flows south into the Sea of Azov. Without stopping to coordinate an attack, some of the Russians and all of the Polovtsy set upon the Tatars, but they were hurled back against the Russian main body. In the confusion that followed, several of the Russian units were wiped out and a number of princes killed or wounded. One of the princes gathered together the remnants and threw up defense works which the Tatars were unable to overcome. The invaders offered for a ransom to allow the Russians to withdraw in peace, but after they marched out of their defense lines the Tatars attacked and slew them. The prince of Novgorod, who had led the defending forces, was placed under a board platform on which the Tatar leaders gathered to feast over the victory, and so was smothered. After sacking a number of border settlements and seizing many captives, the Tatar force was recalled by Chingis Khan, and the Russian land was left to survey its losses and count its dead.

The khan of the Tatars died in 1227, but so firmly had he welded together the tribes under his rule that there was no threat of collapse. Indeed, a convention of tribal chieftains decided to advance against China, Persia, and Russia simultaneously. Batu, who was Chingis Khan's grandson and nephew of the new khan, was assigned to lead the assault on Russia. In the spring of 1237 he assembled 150,000 horsemen on the east bank of the Volga and attacked and crushed forever the Volga Bulgars. Crossing the river he overran the principality of Riazan and wiped out the forces of the prince of Vladimir. The city of Vladimir fell and its cathedral was burned. Driving on through the principality of Tver, the Tatars approached Novgorod, but they turned south before reaching the city. Perhaps the swamps of northwest Russia hampered cavalry maneuvers. Batu crossed Russia from north to south, driving into the Balkans those Polovtsy he did not kill or enslave, and set up headquarters at Sarai on the lower Volga.

In 1240 Batu again moved against the Russian princes and conquered and pillaged Kiev, slaughtering the citizens who had dared to put up a stubborn defense. So thoroughly was the city destroyed that a traveller from the west who visited Kiev six years later reported only two hundred houses left standing and the steppe for miles around littered with skulls and bones. Then the Tatar leader sent a detachment against Poland and defeated a combined Polish-German force sent against him. With the remainder of his force Batu drove through Hungary, destroyed a Hungarian army, and pushed into the suburbs of Vienna. Before the city could be assaulted word came through that the khan had died in the east. Batu halted the advance, turned south and east through Bulgaria, and hurried back into Asia to be present at the election of a new khan. In four years, of which only two were spent in the saddle, Batu had added to the Tatar Empire all the land of Russia, plus the lower Danube and the Balkan peninsula to the shores of the Adriatic.

The Tatars were all but invincible against their European foes. Only the Czechs and Austrians had any success against them. Tatar horsemen could live for a month, so Marco Polo maintained, on mare's milk or on blood tapped from the horse's veins, and could stay in the saddle two days at a time, not even dismounting to sleep or to let the animals graze. Each trooper was provided with a score of horses which he rode in relays. The Tatars took few captives and so were unencumbered by prisoners when on the march. When attacking a walled city they built around it another wall which cut supply lines and provided cover for themselves. Battering rams were brought against stone defenses or the defenders were simply worn to exhaustion by hurling ever fresh troops against them. Once the city fell all were put to the sword and the churches were set on fire while crowded with refugees. Meeting an enemy force in the field, the Tatars surrounded it and overwhelmed it by sheer weight of numbers. The horde was well organized into squads, companies, and brigades, and the men were sternly disciplined not to accept defeat. If some of a group of ten returned to camp with word that part of their number had been taken prisoner, the rest were put to death on the spot.

The Russian historian Karamzin has suggested some of the reasons for the success of the Tatars. The prowess and courage of the individual Russian was probably equal to that of his adversary. Certainly, the Kievans had gained a good deal of military experience in their wars against the Pechenegs, the Polovtsy, and each other. Isolated victories now and again proved that the Russian was a match for the Tatar. But the Kievan forces were overwhelmed by vastly superior numbers. Batu led 150,000 horsemen across the Volga in 1237. Secondly, the well-disciplined cavalry of the invader moved swiftly as one man; there was no straggling. Thirdly, the Tatars found Russia divided. Some of the princes refused to join in a common defense and held back to fight only for their own principalities. They were easily despatched singly, one after another. Fourthly, every man in the Tatar tribes was a soldier, while in Kievan Russia only the boyars and citizens of the towns bore arms. The peasants and slaves met the attack passively, accepting the mastery of the invader or fleeing to the woods. Fifthly, the Tatars had the enormous advantage which always lies with the offensive—the element of surprise and the privilege of choosing the field. Finally, Kiev went down before no ordinary opponent. The Tatars, fresh from a hundred victories, had conquered much of Asia. Indeed, they spent their fury against the Slavs in eastern Europe, first against the Russians, then against the Poles, and finally against the Bohemians and Moravians. It is only a slight exaggeration to say that "the Germans suffered nothing from the invasion of the Mongols but the fear of it" (Rambaud).

ALEXANDER NEVSKY

After the Tatar scourge had passed over the land for the second time and the horde had returned to its camp on the Volga, the grand prince of Vladimir undertook to restore order, to rebuild his towns, to bury the corpses which cluttered the roads, and to comfort and provide for the many refugees who fled to his territory from the border regions. He was ordered to visit Batu's headquarters on the Volga where he was recognized as grand prince, but after reporting to the khan in Asia as he was commanded he died in the desert on the way back. His place was taken by Alexander, a grandson of Vsevolod "Big Nest" and great-great-grandson of Vladimir Monomakh. He was to become immortal as one of Russia's greatest heroes.

Alexander first won fame and recognition as prince of Novgorod. He built up the city's defenses and repulsed the pressure of neighboring tribes of Finns and Lithuanians which threatened to cut Novgorod's contact with the Baltic. In 1240 Novgorodian territory was invaded by Swedes whom the Pope had incited to undertake a crusade against Orthodox Russia. Alexander, with a handful of followers, met the Swedes on the river Neva and put them to rout, destroying many of their boats. For the achievement Alexander was dubbed Nevsky, or "of the Neva." The clergy saw in the exploit a victory of Orthodoxy over the Roman Catholic church of the west, and later canonized Alexander. Instead of showing their gratitude, however, the Novgorodians quarrelled with Alexander, as they did with so many of their princes, and Nevsky left the city. He had been away less than a year when he was frantically called back to defend Novgorod against the Teutonic knights.

The Germans, attracted by its trade possibilities, had moved into the eastern Baltic as early as the middle of the twelfth century. German traders were accompanied by German missionaries seeking to convert the pagan Letts and Lithuanians to Roman Christianity and in so doing to make of them allies in the struggle against Orthodox Novgorodians for control of the area. By the end of the twelfth century many Germans had settled in the region, a Roman Catholic bishopric had been established near the mouth of the Western Dvina, and in 1201 the Germans built the city of Riga where the Dvina enters the Gulf of Riga. The crusading Order of Sword Bearers, sometimes called the Livonian Order, was founded to spearhead the German drive eastward. The white mantle with a red cross on the shoulder worn by the Livonian knights became a symbol of savage destruction. Within a decade the native Lett and Lithuanian tribes had been laid under tribute to the Germans, usually only after their princes had been won over by bribery and their towns and villages stormed and burned. In 1221 the prince of Novgorod led a campaign against the Germans in the lower Dvina and raided deep into German territory, but he was unable to dislodge them completely. Three years later the Germans retaliated by taking Iuriev, built two centuries earlier by Iaroslav the Wise, and re-naming it Dorpat. During the years when the Germans were consolidating their position the Danes were also becoming interested in the eastern Baltic, and Reval, at the mouth of the Gulf of Finland, was founded by them in 1219. In less than a generation's time Estonia had become a Danish province.

While the Livonian knights were winning success in the basin of the Western Dvina, another German crusading order appeared in the valley of the Vistula. The knights of the Teutonic Order, which had crusaded in the Holy Land but had since been expelled, set up new headquarters in Venice and from there sent out applications for new employment. Offers were made to the king of Hungary and to the Polish prince of Mazovia to campaign against their enemies, and Konrad, the prince of Mazovia, agreed to engage the knights. The Teutonic Order was given a block of territory on the lower Vistula from which to move against the Prussians, a Lithuanian tribe which had resolutely resisted all Polish attempts to conquer them and convert them to Christianity. The Teutons moved in and proceeded systematically against the Prussians. One district after another was conquered, its inhabitants slaughtered or expelled. German colonists were brought in and castles and churches erected to impose German rule. A native song, still sung in the nineteenth century, recalled the time when these pagan peasants were brought under the German yoke. "That was the time of massacre, a long time of suffering. . . . Destroying fiends were unchained against us. The priests strangled us with their rosaries, the greedy knights plundered us, troops of brigands ravaged us, armed murderers cut us in pieces. The father of the cross stole our riches, stole the treasure from the hiding place, and attacked the sacred tree." In 1234 the pope granted the territory they had conquered to the Teutonic Order in perpetuity, thus freeing the knights from the suzerainty of the prince of Mazovia. Three years later the Teutonic knights absorbed the Livonian Order and the grand master became the formidable leader of German power in the southern and eastern Baltic. When the subjugation of the Prussians was completed the Teutonic knights turned to new fields of conquest and began to press against Poland, Lithuania, and Russia. "Prince Konrad's move of inviting the Teutonic knights to Prussia proved to be the worst political mistake ever made by a Polish ruler" (Vernadsky).

It was the expanding drive of the knights that Alexander Nevsky was called back to Novgorod in 1241 to halt. The invaders had pressed to within twenty miles of the city, were besieging Pskov, and had built a fort commanding Novgorod's trade with the west. Alexander captured the fort and then raised the siege of Pskov. Advancing against the Germans he met them on Lake Peipus, still frozen on that fifth of April in 1242. The famous "iron wedge" of the knights broke through the Russian center, but the Russian flanks folded together in an enveloping movement and the attacking force was overwhelmed. The German defeat became a rout, and many of the knights were slain in the five-mile pursuit before reaching the shore and escaping into the forest. After saving Novgorod from the German threat, Alexander fought off the Lithuanians who were seeking refuge from German pressure on their homeland, and successfully defended Novgorodian territory from attacks by the Swedes and Finns who attempted to move east across the Narova river which connects Lake Peipus with the Gulf of Finland.

When his father died Alexander Nevsky became grand prince of Vladimir and so titular head of the Russian nation. Understanding the hopelessness of opposing the Tatars in Russia's weakened condition, he accepted the inevitability of their rule and advised the other princes to do likewise. When the khan's deputies appeared in Novgorod to lay the city under tribute Alexander accompanied them through the gates and urged the citizens to submit. They refused, but two years later the khan sent agents to repeat his demands. This time the Novgorodians accepted Alexander's repeated urging that resistance would be useless, and grudgingly accepted the tax collectors. Time and again Nevsky make the long journey to Tatar head-quarters to plead that various Russian towns not be punished for refusal to pay the taxes which the conquerors laid upon the land. On the fourth such journey in 1263 Alexander died, ending his life as he had lived it in the service of his people. The metropolitan broke the news to the congregation assembled in the cathedral of Vladimir: "Know that the sun of Russia has set."

The words of the metropolitan of Vladimir were prophetic. Alexander Nevsky was the last of the princes to make any serious effort to hold together the land that had been Kievan Russia. He had urged the princes and the people not to court destruction by opposing Tatar rule once it had been firmly and inevitably established. He had saved the Russian people from possible inundation by the Teutonic knights, which would have meant the Germanization of Russia. But in accepting Tatar rule he risked no such danger that Russia and the Russians would lose their identity and their culture. The Tatars never made any attempt to impose their customs and their civilization upon the conquered land. By the time of Nevsky's death Tatar rule was accepted if not welcomed. But the unity was gone and the land separated into principalities practically independent of each other. For a long time the only cohesive force in the territory was to be that imposed by the alien conqueror, until a descendant of Alexander Nevsky came forth to provide the leadership that would free the land of foreign rule.

SUGGESTED READING

See *Suggested Reading* at end of Chapter 6.

Kievan Society

RUSSIANS AND RUSSIAN HISTORIANS have always felt a sentimental attachment for the history of Kiev, "the mother of Russian cities." This first capital of Russia has been the subject of romantic affection and has caught the popular fancy much more successfully than either of the later two capitals was able to do. The reason lies perhaps in the fact that popular attention has centered upon the heroic figures from Oleg to Iaroslav, and has found relief from the dreary decline of Kiev in the careers of men like Vladimir Monomakh and Alexander Nevsky. Much that was brutal and narrow and prosaic in Kievan society has been glossed over, and that which was brave and daring and venturesome has received more than justifiable attention. Too little notice has been paid to the institutional side of Kievan history. Too much has been given to the lives of its great leaders.

POLITICAL ORGANIZATION

Before examining the machinery of central and local government, it may be noted that the Kievan experience produced certain socio-political attributes which were to characterize the Russian people throughout their history, regardless of governmental organization. The first of these was a deep sense of attachment to the Russian land. The concept of "Mother Russia" as a land meriting the love and respect of its people, quite apart from the administration or the prince who ruled over it, goes back to Kievan times. In the dismal period after Iaroslav's death a concern for the Russian land was voiced again and again by contemporary chroniclers. In spite of

87

the fact that the area was fast losing its political unity, an awareness of popular unity and national solidarity persisted. The Kievan period was indeed the cradle of Russian nationality. Russians have always spoken affectionately of *"Russkaia zemlia"*—the Russian land—and were doing so no less frequently, perhaps even more stubbornly, in the twelfth and thirteenth centuries when outward semblance of unity had all but disappeared.

The second socio-political attribute that grew out of the Kievan experience was an awareness of the unity of the Russian people. The various tribes of East Slavs were welded firmly together by the early princes of Kiev, and the non-Slav peoples of the area—the Finns, for example—were absorbed so completely that they lost all sense of identity other than Russian. Pressure on the frontier from Swedes, Lithuanians, Poles, Germans, Bulgars, and steppe-raiders contributed to the feeling of individuality of the Russian people. The foreigner was an enemy of the Russian people to be expelled from the Russian land. Here lies the key to the affection in which Vladimir Monomakh and Alexander Nevsky have always been held. They, more than any others, rose above the pettiness and selfishness that characterized the princes and led their people in defense of the homeland. If there grew out of the Kievan period no sense of loyalty to state, there was a deeper loyalty to territory and to people or nation that proved to be more abiding. Even in times of the nation's worst trials, when corrupt governments have lost all popular respect, loyalty to the land and to the nation has never wavered.

Central Government

Until the coming of the Varangians there was no central government in the sense of an administration for the entire land and an authority over the various groups of East Slavs. Each tribe governed itself in matters affecting its own local interest. Passing attempts were made by transient conquerors to organize an area, such as the steppe or a trade route, but no effort to unite European Russia as a territorial unit or the East Slavs as a nation had ever been successful. Ermenrich, the Gothic leader, had sought most precisely to do so, but his experiment lasted less than a generation. Not until Oleg brought together both ends of the water-road and went far toward uniting the East Slav tribes were the foundations laid for building a national state.

For nearly two centuries after Rurik's coming the state was considered as a political unit, to be ruled by one man and handed down inviolate from one ruler to another as a single heritage or patrimony. To hold the territory intact and expand it, to weld the people together and prevent dissension and injustice, and to protect the state from outside pressure and guard its economic interests—these were the responsibilities which the early princes saw clearly in their position as rulers of Kievan Russia. Those responsibilities were as new and strange to the area as were its Varangian princes, for they did not exist as long as tribes and cities clung to their local interests. From the time of Oleg's appearance in Kiev to the end of Iaroslav's reign these tasks were understood and grappled with by the rulers.

After Iaroslav the nature of the executive changed radically. The ruler was not an individual but a family. Ruling out all such complications as the attacks of the nomads and the decline of Constantinople, the change in the executive power alone was sufficient to destroy the likelihood that the responsibilities of the executive would continue to be met. That is precisely what happened. The state territory shrank in size and finally split up into divisions comparable to the tribes and cities of pre-Varangian times; dissension and injustice were rife as civil war pitted locality against locality; the economic interests of the entire area were lost from view as each town fought to salvage its own prosperity from the destruction and depression that others suffered; and the borders of the state were violated and the territory finally overrun by foreign powers. For a short time under the rota system the dignity and power of the office of grand prince survived, and the unity of the family which ruled the land was maintained by princely conferences. But more and more the junior princes came to look upon their graduation to Kiev as simply a step which would bring them richer income and greater prestige. The acceptance of such an attitude marked the disappearance of responsibility for national leadership. As the rota system became a mockery, so, too, did the title of grand prince. Russia became a state without an executive, a sprawling, twitching body without a head. In the latter part of the twelfth century, when the capital was transferred to Vladimir, the grand prince thought not of Russia but of his own principality of Suzdalia. Vsevolod "Big Nest" ignored the plea that he join the other princes in opposing the Polovtsy, thus giving pointed expression to his refusal to think in terms of the Russian state. Monomakh and Nevsky were only passing exceptions to this drift of the Kievan state toward decline of executive responsibility.

There was never any thought in Kievan Russia that the power of the executive was absolute. After the conversion the principle was accepted that the prince must rule according to Christian precepts. Arbitrary rule, in violation of the new morality or without reference to the wishes of at least some segments of the population, was frowned upon and, indeed, was hardly possible in Kievan times. The prince was limited in his authority by a council, or duma, of his boyars, or nobles. When the boyars attended the prince on campaigns they were referred to as his *druzhina.* Since the term duma was not in use in Kievan Russia, the boyars as a group, whether acting as warriors or as a deliberative body, were called the prince's *druzhina.* When Olga besought her son to be baptized, Sviatoslav answered, "My *druzhina* would laugh at me." That is to say, the boyars acting as a deliberative and consultative body would not consent to imposing Christianity upon the nation. The boyar council which advised the grand prince of Kiev occupied somewhat the position of a baronial assembly for the state, but only because the grand prince was the ruler of Kievan Russia. Every prince had his own *druzhina,* who followed him to the wars and advised him in the administration of his principality, no matter how small.

The council of boyars was a body possessing considerable power. The prince had to accept its advice on any important matter, and had to have its approval of legislation, even in the codification of law. Iaroslav's sons prefaced their additions to the *Russkaia Pravda* with a list of the leading boyars who gave their consent to the promulgation of new regulations, and treaties with other nations had to be approved by the boyar council. Leading boyars often sat in the princely conferences which met from Monomakh's time on to arrange peace in the ruling family. On occasion, the council acted as supreme court of the land. Its powers were defined not by law but by custom, but so completely was its right of deliberation and advice recognized that no prince dared to make an important policy decision without its approval. An inner circle or cabinet of three to five members of the boyar council attended the prince constantly, probably assisted him in administration, and advised him in the disposition of routine problems. Any decision involving important matters of state, however, could be taken only in full session of the boyar council.

In the early days of Kiev the council consisted of the retainers of the prince, the descendants of Slav tribal chiefs, and commercial leaders of the towns, sometimes elected by the *vieche* to represent it. The latter were called the "city elders," who were consulted along with the *druzhina* when Vladimir was contemplating baptism. In early times promotion to boyaral status came as a result of outstanding service, military or civil. Later the boyars constituted a hereditary nobility, when land was granted to them as a reward for service. Such grants of land, however, never entailed any obligation of service to the prince as was the case under Western feudalism. Any boyar was free to leave the service of his prince at any time, even though he held land in the principality, and seek employment wherever he chose. What held him in the service of a particular prince was the promise of reward in the form of land, or prospect of plunder when on campaign, or the salary and gifts he might draw from the princely treasury.

There was a second assembly exercising some vague limit upon the princely authority—namely the town meeting, or *vieche,* of the capital city. While the *vieche* concerned itself primarily with local problems, there were times when it raised its voice in national affairs. Frequently it interfered in the succession. The popular assembly of Kiev insisted upon Vladimir Monomakh's becoming grand prince in spite of his junior position in the rota system, and several times after his death the *vieche* demanded that one of his descendants rule in place of the legitimate claimant to the princely throne. At times the assembly was called by the prince to approve a decision which he believed should have popular support. At others it was brought together by the mayor or by leading citizens to register its disapproval of princely policy. Each district capital had its own *vieche,* which dealt only with local or provincial affairs, but that of Kiev frequently influenced national affairs because of the pressure it was occasionally able to exert upon the grand prince.

The prince was entitled to a third of the revenue that came to the central government in Kievan times for the maintenance of his household; the remainder went to meet state expenses. A heavy drain upon the latter was the right of every member of the princely family to an income from the state treasury. Frequently this claim upon state income was satisfied by appointing the claimant to rule over a district or town. The appointee kept the revenue from his district if it equalled the amount to which he was entitled; if there was a surplus, he remitted it to Kiev. Such a prince might invest his income in trade or in land, and so improve his financial position. But no matter how wealthy he became or how much land he came to own, he was entitled, as a descendant of Rurik, to a share in the state revenue.

One of the chief sources of government income was in the form of tribute, or *dan,* which was levied upon the Slav tribes at the time of their subjugation by the early Varangian princes. At first the *dan* was gathered by the prince in person, who made an annual visit to the conquered tribe to collect it. Olga put an end to these annual expeditions and assigned the task of collecting the tribute to agents sent out from Kiev or to locally chosen bodies. The payment continued to be called tribute, although it was no longer levied upon the tribe but became a tax paid by the individual. The *dan* bore most heavily upon the farming population, who were taxed according to the amount of land under cultivation. Inhabitants of small towns paid a lighter tax assessed upon each household. By the twelfth century each taxation district or town was collecting its own *dan,* the amount required being set by the grand prince and the sum being apportioned among the inhabitants of the district as their local government decided. The large cities were exempt from payment of tribute, as were boyars and upper middle class. All classes were subject to fines for criminal offenses, and these were sufficiently heavy to bring in nearly as much revenue as did the tribute.

Taxes on trade produced considerable income. All goods brought into a city had to pay a duty to pass through the city gates. Merchants were required to pay a fee for the right to display their wares in the market place, and another for having their goods weighed and measured. There were charges for use of bridges, ferries, and portages. There were indirect taxes in the form of licenses on taverns and the profit made from the state salt monopoly. Finally, it must not be forgotten that many of the princes were themselves traders, and so enjoyed a profit from their own dealings. Perhaps it was because the prince harvested such a rich income from trade that he made such a sincere effort to defend caravans at portage points and to maintain bridges, roads, and planked passageways over the portages. Other charges upon the state revenue went for the maintenance of schools and institutions for the care of the poor and infirm, although the church shared this cost with the administration. After the conversion the prince frequently assumed responsibility for relieving destitution in time of plague, famine, or war, but again the church bore much of the burden.

The military force available to the prince for defense of the realm and to expand the state territory consisted of two elements, the *druzhina* and the city militia. The *druzhina* was a small force of well-armed and highly trained cavalry of such proven worth and dependability that the prince placed his chief reliance upon it. The city militia was intended primarily for the defense of the town but was called into service occasionally for a major campaign far from home. All able-bodied citizens of the town were subject to militia service, with the prince supplying the mounts and weapons necessary to equip them for field service. Since the militia were not reliable and were poorly trained, the princes often hired mercenaries. Bands of Varangians were brought in by the early Kievan princes, and in the wars following Iaroslav's death Poles, Hungarians, Lithuanians, and even Pechenegs and Polovtsy were employed at various times. The army followed the universal practice of living off the land. This increased its mobility and maneuverability by reducing the size of its supply trains, but made the Kievan columns almost as much of a scourge as the steppe-raiders to the native population.

Local Government

For centuries before the coming of the Varangians Russia had been a land of many towns, and indeed the Scandinavians referred to it as *Gardariki,* or "the Realm of Cities." Nowhere in their wanderings over Europe could the Vikings have come in contact with so many cities as in Russia. The East Slav tribes had tended to gather around certain old towns, and to build others when they moved into new territory. The Poliane settled around Kiev, the Radimichi between Chernigov and Smolensk, the Dregovichi south of Polotsk, the Krivichi and Slovene in the neighborhood of Novgorod and later in the region of Suzdal and Rostov. The land before Rurik's coming was divided among a number of city-states, although their borders were never perfectly coterminous with tribal boundaries because the tribes were constantly moving.

Throughout the Kievan period these major cities continued to dominate the areas surrounding them, because each of them was so situated as to control trade routes. Each major city became in a sense a provincial capital, an administrative center, and its position was recognized and confirmed by being given rank in the rota system. Minor towns of each area were bound to each capital by trade and administrative ties, and were called "junior" or "by-" towns. The rural area associated with each capital was known as its *volost*, a word whose root means power, and so the *volost*, or district, was the rural territory dependent upon and ruled by the capital. Iaroslav's will recognized this city-state arrangement, and soon the Kievan state was divided into a number of principalities, each with its capital city—Kiev, Novgorod, Chernigov, Smolensk, Pereiaslav, Suzdal, and Polotsk. Even after all semblance of unity in the land disappeared, when there was in reality no Kievan Russia, these city-state principalities continued; indeed, their number grew. The city of Vladimir was raised by Andrew Bogoliubsky to the rank of a princely capital, and Moscow later achieved similar status. For perhaps a century before the Tatar invasion Russia was no more than a confederation of city-states. After the invasion each prince divided his land or appanage among his many sons, and the juniors raised their own small towns to the rank of junior capitals. This atomization of the land reduced the power of the princes and paved the way for its reunification under the leadership of Moscow.

The basic unit of local government, in town and country, was the commune, or *mir*, composed of the heads of all families in a neighborhood or town. In cities like Novgorod and Kiev there were many *mirs*, each representing a street or quarter, in which neighborhood problems were settled. The city-wide assembly, or *vieche*, included all the citizens of the town, and the citizens of junior towns also had a voice if they cared to attend. The *vieche* of the provincial capital often influenced national government or policy, as for example on those occasions when the citizens of Kiev determined the choice of grand prince, or when the citizens of Novgorod called Alexander Nevsky to defend the land against the Swedes and Germans.

All freemen in the province who were heads of families were privileged to participate and to vote in meetings of the *vieche*. Practically, the assembly included only freemen of the capital, since distance and irregularity of meetings discouraged attendance from the junior towns. Meetings were not scheduled, but were convened when a problem arose demanding consideration. By ringing the great bell, or by sending criers through the streets, the citizenry was brought together in the market place or in the cathedral square to voice their approval or objection to matters put before them by the prince or the mayor. The final vote had to be unanimous, and the meeting continued until one side won the argument or resorted to blows to impose acquiescence in the will of the majority. Unless that could be brought about, no decision was reached. Many and often bloody were the quarrels between factions in the *vieche* of Novgorod. Usually the mayor presided over the meetings, although at times a bishop sat in the chair. The prince never presided, but attended and participated if, for example, a campaign which he was to lead were under discussion. The power of the city assembly varied from city to city, reaching its apogee in Novgorod and first being rendered impotent in Suzdalia. In none of the Russian cities did the *vieche* ever become representative, in the sense of containing elected delegates either from the freemen of the capital or from the junior towns who had the right to attend it. Consequently, the larger the town grew, the more unwieldy became the assembly and the greater the tendency to circumvent it and to allow the accumulation of power by an oligarchy.

An important official in the city was the *tysiatsky*, literally "head of a thousand," who served as commander of the militia and police prefect. It was his unpleasant responsibility also to serve as spokesman for the citizens in their relations with the prince. Originally elected by the *vieche*, the office of *tysiatsky* was filled in late Kievan times, except in Novgorod, by the prince's appointee, and came to be the object of hatred and violence when the citizens felt their wishes were being contravened. Under the *tysiatsky*, or "head of a thousand," was the *sotsky*, or "head of a hundred," and the *desiatsky*, or "head of a group of ten." These officials constituted a chain of military command. They seem also to have had some relationship to the early tribal organization of the Slavs. The thousand may have corresponded to the tribe, the hundred to the clan, and the ten to the family. In the cities of Kievan Russia the thousand represented the entire city, the hundred the district or neighborhood, and the ten the household. The chief function of these officials was to marshal the populace in time of danger. The head of the city administration, responsible to the *vieche* for all aspects of local government, was the mayor who was elected by the assembly of citizens.

The prince's representative in each province was his lieutenant, or *posadnik*, literally one who "sits in the place of" the appointing official. He was a noble or boyar, often one of the younger members of the princely family, and through the hierarchy of locally-elected officials guarded the prince's interests, assuring the flow of taxes into the princely treasury. The rural districts were divided into hundreds, for the administration and leadership of which the *sotsky*, or "head of a hundred," elected by the freemen of the district, was responsible to the *posadnik*.

In late Kievan times, as many freemen in rural areas were depressed into slavery and as a few merchants in the towns rose to commanding positions of wealth, there was a drift away from the democratic institutions of earlier days. Great landowners assumed political power in the country, and the manorial lord ruled over his great estate and over the slaves who cultivated it. Freemen managed to retain their judicial and political independence, but their numbers declined sharply in the twelfth and thirteenth centuries.

Similarly, those who accumulated fortunes from trade succeeded to positions of power in the cities. Through most of the twelfth century the mayors of Novgorod came from a single family. The mayor, who judged disputes over land, and the *tysiatsky*, who judged disputes over trade, were in a position to favor the great man over the small. Since voting in the *vieche* was by acclamation, the powerful were able to bring pressure upon their dependents and thus place in office men who would protect their interests.

The Appanage System

As the political power of Kiev ebbed away in the twelfth century, the influence of the rota system, which focused princely attention upon Kiev as the national capital, declined proportionately. Andrew Bogoliubsky, who rose to the position of grand prince by dint of military power, scorned Kiev as a capital and preferred his city of Vladimir on the Kliazma, which he sought to make the successor to the old city on the Dnieper. This shift of political direction was a reflection of a movement of population away from the steppe zone to escape the frustrating wars of the princes and the raids of the nomads. Andrew and his brother Vsevolod strove to reorganize Russia by subordinating the princes to the new power center. In the attempt, the rota system fell into abeyance as precipitately as the capital around which it revolved had declined in importance.

In the valley of the upper Volga, where the fleeing population of Kievan Russia found sanctuary, a new political order developed, based not upon the idea of territorial unity but upon the concept of individual princely ownership of the parcel of land over which he ruled. This system which sprang up in north central Russia is known as the appanage system.

Andrew Bogoliubsky was responsible for abolishing the rota system and for laying the foundations of the appanage system which replaced it. His disgust for the old method of settling the succession was sincere and arose out of his honest concern for the nation which that system had done so much to weaken. It will be remembered that under the system inspired by the will of Iaroslav the Wise the death of the grand prince brought to the throne of Kiev the next senior prince, namely the prince of Chernigov. The latter turned over the province of Chernigov to the next senior prince at the time he moved on to the capital. Now when Bogoliubsky became grand prince, instead of removing to Kiev as his predecessors had, he remained in his principality of Suzdalia. Suzdal, which along with Pereiaslav had been part of the heritage of Iaroslav's third son and therefore one of the stepping stones to the capital, was thus withdrawn from the rota system. The province of Suzdalia lost its family significance and came to be considered as the inalienable property of its prince and his heirs. Andrew's successor, Vsevolod, did not bother to journey to Kiev to assume the title of grand prince, but ruled the land of Russia, the grand principality of Kiev, from his capital on the distant Kliazma. The brothers Andrew and Vsevolod succeeded in divorcing political power over the nation from the association with Kiev as the capital. What is even more important here is that they also succeeded in taking the principality of Suzdalia out of the rota system and preserving it as a hereditary province in their own branch line. But to free himself from the restrictive aspirations of the *vieche* of the town of Suzdal, Andrew had created a new capital, Vladimir, which with the neighboring territory soon came to be recognized as a province separate from its parent province of Suzdalia.

The successors of Vsevolod "Big Nest" treated the province of Suzdalia as a heritage of private property. A father would will it to an only son. But when there were several sons, the province had to be divided up among them, each receiving his portion outright to pass on as he chose. The sub-provinces were further subdivided until each heritage was small and poor, but in each case the heritage was passed down vertically from father to sons and not horizontally from brother to brother as had been the case under the rota system. Each inheritor under the new system looked upon his heritage as his patrimony or appanage, as his estate to will to his heirs in turn. With the appearance of the appanage system among the sons of Vsevolod, the movement of princes from one province to another which had characterized the rota system came to an end. The earlier view of the family heritage as possessing integrity and indivisibility gave way to the heir's concern to receive his share in absolute proprietorship.

The appanage system, recognizing the right of all sons to share a father's estate, was responsible for breaking down the new Russia of the upper Volga into scores of microscopic principalities. Vsevolod left five sons who raised twelve grandsons. Thus, in two generations' time the region of Suzdalia was broken into twelve appanages, one of which, it may be noted, was Moscow. One of the twelve was further subdivided into over twenty small parcels in a century's time. This atomization obviously impoverished the princes who succeeded to such an insignificant patrimony. One fifteenth-century prince entered a monastery in preference to sharing with several brothers an inheritance which consisted only of a manor house, a church, and a hamlet.

Another consequence of the appanage system was the complete estrangement of the family which descended from Vsevolod. The rota system, even in its worst days, had given the members of the princely family a sense of family solidarity. Even their fighting for place drew them together at the same time as it pitted them against each other. Seniority in the family and how to enforce it or circumvent it was always foremost in the minds of the princes of Kiev. But in Suzdalia the descendants soon forgot that they were "grandsons of one grandfather," and lost all contact with each other.

The appanage system had the effect of depriving the princes of all political significance and of reducing them to the position of simple landowners. In the best days of Kiev the state on the Dnieper was a nation, bordering upon other nations and having to defend itself against them. It possessed a people, different from other peoples in language and in custom, aware of its individuality and jealous of its independence. But in the fourteenth century the prince of a small appanage was no different from scores of others. His lands were surrounded by those of princes no greater than himself. His people were the same in habit, tongue, dress, faith, work, and play as those of every other prince. He had no foreign relations, but only the relations of one landowner to another. Indeed, he had no people, in the sense of being able to force the freemen of his territory to stay with him and serve him. Only his slaves were bound to him. The freemen who rented from him could leave to rent from another prince when their lease was up. Even his boyars were free to seek service where they chose, as they had always been since Iaroslav's time. Many of them in the fourteenth century chose to serve the grand duke of Lithuania, who paid much better than could a poor appanage prince. Many of them drifted to the court of the prince of Moscow, whose wealth and power were growing rapidly in the fourteenth century. The average small appanage prince had no feeling that anyone was his subject, for the reason that he did not consider himself a sovereign. It was not unusual for a boyar to own or lease land in one appanage and to take service under the prince of another. Holding land did not entail any service to the overlord as it did in western Europe, and so there was no political similarity between the feudalism of the West and the appanage system of North Russia.

Finally, the appanage prince became independent of all other princes, and the only political hegemony over the land was that imposed by the Tatar khan whose capital at Sarai was far away on the lower Volga. All sense of territorial unity disappeared among the princes, to be restored again only in the fifteenth century. Political disintegration under the appanage system was even more complete than it had been under the rota system. Under the latter system there had been at least some semblance of political unity, however slight, in a recognition of family ownership of the grand principality. The appanage system, which reduced the princes to impoverished small landowners, deprived them of all political awareness and all feeling of responsibility to the inhabitants of their small estates. When a strong leader appeared among them, anxious to reunite the land, he found little popular opposition to destroying the appanage prince, for there never had been any spirit of loyalty to him. The prince of Moscow's work of reunification was made easy by the fact that he encountered no political opposition in the system which he swept away.

THE ECONOMY OF KIEVAN RUSSIA

Historians have not agreed on the nature of the Russian economy in the Kievan period. One school, led by Kliuchevsky, insists that trade was not only the most important, but almost the sole, basis of the economy, and holds that agriculture was practiced on so small a scale as to be negligible. Recent Russian historians, led by Grekov, have taken the position that the Kievan state rested essentially upon an agricultural base, and that trade was relatively unimportant. The best opinion (Vernadsky) now is that both Kliuchevsky and Grekov exaggerated, and that the truth lies somewhere between the two extreme points of view. Certainly trade was of vital importance in Kievan times, as it had been for centuries and as the geography of the area would lead it to be. On the other hand, South Russia with its rich black soil had been hospitable to agriculture for at least as long as its rivers had promoted trade, and there is no reason to believe that farming suddenly stopped with Rurik's coming. Indeed, Kliuchevsky, in his analysis of the class structure of Kievan Russia, presents all the evidence necessary to see the basic importance of agriculture, but in his weakness for sweeping generalization he overshot the mark in insisting upon commerce as the mainstay of Kievan Russia.

Commerce on the Water Road

Oleg, the real founder of the Kievan state, brought most of the East Slavs under subjection and imposed an annual tribute upon the various tribes. This tribute, paid in furs, wax, and honey, was collected personally each year by Oleg and his successor Igor on visits to the tribal capitals. Early in November the prince set out from Kiev with his retinue to call at the various cities in the land, in each of which he collected the tribute and settled for a stay to be entertained by the tribal chief. The journey lasted through the winter, for the princely party did not return to Kiev until the ice had left the Dnieper in April. During the winter the Slavs trapped and hunted and built boats of hollowed logs in which to ship the season's catch to Kiev when the rivers opened. Now, in April, their boats were beached near the capital, and the prince and members of his *druzhina* came to the bank to exchange or buy up the furs and other products which the tribesmen brought in, and often to purchase the boats in which they had come. This stock, the tribute which the prince had collected, wheat gathered in from the steppe farmers who had it to sell, and slaves captured in the wars against enemy tribes—all were loaded into the boats for Byzantium. Then the prince and his warrior-merchants, joined by similar fleets of private merchants from Novgorod, Smolensk, Chernigov, and the other towns, dropped down the Dnieper to the Black Sea and edged around it to the great trading center on the Bosporus, Constantinople. A typical convoy carried ten thousand tons of cargo, about half in slaves and the rest in commodities.

The Russian merchants spent the summer trading season in the eastern capital, residing in the suburban quarter of San Mamo and enjoying the food and baths provided at the emperor's expense. Each trading day the Russians were escorted inside the city walls, fifty at a time, and were returned to their compound at the end of the day. Trading was by barter, the Russian furs, wax, honey, and slaves exchanging for Byzantine wines, gold and silver ornaments, glassware, spices, fruit, and silks. At the end of the season the emperor provided the ship's stores necessary for the return voyage, and the Russians set out for Kiev, arriving there shortly before the annual circuit began again in the fall. The prince and his *druzhina* stopped at Kiev, while the merchants from the other towns returned home for the winter to exchange in their own markets the Byzantine wares they had brought with them. At Novgorod the products of the East were sold to Scandinavian merchants who distributed them over the Baltic area and into central Europe.

The fact that the collection of tribute from the provinces and the trading journey to Constantinople took the prince and his retinue nearly the entire year may have been responsible, in part at least, for Kliuchevsky's hasty conclusion that the economy of Kievan Russia was based exclusively upon foreign trade. Certainly, trade was of tremendous importance, and the exchange of goods between Novgorod and the Baltic region on the one hand and between the entire water-road area and Byzantium on the other was vital to the prosperity of the state. After Olga's reform of the collection of tribute made unnecessary the annual journey of the prince to the East Slav tribal capitals, the amount of time the prince had to devote to gathering in the products of the land was reduced. But improving the revenue-collecting machinery simply freed the prince's time and energy for the further extension of the state limits and the trade area. Sviatoslav dreamed of uniting the entire steppe from the Volga to the Danube into one commercial empire, and Vladimir sought to push the western limits of Kiev into the valleys of the Niemen and the Vistula and so to improve access to the Baltic Sea. Several of the princes made an effort to establish firm commercial ties with central Europe by the overland route running west of Kiev. The early princes never gave up the hope of incorporating the Tmutorokan area into the state and so of controlling the "silk road" between the Mediterranean and China. And Andrew Bogoliubsky and his brother Vsevolod strained every effort to create a new trade axis by subduing Novgorod and seeking to break through the territory of the Volga Bulgars and so open up the lower Volga, one highway to the Orient. The vital importance of foreign trade is re-

flected in the sharp decline in Kievan prosperity and power that set in
when the Crusades undermined the position of Constantinople, although
other factors—the interminable civil war and the Polovtsy raids—also
contributed materially to that decline. Throughout the early Kievan period,
and frequently after Iaroslav's death, the princes fought to keep open
the trade exits through which goods could flow between the national territory and the markets beyond.

While Kievan commercial relations with foreigners were of vital importance and certainly spectacular, there was a considerable volume of inter-
regional trade inside Russia itself. The products of the forest moved south
over the Dnieper from Smolensk, and the grain and meat of the steppe
moved north from Kiev over the same river. Furs, wax, and honey from
Rostov and Suzdal could reach Kievan markets with but a single portage,
that between the headwaters of the Oka and those of the Desna, which
enters the Dnieper just opposite Kiev. Novgorod received from the steppe
the grain necessary to feed her large population, and was as dependent upon
the water-road for her own food supplies as for the exotic foreign wares
her merchants displayed in their market stalls. Because of the early growth
of cities, there was always a lively local trade, as the farmers from suburban
areas exchanged their milk, meat, poultry, honey, wax, horses, cows, timber,
furs, grain, salt, and game for the tools, weapons, pottery, clothing, and
leather goods that were manufactured by city craftsmen. While many of the
transactions were between the neighboring farmer or trapper and the local
artisan, every city market was visited by merchants from other towns who
sold wholesale to local distributors or who bought up quantities of goods
to take back home to their own markets. Market day was a weekly event,
usually held on Friday.

The fair, on the other hand, was held annually and often ran for weeks
on end. In general, the fairs brought together the produce of wide areas
and usually were attended by foreign merchants. That held each winter in
Nizhni-Novgorod, at the junction of the Oka and the Volga, was world
famous; merchants came there from central Europe, from the neighboring
Volga Bulgars, from Siberia and Turkestan. Smolensk and "Great" Novgorod
held annual fairs visited particularly by German and Scandinavian merchants. The trade of Novgorod in the tenth and eleventh centuries was in
part a transit trade, for through it passed silks, spices, jewels, and carpets
from the Orient and Constantinople to northern Europe. And Novgorod
and Smolensk were collecting stations for Russian goods which found ready
sale in German markets—for flax, hemp, burlap, hops, tallow, hides, and
silver—and distribution centers in Russia for northern European goods—
for woolen cloth, linen, needles, weapons, glassware, iron, copper, tin, lead,
herring, wine, and beer. Russian merchants travelled abroad to buy and to

sell, in Persia and Bagdad until the Polovtsy put a stop to it, in Vixby and North German towns throughout the Kievan period.

The rights of Russian merchants abroad and of foreign traders in Russia were codified in commercial treaties and in the *Russkaia Pravda*. The latter provided for settlement of a foreigner's claim against a bankrupt Russian before his countrymen could be satisfied. In addition to the treaties between Kiev and Constantinople obtained by Oleg and Igor, trade agreements were also negotiated between Novgorod and her German and Scandinavian correspondents. A most-favored-nation clause in one such treaty provided that the terms Novgorod extended to Germans and Scandinavians might also be enjoyed by merchants of "every Latin [Roman Catholic] nation."

Russian traders organized their own associations for mutual protection. Reference in the treaties with Constantinople to the merchants of "Kiev, Chernigov, Pereiaslav, and the other cities" suggests that the association may have been by town. Novgorodian merchants later were organized in guilds, each with its patron saint as was true in the West. For a particular venture several merchants might cooperate in a partnership arrangement, as when a fleet of boats or a caravan of wagons set off to a distant market. The need for association was great, whether the goods moved by land or by water. A large train of wagons or pack horses was less vulnerable to the highwaymen who plagued the trails through the forest than a single merchant's small party would have been. A flotilla of boats moving over the river net was relatively safe except at the portages. The cataracts which run for forty miles in the lower Dnieper were always haunted by steppe nomads, and on the prince's annual trips to Constantinople a strong guard had to be thrown out to the flank while the slaves destined for sale in Byzantine markets dragged or carried the boats around the rapids.

Money and Credit

Several media of exchange were used in pre-Kievan times, including furs in the forest zone and cattle in the steppe. Silver bars of measured weights constituted the monetary standard, such bars being worth so many marten skins or so many cattle. Arabic, Persian, Roman, and Byzantine coins circulated freely, but no Russian coin was made until Vladimir's time. From the tenth century on gold and silver coins were in common use. In this land where foreign and domestic trade was so highly developed, money circulated among the people to a much greater extent than was true in western Europe at the time.

Credit and investment techniques were quickly learned from Constantinople, and there are many recorded examples of merchants borrowing from a prince, from each other, and from associations. Interest rates in the period were surprisingly low, a sure evidence of the fluidity and availability of investment capital. The *Russkaia Pravda* recognized three categories of loans—those for short terms of less than four months, those for intermediate periods of from four to twelve months, and long-term loans running a year or longer. Interest rates on long-term loans were limited by law to not more than 10 per cent. Presumably, higher rates applied to short-term loans. It may be noted that interest up to 8 per cent was allowed on year-long loans in Constantinople at the same time, by which it may be seen that rates were remarkably moderate in Kievan Russia, an economic frontier. The low interest rates reflected a ready supply of liquid capital and a low element of risk because of the political stability maintained by the early princes. The maintenance by the government of well-traveled roads, of bridges kept in repair, and of portages paved and defended, must have greatly reduced the likelihood of loss.

The princes managed to accumulate large holdings of gold and silver by selling more than they bought in Constantinople or by disposing of Byzantine goods to traders in Russian cities, by gathering plunder in war, and by the collection of tribute and taxes from the land. This reserve was invested in trading ventures, loaned out to merchants, or injected into the economy as the government paid for the various goods and services it needed. Smaller accumulations of treasure were amassed by the boyars from trade and from their share in the booty yielded by war. The church soon found itself in possession of a respectable treasure through gifts from the princes and boyars, and from the tithe which Vladimir had assigned to it. However, church funds were seldom liquid, for the gold and silver which came to it were made into church ornaments, or its money quickly invested in land and buildings. After the decline of Kiev and the removal of the metropolitan to Vladimir and later to Moscow, gifts to the church were usually in the form of land, until it became the largest landowner, next to the prince, in Russia. Much of the capital in later Kievan times was in the form of slaves, a highly liquid investment because of the ready market for them both at home and abroad. Merchants of the leading towns must have grown very wealthy, considering that several of them built churches entirely at their own expense. So much did Kievan Russia come to depend upon trade, domestic and foreign, and so completely did it develop a money economy, that one student has worked out an almost unbroken chain of business cycles that affected the entire nation from 981 to the Tatar invasion two and a half centuries later. The economy of the period may be characterized as one of commercial capitalism, one in which depression followed prosperity with monotonous regularity.

Agriculture

Cultivation of the soil was practiced all over Kievan Russia, in forest as well as in steppe. In the forest zone the preparation of the land required a heavy investment of labor. The trees and brush were burned away before plowing and sowing, the ashes providing the necessary fertilizer, for the land of the taiga is so poor that it must be nourished constantly to assure a sustained yield. After three or four years the soil lost its strength, and the farmer and his family had to move on to another patch, burn it off, and start anew. This movement of the farm population over the land accounts for much of the instability of early appanage times. Later, as northern and central Russia became more congested, the enlarged family of several generations occupied a greater holding, burning off one patch and cropping it for three or four years, then doing the same to another plot while the first again became overgrown and so could be used after the second was exhausted. Thus a two-field or three-field system of rotation was imposed upon the cultivator by the rapid impoverishment of the soil.

The rich black soil of the steppe was so fertile and of such fine texture that it needed plowing only once in several years. The quality of the soil made possible small farms, which were much more common in the south than in the north. But even in the steppe the land could be worked out, and the two- or three-field system, in which one field lay fallow for several years at a time, developed to provide rest for the soil. Oxen- and horse-drawn plows with iron plowshares which turned the sod, instead of just scratching it as earlier primitive plows had done, were in use long before the coming of the Varangians. Wheat and buckwheat were standard grains in the south, while rye, barley, and oats were more popular in the north. Flax and hemp were raised for textiles. A variety of vegetables, including peas, turnips, cabbages, onions, and pumpkins, was grown and found ready sale in the town markets. Poultry was raised by every farm family, and livestock was produced in large numbers. On the prince's estates much attention was given to horse breeding in order to provide mounts for the troops in time of war. Cattle, frequently used as draft animals, provided meat, milk products, and hides, and were popular in the steppe as they had been for centuries before Kievan times.

While small family farms were not uncommon in the south, agriculture in the steppe came more and more to be characterized by great estates owned by princes, boyars, or the church. While the church objected to slavery, the estates of boyars and princes usually were tilled by armies of slaves; free hired labor was also used. Church lands were cultivated by monks or were let out to tenants on a share or cash-rent basis.

The Russian drew some of his food from the forest. Game birds and animals were snared or hunted with bow and arrow. Trapping of fur-bearing animals provided pelts with which to pay taxes or buy essentials and from which to make winter clothing. The *Russkaia Pravda* fixed severe penalties for fouling or robbing another's traps, or for trespassing upon the game preserves of princes and boyars. Bees were kept in tree hollows marked with the owner's name. Again the law provided punishment for defacing an owner's mark or robbing a hive. Wax and honey, the former used in the making of candles, were consumed in great quantity at home and were basic items in the export trade.

The rivers and lakes of Russia teemed with fish, an important element of diet long before the conversion. Indeed, Russians seem to have consumed no more fish as Christians than as pagans. Fish was eaten by all people, but at times of their own choosing, not at times designated by the church. Commercial fishing was an important industry, the catch being sold in the city markets. The walrus was hunted in the Arctic ocean, and his tusks were exported to the Baltic countries in sufficient quantity to merit notice in the chronicles.

Mining and Industry

During the Kievan period the Russians did not maintain sufficient control over the areas rich in mineral deposits to permit their exploitation even if they had possessed the technical skill to put those deposits to use. The land east of the lower Dnieper, and particularly the Donets basin so vital to modern Russian industry, was never securely held by the Kievan princes. The other rich mineral area in European Russia, the Urals, was screened from Russian occupation by the Volga Bulgars and the Turkic peoples who controlled the lower Volga. In the forest zone, however, there were extensive deposits of iron at or very near the surface, and the ore was being smelted and worked into tools and weapons even before "the calling of the Varangians." Throughout Kievan times iron continued to be mined and manufactured into plowshares, hoes, rakes, nails, spears, arrowheads, and shields. Copper, tin, lead, gold, and silver were imported from central Europe, Asia Minor, the Caucasus, and the Urals, to be made into household utensils, church bells and ornaments, coins, bridles, jewelry, and building materials. Craftsmen who worked the metals into usable forms found heavy demand for their workmanship in both domestic and foreign markets.

Because of the plentiful supply of timber the Russians made their houses of wood even in the steppe, to which timber could be floated down the rivers. Russian woodsmen and carpenters were kept busy; Novgorod, famous for its carpenters, even paved its streets with timber. After the Russian conversion, churches often were built of stone, and lay princes aped those of the church by building palaces of brick and stone. To erect these edifices and to circle the towns with permanent walls, bricklayers and stonemasons first were imported from Constantinople, but soon Russia had its own corps of such workers. The city of Vladimir, which Andrew Bogoliubsky did so much to endow with rich churches, came to be as famous for its masons as was Novgorod for its carpenters. Shipbuilding, too, was an important industry in Kievan Russia, and so well were the Russian boats built that many of them were bought by Byzantines. The typical boat, made from a single tree trunk, was fifty to seventy feet in length, twenty in width, and twelve in depth. It was powered by from ten to twenty pairs of oars, and was provided with a mast upon which to hoist a sail when wind was favorable.

Textile industries flourished in Kievan Russia, turning out a variety of products for many uses. Long before Rurik's coming the Slavs had been weaving and fulling. Linen was made from hemp and flax and tailored into light clothing, particularly for the well-to-do. Coarser garments of wool were worn summer and winter by the average Russian. Cordage, burlap, canvas, and sailcloth were manufactured for use by the commercial fleets which sailed the wide rivers and the border seas. Kievan furriers were renowned for their fine craftsmanship in the making of coats and caps. Pottery making, an art almost as old as the land itself, was an important industry. While many of these crafts were practiced in the home, the relatively large size of some industrial organizations indicates a great volume of trade and a considerable degree of specialization.

SOCIAL ORGANIZATION

The size of the population of medieval Russia can only be roughly estimated, since no effort was made to take a census until the eighteenth century. However, it may be conjectured that between seven and eight million people were living in Kievan Russia in the latter part of the twelfth century, in the period immediately after Iaroslav's death. The draining of the population through perennial Polovtsy raids and princely civil wars probably kept the figure static through the second half of the twelfth and the early part of the thirteenth centuries. The Tatar invasion and the awful desolation that came in its train may so have depleted the population that there was no recovery through the thirteenth century. In the middle of the fourteenth century Kievan Russia was stricken by the Black Death, which then swept westward to decimate Europe. By the end of the following century, around 1500, the population of Russia had recovered and grown to between nine and ten million. A century later it had risen to fifteen million.

A relatively high percentage of the population of Kievan Russia was urban, as might be expected from the commercial capitalism stage into which the national economy had developed. City dwellers numbered perhaps a million on the eve of the Tatar conquest, or between 12 and 14 per cent of the national total. Kiev, Novgorod, and Smolensk together contained not less than four hundred thousand inhabitants. The percentage of urban to rural population in Kievan Russia was high in comparison to that found anywhere in western Europe at the time.

Classes in Kievan Society

Before the appearance of the Varangians the East Slavs were organized into tribes composed of several patriarchal clans who had probably come together for protection. The clans, however, were never very firmly knit together and broke down quickly after being conquered by the early Kievan princes. After Olga's financial reforms nothing more was heard of them. The tribe, as an association of clans of blood relatives, simply did not provide the cohesive force that was provided by territorial economic unity, by the city and its trade territory which was the fundamental unit of society in Russia, whether that Russia was Slav, Turkic, or Varangian. The basic element in East Slav society was the *zadruga*, or enlarged family of three or more generations, holding its blood relatives together by common ownership of property and by the need for economic cooperation imposed by life in forest or steppe. The *zadruga*, whose members numbered from twenty to sixty or even eighty, was ruled by the village elder, the oldest man in the community or one chosen to replace him if he were incapacitated. His was the responsibility to maintain peace and order in the family, to assure justice to each member, to assign work, manage the farm, divide the product, and pay taxes. In some districts of Russia, particularly in the south and west, the *zadruga*, somewhat smaller than in early times, was still common in the late nineteenth century.

The boyars, or aristocratic element in Kievan society, sprang from a number of roots. At the top of this class, and in early Varangian times separate from it, were the members of the princely family. Rurik and his successors down to the first generation after Iaroslav constituted a distinct class of royalty. But by the time of the Tatar invasion the family of Rurik had multiplied to such an extent, and the land holdings of the junior princes had become so small, that royalty had merged with and become indistinguishable from nobility; all were in effect boyars, with the princes constituting a sort of upper stratum, often no more wealthy or powerful than the others but possessing the blood of Rurik. The chief but not the only agency through which a man might become a boyar was the prince's *druzhina*, or retinue. The early *druzhina* was a heterogeneous lot. Some of its members were chieftains of Slav tribes; others were Varangian warriors who had accompanied the prince from the homeland or who joined him later. Some were of noble ancestry; others, occasionally even slaves, rose from humble origin through outstanding service to the prince. The senior members of the *druzhina* were the officers of the prince's army and leading servants in his household, such as the steward and the master of the horse, while pages and common warriors made up the junior membership of the retinue. A man might rise to boyar rank without serving in a princely *druzhina*. Leading officials and merchants in the chief towns also were regarded, socially and legally, as boyars. With the possible exception of the latter, the boyars before the decline of Kiev were becoming landowners, and it is their occupation of great estates that distinguishes them in a later period from other social classes.

The boyars never constituted a distinct social class in quite the same way as did the barony of western Europe. Their position was not consequent upon service to the prince, and particularly in the appanage period of the thirteenth, fourteenth, and fifteenth centuries they were free to leave the service of òne prince for that of another at any time without risking loss of land or social status. The class was not strictly a hereditary one, for it was constantly being replenished by recruits from among commoners. And boyars were not the only landowners, for there was no limitation upon purchase and sale of land, and the estate carried with it no requirement of service and no status in society.

The middle class in the cities of Kievan Russia was divided into upper and lower strata, though in what proportion there is no way of knowing. Extremely wealthy merchants probably were not numerous, although there were enough of them, in Novgorod at least, to form a separate guild of their own. Some of the most prosperous families came to dominate city office, and so rose into the class of city boyars. Small merchants and prosperous artisans made up the lower middle class, distinct from the laborers beneath them whom they employed. There was also a rural middle class, freemen who owned small estates but who were clearly distinct from the great landowning boyars above them and the landless peasants—free, half-free, or slave—beneath them. In South Russia this rural middle class succumbed to Polovtsy raids and the Tatar invasion, but it reappeared in central Russia in the thirteenth century and never disappeared from Novgorodian territory.

The laboring element in Kievan cities may be classified as skilled, semi-skilled, and unskilled. Many skilled workers, no matter how modest their income, really belonged to the middle class in the sense that they did not work for others but owned their own shops and sold the product of their own labor. Some carpenters, smiths, masons, saddlers, bakers, potterers, cobblers, butchers, tanners, and other craftsmen sold their labor, and it was these who constituted the skilled labor class. Some skills required only a short time to learn, and men like teamsters, hostlers, and farriers made up the class of semi-skilled labor. Urban and rural workers whose tasks required no training period to learn fell into the unskilled class.

Agricultural workers in Kievan Russia may be grouped into three classes: the state peasant, or *smerd*, who was a freeman; the *zakup*, who was half-free; and the slave, or *kholop*. The *smerd* tilled his own small farm, which fell to his son when he died but which he could neither sell nor will to daughters. If there were no sons, his land reverted to the state—that is, to the prince, who resettled it upon another *smerd*. This free peasant enjoyed the "privilege" of paying the tribute or tax and of furnishing horses to the state in time of war, while the half-free and unfree classes had no such privilege. The prince extended a special protection to the state peasant, who could not be arrested or punished without the prince's consent. On the other hand, the *smerd* could be fined by the prince for infractions of the law, and the right to be fined was a distinction of free men. In the territories of the city-states of the North, in Novgorod and Pskov, the city and not the prince protected and exercised authority over the *smerd*. Legally and personally the *smerd* was free. Economically he was circumscribed, for his right to dispose of his small farm was not unlimited.

Midway between the free peasant and the slave was the *zakup*. Once a freeman, the *zakup* was one who had fallen by debt into a period of indenture or who had voluntarily sold his future labor for a sum of money. When his obligation was paid, he again became a freeman. A small farmer or a town craftsman might borrow money to improve his farm or his business. If he were unable to repay the loan with interest at maturity, he had to work it out with his own labor. The creditor was free to employ the debtor in any way he chose. Most debtors became agricultural laborers. The *zakup* could not be sold as a slave, although he became a slave if he attempted to escape. The creditor was free to impose corporal punishment upon his indentured worker for just cause, but the *zakup* could sue his lord for excessive cruelty or for unjust punishment. He could bear witness in court, the distinction of a freeman, but on the other hand he could not be held accountable for theft. Responsibility for theft by a *zakup* lay upon his master, who could then bind the culprit in complete slavery. It will be remembered that Vladimir Monomakh took steps to protect the indentured worker from falling into slavery by fraud of his creditor and to fix interest rates at a fair level to prevent wholesale loss of freedom by the debtor class. Other half-free men were those who, during war or famine, voluntarily gave up their freedom and worked for a lord in return for protection and for food and shelter.

The slave, or *kholop,* might lose his freedom only temporarily, as when he fell captive to the Polovtsy and was later ransomed or was seized by the Poles and released at the end of a war. Civilians captured and sold to Byzantium could work out their freedom. Treaty arrangements between Kiev and the eastern empire set limits to the amount of ransom to be charged and provided specific lengths of time a member of each class might be worked before being given his freedom. By far the largest number of slaves consisted of those who had permanently lost their freedom—that is, had descended into "full slavery." A freeman might become a full slave in one of four ways: by entering the service of another without a clear contractual understanding that he should remain free; by marrying a female slave without the agreement of her lord that he should remain free; by selling himself into slavery; or by being condemned to slavery as punishment for theft or robbery. An agreement to sell one's self into slavery was only binding if the seller received the minimum legal price and if the registration fee was paid to the town clerk. To prevent fraud, the city official assured himself that the sale was voluntary and that the legal price had been paid. Once the individual descended into the *kholop* class, he could be sold by his owner, with or without his family. Traffic in slaves for speculative purposes was frowned upon by the church and by public opinion, which looked upon the buying and selling of slaves for profit as sinful. The slave possessed no civil rights whatever. He could not appear in court, as suitor or as witness. He could not own property or transact business, and if he did so surreptitiously, the other party could obtain redress for damages from the slave's owner. He could be killed with impunity by his lord, although the church might force the lord to do penance for his crime. The *kholop's* labor could be put to any use the master chose—in the field, in the stable, or about the house. Some were trained in the crafts, and a few even became tutors to the master's children. Escape from slavery was only possible by running away, for which the penalties were severe, or by being freed by the owner. The church constantly encouraged masters to free their slaves, and some provided in their wills that their slaves should be given their freedom.

The Growth of Feudalism

The position recently taken by Russian historians—that Kievan society was feudal in nature—has been challenged (Vernadsky) more in its emphasis than in its proposal. Certainly Russian society in the tenth, eleventh, and twelfth centuries possessed many features not found in the feudalistic society that obtained in western Europe. Those features must be kept in mind if an accurate picture of Kievan society is to be gained. First, it must be noted that slavery, an institution foreign to Western feudalism, existed throughout the Kievan period, and that it tended to become more widespread after the middle of the eleventh century. In the turbulent times that civil war and nomad raids produced, the individual tiller of the soil despaired of providing his own security and sold his freedom in return for protection, or found it impossible to stay out of debt and so sank into slavery to his creditor. Vladimir Monomakh probably provided only a temporary stay to this drift by forbidding landowners to enslave tenants who could not repay loans and by restricting the right of the bankrupt to sell himself into slavery. Second, it must be remembered that Russian landowners held their land outright, free from military or other service, and were free to devise it or sell it at will. Third, the importance of trade to the state was far greater than was true of any feudal agricultural state in the West. The great estates in Kievan Russia, which resembled the latifundia of the Roman Empire in many ways, never approached the degree of self-sufficiency achieved by the English or French manors in medieval times, and their deliberate production of a surplus for sale in the nearest town had no parallel in the West. Russia was in a stage of money economy not matched in western Europe until the fifteenth century. Finally, the significance of cities in this commercial nation greatly exceeded that of urban centers in western Europe during the tenth, eleventh, and twelfth centuries. These cities of Kievan Russia were both cause and result of an economic interdependence quite impossible under Western feudalism.

When all this has been recognized, there is still room for admission that Russia after the beginning of the twelfth century was showing unmistakable evidence of drifting toward economic, if not political, feudalism—a drift which was halted by the Tatar conquest and by the rise of Moscow. The first fact to be noted in support of this contention is the growing disregard of the descendants of Iaroslav, typical of Western feudal barons, for the welfare of the nation. The loss of freedom of a sizable segment of the population is a second indication of Kiev's drift toward feudalism. Whether the individual be called a serf or a slave, whether he be bound to the soil or to a master who farms the same estate generation after generation and must keep his slaves to give the land value, is not important in this connection. The fact remains that Kievan soil was worked by a mass of unfree labor, as was the soil of western Europe. A third fact to note is the decreasing importance of foreign trade after the Crusades and the decline of Constantinople, although it must not be forgotten that internal trade between town and country and between forest and steppe continued to thrive. Finally, it must be noted that cities, some in particular, rapidly lost their relative importance from the twelfth century on. Kiev, Pereiaslav, Chernigov, Polotsk, and Smolensk fell away. Some, notably Kiev, were so thoroughly sacked by the Tatars that they did not recover for centuries. Others, such as Polotsk and Smolensk, were absorbed by Lithuania and so were lost to the Russian state. Not until the early twentieth century did cities rise again to the importance they had maintained in the brightest days of Kiev.

Diet, Dress, and Dwellings

The average Russian probably ate more food and a greater variety of it in Kievan times than at any other until the twentieth century. Bread and meat were staples available to everyone. Wheat in the south and rye in the north were then, as ever since, the bread grains. In monastery and manor house a sweet bread was made by adding honey and poppy seed to ordinary bread. Oats were used in porridge. Mutton, beef, pork, goose, chicken, duck, and pigeon were obtained from domesticated herds and flocks. In time of famine horseflesh was eaten. Game was plentiful, and traps and snares yielded deer, bear, and wild fowl. Fish was always popular even before the Russian conversion, and caviar appeared on the tables of the wealthy. Eggs, milk, cheese, butter, and vegetable oils were common among all classes.

Meats were boiled, grilled, fried, or cured. Vegetables, eaten raw or boiled, included peas, turnips, cabbage, and onions. All sorts of fruits were eaten raw or made into pastries. *Kvas,* a weak beer, had already become a national beverage; mead, made of honey, provided a stronger drink for the poor, while the wealthy drank imported wines. Gold and silver tableware was used in homes of the wealthy, while pewter and wood served in those of the lower classes. Forks were not in use, and each man used his own knife to cut bread and meat.

Although food was more plentiful in Kievan than in later times, drought, famine, and plague struck occasionally and reduced the population, especially the lower classes, to severe hardship. Plagues were particularly violent in the twelfth century, when great numbers died over wide areas, but apparently the entire nation was never afflicted at the same time. Early frost or lack of rain brought famine then as later. Civil war and steppe raids frequently caused a short harvest and drove up grain and bread prices, forcing poor peasants to eat bark, leaves, and straw.

Clothing was worn for comfort and for such adornment as the wearer's purse might allow. The upper classes wore linen clothes in summer, silk and brocade in winter with outer garments of wool or of marten, beaver, and sable fur. Clothing and rugs of fur, usually of bear or wolf skins, were more common among the lower classes than in later times. Homespun flaxen garments and caps of squirrel fur adorned the typical peasant. The wealthy wore boots of fine leather dyed blue, green, yellow, or red, occasionally with long curved toes, while the peasant, in the tenth century as in the nineteenth, wore bast shoes made of willow or birch bark. Finely-wrought leather goods and ornaments of gold and silver set with precious stones were imported from Byzantium for wealthy men and women alike.

The typical peasant hut had three rooms; in the north it was a log cabin called an *izba;* in the south it was a double-walled frame dwelling called a *khata.* The large main room, which contained the brick stove, was used for all purposes—for dining, sleeping, and entertaining. A smaller unheated room was usually used as a storeroom or as a stable for a sick pig or cow, but might be opened to human occupants in summertime. Between the two was the entrance hall. Stables, pens, and barns were built near the house, as was the *bania,* or bathhouse. The Russians' love for an almost unbearably hot steam bath, punctuated by lashings with reeds to stimulate circulation and brought to an end by dashings of cold water or tumbling into a snowdrift, apparently antedates the coming of the Varangians. Simply by adding rooms, heated or unheated, to the basic dwelling unit typical among the peasants, the middle and upper classes provided themselves with more pretentious houses. The palace of the prince was a much more elaborate structure, with large dining hall and tower made of stone. Windows were made of mica, and all dwellings were lighted by vegetable oil- or fat-burning lamps.

Candles were also used by the well-to-do, torches or wood splinters by the poor. Beds, chairs, and tables were made of wood, some of them in upper class homes being ornately carved.

Life in the city, with its richly decorated stone cathedral and its princely palace, was far more colorful than life in the village, with its drab huts and poor parish church. To the town markets and fairs came travelling companies of players and minstrels to sing of the valiant deeds of warriors who fought against the steppe raiders. Church and civic festivals were numerous and gay. Market day provided citizens and villagers from the neighboring countryside with entertainment and the chance to exchange bits of news and gossip. Every provincial capital was equipped with schools, founded by Vladimir and Iaroslav, offering elementary and higher education. Greek and Latin were taught in some schools, and many a prince, boyar, and merchant possessed a respectable library. Thousands of titles of books written in the Kievan period have been noted, in spite of the fact that many libraries must have been destroyed by fire or in the pillage to which the cities were subjected. The rate of illiteracy was lower in Kievan times than at any time until the late nineteenth century.

City life carried with it, however, its own types of hardship and suffering. With its houses built of wood the town was under constant threat of fire. Kiev was almost destroyed by fire in 1124. In the century and a half following Iaroslav's death Novgorod suffered ten particularly devastating conflagrations, one of which destroyed fifteen churches and over four thousand houses. Vladimir in Suzdalia endured three disastrous fires in fifteen years during the reign of Vsevolod "Big Nest." Plague struck down townsmen by the hundreds, while country districts nearby might be passed over. Short harvests that left the farmer with enough for his family but nothing to carry to market brought famine to city dwellers. And in the depressions to which business activity was periodically subject the laboring classes experienced unemployment with all its insecurity and hardship.

KIEVAN LAW AND CUSTOM

Law in Kievan Russia was a composite of pre-Varangian Slav custom and Byzantine law, with some slight additions from Scandinavian-German practice. While there was a tendency in later versions of the *Russkaia Pravda* for Byzantine influence to predominate, the Russian jurists who drew up a particular codification did not hesitate to reject Byzantine practice where it conflicted with Russian interests or custom. For example, they accepted the legality of interest on loans, as Justinian law provided, but did not accept the capital and corporal punishment which that law recognized, substituting for it a scale of fines in keeping with ancient Slavic practice.

There are three versions of the *Russkaia Pravda,* or *Russian Law,* the first dating from Iaroslav's reign, the second from the time of his sons, and the third from about 1160. The three show so many differences that they amount to three distinct codifications. In general it may be said that Iaroslav's *Pravda* reflects little influence of the then recent conversion to Christianity, but shows Varangian–East Slav pagan practice in a nearly pure state, while the later versions indicate in many places the impact of Christian influence.

From the text of Iaroslav's version of the *Russian Law* it would seem that by pre-Christian practice crime was a personal matter in which the state took little interest. By the "law of vengeance," relatives of a murdered freeman were allowed to seek out and kill the murderer. But the *Pravda* of Iaroslav's sons abolished the right of vengeance for murder and replaced it with a scale of fines, or bloodwite, to be paid to the prince in money or in furs, great or small according to the murdered freeman's status in society, and a wergild paid to the relatives, also scaled according to the rank of the deceased. The fine collected by the prince for murder was twice as great for a boyar as for a freeman, four times as great for a freeman as for a *smerd,* and half as much for a woman as for a man. A boyar's wergild was the same as the fine for murdering him, while that of a simple freeman was only a fourth as much as the fine. The appearance of the bloodwite evidenced the prince's interest in the maintenance of peace. Through murder the state lost a taxpayer and a producer. There was no such compunction where a slave was involved, for as a chattel he paid no taxes. If a slave assaulted a freeman, his master must compensate the complainant or turn the slave over to him to be killed. Whether the master chose the one course or the other probably depended on the value of the slave as a piece of property. The law of Iaroslav's sons increased the severity of the punishment by providing that the freeman so assaulted might kill the slave on the spot or sue the master for damages. While freemen, according to the *Russian Law,* were not supposed to be put to death for crime, it is not unlikely that at times the law was ignored even by the princes. Vladimir Monomakh, it may be remembered, counselled his sons not to put to death either "the just or the unjust," the guilty or the innocent, a bit of advice that would have been unnecessary if the law had been strictly observed.

Kievan law distinguished between willful and unpremeditated crime, providing fines four times as heavy for the former as for the latter. A scale of fines was also graduated according to the degree of bodily injury inflicted by an assailant upon a freeman. Insult to a man's honor was visited with a very heavy fine, indicating that *Russkaia Pravda* was the code of the well-born in society.

The emphasis in Kievan law was upon property rather than upon the individual. Penalties for theft, robbery, arson, and horse-stealing increased in the successive versions of *Russkaia Pravda,* until in the "expanded version" of the twelfth century these crimes were punished by confiscation of all property of the thief and his sale into slavery. The same fine was exacted for stealing a beaver out of another man's trap or for ignoring or erasing a landmark as for knocking out a tooth or killing another man's slave without provocation. Damaging another's hunting weapons or nets drew the same penalty as severing a man's finger or striking him in the face or illegally binding a freeman in slavery. One who murdered another's slave must pay the owner the slave's value, just as he must compensate for destruction or damage of any other item of property. A man could kill his own slave with impunity as far as the state was concerned, although the church might impose penance upon the killer.

The law established safeguards for liquid capital and credit. The expanded version of *Russkaia Pravda,* the twelfth-century edition, has been aptly referred to as a "bankruptcy statute" because of the number of provisions designed to protect investors. A bankrupt merchant could be sold into foreign slavery to satisfy the claims of his creditors, but only if his insolvency was due to his own mismanagement and not to misfortune. Interest rates were fixed according to degree of risk and length of maturity, although the church's exhortations against usury suggest that the law at times was circumvented. Perhaps to discourage the freezing of capital in long-term investments, Vladimir Monomakh added to the *Russian Law* the provision that interest exceeding half the amount of principal should not be recoverable at law. Wages, too, were fixed. Twenty-five cents per day plus living costs was the legal rate for carpenters.

Woman enjoyed a respectable position under Kievan law. Her wergild was half that of a man, presumably upon the assumption that her toil was only half as productive as that of a man. Her right to own property in her own name was recognized long before the first codification of Russian law. By Oleg's treaty with Constantinople a woman's property was not to be held liable to satisfy claims against her husband. A widow had the right to a portion of her husband's estate, if there were no children or if they were adults, and was the legal administrator of the estate during the minority of the children. Daughters as well as sons inherited from the father. A man who stole yarn or cloth spun or woven by his wife was subject to fine. In every respect Kievan women enjoyed a more dignified position than did their sisters in the West.

CHRISTIANITY AND THE CHURCH
IN THE KIEVAN PERIOD

Vladimir's conversion in 988 was followed by a half century in which the relations of the Russian church with the parent church in Constantinople were irregular and cool. If the patriarch had promised to send to Kiev a metropolitan bishop, as may be surmised, the promise was not kept and Vladimir went his own independent way. Priests were brought from the Crimea, and the bishops installed in the leading Russian cities were consecrated by the metropolitan of Tmutorokhan, who held sway as head of the new Russian church. This anomalous situation continued until 1037 when the patriarch of Constantinople despatched a metropolitan bishop to Kiev. From that time on, the Kievan church was an autocephalous organization under the titular headship of the Byzantine patriarch. The latter's concern to regularize relations with Kiev and to tie it firmly into his own orbit of influence may be readily understood when it is recalled that less than a generation after the settlement a schism developed between the Patriarchate of Constantinople and the Roman Papacy which has never healed. In 1054 the two excommunicated each other, the Western church henceforth claiming to be the Catholic or universal church, while the Eastern church held itself up as the Orthodox or only true church. When the split between the two Christian churches developed, the Kievan church followed Constantinople, as the Patriarch shrewdly had guessed it must when he won its favor by granting it local autonomy under its own metropolitan. No serious question was raised in Kiev, when the breach between East and West opened, as to whether the Russian church should follow the one or the other. Russia went automatically and without dispute where the Patriarch led her in religious affairs.

The religious break between East and West was fraught with consequences of vast importance to the history of Russia. After 1054 relations between the peoples who embraced the two faiths were frequently strained and always potentially hostile. Popes felt no more scruple in urging crusades against the Orthodox than in sending the faithful against pagans or Mohammedans. The Germans, intermittently at war with the Slavs since the time of Clovis in the sixth century, found in the schism an excuse for their *drang nach Osten*. Prussian secession from the Roman Catholic discipline in the sixteenth century had no effect upon their relations with the Orthodox Slavs, whose lands were the goal of German expansion right down to 1945. On the other hand, Russian churchmen implied that Roman Catholics were not Christian when they spoke of Russians as Christians and Westerners as "Latins," and invariably preached a holy crusade when Russia went to war with Poles or Germans.

The estrangement between East and West after 1054 cut Russia adrift from the West European cultural stream. The stimuli which quickened the thought and life of Western peoples, such as the Renaissance and the Protestant Revolt, did not affect Russia. From this isolation Russia suffered an intellectual and technological handicap which has placed her at a sometimes disastrous disadvantage. Russia's greatest leaders have been fully conscious of this backwardness and they have bent their finest efforts toward overcoming it.

When in 1037 the patriarch of Constantinople ordained and sent to Kiev the first metropolitan, Russia became a metropolitical diocese of the Byzantine church. With only two exceptions all the metropolitans of the Kievan period came from Constantinople, as did perhaps half of the ordinary bishops. The Byzantines sent out to occupy the Russian bishoprics took with them a train of clerks and assistants, and each cathedral city became a center from which the culture of Constantinople spread over the land. At the time of the conversion Russia was assigned eight bishops to sit in the principal cities of the realm. Two and a half centuries later the number of bishoprics had grown to fifteen, including that at Novgorod which had become an archbishopric. While all bishops were ordained by the metropolitan, the selection of those not sent out from Constantinople was left to the grand prince or, as in the case of Novgorod, to the city *vieche*. These princes of the church—the bishops, whose authority and wealth contrasted so markedly with the position of the lower clergy—were chosen from the monastic ranks, the so-called "black" clergy. The parish priests, or "white" clergy, took no vow of celibacy and were, in fact, selected from married men. Since each congregation nominated its own priest, whom the bishop then ordained, the lower clergy represented the class dominant in each particular parish. Most of them consequently sprang from the lower classes of society.

All monks in the Russian church belonged to one order, but not all followed the same pattern of life. In some monasteries the brothers lived, dined, and worked communally, while in others each monk kept to his own cell. By the close of the Kievan period over fifty monasteries and a dozen nunneries had been established, all but one of which were situated in cities. The Monastery of the Caves in Kiev, which became the most famous in the land, did much to promote learning and it was there that the *Primary Chronicle* was written.

In addition to these clerics and their families, the Church, in its own courts over which the bishops presided, exercised complete legal jurisdiction over various categories of Russians who served the church. Among these were sextons, caretakers, choristers, physicians, keepers of inns for pilgrims and homes for the aged, men freed from slavery who tilled church lands, and even the women who baked the wafers for use in the communion service. Furthermore, as in the West, all Kievans came under the authority of church courts in some cases, notably in those having to do with infractions of the moral law. Byzantine law spread quickly in Russia by its application in ecclesiastical courts. While some attention was paid to social services by an occasional prince, the church accepted responsibility for caring for the needy and for promoting education. Its schools were maintained for the education of recruits for the ranks of the clergy, but not a few graduates took service with lay princes. Hospitals, inns, and homes for the aged were operated by monasteries, and the care of the poor was both undertaken by the church and recommended by it to laymen.

The adoption of Christianity brought vigorous stimulation to the pursuit of the fine arts. Choral music was introduced, and the Russians have excelled in it ever since. Following the Byzantine practice, instrumental music was not used in the churches. But in the eleventh century the use of bells was taken up from the West, and in their casting Russians have remained unsurpassed. It was in the field of church architecture, however, that the effects of the conversion were most pronounced. Vladimir began work on the Church of the Tithe in Kiev shortly after his baptism. The Cathedral of St. Sophia, with its richly painted walls and its central cupola surrounded by twelve smaller ones, must have been an imposing sight. Begun by Iaroslav and completed in 1100, it suffered badly from fires and desecrations during times of political instability. The stone cathedral of the same name in Novgorod, begun in 1045, survived until 1944, when the Germans almost completely destroyed it before their withdrawal. In the late twelfth and early thirteenth centuries there developed in the north, centering in Vladimir, a new type of church building known as "Suzdalian architecture." Andrew Bogoliubsky and Vsevolod "Big Nest" imported Westerners to aid in the construction of a number of churches, and the peculiar type which resulted was a blend of Byzantine and Romanesque lines. The princes of Moscow later patterned their churches after those in the Suzdal period. The Eastern church frowned upon sculpture but encouraged painting and mosaics. Painted images substituted for sculptured ones, and the icon "corner," where pictures of the saints were hung and candles lit before them on holy days, was to be found in every Russian home. At first icons were imported from Byzantium, but skilled Russian artists soon were at work in sufficient numbers to satisfy the home market. The literary effects of the conversion, while perhaps not as dramatically evident as were those in architecture, were also considerable. Because the Eastern church did not insist that the service be conducted in a strange tongue, the Slavs learned the new ritual and understood it in their own language. The homilectics of the leading divines and the "lives" of the saints were accessible to all who could read Slavic.

Judaism and Roman Catholicism also existed in Kievan Russia, but chiefly among foreigners who came there to trade. Roman Catholic churches were built in Kiev, Novgorod, and Smolensk to minister to German and Scandinavian merchants, and there was even a Dominican monastery in the capital. Inside the Russian church the "Bogomil" heresy, emphasizing the struggle between good and evil or God and Satan and objecting to the accumulation of wealth by Orthodox clergymen, made some headway. It entered Russia from Bulgaria, and passed on to the west to appear in southern France as the Albigensian heresy.

Russian society in Kievan times developed a number of trends which were projected through the period of Tatar domination into the new Russia that was to emerge under the leadership of Moscow. Perhaps the strongest link between the old and the new was the church, which in times of chaos often seemed the only tie binding East Slavs together. A system of law, welding together Byzantine practice and Varangian and East Slav custom, survived the decline of Kiev. A common language, given stability by the introduction of an alphabet which permitted the tongue to be written as well as spoken, bound all Russians together. A literature handed down to succeeding generations the stories of the great deeds and of the sufferings of the people. A strong feeling of national unity and inviolability of the land, a feeling for "Mother Russia," continued through times when there was no nation in the political sense. Cultural homogeneity characterized the society of Kievan Russia and survived through the period of chaos that followed the collapse of the state, to be caught up again and given political leadership by the princes of Moscow.

SUGGESTED READING

Chadwick, N. K., *The Beginnings of Russian History* (New York, Cambridge University Press, 1946).

Cross, S. H. (ed.), *The Russian Primary Chronicle* (Cambridge, Harvard University Press, 1930).

Fedotov, G. P., *The Russian Religious Mind: Kievan Christianity* (Cambridge, Harvard University Press, 1946).

Grekov, B. D., *The Culture of Kiev Rus* (Moscow, Foreign Languages Publishing House, 1947).

Kendrick, T. D., *A History of the Vikings* (New York, Scribner's, 1930).

Kliuchevsky, V. O., *A History of Russia*, vol. I (London, Dent, 1911).

Lyashchenko, P. I., *History of the National Economy of Russia to the 1917 Revolution* (New York, Macmillan, 1949).

Mavor, J., *An Economic History of Russia* (New York, Dutton, 1925).

McGovern, W. M., *The Early Empires of Central Asia* (Chapel Hill, University of North Carolina, 1939).

Mirsky, D. S., *Russia, a Social History* (London, Cresset Press, 1931).

Pares, B., *A History of Russia* (New York, Knopf, 1953).

Platonov, S. F., *History of Russia* (New York, Macmillan, 1925).

Vasiliev, A. A., *History of the Byzantine Empire* (Madison, University of Wisconsin Press, 1929).

Vernadsky, G., *Ancient Russia* (New Haven, Yale University Press, 1943).

———, *Kievan Russia* (New Haven, Yale University Press, 1948).

———, *Medieval Russian Laws* (New York, Columbia University Press, 1947).

7

Great Novgorod

WHEN THE VARANGIANS WERE INVITED or hired to assume political leadership over the East Slavs, the land was organized into a loose confederation of city-states. Because of their strategic location near opposite ends of the Dnieper water-road, two of these city-states, Kiev and Novgorod, towered above all the rest in importance. The former became the capital of the state which Oleg welded together, and so in a sense lost its identity. But Novgorod did not suffer by the prince's decision to set up his capital at the other end of the water-road. Its economic and even its political importance was never dimmed through Kievan times, and indeed toward their close, when the capital was falling into eclipse, the great city of the north was at work building and developing a distinct economic empire of its own. Long before the end of the fifteenth century, when it came under the rule of the Muscovite state, Novgorod had extended its control over nearly a third of European Russia and was far larger than any of the other principalities.

The city of Novgorod straddled the river Volkhov a few miles downstream from where the river leaves Lake Ilmen. The two banks were connected near the town center by the Great Bridge. On the eastern bank lay that portion of the city known as the "commercial" side, from the fact that near the bridge was located the principal market. Adjoining the market was a great square called Iaroslav's Court, in the center of which stood a rostrum from which leaders addressed the citizens assembled in the *vieche*. Nearby rose the tower containing the great bell which called the people to meet in assembly in the square. This "commercial" side, it may be noted, was the democratic, working-class district of Novgorod. Across the river lay the "Sophia" side of the city, so named because near the bridge in an enclosed

square stood the great Cathedral of St. Sophia which has been referred to
as Novgorod's Westminster. This was the portion of the city occupied by
the homes of the well-to-do merchants and boyars. The city proper, including both banks, was divided into five "quarters," some of which originally had housed particular crafts or trades, such as the "potters' quarter"
and the "carpenters' quarter." The five quarters were surrounded by a ram-
part and ditch. Outside these defenses lay the city's suburbs and a number
of monastic communities, and beyond the suburbs extended a vast colonial
territory tributary to the city.

THE GOVERNMENT OF NOVGOROD

In the early Kievan period Novgorod was little noticed by the princes,
or perhaps it was taken for granted. Their attention was upon Constantinople, and their energy was concentrated upon keeping open the lower
Dnieper and upon winning Russian access to the markets of the great
entrepôt on the Bosporus. After Iaroslav's death Novgorod did not become
a separate principality, as did Smolensk and Chernigov and Pereiaslav, but
was assigned along with Kiev to the senior member of the family. The senior
as grand prince kept to the capital on the lower Dnieper and delegated one
of his sons to rule in Novgorod as his viceroy. None of the princes who
ruled in Kiev after Vladimir Monomakh was sufficiently powerful to maintain his authority undiminished over the northern city. As the princely feuds
brought to Novgorod a rapid succession of princes, each a transient waiting
for promotion in the rota system, the Novgorodian *vieche* won two important
political victories: first, the right of the citizens to name their own administrative officers and, second, the right to wring concessions from their
prince by arranging a treaty with him before he assumed office. The city
began referring to itself as "Lord Novgorod," indicating that, no matter
what lord or prince might rule in Kiev or elsewhere, this giant of the north
was its own master.

The famed Novgorodian freedom referred to the city's relative independence from higher authority and not to any specific liberties supposedly enjoyed by its citizens. That relative independence from princely power arose
from a combination of factors that distinguished Novgorod from the rest
of Kievan Russia. In the first place, the city and province were on the outer
rim of the state both geographically and politically. It had no separate place
in the rota system, and consequently was not a prize to be sought after as
the princes struggled for position in the scale of succession. To serve as
prince of Novgorod offered no attraction to members of the royal family,
one of whom referred to its citizens as a "contemptible small company of
carpenters." Secondly, through the eleventh and twelfth centuries, when the

princely squabbles were at their worst, Novgorod had no need of strong leadership to protect her against powerful neighbors and could manage her own administration. Later, in the thirteenth century, when she did sorely require the military leadership of a strong prince, she had already won the elements of that freedom which subordinated the prince to the city *vieche*. Thirdly, Novgorod was the economic hub of a vast empire so rich and powerful that her importance dwarfed that of any individual prince.

Soon after the death of Vladimir Monomakh Novgorod won control over the selection of its own officials. Theretofore the prince of Novgorod, acting as the viceroy of the grand prince of Kiev whose son he usually was, ruled the city through two officials brought with him from Kiev or sent to him from the capital by the grand prince. These officials, invariably Kievans until 1126, were the *posadnik,* or mayor, and the *tysiatsky,* or military and police prefect. When the prince of Novgorod was replaced or promoted to a spot in the rota system, his *posadnik* and *tysiatsky* necessarily resigned, since the new prince would bring his own officials with him. During the time between the departure of one prince and the arrival of another the city was without administrative officers; it developed the practice of choosing a temporary *posadnik* and asking the new prince to make the selection permanent. This first happened in 1126, the year after Monomakh's death, when the chronicler noted that "the men of Novgorod did award the office of *posadnik* to one of themselves." The practice was allowed to continue, and it changed the pattern of relationships between the citizens and their prince. Henceforth the *posadnik* was chosen in the public square and, instead of guarding the interests of the prince as he had previously done, he represented the citizens by whom he had been elected and who had the power to unseat him. In due time the office of *tysiatsky* also came to be filled by election. Finally, in the latter half of the twelfth century, the citizens won the right to elect their own bishop from among the brothers in the monasteries which rimmed the city, and to send him to Kiev to be invested by the metropolitan. Within a space of thirty years, by 1156, the three heads of the city administration had been brought under the elective control of the *vieche,* and the citizens had freed themselves from princely domination. As the descendants of Iaroslav increased in number and made it possible for the city to choose its prince from among several rivals who had no principality, it became easy to accept a prince only after imposing further restrictions upon his power in the city. One prince scorned the position, saying, "Talk not to me of Novgorod. Let it rule itself as best it may, and seek itself princes where it listeth." Soon the princely family recognized the city's right to choose its ruler from anyone in the royal family who would accept the position. The treatment often meted out to the prince suggests that the citizens were not easily satisfied. In 1136 the Novgorodians seized their prince, imprisoned him for a time, and finally expelled him or "showed him the road," as the chronicler expresses it. His successor was allowed to stay less than a year, and a third prince lasted less than two years. The city went through most of 1141 without a ruler, and when one was finally found he was dismissed after a few weeks. Between 1154 and 1160 seven princes were tried out, all of whom fled in the night or were expelled.

The privileges of the city were specified in charters granted by the princes, and are the closest approximation to a constitution to be found in the Kievan period. The oldest charter extant dates from 1265, just fifty years after the English barons forced King John to accept the Magna Carta. In accepting the treaty or charter of 1265 the prince agreed to rule and "maintain Novgorod according to the custom of ancient times," which suggests that the privileges were of long standing. The prince was named as the supreme administrative and judicial head in Novgorod, but his powers were to be exercised, not as his will dictated, but only with the consent of the elected *posadnik,* or mayor. Without the latter's presence the prince could not hold court; without his approval the prince could not appoint officials to minor administrative posts. Important offices were filled by election in the *vieche.* Only Novgorodians could be named to appointive posts, and none could be dismissed without trial. The prince was obliged to reside in the city and carry out his administrative and judicial functions under the observation of the *posadnik.* "Not from the land of Suzdal shalt thou administer Novgorod," one prince was warned.

The revenue of the prince of Novgorod was adequate but strictly limited. He received "tribute" or direct taxes from the citizens, not in annual payments but in installments, only while he was present in the city. If he should leave the city, even only temporarily, perhaps to inspect his private estate elsewhere, the tribute stopped until he returned. Taxes levied upon the city's colonial districts were collected by Novgorodians and paid over to the prince in the city. While in Novgorodian territory the prince also received a percentage of court fees and tolls upon fishing, hunting, and beekeeping. He was not allowed to own property in Novgorod, to lend money at interest, or to engage in any business, for such income might free him from complete financial dependence upon his office. The prince was looked upon simply as a defender of the city and as protector of its trade, and the charter was carefully drawn to prevent his being anything else. He was the military leader, not the commander, of the citizen army, "alongside of whom the citizens may stand and fight." His residence lay some distance outside the walls. So completely was his power circumscribed that Novgorod was in effect a free commonwealth, even though it possessed a prince just as did other Russian cities.

Just as in the other cities of Russia the political subdivision of Novgorod followed military lines. The city as a whole and its fighting men as a body constituted a *tysiach,* or regiment, literally a thousand, commanded by the elected military prefect, or *tysiatsky*. Each ward made up a hundred, commanded by an elected *sotsky*, which fought as a unit in wartime and in peacetime governed itself through its own assembly, or *vieche*. Two hundreds were assigned to each quarter of the city, and the quarter was administered in civil affairs by a board of leading citizens responsible to the two ward assemblies within the quarter. Finally, the hundred or ward was divided into tens, or streets, led in war by a *desiatsky*, or commander of ten. In civil life each street constituted a *mir* or commune, an assembly of heads of families, organized to govern itself in its own local affairs.

The *posadnik* and the *tysiatsky* were elected for an indefinite term, subject to recall for malfeasance. Not until shortly before the conquest of Novgorod by the grand prince of Moscow was the term of these officials limited to one year. They were paid from the revenue from a tax on agricultural land. The two officials cooperated to maintain the peace and carry out the laws of the commonwealth. The *tysiatsky* as prefect of police kept the watch and seized disturbers of the peace, while he and the *posadnik* worked together in bringing criminals to justice. Both officials sat on a board to decide disputes between Novgorodian and foreign merchants. There was a confusion of courts in medieval Novgorod—courts at the ward level and courts in each quarter, the prince's court, the bishop's court, the *posadnik's* court, and the *tysiatsky's* court. Court fees were an important source of revenue, and a right to a share in fees and fines was a perquisite much sought after.

The Novgorod *vieche* continued, in spite of the growth of the city and the unwieldy size attained by the assembly, to include all male heads of families in the city and its subject territory. In practice only inhabitants of the city proper attended its sessions, for the technique of representation never developed in early Russia. At times the prince called the *vieche* into session, at others the *posadnik* or the *tysiatsky*, and occasionally leading citizens tolled the great bell to organize the townsmen against the officials. The power of the Novgorod *vieche* was greater than that of any assembly in Europe at the time. It could dismiss or imprison a prince and summon a new one. It elected and could recall the leading officials, the *posadnik*, the *tysiatsky*, and the bishop. It voted war and peace and decided all questions of foreign or external relations. It enacted all legislation affecting the city at large and approved all tax changes. Finally, it acted as supreme court to punish all criminals whose offense was serious enough to make them liable to death, exile, or confiscation of property. All decisions of the *vieche* had to be unanimous, and a minority which held out in opposition was cajoled, threatened, or bludgeoned into voting with the majority. Frequently the assembly broke up into two hostile groups, the one continuing to meet in Iaroslav's Court, the other repairing across the Volkhov to organize its own *vieche* in the Cathedral Square. "When there should have been war against the pagans [i. e., the Lithuanians] then they began to fight each other . . .

and then there were *vieches* all through the week." At times the opposing factions met on the Great Bridge, and men were beaten and hurled into the Volkhov until the bishop managed to restore peace.

Because of the size of the *vieche*, its lack of organization, and the fact that it did not hold regular meetings but came together to pass judgment on a given question, the action of the Novgorodian assembly was limited to a simple approval or rejection of a proposal. This gave rise to the organization of the Novgorodian Council of Magnates whose job it was to formulate questions or laws to be put to the *vieche* for passage. The archbishop, most wealthy citizens, and all who had ever held the office of *posadnik* or *tysiatsky* sat on the council, which at one time numbered over fifty members. It was made up exclusively of members of the great merchant families who dominated city office, and gave city government the character of an oligarchy rather than that of a democracy. A dozen different *posadniki*, for example, came from a single family. While the members of the Council of Magnates could not vote in the *vieche,* they could so word the propositions put before it as to obtain the action they desired. For this reason, as well as for the fact of social stratification which is known to have existed, the highly touted Novgorodian freedom had little meaning for the majority of citizens.

Long before the Varangians were called into Russia Novgorod was a city-state, a city upon whose markets a large surrounding district had been brought to depend and which had managed to impose political as well as economic control over a considerable area beyond its walls. Some of the early princes, notably Vladimir and Iaroslav, had led the metropolitan militia to further conquests, and the city had expanded in all directions during the tenth and eleventh centuries. Its most notable strides were made toward the northeast, where bands of armed traders pushed into the sparsely inhabited forests, founded settlements, levied fur tribute upon the natives, and gathered wax and honey in the forests. Such bands had settled east of the Northern Dvina in the eleventh century, and a century later had reached the Pechora and the north coast of the White Sea. By 1200 "Lord Novgorod the Great," as the citizens styled it, was not just a city but a vast colonial empire stretching away to the Arctic Ocean and to the Urals and even beyond.

That portion of this colonial area which was first acquired was divided into provinces, or "fifths," while towns and regions later brought under the city's control or shared with other principalities were administered separately as districts, or "lands." Northwest of the city and west of the Volkhov river lay the province of Vodi, so named for the Finnish tribe of Vodi who inhabited the area. While serving as prince of Novgorod before his father's death, Iaroslav had conquered much of this area and had carried Novgorod's authority to the shores of the Gulf of Finland. Northeast of the city and east of the Volkhov was the province or "fifth" of Obonezh which included Lake Onega and reached for four hundred and fifty miles nearly to the White Sea. East and south of Novgorod, between the Msta and Lovat rivers, lay another "fifth," and southwest of the city, in the direction of Pskov, still another. The last of these "fifths" lay between the Msta and the Volga. Beyond these provinces lay the domains, or "lands" which were conquered last in Novgorod's insatiable drive for territory. Some of these were relatively small areas shared with Novgorod's neighbors. Such was Veliki Luki, near the headwaters of the Lovat, which Novgorod shared first with Smolensk and later with Lithuania; similarly, the towns of Volokolamsk and Torzhok were shared between Novgorod and the princes of Moscow. The land between the rivers Onega, Northern Dvina, and Volga constituted one administrative region or domain; the "land of Permia" covered the valley of the Vychegda, tributary of the Northern Dvina; next east lay the Pechora district, lying along the river of that name; farthest east the Iugra region reached to the Urals and beyond. Finally, the northern and western shores of the White Sea comprised still another domain.

The administration of the "fifths" or provinces was centered in Novgorod, although each was allowed considerable latitude in controlling its own local affairs. Each of the "fifths" was assigned to one of the five quarters of the city. Residents of the provinces paid taxes to the city quarter to which their "fifth" was attached and could arrange contracts only with the citizens of that quarter. Provincial towns were organized on the same pattern that obtained in the capital: each was headed by a *posadnik* sent out from Novgorod, each had its own *vieche,* and each in turn was divided into wards and hundreds where its size justified the subdivision. Leading provincial officials were responsible to the *vieche* of the Novgorodian ward which confirmed their appointment. Provincial courts could marshal evidence and open cases in which provincials were involved, but judgment could only be passed by the appropriate court in the capital. Serviceable men residing in the "fifths" were required to bear arms in the Novgorodian militia in time of need. Aside from these ties and duties to the capital, the provinces were left very much to themselves. However, now and again a provincial town refused to pay taxes to Novgorod, and was punished by execution of some of the local inhabitants and the burning of part of the town. "Lord Novgorod" could be a stern master.

NOVGORODIAN SOCIETY

The inhabitants of this great metropolitan empire of the north may be distinguished as urban or rural, and each of these was further stratified into classes. At the top of urban society was the class of boyars, who insisted upon the same social recognition that fell to those noble servants of the princes who attained boyar status through the *druzhina* and who developed into landowning gentry in late Kievan times. In Novgorod members of the wealthiest families, often moneylenders, who monopolized high office—the "hundred" men or ward aldermen, the mayors and police prefects —came to refer to themselves and to be considered by the prince as boyars. Next to the boyars and closely allied to them was a small class of moderately wealthy merchants, not sufficiently wealthy and influential to be included in the closed circle of magnates from which the chief officials were selected, but towering over the class of small merchants and shopkeepers who stood below them. Members of this class owned spacious and comfortable town houses, but not the palatial sort of residence occupied by the leading families. Many of them owned sizable estates in the country. These were the great traders and wholesale merchants, in whose enterprises the Novgorodian boyars were willing to invest capital but not to take an active part. As "capitalists of a secondary order" they stood midway between the investment banking and important office-holding class on the one hand and the small tradesmen on the other. While this class is hard to distinguish, its characteristic feature was its ownership of country estates which led Moscow later to classify it as composing not merchants or city dwellers but landed proprietors. The third class in Novgorodian society was that which included retail merchants and shopkeepers, the more prosperous of whom were associated in the "corporation of the Merchants of St. John," a merchant guild which maintained mercantile standards and which settled disputes arising out of trade. At the bottom of urban society were the *chernie liudi* (literally black, soiled, or dirty people), composed of the skilled and unskilled wage-laborers who worked for the merchants above them. The society of provincial towns subject to Novgorod included chiefly the third and fourth classes found in the capital itself. The boyars and great merchants preferred the capital, and the nature of their economic and political interests tended to keep them there.

Agricultural land was cultivated for the most part under a system of great estates, the owner of which at times lived on his estate and supervised its operation but at others preferred to leave its management to a bailiff while he followed commercial interests in the capital. At the bottom of rural society was the slave, or *kholop,* who had lost his freedom by debt or by capture in war. For example, some of the troops of Prince Andrew Bogoliubsky of Suzdalia were captured while attacking the city and were paraded through the streets to be sold in the markets of Novgorod for the same price as a loaf of bread. At another time, the chronicler reports, Prince Vsevolod of Vladimir "with the men of Novgorod went against the Chud [Finnish] people in the winter during the Feast; them he slaughtered, their dwellings he burned, and their wives and children he brought home [as slaves]." These very numerous slaves were found only on privately owned estates, for the state lands of Novgorod were worked only by free peasants. Some free peasants also were located as sharecroppers on private lands, where they surrendered to the owner a third or a fourth of the harvest in return for the use of the land. While the peasants whose labor was used on Novgorodian state lands retained their freedom until Novgorod fell to Moscow, the status of those on private estates declined steadily until they were hardly distinguishable from slaves. By the opening of the fourteenth century they were bound to the owner whose acres they tilled, and treaty arrangements with neighboring principalities provided for their extradition should they escape from Novgorodian territory. This was a century and a half before serfdom appeared in the rest of Russia and indicates that the great mass of the rural population toiling on the great private estates of free Novgorod was certainly not free. Finally, in the rural districts around Novgorod there was a small class of peasant proprietors, owning outright and working with their own labor their small farms of forty or fifty acres. They organized associations among themselves to pool labor, seed, and capital and so to protect themselves from the vicissitudes that might drive the individual into bankruptcy and slavery. Some in this class were small city merchants who invested their business surplus in a suburban acreage and then rented it on shares to other peasant proprietors or to landless free peasants.

The turbulent political history of Novgorod in the eleventh, twelfth, thirteenth, and fourteenth centuries reflects the class composition of Novgorodian society and the conflicts it engendered. In the first two of these centuries the serious uprisings, of which there were twelve in the city, were the result of disagreements over the succession which were associated with the question of whether Novgorod's commercial tie should be stronger with Suzdal or with Kiev. The moderately wealthy wholesale merchants, who constituted the entrepreneurial class in business, sought to strengthen Novgorod's economic ties with Suzdal and the middle Volga; in backing a candidate to be prince of Novgorod they gave their support to the descendants of Vladimir Monomakh and his grandson, Vsevolod "Big Nest." The boyar investment-banker class at the pinnacle of Novgorodian society, on the other hand, had investments in Kiev and in the trade with Constantinople, and consequently favored a close tie with the southern end of the water-road; it supported the senior branch of the princely family, the descendants of Monomakh's older cousin Oleg Sviatoslavich. In part, at least, the question was one of promoting domestic trade by closer association with the rising prosperity of the Suzdal area, or of continued reliance upon foreign trade over the water-road to Constantinople even though the security of the outlet to Byzantine markets was being steadily reduced by princely civil war and Polovtsy raids. The fact that Novgorod's two wealthiest and most powerful classes could afford the luxury of intraclass war over the disposition of the succession and the orientation of the city's commercial development suggests that the lower classes may still have been fairly prosperous and relatively free, and had not yet been driven to the point of desperation. Many of them were moving east into the vast hinterland to seek new opportunity on the frontier which served as an escape valve for what might otherwise have developed into social unrest. It hardly needs to be pointed out that during this early period of civil strife the government of Novgorod was firmly in the hands of the two wealthiest classes, the question being simply which faction should fill the chief administrative posts and control the administration. However theoretically free the Novgorodian citizenry may have been when assembled in the *vieche,* every common freeman must have been acutely aware of the presence of members of a few rich families for whom he worked or to whom he owed money. Since voting was by acclamation, his economic dependence was translated into political dependence.

During the thirteenth and fourteenth centuries the character of civil strife in Novgorod changed markedly. Now it was class war between the rich and the poor, between the propertied and the propertyless, between the employing class and the laborers, between the boyar merchant-citizens from the Cathedral side of the Great Bridge and the working-class and small shopkeeper quarter from the "commercial" side of the Volkhov. As the lower classes became more and more liable to loss of freedom through debt and the heavy taxes which they alone could not manage to escape, some of them formed gangs, which were joined by runaway slaves, and roamed and pillaged over the countryside, some operating as far east as the Volga. In 1386, according to the *Chronicle of Novgorod,* the city was forced to pay eight thousand rubles to the grand prince of Moscow "for the guilt of the Volga men," as such gangs were called. Others who could not escape rose up against their masters, surged over the Great Bridge, and beat or killed boyars and sacked their homes, only to suffer an awful vengeance when the boyars recovered and counterattacked. One boyar family came forward to lead the oppressed, and so managed to take over the administration when working-class uprising unseated those who represented the wealthy. The lower classes produced no leaders from among their own ranks, and so through the thirteenth and fourteenth centuries the offices of mayor, police prefect, and ward aldermen continued to be dominated, as they had been in earlier centuries, by two or three great families. The *vieche* became a mob whose meetings no boyar dared attend except those of the renegade family which now led the popular uprising. The propertied classes organized their own assembly on the Cathedral side, and at times there was no central administration in the city. Battles between the two sides sometimes ran for days, when one side would emerge the victor and impose its will over the entire city. When Moscow advanced against Novgorod in 1471, the boyars sought help from "Latin" or Roman Catholic Poland, while the lower classes, staunchly faithful to Orthodoxy, supported Moscow. Thus, in the end, Novgorod's inability to settle her social and political problems brought her downfall, and the great empire was absorbed into the growing territory of the principality which was to become the new nation-state of Russia.

NOVGORODIAN ECONOMY

The economic basis upon which Novgorod depended was "the exhausting exploitation of natural resources" (Fisher). This explains the city's insatiable drive to expand the area under her control, to incorporate within the state ever new untouched expanses which her armed traders might develop. The availability of vast reaches of territory to her northeast, rich in the products of the forest and still lying beyond the borders of any Russian principality, made possible the steady expansion of Novgorod and with it a corresponding growth in her size and wealth. Novgorodian settlers pushed into the area east of Lake Onega and when a number of villages, forts, and trading posts had been established, this "fifth," or province, of Obonezh was attached to "Lord Novgorod." Then other parties pressed on to the Northern Dvina and its tributary the Vychegda, and this new frontier was brought under Novgorodian rule as the "Land of Permia." Still farther into the northeast armed bands drove to the Pechora, and, crossing the Urals as early as the eleventh century, others found their way even into the valley of the Ob. No settlements were built in this corner of Russia, and Novgorod was content to send out annual expeditions simply to collect tribute from the natives.

The forest product which prompted this restless drive into the hinterland was fur, the most important commodity of export from Novgorod. The search for pelts, which involved a heavy outlay of capital for men, equipment, and articles to trade with the natives, was carried on by wealthy merchants and sometimes financed by Novgorodian boyars. The maintenance of villages and trading posts far from the capital and the equipping of large expeditions to penetrate beyond the fringe of settlement was a costly business which no small trader had the wherewithal to finance. Sable was most in demand, but if the natives had not been able to gather enough sable pelts to meet the full amount of their *iasak*, or tribute, they were allowed to make up the difference in ermine, marten, beaver, otter, fox, lynx, wolf, or squirrel. The Novgorodians used every possible method of gathering furs, no one of which alone could satisfy their greed. Armed expeditions were sent out each spring to levy tribute upon the Finnish peoples native to the area, the tribute being payable in pelts and the standard of payment being set in sables, the most valuable fur. These military bands were sent only into territory not yet brought firmly under Novgorodian authority. This method of obtaining fur was used chiefly in Iugria, east of the Urals, which Novgorod never thoroughly conquered. Not all such expeditions, however, met with success. In 1187 the natives on both slopes of the Urals rose and massacred the Russians who came to collect tribute. Six years later a similar force met disaster. Again in 1445 an army of three thousand men sent into Iugria to impose the will of Novgorod was handed a severe drubbing by the natives. In domains closer to the capital, where trading posts were maintained, furs were bartered from the natives in exchange for axes, knives, and trinkets. From these trading posts travelling merchants visited the native villages, loaded on the out journey with articles the natives were willing to buy, and weighted down on the return trip with a rich fortune in pelts. In this area where Novgorodian settlement made life relatively safe, individuals trapped on their own account, as though impatient to wait for the harvest that trade and conquest would produce. Here on the Russian frontier, for four centuries beginning with the eleventh, the quest for fur consumed the energy of every Novgorodian in the area. So important was fur that during those four centuries it occupied the place of currency. *Kuny,* the word for money in use at the time, came from *kunitsa*, meaning marten.

The pelts gathered on the northeastern frontier were brought into Novgorod, sorted, graded, baled, and sold wholesale to the German merchants of the Hanse who maintained permanent offices and warehouses in the city. From Novgorod the furs were shipped out to important markets in western Europe, to Bremen, Hamburg, Lübeck, Ghent, Bruges, London, and even the Italian cities. These shipments were balanced by Novgorod's imports from the west of such commodities as Ypres cloth, fine clothing, weapons, needles, iron, copper, tin, herring, wine, beer, and occasionally salt and grain. To buy up these products and to negotiate contracts for the sale of her own exports, Novgorod sent her own merchants into foreign ports on the eastern and southern shores of the Baltic. The chronicler tells of the loss at sea of seven Russian ships returning from Denmark in 1131. In Visby, on the west coast of the island of Gotland, the colony of Russian merchants was of sufficient size to justify their maintaining a parish church. Later, when the Hanseatic merchants squeezed out the Scandinavian merchants and took over their facilities in Novgorod, the Russian colony in Visby moved to Lübeck. Russia's trade with the west, however, from the thirteenth century to the middle of the fifteenth, was carried on chiefly through the agency of members of the Hanse. Novgorod herself was never a member of the League, the easternmost city actually joined to it being

Riga, but her association with it was very close and her reliance upon it to distribute her furs over Europe was very great. To maintain her own domestic commercial independence from the powerful Hanse Novgorod forbade any Russian to become a member of the German guild and prohibited any retail dealing with the Germans.

German merchants appeared in Novgorod before the middle of the twelfth century, and by 1165 shipments of goods were being made directly to and from Cologne. By 1225 the Germans had won such recognition in Novgorod that the details of their privileges were inscribed in a code which was enforceable in Novgorodian courts. A section of the "commercial" side of Novgorod, called the "Court of the *Nemtsy*," * was set aside for their exclusive use. Here the German merchants had their warehouses, their shops, their brewery, their guildhall, their church, and dwellings for them and their families. The area was walled off separately and its gates locked and guarded at night. The Hanse enjoyed similar privileges in Pskov and Ladoga, towns tributary to Great Novgorod.

Novgorodian exports moved into western Europe chiefly through Hanseatic merchants. The city was the great fur center of the world, and its reputation for high quality fur was universally recognized. Novgorod's importance began to decline, however, after the middle of the fifteenth century, as the grand prince of Moscow moved into Novgorodian territory and usurped control of the fur trade to which the city owed much of her greatness. Her economic decline was well under way as a result of this encroachment when Moscow administered the *coup de grâce* by seizing the city itself after 1471.

Fur was not the only product of the colonial empire which Novgorod brought under subjection, although it was by far the most important. Honey was gathered in large quantity, but most of it was consumed locally or sold in other Russian cities. Wax and wax candles were exported to Catholic Europe, although Orthodox Russia also used an enormous lot. Timber, always the primary building material of the north, was cut even in remote areas where it could be floated downstream to market. Clothing and leather goods were manufactured by city craftsmen, chiefly for the domestic market.

Novgorod, always pre-eminently a market rather than a production center, was dependent upon trade for her very existence. The maintenance of her contact with the west was absolutely necessary to permit her to market the surplus which her colonial empire yielded and to receive in exchange the finished goods which western Europe could provide. There was another aspect, however, of Novgorod's reliance upon the outside which, if not as

---

* *Nemtsy* is the name by which Germans have been known to all Slavs for centuries. In time of war the word expresses otherwise unspeakable contempt, in time of peace something of suspicion. Often it has been applied to all foreigners. *Nemoi,* the root from which it comes, means dumb, mute, speechless, or incomprehensible.

dramatic, was just as vital to her. This was her need to import food, and particularly grain, from distant areas. The great estates which ringed the city brought into her markets a considerable quantity of vegetables and of rye for the making of bread, but at its best this source could not meet the demands of a population that exceeded a quarter of a million. At its worst, when an August frost dashed all hope of a harvest, this source was worthless. The *Chronicle of Novgorod* reveals the hardships which such a catastrophe imposed upon the city. For 1127 there is the entry: "In the autumn the frost killed all the grain and the winter crop; and there was famine throughout the winter." Loss of the crop that year produced even greater misery in the following year:

This year it was cruel; [a pound of gold bought less than three bushels of rye]; the people ate lime tree leaves, birch bark, pounded wood pulp mixed with husks and straw; some ate buttercups, moss, horseflesh; and thus many dropping down from hunger, their corpses were in the streets, in the market place, and on the roads, and everywhere. They hired hirelings to carry the dead out of the town; the serfs could not go out [to work in the fields]; woe and misery on all! Fathers and mothers would put their children into boats in gift to merchants [i. e., give, not sell, them into slavery to foreign merchants], or else put them to death; and others dispersed over foreign lands.

In 1230 an early frost destroyed crops all over Russia except in the Kiev area, and bread riots broke out in Novgorod. The monk who chronicled the city's history left a gripping account of the tragedy wrought by the famine:

A frost killed the crops throughout our district and from that there arose great misery. . . . Our town and our country went asunder and other towns and countries became full of our own brothers and sisters; and the rest began to die. And who would not weep at this, seeing the dead lying in the streets, and the little ones devoured by dogs? And God put into the heart of Bishop Spiridon to do good. He put a common grave by the Church of the Holy Apostles in Prussian Street and engaged a good and gentle man to carry the dead on horses wherever he went about the town and so continuously he dragged them every day; and he filled it up to the top; there were 3,030 in it. . . . For what is there to say, or what to speak, of the punishment that came to us from God? How that some of the common people killed the living and ate them; others cutting up dead flesh and corpses ate them; others ate horseflesh, dogs and cats; but to those found in such acts they did thus—some they burned with fire, others they cut to pieces, and others they hanged. Some fed on moss, snails, pine-bark, lime-bark, lime and elm-tree leaves, and whatever each could think of. And again other wicked men began to burn the good people's houses, where they suspected that there was rye; and so they plundered their property. Instead of repentance for our wickedness, we became more prone to wickedness than before, though seeing before our eyes the wrath of God: the dead in the streets and in the market-place, and on the great bridge, being devoured by dogs, so that they could not bury them. They put another pit outside at the end of Chudinets Street, and that became full, and there is no counting [the number of bodies in it]. And they put a third at Koleno beyond the Church of the Holy Nativity, and that likewise became full, there was no counting the bodies. And seeing all this before our eyes we should have become better; but we became worse. Brother had no sympathy with brother, nor father with son, nor mother with daughter, nor would neighbour break bread with neighbour. There was no kindness among us, but misery and unhappiness; in the streets unkindness one to another, at home anguish, seeing children crying for bread and others dying. . . . Fathers and mothers gave away their children into servitude to merchants for bread. . . . And so has God rewarded us according to our deeds.

Until the middle of the eleventh century the great city could rely upon wheat brought up the water-road from the steppe, but when the Polovtsy raids increased in frequency and severity the Kiev area no longer produced a surplus for export. Occasionally wheat was imported from western Europe, but transportation costs ran high when grain was shipped such a distance in vessels which could carry only a few hundred tons of cargo. To ship grain from the west and sell it in Novgorod for a price which would cover cost was to impose upon the poor such hardship as to invite social unrest. From the twelfth century on Novgorod found a new source of food much closer than either Kiev or the Baltic. This was the valley of the upper Volga, upon which the city came more and more to rely for bread grain, notably rye. So completely did she come to depend upon it that she made herself dangerously vulnerable to attack by any power able to sever her contact with the Volga basin. An enemy from the east had only to seize Torzhok to shut off Novgorod's food supply. The *Chronicle of Novgorod* describes such an eventuality in 1215:

The same autumn much harm was done; frost killed the crops throughout the district; but at Torzhok all remained whole. The Prince seized all the grain in Torzhok, and would not let one cart-load into the city; and they sent Semen Borisovich, Vyacheslav Klimyatich [and] Zubets Yakun to fetch the Prince and he detained them; and he detained whomever you sent. And in Novgorod it was very bad; people ate bark and lime tree leaves and moss. O brothers, then was the trouble; they gave their children into slavery. They dug a public grave and filled it full. O, there was trouble! Corpses in the market-place, corpses in the street, corpses in the fields; the dogs could not eat up the [dead] men!

This was precisely what happened again in 1471, when the grand prince of Moscow, Ivan III, cut Novgorod's connection with the Volga. The city was starved out, and a rising of the population brought Ivan a speedy and costless victory. "Lord Novgorod the Great" and the fur empire which she had built fell almost without a struggle, a victim of her dependence upon a distant source of food.

NOVGOROD, THE PRINCES, AND EXTERNAL RELATIONS

To the city which considered itself the lord and master of its own destiny the prince stood in an ambiguous relationship. The Varangians had been called in primarily to defend Russian cities and to guard their trade, and Novgorod resolved that her prince should never be more than a protector. From the successors of Vladimir Monomakh the citizens were able to exact concessions and to force them to accept a generally subordinate position in the government of the "principality." In periods of peace, then, the prince was a shadowy figure, and at times many were paraded through the princely office only to end a momentary career in dismissal or imprisonment. When the city was threatened, however, the prince became invaluable to Novgorod as a military commander, and those who led the citizens in defense of Novgorodian territory stand out in the chronicles in sharp contrast to the princes whose misfortune it was to sit in Novgorod in times of peace.

The first of these princes to rise above the anonymity to which most of them were condemned was Vladimir, the founder of the Russian Orthodox church. When his father Sviatoslav left to take up his permanent home on the Danube, Novgorod was assigned to the rule of the youngest son, Vladimir. At Sviatoslav's death the succession was disputed by the three surviving sons, and Novgorod gave its active support, military and probably financial, to its own prince in his campaign to win the Kievan throne. Vladimir hired a band of troops from Scandinavia—with funds advanced him by Novgorodian merchants, it may be inferred; he added an army of volunteers from the Novgorod area, and won his father's throne by conquest and by murdering his elder brother.

Vladimir's son, Iaroslav the Wise, ruled as prince of Novgorod during the later years of his father's life and nearly went to war with the grand prince over the taxes assessed against his city. It may be surmised that the initiative came from the Novgorodian *vieche,* and that Iaroslav was only the spokesman for the merchants who refused to pay at the rate which Kiev demanded. Upon Vladimir's death the succession was again fought over by the sons, and again the Novgorodians backed their prince to force the settlement. According to the *Chronicle,* three thousand men of Novgorod and a thousand Scandinavian troops, hired for the purpose with Novgorodian money, marched with Iaroslav against his brothers. When all but two of Vladimir's sons had been killed in the war for the throne, the two, Prince Iaroslav of Novgorod, and Prince Mstislav of Tmutorokan, agreed to share their father's land. For a few years Kiev no longer served as the Russian capital, for Mstislav continued in Tmutorokan and Iaroslav preferred to remain in Novgorod. Now Iaroslav repaid Novgorod for her support by seizing the southern shore of the Gulf of Finland from the Estonians and building an outpost, Iuriev, to hold it. After his brother's death Iaroslav became sole ruler of the land of Kiev and left Novgorod to return to the capital on the lower Dnieper. He continued, however, to support Novgorodian interests, and led a Kievan force to drive the Finns from the northeastern shore of the Gulf of Finland, thus improving still further Novgorod's control over the outlet to the Baltic.

For more than a century after the death of Iaroslav the Wise Novgorod sought no favors of the princes and remained relatively free of their control. There was still no serious threat from the west, and the great city spent her energy in expanding with little opposition into the rich fur-producing lands to the northeast. During the wars of the princes over the succession to Iaroslav's throne Novgorod accepted her own princes only after obtaining concessions from them. This was the period of the founding of the "freedom of Novgorod."

Only Vladimir Monomakh saw the need to restore unity in the land of Russia, and during his short reign a number of Novgorodian citizens was held hostage in Kiev to force the giant of the north to accept the rule of the grand prince. When Monomakh died in 1125 the princes returned to their costly feuds and Novgorod was free once more to impose her conditions upon the princes she condescended to admit inside her walls. Even Andrew Bogoliubsky of Suzdalia was unable to bring the city completely to heel. Novgorod accepted "of their own free will" a prince nominated by Andrew, but only after his assurance that none of the city's "ancient" privileges would be violated. Andrew's successor, Vsevolod "Big Nest," managed to dominate the city, forcing it to accept the princes which he delegated to rule in his stead and demanding that citizens known to be guilty of crime be punished without trial. Novgorod's submission, however, lasted only until Vsevolod's death. His son was unable to hold the city in check. He seized Torzhok and shut off the flow of grain from the Volga, but Novgorodian troops, aided by detachments from Pskov and Smolensk, drove the prince back upon Vladimir and the great republic was saved.

In 1236 Novgorod received as prince the grandson of Vsevolod "Big Nest," Alexander by name, later hailed as Nevsky. In the following spring the Tatars destroyed the capital of the Bulgars at the mouth of the Kama and crossed the Volga into Russia. A year later they were in the principality of Riazan, demanding a tenth of all valuables as the price of peace. "Only when none of us remain then all will be yours," the princes answered, and

Riazan and the neighboring towns were mercilessly destroyed. "They killed the Prince and Princess [of Riazan], and men, women, and children, monks, nuns and priests, some by fire, some by the sword." The scourge moved on to the west and invested Torzhok, the key to Novgorod. "They fenced it all round with a fence as they had taken other towns," says the *Chronicle,* "and here the accursed ones fought with battering rams for two weeks. And the people in the town were exhausted and from Novgorod there was no help for them; but already every man began to be in perplexity and terror. And so the pagans took the town, and slew all from the male sex even to the female, all the priests and the monks, and all stripped and reviled gave up their souls to the Lord in a bitter and wretched death." From Torzhok the Tatars moved westward into Novgorodian territory and drove to within seventy miles of the great city. But Novgorod was saved by the forests and swamps surrounding the city, and the invaders turned away to the south.

Hardly had this awful terror passed before Novgorod was threatened from the west. In 1240 the city's control of the Gulf of Finland was contested by the Swedes. Pope Gregory IX preached a crusade against Orthodox Novgorod because the city had helped the Finns to resist conversion to Latin Christianity. But the chronicler suspected that the Swedes were intent upon conquering the entire republic. "The Swedes came in great strength in very many ships with their Prince and with their bishops, and halted in the Neva, wishing to take possession of Ladoga, or in one word, of Novgorod, and of the whole Novgorod province." Novgorod's Prince Alexander led the city militia against the Swedes and almost annihilated them in their camp on the Neva. This brilliant victory won Alexander the title of Nevsky, immortality as defender of the homeland, and canonization as a champion of Orthodoxy against the Latin West.

For some years the German knights had been pressing eastward from the Gulf of Riga, and in 1224 they had conquered Iuriev west of Lake Peipus and renamed it Dorpat. In 1240, the year of Nevsky's victory over the Swedes, the knights drove southeast of Dorpat, captured Izborsk, and laid siege to Pskov, the "younger brother" of Novgorod. Villages for miles around were sacked and ravaged, and Pskov itself fell to the Germans when some of the leading citizens were won over by bribes. Refugees poured into Novgorod with frightful tales of the terror of German rule. Speeding on to the east the Teutonic knights drove to within twenty miles of Novgorod, seized the goods of merchants travelling toward the city and drove off horses and cattle so that "in the villages it was impossible for any one to plough and nothing to do it with." Another German army raided the Neva region, threatening to surround Novgorod. At this critical time when the German knights were pressing deep into Novgorodian territory, the citizens had quarreled with their prince and Alexander had left the city. Now, with the invaders within twenty miles of the city, the townsmen repented and frantically pleaded for Nevsky to save them.

In 1241 Alexander returned to Novgorod and led the militia against the knights who had attacked the Neva area. He delivered the territory from the invader, recovered the towns which had been lost, and drove the Germans back to the west. In the following year Alexander turned to the southwest, relieved Pskov, hanged the traitors who had delivered the city to the enemy, and packed a number of the knights back to Novgorod in chains. Then on April 5, 1242, the Russians caught up with the German main body and won a decisive victory on the ice of Lake Peipus. "A countless number" of allies of the Germans fell and four hundred of the knights were killed and fifty captured. The enemy sued for peace and agreed to give up his conquests and return to Dorpat. Once again Nevsky had saved Novgorod.

Alexander became grand prince of Vladimir and titular leader among the princes in 1246, and was forced to journey to Sarai, the Tatar capital on the lower Volga, to be confirmed. Even after his promotion he kept in close touch with Novgorod, giving the city his son as prince and coming himself to succor the citizens when the need arose. In 1256 the Swedes returned to the Gulf of Finland, but Alexander again drove them off.

Novgorod had been spared the sight of Tatar troops, but in 1257 the khan sent tax assessors to the city to demand payment of the tithe. The citizens refused, but they sent the assessors away with presents and managed to avoid payment for another two years. When the taxgatherers returned in 1259, however, there was no escape. "The accursed raw [flesh] eating Tatars, Berkai and Kasachik [by name], came with their wives, and many others, and there was a great tumult in Novgorod, and they did much evil in the province, taking contribution for the accursed Tatars." So incensed and threatening were the Novgorodians that Nevsky, who had accompanied the Tatars to the city, had to provide a guard to prevent the taxgatherers being mobbed. To the request that they permit their houses to be numbered for tax purposes the citizens answered that they would die first, "honorably for St. Sophia." Alexander saw the utter futility of opposing the Tatar power and patiently urged the Novgorodians to submit to the tax which all Russia was forced to pay. Finally, the advice of this prince who had given the city so much prevailed over less cautious counsel, and the citizens agreed to the census. The chronicler wrote the bitter words: "And the accursed ones began to ride through the streets, writing down the Christian houses; because for our sins God has brought wild beasts out of the desert to eat the flesh of the strong, and to drink the blood of the citizens. And having numbered them for tribute and taken it, the accursed ones went away, and Prince Alexander followed them." Ignominious and painful as his action must have been, Nevsky had again saved the city from what would have been sure and awful punishment.

Four times Alexander made the long arduous journey across Russia to the court of the khan to intercede for the Russian people, to beg that cities not be destroyed because some rash zealots had murdered the tax-gatherers. From the last he returned broken in health and died in 1263. The chronicler mourned his passing as did all Russians, and prayed: "Grant him, O merciful Lord, to see Thy face in the future age, for he labored for Novgorod and for all the Russian land."

Alexander's victory on the Neva in 1240 halted the Swedes only temporarily, and they continued down to the eighteenth century to press their interest in the eastern Baltic. Ten years after Alexander left Novgorod to become grand prince of Vladimir the Swedes returned to the Gulf of Finland and "began to make a town" called Landskrona, or Crown of the Land, on the Narova river near the modern city of Narva. The *Chronicle of Novgorod* suggests that just the rumor that Nevsky's help was being solicited was enough to frighten away the Swedes: "There came Swedes and a quantity of armed men, and they began to make a town on the Narova. And the Prince [Alexander Nevsky] was not then in Novgorod, and the men of Novgorod sent to the Low Country [that is, to the city of Vladimir] to the Prince for armed men, and themselves sent throughout their province, thus gathering armed men. And they, accursed ones, having heard, fled beyond the sea." There is no further word of the Swedes until 1292, when they managed to erect Kexholm, a fort on the northwest shore of Lake Ladoga inside what was claimed to be Novgorodian territory. But this Swedish effort came to nothing, for "the men of Novgorod went and plundered it, and let no man escape." A few years later the Swedes tried again to plant a town on the Neva, bringing with them "a special master from great Rome from the Pope." But again Novgorodian troops drove off the invader and razed the town.

Novgorod's stubborn defense of her position on the Gulf of Finland convinced the Swedes of the futility of further aggression. The Russians, on the other hand, were forced to recognize Sweden's control of the north shore of the Gulf of Finland west of Viborg. Novgorod attempted in 1322 to conquer Viborg but withdrew after a month's siege. In the following year the two powers agreed to "an everlasting peace," by which Novgorod's right to build a fort at the mouth of the Neva was admitted, and fifteen years later the peace was renewed. Minor Swedish attacks in the Karelian Isthmus in 1395 and 1411 were driven off, and an attempt in 1445 to invade Novgorodian territory by way of the Northern Dvina was also successfully resisted. The Swedes did not again raise any serious threat to northwest Russia until the sixteenth century.

Western Russia's relations with Lithuania and Poland concern not only Novgorod but all Russia, and will be better understood in connection with the rise of Moscow. However, with one other people, the Germans, Novgorod's contacts were frequent and usually hostile. The invasion of the Teutonic knights to within twenty miles of Novgorod in 1242, the most serious challenge to the great republic, was stopped by Nevsky on the ice of Lake Peipus. But the entire southeast coast of the Baltic, from Danzig to the Gulf of Finland, remained in German hands, as did the hinterland as far east as Dorpat. Towns on Novgorod's western border were German towns, and even cities inside Novgorodian territory such as Pskov were occasionally attacked and pillaged by the German knights. But Novgorod managed to keep the German peril at arm's length, and the city itself was never again so seriously threatened as when Nevsky had rescued it in 1242. Northwest Russia was finally relieved of German pressure by the union of Poland and Lithuania in the fourteenth century, and the master of the Teutonic Order became vassal to the king of Poland. The German *drang nach Osten* was brought to a halt by the Poles at the battle of Tannenberg in 1410, and Russia was delivered of German pressure for five centuries.

NOVGOROD'S "YOUNGER BROTHER," PSKOV

Of the many cities which were tributary to Novgorod—including Pskov, Ladoga, Izborsk, Veliki Luki, Rzhev, Staraia Russa, and others—Pskov was by far the most important. Its persistent efforts to win independence from Novgorod finally were successful. After 1322 Pskov chose her own prince and styled herself "Lord Pskov the Great" in imitation of Novgorod. Earlier, in 1242, the city had played the dangerous game of cooperating with the Teutonic knights when the latter invaded Novgorodian territory, but Nevsky had restored it firmly to Novgorod's control and hanged its traitorous leaders. A century later, when the German threat had been contained, the parent city formally recognized Pskov's independence.

As long as Pskov was subject to Novgorod, the senior city sent a *posadnik*, or mayor, to rule over the tributary, and Pskovians might be summoned to Novgorod to appear before civil or ecclesiastical courts. Pskov was relieved of these conditions by the treaty which granted her freedom. The city was divided like Novgorod into wards and districts, and like the parent city it exercised some control over a surrounding area administered from the center. The *vieche* exercised the same powers in Pskov as in Novgorod, but seems to have been much more free of strife and dissension than that of the older city. Pskovian society showed no such sharp division into classes as was found in Novgorod and elsewhere in Russia. Those who tilled the soil in the rural districts were free peasant-proprietors; there were no slaves or half-free peasants in Pskovian territory.

Pskov, in its jealousy to win and guard its independence from Novgorod, drew close to the prince of Moscow when the latter set about to incorporate the great republic into his growing state. Its reward for its loyalty to Orthodox Moscow was to retain its independence forty years longer than did Novgorod. Not until 1510 was Pskovian liberty swept away and the territory brought into the principality of Moscow.

Through the long dismal period of Russian history from the twelfth to the fifteenth centuries, when the nation first was torn asunder by nomad attacks and internal strife and then subjected to the yoke of the Tatars, the republic of Novgorod stood forth as a reminder of a great Russian past and as a harbinger of greatness yet to come. The city managed to stand aloof from the petty brawls of the princes and to retain its independence, tarnished only by the payment of taxes to the Tatars, while the rest of Russia grovelled at the feet of the khan. The best of the early Kievan period lived on in Novgorod through the centuries of chaos and humiliation that lay between the death of Iaroslav and the lifting of the Tatar yoke. What democratic tendencies Kievan cities had nurtured continued to flourish in the north. The spirit of enterprise which motivated early Kievan princes and merchants drove Novgorodians to the conquest of an empire. The foreign contact which had meant so much to Kiev and which was severed for most of Russia in the Tatar period was kept alive by Novgorod's ties with central and western Europe. The conquest of Novgorod by Grand Prince Ivan III of Moscow destroyed the last remnant of the Kievan period and, by virtue of the city-empire's size and wealth, provided Moscow with a firm base upon which to build a new Russia.

SUGGESTED READING

Fischer, R. H., *The Russian Fur Trade, 1550–1700* (Berkeley, University of California Press, 1943).

Kliuchevsky, V. O., *A History of Russia,* vol. I (London, Dent, 1911).

Michell, Robert and Nevil Forbes, *The Chronicle of Novgorod, 1016–1471* (Camden Society, 3rd Series, XXV, 1914).

Pirenne, Henri, *Medieval Cities* (Princeton, Princeton University Press, 1925).

Pokrovsky, M. N., *History of Russia* (New York, International Publishers, 1931).

Vernadsky, G., *Kievan Russia* (New Haven, Yale University Press, 1948).

8

The Rise of Moscow

IN 1147 THE PRINCIPALITY OF SUZ-
dalia was ruled by Iuri, called *Dolgoruky,* or "Long Arm," youngest son of
the famous Prince Vladimir Monomakh and father of that Andrew Bogoliubsky who started the principality on its meteoric rise to dominance over
north central Russia. In that year Iuri invited a neighboring prince to a
"mighty feast" to be held at Moscow, one of Prince Iuri's country villas
situated on a height overlooking the Moskva river. This is the first mention
in the chronicles of the town which was one day to become the capital of a
mighty empire.

Nine years later Prince Iuri built a wall around the few buildings which
crowned the hill on the river's bank, thus making of the villa a walled
town. This *kreml,* or fort, the original Kremlin, was strategically located
near Suzdalia's border to protect it from the neighboring principalities of
Chernigov and Riazan. The town grew, unnoticed again by the chronicler
until 1237 when it was sacked by the Tatars on their way to Suzdal. Because
it had been founded only recently and so was junior to other Russian towns,
Moscow was relegated to a minor position and assigned to junior princes.
Indeed, for years on end it seems to have had no prince at all.

BEGINNINGS OF THE MOSCOW PRINCIPALITY

Before his death in 1263 Alexander Nevsky assigned to his youngest son,
Daniel, the principality of Moscow, which included only the Kremlin and
a few neighboring villages. Daniel bequeathed to his successors an enlarged
territory and a policy of expanding the principality by winning control of

strategic rivers. From a childless nephew Daniel inherited the important town of Pereiaslavl-Zalieski, eighty miles northeast of Moscow, which placed his principality on a tributary of the Volga. From the prince of Riazan, who was taken prisoner and then murdered at Daniel's command, the prince of Moscow seized the town of Kolomna, located where the river Moskva empties into the Oka. Indeed, Daniel would have taken the entire principality of Riazan had not the Tatar khan ordered it returned to its rightful heir. His son Iuri (1304–1325), who had inherited his father's acquisitive proclivities, seized Mozhaisk from the prince of Smolensk. This gave the principality of Moscow control over the Moskva from its headwaters to its mouth. The "river policy" of the Muscovite princes and the later tsars of Russia thus originated with the very founders of the dynasty.

When the office of grand prince fell vacant early in the fourteenth century Iuri of Moscow stepped forward to claim it. His uncle, Prince Mikhail of Tver, had the indisputable senior right to the title, but the final decision had to be made by the Tatar khan, the sovereign ruler of the Russian land whom the grand prince served only as lieutenant or viceroy. Iuri of Moscow hurried off to the Tatar camp at Sarai on the lower Volga, laden with rich presents for the khan. Mikhail of Tver followed along later and arrived to find himself confronted with charges of having shown no respect for the khan's authority. By liberal bribes Iuri obtained a sentence of death against his uncle and apparently volunteered to do the job. Iuri's own attendants attacked the prince of Tver in his tent, stripped him, and cut out his heart. When Iuri and the khan entered the tent later the prince of Moscow showed so little emotion at the sight of his uncle's mutilated body that even the Tatars were shocked. Iuri won the appointment as grand prince but years later was slain by the son of the same Prince Mikhail of Tver. Iuri's brother Ivan had his vengeance in turn when he sacked the city of Tver with fifty thousand Tatar and Muscovite troops because the citizens refused to pay tribute to the khan.

Ivan Kalita, 1325–1341

Ivan, the second son of Daniel, is known as *Kalita*, or "Money bags," because of the gainful use he made of his seemingly plentiful supply of money. His heritage consisted of only four or five town-districts and a few score peasant villages, but it also included the considerable treasury which his predecessors had built up by levying duty upon the trade which passed up and down the Moskva river.

Soon after succeeding his brother as prince of Moscow, Ivan became grand prince of Russia * and received from the Tatar khan the *yarlik,* or

---

* Technically, he became grand prince of Vladimir. The Grand Principality of Valdimir was the name by which the East Slav state at this time was known, as earlier it had been called the Grand Principality of Kiev. To the west lay the Grand Principality

official confirmation without which he would have had no authority. Furthermore, the khan appointed him his collector of tribute from the Russian lands. Ivan turned this thankless assignment to his own good use. While Christian Russia was freed from the humiliation of having Moslem Tatars visit every town each year to demand the tithe, Ivan and his successors proved themselves to be as efficient and as merciless in gathering the levy as ever the conquerors could have been. From Novgorod, whose citizens played the dangerous game of courting the support of the neighboring grand prince of Lithuania, Ivan exacted twice as much as the khan demanded and pocketed the difference. "If unable or unwilling to castigate another prince with the sword, the Lord of Moscow could now castigate him with the ruble" (Kliuchevsky). But Ivan did not hesitate to resort to force if it became necessary. When the citizens of Tver revolted against payment of the tithe, Ivan led an army of Tatars, accompanied by a small band of his own Muscovites, against Tver and laid waste the entire principality.

The profit which he realized from serving the khan as tax-collector Ivan employed to expand his own possessions. He bought Galich, far to the northeast beyond the Volga and close to the rich fur country which belonged to the republic of Novgorod. He found a bargain in the town-district of Beloozero on the lake of that name, a spot even closer to Novgorodian territory. By the purchase of Uglich, north of Moscow, he obtained land on the mighty Volga itself. In all these cases he allowed the princes of those towns to stay on and govern in his name, and the districts were incorporated into the principality of Moscow only in the reign of his grandson. Ivan married his daughters to the princes of Rostov and Iaroslavl, both near neighbors, and by so doing brought those princes under his influence if he could not bring their lands under his control. By such peaceful methods, by purchase of land and by marriage, Ivan and his sons contributed to the growing importance of Moscow. His grandson Dmitry Donskoi was not so patient and resorted to firm pressure and even war when he could win territory in no other way.

Kalita ruled his principality like a landowner managing his estates. There were no town *vieches* to contest his authority or to embarrass him by rising against the Tatars. From the moment of his accession, the chronicler maintains, "there was thenceforth a great quietness throughout the Russian land, and the Tatars ceased fighting against the Russian land." Punitive expeditions against those who refused to pay tribute were sometimes necessary, but they were led by the prince of Moscow in the khan's name. Contemporaries

---

of Lithuania. The prince of Moscow could will his own lands, that is, the principality of Moscow, to his heirs, but the *yarlik*, or appointment as grand prince of Vladimir, might be given to any of the princely family whom the khan of the Tatar horde chose to name. As a matter of fact, the princes of Moscow after Ivan were almost without exception also appointed grand princes of Vladimir.

must have considered Ivan a scoundrel and a renegade. Actually, he exhibited the same good sense that Alexander Nevsky had shown earlier in not risking the complete destruction of Russia by challenging the khan.

The "great quietness" that spread over his principality gave it the character of a sanctuary. Peasants from the south sought refuge there in the hope of tilling the land in peace, and found the well-to-do prince of Moscow willing to advance them money to buy seeds and tools. Boyars left the service of other princes to enlist under him, for there was more prestige and more promise of gain in serving the grand prince whom the khan trusted above all others. From the Tatars Ivan and his successors ransomed thousands of Russian captives and settled them in Moscow. This flow of population raised the productivity and the prosperity of Ivan's territory and brought into it additional taxpayers to fill the prince's coffers.

Under the sound management and shrewd leadership of its prince Moscow gave promise of becoming the most important city in central Russia. But Ivan Kalita may have been jealous of the fact that not his own city of Moscow but Vladimir was the official and the spiritual capital of the grand principality. He must have thought that if the metropolitan could be prevailed upon to settle in Moscow the city's prestige would be immeasurably enhanced.

At the very end of the thirteenth century the then metropolitan of Kiev, alarmed that the population of South Russia was melting away and disappearing into the north to escape Tatar violence, left the city on the Dnieper with all his staff and moved to Vladimir, the new capital of the grand principality on the river Kliazma. From his new home, however, it was necessary to visit the Kievan bishoprics periodically, and on such journeys the metropolitan often stopped to rest at Moscow. There Metropolitan Peter developed a close friendship with Ivan Kalita, who served as governor of Moscow before he succeeded his brother Iuri as prince of Moscow and grand prince of Russia. Peter and Ivan worked together in founding the Cathedral of the Assumption in the Moscow Kremlin. The old metropolitan told Kalita he wished to be buried in the new church and prophesied a great future for the prince of Moscow who had helped to found it. "God will bless thee," he said to Ivan, "and elevate thee above all the other princes, and raise this town above all other towns. Thy race will reign in this place during many centuries; their hands will conquer all their enemies; the saints will make their dwelling here, and here shall my bones repose." The words were spoken just after Ivan became prince of Moscow and nearly three years before he became grand prince. After Peter's death in 1326 a number of miracles conveniently transpired at the site of his tomb, and the spot soon became the goal of pilgrimages from all over Russia. Where Peter had only visited Moscow from the ecclesiastical capital of Vladimir, his successor moved the metropolitical seat permanently to Moscow. Peter's tomb became a national shrine, and the city in which it rested and from which Peter's successors ruled over the Russian church became the religious capital of the land.

Simeon the Haughty (1341–1353) and Ivan the Debonair (1353–1359)

The prince of Tver, supported generally by the other Russian princes, pressed his candidacy to the office of grand prince when Ivan Kalita died in 1341, and appealed to the khan not to settle the *yarlik* permanently upon the princes of Moscow. But Moscow gold and the respect and confidence in which the khan had held Ivan decided the issue in favor of Ivan's son Simeon when the candidates appeared in the Tatar camp on the lower Volga. The prince of Moscow was received with great honor and cordiality and promptly won the appointment as grand prince. Indeed, the khan "put all the Russian princes under his hand," and Simeon claimed the title of "Grand Prince of all the Russias." Because of his domineering attitude toward the other princes Simeon was known to his contemporaries as "the Haughty." To the Tatars he affected meekness and subservience, assuring the khan that Russia was his "faithful province." But he urged the princes to stand together and accept his rule dutifully, for only if the land were firmly united would it some day be possible to throw off the Tatar yoke. His assurances may have been convincing, for the chronicler reports that "all the Princes of Riazan and Rostov—nay, even those of Tver—were so obedient unto him that they did perform everything according to his word." Since the prince of Moscow had the power of the khan to enforce his commands there was nothing the other princes could do but obey him.

Simeon like his father, gave every encouragement to the church and received in return its staunch support. Foreign artists and native painters schooled in Constantinople were employed to decorate the churches in the Kremlin, and bells were cast for the cathedral churches of Moscow and Novgorod. Moscow, the seat of the metropolitan, with its brilliantly adorned churches and its miracle-working tombs, was fast succeeding Kiev in the minds of the faithful as a sacred city. And north of the Volga not far from Moscow, "where he had at first no companion but a bear, on water-courses which were haunted only by the beavers" (Rambaud), St. Sergius founded the Troitsky Lavra, or Monastery of the Trinity. It grew to be one of the richest and most venerated in the land, and the respect in which the monastery and its founder were held added much to the rapidly growing religious importance of the Moscow area.

Simeon the Haughty died of the plague in 1353 in the epidemic known to western Europe as the Black Death. His brother Ivan II, called the Debonair, ruled for six years as prince of Moscow and grand prince of Russia. Ivan's mild and gentle nature was imposed upon by the other princes, who showed no respect for his authority and who warred among themselves and insulted even the grand prince himself with impunity. Anarchy reminiscent of the declining days of Kiev descended over the land. There was civil war among the princes of Tver, and also among those of Riazan. One of the latter invaded Muscovite territory and burned several villages, but went unpunished. The Lithuanians threatened Pskov, but Ivan II did nothing. The Novgorodians spurned his authority and opened their gates to the prince of Suzdalia. Even his own district governors were assassinated, and Ivan let the criminals go free.

Then Metropolitan Alexis stepped forward to steady the government and carry out the tasks that should have been shouldered by the weak Ivan. Alexis prevailed upon the princes of Tver to end their senseless wars, and his subordinate, the archbishop of Novgorod, put down a revolt in the northern republic. The Metropolitan was highly respected by the Tatars, to whose headquarters he journeyed a number of times to propitiate the khan. During the reign the khan bestowed upon the grand prince the power to settle disputes among all the Russian princes. The khan's confidence in the wisdom and justice of this Metropolitan of the Russian church must have been great, for he could not have supposed that the power would be exercised by the weak-willed Ivan II. When Ivan died in 1359 he left a minor to succeed him, and the Metropolitan governed as regent and guardian until the young prince reached maturity.

REASONS FOR MUSCOVITE SUCCESS

Alexander Nevsky's bequest of the insignificant principality of Moscow to his youngest son Daniel had produced unexpected results by the middle of the fourteenth century. By that time the prince of Moscow had risen to a position of command over all the other princes, and four successive rulers of Moscow had held the title of grand prince. Under the *yarlik,* or commission of the Tatar khan, the prince of Moscow served as the khan's lieutenant or viceroy, adjudicating all disputes among the princes and maintaining peace among them. As the khan's tax collector the prince of Moscow gathered all the tribute laid upon the land, receiving a good commission for it and having the khan's troops to back him up against those who refused to pay. By the middle of the fourteenth century Moscow had become the capital of Russia. Less than a century before it had been an unwalled villa, a small group of buildings serving as a resting station for the grand prince on his journeys from Vladimir to the Dnieper.

A number of factors contributed to the rise of Moscow. Perhaps no one of them could have turned the hill on the Moskva into the nation's capital, but all of them working together and supplementing each other contributed to that end.

Moscow's geographical location must be noted first among the factors which gave it importance. The town lay on the Moskva river at the spot where the tributary Iauza flows into it, and the upper reaches of the Iauza river approach very near to the Kliazma. This was a great trade highway long before the building of the Kremlin, for the Kliazma flows east to join the Oka not far from Nizhni-Novgorod on the Volga where the great medieval fairs were held. A more leisurely way to the Volga lay down the Moskva to the river Oka, which bends far to the south before turning northward to enter the Volga at Nizhni-Novgorod. Muscovites who were impatient to get to the Volga might follow still a third and shorter route. They could go up the Moskva and its tributary the Istra, portage over to the Lama at Volokolamsk—a town whose name means "the portage on the Lama"— drift down the Lama into the Shosha, and so reach the Volga a few miles downstream from the city of Tver. The Volga, from its source to its mouth, was always an important highway of communication. Moscow lay almost exactly in the center of the "Russian Mesopotamia," midway between the Volga and the Oka rivers. One could travel from Moscow to the Dnieper by going up the Oka and its tributary the Ugra, and then portaging directly to the Dnieper above the important trade town of Smolensk. At Smolensk the traveller found himself on the ancient water-road "from the Varangians to the Greeks." Finally, Moscow lay on the important overland route which connected Rostov in the north with Kiev in the south.

Moscow was ideally located, then, at the heart of a network of trade routes, both land and water, which could offer rich opportunity to the merchants who chose to settle there. The flow of trade north, south, east, and west through Moscow was encouraged by the early princes of Moscow, but it was also taxed. Goods moving locally up and down the Moskva, or those moving greater distances from Smolensk to Nizhni-Novgorod or from Kiev to the upper Volga, were taxed for the privilege of passing through territory controlled from the Kremlin. Merchants who stayed the night in Moscow paid for their shelter and care and for the security which was assured their boats or their pack trains. Because of its central location and its rapidly growing population Moscow soon became an important market, and those who displayed their wares in its streets paid fees for the privilege. A steady flow of fees and customs fed the treasury of the early princes of Moscow. The money was carefully invested—in buying up land, in endowing the church, in bribing the khan—in ways that brought rich return to Daniel and his successors.

Moscow gained peace and security from its sheltered position in the very center of thirteenth- and fourteenth-century Russia. There was no problem of foreign relations, little need to fear foreign aggression. While the grand prince of Lithuania might occasionally press eastward dangerously close to Moscow territory, it was principalities lying to the west of Moscow, such as Tver and Smolensk, which received the blow. To the east the principalities of Rostov, Nizhni Novgorod, and Riazan absorbed the shock of Tatar fury when it came. To the north lay the protecting screen of Novgorod to shelter Moscow against raids by the native Finns. For a hundred and thirty years after the Tatars burned the town in 1238 Moscow was probably the only spot in North Russia which suffered no serious injury from enemy attack. This immunity from attack encouraged immigration from border areas which enjoyed no such calm.

An important factor contributing to the rise of Moscow was the position and character of its early princes. From the very first the principality was insignificant and it was assigned to junior princes. Moscow was not part of the rota system, and consequently its princes could not look forward to improving their lot by rising in the family scale. They were obliged to accept their miserable heritage and improve it as they might. But these early Muscovite princes made the most of their position, and each of them followed a policy of leaving more land and valuables to his successor than he had received from his predecessor. Each added to his territory—by purchase, by marriage, by diplomacy, or by armed force. Each left a will enumerating in great detail, and, it may be suspected, with great pride, the amount of money in his chests, the number of animals in his flocks and herds, the number of pieces of silverware, and even items of clothing such as his furs, caps, and coats. His acquisition of towns, villages, gold and silver, livestock, and furs gave the prince of Moscow the reputation of being a model administrator at a time when other princes were profligate and wasteful. His careful management of his estates, the peace and good order he maintained, and his favor with the khan attracted settlers of all types— peasants anxious to till the soil and work the forests, merchants seeking to develop the trade which peace and geographical location promoted, and boyars preferring to serve under this prince whom the khan favored. Russians captured and enslaved by the Tatars were ransomed by the early princes of Moscow and settled upon the land. New settlers in his principality meant more taxpayers, more producers, more colonists for the sparsely inhabited lands; those who had not the capital to set up in farming or in business even found it possible to borrow from their prince.

The prince of Moscow gained an enormous advantage over the other princes by winning and keeping in his family the *yarlik,* which set him apart as grand prince. He was much more of an absolute ruler than had been the later princes of Kiev because his authority was backed up by the power of the khan. His absolutism may have been somewhat secondhand, but for all that no one dared question it. When Ivan the Debonair received from the khan judicial authority over the other princes, all the rest had to look up to him, court his favor, beg his mercy, and respect his judgment. What the Russian princes may have gained by having one of them for judge and by avoiding the long journey to Tatar headquarters must at times have been offset by the fact that the prince of Moscow looked upon every dispute, whether he himself was a party to it or not, from the point of view of his own interests. The khan's favor was courted assiduously by the early princes of Moscow. Princes of Tver or of Riazan might tempt disaster by rising against the Tatars, but those of Moscow saw clearly that the khan could only be won over by "peaceful cunning," by fawning servility, and bribes. "No prince more often went to pay his respects to the Tatar potentate than did Ivan Kalita, nor was he ever aught but a welcome guest on his arrival, seeing that he took care never to come empty-handed. Already it was an accepted axiom among the Tatars that a visit from the Muscovite Prince meant much gold and silver for the Khan and for his favorites" (Kliuchevsky).

Moscow profited immeasurably from Daniel's foresight in currying the friendship of the metropolitan of the Russian Orthodox church. The tomb of the Metropolitan Peter became a national shrine, and he and the other early metropolitans of Moscow were beatified. The early Muscovite princes assured the church of their protection, built churches for its edification, and gave liberally to it from their treasuries. In return the princes received the church's support and blessing in their rise to power. The Metropolitan Alexis took over the responsibility of government during the reign of the weak Ivan II and made a number of journeys to the khan's headquarters, as Peter had done before him, to ease the Tatar burden upon the Russian people.

Members of the monastic orders gave support to the growing power of Moscow in their own way. They founded monasteries in the sparsely settled wilderness, and this prompted colonists to follow them. Thus, there was a steady flow of clergy and settlers to the north and east into the rich fur country, and Moscow was early able to contest the area's control by Novgorod. Missionaries from the Troitsky Monastery crossed the Volga to the north of Moscow and built cloisters deep in Novgorodian territory. The settlements which soon grew up around them were filled with Muscovites, giving a later prince of Moscow a claim to the land because it was inhabited by his own people.

An important factor in Moscow's rise to pre-eminence was the absence of dispute over the succession. This was only partly the result of the fortuitous paucity of heirs. When a prince left more than one son, as did Daniel and Ivan Kalita, there was never any warring among the brothers. When Daniel was succeeded by his elder son Iuri, the younger son Ivan accepted the settlement without question, and contented himself with serving as viceroy in Moscow while Iuri held forth at Vladimir as grand prince. Since Iuri left no sons, Ivan's turn came when his brother died. Kalita again left two sons, but there was no disagreement over the succession. Simeon ruled proudly over his brother as well as over the other princes, and the death of his sons before him precluded any contest over the principality when the plague struck him down. There was a single exception to this rule of un-contested succession from the time of the founding of the Moscow dynasty in the thirteenth century to the time the line of Daniel ran out at the end of the sixteenth century, and the exception caused a flurry for less than two years. The reason for these peaceful successions lies in the fact that the princes of Moscow made testamentary provision for all sons, if there were more than one, but were careful always to leave the title and the bulk of the inheritance to the oldest son. Kalita, for example, willed a few small towns to his younger son, leaving the older son and successor the entire course of the Moskva river including the towns of Mozhaisk and Kolomna at its source and mouth, and forbade that the original principality of Mos-cow be divided. From such foresight "the idea of the state as one and in-divisible was certain to gain the day" (Rambaud).

Daniel's original appanage consisted of less than five hundred square miles. A century and a half later the principality of Moscow had grown more than thirty times over to about fifteen thousand square miles. That phe-nomenal expansion, to which every one of the early princes made a con-tribution, was the result of a number of circumstances. Favorable location and good fortune certainly played their part. But the political acumen of the early princes—careful stewardship of their estates, shrewd investment of treasure, keen understanding of the political milieu in which they lived, grovelling before the conqueror when there was no force with which to oppose him—was responsible above all for the accumulation of power with which Tatar domination might soon be contested.

POLISH-LITHUANIAN CHALLENGE

Paralleling the growth of the Moscow state was the rise in the west of the grand principality of Lithuania which by the fifteenth century had gained control over the basin of the Dnieper, the river which had formed the com-mercial axis of the Kievan state. Impelled by pressure from the Teutonic knights in the early part of the thirteenth century, the various tribes of Lithuanians, the "Godless Litva" of the Chronicles, united under Prince Mindovg to prevent being overwhelmed one by one. Mindovg seized Grodno, which became his capital, and drove east up the valley of the Niemen into Russian territory. Pressed on one side by the Russian Prince Alexander Nevsky and on the other by the German knights, Mindovg gave up his paganism and embraced Roman Christianity in the hope that the knights would halt their crusade against his people. When this forlorn hope did not materialize the prince returned to his pagan ways, and took stern ven-geance upon the Teutons by raiding and devastating their province of

Mazovia in Poland. His harsh measures to subdue the other Lithuanian princes provoked stubborn opposition, and Mindovg was assassinated by a disgruntled subject in 1263, the very year of Nevsky's death in Russia.

A half century of civil war and anarchy among the Lithuanians following Mindovg's rule ended in 1316 with the appearance of Prince Gedimin. Not only was Lithuanian territory reunited, but twice as much Russian as Lithuanian land was added to the state. From his new capital of Vilna Gedimin ruled over a principality stretching from the Russian city of Polotsk on the Western Dvina to ancient Kiev on the Dnieper. Not until the latter part of the seventeenth century would Kiev return to Russian control. While he and his people kept to their pagan customs, Gedimin tolerated Russian Orthodoxy and even built an Orthodox church in his capital. The Russians welcomed his coming and opened the gates of their cities to him, not only because of his tolerance, but also because he freed them from the heavy financial burdens of Tatar rule. Russian influence at the Lithuanian court was strong and Russian was the official language. Lithuanians and Russians lived together in peace and intermarried freely. The great threat to Lithuanian independence was the aggression of the German knights, and Gedimin took Mindovg's way of seeking to counteract it. He received Franciscan and Dominican missionaries into his land and expressed his willingness to embrace Roman Catholicism if the Pope could prevail upon the knights to cease their attacks. This the Pope was unable to do, and the missionaries were expelled. Gedimin was given a pagan burial in 1345.

Gedimin's son Olgerd pushed the Lithuanian border far to the east and south, gathering in the Russian towns of Vitebsk, Mogilev, Briansk, and Novgorod-Seversk on the river Desna. The conquest of the district of Podolia on the Southern Bug from the Tatars carried the Lithuanian frontier to the shores of the Black Sea between the Dnieper and Dniester rivers. He attacked the great republic of Novgorod and encouraged its vassal Pskov in its efforts to win independence. He sought an alliance with Prince Simeon the Haughty of Moscow, but then attacked Simeon's nephew Dmitry and advanced almost to within sight of the Kremlin.

The reign of Olgerd's successor, his son Iagailo, is noted for the overwhelming defeat he administered to the Teutonic knights and for the union of Poland and Lithuania by his marriage to the Polish queen. Poland, suffering from internal dissension and the encroachments of her nobles upon the central authority, was under pressure on the south by the Lithuanians and on the north by the German knights. Polish leaders proposed to absorb the one enemy, Lithuania, and concentrate their combined strength on the other, the Teutonic Order. In 1386 the terms were arranged and Iagailo, converted to Roman Christianity for the occasion, married Queen Jadwiga of Poland. Iagailo changed his name to Wladyslav II, king of Poland, and moved his capital to Krakow. Roman priests were brought in to convert the Lithuanians to Christianity and Polish nobles were given estates in Lithuania. Their king's acceptance of Polish customs and religion irritated the Lithuanians, and a cultural cleavage, particularly between Roman Catholics and Russian Orthodox, long endured in the eastern districts which had only recently been peaceably absorbed into the Lithuanian state.

Iagailo's attempt to force Polish customs, Polish landowners, and "Latinism" upon the Lithuanian and Russian people under his rule provoked bitter opposition. His nephew Vitovt united the dissident elements in the eastern districts and declared war upon Iagailo and the Poles. The Battle of Tannenberg had not yet settled the German problem and the king of Poland was forced to give way. Vitovt was recognized as grand prince of Lithuania, technically subordinate to the Polish king but in effect completely independent. The union of Poland and Lithuania was declared to be purely dynastic, and the two might even have gone their separate ways again had it not been for external pressures which later forced them into a firmer union.

Vitovt set about to restore the former brilliance of Lithuania and to conquer new territory to the east and south. He seized the Russian principality of Smolensk, and so became next door neighbor to the princes of Tver, Moscow, and Riazan. Only these lands and those of Novgorod and Pskov remained in Russian hands, and Vitovt had hopes that even they some day would be part of Lithuania. In the meantime he proposed to conquer the Golden Horde, the Tatar power which ruled all Russia from its headquarters at Sarai. The Tatars on the lower Volga, known as the Golden Horde, had won their independence from the great khan in Central Asia, and this division of the Tatar power gave Vitovt reason to hope that he might defeat them. Earlier he had fought against the Tatars on the Sea of Azov and taken many prisoners, so he knew they were not invincible.

But the Lithuanian prince soon ran into unexpected complications. A new conqueror, Timur the Lame, or Tamerlane, rose to the throne of the great khan in Asia and determined to reunite all the Tatars and expand their empire. The rebellious khan of the Golden Horde in southeast Russia was driven from his capital at Sarai and, with many of his Tatar followers, sought refuge with Vitovt. Ambitious himself to absorb the Golden Horde's territory and to add it, together with Moscow and the rest of Russia, to his expanding principality, Vitovt gathered a mighty army at Kiev in 1399. His Lithuanian force was joined by Polish troops sent by Iagailo, by detachments contributed by several Russian princes, by the Tatars of the Golden Horde who had fled from Timur the Lame, and even by five hundred Teutonic knights, for this was a crusade of Christians against the infidel. On the banks of the river Vorskla, which enters the Dnieper above the cataracts, the formidable array met the Tatars. So fearsome was the western host that Tamerlane offered to arrange a peace, but Vitovt proudly claimed that God meant him to rule the world and ordered the great khan to surrender. In the battle that ensued Vitovt's mighty army, whose two hundred thousand men were outnumbered and outmaneuvered, was badly beaten and two-thirds of it was left on the field. The rest fled beyond the Dnieper, and Timur laid a heavy indemnity upon Kiev.

After the disaster on the Vorskla Vitovt gave up his plan to subdue the Golden Horde and conquer Russia. But his greatest triumph still lay before him. When the Prussians, a Lithuanian people, rebelled against the oppression of the Teutonic knights who ruled over them, Vitovt went to their relief. Again a mighty army gathered under him, for his fame as a fighter won him widespread respect. Forty thousand Tatars came from the Golden Horde to serve with his hundred thousand Poles and Lithuanians, and twenty thousand Czechs, Moravians, Hungarians, and Russians joined the host. While technically Iagailo, or Wladyslav II of Poland, commanded the force, it was Vitovt's leadership which was most responsible for the victory that followed. At the Battle of Tannenberg in 1410 the Teutonic knights, outnumbered nearly two to one, were decisively beaten, and the grand master and many of the knights were slain. The Russians and particularly those from Smolensk distinguished themselves in this great victory of Slav over German. The power of the Teutonic Order was broken and eastern Europe was delivered from the *drang nach Osten* for five centuries.

The cooperation of Poles and Lithuanians on the field of Tannenberg led to closer political ties between the two nations. Three years after the great victory Vitovt led his Lithuanian nobles to a conference with Iagailo and his Polish lords to work out a union of their subjects. The terms agreed upon provided that Lithuanian nobles who embraced Roman Catholicism should enjoy the rights and privileges of the Polish nobility, and that a council of Polish and Lithuanian lords should settle common issues and elect Polish kings and Lithuanian grand princes. Vitovt later was pressed by his spirited subjects to renounce the agreement and to seek recognition as king of Lithuania, but the move was blocked by the Poles with papal backing. In his concern to be independent of Moscow as well as Poland, Vitovt had named an Orthodox metropolitan bishop of Kiev, and his sympathy for the eastern faith had won him papal as well as Polish enmity. The old man died in 1430 at the age of eighty, and with his passing Lithuania speedily declined. Finally, at the Union of Lublin in 1569, Lithuania and Poland became one, and soon thereafter their combined strength was thrown once more against Russia. Vitovt's dream of absorbing Russia was momentarily realized early in the seventeenth century when a son of the Polish king served two years as tsar of Russia before being driven back to his homeland.

DMITRY DEFIES THE TATARS

Ivan the Debonair, prince of Moscow and grand prince of Russia, died in 1359 leaving two minor sons. The older of the two, Dmitry (1359–1389), was proclaimed prince of Moscow and the land was ruled in his name by his guardian, the metropolitan of Moscow. But a child of ten, even with the church's blessing, could not command the respect of all the Russian princes, many of whom had scorned the authority of the child's weak father. The prince of Suzdalia, also named Dmitry, secured the *yarlik* after the death of Ivan II and with it the title of grand prince. His own brother rebuked him for it, for many, if not all, of the princes were convinced that only under Moscow's leadership could the alien yoke be lifted. Now the Metropolitan put the young prince of Moscow at the head of an army which marched on the capital city of Vladimir and literally captured the title of grand prince from the grasping prince of Suzdalia. The two Dmitrys signed a treaty which left the *yarklik* with Moscow. The young prince of Moscow married the daughter of Dmitry of Suzdalia, and in the following reign the principality of Suzdalia was quietly absorbed by Moscow. Young Dmitry purchased his bride with the promise that Nizhni-Novgorod should go to her father. That the great trade center at the mouth of the Oka did not belong to Moscow made no difference to Dmitry. When the citizens objected to the arrangement, the prince of Moscow prevailed upon the Metropolitan to lay Nizhni-Novgorod under an interdict, and the opposition was broken. In the reign of Dmitry's son Nizhni-Novgorod along with Suzdalia was swept into the Muscovite state.

When civil war broke out among the princes of Tver, one of them, a Prince Michael, called to his assistance his brother-in-law Grand Prince Olgerd of Lithuania. Dmitry of Moscow backed Michael's opponents and so came to blows with Olgerd. A Lithuanian army burned and pillaged its way to the outskirts of Moscow, but there was no pitched battle. Olgerd chose not to risk disaster so far from home and Dmitry was willing to await the Lithuanian withdrawal before pressing his interest in Tver. After Olgerd's death Dmitry led a strong army made up of Muscovites, Novgorodians, and detachments from allied and vassal princes against the city of Tver. Prince Michael, deserted by Lithuania, then agreed to recognize Dmitry of Moscow as his "elder brother," gave up an earlier claim to Novgorod and Vladimir, and promised to cooperate with Dmitry in his relations with the Tatars, whether he should pay them tribute or attack them. Dmitry has been criticized for not absorbing Tver completely, but the city was to fall to Moscow in good time and by his firm but not vindictive treatment of Michael he avoided later insurrection, which would have been costly had it come when Dmitry was battling the Tatars.

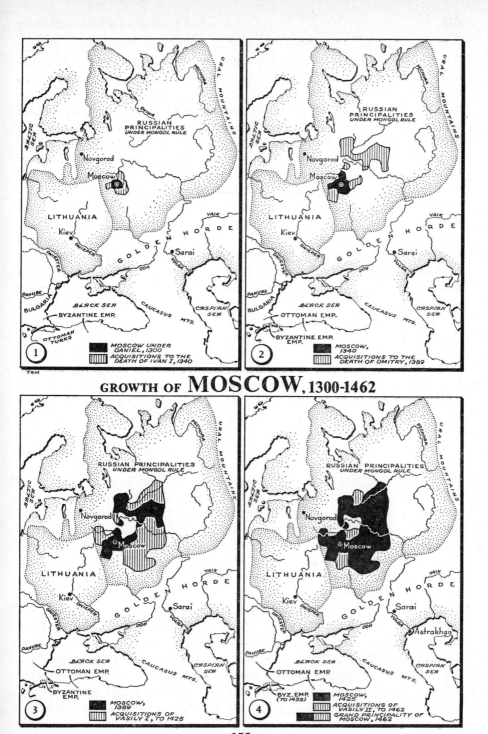

GROWTH OF **MOSCOW**, 1300-1462

Map 1:
MOSCOW UNDER DANIEL, 1300
ACQUISITIONS TO THE DEATH OF IVAN I, 1340

Map 2:
MOSCOW, 1340
ACQUISITIONS TO THE DEATH OF DMITRY, 1389

Map 3:
MOSCOW, 1389
ACQUISITIONS OF VASILY I, TO 1425

Map 4:
MOSCOW, 1425
ACQUISITIONS OF VASILY II, TO 1462
GRAND PRINCIPALITY OF MOSCOW, 1462

Dmitry had trouble with still another important principality, that of Riazan. The old princely family in Riazan often worked to secure the favor of the khan of the Golden Horde and managed by subservience and bribes to win the khan's protection against the growing demands of Moscow. But its efforts were not always successful, for bands of Tatars frequently raided Riazan territory. Now Dmitry of Moscow drove the prince of Riazan from his throne and installed a puppet in his place. Soon the old prince was back in power, and he later had his revenge against Dmitry by opposing Moscow in its war against the Golden Horde. Moscow's princely enemies to east and west betrayed the national cause of Russia to foreign foes.

The Golden Horde was beginning to disintegrate in the latter half of the thirteenth century. Contests for the throne were frequent and there already were signs that segments might fall away and become independent, as the Golden Horde itself had become practically independent of the great khan in Asia. The Russians were quick to grasp the significance of this Tatar decadence, and by Dmitry's time a number of Russian princes were ready to try their strength against the oppressor. The prince of Riazan gathered a small force and dared to punish the Tatars for having ravaged his principality. The prince of Nizhni-Novgorod put to death the khan's envoys and fifteen hundred troops who accompanied them, although the town was sacked the following year in retaliation. Dmitry himself defied the khan on a number of occasions. He attacked Kazan and withdrew only when the Tatars paid him to do so. In 1378 he attacked the khan's army with a large force and won a signal triumph. "Their time is past and God is with us!" Dmitry boasted after the victory.

To punish such insolence and to restore the payment of tribute which Dmitry now refused, Khan Mamai assembled a great army of Tatars, Turks, Polovtsy, and even Genoese from their trading towns in the Crimea. The prince of Riazan aided the cause of Russia's enemies by arranging an alliance between the khan of the Golden Horde and Iagailo, at that time grand prince of Lithuania. The two were to attack simultaneously, and Dmitry of Moscow would be crushed between them. But Iagailo's own brothers and many of his boyars joined the Russian host. Dmitry called for all the Russian princes and every fighting man to join in a glorious crusade to lift the foreign yoke. St. Sergius of the Trinity Monastery blessed the mission and forecast a bloody but victorious battle. From all over Russia the princes led their contingents into Dmitry's camp—from Pskov in the northwest, from Beloozero in the north, from Nizhni-Novgorod in the east, and even from Volynia far to the southwest. The immense army, estimated to number between 150,000 and 400,000 men, consisted almost entirely of Russians, for this was something more than a crusade of Christian against infidel. It was a national effort among princes who were willing to set aside their differences temporarily to rid the land of alien rule. Not all, however, could rise above their pettiness. Novgorod apparently sent no troops, and the princes of Tver and Riazan remained neutral.

In August, 1380, Dmitry led his army through the principality of Riazan to meet Mamai and his Tatars and beat them back from Moscow. Word came to him enroute that the Tatars were turning westward to join forces with the Lithuanians, so Dmitry marched south to put himself between the two enemies. When the Russians came to the headwaters of the Don, Dmitry called a council of war to decide whether to cross the river and press on to meet the Tatars or whether to wait and defend the river line. A courier arrived with warning that the Lithuanians were only a day's march to the west. The information put an end to indecision, and the Russians crossed the Don east of present-day Tula and lined up on a meadow known as *Kulikovo Pole,* or "the snipe field." Soon the Tatars came up and attacked. The fight was bloody and long in doubt. Dmitry's own bodyguard was scattered and the grand prince himself was roughly handled. But when the Russian reserves were brought in the issue was quickly decided. The rout of the Tatars was complete, and much equipment and many camels and horses were abandoned in the precipitate flight. Khan Mamai lost a hundred thousand men; the Russian losses, of which there is no estimate, must have been equally severe.

Dmitry, henceforth called Donskoi in honor of his victory on the river Don, was acclaimed a hero not only by Moscow but by all Russia. He had proved that the terrible Tatar was not invincible and inspired his people with the hope that the oppressive rule of the conqueror might soon be lifted. As the abbot of the Trinity Monastery had foretold, the victory was won only at a terrible cost. While the Tatars could quickly refill their ranks, Dmitry had suffered irreparable loss. And it was his great misfortune to beat back the Golden Horde only to come upon a new threat in the person of Timur the Lame. Timur, engaged in reuniting the Tatars, welcomed the defeat of Mamai and congratulated Dmitry upon having beaten their common enemy. Mamai was executed at Timur's command and the Golden Horde was brought once more under the authority of the great khan.

Then Timur called upon the Russian princes to appear at Sarai, but Dmitry refused. Marshalling another vast army Timur sent his finest general, Tokhtamysh, to punish the prince of Moscow. Dmitry left his capital to gather another army, but met only with indifference among the princes, who had had enough. While he was gone Tokhtamysh captured Moscow and laid it under fire and sword. The city was razed and over twenty thousand of its inhabitants were slain. Mozhaisk, Vladimir, and other towns belonging to the prince of Moscow received similar treatment. Unable to win support for another campaign, Dmitry was forced to resume payment of the Tatar tribute and to admit the khan's sovereignty over the Russian land.

Dmitry Donskoi salved his disappointment by wreaking vengeance upon the traitorous prince of Riazan. The prince managed to escape, but his capital was sacked as thoroughly as though the Tatars themselves had done it. The prince of Riazan fought back, but the abbot of the Trinity Monastery threatened him with anathema unless he arranged a peace with Dmitry. Donskoi had been so weakened at Kulikovo that he was unable to triumph even over the prince of Riazan.

He was more successful, however, in punishing Novgorod for the depredations of the "Volga men," those bands of Novgorodian outlaws who pillaged Muscovite settlements in the territory north of the Volga. In 1386 the grand prince led an army against the great republic, forced it to pay an indemnity of eight thousand rubles, and laid it under an annual tribute to Moscow. By her refusal to join in the crusade against the Tatars and by the frequent enlistment of her boyars in the service of Lithuania, Novgorod had merited little sympathy. Less than a century of independence lay before her.

Dmitry's tilts with the Tatars are perhaps the most spectacular and dramatic events of his reign, but they do not tell the whole story. He continued his predecessors' policy of aggrandizement of his position and territory. He exalted his authority over the other princes and took the attitude that the succession to the grand principality was not open to question, that it must go as a matter of course to the prince of Moscow. With the exception of Tver and Riazan the princes of north central Russia recognized him as "elder brother." He treated the territory of Vladimir which went with the title of grand prince as though it were part of his patrimony. Dmitry added more territory to the principality than he had received as his inheritance, and he continued the river policy of his predecessors by adding lands of strategic and commercial importance. Nearly the whole left bank of the Volga from Kostroma almost to Kazan came under his rule. The entire course of the Sheksna, an important tributary of the Volga connecting it with Beloozersk, was absorbed. The valley of the Tsna entered the Muscovite principality, as did part of the upper Oka. Thus the principality of Riazan was all but surrounded by Muscovite land, as were the principalities of Rostov, Suzdalia, and Nizhni-Novgorod. Moscow even moved into the Don river system when Dmitry won control over the headwaters of its tributary, the Voronezh. His successors had simply to fill in the gaps in order to make the territory of Moscow contiguous and in absolute control of the strategically located river network of north central Russia.

Donskoi's greatest contribution to the rise of Moscow, however, was his daring to defy the Tatars. Kulikovo made him a legendary hero whose later defeats were forgotten in the glory of that great victory. Russians knew that they could beat the Tatars in battle; they never forgot that they had done so under Dmitry's leadership and looked forward to the time when the foreigner's grip would be broken. All looked to Moscow, whose prince had the church's blessing, to lead the nation to revival and unity and independence. All felt scorn and contempt for those princes who stood aside when Dmitry marched to Kulikovo. If there had been any doubt about who would lead the Russian people to victory over the conqueror, there was none when Dmitry died in 1389.

THE GROWING STRENGTH OF MOSCOW

Dmitry left two sons of whom the elder, Vasily I (1389–1425), succeeded to the throne without dispute. He did not travel to the Horde to be confirmed, but took over his patrimony and his title of grand prince in full confidence that they were rightfully his and that his father had left no doubts about either. Indeed, throughout his long reign Vasily journeyed only once to Tatar headquarters, and then only to obtain sanction for an important acquisition of territory.

A few years after his accession Vasily set out to fill in the remaining gaps in his territory. The land of the prince of Suzdalia covered the entire lower course of the Kliazma, and also the confluence of the Oka and the Volga where lay the important commercial center of Nizhni-Novgorod. Vasily determined that this important section should be brought under Moscow. In 1392 he set off for Sarai accompanied by a large band of attendants, and ceremoniously and with great pomp he presented himself to the khan. With rich presents he prevailed upon the khan to grant him possession of the principalities of Suzdalia, Nizhni-Novgorod, and Murom. The latter, astride the lower Oka and running along the right bank of the Volga from Nizhni-Novogorod nearly to Kazan, would round out Vasily's territory on the east and carry his authority nearly to the bend of the Volga. When the grand prince left the Tatar camp an envoy of the khan went with him, and the party stopped at Nizhni-Novgorod to announce the khan's will. The prince of Suzdalia, who owned Nizhni-Novgorod, refused to receive the announcement, but he was betrayed by his own men and turned over as a prisoner to the grand prince. In a pompous ceremony Vasily was hailed as prince of Suzdalia and Nizhni-Novgorod. Murom was not contested, and with its absorption Moscow won complete control of the lower Oka.

This last decade of the fourteenth century witnessed the attempt by Vitovt, grand prince of Lithuania, to destroy the Golden Horde and absorb it and its vassal Russian lands into his projected East European empire. At the same time Tokhtamysh, formerly favorite of Great Khan Tamerlane and now khan of the Golden Horde, rebelled against his former patron and joined Vitovt. Dmitry Donskoi had been humiliated by the terrible Tatars, his capital pillaged and tribute again imposed upon a Russia that had dared momentarily to refuse it. Now Dmitry's son, Vasily I, again refused to pay tribute to the khan and Timur the Lame himself advanced into Russia to strike terror into the hearts of his rebellious subjects. His army plundered its way to the upper reaches of the river Don, but the land so recently devastated provided little booty. The Muscovites sent to Vladimir for its wonder-working icon of the Virgin Mary and were preparing to make a desperate stand when the good news came that the Tatars had moved away. Turning off to the south the raiders sated their lust for plunder on the rich Venetian and Genoese trading centers around the Sea of Azov; they even pillaged Sarai, the capital of the Golden Horde, in 1395.

Vitovt of Lithuania thought to capitalize the dissension among the Tatars and welcomed Tokhtamysh, the khan of the Golden Horde, as an ally against their common enemy Tamerlane. Vitovt's formidable army met Timur on the Vorskla in 1399, but the Lithuanian's presumptuous demand that the great khan bow to him as overlord brought about a battle in which Vitovt's army was destroyed. His hope of incorporating the territory of the Golden Horde was completely dashed.

In this struggle between Moscow's enemies Vasily I was content to stand aside. There was nothing to choose between them. A few years after Timur had disposed of the Lithuanians he sent an army once more into central Russia to demand tribute of Moscow. The Tatars advanced to the suburbs of the city and destroyed the villages around it; but they raised the siege after a month of feints and threats when Vasily paid them off with three thousand rubles.

In spite of the fact that he had married Vitovt's daughter, Vasily I faced in Lithuania a greater threat than that posed by the Tatars. Vitovt seized Smolensk, which did not return to Russia for over a century. He encouraged the prince of Tver in his opposition to the grand prince of Moscow, and supported the anti-Muscovite parties in Pskov and Novgorod. On three different occasions Vitovt raided deep into the principality of Moscow, but he was never able to take his attention away from his more formidable enemies for long enough to attempt the conquest of Moscow. Vasily I and Vitovt finally agreed upon the line of the river Ugra east of Smolensk as a common boundary, a line dangerously close to Moscow. After Vitovt's death the Lithuanian pressure upon Moscow relaxed, and Vasily's grandson began a Russian march westward which recovered Smolensk early in the sixteenth century.

Dmitry Donskoi had decreed that "when my son Vasily dies, his territory shall go to the brother next after him." Vasily died in 1425, leaving a brother and a ten-year-old son. The brother, Iuri, insisted that Donskoi's will meant that he should become grand prince. By long tradition ever since the time of the first prince of Moscow, however, the throne had descended from father to son when there was a son to receive it. For the time being Iuri was unable to gain the princely title because the dead Vasily's son, Vasily II (1425–1462), known as Vasily the Dark, had as his guardian his maternal uncle, the powerful Vitovt, grand prince of Lithuania. When the guardian's death in 1430 left Vasily II to his own devices, envoys of both Iuri and the young prince went before the khan to settle the matter. Vasily's delegate said to the khan, "My master, the grand prince, prays for the throne of the Grand Principality which is thy property, having no other title but thy protection, thy investiture and thy *yarlik*. Thou art master and canst dispose of it according to thy good pleasure." By such grovelling flattery the grandson of Dmitry of the Don won the contest and was named grand prince. But for the next twenty years there was civil war between Iuri and his sons on the one hand and Vasily II on the other over who should hold the title of grand prince.

During most of that time Vasily II ruled in Moscow whose citizens gave him their unqualified support, not because of any lovable qualities he possessed and certainly not because of his vigorous policies, but simply because he was his father's rightful heir and the interest of the state seemed to them to demand allegiance to him. For brief moments Vasily II was driven from his capital and his place occupied by his uncle or one of the uncle's sons. So divided was the territory of Moscow that Vasily could muster only fifteen hundred men against the Tatars when they raided his land and carried him away prisoner to the new Tatar city of Kazan on the middle Volga. The prince of Tver raided Muscovite territory when he chose, and armed bands of Lithuanians, Tatars, and Novgorodian outlaws roamed and plundered the land at will. On one occasion Vasily was captured and blinded by Iuri's son, and came to be known as Vasily the Dark or the Blind.

Iuri's son, petty, selfish, and utterly unscrupulous, so enraged the Muscovites by his complete disregard for the state's welfare that by 1450 he was driven into retirement and died soon after. Only then was Vasily the Dark free to take up the work of the earlier princes of Moscow. During the last twelve years of his reign he added much to the state territory. Petty princes who still held small independent appanages were ruthlessly dispossessed or forced into the service of the grand prince. A block of land at the confluence of the upper Don and its tributary the Sosna was thus added to Moscow, and the encirclement of the principality of Riazan was completed. When that principality was inherited by a minor, Vasily brought the young prince to Moscow, ostensibly to rear him. But Vasily sent a deputy to rule Riazan and the young prince never was allowed to return. In the next reign the principality was incorporated into the territory of Moscow. Vasily held the city of Pskov firmly under his control by forcing it to accept his nominee for prince. Novgorod, which had given sanctuary to his enemies during the civil war, was again forced to pay tribute to Moscow and to promise to trim the acts of its *vieche* to Vasily's will.

During the reign of Vasily II the territory of Moscow expanded far to the northeast. It was conquered not by the military exploits of the ruler but by the peaceful settlement of Muscovite colonists, some fleeing the civil war which made life in the neighborhood of Moscow unbearable and others simply seeking opportunity in the fur country beyond the Volga. Often some wandering monk in search of solitude would build a rough hermitage deep in the forest, and refugees from the war-torn south would gather around him and found a settlement. Great numbers poured across the Volga and on to the Sukhona and even to the Northern Dvina. The Muscovites came as settlers, hunting and trapping but also clearing away the forest and tilling the soil. Novgorod, which claimed the district, sent into it only a few traders and fur-gathering expeditions, and soon her hold was broken by the colonists from Moscow who came to build homes. Novgorod protested and tried to get Vasily to agree to a division of the territory along boundaries which both would respect. But no settlement was possible, for the settlers from Moscow kept spilling over any line that could be drawn. By the end of his reign his colonizing people had brought to Vasily the entire valley of the Sukhona and a strip of land beyond the Northern Dvina.

The reign of Vasily the Dark was an important one in the development of the Russian Orthodox church. In 1438 the Byzantine emperor at Constantinople, hard pressed by the Ottoman Turks who were driving against his borders, suggested to the pope at Rome a union of the Eastern and Western churches to heal the schism that had divided them since 1054. The emperor hoped that religious union might pave the way for cooperation of East and West in a great crusade to save his empire. A Church Council was called to meet at Florence in 1439, and to it went a great concourse of Eastern patriarchs, bishops, and metropolitans, including Isidore, the metropolitan of Moscow. The terms proposed by the Western churchmen left the Orthodox free to follow their different ritualistic practice but insisted upon recognition of the headship of the pope over all Christendom. Although the Eastern churchmen refused to unite with the West on such grounds, the metropolitan of Moscow accepted them and announced his acceptance in Kiev and Moscow. Vasily the Dark and the bishops of the Russian church, however, would have nothing to do with the settlement, and the metropolitan was driven from Moscow.

A few years later, when Constantinople fell to the Turks, in part because the failure of religious union prevented political cooperation between East and West, the Russian church severed all connection with the patriarch of Constantinople. A council of Russian bishops elected its own metropolitan to rule over the Russian church as an independent body. After the fall of Constantinople the Orthodox faithful all over Eastern Europe came to look upon the metropolitan of Moscow as the head of the Eastern church and upon Moscow as their religious capital.

Anxious that his son should not have to endure his own tragic experience of civil war, Vasily the Dark took Ivan, the heir apparent, into the administration long before his death and accustomed his subjects to regard the son as ruler in Moscow. Ivan's practical experience thus paved the way for an easy transition to the new reign after the death of his blind father. In 1462 Ivan succeeded to the grand principality without incident and to a territory far larger than that of any other prince in northern Russia. Only decadent Novgorod controlled more territory, and the internal disturbances to which it was chronically subject presaged its early demise.

SUGGESTED READING

See *Suggested Reading* at end of Chapter 9.

9

The Birth of Modern Russia

WHEN VASILY THE DARK LEFT HIS throne to his son Ivan, a number of large states shared the land of European Russia. In the north sprawled the republic of Novgorod in uneasy possession of a vast territory stretching from the Gulf of Finland to the Urals and from the Arctic nearly to the Sukhona and Kama rivers. Vaguely subject to the grand prince of Russia, who in turn was vassal to the khan of the Golden Horde, Novgorod was semi-independent, accepting the rule of the grand prince when she was forced to do so but frequently toying with the idea of attaching herself to Lithuania to escape pressure and tax levies by Moscow and the Horde. In the southeast and south of European Russia were the Tatars, scattered over the steppe from the Dnieper east beyond the Caspian. But the Tatar power was in process of breaking up. While the khan of the Golden Horde still controlled the lower Volga, the khanate of Kazan astride the middle Volga and the Kama, as well as the khanate of Crimea in the Crimean peninsula and the valley of the lower Dnieper, had broken away from the Golden Horde during the first part of the fifteenth century. On the west was the grand principality of Lithuania, whose eastern border rested approximately on the Black Sea and the rivers Dnieper, Vorskla, Ugra, and Western Dvina. The grand principality of Moscow lay in the center surrounded by the other states. In this center there were bits of territory—Riazan, Rostov, and Iaroslavl—that the grand prince had not yet absorbed, but he had encircled them with his own domains and could incorporate them at will. Tver was wedged between Moscow, Novgorod, and Lithuania. It must be borne in mind that all East Slavs at this time were subject either to the Tatars or to the grand prince of Lithuania.

The principality of Moscow constituted an almost solid block of territory straddling the upper Volga and the Oka, stretching away to the Northern Dvina in the northeast, nearly to Lake Onega in the northwest, almost to Kazan in the east, and into the Don basin in the south. The Lithuanian border was less than a hundred miles to the west of the city of Moscow, and Tver was even closer on the northwest. Moscow had just about reached the limit of expansion possible without encroaching upon the possessions of the large states which surrounded her. Her princes had developed a habit of adding territory to their heritage and were coming to be known as "collectors of Russian soil." Would they be satisfied now with the control of central Russia or would they press for further acquisitions? The Russian people wherever they might be living had come to look upon the princes of Moscow as national leaders, as champions of the cause of national independence, as harbingers of national unity. The Russian church had supported and encouraged the princes of Moscow in their gathering of the Russian land. Would the prince, the people, and the church be willing to stop now? Or would the new grand prince continue along the course marked out by his predecessors? This was the problem facing Russia when Ivan III came to the throne in 1462.

IVAN III, THE GREAT (1462–1505)

Ivan, at twenty-two, was no stranger to the problems of governing his principality. For a number of years he had been associated with his father in the administration, and during that apprenticeship he had "penetrated the secret of autocracy." Loyally devoted to the church as an institution but little troubled by the principles it taught, Ivan did not hesitate to put to death his brother and nephews who had conspired against him, although he wept copious tears at their passing. Torturing boyars, condemning Poles to be burned alive, sending princes and even monks to the whipping post, Ivan might have been known to history as "the Terrible," had his cruelty not been eclipsed by that of his grandson. So lacking in courage that he laid himself open to the charge of cowardice, Ivan avoided war whenever possible or sent lieutenants to lead his troops into battle. A contemporary ruler said of him, "Ivan is a strange man; he stays quietly at home and triumphs over his enemies while I, though always on horseback, cannot defend my country." He inherited from his forbears a mastery of diplomacy, trickery, and double-dealing by which he often accomplished his purpose without the expense of a costly campaign. Like Ivan Kalita he kept careful watch over the treasury and opened his purse only when there was promise of good return. The nineteenth-century Russian historian Karamzin aptly compared Ivan with his contemporary, Louis XI of France, and observed that "economy, deliberation, caution, keen distrust of bold measures which may accomplish everything and which may spoil everything; at the same time resolution in carrying to the end whatever he had once begun, and finally absolute cool-ness—such were the leading traits of the character of Ivan III."

The Fall of Novgorod

The expansion of Lithuania under Olgerd and Vitovt had freed the Dnieper water-road from the Tatars, and in the mid-fifteenth century that great highway was controlled by Lithuania from Smolensk to its mouth on the Black Sea. This was one reason why Novgorod was tempted to offer herself to the grand prince of Lithuania, for only by so doing could her mer-chants obtain the right to trade up and down the Dnieper. Kiev would once again be opened to Novgorod merchants, and from it Russian furs could pass by the overland route into Galicia, Hungary, Austria, Bohemia, and South Germany. For centuries the furs of Novgorod had been sold in west-ern Europe by the Hansards. Now once more, if the great republic were to join Lithuania, Novgorodians themselves might control that profitable trade.

To break away from Moscow would mean excommunication from Ortho-doxy, but there was a remedy for that. Kiev now had its own metropolitan— a heretic, it was true, who recognized the headship of the Pope, but never-theless a metropolitan—who could invest the archbishop of Novgorod if the metropolitan of Moscow should refuse to do so. Indeed the commercial attraction of the Dnieper and Kiev as a gateway to central Europe was so strong that a number of wealthy Novgorodians hailed the metropolitan of Kiev as the only bona fide church leader in the Russian land, and denounced the metropolitan of Moscow for serving a grand prince who was a vassal of the infidel khan of the Golden Horde.

Finally, there was sound political reason for Novgorod's interest in be-coming part of Lithuania. After Vitovt's death in 1430 the power of Lithu-ania and the vigor of her rulers waned, while Moscow was becoming more and more formidable and threatening. Novgorod's fur empire to the north-east was suffering encroachment by Muscovite settlers. The eventual inun-dation of her territory and the loss of her freedom seemed inevitable if Novgorod continued her tie with northern Russia. But, after all, there were many Russians, people and princes, who were part of Lithuania. Why should Novgorod not join them? It would not be as if she were completely desert-ing the Russian land. Perhaps, if her own declining power were added to the waning force of Lithuania, the union might prevent all Russia's being en-gulfed by the insatiable prince of Moscow. By such reasoning some Nov-gorodian leaders may have justified their hope to tear away from Moscow and join Lithuania. That the prince and metropolitan of Moscow would accuse them of treason to the land and the church they could have no doubt.

The Novgorodian leaders must have been fully aware that desertion to Lithuania and the metropolitan of Kiev would precipitate rebellion among the faithful Orthodox lower classes of the republic. But the religious factor was not the only one impelling Novgorodian commoners to oppose their leaders. Politically, they were pitted against the boyar class in the city, for the "freedom of Novgorod" meant little to the lower classes. Economically, too, there was cleavage, for the wealth of Novgorod went chiefly to the boyars and the commercial magnates; the mass of urban and rural laborers was drifting toward pauperization. The lower classes tended to support Moscow because they hoped that Moscow would curb the economic and political power of the Novgorodian merchants.

Vasily the Dark had exacted from Novgorod a promise not to shelter any prince who opposed his suzerainty over the city. But hardly had Vasily turned his back upon the republic than the leading citizens, who constituted a pro-Lithuanian party, brought in a Lithuanian to become the city's prince. He stayed only a short time, and another Lithuanian brought in a few years later also left soon after arrival. But Novgorodian leaders must have known that there could be no drawing back once Lithuanians had been called to the princely office. The city had broken its agreement with Moscow and revenge was sure to follow. In 1470 the city's leaders went the whole way, recognizing the king of Poland as their sovereign and promising him as much in taxes as they had been paying in Tatar tribute to Moscow. In return, they received his guarantee to safeguard the "ancient liberties" of Novgorod and not to restrict Orthodoxy. Moscow's answer to this precipitate step followed immediately.

Ivan III considered Novgorod to be part of his "patrimony," for the grand princes of Moscow had long insisted upon the right to name the princes of Novgorod. The khan of the Horde, Moscow's overlord, recognized that right. So in 1471 Ivan led an army against Novgorod to put the rebellious republic in its place. Until then he had been amazingly patient and forbearing of the city's duplicity. The *Chronicle of Novgorod,* written by an Orthodox monk whose sympathies were all with Moscow, reported: "The pious sovereign and Grand Prince of all Russia, Ivan Vasilievich,* has frequently sent his messengers to them [the citizens of Novgorod], calling on them to keep his patrimony from all harm, to improve themselves in all things within his ancestral estates, and to live according to old custom. [He warned them that] he suffered much in these things from their vexatious ways and contumacy within his paternal domains, while he expected from them a thorough amendment of their conduct towards himself and a respectful submission." In 1470 Ivan had warned Novgorod again. "Mend your ways towards me, my patrimony, and recognize us; keep my name of Grand Prince in strictness and in honor as of old; and send to me representatives to do homage and to make settlement. I desire to keep you, my patrimony,

---

* That is, Ivan, the son of Vasily. Russians are referred to by their Christian name and patronymic.

in good favor, on the old conditions." The Moscow party in the city, led by the archbishop of Novgorod, demanded reconciliation with Ivan, but the Lithuanian party had won out. "We are free, we are no patrimony," some had shouted in the *vieche,* and the arrangement with the king of Poland passed the assembly. Thereupon, says the chronicler, Ivan "informed his patrimony that his power of endurance was exhausted, and that he would not suffer their misbehavior and contumacy any longer." The metropolitan of Moscow also had written repeatedly to Novgorod, urging the citizens not to give in to "Latin" blandishments and calling upon them to stand firm in the true faith. His pleas probably were not read to the *vieche* and made no impression upon the wealthy boyars who favored the union with Lithuania. Novgorod severed her connections with Moscow and braced herself against Ivan's wrath.

The campaign against Novgorod in 1471 was carefully planned. At the last minute Ivan sent another warning, "but the wicked people minded him not, and clung to the intention of abandoning Orthodoxy and giving themselves over to the King [of Poland]." When his armies were ready to march Ivan "dispatched to Novgorod the Great a challenge in writing, exposing the malpractices of the people and their treason, and announcing that he was himself marching with a force against them." This was not just an act of bravado. By reviewing the "malpractices of the people" and charging Novgorod with treason Ivan justified himself in the eyes of all Orthodox Russians and at the same time appealed to the lower classes in Novgorod to rise against their traitorous oppressors and welcome him as a deliverer.

Ivan delivered the attack in two simultaneous blows, one aimed at the city of Novgorod and the other at the center of her fur empire far to the northeast. The second was sent on ahead so that it might arrive at its destination and attack at about the time the assault was delivered against Novgorod. The defending forces were thus divided and prevented from combining to defend the capital. The army dispatched to the northeast moved first to Vologda where the troops from Moscow were joined by "the men of Vologda." Then the force moved down the Sukhona to Ustiug, where it picked up contingents from that area and from Moscow's ally, the republic of Viatka. Then the Muscovite army, with its colonials and allies, burned Novgorodian villages and trading posts and ravaged "all the territories of Novgorod" in the basin of the Northern Dvina. The defending forces were beaten time and again, their commander so seriously wounded that he had to be evacuated, and "a large number of the men of Novgorod slain and others captured." The valley of the Dvina was added to the grand principality of Moscow.

In the meantime the main attack was delivered against the capital itself by a combined force of Russians and Tatar mercenaries from east of the

Oka. While Ivan and his court followed along at a safe distance, this large army seized Torzhok and cut off the supply of grain upon which Novgorod depended to feed her populace. Detaching a guard to hold Torzhok, Ivan sent the main body against Staraia Russa, burning towns, driving off livestock, and "visiting every part of the Novgorod country with the dread powers of his fire and sword." Even the weather favored Orthodox Moscow, for not a drop of rain fell from May to September and the swamps which had saved Novgorod from the Tatars all dried up. "The troops of the Grand Prince found no impediments," the chronicler observed, "and could ride in every direction over the country, driving the cattle over dried ground; thus did the Lord God through this desiccation punish the men of Novgorod for their evil-doing and subject them to the strong hand of the pious sovereign and Grand Prince Ivan Vasilievich of all Russia."

While detachments moved against villages and farms, the main body continued on to the west, circling Lake Ilmen to join the citizen army of Pskov which had been ordered to support Moscow, and thus intercepting any possible relief from Poland-Lithuania. But the king of Poland had no inclination to go against Ivan. His only move to assist his recently acquired subjects was to suggest to the khan of the Golden Horde that it would be a good time to attack Moscow when Ivan was involved against Novgorod. But when the khan's men advanced to the Oka they showed no disposition to attack the one hundred eighty thousand Russian troops which barred their way, and Novgorod was not relieved.

The Novgorodians lost one skirmish after another and finally took a stand on the river Shelon, facing the attackers on the opposite bank. "The troops of the Grand Prince plunged into the river on their horses, not one of their horses stumbling in descending the steep bank, nor floundering in the water, and closing up they rushed upon the whole body of the men of Novgorod and they joined in battle." Artillery, mentioned in Russian history for the first time, served Ivan well and in an hour's time the battle was decided. The defenders "threw down their arms and fled back whence they had come; they ran in disgrace, casting away their armor to relieve their horses of weight, and a great number of them fell dead, for their lawlessness and for their rebellion against their sovereign the Grand Prince." Those who had come from Novgorod by water over Lake Ilmen overcrowded their boats in their panic to get away, and many of the craft were swamped. Ivan's horsemen pursued the mounted Novgorodians for fifteen miles, killing many of them and taking many prisoners.

The monk who wrote the *Chronicle of Novgorod* was as pleased as when Alexander Nevsky defeated the Teutonic knights: "Thus was God's favor bestowed on the troops of the Grand Prince, maintaining his just cause; even as God helped Gideon against the Midianites, and Abraham against the king of Sodom, so did he aid the troops of the Grand Prince against these unrighteous backsliders, the men of Novgorod." After the rout on the Shelon Novgorod capitulated. The lower classes, starved when the city's access to grain was cut off by the earlier seizure of Torzhok, rose against the officials and opened the city's gates.

Ivan's justice against those who were responsible for Novgorod's defection was stern but not vindictive. Only a few leaders of the pro-Lithuanian party in the capital, including the infamous traitor Marfa, widow of a former mayor, were beheaded "for their conspiracy and crime in seeking to take to Latinism." A number of others were imprisoned and many families of "boyars and men of substance" who had held high office were removed to towns nearer to Moscow. The rest of the populace, led by the clergy, begged Ivan's forgiveness and received it. "He withdrew from them the anger of his heart, and withheld his sword and his menace over the land." The prisoners were freed without ransom, the raiding parties called in from the country-side, and the army withdrew to Moscow. Novgorod had to pay a heavy indemnity, admit Ivan's supreme judicial authority over its courts, and promise to have nothing to do with Poland-Lithuania.

The Lithuanian party in Novgorod was not completely destroyed in the campaign of 1471. Only its leaders had been put to death, imprisoned, or exiled to other Russian cities. Other leaders rose to take their places, for as long as this border town retained control over its own actions there was bound to be a group who honestly believed that the city's salvation lay in playing off one strong neighbor against the other. Ivan III returned to Novgorod in 1475 in his capacity as supreme judge in the city, put a number of the pro-Lithuanian party to trial on charges of treasonable intent and sympathy for Poland and Roman Catholicism, and packed them off to Moscow as prisoners. Many Novgorodians who sympathized with Ivan moved to Moscow and there pressed their charges of duplicity and treason against those who still favored Lithuania.

Ivan demanded complete submission of Novgorod to his will and an end to pro-Lithuanian activity. When the warning was ignored he sent an army against the city and put an end to its independence. This time the penalty was more severe. Again the leaders were put to death, and many were tortured to obtain confessions or incrimination of others. Scores of leading families were scattered among other towns, their estates confiscated and turned over to families from Moscow who were moved to Novgorodian territory in large numbers. "In this way the aristocracy of Novgorod disappeared completely, and with it perished the very memory of Novgorodian liberty. The 'lesser people,' i. e., peasants and other land laborers of Novgorod, were freed from the oppression of the boyars and organized in tax-paying peasant communes as in Moscow. On the whole, their condition was ameliorated, and they had no cause to regret the passing of the old order"

(Platonov). In 1478 the republic was added to the territory of the grand principality of Moscow, and the great bell which had called its citizens to assembly was moved to Moscow in token of the end of the freedom of Novgorod.

Absorption of the Appanage Principalities

During the reign of Ivan III the power of the appanages of central Russia declined more and more until their rulers could not avoid incorporation with Moscow. Some found their territory surrounded by that of the grand prince. Others fell hopelessly into debt to Ivan for the Tatar tribute and could settle it only by willing their debts and their lands to Moscow. Some thought to take service with the grand prince of Lithuania, but any prince who tried to do so knew that he risked Muscovite wrath. Princes who entertained such thoughts found it safer and wiser to seek service with the grand prince of Moscow and to leave their estates to him. Where earlier appanage law had allowed the prince to settle his heritage upon whomsoever he chose, now Ivan commanded that the lands of an appanage prince who died without heirs must pass to the grand prince. If these measures did not provide for every contingency there were still other ways to deal with an appanage prince.

The princes of Rostov and Iaroslavl offered their lands to Ivan III and took service at his court. Others with smaller estates—the princes of Viazma, Odoiev, Bielev, Mtsensk, Novosil, Vorotin, and others—followed suit. The addition of their domains to Moscow gave Ivan authority along the entire right bank of the Desna to its mouth just above Kiev; it pushed the Lithuanian frontier far to the west, for some of these princes had been vassal to the grand prince of Lithuania since Vitovt's time. The last two princes of Riazan were Ivan's nephews who were completely amenable to his will. One of them died without heirs, leaving half of the territory to Ivan, and the rest of it fell similarly to Moscow in the next reign. Perm on the Kama, a republic distinct from Novgorod's "land of Permia," joined Moscow in 1472.

The prince of Tver, who loyally supported Ivan against Novgorod, later sought an alliance with Lithuania in an effort to recover his freedom of action. In the meantime many of the Tveran boyars deserted their prince to join Ivan, won over by bribes or simply by the advantages of serving the wealthiest and most powerful among the Russian princes. Ivan accused the prince of treason and sent an army against him. The rest of the Tveran boyars deserted en masse, the prince fled to Lithuania, and the principality was added to Moscow in 1485 without striking a blow in its own defense. At the same time Viatka, an independent republic in the rich fur country to the northeast which had been allied with Moscow during the campaign against Novgorod, was absorbed without opposition. At the time of his death in 1505 Ivan passed on to his son a territory three times as extensive as that which his own father had bequeathed to him forty-three years earlier.

The End of the Tatar Yoke

Vasily the Dark had appointed a Tatar friend to govern the region of the lower Oka, and this small, subject khanate of Kasimov provided a shield against raids into Muscovite territory from the east. Now Ivan III proposed to use his vassal, the khan of Kasimov, against the hostile khan of Kazan on the middle Volga. A rebellious party in Kazan, possibly motivated by Muscovite bribes, plotted to overthrow their ruler and replace him by the khan of Kasimov, whom they called to take over the throne. Ivan sent an army from Moscow in 1467 to help his vassal, but the attack failed. Two years later the grand prince sent a formidable army to the outskirts of Kazan, whose khan begged for peace and agreed never again to raid Muscovite territory. Tatars from the subject khanate of Kasimov marched with Russians to the attack. The fact that his vassal candidate for the throne of Kazan had died in the meantime did not swerve Ivan. He accomplished his purpose of weakening Kazan to free his hand for action elsewhere, and the khanate on the middle Volga was left to be added to Moscow later by his grandson.

Ivan's support of the Tatar khanate of Kasimov and his reduction of the power of the khanate of Kazan were part of an elaborate scheme which aimed at nothing less than the destruction of the Golden Horde, or at least the elimination of its titular control over the grand principality of Russia. Less than two years after his accession Ivan began to weave a diplomatic net designed to encircle and isolate the Golden Horde. In 1464 a delegation from Moscow visited Herat. Two years later Ivan received envoys from the ruler of Baku beyond the Caucasus and sent an embassy to repay the call the same year. Only the year before, the khan of the Golden Horde had prepared a raid against Moscow but was kept at home by an attack of the khan of the Crimean Tatars.

For some years Ivan's hope to encircle the Golden Horde lay in abeyance while the grand prince faced the more immediate task of dealing with Novgorod. The cautious Ivan was not so rash as to embroil himself simultaneously with the Horde, with Novgorod, and possibly with Lithuania. Moscow was not yet powerful enough to deal with more than one enemy at a time. But when Ivan returned to his capital in 1472 after the campaign against Novgorod, he took up once more his earlier plan to isolate and destroy the Golden Horde. He concluded an arrangement with the khan of the Crimean Tatars who agreed to immobilize Poland while Ivan attacked the Horde. By 1475 everything was in readiness for the assault upon Sarai which would end Tatar dominion over Moscow. Stripped of allies by Ivan's diplomatic triumphs, the Horde would have to fight alone. But at the very moment when victory seemed assured the situation in South Russia changed completely. The Ottoman Turks entered the Crimea, overran the Genoese trading posts in the peninsula, and took the khan of the Crimean Tatars prisoner to Constantinople. He was freed to return to his people only when he agreed to recognize and obey the Ottoman sultan as his sovereign. His commitment to Moscow could not for the time being be fulfilled.

Ivan could not now move against the Horde until he could rebuild a system of alliances. He set about immediately to do this. A mission, headed by an Italian in the service of Moscow, crossed the Caucasus to Tabriz to engage the benevolent neutrality of the Turkoman chieftain in Persia in the event of a war between Moscow and the Golden Horde. Then Ivan secured an alliance with the khan of the Nogai Tatars, whose control of the valley of the Ural made him particularly valuable to the grand prince in the coming struggle. Before the attack could be launched against the Horde, however, there had to be a final settlement with Novgorod. In 1475 Ivan returned to that city to overturn the Lithuanian party, but he came to the conclusion shortly thereafter that Novgorod could not be trusted and that the only way to put an end to the danger that it might turn against him at a critical time was to take away its freedom. Only after the absorption of the republic by Moscow in 1478 was Ivan again free to concentrate his attention upon the Horde.

In the meantime Ivan, urged on by his imperious wife, handed the khan of the Horde one insult after another. His then ally, the republic of Viatka, sent a force down the Volga and pillaged the khan's capital Sarai. A strong Muscovite army held the Tatar host at arm's length while Ivan worked his will against Novgorod in 1471. In 1476 the khan ordered Ivan to resume the payment of tribute immediately and to present himself at Sarai, for the grand prince was still the khan's vassal. But Ivan sent back a scornful answer. When another embassy from the lower Volga came to Moscow with a picture of the khan and asked only that he kneel to the khan's likeness, Ivan hurled the picture to the ground and trampled on it. Then all the khan's envoys but one were slain, and that one was ordered back to Sarai to report the contempt which Moscow showed for the Tatars. Sooner or later, when the opportunity came, the ruler of the Horde would have to punish such insolence or admit that the grand prince of Russia was no longer his subject.

The king of Poland, confident that the Crimean Tatars would not attack him now that they had been brought under the suzerainty of the Ottoman sultan, arranged with the khan of the Golden Horde for a combined attack upon Moscow in 1480. Both had recent grievances to settle with the grand prince of Russia. Ivan had recently added to his domain the republic of Novgorod, whose officials had sworn allegiance to the king of Poland, and the khan's envoys had suffered humiliating insults in Moscow. But, unfortunately for the allies and fortunately for Russia, this cooperation between Poland and the Horde came too late, and even now the two could not get together. Now Ivan was free of the threat to his rear from Novgorod. And the coming war with Poland and the Horde aroused immense popular enthusiasm for a crusade against foreign heretic and foreign infidel.

In the autumn of 1480 the khan led his troops north against Moscow. Finding the Oka river well defended the horde turned west, hoping to join forces with the king of Poland. But the Polish army never appeared, for at that moment the Crimean Tatars attacked in the south, and the king could not spare troops for the war with Moscow. The khan pitched camp on the banks of the Ugra, the border between Muscovite and Lithuanian territory, to wait for his western allies. Ivan posted an army on the opposite bank, ordered Moscow to look to its defenses, sent his wife north to safety should the Tatars assault the city, and prepared to follow her. The churchmen shamed him with the memory of Vladimir Monomakh and Dmitry Donskoi, and the people of Moscow protested loudly against such cowardice. Ivan joined the army on the Ugra, his spirit restored by the metropolitan's blessing and assurance of victory. Always cautious, he refused to order the attack and contented himself with "sending arrows and insults across the river" (Rambaud). But he did find the courage to spurn the khan's offer of peace and pardon if he would send one of his men to kiss the khan's stirrup. One morning the two armies awoke to find the river covered with ice, and each feared that the other might cross. Ivan ordered a withdrawal. The bustle of breaking camp convinced the Tatars that the Russians were about to attack, and they turned and fled away to the south, not stopping until they reached the Volga. The Tatar yoke had been lifted.

The following year the Horde was attacked by the Crimean Tatars, and the khan who had fled from the Ugra river line was killed by one of his own men. By the end of the century the Golden Horde was completely broken up. For nearly three centuries more, Russia was to know little peace from raids by Crimean and Nogai Tatars. But devastating and exhausting as these raids were, the Tatars made no attempt to dominate Russia politically. Ivan, by conduct that was far from heroic, had brought nearly two and a half centuries of subjection to foreign rule to an end in 1480. Russia was strong and independent for the first time since Alexander Nevsky had bowed to the conqueror. After 1480 Ivan added the word "Autocrat" to his title to signify that he was now independent.

Some years after the "victory" on the Ugra a son of the late khan of the Golden Horde attempted to halt the Horde's drift toward oblivion by winning control of Kazan. He was supported by a party within Kazan which aimed at fighting off the imminent control of Moscow by allying with the Horde. It will be remembered that in 1469 Ivan III had sent an army against Kazan and had forced it to beg for peace and to promise not to raid Moscow territory. But that submission could be taken as a sign of weakness, an invitation to later conquest, and some of its people feared Kazan might go the way of Novgorod. Civil war broke out in Kazan between those on the one hand who favored uniting with the Golden Horde against Moscow and those on the other who sensed the decline of the Horde and hoped by coming to terms with Moscow now to avert annihilation later.

Ivan sent a powerful army against Kazan in 1487, the city fell before the Russian assault, and the candidate of the Moscow party became khan of Kazan, taking an oath of loyalty as vassal to Ivan. But it was not Ivan's disposition to hurry such a matter. He was satisfied with Kazan's subordination to Moscow and made no effort to absorb it. There was good reason to believe that in good time the khanate would fall like ripe fruit to Moscow, as had Novgorod. When Ivan IV later brought to an end the separate existence of Kazan and added its territory to Russia, as the grand principality of Moscow must now be called, his task was made easy by Ivan III's earlier reduction of the khanate almost to impotence.

After bringing Kazan more firmly under his control Ivan III turned against the Golden Horde. With an army of Russians and troops from his vassal khanates of Kasimov and Kazan, and allied with the khan of Crimea, Ivan almost completely crushed the Horde in 1491. The Crimean Tatars administered the final blow in 1502 and the Golden Horde collapsed. A small remnant of its once mighty power managed to survive as the khanate of Astrakhan at the mouth of the Volga, but this, too, was added to Russian territory by the grandson of Ivan III.

The Western Frontier

With the absorption of Novgorod and the declaration of independence from the Golden Horde, Moscow, now Russia, became a nation-state. Henry VII in England, Louis XI and Charles VIII in France, and Ferdinand and Isabella in Spain were contemporaries of Ivan III in Russia. After 1480 this nation-state of Russia had to concern itself with foreign affairs, to take notice of its relations with other sovereign states, not simply as a matter of national pride, but as a vital matter of national survival. There had been no problem of foreign relations when Russia was vassal to the Horde, nor could there have been until she had won her independence. And not until the power and wealth of Novgorod came under the control of the grand prince did the state have the strength to win the respect of other nations, even if it had been independent before then. The dual task of uniting all of north and central Russia under one leadership and winning independence from foreign rule occupied the grand princes fully until its fulfillment in 1480.

Ivan III applied the same tactics to Poland-Lithuania after 1480 that

he had used earlier with such success against the Golden Horde. He sought
to neutralize Poland diplomatically by surrounding her with states friendly
to Moscow. In 1482 a diplomatic mission from Hungary visited Moscow,
and Ivan sent his chief diplomat to return the visit. At the same time he
married his oldest son to the daughter of the prince of Moldavia. By these
moves Poland was flanked on the south and Lithuania on the southwest by
Russia's allies. Southeast of Lithuania lay the khanate of Crimea, long
friendly to Moscow. To strengthen the reliability of that friendship Ivan
opened negotiations with the Ottoman sultan, to whom the khan of the
Crimean Tatars owed allegiance. The Jews in Lithuania, suffering under
government persecution, were given to hope that their religion might expect
more tolerance from Orthodox Russia than from Roman Catholic Poland-
Lithuania; they, too, became active supporters of Moscow. Finally, the
German emperor sent an embassy to Moscow to offer Ivan the title of
king. Ivan refused, saying that his title needed no confirmation from anyone
else. However, Ivan gladly accepted the German emperor's offer to support
Russia in the event of a war with Poland, in return for a similar promise
of assistance. By this agreement in 1490 Ivan completed the encirclement
of Poland. To discourage Sweden from going to Poland's assistance in case
of war, Ivan arranged a treaty of friendship and support with Denmark.
One provision of the treaty, by which Ivan agreed to expel the Hanseatic
merchants from Novgorod, profited both Russia and Denmark. Henceforth
Russian merchants would do their own trading with western Europe.

With the death of the king of Poland in 1492 the union between Poland
and Lithuania came temporarily to an end. The Lithuanians insisted that
a younger son of the late king rule them separately, while the Poles chose
the older son to succeed the father. Ivan III took the end of the dynastic
union between the two countries as his cue to attack Lithuania. At the
same time his ally, the khan of Crimea, raided through southern Lithuania
and into Poland with such force that the new king of Poland was unable
to help his brother in Lithuania against Moscow. Russian victory came
easily in 1494 and the grand duke of Lithuania was forced to give up all
claim to Novgorod, Pskov, and Tver. But the treaty was only a truce.
Lithuanian persecution of Greek Orthodoxy drove some of the border princes
in the valley of the lower Desna to desert Lithuania and carry their loyalty
and their lands to Moscow; this gave Ivan III an excuse for going to the
relief of his coreligionists. Again his armies were victorious, but his success
drove Poland and Lithuania to restore their union and to call in the Teutonic
knights to assist them against Moscow. The Russians were stopped, but the
border principalities remained with Moscow when Ivan III's last war came
to an end.

Ivan's aggressive policy in the west added territory to the state and
contributed to the decline of his enemy Poland-Lithuania. While the Polish

gentry were encroaching upon the power of their king and adding to their political as well as economic rights over their own estates, Ivan III gave the Russian Orthodox peoples living beyond his borders to understand that they could look to Moscow for deliverance from religious persecution. Irridentism henceforth would embarrass Poland-Lithuania and serve the hope of Russia's rulers that the "Russian land" might be brought once more under Moscow. Indeed, Ivan III insisted that until "all the Russian land which now doth appertain unto Lithuania" became part of Moscow, there could be between the two countries no more than an armistice "for the gathering of fresh strength and the drawing of fresh breath." In 1503, at the end of one of these perennial wars, the grand prince of Lithuania asked for the return of his border lands occupied by Moscow, saying that he "doth desire but his own patrimony." Ivan III answered him: "And do I not also desire mine own patrimony—the Russian land which until now hath been held by Lithuania, and which doth yet include both Kiev and Smolensk and others of our towns?"

Moscow, the Third Rome

His first wife died five years after his accession and Ivan began casting about for another. At that time Sophia Palaeologus, the orphaned niece of the last Byzantine emperor, was living in Rome as a ward of the pope, who gave her refuge after the fall of Constantinople to the Turks in 1453. Religious leaders in Rome, hoping that the Orthodox church might be brought to accept the headship of the pope now that the eastern capital had been conquered, knew that Russia and the metropolitan of Moscow must be won over before Christian unity in Europe could be restored. The pope offered his ward to Ivan of Moscow along with the suggestion that the union of East and West be considered. Ivan accepted, and Sophia started for Moscow in 1472 along with a train of Italians and Byzantine refugees and a Roman cardinal who was to argue the case for church union. The party arrived outside Moscow and arranged itself in procession to enter the city, the cardinal leading the way bearing the Latin cross. But the metropolitan warned Ivan that unless the cardinal lay aside the Latin cross "then he comes into the city by one gate and I am out of it by another." Ivan yielded to the ultimatum and the party passed through the gates without the hated symbol of the West. In the debate that ensued over the proposed union of the churches Russian clergymen staunchly defended Orthodoxy and bitterly condemned the papacy. The cardinal was forced to return to Rome with the report that Moscow would not yield.

Sophia, renowned all over Europe for her intelligence and wit, was an ambitious woman who came to exert great influence over her husband. Proud of her ancestry and contemptuous of the grand prince's modest position as vassal of the khan of the Golden Horde, she taunted Ivan with the contrast between the brilliance of the imperial court where she had grown up and the humble and homely situation she found at Moscow. Sophia continued after her marriage to sign herself as "Imperial Princess of Byzantium," and insisted upon receiving ambassadors who came to Moscow. She would not be simply the wife of the ruler; she wanted to share the throne. As heiress of the eastern emperor she was bringing to Russia the imperial authority and dignity of Byzantium. In his correspondence with foreign rulers Ivan now signed himself Tsar or Emperor, and Sophia was Tsarina or Empress in her own right. At her insistence letters sent abroad took on a formal and imperious tone, and Ivan presumed to call himself "Tsar of all Rus," implying a claim to Russian lands still under foreign rule. After 1480 he added to his title the word "Autocrat," which at that time indicated only that he considered himself an independent sovereign. As successor to the position of the eastern empire, Moscow added the double-headed eagle of Byzantium to the state crest and seal.

Down to the time of Ivan III central and western Europe had looked upon Moscow as just another insignificant principality, an attitude fully justified by the facts. Indeed, many Europeans had never heard of Moscow, and "Rus" to them meant Poland-Lithuania. In 1486 a wandering German knight stumbled upon Moscow and upon his return home reported to the Holy Roman Emperor Frederick III that east of the "Rus" of Poland and Lithuania there was still another "Rus" of Moscow. The emperor sent the roving knight back to the Kremlin as ambassador with a request for one of Ivan's daughters to marry his nephew and an offer to raise the prince of Moscow to the rank of king. Ivan, who had recently won independence from the Golden Horde, haughtily answered the ambassador: "Touching what thou hast said unto us concerning the kingship, we, by grace of God, have been Emperors of our land from the beginning, and from our earliest forefathers, and do hold our commission of God himself. Therefore we pray God that He may grant unto us and unto our children to be Emperors of our land forever, even as we are now, and that we may never have need to be commissioned unto the same, even as we have not now." Of the inaccuracies in the statement the German emperor would not be aware, but there could be no doubting Ivan's disdain for a delegation of authority from anyone less than God.

Sophia detested the lack of ceremony and the egalitarianism that characterized the court at Moscow. Among his courtiers, if they can be called that, Ivan was just a prince among other princes and boyars, some of whom also could trace their ancestry as far back as Rurik. The prince of Moscow was treated as only first among equals; the boyars came and went at will in the palace, if it can be dignified by that name, and subjected Ivan to "many words of reviling and abuse." Soon after she came to Moscow Sophia insisted upon the adoption of a court etiquette in keeping with the exalted position which she urged upon her husband. Byzantine ceremony and pomp came to characterize the court of the Kremlin. No longer did the boyars come and go as they pleased or treat the prince of Moscow as one of them. Now Ivan was "Tsar of all Rus" and successor to the Caesars of Constantinople. His old wooden dwelling in the Kremlin was unsuited to his new position, so Ivan brought Italian architects to Moscow to build a fine new palace of stone.

After freeing Russia from the Tatar yoke Ivan became the sole independent ruler in the Orthodox world. Heir to the political position of Byzantium, Moscow also claimed succession to the religious leadership of the East. The metropolitan of Moscow was the rightful ruler over true or Orthodox Christians. Moscow, according to the church scholars who twisted history to fit the city's new pretense, became the third Rome. Western Rome had succumbed to heresy and papal domination. Constantinople, the second Rome, had fallen into heresy when her patriarch had accepted union with the West at the Council of Florence, and soon thereafter the city had lost its political independence as well. Now Moscow, the third Rome, was the capital of the true Church, and politically and religiously she would survive forever. There would never be a fourth Rome.

Sophia did not limit her influence over her husband to insisting upon formality at court, urging him to take new titles upon himself, or hailing Moscow as the successor to Byzantium. Just how decisive her influence was, or in what specific instances it was applied, there can be no way of knowing. From what is known of her nature and background, however, and from evidence of her actions on a few occasions, it seems safe to assume that she dominated her less strong and forceful husband completely. In 1498, when Ivan was nearly sixty years old, he had his grandson by his first wife crowned tsar in a pompous ceremony. By primogeniture the grandson had the right to succeed Ivan, and in the preceding reign Moscow had had a taste of the civil war that might follow a setting aside of the succession in the senior male line. So Ivan accepted the counsel of his advisers that the grandson should be crowned. But later Sophia's influence over her husband won out, and in another ceremony her own son, Vasily, was crowned as co-tsar and successor.

It is probable that the termination of Novgorod's freedom was hurried at Sophia's suggestion. The city had owed allegiance to the grand prince since the tenth century, and when the princes of Moscow became grand princes, it was to them that Novgorod's loyalty was due. When the city officials took an oath of allegiance to the king of Poland, they thereby made Novgorod guilty of treason. Sophia would not have hesitated to remind Ivan of the fate of traitors in Constantinople and to taunt him because Novgorodian freedom had not earlier been suppressed. And that she was capable of taunting him is known from the record of her flare of temper in

1480 when the khan, riding at the head of his troops, called upon Ivan
to renew his pledge of allegiance and to resume payment of the tribute. "I
lost my inheritance rather than submit," she flung at her husband when
his own weakness and dread of battle prompted him to draw back from
inviting the khan's anger. Sophia must have urged Ivan constantly to
strengthen his alliances with the enemies of his enemies, for Byzantium had
a centuries-long record of diplomatic triumphs, not all of them entirely
honorable. Once Novgorod and the Tatars had been disposed of, it was
like Sophia to urge Ivan to press on against Poland, to attack Lithuania
at the moment when the union with Poland was dissolved, and to champion
the cause of the Orthodox Christians who suffered persecution under foreign
heretical rule. Indeed, in every move that Ivan made the strong hand of his
willful and intelligent wife is discernible. Her influence over her husband
was considerable and, for the future of Moscow and of the Russian national
state, almost entirely beneficial.

Internal Developments

So spectacular were Ivan III's achievements in conquest and diplomacy
that Russia's strides in the domestic field during the reign are sometimes
overlooked. But the accomplishments in the field of foreign relations brought
about a considerable degree of internal change. Sophia's effect upon court
ceremony and etiquette has already been noted.

Ivan showed an interest in contact with the West which was prophetic
of Peter the Great, and it seems in both cases to have grown out of an
awareness of Russia's backwardness and of how much the nation might
gain by that contact. In Sophia's train in 1472 came both Greeks and
Italians who brought to Russia skills which could only be found abroad.
Some of them became Ivan's counsellors in matters of government, such
as the need to establish a regular diplomatic service. Others, like the Italian
Marco Ruffo and the Greek Demetrios Ralo, served him as ambassadors
to foreign courts. Alberto Fioraventi became his military engineer and master
of artillery; with Pietro Antonio, he designed and built the new imperial
palace and the Uspenskii Cathedral. Italian artists redecorated Moscow
churches, Italian architects built new ones, and Italian engineers surrounded
the Kremlin with a stone wall. The Italian metal-founder Paul Bossio, and
the gunsmiths who came with him, taught the Russians improved methods
of arms manufacture and made them less dependent upon foreign producers
for war equipment. Italian die-makers improved the minting of coins, and
the effect of this, together with Ivan's order forbidding the appanage princes
to coin money in their own principalities, was to establish one currency
for the nation. Ivan was always interested in the work of these foreign
artisans, and time and again sent emissaries to the West to bring more of
them to Moscow. German doctors served the court and a few German

craftsmen joined the Italians from Venice and Rome, although Ivan seems to have had the greatest confidence in his Venetians.

The absorption of the appanage principalities brought into the service of Moscow a number of petty princes who theretofore had exercised certain local governmental authority, particularly in matters of coinage, foreign affairs, and justice. When they came to the court of the grand prince their control over such matters fell to Moscow. Taking over the powers of coinage and dealing in foreign relations raised no problems for the central government; in fact, it eliminated them. But wiping out the judicial authority of the petty princes raised the question of what to put in its place. The definition of crime, punishment for various crimes, and court procedures varied from one principality to another, and all differed from practice in Moscow.

To establish judicial uniformity over the land Ivan III published the *Sudebnik,* or code of law, drawn up in 1497 by a corps of Russian and Greek legal experts. This was the first codification of Russian law since the old *Russkaia Pravda* of Kievan times, and its appearance was striking evidence of the fact that Russia had become a nation-state. Byzantine influence over the new code was very strong, as had been true of the earlier code, but between the tenth century and the fifteenth Byzantine practice had become more harsh and cruel. In the *Sudebnik* of 1497 punishments were more severe than they were in the Kievan period. Murder was punishable by death, and theft by public whipping. Torture to obtain evidence was given legal sanction, with certain limitations, and trial by combat was recognized in cases involving personal honor. Government representatives were assigned to provincial courts and each court was required to have a scribe take down the evidence and proceedings. Safeguards were provided against bribery of judicial officers, for the people of the newly acquired territories looked to Moscow for justice and protection. By the provision that peasants might move from one landowner's estate to another only during the two weeks around St. George's Day, the 26th of November, Russia took the first step toward serfdom. Poland, it may be noted, had first moved in the direction of serfdom some forty years earlier.

Serious effort was made at the end of the fifteenth century to increase the ruler's revenue, for the new responsibilities of statehood, relations with other nations, the increase in court expenses, the new building in the capital, and the modernization of army equipment laid a heavy financial burden upon the treasury. Assessors were sent over the land to determine more precisely the taxpaying ability of the people, and each landowner's name and the size of his estate were entered in a great book listing assessments. Revenue from levies upon trade, which had always brought good income to Moscow, increased not so much by raising rates as by the fact that new markets with their fees and new commercial avenues with their tolls came under Muscovite control in the great expansion of the state territory. By far the richest addition to Ivan's revenue came from the absorption of the fur-bearing reserve of northeast Russia, for every trapper and trader had to forfeit the best pelts to the state. But still the crying need for revenue was not satisfied. To meet it Ivan gave serious thought to the secularization of church lands, in which he was encouraged by sectarians who frowned upon the growing wealth of the Russian church and urged a return to apostolic poverty and purity. But a council of church leaders protested against secularization, and the step was postponed for four centuries.

The state's need for men to serve in the military and in government service was much greater in Ivan's time than it had ever been before. At the same time there was not the wherewithal to pay them in cash, even if Ivan had not found so many other uses for his money or had been less penurious than his predecessors. His father had hit upon the scheme of paying those who served him in land rather than in money, and Ivan enthusiastically continued it. The practice, now elaborated into a system and used consistently by Ivan and his successors, was known as *pomiestie,* by which a man was given land in return for military or some other kind of state service. Such a landholder, called a *pomieshchik,* received no hereditary title to the land, but held it only during such service. Upon his death the land reverted to the sovereign unless there was an heir who could take up the service responsibility which attached to it. When the territory of Novgorod fell to Moscow an enormous expanse of land, only part of which was habitable or arable, became available for *pomiestie* grants. In fact, the Muscovite families transplanted to Novgorod after the city's reduction were placed upon that basis, as were the Novgorodian boyars who were evicted and settled nearer Moscow. Boyars who deserted their appanage princes to serve with Ivan were put on the same footing; they became landholders who had no better claim to their estates than the grand prince's revokable grant in return for faithful service.

In providing the state with civil and military servants the system was extremely efficient. The *pomieshchik's* loyalty and devotion to duty were assured by his tenuous title to his estate. It could be withdrawn and he could be pauperized by the loss of the ruler's favor. As Russia in later years moved south into the sparsely settled steppe, the *pomiestie* system of granting land followed the advance of the frontier. While there were many in Ivan's time who held land by hereditary right, the percentage shrank from then on as such landowners died without heirs and their estates reverted to the crown, and as new grants of land were made only on condition of service, —on terms of *pomiestie.* Peter the Great later erased all distinction between the two types and placed all landholders on a *pomiestie* basis. Not until late in the seventeenth century did the *pomieshchik* receive the right to sell his estate, and only then if the purchaser was physically able to shoulder the burden of state service.

The autocratic nature of Muscovite rule was enormously enhanced by the adoption of Byzantine ideas of government consequent upon Ivan's marriage with Sophia. At the same time a strange check upon the autocracy developed, at least as far as the boyars and appanage princes were concerned. As each successive petty prince surrendered his lands to Moscow and moved to court, or as each boyar deserted his prince to join Ivan, he was assigned a rank in state service and court functions commensurate with the date of his removal to Moscow or with his hereditary seniority. If two princes descended from Rurik entered Moscow service, the one descended through the senior line took precedence over the one descended from the junior. The boyar whose ancestor had come early to Moscow enjoyed preferment over one whose forefather had come later, and the boyar whose family had served the prince of Moscow since the beginning of the principality took precedence over all other boyars and even over some junior princes.

This system of seniority, the *miestnichestvo* system, or schedule of rank, required that all state offices be assigned in order of importance to members of the nobility in corresponding order of their genealogical position. If a prince descended in a junior line of Rurik, for example, was appointed to command an army, no prince genealogically his senior could be forced to accept a post under him. Regardless of size every army sent into the field marched in five divisions or regiments, namely the main body, right wing, advance guard, rear guard, and left wing. Why the left wing should rank last is not clear, but this was the order of importance and the order of seniority which governed the assignment of officers. The main body had to be commanded by the genealogical senior, the right wing by the prince or boyar next senior, and so on. If a noble were asked to serve under someone junior to him in the *miestnichestvo* system, he could refuse with impunity. The grand prince had no recourse, for the system enjoyed full legal sanction. Family pride may have operated to assure the individual's giving the best that was in him, but under such an arrangement there could be no assurance that the appointee had any qualifications for the job to which he was assigned.

The ruler thus had little freedom of choice in appointments made from the ranks of the nobility. The only alternative open to the ruler was to give an important post to a foreigner or commoner, who had, of course, no position in the *miestnichestvo* system. Indeed, Ivan III named many of the middle class and foreigners to office, and his grandson Ivan IV carried the practice much further.

The Greatness of Ivan III

The Russian historian Solovev has said that "it is to the glory of Ivan III that he understood how to make the most of his opportunities and the fortunate circumstances in which he found himself throughout his whole life." If Ivan had any claim to the title "the Great" which history has added to his name, it lay in this ability to make the most of his opportunities. Certainly there was nothing great about his character, his manner, or his appearance. Russia accomplished great things during his reign, sometimes as a result of his foresight or understanding, but seldom because of any strong leadership. The lifting of the Tatar yoke was accomplished almost in spite of Ivan, although it must be remembered that he had previously undermined the power of the Tatars by his diplomatic encirclement. It may be that he hoped to free Russia from the khan without striking a blow, and that his fear of facing the Tatars in battle was simply a matter of personal cowardice. If "always, by preference, he made two bites at a cherry" (Pares), it must be borne in mind that Ivan could look back upon some princely heroes—Vladimir Monomakh and Alexander Nevsky, among others —in whom caution was recognized as one of their chief virtues, and upon others—Sviatoslav of Kiev and Vitovt of Lithuania, for example—whose rashness had cost them dearly. Whatever the judgment of Ivan's character may be, the fact remains that at his accession Moscow was only a dependent principality and that by the time of his death it had become a sovereign nation-state.

By the destruction of Novgorod Ivan eliminated the last East Slav state capable of checking the unification of Russian territory. When Novgorod and the appanage principalities, with a few minor exceptions, all were swallowed up, there was one Russia, not many, as there had been at the time of his father's death. Foreign powers still controlled much of the Russian land, it is true, but it remained to his successors to move against alien, non-East Slav states. Division among the East Slavs had disappeared, and a united nation could take up the struggle against those foreigners who still occupied the Russian land and held Russian people in subjection.

When the Russian border line had been drawn around the last of Ivan's acquisitions, the state territory was nearly treble the size it had been when he had moved to the first conquest. Moscow now ruled over an expanse reaching from the southern edge of the forest zone a few miles east of Kiev to the White Sea and the Arctic Ocean on the north, from Chernigov, the Gulf of Finland, and the region of modern Murmansk on the west to the Urals and, at a few points, even beyond. Ivan's conquests, particularly of Novgorod, made available a vast wealth to be exploited by the merchants and the government of Moscow. Silver from the mines of Iugria now poured into the state treasury. Timber, wax, and honey flowed in great volume into the capital, there to be sold to central and western European merchants or shipped across the Baltic. Above all, the tribute in sable and other furs which Novgorod had levied against the Lapps, Samoieds, Voguls, Pechorans, Zyrians, Permiaks, Iugrians, and other natives now came to Moscow, and Muscovite traders and trappers added many more pelts of their own for sale to the German, Flemish, Scandinavian, Polish, Lithuanian, Italian, Tatar, and Persian merchants who came to the Russian fairs. Moscow became an important center for the export of fur, which moved into central Europe by overland routes; it was surpassed only by Novgorod, which continued to be the chief entrepôt of the fur trade until Russia lost her foothold on the Baltic.

When Ivan the Great moved diplomatically and militarily against the Golden Horde, his decision evidenced much more than a simple desire to be rid of foreign rule. The days of the Horde were numbered even without Russian pressure, for centripetal forces were exploding it into a number of small independent khanates, and Russian interference simply hurried the process. It is easy to exaggerate the importance of the campaign of 1480. Complete independence would have come sooner or later to Russia just by default. Indeed, the grand princes had been paying tribute to the khan only very intermittently for many years before Ivan's accession, and the time would have come when the Tatars could no longer enforce it at all. Ivan's diplomatic pressures upon the Horde before 1480 had the effect of forcing the khan into a corner and making him fight back. Even more important than the lifting of foreign rule, Ivan's moving against the Tatars signaled the opening of the drive to return to the steppe. While Ivan the Great did not accomplish much in this respect, every one of his successors, with the exception of Elizabeth, advanced the frontier farther to the south until near the end of the eighteenth century the border rested on the Black Sea.

The attack against the Tatars was significant, too, in that it opened the drive against foreign powers. Until then, with unimportant exceptions, Moscow's advance had been against other Russian principalities. From that day forward Russian territorial advance meant Russian encroachment upon land ruled by a non-Russian state. From that day on, not counting periods of civil war, only four Russian sovereigns failed to add to the state territory, and three of them were on the throne for only a year or two.

Much of Ivan's right to claim greatness grew out of the consequences of his second marriage. The idea of Moscow as the successor to the political and religious glory of Byzantium was born of Sophia's coming to Russia. And Ivan came to share the sense of pride and ambition which this emperor's daughter felt so deeply. The court took on the ceremonial aspect of a court whose ruler demanded obeisance from his subjects and recognition by foreigners. Foreign artists and artisans were brought in to dress up the Kremlin so that visitors would be duly impressed with Moscow's greatness. Ivan took personal delight in corresponding with other sovereigns and in concluding agreements with them. His contacts with foreigners, and particularly with westerners, taught him that Russia had to learn the technical skills of the West if she were to maintain her new position as one of the family of nations. But with all this interest in Western civilization, Ivan rose to greatness in Russian eyes when he refused to accept religious subjection to the Western church and dignifiedly maintained the independence of Russian Orthodoxy.

Ivan was great not least of all in that he indicated to those who followed him many of the lines along which Russia had to develop. When his successors showed an interest in winning access to the Baltic, they could recall that Ivan the Great was the first of the princes of Moscow to reach that sea. When Russian pioneers first looked out over the Pacific in 1638, they may have remembered that Ivan first crossed the Urals. When Ivan IV and Alexis and Nicholas I recodified Russian law, they could look back upon the *Sudebnik* of 1497. Many more such lines project from the fifteenth into later centuries. But above all, every Russian ruler from that day to this who has felt keenly Russia's need to maintain contact with the West and to learn from it could remember that it was Ivan the Great who first sensed the need and took steps to meet it.

VASILY III (1505–1533)

Vasily III, the son of Ivan and Sophia, was much more like his mother than his father. From her he inherited a preference for autocracy rather than compromise. He rarely consulted his council, or duma, the descendant of the *druzhina* of Kievan times which once had had a right to give advice to the prince. Individual boyars who questioned his actions were quickly silenced; some went to prison and one who dared to complain because Vasily settled all matters alone was beheaded. The German ambassador reported that the Muscovite ruler enjoyed more power over his people than did any other sovereign in the world. "He uses his authority as much over ecclesiastics as laymen, and holds unlimited control over the lives and property of all his subjects" (Herberstein). The court became more brilliant than ever, and the sovereign lived in unprecedented luxury. Where Ivan III had been attended by dozens, hundreds waited upon Vasily III. Sons of boyars in rich costume were ranged about the throne; cupbearers by the score wandered through the palace; literally hundreds of horsemen rode with the sovereign when he hunted. Westerners continued to come to Moscow, many of them fresh from studies with leaders of the Renaissance. Russian embassies appeared at every court in Europe except France and England. Vasily corresponded with popes and German emperors and Moslem sultans and Indian princes, and called Charles V his brother.

The "gathering of the Russian soil" continued under Vasily, and the last of the appanages were swept into the growing state. In Pskov there developed the same schism between upper and lower classes which had cost

Novgorod her independence, and in the same way the Pskovian nobility and great merchants leaned toward Lithuania and Poland. Vasily summoned the leading citizens to Moscow and imprisoned them. Deprived of leadership the anti-Moscow party was unable to sway the *vieche,* and Pskov surrendered without lifting a hand in her own defense. The town bell, symbol of freedom, was removed in 1510, and a Moscow garrison was stationed in the town. Hundreds of leading families were transported to the vicinity of Moscow, and Muscovite settlers were brought in to replace them. The last prince of Riazan was charged with conspiring with the khan of the Crimean Tatars, and when he fled to Lithuania his principality fell to Moscow. Now there remained only one appanage principality, that of Novgorod-Severski on the river Desna. One day a monk with a broom paraded through the streets of Moscow, saying, "The Empire is not yet wholly cleansed. The time hath come to sweep up the last of the dust"; the reference, of course, was to this last of the appanages. Soon afterward its prince was accused of seeking an alliance with Poland and "the last of the dust" was added to Moscow.

With occasional interruptions the war with Lithuania continued, as Ivan III had predicted it must. Upon the death of one Lithuanian prince, Vasily put forward his candidacy to the throne. But the Lithuanian nobles chose the king of Poland, and again the two united. Had Vasily been successful in joining Lithuania to Russia, the future of eastern Europe might have been much different. Vilna would thereby have become a Russian city and the Niemen a Russian river. Already Russian was the official language in Lithuanian court circles and the people were Greek Orthodox in faith. The war which followed Vasily's failure to gain the Lithuanian crown ended in the declaration of a "perpetual peace" which lasted three years, and in the next campaign Vasily seized Smolensk, whose citizens opened the city's gates to him. This strange war found the khan of Astrakhan, the king of Denmark, the Teutonic knights, the Ottoman sultan, and the prince of Wallachia supporting Russia, while Poland-Lithuania enjoyed the friendship of the Crimean Tatars, the Dnieper Cossacks, and Sweden. Pope Leo X urged Vasily to come to terms with Lithuania and to turn his strength toward recovering his mother's inheritance, Constantinople. When the war ended, through the mediation of the Pope and the Holy Roman Emperor Charles V, Russia kept Smolensk.

Vasily's father Ivan the Great had had considerable success in dealing with the various Tatar powers, but the son lost much of the gain. The Crimean Tatars, who had always been friendly to Ivan III, now supported Poland and at one time mounted a devastating raid through Vasily's territory up to the very walls of Moscow. Vasily bought them off with rich presents, but the Tatars carried away thousands of Russian women and children to sell in the slave markets on the Black Sea. The next year Vasily gathered an army well equipped with artillery and advanced into the steppe to punish the khan, but the Tatars refused to fight and disappeared in the limitless sea of grass. Vasily dared not leave Moscow too long, for earlier the khanate of Kazan, which Ivan the Great had kept in subjection, had thrown out its ruler who had been sympathetic to Moscow. Attempts to force Kazan back into allegiance to Vasily had been unsuccessful, and the khanate on the middle Volga retained its independence until the following reign. The commercial position of Kazan was undermined, however, when Vasily organized a fair at Makarievsky farther up the Volga.*

Vasily divorced his first wife for bearing him no sons and married Helen Glinsky, daughter of a Russian prince who had deserted the service of Lithuania to join Moscow. In 1530 Helen bore a son who was named Ivan. Three years later Vasily died, and the child became ruler of Russia as Ivan IV.

Between 1462 and 1533, in the reigns of Ivan the Great and his son, Russia changed from a land divided against itself to a powerful nation-state. Great things had been accomplished in that time, but there were still great problems to be met. The grand princes had done a fine job of gathering in the Russian soil and of bringing all the Great Russian people under one rule. But their attitude had been not so much that of heads of state as that of landowners seeking to add acres to their estates and tenants to their rent-rolls. A wide expanse had been swallowed but not digested, for little thought had been given to organizing a state administration. To knit that wide expanse into a political as well as a territorial and ethnical unit was the problem facing Russia when a three-year-old boy fell heir to the throne in 1533.

SUGGESTED READING

Beazley, R., N. Forbes, and G. A. Birkett, *Russia from the Varangians to the Bolsheviks* (Oxford, Clarendon, 1918).

Cross, S. H., *The Russian Primary Chronicle* (Cambridge, Harvard University Press, 1930).

Herberstein, Baron S., *Notes upon Russia* (London, Hakluyt Society, 1852).

Kliuchevsky, V. O., *A History of Russia,* vol. II (London, J. M. Dent, 1912).

* Later the fair was moved to Nizhni-Novgorod, where it became one of the richest in the land. To it came thousands of merchants from all over Europe and Asia, from as far west as Germany and Italy and from as far east as China.

10

Ivan the Terrible

At THE AGE OF THREE IVAN IV (1533–1584) succeeded Vasily III, and for the next fourteen years the nation was governed by a succession of regency councils in which the leading boyar families contested for power. Neglected and deprived of family affection, the child-tsar grew up in an atmosphere of loneliness that made him suspicious of men in general and of boyars in particular. At seventeen he ordered his coronation and married Anastasia Romanov, the daughter of a poor boyar, a choice perhaps deliberately intended to incense the great princely families.

Through the early years after the coronation Ivan ruled with the advice of a "selected council," most of whose members were taken from the middle class. A number of reforms were put through in this happy period of the reign. A new law code was adopted and a church council assembled to consider rectification of abuses in church administration. The tsar reduced the authority of provincial governors, turning many of their functions over to elected officials, in an attempt to reduce corruption in local government. A *Zemskii Sobor,* or national assembly, was convened, attended by representatives of all classes with the exception of the peasants.

In 1564 Ivan divided each province into two portions. In one portion, the *oprichnina,* the tsar would govern with trusted subordinates to give the district a modern, efficient administration. In the other portion, the *zemshchina,* the old landholding gentry would continue to dominate local government in the old, inefficient, corrupt way. Ivan's purpose was to hold up to ridicule the political influence of the boyars. A loyal army of *oprichniks* harried the *zemshchina,* subjecting the boyar families, especially, to frightful persecution and terror. This was the tsar's way of forcing all his subjects, many of whom he suspected of disloyalty, of accepting the autocratic power which he was convinced God had granted him. Under the rule of the *oprichniks* untold thousands of Russians were driven off their land and transplanted or were flogged, tortured, and executed.

The early reforms and the *oprichnina* were designed, to the extent that there was design in Ivan's cruelty and madness, to reduce the influence of the boyars as a class, to assure the triumph of absolutism, and to prevent Russia's becoming a "constitutional anarchy" like Poland, where the growing power of the aristocracy was making a mockery of royal authority. Even the clergy, a few of whom were brave enough to challenge the tsar's violence, were persecuted and held up to ridicule.

Ivan's most constructive achievement was his incorporation into the Moscow state of the basin of the middle and lower Volga and western Siberia. But his effort to carry the western frontier to the Baltic failed miserably. Poland-Lithuania, Sweden, Denmark, and the Livonian knights joined forces to keep Russia from winning warm-water ports through which she might obtain the equipment and the skills of the West. English merchants made their way to Moscow through the White Sea, hoping to find through Russia easy access to the riches of the Middle East. But England's Queen Elizabeth rejected the tsar's proposal for an Anglo-Russian alliance against his enemies in the Baltic, and Ivan's offer to take an English wife received no serious consideration in London.

The mad terror to which Ivan subjected his people and the administrative chaos in which he left the nation practically foredoomed Russia to a period of unrest and weakness after his death. Such a tragic consequence was assured when the tsar killed his oldest son and committed the succession to a simpleton.

CHILDHOOD AND CHARACTER

The death of Vasily III left the grand principality of Moscow under the titular headship of a three-year-old child in whose name the mother, Helen Glinsky, ruled the land. Her chief advisers were her lover Prince Ivan Obolensky and her uncle Prince Michael Glinsky. In the first five years of the reign these three managed by their capricious and selfish actions to stir jealousy and intrigue among the princes and boyars, to drive some of them into conspiracy with Lithuania, and to provoke others to plot the assassination of the ruling clique and even of the young prince. The imprisonment of Ivan's uncles did not halt the plotting and his mother died suddenly, by poison it was rumored, in 1538. Those who had supported her, including Obolensky and her uncle Michael, were quickly dispatched or allowed to starve to death in prison. In the purge the child ruler was overlooked and managed to survive.

For another five years the regency council was controlled alternately by the princely families Belsky and Shuisky. The defeat of one party would be followed by the imprisonment, torture, execution, or banishment of its members, but after a few short months the victors would suffer the same treatment. The bloody brawls in the Kremlin even reached the imperial palace and stormed round the person of the youthful prince. Late one night a band of boyars broke the palace windows and crowded into Ivan's bedroom in search of the metropolitan bishop who opposed them. The boy's companions and even his nurse were taken from him, and Ivan was left alone to suffer the indignities heaped upon him. He never forgot the sight of drunken boyars lurching through the palace and of Prince Andrew Shuisky propping his feet upon the bed of Ivan's dead father. On state occasions, when Western ambassadors were present at court, those who ruled in his name prostrated themselves before the ermine-robed child and called themselves his slaves. The ceremony over, Ivan was ignored and neglected to the point of suffering for want of food and clothing. He found solace in his books, reading over and over again the Old Testament, Byzantine history, the Russian chronicles, and the writings of the church fathers. Here he learned and memorized the stories of powerful rulers and of wise men who championed the cause of good against evil, and stored up these examples against the day when he would rule and stamp out the sin which plagued the nation, and from which he suffered most of all.

These years of insult and neglect twisted the mind and warped the character of the young prince. Early deprived of his father and abandoned by his wanton mother, he always felt himself alone and isolated. He wanted desperately to be loved and gave his own love completely, first to his mother who neglected him so shamelessly and then to his first wife and a few intimate advisers. After these few were gone he was left alone again, surrounded by enemies. Moody and morbid he was, with an insane temper which drove him to kill even his own son, and so he deprived himself of the last of those he loved.

Always distrustful of others, Ivan looked from his squinting little eyes suspiciously upon those who fawned over him and sought his favor. He was viciously cruel in an age renowned for its brutality, and even as a child amused himself by hurling dogs from the palace roof. Men were flayed and impaled and roasted at his order and he took keen delight in igniting the beards of his enemies. With the sharply pointed walking stick he always carried he once pinned a messenger's foot to the floor and then ordered the man to read the long letter he had brought. And when he received an elephant as a gift he condemned it to death because it would not kneel before him.

After the death of his first wife, Ivan IV lived a life of the grossest immorality, relieving the boredom of his other six marriages with countless mistresses and bouts of drunkenness that lasted for days. But he was an intensely religious man in a formal way who sought to atone for his debauchery with hours of prostration before the altar, beating his head upon the stone church floor until his face was a mass of bruises.

Through the impressionable years of his youth and early manhood a succession of emotional shocks disturbed Ivan's mental balance. There was the death of his father and mother, the plague that carried away thousands in the city of Novgorod, the fire that levelled Moscow, the death of his first son and then of his beloved wife, his own near-fatal illness, the apostacy of his friend Kurbsky. In all of these except the last he saw the vengeance of God for his own sin and weakness and resolved to turn away God's wrath by killing infidels or by striking down those who opposed the government God had put in his keeping. Wavering between insanity and clarity after his first wife's death, his moments of madness came upon him more frequently and lasted longer with his advancing years. When in a passionate rage he mortally wounded his own son his sanity left him completely, and he died in a fit of inhuman howling. He had earned among his own people the title "the Dread" or "the Terrible."

Until his madness overcame him Ivan showed himself one of the most intelligent and one of the best informed of all Russian rulers. His letters mark him as a man of considerable literary ability and in his disputations with churchmen, Orthodox or Lutheran, he often confounded his opponents. He had only scorn for illiterate priests who knew the liturgy only half so well as he. Ivan took keen delight in the literary debate with the renegade Kurbsky, filling his long rebuttals with quotations from scripture.

Ivan developed a sympathy for strong monarchy from his reading of the lives of strong rulers and from his determination to avenge himself for the insults of the boyars in his childhood. He regarded himself as divinely appointed and responsible only to God, as head of the church as well as of the state. In his handling of affairs he would allow no interference by any man or group, layman or churchman, bishop or boyar. He referred to his officials and court functionaries as slaves of whose lives and fortunes he could dispose as he pleased. He looked upon the ambition of the boyars as a threat to good government, as the example of the Polish nobles on his western frontier indeed proved it to be. Like the Tudors in contemporary England he sought, but with less success than they, to undermine the power of the aristocracy and to assure its subservience to the throne. His failure was attributable to the fact that he attacked the boyars as individuals and not as a class.

CORONATION AND MARRIAGE

Thrown as he was upon his own resources Ivan matured rapidly. At thirteen he asserted his authority by ordering the keeper of his hounds to get rid of Andrew Shuisky, the leading boyar at court, who had fouled his father's bed with his feet. The old prince was thrown in prison and later strangled. The Glinskys, relatives of Ivan's mother, replaced the Shuisky party in control of the regency council, but they were imprisoned or murdered four years later soon after Ivan's coronation.

In 1547 Ivan was crowned as "Tsar of All the Russias," the first ruler to assume the title at the time of his coronation. With a scholar's care he examined the historical precedents for the ceremony and, with less concern for accuracy, claimed to be descended from Caesar Augustus, whose title he appropriated. It fitted in well with the preposterous "Third Rome" doctrine which the churchmen preached and to which Ivan IV subscribed.

Then the tsar, whose licentious living had become a scandal, announced that he would marry. He would not have a foreign princess but one of his own subjects. Beauties of noble birth from all over Russia were paraded before him and he chose Anastasia Romanov. Her family was esteemed by the poor of Moscow but, perhaps for that very reason, was hated and envied by the great boyar families. Ivan's choice may have been inspired by his bitterness toward the older families, and now their resentment must have given him keen satisfaction. He loved Anastasia deeply, and she was the only person who ever was able to restrain his savage cruelty toward others. Time and again he gave in to her pleas for the release of prisoners or for the commutation of a severe sentence. He always attributed her mysterious death to some boyar's poison, and for it he took frightful vengeance. Toward the end of his life he insisted that he would not have slaughtered so many boyars "had they not taken from me my little heifer."

EARLY REFORMS

Soon after the tsar's coronation and marriage a succession of fires swept through Moscow, burning even into the Kremlin and scorching the royal palace. The wooden houses of the common people kindled like firewood and thousands lost their lives. The citizens blamed the fires on sorcerers and, at the incitation of the Shuiskys and Romanovs, demanded punishment of the Glinskys, the boyar family then most influential at court. Some of the Glinskys were lynched by a mob, others were imprisoned, and the rest were driven from the Kremlin.

For several years after the Moscow fire of 1547 and the purge of the Glinskys Ivan ruled with the advice of a "selected council" whose membership was chosen for the most part from the middle class. Alexis Adashev was appointed head of a new "office of petitions" which would receive appeals from the people to correct the abuses of local government officials.

The new court chaplain, the priest Sylvester, suggested to Ivan a program of church reform. The old Metropolitan Makary, another of the group, softened the tsar's passion for cruel punishments, urged him on to crusade against the infidel Tatars, and argued against war with Poland. These men could disagree with Ivan without exciting his suspicion, and for a while he did nothing contrary to their advice.

During the twelve or thirteen years when Ivan was under the wholesome influence of the "selected council" several governmental reforms were inaugurated. A new law code, the *Sudebnik* of 1550, sought to improve the administration of justice by eliminating antiquated practices in court procedure and making local governors answerable for the misdeeds of their subordinates. The following year the tsar assembled a council of leading churchmen and challenged it to put an end to the ignorance, sloth, and licentious living of the clergy. Obediently the council ordered the founding of schools for the education of priests, condemned the immorality of which many churchmen were guilty, promised a scholarly examination of the holy books to eliminate errors that had crept in through centuries of bad copying and translating, and considered minor alterations in church ritual. The problem of halting the acquisition of land by the church and the possibility of forcing it to surrender the estates it had already acquired were discussed but not decided. Nor were any of the reforms ordered by the church council carried out. A century later the problem of church reform had to be undertaken from the beginning, as though the pious pronouncements of 1551 had never been made.

In 1566, in the midst of war in Livonia, Ivan convened the first *Zemskii Sobor*, literally land or national assembly, composed of men chosen from every class except the peasants. The grand duke of Lithuania, hard-pressed by the Russian invasion, offered to surrender the land Ivan's armies had overrun in exchange for a guarantee of the rest of his territory. Wanting the advice of a broader representation than the nobles in their boyar duma, or advisory council, could provide, and perhaps contriving to impress upon the boyars how easily their advice could be ignored or overridden, Ivan called together representatives from the clergy, the lesser gentry, and the merchant class to sit with the boyar duma to consider whether Lithuania's terms should be accepted. The members of this enlarged assembly, the *Zemskii Sobor*, were not elected by the various social groups but were named to it by the tsar. Most of them were government officials who could provide information on the feasibility of continuing the war. The 1566 assembly was the only one to meet during the reign of Ivan the Terrible, although the *Zemskii Sobor*, more truly representative, would be called frequently during the century following Ivan's death.

Ivan moved to end corruption in local government. Heretofore provincial governors, appointed from the boyar class, had headed local administration, dispensed justice, and gathered taxes, keeping a part of what they collected for themselves. This practice, called "feeding," understandably encouraged abuses. Now Ivan assigned the police and judicial duties formerly handled by the governors to elected local officials chosen from among the freemen of the locality. Collection of taxes was taken out of the hands of the governors and assigned to locally elected elders. But the transfer of these functions from the governor to district officials chosen by all freemen was not an unmixed blessing to the people. Ivan made the district and each community answerable for the proper conduct of the elected officials and made each locality collectively accountable for the maintenance of order and the payment of taxes.

The tsar encroached upon the rights of hereditary landowners by making them subject to the same obligations as those who held their land by service tenure. Henceforth all landowners, regardless of the nature of their title to the land, would retain their holdings only so long as they rendered military service. A son might inherit an estate, but along with it he assumed the service obligation which attached to the land. He began his military career at the age of fifteen and continued it as long as he was physically able to do so. Daughters might inherit the estate if they married someone able to fulfill the service obligation. If a landholder had more sons than the size of his estate would warrant enrolling in service, his estate was enlarged from the public lands or the extra sons were provided with their own holdings. No son could escape his obligation to defend the nation.

Ivan's early reforms—his reliance for advice upon commoners, his transfer of authority in local affairs from the governor to elected officials, his calling the *Zemskii Sobor*, his fastening of the service obligation upon all landholders—were inspired by his determination to reduce the power of the nobility. He hated the class whose members had treated him with such contempt as a child and which he blamed for his mother's death. He suspected the boyars of wanting to bring down the authority of the crown to a position of impotence. Further, when many of the nobles escaped to Poland, where the influence of their class was waxing, in Ivan's eyes they committed the worst of all treasons—forsaking Orthodox Russia and joining her Catholic enemy.

Ivan fell dangerously ill in 1553. It was expected by many and hoped by some that he would not recover. The tsar demanded that the boyars swear to support the accession of his son Dmitry. Most of them demurred, preferring Ivan's cousin Prince Vladimir to an infant whose accession would mean the continued influence of his mother's family, the Romanovs. Even the commoners Adashev and Sylvester opposed Dmitry. When Ivan ordered his advisers and the boyars to swear allegiance to his son they did so grudgingly, expecting to order affairs to their own liking after the tsar's death. But Ivan recovered, and he never forgave those who within earshot of his sickbed mumbled their plans to dispose of the succession in their own selfish interest.

With the tsar's recovery from the near-fatal illness, some of the boyars who had opposed swearing allegiance to the child Dmitry fled to Poland and Lithuania to escape Ivan's insane wrath. Those who remained at court tried to undermine the influence of the Romanovs, the tsaritsa's relatives. When, in 1560, Anastasia died after a lingering illness, Ivan suspected that she had been poisoned by plotters anxious to succeed to her kinsmen's preferment. Sylvester and Adashev, whose counsel he had listened to for a dozen years, were banished from court. Tension between the tsar and those allowed near him mounted steadily. In 1564 one of his army commanders, Prince Andrew Kurbsky, whose advice Ivan had long respected, deserted to Lithuania in the midst of a war with that duchy.

During the next fifteen years, while stirring Poland and Lithuania and the Crimean Tatars to attack Moscow, Kurbsky addressed several long, bitter letters to his former sovereign. He compared Ivan to the Old Testament tyrant Rehoboam and charged him with fiendish cruelty from which it was only right to escape. He warned that God would avenge those who had suffered inhuman tortures, particularly those who had been pursued into the churches and struck down in sanctuary. He protested that monasteries were becoming no better than dungeons where men and women whom the tsar disliked were forcibly tonsured. He reasoned that Ivan had committed heresy by presuming himself to be above the law of God and called the tsar antichrist.

Ivan could not let such charges go unchallenged. In long answers filled with biblical references the tsar insisted that his power came from God alone and that no man could question his use of that power. He flung back the charge of treason and the sterner charge that Kurbsky had committed apostasy in fleeing the service of God's annointed ruler on earth. He warned that the prince had condemned himself and all his family to eternal damnation for violating his oath of fealty, sworn upon a relic made of the wood from the cross of Christ, and so had committed an unforgivable "crime against the cross." He protested that he had only done God's work in sweeping away those who had plotted against the power which God had given him. He had invoked God's blessing on all his actions and had even paid the clergy to pray for the repose of the souls of those he had executed. He argued that in attacking the boyars he was only defending the throne God had placed in his keeping and pointed to the fall of Constantinople as an example of what happened to those who did not guard their inheritance.

OPRICHNINA

A few months after Kurbsky's desertion Ivan packed his family, clothing, valuables, and icons into a train of sledges and drove out of Moscow, telling no one where he was going. The capital and the nation were left without a governing head. From the village of Alexandrovskoe, where he came to rest fifty miles away, he sent two letters to the metropolitan bishop of Moscow. One charged the boyars and the clergy with treason, graft, and corruption and announced the tsar's decision to rule no longer in a land of traitors. The other, addressed to the people of Moscow, assured them that they were in no way the cause of his dissatisfaction and swore that he was their friend and protector. When the letters were read to the multitude in Red Square the people protested their loyalty to the tsar, clamored to support him in ridding the nation of its enemies, and begged the metropolitan to visit Ivan with a plea to return and govern as he pleased.

Ivan consented to return to Moscow only on certain conditions. He wanted complete freedom to deal with traitors as he deemed necessary and he proposed to establish, in part of the realm at least, a new administration responsible only to himself. The terms were granted without demur and Ivan came back, marking his return with the execution of several boyars, including Kurbsky's wife and family.

A part of each province and of each city and even of Moscow now became Ivan's own personal domain, the *oprichnina*—a word meaning reservation or the widow's portion of an inheritance. The rest of each province and city made up the *zemshchina*—literally the old land to be governed in the old way by the boyars. In the *oprichnina* the tsar would head a new well-ordered administration staffed by officials sworn to serve him without question. Thousands of landowners were driven off their estates, which now were awarded to the *oprichniks*—the citizens and administrators of the *oprichnina*. A new administration, backed by a special army of *oprichniks* six thousand strong, governed in the land the tsar set apart. His object was to hold up to ridicule the *zemshchina* with its ancient, inefficient, and corrupt administration and to contrast with it the new, efficient, loyal administration of the *oprichnina* which, by implication, would bring order, prosperity, and strength. The *oprichnik* army, robed in black and riding black horses, each rider with a dog's head fixed to his saddle and carrying a broom symbolic of the tsar's determination to sweep corruption from the land, rode at night through the *zemshchina* terrorizing the families of the old boyars. But not all boyars suffered Ivan's fury nor were all commoners immune, for this was no class war which the tsar incited. He was concerned simply to establish a regime based upon undiluted loyalty to the sovereign.

To dramatize the contempt he felt for the old Russia Ivan arranged the mock coronation of a new "tsar," naming a contemptuous renegade Tatar to be "Tsar and Grand Prince of all Russia." Calling himself simply "Prince of Moscow," Ivan prostrated himself before the figurehead and professed himself only another "loyal boyar." Ivan soon tired of this play acting and swept aside the foolish Tatar whom he had raised to the throne. Meanwhile, of course, he had dictated every governmental order the Tatar had been allowed to sign.

The *oprichniks* constituted a security police whose primary aim was to purge the land of treacherous elements. Ivan's victims were subjected to heartless torture. Many were drowned or strangled or flogged to death; some were impaled, others roasted on a spit, still others fried in large skillets. The entire city of Novgorod was put to torture on the charge that its archbishop was planning to turn over the city to the Lithuanians. Tens of thousands of its citizens were butchered in a week-long orgy. But church-men, boyars, and merchants whom Ivan suspected of treason were not the only ones to suffer. His favorites, the *oprichnik* leaders, died in an agonizing torture more fiendish than anything they had devised for their victims.

Ivan gathered around him at the Alexandrovskoe Monastery, which be-came his headquarters and residence, a picked bodyguard of three hundred *oprichniks* whom he clothed in monk's garb and whom he commanded as abbot. His prodigious drinking bouts with his companions were punctuated by courts of cruelty where new methods of torture were tried out against his unfortunate victims. On occasion the tsar himself led the church service, preaching temperance and virtuous living to his *oprichnik*-monks and offer-ing prayers for those he had condemned to death.

The *oprichnina* may seem to be the work of a man gone mad or of one who could not control his sadistic tendencies, though he occasionally felt contrition for his excesses. It may be contended, however, that Ivan pro-ceeded deliberately in his determination to destroy the political influence of those boyars and church leaders whose meddling he saw as a threat to monarchy and good government and even the safety of the nation. Thou-sands of leading families were transplanted from one district to another in an obvious effort to destroy their influence. That he was not successful in ending the political ambition of the boyars and their threat to orderly suc-cession to the throne became apparent almost immediately after his death.

IVAN AND THE CHURCH

His protestations that only he sought to do good and that all men were against him must have puzzled many who watched Ivan at his fiendish crimes. His frequent participation in long church vigils and his strict ob-servation of ritual mark him as a man concerned about the formalities, if not about the substance, of his religion. Even though it be assumed that he tortured and slew not because he enjoyed the sight of suffering but to serve the state as he understood its needs, still his moral excesses show that he paid no heed whatever to Christian precepts.

Ivan had strong convictions about the church as an institution and the men who staffed it. He believed that the church should give up its vast holdings. While he never took the step of confiscating all church property, he often laid the church under heavy fine and taxation. At the tsar's order the church council of 1580 forbade monasteries to accept further gifts of land, although the growth of church estates went on surreptitiously. Convinced as he was of the divine right of monarchy, he felt that the state should be supreme over the church. The Metropolitan Makary felt similarly and managed to lose neither the tsar's friendship nor his own position for twenty years. After his death a succession of men served only short terms as metropolitan, for if they did not please Ivan they were dismissed. One, Philip, braver than the rest, dared to warn Ivan of punishment for his sins. The tsar had Philip returned to his monastery and later strangled.

Ivan felt only contempt for the great majority of the clergy for their selfishness, their sinful living, and particularly for their ignorance. While it is true that most of his own administrative officials could barely read and write, he had little patience with an illiterate priest. And the strict rules of conduct he drafted for his order of *oprichnik*-monks may have been intended as an indictment of the profligacy of Orthodox monks. His delight in pushing aside celebrants in parish churches and conducting the service himself may have been inspired by his contempt for most priests.

Ivan, who assumed that his every public act was sanctioned by divine approval, did not hesitate to work the same cruel punishment upon wayward clergymen that he imposed upon laymen. Priests were dragged from their altars to be flogged, flayed, or broken on the rack with no regard for the sanctity of their position. During the sack of Novgorod in 1570 the city's archbishop was trussed up in a bearskin and fed to the hounds. And yet Ivan, knowing no peace of mind after he killed his own son, abdicated and became a monk a few moments before his death.

EASTWARD EXPANSION

The one enduring thing that Ivan accomplished was to move the frontier of Moscow far to the east to incorporate the middle and lower Volga and western Siberia. He set the course of Russian expansion, and before the middle of the following century the Moscow state had brought its boundary to the Pacific.

At the bend of the Volga lay the khanate of Kazan, a Tatar state that had seceded from the Golden Horde. Its government was often in turmoil from interference by Moscow or by the Tatar khanates to the south. Its nearness to Moscow and its accessibility by way of the upper Volga made Kazan a natural prey as soon as the Russian state could muster the strength to attack it.

Taking advantage of a dispute over the succession, Ivan led a hundred-thousand-man army against Kazan in 1552. Almost at that very moment, the Crimean Tatars thrust north into Moscow territory as they did every year in search of plunder and captives. This time they attacked Tula and might have advanced on the capital itself had not Ivan turned back to drive them off. Then he pressed on to Kazan, where he prayed for a great Christian victory over the infidel. For months the Muscovite army besieged the great fortress, which was stubbornly defended. Ivan used over a hundred cannon to breach the walls—the first time artillery figured prominently in a Russian campaign. Kazan fell to Moscow, and with it went command of the middle Volga and the easy pathway up the Kama and through the Urals into western Siberia.

Three years later Ivan sent an army down the Volga to attack the khanate of Astrakhan, and in 1556 that Tatar stronghold was annexed to Moscow. Now Ivan ruled over the entire course of the Volga; now the Caspian Sea, and across it the Middle East, invited the attention of Russia merchants.

But the southern frontier of Muscovy was not yet secure from Tatar raids. The khanate of Crimea, which had come under Turkish rule eighty years earlier, annually sent raiding hordes north out of the peninsula to pillage and take women and children for sale in the slave markets in the Crimea and Constantinople. A Jewish money-changer, watching the endless stream of captives pass through the Isthmus of Perekop, asked whether there were any people left in the land of Russia. To defend the land against these terrifying incursions Ivan strung a line of fortifications and observation posts along the northern steppe from Voronezh nearly to Kiev. But the raiders occasionally slipped through the defense line, as they did in 1571, when they reached Moscow and dragged off over a hundred thousand Russians into slavery. At the time of the assault upon Astrakhan Ivan had turned aside momentarily to strike at the Crimean khanate, but the 1555 campaign had accomplished nothing. Backed by the power of their overlord, the Turkish sultan, the Crimean Tatars were much more formidable than their cousins at Kazan and Astrakhan.

In 1583, just a year before his death, Ivan received all western Siberia to the Ob and the Irtysh and north to the Arctic as a gift from the Cossack Ermak. The tsar had not planned the annexation. Rather, he had hoped for peace with the wild Siberian tribes who might threaten newly-acquired Kazan. Indeed, Ermak and his Cossacks were warned of execution if they stirred up the Siberian tribesmen. Ermak was employed by the Stroganov family, which held rich salt and mining interests in the Urals, to defend its holdings and explore east of the mountains. The Cossack band drove eastward to the Irtysh, captured Sibir, the capital of the khanate, and forced the Tatars throughout the Ob basin to recognize Russian rule. Now the tsar forgave Ermak and added the new territory to his dominion. Ivan's acquisitions in the east had doubled the size of his territory.

RELATIONS WITH THE WEST

Soon after the capture of Astrakhan Ivan's attention shifted to the northwest and the Baltic. He may have been inspired to do so by the thought of winning a victory for Orthodoxy over its enemies the Livonian knights, Sweden, and Poland. His adviser Sylvester urged another campaign against the Crimean Tatars and warned Ivan that warring against other Christians would not meet with divine favor. Adashev, too, opposed war in the west, but both of these friends of the tsar were banished from court. Ivan may have turned to the Baltic in the hope of improving communications with England, whose military goods and technical skills the tsar was anxious to acquire and to whose merchants he had recently extended a cordial welcome to trade in Russia. He may have looked upon the German knights, whose power in the eastern Baltic had been waning for over a century, as less formidable than the Crimean Tatars, who could rely upon Turkish backing against any determined attack from Moscow.

The Knights of the Sword, or the Livonian Order as they came to be called, had moved into the eastern Baltic in the thirteenth century and had quickly subjugated the coast and hinterland as far north as Narva. In alliance with the Teutonic knights the Livonian Order had suffered a disastrous defeat by a Polish-Lithuanian army at Tannenberg in 1410. Thereafter, the remaining strength of the Order was sapped by dissension among its leaders and by rebellion among its Baltic subjects against the repressive rule imposed upon them. Ivan III had fought against the Livonian knights who stood with Poland and Lithuania to repel Moscow's westward advance. As the strength of the Order waned a struggle developed among the other Baltic powers to decide who should acquire its territory.

In 1558 Ivan IV advanced into Livonia—known in the twentieth century as Estonia—and subjected the land to frightful pillage and torture. Narva and Dorpat were captured, the former giving the Russian ruler an outlet on the Baltic for the first time since the days of Kiev. The Livonian knights, not wanting to lose their lands to an Orthodox prince, turned over Courland, or Latvia, to Poland; Estonia to Sweden; and the offshore islands to Denmark. Now Ivan, if he wanted to press his claim to the eastern Baltic, would have to fight all three heirs of the Livonian knights or play off one against the others for part of the spoils.

A Russian army advanced south and west into Courland, forcing Poland to defend this land she had recently acquired. For several years Ivan's drive was successful, and the grand duke of Lithuania offered to surrender the territory the Russians had overrun if he might keep the rest. In 1566 the tsar called a *Zemskii Sober* to consider whether the Polish peace proposal should be accepted. The advice he received was that the war must go on until "all the Russian land"—that is, all the land ever claimed by the Kievan princes—was recovered. It was this continuation of Russian pressure that brought the grand duchy of Lithuania and the kingdom of Poland to agree, in the Union of Lublin of 1569, to join under a common sovereign to be elected by an assembly of the Polish and Lithuanian gentry.

Three years after the Union of Lublin the hereditary line of Polish rulers died out, and an election was held to choose a successor. Ivan IV put forward his candidacy, but the Polish assembly elected Henry of Valois, brother of the French king. Henry abdicated a year later to succeed his brother as king of France, relieved to be rid of a throne whose prerogatives were so circumscribed by the privileges of the Polish nobles. Again Ivan was a candidate, but the election went to Stephen Batory, a Transylvanian prince renowned for his military ability. Had the Russian tsar won the election Polish national identity might have been snuffed out and the history of eastern Europe might have taken a far different course than it was to pursue. But there was never any possibility that Ivan would be chosen by the Polish gentry. His autocratic treatment of his own nobles made him wholly unacceptable to the nobles of Poland who were already winning the struggle against royal power and in doing so destroying their nation's strength.

Ivan's effort to seize the east Baltic littoral involved him in a war that dragged on intermittently until 1582. Russia's drive to the open sea was opposed by the Livonian knights, Poland-Lithuania, Sweden, and Denmark. The superior military equipment of the West and the fine leadership of the Polish king, Stephen Batory, decided the contest. Ivan lost all he had won— his gains in Latvia went to Poland, and he surrendered to Sweden all of Estonia, the south coast of the Gulf of Finland, and the Karelian Isthmus which separates Lake Ladoga from the Baltic. Russia's enemies in the Baltic had succeeded, at least temporarily, in their determination to prevent her from establishing contact with the West and equipping herself with the Western knowledge and technique that would make her a formidable military power. And they had whetted that appetite for Russian land which they would seek to satisfy in the days of Russia's weakness after the old tsar's death.

During the reign of Ivan the Terrible England established intimate relations with Russia, the first Western nation to do so. In 1553 two explorers, Willoughby and Chancellor, sailed from England in search of a northeast passage around Europe and Asia to the East. Willoughby and his crew froze to death on the Lapland coast, but Chancellor, in a "great ship" of a hundred and sixty tons, sailed into the White Sea and landed near Arkhangelsk. Four months later Chancellor and the London merchants who had come with him arrived in Moscow to be warmly welcomed by the tsar. When the English returned home early the following year they carried with them Ivan's offer to Queen Mary to allow English merchants complete freedom to trade in all goods anywhere in the tsar's dominions.

Chancellor arrived back in Moscow in 1555 with full power to negotiate a commercial treaty. Over the objections of Russian merchants Ivan agreed that the merchants of the Muscovy Company of London might carry on trade in Russia free of the dues and duties that even Russian merchants had to pay. The tsar proposed an alliance between the two governments and was piqued that Chancellor was empowered to arrange only commercial relations. Ivan sent an ambassador to London, where Queen Mary granted Russian merchants reciprocal privileges to trade in England, privileges of which they had no opportunity to avail themselves. The Russian ambassador returned to Moscow with a number of craftsmen, doctors, and engineers, thus inaugurating a policy of importing Western technical knowledge which Russian rulers would continue to pursue well into the twentieth century.

When the Polish-Lithuanian union in 1569 threatened the security of Russia's western frontier Ivan sent Queen Elizabeth a proposal for an offensive and defensive alliance with England. An English fleet in the eastern Baltic might have assured the tsar success in his Livonian war. He urged that English merchants not be allowed to trade with Poland and asked Elizabeth to send him experts in shipbuilding and the manufacture of artillery. The Polish king then besought the English queen not to honor the tsar's request, admitting frankly that Russia could be beaten only if denied Western knowledge and skills.

In the correspondence that passed between London and Moscow Ivan offered Elizabeth sanctuary in Russia if she should lose the throne and asked in return for asylum in England if he should need it. The *oprichnina* had brought the tsar so many enemies that there was good reason for him to make the request. At the same time Ivan apparently knew that Elizabeth, too, was the subject of interminable plots. However, the English queen showed no interest in escaping to Russia and none in having the mad tsar reside in England. It is possible that Ivan proposed marriage to Elizabeth after the death of his second wife. But the queen was interested only in the trade privileges her merchants might enjoy in Russia and in obtaining free passage for them over the Russian river system into the Middle East.

Two years before his death Ivan proposed marriage to Mary Hastings, Queen Elizabeth's niece. The fact that he was already married at the time to his seventh wife made the offer anything but attractive to Lady Mary. An English ambassador arrived in Moscow to drag out the negotiations, seeking to win for English merchants a monopoly of foreign trade in Russia and expulsion of the Dutch traders who had moved into the White Sea. Nothing came either of the marriage proposal or of the efforts of London merchants to improve their position. Ivan seems to have had his heart set on an English marriage and to have been deeply disappointed that his proposals were spurned. He avenged himself upon the English merchants, imprisoning some, seizing their goods, and suspending their right to trade. While the restrictions he imposed upon them were soon lifted, the English were not awarded the monopoly that Queen Elizabeth negotiated for twenty-five years to obtain.

THE LEGACY OF IVAN THE TERRIBLE

Two years before his own death in 1584 Ivan quarreled with his oldest son and in the heat of argument stabbed him to death with the pointed staff he always had with him. He never overcame the grief his vicious temper had brought him. The murder doomed the dynasty to extinction, for Ivan's sole remaining heir, his younger son Fedor, was a simpleton whose marriage was barren.

The end of the dynasty would bring turmoil. The chaos in which Ivan left the administration, the bitter resentment of the boyars who had survived his purges, the sense of insecurity and fright which was felt by men of every class, the foreign enemies whose hatred of Russia had been sharpened by Ivan's campaigns of pillage, torture, and desolation—all compounded to leave the land weak and divided. For many years there would be serious question whether the nation could survive.

SUGGESTED READING

Eckhardt, H. von, *Ivan the Terrible* (New York, Knopf, 1949).

Fennell, J. L. Z., *The Correspondence Between Prince A. M. Kurbsky and Tsar Ivan IV of Russia, 1564–1579* (New York, Cambridge University Press, 1955).

Fletcher, G. and J. Horsey, *Russia at the Close of the Sixteenth Century* (London, Hakluyt Society, 1856).

Graham, S., *Ivan the Terrible* (New Haven, Yale University Press, 1933).

Herberstein, S. von, *Notes upon Russia* (London, Hakluyt Society, 1852).

Jenkinson, A., *Early Voyages and Travels to Russia and Persia* (London, Hakluyt Society, 1886).

Kliuchevsky, V. O., *A History of Russia,* vol. II (London, Dent, 1912).

Waliszweski, K., *Ivan the Terrible* (Philadelphia, Lippincott, 1904).

Wipper, R., *Ivan the Terrible* (Moscow, Four Continent Publishing House, 1947).

II

The Time of Troubles

Upon THE DEATH OF IVAN THE TER-
rible the throne of Moscow passed to his simple-minded son Fedor, whom
no one expected to take an active part in government. In his name the
land was administered by a regency council headed by Fedor's brother-in-
law Boris Godunov. The ambitious Boris soon scattered the other councillors and became the sole regent.

In Fedor's name Boris put an end to the brutal persecution the nation
had suffered under Ivan the Terrible. He obtained the elevation of the
Russian church to a patriarchate. He firmly established Russian control
in western Siberia and extended Moscow's influence beyond the Caucasus
Mountains. And he won back some of the lands in the Baltic region that
Ivan IV had lost, although he was not able to advance the Russian
frontier to the sea. He increased restrictions on the peasants' freedom of
movement from one estate to another and so speeded the approach of
serfdom.

After Fedor's death without heirs Boris was elected tsar. Opposed by the
great boyar families and suspicious that many envied him his title, Boris
filled the land with spies and practiced much of the cruelty and arbitrari-
ness that had characterized the reign of Ivan IV. He became obsessed with the
desire to keep the throne and pass it on to his heirs. To eliminate potential
contestants he exiled and imprisoned entire families of suspects, notably
the Romanovs, kinsmen of Ivan IV's first wife. He died suddenly in 1605,
perhaps by his own hand.

The succession now passed to the so-called False Dmitry, an adventurer
who professed to be Ivan IV's son by his seventh wife. Discontented elements in the population refused to accept Boris's story that the true

Dmitry had died as a child; they supported the new tsar in the hope of ending the recent oppression and halting the advance of serfdom. But Dmitry's profession of sympathy for the lower classes and his promise to his Polish allies that he would make Russia Catholic turned the boyars and the church against him. He ruled less than a year, and was assassinated by a boyar conspiracy.

The next tsar, Vasily Shuisky, was a member of an old and influential boyar family. He was elected by the boyars and was forced to surrender much of the royal authority to the boyar duma and to govern in the interest of the great landowners. His conservatism and his lack of concern for the lower classes were responsible for the appearance of another false Dmitry, whose banner became a rallying point for the downtrodden masses, particularly for the vaguely democratic Cossacks. The Romanovs conspired with the Polish king to overthrow Shuisky, who was forced to abdicate under the combined pressure of the Poles and the second Dmitry.

Wladyslav, the son of the Polish king, was elected tsar; but his father sought to win the Russian crown for himself. His known intention to turn Russia Catholic turned the clergy against Wladyslav, and the patriarch of Moscow inspired a national rising to drive out the Poles. The period of upheaval which the Russians call the "Time of Troubles" ended with the election by a national assembly of young Michael Romanov to be tsar.

THE GOVERNMENT OF THE TSARDOM OF MUSCOVY

While Ivan IV left the government of Russia—or Moscow, as it was still called in the sixteenth century—in turmoil if not in chaos, the framework of the central administration remained essentially what it had been under Ivan III. The grand prince, become a tsar at the coronation of Ivan the Terrible, was customarily the oldest surviving son of the late ruler. The same dynasty—called variously the line of Rurik or the line of Daniel or the line of Monomakh—had succeeded in unbroken descent since the time of Daniel, the youngest son of Alexander Nevsky.

While Ivan IV claimed to rule by divine right and fought every check on his authority, custom required the prince or tsar to seek the advice of the boyar duma which met frequently, sometimes daily, with the tsar presiding. The *Sudebnik,* the law code which Ivan IV issued in 1550, even declared that the duma's approval was required for all important decisions. Laws or *ukazes* declared in duma meetings began, "The tsar has directed and the boyars have agreed." There can be no doubt of Ivan's ability to cow any who might oppose his will in the duma. Yet it was, in part at least, to free himself from even this mild restraint that the tsar convoked the *zemskii sobor* to still the voice of the boyars in a chorus of commoners' votes, and then organized the *oprichnina* to avoid meeting with the duma altogether.

As the small principality of Moscow grew into the Russian state and acquired enormous territory, the household officials who had served the prince when his patrimony was hardly larger than a great landowner's estate could not handle the multiplicity of problems facing the nation-state. New government bureaus called *prikazes* were set up, each headed by an appointee of the grand prince and staffed with a corps of clerks. Some of these bureaus dealt with particular governmental functions, while others were created to administer new lands added by conquest. One *prikaz* handled receipts and disbursements like any treasury department in the West; another supervised embassies sent abroad and foreign missions received in Moscow like any foreign ministry in western Europe; still another dealt with military matters like any western war office. Alongside these bureaus created on functional lines were other bureaus whose responsibility it was to deal with all types of administrative matters in a given territory, particularly in one recently acquired. A *prikaz* for Novgorod was set up to govern that wide area after its absorption by Ivan III. When the principality of Tver was added to Moscow a *prikaz* was created to administer it. The conquest of Kazan added another to this growing list, and late in the sixteenth century another *prikaz,* or bureau or colonial office, came into existence to govern Siberia. There was no order and little logic in the way in which these bureaus proliferated. A new function added or a new district conquered seemed to dictate the creation of another *prikaz*. By the end of the sixteenth century there were thirty such departments; by the time Peter the Great a century later swept them away and set up a new administrative pattern the number had doubled. Often their functions overlapped; several of them, for example, gathered and spent revenue.

The government's income, much of it in goods and services and a small percentage in money, came from a variety of sources. There were customs dues, taxes on internal trade, fines, confiscations, occasional impositions on communities or groups, and produce from crown estates. Conquered areas, often sparsely inhabited, provided what amounted to a treasure in the form of land with which the tsars paid obligations to those who had rendered them service, civil or military. From the time of Ivan III on there was a rapid growth in the number of *pomeshchiks,* men who received land from the government in return for service and who retained it only so long as they and their heirs rendered the obligation for which the land was assigned.

Every year the tsars gathered a huge army, sometimes to lead against the West but most often to fight off the incursions of the Tatars from Crimea. Frequently mercenaries were hired from enemies with whom Moscow at the moment was not at war—Swedes, Poles, and even Tatars—

and these had to be paid in coin. A picked corps of Russian sharpshooters, the *streltsy*, were privileged to live in their own quarter of Moscow and, when not in the field, to carry on trade free of the taxes which merchants had to pay. They numbered a thousand men in the sixteenth century, several thousand in the seventeenth. Stationed as they were in the capital and constituting the most effective unit in the army, the *streltsy* became an important political force, a Praetorian Guard, and dared in the seventeenth century to influence the succession.

MUSCOVITE SOCIETY

No class had completely escaped the violence and the terror which had swept over the land in the last twenty-five years of the reign of Ivan IV. It was against the nobility, the boyars, however, that the tsar had concentrated most of his fury. The old princely families, descendants of appanage princes who had entered the service of Moscow, mostly during the period of the Mongol domination, had not all been slaughtered. But many of them had been deprived of their estates and transplanted, scattered from one end of Russia to the other. Their political influence had been reduced, but not destroyed. While the princely families had not dared to challenge the capricious doings of Ivan IV, those who survived the terror nursed grievances against the monarchy so bitter that it was a surety they would seek vengeance if ever there was an opportunity.

The second rank of the nobility, the boyars proper, made up of those who had grown up as attendants or boyars in the service of the early Moscow princes and those who had moved to Moscow from boyar service under other appanage princes, had fared little better. Some like the Romanovs and the Godunovs had retained the tsar's favor, but many had been banished or had died. Many who had avoided persecution had been impoverished by heavy taxes and the crushing burden of service, or by having their peasants flee to the southeastern frontier and so losing the labor force without which their land was worthless. The gentry, the *pomeshchiks* who held their land by service tenure, often held too little land or land too thinly populated to provide a decent living. Some had only one peasant family living on their estates—"one-yarders," they were called—and had to till their acres themselves when they were not on campaign. Others had their peasants stolen from them by great landlords whose power they were too weak to challenge. The nobility and the gentry, sometimes poles apart economically, had one thing in common—their service obligation to the state.

The merchants as a class felt the oppressive burden of taxation imposed by Ivan the Terrible to finance the endless war against the Tatars and the

fruitless effort to push through to the Baltic. The middle class was beginning to show the same cleavage that separated the rich from the poor
gentry. Wealthy merchants, appointed to collect the government's taxes,
were given special trade privileges and exempted from paying taxes themselves. This increased the burden upon the lesser merchants, many of
whom fled the cities and the strangulation which threatened them. The
state sought to halt the depopulation and the decline of the cities by binding members of the middle class to their occupations and forbidding them
to move.

Economically, the church suffered least of all in the tumultuous reign of
Ivan the Terrible. While individual churchmen suffered cruelly—an occasional bishop or the priests of an occasional church or all the clergy in a
particular town like Novgorod—the church as an institution grew increasingly wealthy. It avoided taxation even after the church council of 1580 at
the tsar's order expressly forbade churches and abbeys to shirk their tax
responsibility. It continued to receive gifts of land even after the same
council had forbidden such acquisitions. By the end of the sixteenth century the great abbeys held tens of thousands of acres of land and even
maintained their own markets to dispose of surplus produce. Even more
important, church estates prospered as peasants, anxious to escape the
unsettled conditions that disturbed farming under a lay lord, flocked to the
relative quiet of monastery holdings. An occasional clergyman spoke out
against the church's mounting wealth and the profligate living it encouraged. But most churchmen defended ecclesiastical holdings, and one even
argued that sons of the well-born would not enter the clergy if the church
were poor.

THE APPROACH OF SERFDOM

Many areas of Russia were being drained of their peasant population in
the sixteenth century. The wars of Ivan IV took heavy toll, for the armies
a hundred thousand strong he gathered year after year melted away because of desertion, the taking of prisoners, and the frightful slaughter.
There was a still greater leakage to the Tatars who raided Muscovy every
spring with baskets fastened to their saddles to carry off children and
young women by the tens of thousands. Finally the tsardom of Muscovy
lost untold thousands of peasants who ran away to the frontier and beyond
in the south and southeast to escape enserfment.

The great mass of Russian peasants consisted of small farmers who
rented the land they tilled from the landholding gentry, from the church,
or from the state. These tenants rented the soil and buildings and borrowed
from the landlord for seed, equipment, and livestock at high interest rates,

normally 20 per cent. Those who could not pay the interest in money or in produce had to work it off in compulsory labor, or *barshchina,* in the proprietor's fields. The peasants had an ancient right to terminate their tenancy at any time and settle under another landlord. Many did so in the fifteenth and sixteenth centuries, sometimes attracted to a new estate by promises of lower rent under a landholder who had just received a grant and needed peasants to cultivate it. Ivan III had moved to protect landlords from loss incurred when tenants moved to another estate without settling their debts and arrears in rent, and the law code of 1497 had limited the peasants' right to move to the week before and the week after St. George's Day, November 26th, when the harvest was in. As the service obligation of the gentry increased there was all the more reason for preventing a landlord's being suddenly deprived of his peasants. Furthermore, the landholder gathered the state taxes from the peasants on his estate, and the government insisted that no peasant whose taxes were in arrears be allowed to move.

On state-owned lands the peasant villages were communally responsible for taxes and for the money or produce which went to the government for use of the land. This joint accountability made possible the early development of local self-government among the state peasants, a privilege which later made their lot far more endurable than that of peasants on private estates. But the joint responsibility for taxes and rent made the state, and indeed the peasant communities themselves, resist the movement of individual peasants or families away from crown estates. Since each village paid a fixed sum in taxes and rent the removal of one peasant family left its share of the burden to the families left behind. Increasing restrictions were placed upon the freedom of state peasants to leave the village, and those who left without permission were pursued and brought back.

In the sixteenth century rising taxes and the growing burden of debt made it increasingly impossible for peasants to leave the estates of private landholders legally. But small proprietors, who constituted a majority of the *pomeshchiks*—those who held their land by service tenure—lost their workers to great landowners who enticed the peasants with promises of easier conditions or who simply stole them away. Landlords often fought for possession of the peasants, for there were not enough to man every estate.

Landholders whose peasants had run away leaving debts or unpaid interest had the legal right to track down the fugitives and return them. Threatened with ruin, the owners of small estates—those having only a village or two—pressed the government to tighten the restrictions upon the peasant's freedom of movement and to lengthen the legal period for forcibly returning a runaway. In 1597, during the reign of Fedor I, the government extended to five years a landlord's right to track down and bring home any peasant who had left the estate illegally. Later the five-year limitation was withdrawn and the peasant lost his former right to move from one estate to another, on St. George's Day or at any other time. From then on he was no longer a free peasant but a serf, bound at first to the estate where he was born but bound later only to the estate-owner whose chattel he became. By the middle of the seventeenth century the law recognized no peasant rights whatever. To assure itself of collection of taxes from the peasants and their conscription into the army the government forced the agricultural population into bondage to the landlord, who might be a member of the gentry, a monastery, or the state itself.

THE COSSACKS

Beyond the line of fortifications and outposts which Moscow threw up along the southern rim of its populated lands in an attempt to halt Tatar raids, in the no-man's-land between the tsar's dominions and the Crimea, there sprang up in the sixteenth century several free communities of adventurers and fugitives known as Cossacks. The most famous of the bands were the Zaporozhian Cossacks—staunchly Orthodox Russians, for the most part, who had fled from the exactions and impositions of the tsar of Muscovy and the king of Poland. With the approach of serfdom, with the increasing restrictions upon freedom to till the soil and move about, strong young men ran away to the frontier and banded together in a loosely knit, jealously free, and fiercely democratic association to live by fishing, hunting, trading, and plundering occasionally from Moscow, often from Poland, and incessantly from the Crimean Tatars.

The Zaporozhian Cossacks kept their camp on one of the many islands in the Dnieper at the cataracts, moving to a new island from time to time to escape detection. In the circle around the campfire where all important matters were decided by vote all men were equals loyal to each other and to the community. Every year they elected a new chief, or "hetman," who led them to war and who had dictatorial authority over the band when on campaign. At the end of his year of leadership the hetman returned to the circle, as an equal but no more, and a new hetman was chosen. When a Cossack married he was forced to leave the circle, for no women were allowed in the fortified camp. He and his family settled on the Dnieper bank to till the soil under the protection of the band or "Host" of warriors who lived a spartan life in the island camp.

The favorite target of the raids of the Dnieper or Zaporozhian Cossacks was the Tatar nest in the Crimea. But they also ranged over the Black

Sea in their longboats and dared to raid the land of the sultan. Then Turkey would complain to Moscow, only to be told that these were not subjects of the tsar and that the sultan should settle the matter himself. But the tsars provided the Cossacks with arms and at times hired them as mercenaries. When the Cossacks raided Moscow or Poland to seize cattle and were threatened with punishment, they might even ask the sultan for protection. Sometimes they were hired to fight for the Polish king; often they fought against him. So bothersome did they become that the Polish king tried to limit the size of the Cossack band in the Dnieper, whose right bank he claimed as part of the grand duchy of Lithuania. In 1570 only a few hundred Zaporozhian Cossacks were "registered," or enrolled on the approved lists maintained by the Polish government. As serfdom crept over Russia and Poland many fled to the frontier to join the Host and by 1625 there were six thousand registered Cossacks beyond the Dnieper rapids. Thousands more lived with their families on the river banks north of the rapids, part of the Cossack community although not officially "registered."

In the sixteenth and seventeenth centuries other bands of Cossacks appeared in the valleys of the Don, the Volga, and the Yaik or Ural rivers. As the Russian frontier moved south and east still others sprang up in the valley of the Kuban and in Siberia. All but the Zaporozhian Cossacks professed loyalty to the tsar of Russia—all the while successfully maintaining their freedom from tsarist control, at least until the eighteenth century. Even the band in the Dnieper finally chose the protection of Orthodox Moscow in preference to domination by Catholic Poland. The Cossacks were reputed to be the world's finest horsemen, and the cavalry regiments which they later supplied to the Russian army were feared wherever they rode.

FEDOR, THE BELL-RINGER

Ivan the Terrible's murder of his oldest son, Ivan, left the succession to his imbecile second son Fedor (1584–1598). The old tsar realized too late the tragedy he had brought upon his house, for he showed only contempt for Fedor and observed that he was better fitted to enter a monastery than to occupy the throne. A silly smile proclaimed Fedor's feeble-mindedness, and at formal court receptions he played with his sceptre as though it were a toy. His only interest was the church, not in its deeper meaning, of course, but in the observance of its ritual. He especially enjoyed tolling church bells and wandered the streets of Moscow entering one church after another to pull at the bell ropes. The common people loved him, for the Orthodox church had long taught that the saintly fool was particularly beloved and protected by God.

Before his death Ivan IV had appointed a regency council to guide the witless Fedor. Prince Ivan Shuisky, Prince Ivan Mstislavsky, the boyar Bogdan Belsky, and Nikita Romanov, an uncle of the young tsar, were members of the council. The fifth was Boris Godunov, son of a minor boyar of Tatar descent but Tsar Fedor's brother-in-law and Ivan the Terrible's last favorite companion. Cunning and intelligent, although nearly illiterate, ingratiating and ambitious, Boris played off the other four one against another until they all had been forced into exile. Within three years of the accession Boris had taken into his own hands the power of governing Russia in the name of the foolish tsar.

During the last fifteen years of the reign of Ivan IV Boris had been intimately associated with the tsar and had married the daughter of one of the chief torturers in the *oprichnina*. Yet he had taken no part in the brutality and had obtained freedom from prison and exile for thousands of victims soon after Fedor's accession. He had won considerable popularity among the people through his reputation for gentleness and his known squeamishness at the sight of blood. But the great boyar families hated him for the favoritism bestowed upon him by the tsars, father and son, and for the dominating influence he quickly achieved over Tsar Fedor through the latter's wife, Godunov's sister.

Boris made no effort to mask either his power or his ambition. He grew immensely wealthy through the gifts the tsar showered upon him. He held a lavish court and dispensed favors as though he were the real ruler of Russia, as in practice he was. Foreign ambassadors sought to win his support, seeing that Fedor was but a shadow of a tsar.

During Fedor's fourteen-year reign there were several important developments that would influence the nation's future. Since the tsar had little reason or will and no interest in matters of state, government policy was determined by Boris. Indeed, Fedor's own life and actions merit no attention whatever, aside from the fact that he left no heirs and so closed out the Rurik dynasty with his own death.

Ivan IV had left a third son, a child by his seventh wife. But the Russian church, which would bless a third marriage but no more, would not recognize either the union or the child as legitimate. This infant Dmitry and his mother were driven into exile by the regency council before Fedor's coronation. Seven years later he was killed, some said by the ambitious Boris, although the government gave out the story that he had stabbed himself during an epileptic seizure. The incident was forgotten until the death of Fedor, when Dmitry's illegitimacy was overlooked and his death deplored and then denied.

In 1589 the patriarch of Constantinople, then in Moscow appealing for funds, was urged not to return to his home in a land ruled by infidels but to take up his residence in the Russian capital. He refused but consented to endorse the creation of a Russian patriarchate. The tsar chose the candidate, who was a close friend of Boris Godunov, and the other patriarchs of the Eastern church grudgingly recognized the new patriarch, Job of Moscow.

In the last year of Fedor's reign serfdom was brought closer when the government extended to five years the length of time in which a runaway peasant—one who had moved without settling his debts to the landlord—could be forcibly returned. Perhaps Godunov's intention was to protect small landholders against the loss of their peasants to the owners of large estates, the great boyars of whose irritation at his growing power Boris could have had no doubt. The regent allowed the church to continue to acquire land and escape paying taxes in violation of Ivan IV's orders against such practices. The crafty Boris hoped to win clerical support of his own candidacy for the throne should Fedor die without heirs.

The Russian advance into Siberia continued after the Cossack chief Ermak's victory in the year of Ivan's death. But the khan of Siberia struck back at the Cossack band and Ermak was killed. The regent Boris then sent regular troops east of the Urals, and western Siberia was recovered. Several fortified posts were established along the Ob and Irtysh rivers, among them the fort later named Tobolsk. Russian influence also pushed down the west coast of the Caspian Sea around and beyond the Caucasus Mountains, where pockets of Christian peoples asked the tsar's protection against the Moslems. The Turkish sultan, whom the khan of the Crimean Tatars recognized as suzerain, was thus threatened at the back door. This edging down the Caspian shore did not deter the Tatars from their annual raids into the heart of Muscovy, however. In 1591 they pressed to the gates of Moscow. Russian troops drove them off, and Boris, who was not with the defending army, took credit for saving the capital.

Stephen Batory, the troublesome king of Poland, died in 1586. Boris put forward Tsar Fedor to succeed him. The candidacy of the Russian was more seriously considered this time, for the tsar was no Ivan the Terrible. However, the Polish gentry chose Sigismund III, who was heir to the throne of Sweden. When he succeeded to that throne Russia's enemies in the west—Poland, Lithuania, and Sweden—were united under one ruler. Fortunately for Russia the Lutheran Swedes soon forced Catholic Sigismund to leave the country, and the union of the three Baltic powers most hostile to Russian interests came to an end. Boris then obtained a promise of Polish neutrality and attacked Sweden in the hope of recovering the foothold on the Baltic that Ivan IV had secured and lost. He did win back some of the towns Ivan had been forced to surrender and so edged closer to the Baltic. But Sweden retained the ports, and Russia's window to the West remained closed for another century.

TSAR BORIS

Fedor's death without heirs in 1598 left the nation in a state of bewilderment that might have produced a panic. For nearly three centuries the descendants of Daniel, the son of Alexander Nevsky, had ruled in Moscow. For well over seven centuries the Russian land and the Russian people had served the dynasty of Rurik. When Fedor's wife refused the crown and entered a convent the nation was faced with a crisis.

Boris Godunov (1598–1605) was now offered the crown by his creature, the Patriarch Job. No other man could have accepted the charge and eased the transition to a new dynasty with so little prospect of turmoil as could Boris. He had served closely with the last two tsars for nearly thirty years. He had been the real ruler of Russia for the past fourteen years, during which time he had handled matters ably and fairly and had healed the wounds left by Ivan the Terrible. Now Boris refused to accept the crown from the Patriarch and called for a meeting of the *Zemskii Sober* to elect a successor. There were several aspirants, the most serious threat to the candidacy of Boris coming from Fedor Romanov, nephew of Ivan IV's first wife Anastasia. But the *Zemskii Sobor,* made up of government officials many of whom owed their position to Boris and of those boyars who had avoided imprisonment or exile in Fedor's time, unanimously chose the man who for fourteen years had had all but the name of ruler. The mob in Moscow's Red Square shouted approval, and Boris's agents mingled in the crowd to prod the lukewarm into joining the chorus. A few days later Fedor Romanov was shorn and driven into a monastery to become the monk Filaret. His wife was forced to become a nun, and his son Michael and the rest of the family were exiled.

Boris's chief concern from the moment he was proclaimed tsar was to entrench himself as ruler and assure the succession of his house. He knew that many of the boyar families resented his election, although few of them had dared to fight it openly. He hoped that by lopping off the tallest heads he might reduce the rest to submission. So the Belskys and the Romanovs were exiled or thrown into prison where some of them were killed by the guards, possibly at Godunov's order. Others like the craven Prince Vassily Shuisky, whose kinsman Ivan Shuisky had been murdered by Godunov's henchmen in Fedor's reign, accepted employment under the new tsar.

Simeon Godunov, a relative of Boris, headed a network of spies whose job it was to report to the tsar any whisperings of discontent. These spies shadowed every important official, civil or military, particularly watching men like Vassily Shuisky, whose name and rank among the boyars might win him a following. Informers were prompted by promise of rich reward to report suspicions and rumors; slaves were encouraged to testify against their masters, peasants against their landlords.

Boris gambled on the support of the middle and lower classes to remain in power. He freed the slaves of the boyars whose lands he confiscated. He ordered that peasant tenants on great estates might move on St. George's Day to the estates of small landowners but forbade any transfer of tenancy from small to great holdings. In so doing he risked the hostility of the wealthy boyars in exchange for the support of the lesser gentry. When famine swept the land in 1601 and continued for three years Boris offered relief to starved-out peasants by distributing grain and putting men to work on public projects. But the drought and famine were too severe for the government to meet. Hordes of starving peasants roamed the land in search of food and many died.

Godunov soon lost the reputation for mildness which he had won in the time of Ivan the Terrible and maintained through Fedor's reign. Men suspected of disaffection were brought to the torture, and once again victims were flogged and flayed and roasted and impaled. When Ivan IV practiced such cruelty no one dared oppose him. But Boris's position—the fact that he had won the throne by election and not by hereditary right—made him vulnerable to criticism. Discontent mounted rapidly; men awaited only the call of a leader to rise against the new tyranny.

THE FALSE DMITRY

Boris had occupied the throne only a year before it was being whispered about that Dmitry, Ivan IV's son by his seventh wife, was still alive. The rumor had it that a priest's son, and not Dmitry, had been killed at Godunov's command back in 1591, and that Dmitry had escaped.

In 1603 a Russian, about whose identity historians still disagree, appeared at the home of a Polish landlord in Galicia and announced himself as the true Dmitry, son of Ivan IV. He was introduced to the Polish king, Sigismund III, who together with his Jesuit advisers accepted the claim of the Russian, whoever he was, in order to use him to further Polish and Catholic interests in Russia. When word of the adventure reached Moscow Boris ridiculed the claimant as a former monk, Gregory Otrepev, who had once been a serf belonging to the Romanov family. The Patriarch Job anathematized this unfrocked monk and Prince Vasily Shuisky, who at Boris's order in 1591 had investigated the circumstances of Dmitry's death, repeated again that the true Dmitry was dead. But Dmitry's mother insisted that her son had escaped. For her impertinence she was forced into a convent and her name changed to Sister Martha.

After being baptized a Roman Catholic and promising to work for the conversion of Russia to Catholicism, Dmitry received assurance of Polish support in an attempt to seize his "rightful inheritance." However, the assembly of the Polish gentry, fearing Russian vengeance, refused to consort with the adventurer. Dmitry's support came from Sigismund III, his Jesuit advisers, a few Polish nobles, and, most especially, from Russian malcontents. For a year the Pretender lived off the bounty of his Polish host George Mniszek; he even fell in love and later married Mniszek's daughter Marina.

In the autumn of 1604 Dmitry led a small army of Polish adventurers and Russian refugees across the frontier and started for Moscow. The Zaporozhian Cossacks went over to the invader, and later the Don and Volga Cossacks imprisoned Boris's envoys and forsook their loyalty to Moscow. Runaway peasants welcomed Dmitry as a deliverer, as did townsmen threatened with bondage and small landholders impoverished by drought and the loss of their peasants. Exiled boyars came into the Pretender's camp; others slipped away from Moscow to join the motley army. Garrison after garrison surrendered without a pretense of opposition. Dmitry had crossed the Dnieper with only three squadrons of Polish cavalry and a sprinkling of experienced foot soldiers among a few thousand undisciplined and unorganized adventurers. But the number of his followers multiplied several times over as he advanced through southwest Russia. The movement had become a Russian uprising—a rebellion against oppression and a revolt against the approach of serfdom.

Tsar Boris died suddenly in 1605, probably of poison—a suicide, it was widely believed. The Patriarch Job, reluctant to call a *Zemskii Sobor* when the land was in ferment, proclaimed Boris's sixteen-year-old son as Tsar Fedor II. Ten weeks later this pretense of a reign ended when Dmitry led his army through the gates of Moscow. A mob broke into the Kremlin and strangled Fedor Godunov and his mother.

Dmitry (1605–1606), who was highly intelligent and well read, soon lost his enthusiasm for the Polish cause and even for the Catholic religion which he had recently embraced. He seems honestly to have deplored the plight of the Russian people and to have wanted to institute reform. But he was given little time. The household slaves expected immediate liberation. The peasants demanded an end to restrictions on their freedom to move from one estate to another. The lesser gentry hoped for more land and further assurance that their peasants would not be allowed to leave their estates. The boyars insisted that Russia be governed by the boyar duma in the way that the gentry ruled in Poland. The Jesuits who came to Moscow with Dmitry urged him to establish Catholicism immediately as the official religion and were disappointed when he consented only to proclaim toleration for both Orthodoxy and Catholicism. The Russian clergy were furious at losing their monopoly and outraged when Dmitry married Marina, a Catholic Pole. And the Poles at court resented the Russian boyars who were released from prison and restored to favor.

The Pretender refused to accept the crown of Russia until his presumed mother, the nun Martha, came to Moscow and recognized him as her son. This she did in an emotional spectacle which doubters insisted was staged. The treatment she had received from the Godunovs was enough to win her support for their overthrow. The few Romanovs who had survived imprisonment returned, but the head of the family, Fedor Romanov, now the monk Filaret, refused to leave the church and became a bishop.

Prince Vasily Shuisky, who had sought to gain favor by denying his earlier testimony and proclaiming that the child Dmitry had really not been murdered in 1591, sulked over the preferment shown the Romanovs and resented the fact that Polish advisers surrounded the new tsar. Now he reverted to his earlier stand, announcing that Dmitry had indeed died in 1591. He organized a plot among the boyars to overthrow Dmitry, and in the spring of 1606 a mob incited by Shuisky stormed the palace and killed the tsar. Dmitry had been crowned, married, and murdered in eleven short months.

VASILY SHUISKY

The void left by Dmitry's assassination made easy Prince Shuisky's assumption of the crown. He claimed it not by election, which he spurned, but by right of birth, for he was a descendant of Rurik through a junior line. To destroy the popularity of the False Dmitry the body of what was sworn to be the true Dmitry was disinterred and brought to Moscow for a pompous burial alongside the tombs of the tsars. The church obliged by proclaiming the child a saint and miracles were soon being wrought conveniently over his grave. The nun Martha now declared that her son Dmitry had in fact died in 1591. But the story spread over the land that Tsar Dmitry had not been assassinated in 1606, that he would soon return to claim the throne again.

The four-year reign of Vasily (1606–1610) marked the flood tide of boyar influence and the ebb of royal authority. Shuisky was forced to make certain commitments in return for the backing of the boyars who had helped him to the throne. He promised that boyars would not be arbitrarily punished, that those accused of crime would be tried openly and fairly without torture, that property of those found guilty of less than capital crimes would not be confiscated, and that relatives of a guilty boyar should not be punished unless they too were found guilty. He swore to consult the boyar duma on all important matters. In an obvious appeal for gentry support he restored and increased restrictions on the freedom of the peasants to move from one estate to another and extended from five to fifteen years the length of time a runaway peasant might be hunted down. To the mass of the people it soon became clear that Vasily would rule in the interest of the landowners and that serfdom or bondage would be the fate of the farming population.

The False Dmitry had driven the Patriarch Job back to his monastery and named another to the high office. Now Filaret, the former Fedor Romanov, was elected patriarch. But the tsar refused to confirm the choice and insisted upon the election of the eighty-year-old Metropolitan Hermogen, bishop of Kazan. Filaret, always ambitious for himself and his family, never forgave the slight.

Half of Muscovy refused to accept the rule of Vasily Shuisky. The Volga from its bend to its mouth withheld recognition, as did the Cossack lands of the south. Pretenders appeared in profusion, each claiming descent from the old dynasty. The most fantastic fabrication of all was that the dead daughter of the saintly Tsar Fedor had not died and had not been a girl but a boy named Peter, who now providentially reappeared. Few could have been fooled by such nonsense, but the appearance of each pretender and the creation of a court around him amounted to a call to all who had any reason to hate the government to join the standard of revolt.

Vasily had worn the crown only a few months when an army dedicated to the restoration of Dmitry, who was supposed still to be alive, advanced out of South Russia toward Moscow. Its leader was Ivan Bolotnikov, a former household slave who had spent years in Turkish captivity. Bolotnikov preached violent social revolution, urging the slaves and serfs to kill their masters and seize the landowners' land, goods, and women. Many of the impoverished gentry sided with him until the class hatred which the movement engendered drove them to desert to Moscow. There remained an army made up of runaway peasants and of Cossacks from all the river valleys of South Russia who were determined to halt the approach of bondage and restore freedom to the land.

The threat to their privileges united the boyars and gentry firmly on the side of Shuisky. A Moscow army marched into South Russia to wreak savage vengeance upon the rebels. Bolotnikov was taken and executed, but the gospel he preached long continued to stir the blood of the Russian peasants. The government attempted to stifle opposition by fastening every peasant to the land and binding every last member of society to his occupation and his class.

Shuisky had little time for elation at his triumph over Bolotnikov. Another pretender calling himself Dmitry, the "second False Dmitry" history has named him, won the backing of the Polish king Sigismund. No one who knew him was fooled about his identity, but to maintain the pretense among the gullible, the nun Martha embraced him as her son, as she had done with the first False Dmitry, and Marina even accepted him as her husband. This pretender was well supplied with Polish troops. The Cossacks supported him and again the discontented of South Russia flocked to his banner, for the name of Dmitry promised relief from oppression.

The rebel army laid siege to Moscow, and Dmitry established his own capital at Tushino a few miles away. Filaret joined him there and was named patriarch of Moscow. Now the suffering land of Russia had two patriarchs, two tsars, two capitals, two administrations seeking to govern the nation. South, central, and west Russia recognized Dmitry, while Moscow and the provinces north of it remained loyal to Vasily. There was also a vertical division of loyalty. The masses idolized the name of Dmitry, while the conservative landed interests supported Shuisky against the danger of social upheaval.

The second False Dmitry, who came to be called "the thief of Tushino," lost all chance to unite the land behind him when his lawless supporters ravaged and plundered the central and northern provinces. The people organized an army of their own, quite independent of government control, to defend their homes. Once they had rid their own districts of the Pretender's brigands they marched south to succor Moscow. Meanwhile Shuisky had convinced Sigismund of the danger of trafficking with revolutionaries, and the Polish contingents under Dmitry were called back home. In return for a strip of the Russian frontier in Estonia Sweden promised help to Shuisky's cause. A relief army of Swedes and mercenaries from western Europe approached Moscow and broke up the siege. Forsaken by his Polish allies and deserted by lawless elements interested only in plunder, Dmitry abandoned his capital at Tushino and withdrew with his Cossacks.

Filaret and a few dissident boyars who opposed Shuisky now prevailed upon King Sigismund of Poland to advance against Moscow and place his son Wladyslav on the Russian throne. This patriarch of Moscow, as Filaret had been named by the second False Dmitry, soothed his conscience with a Polish promise that Orthodoxy would not be disturbed as the state religion. The boyars with him were comforted by the assurance that there would be no relaxation of the restrictions upon the Russian peasants and by the promise that the Pole would rule with the advice of the boyar duma. A Polish army marched on Moscow while the Swedes held Novgorod and Dmitry and his Cossacks returned to the attack. Shuisky was forced to abdicate by the Moscow mob, incited by the boyars who now deserted the tsar. He was forced to enter a monastery, and Russia was rid of his disgraceful rule. Now there was no tsar. Moscow was governed by the boyar duma.

THE POLES IN MOSCOW

In midsummer, 1610, two armies, each with its own candidate for the Russian throne, camped under the walls of Moscow. One was the Polish army, which if invited in could be expected to continue the conservative policies of Shuisky and defend the interests of the gentry against social revolution. The other, led by the second False Dmitry, was made up chiefly of Cossacks who would insist upon a generally democratic social order which would defend the rights of the peasants against the landlords. For the boyars and other influential but conservative men in Moscow the choice was clear and simple. Wladyslav, the fifteen-year-old son of the Polish king, was elected by a hastily gathered assembly that passed for a *Zemskii Sobor*. Dmitry was driven off and later murdered, and the Polish army entered Moscow.

With Polish troops in control of the Russian capital, King Sigismund now withdrew his son's candidacy for the Muscovite throne and insisted upon his own election. Even the Moscow nobles, selfish as they were, took alarm at this turn of events. While they were confident they could control the youthful Wladyslav, there was little likelihood that they could manage his willful father. The prospect was that Sigismund on the Moscow throne would be advised by Poles and Jesuits and that Russians would receive little hearing. The clergy were most disturbed, for Sigismund, an ardent Catholic, was known to favor Russia's return to the Roman church.

The patriarch of Moscow, Hermogen, led a movement to awaken a national revival in the land, sending out letters to Russian cities calling upon the faithful to resist the Polish invaders. The Poles imprisoned the old man and starved him to death, but he had accomplished his purpose. An army of Cossacks and gentry stormed into Moscow and drove the Polish garrison back into the fortress of the Kremlin.

Kuzma Minin, a butcher of Nizhni-Novgorod, gathered contributions and assembled a sizeable army made up of all classes to save the nation from foreign rule. A Polish army sent to relieve the garrison in the Kremlin was driven off, and the Poles in the capital were forced to surrender. By the end of the year 1612 Moscow was again under Russian control. Three months later a broadly representative *Zemskii Sobor* elected a new tsar. He was Michael Romanov, the son of the Patriarch Filaret, who in turn was the nephew of Ivan IV's beloved "little heifer," Anastasia.

SIGNIFICANCE OF THE TIME OF TROUBLES

Through century after century, from Kievan to Communist times, the course of Russian history has been set by its strong rulers. The story of the nation's past often seems to be simply the history of the state. The history of the Russian people is elusive. For years and decades on end they go unnoticed, serving the needs of the state anonymously, working and dying without identity. Occasionally, however, the people rise up and dominate the story, pushing the state into the background. Momentarily the observer's attention focuses upon the Russian masses and upon the leaders who arise from their midst to lead them. Such moments would come with the rising of Stenka Razin in the seventeenth century and with that of Pugachev in the eighteenth. Such a moment would come in the twentieth century with the overthrow of the monarchy. And such a moment was the Time of Troubles.

The deep-seated social unrest that followed upon the death of Fedor I in 1598 had been mounting throughout the reign of his father Ivan the Terrible. The increasing burden of state service, the sacrifices of goods and labor and life itself which the demands of the state imposed, brought the patience of the people to the breaking point. Men had borne the burdens and suffering to the limit of human endurance because the grand prince or the tsar, as God's annointed, had asked it. But with the end of the dynasty every class in society rebelled against the tyranny which the nation had endured so long. Men fought against autocracy, against the approach of serfdom, against the bondage that was creeping over all classes. They fought against oppression—the oppression of peasants by landholders, of lesser gentry by great boyars, of boyars by the ruler, of church by the state, and, finally, of Russians by foreigners.

The Time of Troubles was a period of national tragedy. Not only was the land scourged and the people bled white by the civil war, but the tragedy lay in the fact that these sufferings accomplished nothing. Serfdom did come to the land, perhaps even sooner than it might have come had there been no Time of Troubles. Bondage did spread over all classes and it would take centuries to cast off its yoke. And autocracy did settle again over the nation, an autocracy more complete and more demanding than anything Ivan IV had tried to impose.

There would be social upheaval again. Men never forgot Bolotnikov, and some would try to emulate him. But the ex-slave's brief career so terrorized the gentry that they were willing henceforth to serve the ruler and the state meekly, lest a decline in royal authority should allow the spark of social revolt to kindle anew.

SUGGESTED READING

Cresson, W. P., *The Cossacks* (New York, Brentano's, 1919).

Fletcher, G., *Of the Russe Common Wealth* (London, Hakluyt Society, Series I, 1856).

Graham, S., *Boris Godunof* (New Haven, Yale University Press, 1933).

Kliuchevsky, V. O., *A History of Russia*, vol. III (London, Dent, 1913).

Platonov, S. F., *History of Russia* (New York, Macmillan, 1925).

Pokrovsky, M. N., *History of Russia* (New York, International Publishers, 1931).

12

The First Romanovs

THE FIRST ROMANOV, THE WEAK-willed, uneducated Michael, let his ambitious father, the Patriarch Filaret, govern for him. Order returned to the land only after years of hunting down the Cossacks and marauders that roamed the countryside. Michael's government bought peace with Sweden and Poland at the cost of surrendering the Baltic lands to the very gates of Novgorod and the White Russian provinces of Smolensk and Chernigov. Filaret tightened the collection of revenue and tried to bind men of all classes to their inherited occupations and homes to insure the state of income and service. He invited West Europeans to settle in Moscow to teach Russians their manufacturing skills, to erect factories, and to train the army. With little education himself, Filaret appreciated the need for schools for the clergy and imported Greek scholars who prepared the way for church reform in the next reign.

The second Romanov, the gentle youth Alexis, was as willing as his father that favorites should manage affairs. The reign is most notable for the adoption of a new law code, the *Ulozhenie,* which legalized bondage for all society. The peasants and former slaves all became serfs, bound to the landlord who collected their tax payments and sent them to the army when the government called for recruits. The law bound Russian townsmen to practice the trades and skills of their fathers and to live where the 1649 census found them. Even the gentry lost all freedom to avoid the burden of military service which the new code imposed upon all landholders. But for the gentry there were privileges—the right to own serfs, the right to own land, preferment in government service. For the nonproprietary classes there were only obligations.

Alexis supported the Patriarch Nikon in forcing upon the Russian clergy a revision of the liturgical books which, through faulty translation, had encouraged minor errors in church ritual. The fact that the corrections were made by scholars who had learned their Greek and Latin in Western schools tainted the new texts with heresy in the minds of many bigoted churchmen. Nikon's impatience and lack of tact in forcing the adoption of the corrected ritual drove many into opposition whom gentler methods might have converted. The Old Believers—those who persisted in the old religious practices —suffered persecution for their treason to the church and to the state which dominated it.

Poland, in her constitutional anarchy, grew steadily weaker. Russia and Sweden attacked her and the Zaporozhian Cossacks shifted their allegiance to Moscow. Alexis recovered the left bank of the Dnieper; Kiev on the right bank once more became a Russian city.

The war with Poland was attended and followed by uprisings in South Russia against the bondage which the *Ulozhenie* had made legal. Bogdan Khmelnitsky raised the Dnieper Cossacks and Stenka Razin the Don Cossacks against the rule of Moscow. Swarms of peasants joined both in a class war against the landlords who symbolized the hated institution of serfdom.

Sympathy for Western ideas and customs ran high at the court of Alexis. The foreign quarter of Moscow filled with West Europeans employed to teach Russians their technical skills. A succession of advisers to the tsar encouraged the importation of Western knowledge and manners.

The third Romanov, like the first two, was a weak youth of fourteen. During his short reign the *miestnichestvo* was abolished and civil and military ranks were thrown open to those with merit, or at least to those whom the tsar chose to appoint. Fedor's death raised the question of whether he should be succeeded by his idiot brother Ivan or by his strong, healthy younger half brother Peter.

THE TSAR MICHAEL

The *Zemskii Sobor* of 1613 elected a thoroughly colorless youth of sixteen, weak in body and in spirit, who was completely dominated at first by his strong-willed mother, the nun Martha, and later by his ambitious and power-greedy father, Filaret. Michael (1613–1645) greeted the news of his election with tears and pleadings to be let alone, and his mother refused her permission for his coronation until assured that the nation would unite behind him. Numerous relatives and favorites contested for influence at court during the first five years of the reign. Then Filaret joined Michael as co-tsar, a situation which recognized the helplessness of the young man to manage affairs alone.

Michael was too young to have taken sides in the recent violence and thus had done nothing to make enemies for himself. In fact, he had spent much of the Time of Troubles in prison. He had no education, although he could read and write. His distinguishing traits were a lack of will of his own and a satisfaction to let others handle matters for him. His lack of character and strength was probably one of the things that made him attractive as a candidate for the throne.

Michael's chief recommendation for the position of tsar came from the name he bore. The ancestors of the Romanovs had entered the service of Moscow in the time of Ivan Kalita, and the family had served its masters faithfully. If Filaret's conduct during the Time of Troubles had at times been questionable, at least he had sided with the masses against the boyars rather consistently. But in 1613 the glory in the name Romanov stemmed from the fact that Michael's great-aunt had been the first wife of Ivan IV. The *Zemskii Sobor* clung to a thread of hereditary descent when it chose the young man whose family had married into the old dynasty.

The Nation Exhausted

Russia had just passed through the most trying ordeal in her history, a period even more painful than the revolution and civil war in the twentieth century, which lasted not half so long. The land had been ravaged by contesting native armies, plundering Cossacks, and pillaging foreigners ever since 1604, and the fighting would go on sporadically for another four or five years after Michael's election. Whole districts had been depopulated as families fled or were driven away. Crops had been destroyed year after year, until men had given up planting and countless estates had passed out of cultivation. Towns had been deserted and many of them destroyed. Markets had closed down; trade disappeared. There was no money in the treasury, for taxes had long been uncollectible. How many men, women, and children had died horrible deaths no one would ever know. To put the nation back on its feet would require years of peace and rebuilding.

The reign of Ivan IV and the Time of Troubles put Russia several generations behind Western Europe technically and intellectually. While the Renaissance spread from Italy over Northern Europe, while the Reformation forced a soul-searching upon the Western church, while the nations on the Atlantic were exploring the seas and developing commerce, while the West was making enormous technological strides, Russia was standing still and then slipping below the level she herself had reached earlier. If in the early sixteenth century Russia was not far behind the West, from then on she rapidly lost ground while Europe moved ahead. Some say that Russia had fallen behind the West by a century, others say two centuries or more, in the sixty years prior to Michael's election.

This loss of ground continued after 1613, for the settlement of the succession did not bring peace to the desolated land. The Swedes had pushed in from the Baltic shores and were occuping the Livonian towns which they had recently lost to Russia. Novgorod, still an important trade center, was in Swedish hands. The Poles were in Smolensk and Wladyslav, the son of their king, announced his determination to press his claim to the Muscovite throne. A Cossack chieftain, Ivan Zarutsky, picking up the claims and ambitions of earlier pretenders, now posed as the true Dmitry and married the adventuress Marina. He and Marina proposed to establish a kingdom of their own on the Volga. Bands of Cossacks and deserted soldiers of several nations swarmed looting, burning, and slaughtering over the countryside.

The Return to Peace

The *Zemskii Sobor* which elected Michael sat continuously for the first nine years of the reign, deciding state policy and giving direction to the mild-mannered tsar and the relatives who advised him. Along with the *Zemskii Sobor,* the boyar duma met in daily sessions to draft proposals to be submitted to the larger body and to answer the tsar's questions on matters of detail. Neither the *Zemskii Sobor* nor the boyar duma enjoyed any right to initiate legislation. They simply discussed propositions the tsar put forward and, when he asked for it, gave him advice that he need not accept. When something like order returned to the land and Michael's father neither needed nor wanted such consultations, the *Zemskii Sobor* was dismissed. From time to time others were elected to give an opinion on vital questions of foreign policy. If this assembly of the land behaved only remotely like a Western parliament, it was the closest Russia was to get to such an institution until the twentieth century. The *Zemskii Sobor* met occasionally during the reign of Michael's son Alexis, and again, for the last time, in 1682 to settle the succession upon Peter and his half brother, Ivan.

The government's first concern was to put down the marauding bands that infested the nation, to restore the order without which trade could not revive nor agriculture recover. Since there was no money in the treasury with which to finance the effort, the state sent groups of agents, guarded by soldiers, into the countryside to gather "voluntary" contributions. The church added pressure by threatening with excommunication those who did not contribute according to their means.

The Cossack Zarutsky led an army north from his "capital" Astrakhan and captured Samara and Kazan. From there he turned against Moscow, but was defeated, brought a prisoner to the capital, and there impaled. The serious danger from the southeast was removed, although pillaging bands kept the valley of the Volga in turmoil for years to come.

In the years after 1603, when Poland first used the False Dmitry to try to dominate Russia, Sweden joined Moscow to protect her own interests, which would surely suffer if the two great Slav countries were united under the leadership of Catholic Poland. Vasily Shuisky encouraged the Swedes in their ambition to dominate northwest Russia, since their presence there as allies tended to hamper Polish operations. So the Swedes built a fortress at the mouth of the Neva, near the site where St. Petersburg later would stand, advanced south and east of the Gulf of Finland, and seized Novgorod. The citizens of Novgorod, much preferring the rule of the Lutheran Swedes to that of the Catholic Poles if there was to be no other choice, listened sympathetically to the proposition that North Russia from the Baltic to the White Sea should be organized into a duchy to be administered by the brother of the king of Sweden. With Michael's accession Swedish King Gustavus Adolphus dropped the pretense that North Russia should become a Swedish duchy and demanded the cession of the territory to Sweden outright in lieu of promised Russian subsidies which had not been paid. Gustavus even considered moving his capital from Stockholm to Narva to be nearer the center of his growing empire.

Negotiations for a settlement dragged on for years until the Peace of Stolbovo was agreed upon in 1617. Michael was recognized as the rightful tsar of Russia. Sweden received an indemnity, won the Karelian Isthmus and the west shore of Lake Ladoga, and recovered the lands near the Baltic which Ivan IV and later Boris Godunov had won temporarily. Russia's exclusion from the Baltic thus was confirmed, although at the time the weakened Moscow was happy to recover Novgorod.

Gustavus Adolphus told his parliament what control of the entire coast of the Gulf of Finland meant to Sweden: "The Russians have been cut off from the shores of the Baltic. Henceforth they are forbidden entrance to the Baltic at any point, and cannot use it for their ships for their own accommodation, either for war purposes or for trade, without our special permission." He urged Swedes to move to this new frontier, which lay close up against Novgorod, and to profit from the overland trade between Russia and the Baltic.

As soon as the Swedish problem was settled the Moscow government was faced with a renewal of the war with Poland. Wladyslav had not dropped his claim to the Russian throne, and as soon as he could gather the money and men to try to recover it he set out from his base at Smolensk to storm Moscow. Twenty thousand Zaporozhian Cossacks joined him in the assault upon the Russian capital, but Moscow withstood the attack. Meanwhile Russian envoys in Constantinople tried to persuade the sultan to attack Poland, but the Turkish government, resentful of raids by the Don Cossacks on the south shore of the Black Sea, refused to succor Moscow.

Wladyslav's army melted rapidly away after the failure to capture Moscow and in 1619 he accepted the terms of the Truce of Duelino. The Poles acknowledged Michael to be the tsar of Moscow for the time being, although Wladyslav refused to renounce his ultimate right to the Russian throne. Poland received the provinces of Smolensk, Chernigov, and Seversk, a considerable addition of territory which marked the farthest eastward advance in Polish history. With the conclusion of the armistice with Poland, which was satisfactory to neither signatory but which promised no hostilities for fourteen years, Russia obtained peace for the first time in a generation.

The Dyarchy

Filaret, the tsar's father, had served the second False Dmitry who had named him patriarch, but he had returned to Moscow after Shuisky's abdication. He had gone as an envoy to the Polish court to implore King Sigismund to consent to the conversion of his son Wladyslav to Orthodoxy as a condition of election to the Russian throne. He had comported himself with dignity, spurning any compromise on the religious issue and refusing to support Sigismund's plan to seize the throne for himself. For his obstinacy he was held a prisoner by the Poles for the next eight years and only released by the terms of the Truce of Duelino.

From the time of his return to Moscow in 1619 Filaret, now duly installed as patriarch of Moscow, ruled jointly with his son as co-tsar. The two, sitting side by side on two thrones, received envoys from foreign governments, greeted them each in his own name, and separately received gifts from each ambassador. Important public documents were signed by both men. But in his weakness Michael left many matters to be handled entirely by his father and submitted meekly to the patriarch's will whenever problems had to be decided by both of them. Until his death in 1633 Filaret determined the course of government policy.

Filaret first set about to increase the revenue and to see that everyone paid his fair share of taxes. Theretofore government tax collectors had dealt softly with those who could bribe them, shifting the burden to those too poor to buy gentler treatment. Now new tax lists were compiled and tax groups were allowed to choose their own assessors. So needy was the government that Filaret allowed London merchants to retail goods in Russia without payment of dues in return for occasional small loans. Russian merchants were charged heavy fees for the right to operate taverns and even laundries. The salt tax was increased until the tax was several times more than the price of the salt. The greatest revenue came from the direct taxes which all classes paid but of which the peasants paid by far the most because they made up 95 per cent of the population. Men were forbidden to sell themselves into slavery, for slaves paid no taxes. Peasants were threatened with dire punishment for running away, for unless the state could bind its population to a definite location where men could be found when needed for tax payments or army service the nation's income and the nation's defenses would suffer.

The military campaigns during the Time of Troubles had been fought
with irregular levies and mercenaries. The Russian army, except for a few
picked units, had proven itself of little worth, particularly in action against
better-equipped, better-led, better-organized Western armies; it often performed miserably even against the Tatars. Some of the infantry were
armed with antiquated muskets that had been obsolete in Western Europe
for a century; other units carried spears and axes. The cavalry was poorly
mounted and much of it armed with bows and arrows. Desertion from such
militia units was common, and the troops panicked and fled at the first
contact with the enemy.

The *streltsy,* twenty thousand strong, were picked musketeers who
received a regular wage and clothing allowance, living with their families
in special quarters near designated towns where they tilled the soil and
traded free of duty to the annoyance of the local merchants. When not on
campaign the soldiers served as local police and firemen. Some *streltsy* regiments fifteen thousand strong were stationed near the capital to serve as
royal household troops and guards for the tsar. The chief officers were
nobles; the men in the ranks were recruited from among city dwellers. The
streltsy constituted the chief element in the standing army, the rest of it
being made up of mercenaries. Only in time of serious threat were commoners drafted. The gentry owed military service to the state, but peasants
and townsmen usually were deemed more valuable to the government following their civilian pursuits of farming and trading and paying taxes.

With the restoration of peace in 1619 and the realization that the nation
had done poorly against the Swedes and Poles, Filaret undertook to raise
the efficiency of the armed forces. He hired foreigners, usually from Protestant countries, to serve as officers in the Russian army and to teach native
troops something of Western methods. Over four hundred of them were
engaged, a third of them Poles, a fourth Germans, a seventh Irish, with
Swedes, Scots, Englishmen, Greeks, and Serbs in lesser numbers. They
received very high wages, some in money, others in land upon which they
settled to rear their families in Russia. But the task of modernizing the
Russian army was too formidable and too costly to be accomplished in a
short time by a still weak government. The gentry shirked their service
responsibility and hurried back to the easy living of their estates as soon
as a campaign was over, sometimes even before.

If the army were to be modelled after those in the West and equipped
with modern weapons, then Russia had to import Western arms and equipment or learn to make such things herself. Since buying them abroad was
out of the question—access to Russia through hostile countries anxious to
keep her backward was often impossible and always expensive—Filaret
planned that Westerners should be hired to establish armaments and equipment factories in Russia. The first Russian weapons factory was built in

Tula in 1632 by Andrew Vinnius, the Russian-born son of a Dutch immigrant. Filaret died the next year, but he had laid the foundation of a war industry upon which Peter the Great would later build.

Westerners who could erect munitions plants were not the only ones who found welcome in Moscow. Filaret hoped that Russians might learn many skills and establish industries which would stimulate the economy and so produce revenue for the treasury. Swedes, Germans, and Dutchmen came from the West to tutor Russians in goldsmithing, bellmaking, leather-tanning, masonry, clockmaking, and the manufacture of glass. The foreigners were given their own quarter of Moscow for the location of their own homes and churches, the "German" or "foreign" quarter—the Russian word *nemets* means German, but at this time any foreigner was called a German. Before Michael's death over a thousand foreign families were living in the German quarter of Moscow, and it was here that Peter the Great as a child learned to respect Western knowledge and techniques.

Although he was a layman with no religious education Filaret appreciated the need for better training of the clergy. He ordered every archbishop to open a seminary for the education of priests, and he expanded the printing of church books, some of which he himself revised. He established a clerical institute to train Latin and Greek scholars, borrowing teachers from the recently-founded seminary for Orthodox clergymen in Kiev. He brought learned Greeks to Moscow to inspire the ignorant clergymen of the Russian Church with an interest in the Greek language from which their own sacred books had been badly translated. In much that he did Filaret prepared the way for the reformers of the next reign, and they in turn made possible the modernization program of Peter the Great.

The Second Polish War

The loss of territory which Russia was forced to concede in the Truce of Duelino made certain that the war with Poland would be renewed at the first favorable opportunity. That opportunity arrived in 1621 when both Sweden and Turkey proposed an alliance with Russia to destroy Poland. The *Zemskii Sobor* urged the co-tsars to take up the offer and preparations were made for war. But before Russian troops could take the field the Turkish army was convincingly defeated by the Poles, and Russian ardor subsided.

Eleven years later old Sigismund III died and Moscow determined to take advantage of Poland's weakness during the confusion over the succession. Alexander Leslie, a Scot in the service of Moscow, hurried off to Stockholm to employ thousands of mercenaries and to bring back smiths, wheelwrights, carpenters, and munitions makers to stimulate Russia's production of war equipment, while an enthusiastic *Zemskii Sobor* encouraged prompt action and liberally appropriated funds to finance it.

The Russian army invested the Polish stronghold of Smolensk, but it was routed by a relief force of Poles and Zaporozhian Cossacks led by the new King Wladyslav IV, Sigismund's son and claimant to the Russian crown. With the fighting over, the two governments pledged "eternal peace." Poland surrendered no territory and received a large indemnity, in return for which Wladyslav gave up all claim to the Russian throne. The Poles remained in Smolensk.

Perhaps the chief consequence of the so-called Second Polish War was to destroy Michael's confidence in his army. He beheaded the commander and exiled the subordinates to Siberia, but never again risked humiliation. Whenever the sultan upbraided Moscow for the raids of the Don Cossacks—they were once at the outskirts of Constantinople—Michael's government humbly apologized. The Don Host seized Azov in 1637 and held it for five years. Then, when a Turkish army threatened to recover it, the Cossacks offered Azov to the tsar. A *Zemskii Sobor* called in 1642 to advise Michael on the matter urged him to accept the gift. The members took the opportunity to complain about the dishonesty of the tsar's officials and suggested that if all classes, particularly the clergy, paid their fair share of taxes there would be sufficient means to hold Azov. But Michael succumbed to Turkish threats and ordered the Cossacks to surrender the Black Sea port. They did so after levelling it to the ground.

The First Autocrat

At the ceremony of his coronation Michael assumed the title of "Autocrat," the first of the tsars to do so at their coronation. In their personal conduct of affairs, however, there was nothing of the autocrat in either Michael, his son Alexis, or his grandson Fedor. If the title meant anything in the seventeenth century it did so because of the strengthening of the royal authority by those men, of whom Filaret was the first of several, who exercised power in the tsar's name. The term came to have meaning for the mass of the Russian people, every man of whom by the middle of the century was bound in service to the ruler. If the tsar dealt gently with the landowning aristocracy, if the burden of bondage fell most heavily upon the peasants, nevertheless long before the century was out few would question the fact that the power of the tsar was that of an autocrat. Men went to the block, to prison, or into exile at the autocrat's order, regardless of the social class from which they came. Indeed, it was rare for a member of the lower classes to be favored with such punishment. Most often the victim was one of the gentry who took his service obligation lightly or who failed in a task he had been ordered to shoulder.

After the death of his father, the patriarch, Michael again fell under the influence of court favorites. Even through the years of Filaret's tutelage the tsar had not developed the confidence and strength to wield the power

that was his. He died in 1645 at the age of forty-eight, leaving the throne
to his sixteen-year-old son with an admonition to the child's tutor, the boyar
Boris Morozov, to guide and protect him.

ALEXIS

Michael's successor was even more harmless and gentle than his father.
His kindness and generosity made him an easy prey to the relatives,
favorites, and hangers-on with whom the court abounded. A host of beggars,
dwarfs, buffoons, and simpletons lived off the tsar's bounty and entertained
the court. The number of these fools mounted until it reached a formidable
figure, but Alexis was too kind to turn them out. He was humane and con-
siderate to an absurd degree, less mindful on one occasion that his troops
had been ignominiously defeated in battle than that there were so many
casualties.

Unlike his father, Alexis (1645–1676) had received some education. Perhaps Filaret, who was keenly aware of his own educational weakness, had
made provision for the instruction of the heir to the throne. While his own
schooling ended at the age of ten, Alexis determined that his children, or at
least those by his first wife, should do better. He shocked conservative circles
by abolishing the *terem,* the isolation of women at court, and by encouraging
the education of his daughter Sophia. He was intensely pious and devoted
much of his time to practicing the formalities of his religion. He was
puritanical, as was his father, who had slit the nostrils of men caught smoking
tobacco. More able and certainly more intelligent than his father, still he
was superstitious in the extreme, at one time forbidding his subjects to gaze
at the full moon.

The *Zemskii Sobor* was convoked to applaud, not to question, the succession of Alexis; then it was dissolved. For the next three years the tsar
was content to let Morozov handle affairs. The favorite, who married the
tsar's sister-in-law, was as sympathetic to Western ideas as was Alexis. After
three years he was dismissed at the demand of a riotous mob but slipped
back to the Kremlin and secretly lived out his life there as one, if not the
chief, of the tsar's advisers. His place of influence over Alexis was taken
by the Patriarch Nikon, who fell from favor ten years later because of his
pompous and domineering manner. Then came the statesman Athanasy
Ordyn-Nashchokin. Throughout his life the tsar was satisfied to reign and
to leave the ruling to others. He amused himself with his dwarfs and fools,
watched ballet or dramatic productions or orchestral performances, all of
which he introduced to the Russian court, or rode about in the luxurious
European carriages which were a gift of his last favorite, Artamon Matveev.

Unrest

The first serious problem which Morozov had to face was the dissatisfaction of Russian merchants. English traders enjoyed such favorable treatment in the capital that their activity threatened to bankrupt the Moscow merchants. In other towns the burghers felt the pinch of competition from *streltsy,* churchmen, and even members of the gentry, none of whom had to pay the trading fees which were levied on members of the mercantile class. Morozov answered the pleas of the merchants for relief by trying to force all who sold at retail to pay the traders' fees. He withdrew the privileges from the London merchants, who were expelled from the land in 1649, ostensibly because the English had beheaded their king, Charles I. They were later allowed to ship goods into Arkhangelsk but not to land.

Morozov sought to ease the burden on the treasury by reducing court expenses, cutting salaries, and abolishing unnecessary posts. His sale of grain to Germans and Swedes at a time when many were suffering from want was attributed to a sympathy for foreigners and a callous lack of concern for Russians. He was blamed for peculation by tax collectors and accused of harboring fortune-hunters at court. Petitions against misconduct of public officials seemed never to reach the tsar—at least they went unanswered.

Riots broke out in Moscow in 1648, the leaders demanding that Morozov be banished. The participation of the *streltsy* in the disturbances was ominous. Morozov was dismissed, but the disturbances continued and spread to many cities. The most formidable riots occurred in the commercial cities of Pskov and Novgorod, where the mob held out for four months against a punitive force from Moscow. When the rioters surrendered on the promise that they would not be punished, the nation must have been amazed that the tsar did not go back on his word and work a grim vengeance as Ivan IV would surely have done.

Bondage

The burden of military service and the growing need for revenue, both of which increased enormously in the seventeenth century as Russia fought the powers on her western frontier and expanded her commitments in the Black Sea region, bore down heavily upon a population impoverished by the Time of Troubles. At every meeting of the *Zemskii Sobor* there were persistent complaints against the ruinous taxes and against the venality of public officials which made the financial burden even more unbearable. As the peasants in ever greater numbers fled to the frontier to escape the tax-gatherer and the recruiter, the state faced the danger not only of losing taxpayers but of witnessing the impoverishment of those who stayed behind. The peasants who could not flee were left with the added responsibility of paying the share of those who had deserted. Some chose to surrender their freedom, to become household slaves, in preference to growing insecurity and the threat of starvation. Soon the tax levy upon those who could not run away but who refused to volunteer themselves into slavery became impossible to meet.

The gentry, whose land was valuable only so long as there was adequate labor to till it, were threatened with ruin when their peasants slipped away. Yet they could neither avoid nor reduce their obligation of military service to the state lest they lose their claim to the land. Occasionally even members of the gentry accepted slavery as an easy way out of the obligations they could not meet with their shrinking labor force. Threatened with bankruptcy by the freedom to trade allowed foreigners and privileged Russians, towns-men, too, sought the same escape which the peasants found attractive. They fled to the frontier or volunteered to become slaves.

The pinching loss of revenue and the alarming possibility that there would not be enough manpower to meet military requirements forced the state to bind every class of society to its appointed task and its allotted location. A *Zemskii Sobor* in 1649, most of whose members were of the gentry, appealed to the government for relief from the problems brought about by the vanish-ing population. The government drafted a new law code, the *Ulozhenie* of 1649 which would be the last for nearly two centuries, which legalized bondage in Russia.

The *Ulozhenie* removed the time limitation upon the right of a land-holder to track down and return his peasants to his estate, and assured the gentry that the police power of the state would assist them in doing so. The law provided harsh penalties for those found guilty of sheltering run-aways, and subsequent edicts imposed even more severe punishments upon those who ran away. The peasant, thereafter a serf, was bound not to the soil or to any particular estate but to the landholder. The landlord could sell his serfs off the land, give them away, or lose them in a card game, but he could neither free them nor turn them into slaves. He alone administered justice among them; he even owned the personal effects which they used, for legally they could not own property. The greatest of serf-owners, the state and the church, allowed a degree of self-government to their serf villages. But no serf, no matter who his owner, henceforth would enjoy any rights whatever. He lived outside the law, beyond the protection of the courts which existed solely for the benefit of the proprietary classes. And this deprivation of all their rights was fastened upon the former peasants for all coming generations, for serfdom became hereditary.

The landlord was obliged by the government to collect and transmit the taxes which his serfs continued to pay even though they had lost their status as free peasants. He also had to hold them ready to serve in the army in time of need. Consequently, he was supposed to treat them at least well enough so that they would not run away and to look after their health and well-being. It was assumed that the landlord would feed his bondsmen in time of dearth. By the latter half of the eighteenth century, however, the gentry were ignoring these obligations to their serfs with impunity.

The 1649 code also imposed bondage upon Russian townsmen. All had to remain in the town where they were living in 1649, and restrictions were imposed upon movement from one district to another. Townsmen were forbidden to become slaves. They could not even marry women from another town. On the other hand, the government sought to ease the plight of the merchant by giving him the exclusive right to trade at retail.

The *Ulozhenie* froze the gentry in their status, just as it imposed bondage upon the rest of the population. No member of the class might henceforth become a slave. None might avoid his obligation to render military service. The class became hereditary, since all were born into the class and, with unimportant exceptions, none might enter it except by birth. Only the gentry could own serfs and no other could own land tilled by serf labor. All preferment in the army and in government was reserved to the gentry. From 1649 all distinction between boyars and princely families and gentry tended to break down, for all bore the common duty to serve in the army. Similarly, distinctions between those who held their land by service tenure and those who held it by hereditary right tended to disappear. All came to hold their land by hereditary right and yet were obliged to render military service.

The *Ulozhenie* of 1649 produced little that was new. It codified, and therefore clarified, conditions that had been developing for years and which had tended to crystallize during Michael's reign. Bondage now had full legal recognition. It would continue for over a century for the upper classes and for well over two centuries for the serfs.

Church Reform and Schism

The tsar's favorite churchman was a Moscow prior named Nikon, a man of matchless eloquence and some learning. The boundless ambition of this son of a peasant carried him to the highest church office before he was fifty. In 1652, at the tsar's insistence, Nikon was elected patriarch of Moscow.

Nikon's election heralded a program of reform in the Russian church which Alexis had been considering for some time. A pious man himself, the tsar had been listening for several years to the protest of learned churchmen, particularly of Greek and Latin scholars, that errors had crept into church practice through faulty translation of liturgical books. Through such errors, which had received official sanction in the church council of 1551, Russian priests had fallen into the practice of using two fingers instead of three in the benediction and even justified it as symbolizing the divine and the human nature of Christ. Faulty translation from the Greek had produced a misspelling of the name Jesus, and Russian churchmen persisted in perpetuating the mistake. Attention to the form rather than the substance of Christianity, which had long characterized Russian Orthodoxy, brought stubborn support for the strange practices even when they were shown to be without scholarly foundation.

Soon after his elevation to the patriarchate Nikon ordered the correction of the ritual to conform with the best translations from Greek to Russian of the Byzantine liturgical books upon which Orthodoxy rested. There can be no question that Nikon was right in undertaking the elimination of stupid errors. But, showing neither patience nor tact nor prudence, the patriarch overrode all opposition in the most high-handed way. Churchmen who protested were driven from the pulpit; some were tortured or exiled. Squads of Nikon's henchmen broke into homes to remove and destroy icons or holy images painted in a way which the patriarch considered heretical.

Nikon was not satisfied to order reform of church practice. He presumed to dictate to the tsar in matters having nothing to do with religion, and even claimed the title of sovereign, insisting upon signing state documents as Filaret had done in the previous reign. Alexis finally lost all patience with the patriarch's presumptuous manner and allowed Nikon to be tried by a church council which deposed him and returned him to the monastery. The reforms which he had pushed through were allowed to stand; in fact they were ignored, for the charge upon which he was tried was that he had presumed to put himself above the tsar.

The state church continued ever after to follow the ritual as corrected by Nikon. But many Russians refused to accept the reforms. The Old Believers, or Old Ritualists, as they came to be called, clung to the old erroneous service and looked upon Nikon and the tsars who upheld his way of doing things as devils incarnate. While their religious position could hardly be maintained by intelligent people, the Old Believers in later years were joined by men who resisted tsardom on political grounds as the Old Believers themselves resisted tsardom on religious grounds. Millions embraced the faith that bordered on treason, and in the nineteenth century they were viciously persecuted.

Poland, the Cossacks, and Sweden

A sustained effort by the Polish government to bring the unruly Zaporozhian Cossacks under control culminated in 1638 in termination of the autonomy which Warsaw had allowed the Host. The Polish government named its own officials to replace the traditionally elected hetman and his officers.

By this time Warsaw had awarded much of the fertile steppe to Polish nobles who had brought their serfs with them and who now attempted to impose serfdom upon the Cossack families they found farming the land.

Catholic missionaries had attempted forcibly to convert the Cossacks away from Orthodoxy and, meeting resistance, had won the pope's consent to make Uniats out of the Cossacks. A Uniat practiced his religion according to Orthodox rites but accepted the headship of the pope. Some Cossacks became Uniats, but many became more staunchly Orthodox against this subtle effort to undermine their faith. To the mounting political and economic pressure from Warsaw the addition of the religious issue was enough to provoke rebellion.

In 1649 the Zaporozhian Cossacks chose as their hetman Bogdan Khmelnitsky, whose family had suffered cruelly at the hands of Polish noblemen, to lead them in a fight to recover their autonomy. The entire Ukraine rose in revolt against Polish domination. Peasants fearing the approach of serfdom and even Tatars from the Crimea joined the hetman and his Zaporozhian Host. Khmelnitsky was successful, at least for a while, in obtaining the restoration of Cossack autonomy and raising the number of Cossacks which Warsaw consented to register to forty thousand.

Since the Cossacks could not hope to maintain their independence of the Poles for long, Khmelnitsky offered the Ukraine to Alexis as a protectorate of Russia. But, with the Polish frontier no farther away than Smolensk, Moscow hesitated to receive the gift for fear of inviting attack from the west. Khmelnitsky prodded Alexis to action by threatening to offer his allegiance to the Turkish sultan and even talked of joining the Poles in a war against Russia should Moscow spurn his offer. A *Zemskii Sobor* urged Alexis to receive the Ukraine and, in 1654, Khmelnitsky and the tsar came to terms. Moscow granted autonomy to the Host, recognized sixty thousand registered Cossacks, and received the oath of allegiance. Serfdom was legally extended over the Ukraine as it recently had been approved for Russia. The hetman promised not to deal with Poland or Turkey except through Moscow.

The *Zemskii Sobor* which urged the incorporation of the Ukraine did so in full knowledge that the challenge to Poland would bring war. With enthusiastic national backing and with the help of the Cossacks the Russian armies were everywhere victorious. Vilna, the Lithuanian capital, surrendered to the Russians as did Kovno, Grodno, and Lublin. Smolensk fell. While Muscovite armies ravaged central Poland Khmelnitsky and his Cossacks overran Galicia. King Charles X of Sweden joined the war, seized Warsaw, and claimed the Polish crown. Threatened with annihilation, the Poles asked Alexis for terms. The tsar thought to demand Lithuania but his chief adviser, Nikon, pressed him to take all of Poland as well.

Poland was saved when Russia turned against Sweden. Khmelnitsky deserted Moscow for a Swedish promise of an autonomous duchy of the Ukraine. Russia ultimately lost the Swedish land on the Baltic, including Dorpat, which her armies had captured. When Moscow resumed her war with Poland the Zaporozhian Cossacks, under a bewildering succession of

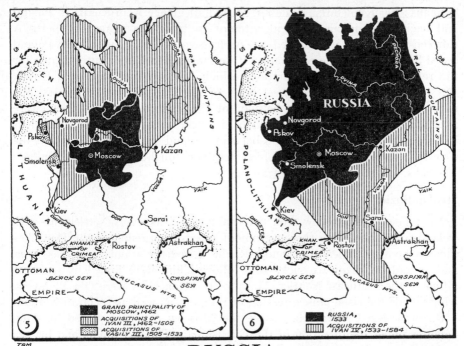

GROWTH OF **RUSSIA**, 1462-1676

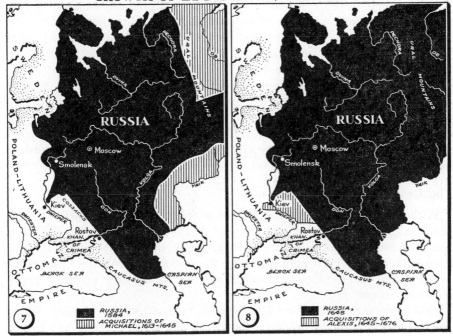

hetmans after Khmelnitsky's death, shifted allegiance from Russia to Poland and back again in an apparent attempt to force the respect of both. A thirteen-year truce was signed at Andrusovo in 1667 by which Poland ceded Smolensk and the east bank of the Dnieper to Russia in exchange for the return of other Polish territory which Moscow had captured. Russia was to occupy Kiev, on the west bank of the Dnieper, for two years. She never gave it up. Again the hetman of the Zaporozhian Cossacks swore allegiance to Moscow, an oath which his successors repeated or refused as it suited their purpose. The wars between Poland and Russia, in which the Crimean Tatars occasionally joined with or fought against the Dnieper Cossacks, left the Ukraine prostrate.

Stenka Razin

No sooner had Moscow won "eternal peace," as every settlement with Poland was called, then the government faced an uprising of the Don Cossacks. One of their leaders, Stenka Razin, raised the standard of class war, and he and the many Cossacks who followed him were joined by peasants all along the southeast frontier. Many of the Don Host were Old Believers, which made the rising an expression of religious as well as social discontent.

Razin besieged Astrakhan, where the Moscow governor placed his land defenses under the direction of the Englishman, Thomas Boyle, and his sea approaches under an Irishman named Butler who commanded the first Russian warship, which had only recently been floated on the Caspian Sea. But Astrakhan fell and Razin made it his capital. From there he extended his control over the Volga and Don basins and even into the Oka toward Moscow. The villages rose to greet him and butchered the neighboring landlords to celebrate their freedom.

For three years Russian armies fought against the risings which Razin's class hatred inspired. At last, the provinces which had joined him were "pacified" after a hundred thousand peasants had been killed. Razin was captured and quartered alive. But the social upheaval which he had led was not soon forgotten either by the landlords whom it had threatened or by the masses whom it had stirred.

The Growth of Western Influence

Without exception the chief advisers to Tsar Alexis were men who appreciated Western technical and cultural superiority over Russia. The number of Westerners brought into Russia to ply their crafts and teach the natives their skills grew rapidly during the middle years of the seventeenth century, and the German, or foreign, quarter of Moscow attracted many Russian visitors.

One contact with the West lay through Poland by way of Kiev, where the theological academy produced the Greek and Latin scholars who helped correct the liturgical books for the Patriarch Nikon. Trade with Sweden provided another important contact with the Western world. By 1665 business relations with the Netherlands had become so important that the government hired an English agent to handle Russian commercial interests there. Dutch shipwrights, carpenters, and sea captains entered the Russian service to instruct, build, and direct the work of Russians assigned to learn Western skills.

The foreign quarter of Moscow set before those who visited it a way of living that attracted some Russians and horrified many others. Western men were clean-shaven or wore only moustaches. Their knee breeches, silk stockings, and shoes contrasted with the long bulky robes and boots which burdened Russians. Their homes were neat and attractively decorated. Their conduct was less coarse and crude than that of Russians. Their women appeared in public gatherings with men. They rode about in fine light carriages and lived in brick houses adorned with flower gardens. There dwelt the families of many Dutch, English, Danish, and German traders, doctors, artisans, and schoolmasters. Many French Protestant refugees lived there along with three thousand Scots—Gordons, Grahams, Hamiltons, Drummonds, Dalziels, Crawfords—who had fled England when Charles I lost his war with Parliament.

A few Muscovites dared to imitate the living they had come to know in the foreign quarter. Not many shaved their beards or set aside their Russian garb, for to do so would have made them conspicuous and perhaps have invited bodily harm. But some redecorated their homes in the Western style and a daring few bought Western carriages. In such homes the seclusion of women came to an end with the abolition of the *terem,* the oriental custom of keeping women in well-born families from the sight of men until their marriage.

The tsar himself sympathized with Western customs. He shocked old Muscovites by introducing his second wife and his daughters to capital society. He hired a German orchestra. He rode through the streets in a Western carriage. But, most ominous of all to those who regarded Western manners with suspicion, he consorted and took counsel with men who believed Russia had much to learn from Western Europe. His chief advisers one after another—Morozov, Nikon, Ordyn-Nashchokin and Matveev—were men of such conviction. Their choice was no accident. Alexis wanted such men around him.

Of those near the tsar who symbolized this fascination with things Western the most outspoken was Athanasy Ordyn-Nashchokin. As head of the *prikaz,* or office of foreign affairs, he arranged peace with Sweden and Poland but left the service rather than condone the retention of Kiev beyond the two years agreed upon in the Truce of Andrusovo. As governor of his native Pskov he sought to remove the preferment which German traders enjoyed in the area and encouraged a combination of Russian merchants to develop trade with Sweden. He was convinced of Russia's need to gain an outlet on the Baltic through which she could establish direct contact with the West. He sought to develop trade relations with Persia over the Caspian and directed the construction of the ship which Stenka Razin later destroyed at Astrakhan. He organized postal communication with Poland.

The old Muscovites, who called him "the foreigner," hated Ordyn-Nashchokin for his respect for Western customs and for his endless criticism of inefficient Russian ways of doing things. He insisted that Russians might learn improved techniques even from their enemies. He deplored the Russian's reliance upon superior officials and urged subordinates to develop initiative of their own. He learned German, Latin, and Polish the better to deal with foreigners. In his unselfish and conscientious devotion to the state in war and peace and as an administrator who sought to bring order to governmental processes, Ordyn-Nashchokin was an outstanding servant to the crown. In his awareness of Russia's backwardness and inefficiency, in his conviction that there need be nothing shameful in "borrowing what is good" even from the heretical West, in his belief that Russia must win an outlet on the Baltic, he was a forerunner of Peter the Great.

FEDOR III

Upon his death in 1676 Alexis was succeeded by his fourteen-year-old invalid son Fedor (1676–1682). The dead ruler's chief adviser, Matveev, proposed that the succession pass over the helpless youth and also his idiot brother Ivan in favor of vigorous young Peter, four-year-old son of Alexis by his second wife. But the boyar duma suspected the proposal was a way of assuring Matveev's continued influence and insisted upon the coronation of Fedor. The new tsar exemplified the growing interest in Western culture, for he had learned Polish and even Latin. Prince Vasily Golitsyn, who managed affairs for the bedridden ruler, knew German, Latin, and Greek.

While leading troops against the Turks and Tatars Golitsyn became convinced that the ineffectiveness of Russian armies was attributable to the *miestnichestvo,* the practice by which military and civil rank in the Moscow state was assigned to boyar families according to their seniority in the service of the tsar. Fedor agreed, and the official book of ranks was publicly burned. Henceforth the tsar's will would determine all official assignments.

Fedor surrounded himself with men of Western sympathies, and his wife even urged courtiers to shave and dress in Western style. But such heresies were still suspect among the vast majority of Russians. Many whispered that Fedor was antichrist for defending such actions, just as they had called his

Ivan III, the Great

Ivan IV, the Terrible

Peter I, the Great

Catherine II, the Great

The Zaporozhe Cossacks drafting a letter to the sultan—from the painting by the Russian artist, Repin.

father and Nikon antichrist for permitting the sacred books to be rewritten by men suspected of knowing Latin.

The reign of Fedor lasted only six years. His death in 1682 again raised the question of the succession. Ivan, the last surviving son of Alexis by his first wife, was witless. There was also Peter, by this time ten years old. And there was a court party to support each of the remaining sons.

SUGGESTED READING

Bain, R. N., *The First Romanovs* (London, Constable, 1905).

——, *Slavonic Europe* (New York, Cambridge University Press, 1908).

Coates, W. P. and Z. K. Coates, *Six Centuries of Russo-Polish Relations* (London, Lawrence & Wishart, 1948).

Conybeare, F. C., *Russian Dissenters* (Cambridge, Harvard University Press, 1921).

Fischer, R. H., *The Russian Fur Trade, 1550–1700* (Berkeley, University of California Press, 1943).

Kliuchevsky, V. O., *A History of Russia,* Vol. III (London, Dent, 1913).

Lantzeff, G. V., *Siberia in the Seventeenth Century* (Berkeley, University of California Press, 1943).

Lyaschenko, P. I., *History of the National Economy of Russia to the 1917 Revolution* (New York, Macmillan, 1949).

Mavor, J., *An Economic History of Russia* (New York, Dutton, 1925).

Palmer, W., *The Patriarch and the Tsar; Testimonies Concerning the Patriarch Nikon* (London, Trübner & Co., 1905).

Vernadsky, G., *Bogdan, Hetman of Ukraine* (New Haven, Yale University Press, 1940).

13

Peter the Great

For seven years after Fedor's death Russia was ruled jointly by Alexis' two young sons, the half brothers Ivan V and Peter I, with Ivan's sister Sophia serving as regent. When Sophia schemed to remove the brothers and become ruler in her own name, Peter drove her into a convent and had his mother assume control. Meanwhile, he spent his days as he had during the regency in the German quarter of Moscow listening to wondrous tales by Swiss, Dutch, Germans, Englishmen, and Scots of what life was like in Western Europe. And he continued playing war games with "play regiments" of his companions in the nearby village of Preobrazhenskoe. There he developed a consuming passion for boats and the sea which made him determined that Russia must have a seacoast.

Peter (1682–1725) captured the Turkish stronghold of Azov on the Dnieper and built a naval base on the Sea of Azov to shelter the new fleet which had helped him win the campaign. But to gain and hold a footing on the Black Sea he must have allies as well as more men skilled in shipbuilding, gunnery, and fortification. He decided to send a great embassy into Western Europe to employ skilled craftsmen and even to go along himself to learn Western techniques and try to win allies.

The tsar and his entourage visited Swedish ports in Germany, Prussia, Holland, England, and Austria. He hired hundreds of craftsmen to return with him to teach Russians the technology of the West. He himself studied mathematics, astronomy, navigation, gunnery, and fortification and learned more of shipbuilding by working with his own hands in Dutch and English shipyards. But he found no one willing to join him in a war with Turkey. On his way home he discussed with the Polish king the feasibility of a war with Sweden. His journey was cut short by news from Moscow of another revolt of the *streltsy*.

Peter completely destroyed the political influence of the *streltsy* by executing hundreds of them and scattering the rest. Then he began a succession of reforms, furiously imposed in the usual way of a benevolent despot, the deliberate intent of which was to modernize and Westernize the nation. He tried to make his subjects Western, at least in appearance, by proscribing beards, ordering the wearing of "German" dress, encouraging the use of tobacco. He even ordered residents of the capital to entertain at gatherings where men and women might dance, play cards, smoke, and drink together. He replaced the old Russian calendar with the Julian calendar, simplified the alphabet, and ordered the printing of books on lay subjects for the first time.

In an attempt to improve the efficiency of the central administration Peter overhauled the machinery of government. He created the Senate to coordinate the offices of administration and to serve as executive in his stead when he had to be away from the capital. He organized a secret police agency charged to reduce tax evasion, check official corruption, and uncover rumblings of discontent. He replaced the old regional *prikazes* with modern functional administrative departments, each headed by a board rather than by an individual, in a vain hope of increasing executive wisdom and reducing peculation. He applied the same principle to church administration, abolishing the patriarchate and replacing it with the Holy Synod presided over by a layman.

In the hope that decentralization might improve tax collection and the drafting of recruits for the army Peter divided the nation into provinces, counties, and districts. Local administrators were responsible to the provincial governors for collection of taxes, recruitment of soldiers, maintenance of order, and dispensation of justice. City councils, elected by the merchant class, were set up to administer similar matters in urban areas.

Peter modernized the army along Western lines and built up a standing force of three hundred thousand men, the largest in Europe, by the year of his death. He created the Russian Navy by building or buying eight hundred vessels and manning them with thirty thousand sailors. To reward merit and improve command he granted hereditary nobility to all regardless of social origin who became commissioned officers.

To finance the armed forces and the wars which went on during every year of the reign but one, the government debased the coinage, monopolized the sale of many commodities, and levied excise taxes on a host of goods and services. The greatest producer of revenue, however, was the new "soul tax," a direct levy upon every male serf. Each landowner collected the tax from his serfs and received the right to forbid their leaving the estate without his written permission. To reduce Russia's costly reliance upon foreign sources of finished materials Peter established factories to turn out weapons and equipment and even consumers' goods which Russians would otherwise buy abroad. By developing the navy he hoped that imports would enter the country in Russian ships. His new capital, St. Petersburg, became a thriving port. Peter organized a rudimentary school system, whose curriculum emphasized practical subjects, for the primary purpose of teaching Russians the skills necessary to make the nation economically and militarily independent of foreign instruction and production.

Poland and Denmark joined Russia in 1700 in an attack upon Sweden, but his two allies were knocked out of the war or driven on the defensive and Peter was left to fight on alone. A Russian effort to capture the Swedish fort of Narva failed and the Swedish King Charles XII scattered Peter's army. For the next several years the tsar patiently reassembled a better army, bought new artillery, and launched a fleet on the Baltic. He overran Swedish provinces on the Gulf of Finland with little opposition while Charles XII was busying himself with Polish affairs. Peter started to build St. Petersburg, and then offered Charles peace if he could keep the site of his projected capital. The Swedish king spurned the offer and the war went on.

In 1707 Charles advanced toward Moscow but was forced to turn south by Russian resistance, by the failure of a subordinate to bring supplies from the Baltic, and by the invitation of the Cossack hetman Mazeppa to rouse the Ukraine. At Poltava Peter caught up with the Swedes and routed them. Charles escaped to Turkey, with whom Russia was soon at war when the sultan refused to surrender him. Peter's march into Turkish territory ended disastrously, and the tsar bought peace by returning Azov to the sultan.

The war with Sweden dragged on another dozen years after Poltava, during which the Russians had things their own way. There were naval victories over the Swedish fleet, and Russian armies overran Finland, occupied all the Swedish provinces on the southeastern Baltic coast, and drove to within sight of Stockholm. By the Peace of Nystadt in 1721 Russia returned Finland to Sweden but kept Livonia, Estonia, Ingria, and the Karelian Isthmus. Peter had his window on Europe. He celebrated the victory by accepting the title of emperor.

The Turkish and Swedish wars and the speed with which the reforms had been applied had settled a heavy burden upon the nation. Masses had run off to the frontier to escape the recruiter and the taxgatherer. There had been several revolts that had required organized expeditions to suppress. After Poltava many who resented Peter's policies looked to his son Alexis to undo the revolution that his father had forced upon the nation. Probably without meaning to, Alexis encouraged that hope. He ran away, but Peter brought him back and tortured him to reveal names. Hundreds were executed and Alexis was sentenced to death.

Peter altered the succession law to permit the sovereign to decide who should follow him. But he died in 1725 without indicating his own choice. Catherine's coronation as empress in 1724 was taken to indicate that Peter wanted his wife to rule after him.

THE REGENCY

Fedor left behind a brother Ivan, a sickly idiot subject to fits and nearly blind, and six healthy sisters, all children of Alexis by his first wife Maria Miloslavsky, as well as Peter, Alexis' son by his second wife Natalia Naryshkin. The Patriarch Joachim asked the crowd gathered in Red Square which of the sons should become tsar and the people, probably prompted by pressure from Naryshkin supporters, named Peter. His mother and other relatives and the patriarch promised a rule of favorites similar to the situation which had become so familiar under the early Romanovs.

A few days later some of the *streltsy* regiments massed outside the Kremlin to demand the punishment of their commanding officers for supposedly withholding their pay. The government meekly gave in to their demands, thereby encouraging others to take advantage of its weakness. The Miloslavsky clan, led by Alexis' twenty-five-year-old daughter Sophia, saw an opportunity to drive the Naryshkins from the palace. Sophia promised the *streltsy* pay increases and whispered that the rightful tsar, her brother Ivan, was in danger of being murdered by the Naryshkins. The *streltsy* stormed the Kremlin, ignored the fact that Ivan was obviously safe, hacked to pieces their unpopular officers, and cut down many of Peter's supporters, including most of the Naryshkin family, while Peter and his mother huddled in fear for their own lives. The soldiers roamed the streets of Moscow killing boyars and urging the masses to rise against bondage. At the insistence of the *streltsy*, a *Zemskii Sobor* was called to reorder the succession. It was the last time the assembly of the land would ever meet. Ivan and Peter became co-tsars by acclamation. The fat, hairy-faced, repulsive Sophia consented to serve as regent. For their service to the Miloslavskys the *streltsy* received a gift of money and an increase in pay.

Throughout the seven-year regency of Sophia the *streltsy* were a constant threat to stable government. They encouraged unrest among the Cossacks. They called for an end to the reforms of Nikon, for many of them were Old Believers. They threatened the extermination of the boyars as a class and demanded an end to serfdom. They fought pitched battles with other regiments led by officers loyal to the government. They threatened to drive Sophia into a convent and raise to the throne their own favorite commander. They seized the Kremlin and forced the regent and her brother Ivan to seek refuge in the Trinity Monastery north of Moscow. Finally, loyal troops subdued the *streltsy* and they were let off without serious punishment as though the government did not dare to put them in their place.

Aside from her unattractive features Sophia was a remarkable woman. Her father Alexis had allowed tutors to enter the *terem* to teach his daughter Polish and Latin. Her shameless love for Prince Vasily Golitsyn, her chief adviser, may be attributed to the Prince's known enthusiasm for Western learning. The two were suspected of wanting to return Russia to the Roman church. Sophia's consuming ambition led her to assume the title of sovereign along with her brothers and finally to contemplate the removal of Ivan and Peter to leave herself alone upon the throne.

In 1683 the Polish king, Jan Sobieski, joined with Austria to stop the Turkish drive into Europe at the very gates of Vienna. Determined to organize a Christian crusade against the Moslems, Sobieski brought Venice and the Pope into the alliance. Russia joined the league in 1686 in return for another "perpetual peace" with Poland. Moscow promised to attack the Porte and, by the payment of a hundred and fifty thousand rubles, received clear title to Kiev, which she had taken temporarily at the Truce of Andrusovo a generation earlier.

Golitsyn, Sophia's paramour and foreign minister who had arranged the alliance with Poland, led a hundred thousand Russians to attack the outpost of Turkish power in the Crimea. When the enemy fired the steppe grass, Golitsyn fell back in confusion leaving a third of his force behind. Early in 1689 Sophia's favorite led another army through blizzards and across floods to the gateway of the Crimean peninsula. Then he withdrew without accomplishing anything more than warning the Tatars and Turks by his appearance there that they must some day lose control of the steppe. Sophia only made herself ridiculous and unpopular by acclaiming her lover a victorious hero. The Western Europeans who accompanied Golitsyn knew, and soon all Moscow knew, that the prince had only managed to avoid disaster and had achieved nothing.

This year of 1689 brought another military and diplomatic defeat to the regent's government. By the Treaty of Nerchinsk Moscow surrendered the basin of the Amur, to whose banks her troops and pioneers had driven only to be turned back by the Chinese. However, the treaty with China, which would last for a century and a half, provided for trade relations across the frontier. Tea, the chief import after 1689, became the Russian national drink. The treaty also had the effect of turning Russian interest in East Asia toward the northeast corner of the continent, toward the Bering Strait, and eventually across it to Alaska.

Sophia thought to save herself and her lover Golitsyn by unseating Ivan and Peter and seizing the throne for herself. In 1689 she planned that the *streltsy* who had brought her to power seven years earlier should murder her brothers if that should be necessary and proclaim her tsarina. Peter escaped and quickly marshalled the force sufficient to thwart his sister's plans. Sophia was driven into a convent. With the *streltsy*, who had threatened to interfere with the succession, the young tsar would deal later in his usual decisive way.

PETER'S YOUTH

Peter was not quite four when his father died. It is likely that had Alexis lived another decade the child would have received an excellent education, probably directed by Western tutors. Fedor placed Peter under the instruction of Nikita Zotov, a man of modest intellect recommended by a conservative churchman who praised Zotov's familiarity with the religious works which prospective tsars normally were expected to learn. The tutor, whose chief skill lay in the consumption of prodigious quantities of liquor, taught his pupil how to read and write and little else. After four years of such instruction Zotov was withdrawn; Peter's formal education had come to an end.

Fedor's death brought Peter into the midst of the struggle for power between the Miloslavskys and his mother's family, the Naryshkins. During the *streltsy* revolt which followed his election as tsar, the child witnessed atrocities which gave him nightmares ever after. He stood quaking in his mother's arms while one of his uncles was dragged into the streets and savagely butchered. He watched horrified while a courtier of whom he was fond was hacked to bits by the mob. There can be little wonder that he developed a nervous twitching which stayed through life with him. From that time on he was never able to sleep alone, but needed some strong man to cling to for comfort and reassurance.

While Sophia ruled, Peter and his mother—unwelcome at court—lived just outside Moscow on a royal estate in the village of Preobrazhenskoe. Only on rare occasions, when the tsars had to preside at a formal reception, did Peter return to the Kremlin to sit splendidly robed beside his imbecile brother on the dual throne behind which Sophia crouched, screened from view, to prompt the youthful rulers with the proper remarks. Between such state appearances, which Peter hated, the boy played and roamed the neighborhood of Preobrazhenskoe free of all restraint. His mother could not control him, and Sophia showed no concern for his welfare or conduct.

Peter gathered about him a band of boys his own age, some from noble families but most of them from servant or middle-class homes. These playmates—"stableboys," some people contemptuously called them—Peter led on riotous pranks and escapades that terrorized the neighborhood. The next year, when Peter was eleven, he organized his friends into a "play regiment" which he drilled and later accompanied on maneuvers. He ordered arms and uniforms and even artillery from Moscow, and Sophia, satisfied to keep him occupied, met every request he submitted. The boys built a wooden fort which they named Pressburg, complete with bastions and ditches. As the "regiment" grew older the play became more serious, and the assaults on the "fortress of Pressburg" often produced casualties. "Bombardier Peter," as the young tsar called himself, enjoyed setting off fireworks and later firing cannon. From a Dutchman, Franz Timmerman, Peter learned the fundamentals of geometry, military engineering, and artillery. He became an enthusiastic drummer and to the end of his life liked to march in parades beating on his drum while others rode in state.

When Peter was fourteen he and his companions found an old English sailboat in storage. Timmerman explained its operation, and Peter launched the rotting craft in the river that flowed through Preobrazhenskoe. Later he moved the new toy to a lake eighty miles away and there, under the direction of the German shipmaster Brandt, built other boats, toiling at the work alongside Dutch carpenters brought from the foreign quarter of Moscow.

Such radical and dangerous pastimes alarmed Peter's mother, who thought to turn her son to a settled life by having him marry at the age of sixteen. But the match with Eudoxia Lopukhin distracted Peter only momentarily, and within a few weeks he had left his wife to return to his boats. Five years later the young tsar stood at Arkhangelsk and looked out fascinated upon the sea. He went on board foreign ships in the harbor, talked and drank with Dutch seamen who called him "skipper," and labored on a ship of his own, the "St. Paul" which was launched in 1694. Meanwhile he ordered a forty-four-gun frigate from a naval yard in Holland. He learned the Dutch language, wore the dress of a Dutch sailor, and affected the walk and the manner of a sailor the rest of his life. He travelled by sea rather than by land whenever there was a choice, and slept on board rather than on land whenever he was near the water.

From Preobrazhenskoe Peter often visited in the foreign, or German, quarter of Moscow and became fascinated with Western manners and the endless stories of Western life. Of the many close attachments he made there, one was with the Scottish adventurer Patrick Gordon. Now a Russian general nearly forty years older than Peter, Gordon had served the tsars since the time of Alexis, at times as a diplomat and at others as a military adviser. Another of Peter's intimate friends was the Swiss Francis Lefort, twenty years older than Peter, a man notorious for his drinking prowess in an age renowned for drunkenness. From 1690 on these foreigners were the tsar's constant companions; he appointed them admirals in spite of the fact that neither had any experience with the sea.

Peter chose his friends from all nationalities and all classes. Some of his Russian companions—men like Fedor Romodanovsky and Michael Golitsyn and the Dolgorukys—were from princely families which had served Moscow for centuries. Others were from humble homes. Alexander Menshikov, who became one of the most wealthy and influential men of his time, had sold pies in the streets of Moscow before Peter noticed him. Most of these men served the tsar, drank with him, and took his violent abuse until their death, for Peter did not often degrade and destroy those around him as Ivan the Terrible had done.

THE DRUNKEN COUNCIL OF FOOLS

Before he was twenty Peter proved himself an accomplished drinker. Visits to the German quarter or gatherings at Gordon's big house in Preobrazhenskoe usually ended as drunken revels. He found keen delight in forcing some man or girl who could not keep up with him to drain a huge glass of vodka without removing it from the lips.

Always something of a mocker, a jester, a drunkard, and a profligate, Peter gave full rein to excess of every kind when at eighteen he organized the "Drunken Council of Fools." He himself drafted the detailed ritual for its drunken spectacles. As "Pope-Patriarch," his former tutor, the stupid Nikita Zotov, led the group in its celebrations dedicated to Venus and Bacchus. A group of stutterers dressed in cardinal's robes waited upon Zotov, whose house was called "the Vatican." Zotov presided from a throne made of wine casks and decorated with bottles. His "election" was celebrated in a parade of mockery, the "Pope-Patriarch" riding on a huge wine vat drawn by four oxen, preceded by Peter dressed as a sailor beating the drum, attended by dwarfs dressed as monks, and followed by a train of assorted carts pulled by goats, pigs, bears, and reindeer.

Another important official in the "Drunken Council" was Fedor Romodanovsky, who was crowned "Prince-Tsar, King of Pressburg" after the play fortress built at Preobrazhenskoe. Throughout his life Peter maintained the pose that Romodanovsky was the real ruler, addressing him as "Your Majesty" in correspondence which Peter signed "Bombardier Peter" or "Rear Admiral Peter Mikhailov." Peter reported to the "Prince-Tsar" on the success of campaigns and received in mock gratitude from the "King of Pressburg" an occasional promotion in naval or military rank.

The sessions of the "Drunken Council" were conducted in mock seriousness and rigid formality. A precise and lewd ritual was performed when the "Princess-Abbess" passed around the ballots for the election of a new "Pope-Patriarch" after Zotov's death. The lowest sort of fun appealed to Peter—belching contests, filthy jokes, comical funerals—and the cruellest sort of punishments—impalings, floggings, roastings, and beard-burnings. He loved pageants and triumphs and fireworks displays, always working at some new rocket whose discharge might decapitate an onlooker. He surrounded himself with fools, misshapen and disfigured oddities both man and beast, idiots, and a score of dwarfs—one of them named Lenin. Peter himself was six feet nine inches tall. He took cruel pleasure in embarrassing his dwarfs, whose antics fascinated him. The contrast must have been striking when the giant Peter walked in parade followed by midgets riding in tiny coaches drawn by ponies.

Peter had many mistresses, one of whom, Catherine, had been mistress to Menshikov and many other men before Peter appropriated her to himself. He later married her—two of their daughters served as flower girls at the ceremony—and raised her to be empress after he had accepted the title "Emperor of All the Russias."

Peter's admirers have insisted that there was method in all this madness. They reason that the orgies of the "Drunken Council of Fools" were calculated to hold up to scorn both the Roman church and the Orthodox. They point to Peter's probable preference for Lutheranism and his lusty singing in church choirs to prove that he wanted to ridicule not all Christianity but only those branches which entertained political ambitions. His mockery of the institution of monarchy, in quite the same way that Ivan IV had mocked it, is not so easily accounted for. The apologists explain Peter's enthusiasm for work with his hands and his insistence on "going through the ranks" in everything he took up as deliberate attempts to set his people an example of hard work and persistence. They count up the professions which he claimed to master—gunnery, carpentry, engineering, shipbuilding, joinery, dentistry, surgery, and others—as though his interest in them were a matter of studied policy. They look for calculated results in the tsar's every word and action.

Peter's detractors on the other hand have insisted that the man never did anything by plan, that there was no sense or order in some of his so-called reforms, that his drunken revels simply reflected the depth of his debauchery, that he was simply a debased and cruel despot. But even these do not deny that the impact he made upon his country was greater than that of any Russian ruler before or since his time.

THE TURKISH WAR

With the backing of the *streltsy* regiments in Moscow Sophia made a move in 1689 to set aside Ivan and Peter and seat herself on the throne. Peter escaped to the Trinity Monastery and called his "play regiments" to his side. The plan collapsed when Sophia's lover Golitsyn, the Patriarch Joachim, and even some of the *streltsy* deserted the regent. Sophia was packed off to a convent and the nation continued under the two tsars.

For a while the government was directed by Peter's mother Natalia and her Naryshkin relatives while Peter, seventeen years old, returned to his war games, his fireworks, his ships, and his drinking bouts. Natalia died five years later and Peter drowned his grief at the news by a wild orgy at Lefort's house. Now Peter had to leave his play and take over the direction of affairs in Moscow. But the "play regiments" went with him to become the first of the Guards, the Preobrazhensky and Semenovsky regiments being named for the villages where they had fought their sham battles.

Immediately Peter decided, evidently upon Lefort's advice, to challenge Turkish power on the Black Sea. He may have wanted simply a more suitable sea for sailing his ships than the White Sea, which was frozen over nine months of the year. The Baltic was firmly in Swedish hands. Golitsyn's campaigns in Sophia's time had shown the futility of trying to drive the Tatars, the sultan's vassals, from the Crimea by crossing the Isthmus of Perekop.

In the spring of 1695 Peter opened his drive to the Black Sea with a feint by Cossacks and old-fashioned militia against the Ukraine. The main force, made up of *streltsy* and the former play regiments, moved down the Volga and into the lower Don to besiege the Turkish stronghold at Azov. This suggested to Peter a canal to join the Volga and the Don, but the project was completed only by the Communists after World War II. Lefort and Gordon led the infantry against Azov while "Bombardier Peter" commanded the artillery. Attempts to storm the fortress failed and the siege was abandoned in the fall.

Peter returned to Moscow, not to carouse and play with fireworks, but to prepare for another campaign against the Turks, determined that this one must succeed. He sent off to Austria and Prussia for engineers, miners, and sappers. He ordered a galley from Holland and proposed to build others like it along the lower Don for a combined land-sea assault upon Azov. He sent the Guards regiments, along with all the workers he could round up, to Voronezh to fell trees and build boats. Peter moved into a two-room hut at Voronezh to supervise the project, working hard alongside the men by day and drinking hard with Lefort and the others at night.

The fleet, with Peter commanding a squadron, slipped down the Don into the Sea of Azov and blocked off the port from any possible Turkish relief. The fortress of Azov surrendered after a two-months' siege. Peter's new army and navy had won a notable victory. There was a parade of triumph in Moscow led by the naval and military commanders, Admiral Lefort and "Generalissimo" Shein, in magnificently gilded sledges. "Captain Peter" followed on foot.

Peter ordered construction of a naval base near Azov, naming it Taganrog. And he swore to launch a great fleet on the Black Sea to station at the new base. This, of course, would mean long bitter war with the Turks. Young Russians must go west to England and Holland to learn more about shipbuilding and fortification and gunnery. Fifty sons of good families were sent off at once. But the nation also needed allies. An embassy must visit the Western courts to urge a European alliance against the infidel Turk. Peter would go himself.

Only days before Peter and his entourage left for the West a plot against his life was uncovered. Several officers of the *streltsy* and some boyars, most of them Old Believers who abhorred Peter's consorting with foreigners and his decision to leave the country, schemed to assassinate the tsar and to restore Sophia as regent for Peter's young son Alexis, for the witless Ivan had died the year before. Under torture, six of the ringleaders confessed the plot and added that Sophia's late uncle, Ivan Miloslavsky, had urged the regent to kill Peter. The six were beheaded and the blood of these traitors allowed to flow down upon Miloslavsky's body, which had been dug up and dragged by pigs through the streets to the place of execution.

THE WESTERN JOURNEY

A great embassy of two hundred well-born Russians, servants, guards, chaplains, clowns, and dwarfs crossed the frontier in March, 1697, and headed for the Swedish port of Riga. Lefort officially led the embassy; the tsar went along incognito as "Peter Mikhailov" who wanted to learn ship-building. The Swedish commander at Riga respected the tsar's incognito so carefully that Peter was not formally recognized and was not allowed to tour the fortifications. He so resented the affront that he later recalled it as an excuse for war with Sweden. At Libau, in Courland, Peter first looked out upon the Baltic.

The embassy moved on to Koenigsberg, the tsar travelling by sea while the rest moved overland. There a Prussian colonel gave the tsar lessons in gunnery and awarded a certificate of proficiency to his royal pupil. Peter was fascinated with strange instruments of torture he had never seen and was disappointed that there was no offender upon whom to demonstrate their use. He lingered in Koenigsberg waiting for news of the election of a new king of Poland and wrote to Romodanovsky, his "King of Pressburg," to move Russian troops to the Polish border if Augustus, the Russian candidate, should lose the election.

When the Polish election turned out to Peter's liking the tsar moved on to Berlin, where he took another short course in military tactics and received another diploma. Near Hanover he dined with the beautiful electress of Brandenburg, who was fascinated by this giant of a man with a wart on his cheek and a tic in his face, whose head jerked and whose eyes rolled, who affected the slouching walk of a sailor and who proudly displayed the work callouses on his rough hands that were never still. He did not know what to do with his napkin and was awkward and shy. He drank too much, but the wine relaxed him and gave him confidence. He talked of his passion for fireworks and told of his plans for a fleet. Then he called for his dwarfs but drove them off with a broom when their ribaldry shocked his hostess.

Now Peter was impatient to visit Holland, the home of many artisans in

Russian service. He passed through Hamburg, spurning the formal reception arranged for him, and boarded a ship for Zaandam near Amsterdam. There he lived in the cottage of a blacksmith who had worked at shipbuilding in Voronezh the year before. For a few days "Master Peter, carpenter of Zaandam," as the tsar was pleased to be called, worked in the shipyards and drank Dutch beer at the local tavern.

After a week in Zaandam Peter went to Amsterdam, where he stayed four months. There he studied mathematics, architecture, astronomy, navigation, and fortification. He visited museums and bought stuffed swordfish, crocodiles, and embalmed human freaks with which to start a museum of his own. He learned a little of engraving and printing. He visited hospitals and attended the anatomy lectures of a famous surgeon. He watched a dentist at work and supplied himself with instruments with which he later practiced on his own subjects. He filled notebooks with information on ship construction, sailed small boats on the inland sea, and worked as ship's carpenter on a galley for himself. He visited with the Duke of Marlborough and met the English King William III, who invited him to London to learn more of shipbuilding.

Peter crossed the Channel to England in January, 1698, and stayed there another four months. He attended the opening of Parliament, received the Doctor of Laws degree from Oxford University, visited the Mint, the Greenwich Observatory, and the Tower of London. He bought a coffin to send home for the edification of Russian coffin-makers. He had his portrait painted by Kneller. He studied clockmaking, discussed theology with Anglican bishops, visited the arsenal at Woolwich, and roamed the shipyards at Deptford. He and his companions occupied the house of John Evelyn on the Thames and reduced it nearly to ruins with their drunken frolics.

From London Peter and his company travelled to Vienna, where again his incognito was so faithfully observed as to irritate the tsar. He expected to go on to Venice to learn still more about shipbuilding and to urge the government to hold fast to the alliance against the Porte. But word came to him in Vienna that the *streltsy* were again in revolt. Romodanovsky had the uprising under control, but Peter hurried home to punish the leaders. He had been gone from Russia eighteen months.

In the capitals of the West Peter found no one to listen to his appeal for a Christian crusade against the Turks. William III and his allies were between wars in their determination to thwart the ambition of Louis XIV, but the War of the Spanish Succession would soon embroil the powers once again. London even hoped that Vienna would come to terms with the Porte and join the alliance against France. The powers were willing to encourage Peter to continue his war with Turkey, for then the sultan would not be able to help his friend, the French king, but they would give Russia no aid.

As an educational venture for the tsar himself, the western journey was a great success. Peter returned to Russia determined to impose upon his people the techniques and even the manners of the West. He left scores of his companions in England and Holland to continue their schooling, and he hired hundreds of Scottish, English, Dutch, and German carpenters, shipwrights, sailors, doctors, teachers, cooks, musicians, and gardeners to return to Russia with him.

In August, 1698, Peter was back in Moscow. He had been the first Russian ruler to travel abroad in nine centuries. And he would again visit the West, which symbolized to him the skills and the learning in which he knew his own land to be so backward.

SUPPRESSION OF THE *STRELTSY*

The *streltsy* decided in the spring of 1698 to take advantage of the tsar's absence in Western Europe to restore the relatively gentle government of the regency. Where these privileged regiments had grown accustomed to a life of ease and indolence through long periods between occasional short campaigns, Peter kept them away from their families always busy at something. When not fighting the Crimean Tatars, the *streltsy* were set to building ships at Voronezh or throwing up fortifications on the Sea of Azov or marching to the western frontier to interfere in Polish politics. They saw their influence at court slipping away as Peter favored the new Guards regiments which were intensely loyal to him and infinitely more reliable. The crowning insult came when the *streltsy* regiments were moved from Moscow to new posts around the Sea of Azov.

Leaders of the plot read out to the *streltsy* regiments in South Russia a letter purporting to come from Sophia asking them to join her in reviving the regency. The men set off for Moscow determined to raze the German quarter and to kill the government leaders.

Patrick Gordon met the *streltsy* south of Moscow with a well-armed force of loyal troops and captured the rebels without losing a man of his own. Scores were tortured to death on the spot and others were strung on gibbets along the highways as a warning to any who would challenge the regime. The rest were thrown into dungeons to await the tsar's return.

Preobrazhenskoe, where the trials took place, became a scene of unspeakable horror for two months during the autumn of 1698. Peter set up fourteen torture chambers to deal with the rebels and even with their families. For days on end men and women were flogged or roasted or garroted or buried alive. Hundreds were beheaded, Peter occasionally swinging the axe himself and immensely enjoying the bungling efforts of his favorites, whom he ordered to assist him in the gory task. Then there would be days of feasting and drinking, after which the tsar would return to the torture chambers and the scaffolds. For five months a thousand bodies lay where they had been cut down from the gibbets or kicked aside from the headsman's block. Early in 1699 in South Russia Peter settled in the same vicious way with the mutinous *streltsy* who had stayed behind at Azov while the others had marched on Moscow. Hundreds more died before Peter's rage was satisfied.

The sixteen *streltsy* regiments involved in the mutiny were disbanded, and their men and officers alike were denied the right to enlist in any branch of the service. Families of the executed men were driven from their homes and sent wandering over the land. Only a few of the regiments were allowed to survive a little while longer until 1705. But the political power of the *streltsy* was completely destroyed.

THE PETRINE REFORMS

Peter was so impatient to pattern the ways and manners of his own land after those he had seen in the West that he began shaving beards even before he settled with the *streltsy*. Aside from the fact that Peter could raise no beard of his own, he reckoned the beard to be the foremost symbol of Russia's backwardness and superstition. The day after his return home he gathered the men at court about him and, with a large pair of shears, cut away their beards. Those who were not available for this first trimming were invited to a banquet and there were shorn by the tsar's favorite buffoon, Turgenev. Peter realized that he could not personally shear every Russian man and keep him shorn. So he issued an *ukaz* that men of the gentry who chose to keep a beard must pay a tax of a hundred rubles and wear a badge showing that they had paid the tax, and that every peasant who entered the gates of a town must pay a kopek or surrender his beard. The beard quickly lost all popularity among the upper classes; it became the mark of a peasant down to the twentieth century.

On the journey across Europe Peter had noticed that Westerners had mocked and jeered at the bulky, uncomfortable Russian clothes—the Russian who carried a handkerchief hid it under his hat because he had no pockets; his wide sleeves were forever dipping into the soup; his bulky garments impeded his freedom of movement. When the tsar finally tired of lopping off the heads of the *streltsy* he set about—with his own hands, as was always his way—to alter the cut of Russian attire. He snipped off the long sleeves of his attendants' robes and ordered those around him to adopt Western dress. Police officials in every town Peter visited received orders to cut at knee length the long belted gown of every man who entered the town gates. The wearing of Western-style clothing became obligatory for government workers and members of the gentry. Peter himself preferred the garb of a Dutch sailor but occasionally appeared at receptions wearing buckled shoes, breeches, and the Western short coat. Within a year or so this "German manner" of dress was popular in the capital and among the upper classes generally. But to the end of tsardom the peasant continued to dress as he had done for centuries in a long shirt and baggy trousers stuffed into high boots.

All Russians, without distinction of class, took more readily to another of Peter's innovations. The tsar picked up pipe smoking from the Dutch and English merchants in the foreign quarter of Moscow and broke convention by allowing the importation of tobacco even before his trip to the West. When in England he sold a monopoly of the right to import tobacco into Russia to Lord Carmarthen for eighteen thousand pounds sterling. Peter dismissed the warning that the patriarch might object to this invitation to use tobacco with the comment that the patriarch was not a customs officer.

Peter's father Alexis had abolished the *terem,* the isolation of women of the royal family. Now Peter extended the emancipation of women to all classes of capital society. To insure the social mingling of women with men and to force the adoption of Western manners Peter drafted regulations for gatherings of men and women for conversation and entertainment. Three times a week, at any large house in St. Petersburg chosen by the tsar or by the police who saw that his orders were obeyed, the host must open his home to nobles, merchants, army and navy officers, and even workmen and their wives. He must provide refreshments, playing cards, and music and make available a room for dancing, another for conversation and smoking, another for chess and card games. The guests were required to busy themselves at one of the pastimes offered or be condemned to drain "the eagle," an enormous goblet filled with wine or vodka.

On January 1, 1700, Peter ordered the celebration of New Year's Day and proclaimed the Julian calendar. Theretofore Russians had observed the first of September as New Year's and had dated time from the supposed creation of the world. The year 7208 according to the ancient Russian calendar became the year 1700 by the Julian calendar. Peter's prejudice against the papacy was too great to allow him to adopt the Gregorian calendar. By 1700 the Julian calendar was already incorrect by eleven days, but from then on Russians at least had the year right. The nation clung to the Julian reckoning until after the 1917 Revolution, by which time the error had spread to thirteen days.

Soon after his return from the West Peter ordered several books in Russian from a Dutch publisher. The difficulties of setting type in Slavonic characters discouraged the Dutchman and Peter set up a publishing house of his own. At the same time he simplified the alphabet by eliminating useless characters and making the letters more nearly like Latin. The new characters were to be used in all lay books. From that time on only religious publications appeared in the old style, which came to be known as "Church Slavonic." It was typical of Peter's concern with practical things that the first book to appear in the new orthography was a geometry text. In 1703 the first Russian newspaper, the Moscow *Journal*, began to acquaint the people with the new alphabet.

From the moment of his return from the West to near the time of his death Peter was busy changing Russian ways of doing things in one fashion or another. Some of the reforms were far-reaching, others trivial. Some of them failed or were abandoned by Peter himself, while others lasted to the end of tsardom and beyond. Some were only mildly, others completely successful. Many were ordered with little thought of their effect, for Peter seldom planned far ahead or considered consequences, but acted often on impulse. Many of the reforms were adopted during the long war with Sweden in an effort simply to win that war. With few exceptions, the reforms were of a practical sort or aimed at a practical result.

Reforms in the central and local administration were scattered over many years and make sense only when arranged in a pattern. Peter spent more time than any other Russian ruler moving from one end of the country to the other and travelling abroad. His absence from the capital often left the administration in chaos, since the center of authority was wherever the tsar happened to be, and allowed officials to settle back into their usual sloth. The *Zemskii Sobor* never met again after 1682. The boyar duma, for which Peter felt only contempt, ceased to meet and simply faded out of existence. It was replaced temporarily by an "intimate council" of the tsar's favorites who gave him advice when he asked for it. But Peter saw the need for a permanent body to head the administration in the capital when he was away at the front.

When Peter left for the Turkish campaign in 1711 he created the Senate of nine appointees whose task it was to head the administration during his absence. The Senate was to act in a judicial capacity, serving as a sort of supreme court. Its chief concern, however, was to centralize the gathering of taxes and the levy of troops, for Peter expected the Senate to improve the marshalling of the country's resources for war. The Senate was supposed to receive an accounting from the "chief fiscal," the head of a body of five hundred men who served as combination revenue agents, secret police, and spies, whose main function was to wring every last bit of taxes from the people. Finally, the Senate was to direct and supervise the governments of the eight provinces into which Russia had been divided in the hope of improving the collection of taxes and the levy of troops. But the power of some provincial governors who happened to be the tsar's favorites—Menshikov was governor of St. Petersburg province and Romodanovsky of Moscow— was greater than that of the Senate, which was unable to check Menshikov's peculation or Romodanovsky's capricious cruelty. The inability of the Senate to cope with the many tasks assigned to it led Peter to refashion the entire structure of the central government.

Peter swept away the old administrative offices, the *prikazes* which had multiplied in such random profusion while Moscow was growing from a small princely domain to a national state with a huge sprawling territory. In their place he created modern government departments, called colleges, to deal with the various functions of administration. Each college was staffed at first with a Russian president and a non-Russian vice president and clerks—Western Europeans imported for the purpose, Baltic Germans conscripted in districts conquered by the army, and even Swedish prisoners of war. As fast as Russians learned the work from these foreign experts, the foreigners were dismissed or assigned elsewhere. Each college was headed by a board of several men, usually eleven, rather than by one man as had been the case with the *prikaz*. Peter supposed that many heads would be wiser than one and that there would be less dishonesty when all checked on each other. There were nine colleges at first, three to handle financial matters, another for interior and justice, and one each for industry, commerce, foreign affairs, war, and the admiralty. Others were added later. While the collegial principle was used in Denmark, Prussia, and occasionally in England, Peter borrowed it from Sweden and closely followed the Swedish regulations in setting up his own offices. That he was at war with Sweden at the time did not in the least deter him from appropriating his enemy's customs when he found them best suited to his own needs.

With the reorganization of administrative departments the Senate assumed a new character. No longer need it bog down in details. One of its functions was to coordinate the work of the various colleges and to supervise the operation of each. Another was to serve as a supreme court to which cases judged by the College of Interior and Justice might be appealed. A third important task which the Senate now could accept was the drafting of legislation, for the orders which rolled off Peter's tongue in an endless stream were often no more than ideas which had to be thought out in detail before they could be applied.

To insure that the senators would not shirk their responsibilities Peter appointed an inspector-general whose job it was to keep the members of the Senate steadily at their work and to see that their decrees were carried out. When this precaution did not always prove effective Peter ordered officers of the Guards to be stationed in the council chamber to warn the senators when they grew lax and to report repeated laxity to the tsar. But there were powerful men in the Senate, the most influential in the land, who might overawe even an officer of the Guards. So Peter finally created the office of procurator-general of the Senate, a sort of viceroy who presided over Senate meetings, kept things moving along, and signed every decree. The procurator-

general had a procurator responsible only to himself assigned to each college
to check upon its operation. This viceroy also controlled the "fiscals," or
secret police, and so had sources of information not available even to the
Senate. Paul Yaguzhinsky, the first procurator-general, came to wield more
power than any other man in Russia except Peter, whose authority he represented.

The collegial principle later was applied to the administration of the Russian Orthodox church. While the Patriarch Joachim had engineered Peter's
succession in 1682, both Joachim and his successor Adrian covertly, and
sometimes openly, opposed the tsar's actions. Both had reviled the foreign
quarter and all it stood for. Adrian had disapproved of Peter's consorting
with foreigners and his trip abroad and had spoken out against the sacrilege
of shaving. When Adrian died in 1700 Peter chose not to appoint a successor
but named Stephen Yavorsky, who had been educated in Jesuit schools in
Poland and who had strayed from Orthodoxy to Catholicism and back again,
to be "administrator of the patriarchal see."

The government took other steps to curb the independence of the church.
Ecclesiastical lands were seized, but not confiscated outright, and administered by a "monastery bureau." A fraction of the income from church
estates was doled out to the church to meet its expenses and the rest was
spent on the army. When the Senate came into existence it received the
right to veto the election of any bishop.

Yavorsky owed his appointment as "administrator of the patriarchal
see" to his known sympathy for things Western and his approval of Peter's
reforms. However, he was impatient to be named patriarch. When it became apparent that Peter was satisfied with the settlement he had made of
church leadership, Yavorsky became bitter against the tsar. He condemned
the "fiscals," the spies or secret police, and disapproved of Peter's sinful life
with his mistresses. He sided with Alexis when Peter brought his son to
trial on charges of plotting to sweep away the reforms after Peter's death.

The headship of the church was settled finally in 1721 when Peter approved the creation of the Holy Synod. The patriarchate was abolished,
frankly, in the words of the *ukaz,* because simple people looked upon a
single head of the church as God's vicar on earth and this popular confidence
gave him the power to encourage revolt. From then on the church would be
administered by the Holy Synod, a college or board of bishops and monks
named by the tsar and presided over by a "procurator-general of the Holy
Synod," a layman appointed by the tsar.

From the moment of its creation the Holy Synod became a tool of the
civil government, and so Peter meant it to be. Its procurator-general became
a powerful official, often more influential than the procurator-general of the
Senate. The church itself became an agency of the government. Peter forced
Russians to attend church regularly, and it was there the priests read out

proclamations and *ukazes* which the government wanted all people to hear. The patriarchate was only restored after the fall of the monarchy, and then it was swept away a few months later by the Bolsheviks.

Peter himself was a religious man in the way of Ivan the Terrible. He attended service regularly and enjoyed singing in the choir. But he had little respect for churchmen, particularly for narrow and superstitious ones, and hated the monasteries, which he looked upon as dens of sloth and wickedness. He rather favored Lutheranism and was inclined to be tolerant of all sects who did not oppose his reforms. Those who did he punished, and he even ordered the Old Believers to wear distinctive dress. Otherwise, particularly if the sectarians were hard-working, he was inclined to "let them believe what they like." He toyed with the idea of reuniting Orthodoxy and Catholicism but would never have accepted the Pope's terms or condoned his interference in lay matters. The scheming Jesuits he banished from the land.

In local as in central government, Peter's initial reforms had to be modified when foreign ideas and institutions proved disappointing or unworkable in the Russian setting. In 1707 the nation was divided into eight huge provinces—Siberia was one province, Kazan and the entire middle Volga another, Azov and South Russia a third. Each governor appointed by the tsar had to reside in his provincial capital. Peter hoped that this decentralization would reduce the inefficiency of tax collection and the drafting of men for the army which characterized the administration of everything from Moscow. In addition to the governor each province was to have appointed supervisors for the collection of taxes and grain, for the drafting of troops, and for the administration of justice. Later the provinces were divided into counties and the counties into districts, each subdivision administered by an official responsible to the provincial governor for the collection of men and taxes, the maintenance of order, and the administration of justice in his county or district. But the parish, the basic unit in the Swedish pattern of administration followed by the tsar, was not created because there were not enough "intelligent men among the peasants" to man the parish offices.

In 1715 Peter attempted to improve the recruitment and financing of army units by creating the *dolia,* an area which contained 5,536 households, the number necessary to provide the recruits and the taxes to support a regiment. The *dolia* cut across district and even provincial boundaries, for its territorial extent depended upon density of population. Since the regiment which such a district was charged to maintain ordinarily was stationed or fighting hundreds of miles away, the *dolia* often neglected its responsibility to forward money and provisions and the troops often went without pay and food. Regimental officers were supposed to cooperate with elected representatives of the landowners in the *dolia,* but the cooperation seldom worked out. The overlapping jurisdiction of the War College, the provincial governor, the district officials, the *dolia* representatives, and the army officers produced only hopeless confusion. Peter readily admitted as much and abolished the *dolia* only five years after creating it.

Peter's concern to improve the collection of taxes lay behind his alterations in municipal government. In 1699 the tsar granted cities, in return for paying twice as much in taxes, the privilege of electing their own officials, thus enabling them to escape the jurisdiction of the old governors, or "feeders," whose voracity Ivan IV had tried unsuccessfully to curb. Cities who chose to double their tax contributions could elect burgomasters with power to levy and collect taxes and to dispense civil justice. Few towns availed themselves of the privilege at such a high price, however.

The new capital, St. Petersburg, received a model city council in 1720, and a College of Municipal Affairs was ordered to extend the model to other Russian cities. Each town's inhabitants were divided into three groups—a "first guild" of wealthy merchants and professional men, a "second guild" of small traders and craftsmen, and the remainder of the inhabitants lumped together as commoners. A city council of members of the first guild was to be elected by citizens of the first and second guilds only. The common people, who made up from half to 90 per cent of the population of Russian towns, had no right to vote. The city council was responsible for the collection of whatever taxes the central government imposed, administered justice, maintained order, and promoted industry and trade. It was accountable to the appropriate colleges and ultimately to the Senate for fulfilling its various functions—police, financial, commercial, and judicial. Soon after Peter's death the city council was made responsible to county officials and through them to the provincial governor; the College of Municipal Affairs was abolished.

Peter's first concern in reorganizing central and local administration was to improve the state's potential for war. His hopes for increased revenue were in part disappointed by the corruption of officials high and low. Peter carried an oaken cane about with him and brought it down mercilessly upon the back of those he heard were robbing the treasury. A governor of Siberia was hanged and the head of the secret police broken on the wheel for amassing fortunes at the state's expense. The procurator-general told Peter to his face that he could never wipe out corruption: "In the end you will have no subjects at all, for we all steal."

Attempts to build up the nation's military effectiveness by increasing the financial and manpower support of the armed forces would have been quite fruitless without a fundamental reorganization of the military establishment itself. Filaret had done his best to improve the defense force by building up a standing army whose members received some training from foreign officers imported to reorganize the Russian Army along Western lines and drill it in Western practices. The *streltsy* had formed the core of the new standing army. Regiments of foreign mercenaries were employed on occasion. Sometimes as many as a hundred thousand Cossacks fought in the service of Moscow. But by the end of the seventeenth century, when Peter attacked first the Turks and then the Swedes, the modernization of the army had to be undertaken all over again. The *streltsy* had grown soft in easy garrison life and had shown a determination to maintain their privileges even at the cost of embarrassing the government. The Cossacks were not always reliable and made a profitable business of treason by trading off their services now to Moscow and now against it.

Peter's campaign against the Crimea in 1695 failed largely because of the inefficiency of the old-fashioned militia and the *streltsy*. The success of his attack upon Azov the following year was in part a naval achievement and in part the work of his "play regiments" and foreign leaders. But the rout of his army at Narva in the opening campaign of the Swedish war indicated that there was much to be done if Russian troops were to stand up against Western Europeans.

The Guards regiments were expanded until they contained in all nearly four thousand men, all sons of the gentry enrolled for life. They constituted a small but thoroughly dependable core for the new army the tsar proposed to build. For the bulk of the new force Peter conscripted recruits from among the peasants. Approximately every twenty households were compelled to provide one soldier and to replace him if he died or deserted before the end of the twenty-five-year enlistment period. Before being assigned to units the recruits were trained in camps by foreigners hired for the purpose or by Russian veterans.

All landowners were required to serve in the army. Improved artillery and flintlocks with bayonets were imported from England. Infantrymen learned to attack with the bayonet rather than to use it only in defense as Western armies used it. Cavalry units were better trained and taught to be more aggressive than in the old army.

Once the new army was brought together and adequately trained Peter never let it go. The troops were never demobilized but were garrisoned on the frontier or quartered in the provinces. By 1725 Russia had a well-drilled and well-equipped standing army of two hundred thousand men, the largest in Europe, plus a hundred thousand registered Cossacks, whose loyalty Peter had firmly won, and a host of Asiatic horsemen, chiefly Bashkirs and Kalmyks whose fearlessness and cruelty made them the most dreaded cavalry in the world.

Peter was the founder of the Russian Navy and he remained sentimentally solicitous of it to the end of his days. The early building of ships at Preobrazhenskoe, at Arkhangelsk, and even at Voronezh had no more lasting effect than to give Peter experience in the construction and use of naval craft. These early vessels did not become part of the permanent fleet. With his seizure of the mouth of the Neva from the Swedes in 1703 Peter concentrated his attention upon building a Baltic fleet. He constructed the naval base of Cronstadt at the mouth of the river and established shipyards in St. Petersburg almost before there were houses for the workers. There were eight hundred ships in his Baltic fleet by 1725, a number of them built in England and Holland, and nearly thirty thousand men. But Peter's successors let the fleet rot rapidly away. Within a decade of his death only a few ships were serviceable and there were no officers to man them.

Peter sought to staff his military and civil service, and at the same time destroy forever the political threat of the nobility as a class, by opening the ranks of the nobility to anyone whose merit could carry him to a certain level in government service. He drew up a Table of Ranks in 1722 which listed all officer ranks in the army and navy and paralleled the list with a similar ranking of all civil offices. The table arrayed fourteen civil and military classes side by side, and the government ordered that every official must begin at the bottom and work his way up the scale as Peter himself had done in the army and navy. Every civil official who reached the eighth rank and every soldier or sailor who became an officer acquired the status, the title, and the privileges of a hereditary noble. The four highest levels in both civil and military service carried with them the title of general, and the men who filled them came to be called "the generality." The Table of Ranks continued to function until the end of the monarchy, although Peter's intention to reward merit and to force his servants to begin at the bottom of the ladder was not followed by his successors.

While Peter had no scruples against raising men of any class to noble rank, he seemed to expect that the government's military and civil officials would come primarily from families of the gentry. To assure that sons of the gentry would seek government service and to guard against the impoverishment of noble families, Peter forbade the division of landed estates among several heirs at the death of their owner. A noble might settle his inheritance upon any of his sons, but only upon one. The rest would in most cases have to enter government service in order to live. Peter thus forced the service obligation upon the landowners in a way and to an extent that none of his predecessors had dared attempt. While the restriction on inheritance was abandoned soon after Peter's death, the monopoly by the gentry of officer rank in the army and, to a lesser extent, of high civil office continued to the end of the monarchy.

Peter's new army and navy were costly. Native Russian men and officers could be forced to serve at a small fraction of the wage foreigners would demand, and even civil servants could be forced to take part of their pay in grain and in goods produced in government-owned factories. But instructors and equipment imported from Western Europe were expensive and had to be paid for in specie. Government revenue, less than a million and a half rubles in 1680, doubled in the next twenty years and then trebled again in the next quarter century. Eighty per cent of the income was spent on the army and navy. The government strained at every possible source of revenue and still could not avoid deficits. Over and over again Peter debased the coinage, until the value of the ruble fell to half its former level. He imposed taxes on stamps, hats, leather, shoes, harness, scythes, fuel, chimneys, troughs, baths, leases, boats, melons, cucumbers, nuts, meat, inns, mills, loans, beehives, beards, marriages, births, and the religious beliefs of dissenters. The government profited from the monopolies of the sale of salt, tar, fats, caviar, and tobacco which it had taken over from an English company. Even oak coffins were bought by the government and forcibly sold to monasteries at four times their cost.

A direct tax on every peasant household brought in considerable revenue, but still not enough. Since the census upon which its collection was based was thirty years old, the government decided in 1710 to take another census to bring in the new taxpayers that the increased population should have produced. The census takers were shocked to find, however, that the number of households in European Russia had fallen by a fifth in the previous thirty years. Some of the shrinkage might reasonably be accounted for by government conscription of troops and laborers to work on canals and in shipyards and in the new capital. Some households were known to have disappeared as peasants by the thousands fled to the southeast frontier and into Siberia to escape taxes and military service. But the greatest shrinkage in the number of taxable households seems to have come about from the practice whereby two or three families moved into a single house to reduce their tax burden by a half or two-thirds.

To halt the loss of revenue occasioned by the decline in the number of households the Senate, in 1718, adopted a new basis of direct taxation. Thenceforth every male "soul" was to be charged an equal share of the estimated cost of maintaining the army. The gentry, the merchants, and the clergy were exempted from this "soul tax," the payment of which came to be the exclusive privilege of the peasants. The results were gratifying to the treasury. Receipts from the soul tax were two and a half times as much as from the former household tax. To be sure that no one escaped the burden a new census was taken in 1718, at which time all remaining legal distinctions between serfs and slaves disappeared. From that time on all were serfs, or "souls," who alone paid the soul tax. Their owners were responsible for collecting it, and now, clearly, the serf was bound not to the land but to his master. By an *ukaz* of 1722 the serf was forbidden to leave the landowner's estate without his master's written consent. This inaugurated the passport system which continued in operation into the twentieth century. Peter had fastened bondage firmly upon the peasant masses for whom he professed so much sympathy.

The census of 1718, made necessary to discover the names of the new individual taxpayers, was sternly resisted; army units had to march into the countryside to force registration and to threaten with death those who tried to conceal themselves. Thereafter, a "revision" of the census was taken every generation or so to bring the lists up to date. Between revisions the landowner simply collected from his peasant villages the amount owed by those whose names were on the last census list, regardless of who had died meanwhile or how many were born.

Peter bent every effort toward reducing the nation's dependence upon outside sources of military materiel. Except for the narrow entry through Arkhangelsk Russia was still landlocked, and the barrier of hostile states across her western frontier made importation of Western goods difficult and at times impossible. Even with easy access to the factories of Western Europe the cost of buying goods abroad would have been prohibitive. His predecessors had laid the foundations for an industrial plant to serve the nation's needs. Now Peter carried on from where his timid predecessors had left off.

During his western journey in 1697 Peter had employed hundreds of Western craftsmen of all sorts to develop Russian industry and teach their skills to Russians. Throughout his reign he ordered young Russians abroad to work and study in the shipyards and the foundries of the West. He welcomed all foreigners except Jews, for Peter was bitterly anti-Semitic. By a proclamation issued in 1702 and published all over Europe, he invited Western military men and craftsmen to join the Russian service, offering to pay transportation and promising high wages, religious toleration, and extraterritoriality. At home he sent out exploring parties to discover new mineral deposits.

The government organized new plants to make arms, uniforms, and other military equipment, sometimes continuing to operate them itself for generations, sometimes turning them over to private companies after the enterprises had become going concerns. To encourage individual merchants or firms to go into manufacturing the government exempted them from taxation and from military service, gave them state serfs as a labor force, allowed them to buy machinery and materials abroad without payment of duty, and granted them a monopoly of the home market or sufficient tariff protection to exclude foreign competition.

At first, Peter concerned himself with developing plants to turn out the military equipment which his new modern army needed. He had bought forty thousand expensive flintlocks and bayonets in England in 1698, and their price had made him determined that Russia should produce her own. He immediately erected plants for their manufacture, and by 1701 Russia was turning out 6,000 muskets and bayonets a year. Production rose to 30,000 five years later and to 40,000 annually in 1711, only ten years after the birth of the industry. During those same years new iron foundries were established, especially in the Urals, where the Demidov family rose quickly to a prominence it did not relinquish until the Bolsheviks took over its plants. Native ordnance plants began to turn out excellent field artillery, which the nation had previously had to import and had not yet learned to use effectively. Textile mills were soon turning out sufficient uniforms to dress the new army respectably. Sail works were established to provide the cloth for the new navy. During Peter's reign the nation discovered its richest ore deposits.

Once heavy industry had moved ahead and war plants had started to equip the army, Peter turned to the promotion of consumer-goods, and even luxury-goods, industries. Brickyards were opened and stone quarries developed to make possible the building of fireproof dwellings in St. Petersburg. Factories started to produce china, glassware, linen goods, velvet, brocade, lace, ribbons, and stockings, and the owners were protected from foreign competition by a high tariff. Peter tried to provide a native source of raw materials for such firms by encouraging the raising of hemp and flax and by experimenting to improve the breed of sheep and the grade of wool. He had hopes that the nation might raise its own silkworms, but his efforts to establish a silk industry failed.

Those merchants who were willing to undertake the management of an industrial plant received every encouragement, from government loans and tax exemptions to a labor force which cost them nothing. State serfs were torn from their villages and given to the factory owners to "possess" and use, but not to own. Such serfs came to be known as "possessional" peasants. The government also assigned criminals, beggars, and orphans to private factories, for Peter, like his contemporary Frederick William of Prussia, could not bear to see anyone idle. A decade after Peter's death the government imposed permanent bondage upon such factory workers, who then became a hereditary class of industrial slaves.

Peter sought to stimulate domestic commerce by permitting anyone to trade who would pay the taxes which those of the merchant class had to pay. On the other hand he allowed some merchant firms a monopoly of wholesale and retail trade in certain commodities. The tsar was not interested in protecting anyone's rights or privileges. If he could obtain more tax revenue by encouraging competition he would do so, but when monopoly promised a greater return to the treasury he willingly allowed it.

Peter's most dramatic achievement in the field of foreign trade lay in his forced shifting of ocean-borne traffic from Arkhangelsk to the new Baltic port of St. Petersburg. Russian and foreign merchants who had used the White Sea port for generations moved only slowly when ordered by Peter to transfer their activities to the mouth of the Neva. But they had little choice when the tsar demanded that they move to St. Petersburg and erect new houses for themselves or else be forbidden to trade. Peter charged lower rates for ships loading and unloading in his new port than for trafficking through Arkhangelsk. Then he forbade certain commodities to move through any other port than St. Petersburg. To promote the use of the new port he proposed to grid the town itself with a system of canals on the order of his beloved Amsterdam. He began construction of a canal, finished after his death, which joined the Neva with the headwaters of the Volga and so linked the Baltic with the Caspian. By 1725 nearly two hundred ships a year were calling at St. Petersburg, while Arkhangelsk quickly declined to insignificance. Russia's foreign trade increased four times over during Peter's reign, and by the year of his death most of it was passing through his "earthly paradise," as he called the new port on the Baltic. He established permanent Russian embassies abroad to promote commercial transactions, although he grossly underpaid his ambassadors, who often received less than half their expenses.

Peter was so conscious of the value of money that he kept strict account in his notebooks of the amount of pay he received each day as a carpenter in the shipyards of Voronezh. He was never able to ignore for a moment the perennial plight of his treasury, and many of his reforms were aimed at reducing the pressure on the budget. Similarly his creation of an educational system was designed to relieve the treasury of the burden of hiring foreigners and of sending Russians abroad to school, although many of the gentry were forced to finance the educational tours of their own sons.

The nation's first school not to be operated under church auspices was established in Moscow in 1701 to teach mathematics and navigation to sons of the gentry who wanted to become naval officers. Some years later it was transplanted to St. Petersburg as the Russian Naval Academy. By the end of the reign its enrollment ran to four hundred, all sons of the gentry. Two smaller schools soon were offering courses in gunnery and engineering for prospective army officers.

A *gymnasium* was founded in Moscow in 1705 by Ernest Glück, a Lutheran pastor taken prisoner in the Swedish war. It offered courses in modern and classical languages, literature, philosophy, and rhetoric. Foreigners staffed the school, which was designed to accommodate a hundred students. When enrollment fell to five in the tenth year of the Gymnasium's operation, the school was closed.

An elementary school system was launched in 1714 when an *ukaz* ordered two "cipher" schools to be opened in every province. The students, ten to fifteen years of age, were to be conscripted from merchant families and were to learn arithmetic, geometry, and trigonometry. Fourteen hundred students were enrolled in these schools during the first ten years of their existence, but less than a hundred graduated. The rest all ran away. A generation after Peter's death the cipher schools became "garrison" schools staffed with army officers, and their curriculum aimed at training men for the army.

The Holy Synod, the new governing body of the Russian church, set up a system of parochial schools which by 1725 were catering to nearly three thousand students, most of them children of the clergy training for the priesthood. In later years, with the expansion of the educational system and the appearance of the first university in 1755, graduates of these elementary parochial schools went on to advanced study in both clerical and lay schools.

Just before his death Peter arranged for the creation of the Russian Academy of Science to promote the study of science and, at the same time, to offer advanced courses in humanistic studies approximately on the university level. A staff of seventeen professors was hired in Germany and, since there was no one in Russia prepared for university work, eight students also were brought in from Germany. Since the professors were required to lecture a certain number of times to a certain number of students, they soon found themselves lecturing to each other. In spite of its comical beginnings, the Russian Academy of Science came in the nineteenth and twentieth centuries to enjoy the respect of similar bodies the world over.

Early in the eighteenth century the first Russian hospital opened in Moscow, and a Dutch doctor became director of the first medical school. Orphans' homes were founded at state expense and later turned over to the monasteries to operate. But Peter had no patience with beggars and assigned them to factory-owners who needed laborers.

Perhaps the most typical of all the Petrine reforms was the abandonment of the old capital and the building of the new. Peter always hated Moscow as a symbol of the old backward Russia. The very word Muscovite, applied by Western Europeans to all Russians before 1700, implied non-European and even oriental. Peter regarded Moscow as a center of superstition and as a bulwark of resistance to the reforms which were necessary to bring the nation out of its torpor. Moscow was an inland town shut off from the sea over which all that was modern and enlightened and efficient might come to Russia.

Peter laid the foundations in 1703 for his new capital, St. Petersburg, at the head of the Gulf of Finland deep in Swedish territory. This was eighteen years before a peace treaty with Sweden gave him legal title to the land on which he located the new city. The site was hardly an attractive one aside from its nearness to the sea. The land was all swamp, and every building had to be set upon piles driven deep into the ground. The city took a decade to build and then was almost impossible to reach over the marshes which surrounded it. State peasants and landowners' serfs were conscripted from all over Russia to work at the brutal task of raising the new capital. Perhaps a hundred thousand of them died of disease and exhaustion.

In 1714 Peter ordered the Senate to move to St. Petersburg. Soon other government offices and foreign embassies followed, cursing the tsar when their horses and carriages became mired in the outskirts. Peter then ordered nobles and merchants to move to the new capital and build themselves expensive houses. Determined that the city should not be subject to the fires that had so often ravaged Moscow, he ruled that houses must be made of stone and forbade the building of stone houses anywhere else in Russia until the needs of the capital had been satisfied. The Admiralty, the Hall of the Twelve Colleges, the Fortress of St. Peter and St. Paul, the Winter Palace, the Orthodox and Lutheran churches, the mansions of the nobles, the shops of the merchants, the busy wharves, and the wide boulevards, or "prospects," made the city seem to a foreign observer in 1714 one of the wonders of the world.

St. Petersburg became and remained to the end of the monarchy a city foreign to the Russian land, more Western than Russian. French and Italian architects worked on its design and on its buildings. Western gardeners laid out its flower beds and orangeries. Western sculptors carved the statues and fountains that dotted its parks. Peter meant his capital to be "a window on Europe." Through that window Russia would breathe Western air. Significantly, the fine equestrian statue of Peter that stands at the mouth of the Neva faces westward.

THE NORTHERN WAR

On his first journey to the West in 1697 Peter had failed to win allies for his war with the Ottoman Empire, which at that time was halted momentarily by a truce. Indeed, Austria was negotiating a peace with the Turks at the very moment the tsar was pleading his case for a Christian crusade. Fresh from the insults of the Swedish governor of Riga, Peter discussed casually with the elector of Brandenburg the profit to be gained from a war against Sweden, whose new king was only sixteen years old. On his way home the tsar stopped off in Poland and listened to the proposal of the ambitious King Augustus II that Sweden should be dislodged from the south shore of the Baltic. A year later Poland, Denmark, and Russia agreed formally to attack Sweden, although Peter committed himself to march only after the Turkish war was settled.

In the spring of 1700 Poland and Denmark opened the campaign, but the Swedish King Charles XII immediately knocked Denmark out of the war in the first of his brilliant victories. At that moment the peace with

Turkey was finally arranged, and a Russian army immediately advanced into Swedish Livonia, besieging the fortress of Narva on the Gulf of Finland. The forty thousand Russians were getting nowhere with the siege when Charles XII attacked them with an army of only eight thousand men. Peter ran away before the battle started but his generals, his artillery, and most of his troops were captured. Narva was one of the most ignominious defeats ever suffered by a Russian army, and Peter, who had surprised Europe with his recent victory over the Turks, became the object of general derision. Once the shock of defeat had numbed, Peter determined to assemble a better army, launch a fleet, and obtain some new cannon, for the old ones had been of little value.

After Narva Charles XII completely ignored Russia and concentrated upon Poland. After six years of pursuit he finally drove Augustus II from the Polish throne and installed his own favorite who came to terms with Sweden, leaving Russia to fight on alone. Meanwhile, Peter, with a new force, had invaded Ingria and Livonia without much opposition and in 1703 had presumptuously marked out the site of St. Petersburg. The tsar now had a Baltic port, which was really all he wanted, and offered peace to Charles XII. But when the Swedish king demanded the return of the districts occupied by the Russians, including St. Petersburg, the negotiations fell through.

Charles led a fine army into the heart of Russia in the late fall of 1707, driving straight for Moscow where, he announced, he would dictate terms. Meanwhile he sent another army under General Löwenhaupt to recover the Baltic provinces and gather up supplies before joining the main body for an assault on the Russian capital. Charles occupied Mogilev on the Dnieper and then advanced toward Smolensk on the road to Moscow, but the Russians stopped him. In the summer of 1708 the Swedish king decided to turn south and join hands with the rebellious Cossacks. A few months later a Russian army met General Löwenhaupt on equal terms and annihilated his force. When he joined Charles on the lower Dnieper he had only a few men and neither artillery nor supplies.

Mazeppa, the hetman of the Zaporozhian Cossacks, offered for a price to join the Swedish king. Charles turned hopefully to join Mazeppa, needing the supplies that South Russia could provide and expecting to be welcomed as a deliverer from Peter's rule. He had reason to believe so, for there had been a last mutiny of the *streltsy* at Astrakhan two years before, and within the previous year the Don Cossacks had been up in revolt. Both risings had been put down only after strenuous campaigns, and Charles hoped to capitalize upon the discontent he knew still smouldered.

Only a small force of Cossacks followed Mazeppa when he joined the Swedish king. Peter's troops stormed the Zaporozhian fastness in the Dnieper and subdued the rest, who elected a new hetman loyal to Russia. From that time on the Cossacks were governed jointly by their hetman and an official sent out from Moscow, and later Peter even appointed Russian colonels to command the Cossack regiments. Toward the end of his reign he abolished the office of hetman and put an end, at least temporarily, to the political ambitions of the Cossacks.

By the spring of 1709 Charles's once splendid army had been reduced by lack of supplies and a severe winter. Little strength had been added when Mazeppa's two thousand Cossacks and Löwenhaupt's stragglers came into camp. Opposed to Charles's pitifully small force Peter had a large, well-trained, and well-equipped army. At the battle of Poltava in June, 1709, the Russians completely destroyed the Swedish army. Charles XII escaped across the Dnieper into Turkish territory with a few attendants. That night Peter dined with the captured Swedish generals and offered a toast "to my teachers in the art of war."

In the following year Peter's troops, now meeting with little Swedish opposition in the absence of Charles XII, occupied Viborg, Reval, and Riga on the Baltic. Meanwhile the Swedish king was urging his Turkish hosts to assert themselves in the Black Sea, and the Porte answered Peter's demand to surrender Charles XII by declaring war against Russia. Peter led an army to the Pruth river, but he ran out of supplies and was not greeted by a rising of Balkan Christians as he had expected. A much larger Turkish force surrounded the Russians, and Peter had no choice in 1711 but to accept the sultan's terms. The tsar would have been willing to surrender all his Swedish conquests except the neighborhood of St. Petersburg, but the Turks were surprisingly generous. Turkey recovered Azov, and Peter allowed Charles XII safe passage through Russia back to Sweden.

For the next several years Russian armies and the new fleet won a succession of substantial victories. One army overran Finland and another occupied the Aland Islands a few miles from Stockholm after the Baltic fleet had won a resounding victory over the Swedish fleet at Hangö. Other Russian forces crossed North Germany and occupied the Swedish-owned ports of Lübeck and Hamburg.

Beyond all question, Russia had become the dominant power in northern Europe. Poland, now again ruled by Augustus II, was rapidly waning, and both the king of Prussia and the Holy Roman Emperor were urging a partition of Poland. Sweden would never recover her importance in eastern Europe and had sunk so low that Russian troops could advance to the gates of Stockholm with impunity. Prussia was ruled by a cautious king who wanted territory but was unwilling to risk anything to gain it. Denmark certainly was too weak to challenge Russian dominion.

Peter now sought to strengthen his position diplomatically by arranging marriage alliances that might bring him influence and would, at least, bring him recognition. Down to the eighteenth century the royalty of Central and Western Europe had spurned Russian marriages. Now Peter seemed to consider it part of the courtesy due him that his relatives should be admitted into the families of Western rulers. From the time of his victory at Poltava to the day of his death Peter was busy arranging marriages for his children and nieces. His son Alexis was married to Princess Charlotte Wolfenbüttel, whose sister was the wife of Emperor Charles VI. Anne, the daughter of Peter's half brother Ivan, was married to the duke of Courland, and her sister Catherine became the wife of the duke of Mecklenburg. The tsar's own daughter Anne was affianced to the duke of Holstein-Gottorp, an heir to the throne of Sweden. When Alexis' wife died, Peter proposed to the French court that his son should marry the daughter of the duke of Orleans. His most ambitious hope was that his daughter Elizabeth should marry Louis XV of France, but nothing came of it in spite of Peter's journey to Paris to urge the suit.

No good came of the Russian marriage alliances with the petty courts of North Germany. In subsequent years St. Petersburg was often embroiled in minor German squabbles that she would have done well to avoid. These involvements only encouraged the suspicion that Russia was trying to interfere in German affairs to her own advantage, a suspicion that was rarely justified. The involvements usually were more costly than they were profitable.

Meanwhile Russia and her allies—Poland, Saxony, Prussia, Denmark, and Hanover whose elector was King George of England—took over Sweden's possessions in North Germany. Russian troops landed at will in southern Sweden to burn the coastal villages, and at one time Cossacks galloped to within two miles of Stockholm. After Charles XII was killed in battle in 1718 Russia's allies one after another came to terms with the Swedish government. Peter had been anxious for peace ever since the battle of Poltava, and now the Swedes were willing to grant acceptable terms.

By the Peace of Nystadt signed in August, 1721, Peter received Livonia, Ingria, and the Karelian Isthmus including Viborg. He returned Finland to Sweden. Russia had her outlet on the Baltic.

When the tsar returned to St. Petersburg the victorious peace was celebrated with great festivities and the usual heroic drinking bouts. An ingratiating bishop acclaimed him Peter the Great and the Senate conferred upon him the title of emperor.

OPPOSITION TO THE PETRINE REFORMS

Many of the reforms of Peter the Great were inaugurated in an attempt to further the nation's war effort against Sweden. As the war dragged on for over twenty years the people became increasingly weary and resentful

"Napoleon's retreat from Moscow," by Vereschagin.

Alexander I

Nicholas I

Alexander II

Alexander III

of the tsar who drove them relentlessly on to greater sacrifice. The burden of taxes and of conscription, both of men for the army and of laborers to build the fleet and raise St. Petersburg, fell chiefly upon the peasants. The nation literally had to be driven with the knout to work and to war. Perhaps the people objected less to the actual reforms than to the speed with which they were applied. Peter was an impatient man. And he insisted that all men serve the needs and the interests of the state as he himself served them.

Resistance to the rule of the tsar and his reforms was shown by every class and took many forms. Occasionally, church leaders spoke out against Western dress and Western manners and were punished for their insolence. Priests whispered that Peter was not really the son of Alexis but one of Lefort's bastards. Old Believers swore that he was antichrist. Peasants hid from the recruiting officer or deserted from the ranks if they could not avoid enlistment. Others ran away in a steady stream to the frontier to take up new land beyond the reach of the tsar's officials. The gentry, who resented the opening of their ranks to commoners, constantly shirked their responsibilities. The *streltsy* never gave up trying to recover their former influence until the last of them had been slaughtered. The Cossacks of the Don and the Dnieper were in revolt on more than one occasion. Even those in whom the tsar placed his greatest trust stole from the treasury. Peter must often have felt that everyone in the land was against him.

After Poltava, the opposition clustered around the person of Tsarevich Alexis, the tsar's oldest son. At the age of sixteen Peter had married Eudoxia Lopukhin, a boyar's daughter, apparently on the order of his mother, who hoped that marriage would turn him away from his wild and dangerous games at Preobrazhenskoe. The restraint lasted for only two months; then Peter returned to his friends in the foreign quarter of Moscow and to the low-born women of easy virtue he knew there. Alexis, the only son of the disappointing marriage, was born in 1690.

Peter took no interest in the child, who was raised by his disgruntled mother and weaned on her bitterness toward her unfaithful husband. After the *streltsy* revolt the tsar forced Eudoxia into a convent, the acceptable way in the eyes of the church for a man to free himself from an unwanted wife. Alexis was taken into the home of his aunt, Peter's sister Natalia, whom he thoroughly disliked. German tutors taught him French and German, and his father dropped in occasionally to set the boy problems in navigation. Peter made no effort to conceal his disappointment that the child showed little aptitude for such subjects as gunnery, fortification, and shipbuilding. That the sensitive Alexis was interested in religion only disgusted the tsar. The boy was a toper and, when under the influence of alcohol, was inclined to let others know of his resentment toward his father.

At the age of nineteen Alexis went abroad at his father's orders to further his education. Again at his father's orders, he married Charlotte Wolfen-büttel. The son had Peter's weaknesses without his strength, and an interest in mistresses and a fondness for liquor made his son's marriage as unhappy as Peter's own. Alexis was not long burdened with Charlotte, however, for she died at the birth of a son Peter, who later became Emperor Peter II. Within a week the tsar's second wife also bore a son, who was also named Peter, as if to warn Alexis that he might be excluded from the succession.

Peter the Great formed many casual attachments in the riotous life of the German quarter before he fell in love with Anna Mons. Anna was Lefort's mistress at the time, the daughter of a German innkeeper and herself a barmaid. He lavished gifts upon her and thought of marrying her before he fell completely in love about 1703 with a peasant girl, Catherine Skavronsky. An orphan, Catherine was reared by a German pastor and put out to earn her own living at an early age. As laundress and mistress she passed through many homes until she settled down with the tsar's favorite, Menshikov. Peter appropriated her for himself, and she bore him eleven children, at least five before they were married in 1712. Ugly, buxom, coarse, common, and gay, she accompanied Peter on campaign, patched his clothes and laundered his linen and stroked his brow to soothe him when violent fits of rage overcame him.

In 1715, when Catherine and Charlotte both bore sons named Peter, the tsar wrote a stern warning to Alexis that he must show some interest in preparing himself for the succession or resign himself to entering a monas-tery. Alexis had neither the strength nor the taste for following the army or learning the chores of monarchy and wrote back confessing himself "your useless son," renouncing his rights to the throne and asking to be allowed to retire to a country estate. A year later Peter wrote from Denmark that Alexis must come to army headquarters immediately or prepare to enter a monastery. Alexis consulted a friend and may have smiled when told that the monk's cowl would not be nailed to his head. He admitted to his confessor that he wished his father were dead and the confessor answered, "We all do."

A year later, when Peter wrote from Holland demanding an immediate decision, Alexis fled to Vienna and asked his brother-in-law, Emperor Charles VI, for sanctuary. Charles hid the tsarevich in one retreat after another, but Peter's agents finally tracked Alexis to Naples and promised his father's forgiveness if he would return home.

Back in St. Petersburg in 1718 Alexis was forced to renounce the suc-cession. But Peter insisted on knowing who had helped the son escape and who was involved in the suspected plot to repeal the reforms and turn Russia back to the old ways after his own death. Nuns were flogged in an attempt to force them to testify that their sister, the mother of Alexis, was party to the plot. A bishop was broken on the wheel for knowing too much.

Hundreds were tortured or executed or banished as the evidence of treacherous thoughts and words mounted. Alexis was tortured repeatedly and finally condemned to death for allegedly having schemed to overthrow the tsar. Peter was not yet satisfied. He insisted upon watching his son tortured again to reveal still more names. Later Alexis was tortured once more, and the next day the government announced that the tsarevich was dead.

Historians still dispute the extent of the tsarevich's complicity in the plot to overthrow Peter—and even whether there was, in fact, a plot. There can be no doubt, however, that many, perhaps a majority of Russians, desperately wanted an end to Peter's violent rule. Nor can there be any doubt that such men looked to Alexis, renowned for his mildness and conservatism and known to detest most of the reforms, to restore the easy ways of old Moscow. Peter was so determined that Russia must continue along the road he had marked out for her that he would let nothing, not even his own son, stand in the way.

THE END OF THE REIGN

There is no evidence that Peter felt any such sense of remorse at the death of Alexis as Ivan the Terrible had known after the death of his son Ivan. That Russia should triumph in the war with Sweden seemed more important to him than the nation's loss of one of several heirs. And new reforms continued to flow from Peter's increasing restlessness and determination to finish the job.

Not for long did Nystadt bring peace to the Russian people. Within a year Peter had opened a campaign in Persia aimed at quieting the area for Russian traders and preventing the western shore of the Caspian Sea from falling to Turkey. With Catherine along, he led a hundred thousand men down the Volga to Astrakhan. There the force parted, most of it continuing by land while Peter went by sea. The Russians took Derbent and Baku with little trouble. The peace settlement in 1723 gave Russia the entire west and south coast of the Caspian Sea. Ten years later, however, Russia returned the land to Persia in return for her support in another Russo-Turkish war.

There was no limit to Peter's territorial imagination. Three months after the Caspian venture two Russian ships left the Baltic with instructions to take the island of Madagascar and then to sail on to India. The fantastic expedition accomplished nothing, however, for the ships were leaky and had to return home. The next year the emperor ordered Captain Bering to discover whether Asia and America were joined together. Four years later, after Peter's death, Bering located the straits which bear his name.

Four years after the death of Alexis and three years before his own Peter issued an *ukaz* giving the sovereign the right to name his own successor. But

he never made use of the law himself. His health failed rapidly after the
Persian campaign, and in 1724 his weakness was complicated by a cold
he caught when he dashed into the Baltic to rescue some soldiers whose
boat had overturned. Late in January, 1725, he sat down to write out his
final instructions but he was unable to complete them. He called his daughter
Anne to finish the testament orally, but he could say no more than, "Give
all to ———." His death left the succession unsettled. A few months earlier,
however, Peter had ordered his wife's coronation as empress, which was later
taken to mean that he intended the illiterate Lithuanian peasant girl to
succeed him. Certainly, he knew too much of Russia's history to leave the
throne to a child.

The impact of Peter the Great upon Russia was cataclysmic. The effect
of the reign was no less than to divide ancient Russia from modern Russia.
Russian society remained for two and a half centuries essentially in the form
in which Peter had molded it. To the end of the monarchy the governmental
structure of the state remained fundamentally what Peter had made it. He
brought Russia out of oriental barbarism into contact with Western civilization. The fact that the transformation was not complete left the nation
half Eastern and half Western, half medieval and half modern, half superstitious and half enlightened. From the reign of Peter I on, Russia as a nation
and the Russians as a people seemed to Westerners full of contradictions and
paradoxes.

SUGGESTED READING

Bain, R. N., *The First Romanovs* (London, Constable, 1905).

———, *The Pupils of Peter the Great* (London, Constable, 1897).

Coates, W. P. and Z. K. Coates, *Six Centuries of Russo-Polish Relations* (London, Lawrence & Wishart, 1948).

Grunwald, C. de, *Peter the Great* (London, Douglas Saunders, 1956).

Mitchell, M., *The Maritime History of Russia, 848–1948* (London, Sidgwick &
Jackson, 1949).

O'Brien, C. B., *Russia Under Two Tsars, 1682–1689* (Berkeley, University of
California Press, 1952).

Oudard, G., *Peter the Great* (New York, Payson & Clarke, 1929).

Schuyler, E., *Peter the Great, Emperor of Russia* (New York, Scribner's, 1884).

Sumner, B. H., *Peter the Great and the Emergence of Russia* (London, English
Universities Press, 1950).

———, *Peter the Great and the Ottoman Empire* (New York, Wm. Salloch,
1949).

Waliszewski, K., *Peter the Great* (New York, Appleton, 1897).

14

The Successors of Peter the Great

Fʀᴏᴍ 1725 ᴛᴏ 1762 ᴛʜᴇ sᴜᴄᴄᴇssɪᴏɴ was hopelessly confused by Peter's order allowing the ruler to choose his heir and by the ability of favorites, a few officials, and the Guards to make and unmake rulers at will. The crown was tossed about with cynical disregard for seniority or even for the legality of the claims of those who wore it. Of the seven who ruled during that thirty-seven years, two had no blood claim to the throne whatever. The succession passed first to Peter's second wife, then to his grandson, then to his stepniece, then to his half brother's great-grandson, then to his daughter, then to another grandson, and finally to that grandson's wife. One reign lasted a generation, another for just over a year, a third for less than six months. But, in a sense, this was not a period where ruler succeeded ruler so much as one where favorite succeeded favorite. With the exception of Elizabeth, those who occupied the throne showed little interest in directing affairs of state.

Two distinct periods with contrasting characteristics suggest themselves. The first period, from the death of Peter the Great to the accession of his daughter Elizabeth, might be called the German period. The court swarmed with petty German princes and their lackeys, with German nobles from the Baltic provinces recently taken from Sweden, and with Germans who had lived in Russia for generations or who had been imported by Peter the Great. This was a period of intrigue when the land was governed or misgoverned by those who jostled each other for the favors of rulers who cared nothing for the country's misery. During this first period many of the reforms of Peter the Great were allowed to lapse or were deliberately altered, particularly those affecting the central administration.

The second period, the reign of Empress Elizabeth, might be called the

Russian period. Elizabeth restored the administrative machinery her father had created and sought within her modest limitations to rule in her father's spirit. She drove the German parasites from court and named Russians to the offices that for seventeen years had been occupied by unscrupulous foreigners. She restored the prestige of the Russian Army by victories over the great Frederick II as impressive as those her father had won over Charles XII.

Through both periods the mass of Russian people settled more firmly into bondage and the serfs lost the last shred of freedom which Peter the Great had allowed them. Toward the end of the second period they began to show their resentment in the only way left to them—revolt. The church lost what little freedom Peter had left it and became completely dependent upon the state even for the salaries of its officials. But one class, the gentry, began to emerge from bondage when Peter III freed the landowners from their service responsibility.

With the accession of Catherine II the rule of favorites ended, for the empress prided herself on personally directing the administration. The interest in reform that had distinguished the reign of Peter the Great also returned.

CATHERINE I

Alexander Menshikov, the former pieman become a prince, had good reason for wanting to see Peter succeeded by his wife. Catherine, the illiterate peasant girl, had been Menshikov's mistress before Peter appropriated her, and she had always defended the man whose origins were as humble as her own. Menshikov had used his influence with the tsar to acquire a fabulous fortune and an impressive list of titles. But Peter had rebuked and threatened him time and again for robbing the treasury. While Menshikov's accomplices had been tortured and exiled, the prince himself had gone free with no more than a few blows of Peter's cane and a fine of half his fortune; he had even managed to retain the tsar's favor. He owed his immunity to Catherine's frequent intercessions in his behalf, and he knew that his continued good fortune depended upon her succession.

Peter's law on the succession and his failure to avail himself of it left the choice to be settled by intrigue and influence, for there were many claimants with some shred of right to the throne. Alexis' son Peter had the best hereditary claim, and the fact that he was only ten recommended him to the conservative gentry, who hoped to dominate him and undo many of Peter the Great's irritating reforms.

Prince Dmitry Golitsyn, who had studied in Italy and who had come to admire Western constitutions, especially the Venetian and the English, urged that the boy Peter be made emperor under the regency of Catherine and the

Senate. Although in favor of westernizing Russia, he felt that many of the late emperor's reforms had come in such a torrent that they could not be digested. There was need to slow the pace.

While Peter the Great lay dying Menshikov, Yaguzhinsky, and other favorites, some senators, and some members of "the generality" gathered in the palace to discuss the succession. When there seemed a possibility that Golitsyn's views might prevail, Menshikov let in some of the officers of the Guards who loudly announced their preference for Peter's wife, Catherine. While the drums of the Guards regiments rolled threateningly in the square below, the Senate and the generality went through the pretense of electing the former laundress to be Empress Catherine I. The pattern would be followed again and again. When ordered to swear allegiance to the tsaritsa, the serfs in the capital joked that their wives should be the ones to take the oath.

The Senate lost all dignity and influence during the short reign (1725–1727) while a new body, the "Supreme Secret Council" of six of the late emperor's favorites presided over by Catherine and dominated by Menshikov, directed the administration. There was an ominous appearance of Baltic Germans and petty German princelings near the throne, not in the capacity of consultants and teachers, as Peter had used them, but as favorites and intriguers. Baltic nobles jostled each other for Catherine's favors. Baron Andrew Ostermann, a born intriguer who had humbly served Peter on diplomatic missions, became vice-chancellor and sought to undermine Menshikov's influence. Anne, Catherine's oldest daughter and the first of her illegitimate children by Peter, married Duke Charles Frederick of Holstein-Gottorp, who was heir presumptive to the throne of Sweden. Then she brought him to court to scheme his succession to the Russian throne.

The empress spent enormous sums on carousals and paramours until Menshikov had to warn her that the serfs were being threatened with starvation by the intolerable tax burden. Catherine's health failed rapidly from the dissolute life she led, and she died after reigning only two years. Anticipating her death, Menshikov thought to insure his continuance in power by marrying his sixteen-year-old daughter to Peter the Great's twelve-year-old grandson Peter, who was the obvious successor. The Supreme Secret Council, the Holy Synod, and the Senate dutifully elected the young Peter while the Guards, prompted by Menshikov, shouted their approval.

PETER II

As the new tsar's father-in-law Menshikov felt himself secure. Anne and her husband were sent back to their duchy of Holstein, where a son, the future Tsar Peter III, was born to them. But Menshikov, of whose haughty and domineering manner everyone had tired, soon followed the duke and duchess into exile. Peter II (1727–1730) quickly wearied of his wife and her father's interference and, encouraged by his tutors Ostermann and Prince Alexis Dolgoruky, stripped Menshikov of his offices and titles and sent him to Siberia.

Now the Dolgoruky family dominated the youthful Peter II. The tsar, whose first wife had died, consented to marry the daughter of Prince Alexis as the dreary play of intrigue went on with new actors. It was the Dolgoruky family, whose members represented the old boyar point of view, who prevailed upon Peter II to transfer the capital back to Moscow. In 1730 the young emperor died suddenly of smallpox, and the question of the succession had to be decided all over again.

THE EMPRESS ANNE

The Supreme Secret Council, made up chiefly of various members of the Dolgoruky and Golitsyn families, gathered to consider the various candidates for the throne. The Dolgorukys, who were officers in the Guards, offered Peter II's bride, a Dolgoruky, as the new ruler, but the rest of the council refused to accept her. The most appealing of the candidates, because she was a widow without children, which meant that the council would be able to decide the succession again at her death, was Anne, duchess of Courland, second daughter of Peter the Great's simple half brother Ivan V. Anne was offered the throne but only on condition that she accept certain restrictions.

The conditions offered Anne seemed on the surface to aim at providing Russia with a constitutional government. In reality they were intended only to perpetuate the influence of the Supreme Secret Council and of the princely families who dominated it. Anne was asked to promise to retain the council as then constituted and not to marry again or to name her successor without the council's approval. She would not be able to make war or peace, levy any new taxes, create any new nobles, raise any civil or military officer to general rank, or make any court appointments without the consent of the council. She must agree not to spend more than the council allowed her to maintain the court. She must not condemn any member of the gentry without trial. She must not attempt to control the Guards, which were to be responsible only to the council. Anne accepted the conditions without question, although probably without any intention of fulfilling them, and left Courland for Moscow.

Before Anne started for Moscow, however, Yaguzhinsky arrived to tell her that the conditions did not represent the wishes of most Russians and to urge her to reject them. There can be no doubt that Yaguzhinsky was correct in believing the stipulations to be unpopular. Most of the gentry favored a return to autocracy rather than the rule of a self-perpetuating oligarchy, the Supreme Secret Council, which they looked upon as "ten tsars instead of one." Prince Dmitry Golitsyn came forward with another plan to insure against the domination of the Supreme Secret Council. He suggested a restoration of the power of the Senate, the retention of the council as an advisory group, and the creation of a two-house legislature with an upper house of gentry and a lower house of merchants. There were other proposals, their number making it clear to Anne that the gentry were suspicious of the great families and the great families suspicious of each other.

Just outside Moscow Anne received and entertained a delegation from the Guards, and, probably at Ostermann's advice, she declared herself colonel of the Preobrazhensky Guards. A few days after entering the old capital she dined with the Supreme Secret Council to hear a discussion of the various constitutional programs that had been suggested. But the Guards were demonstrating in the courtyard in favor of a revival of the autocracy. When a delegation of officers broke in and petitioned Anne to renounce the conditions she had accepted, sweep away the council, and restore the autocratic power, the empress gave way to what she chose to regard as the popular will and tore up the conditions while the disappointed councillors looked on. The Supreme Secret Council was disbanded and its members imprisoned or exiled. To symbolize the restoration of the autocracy Anne moved the capital back to St. Petersburg.

Some members of the princely families, the gentry, and the merchants had opposed the schemes to limit the sovereign power because they feared the vengeful rule of a few oligarchs more than they feared autocracy. So it was in their own defense that they supported the revival of absolute monarchy. Such men must have questioned their own wisdom, however, once the nature of Anne's rule became apparent.

Anne (1730–1740) was a boorish, fat woman of sour disposition, as unattractive in her manners as in her appearance. Her morals were as low as those of Empress Catherine I. Like Peter I, she was fond of human and animal freaks and surrounded herself with dwarfs, giants, and misshapen idiots. If such tastes were unseemly in a man, they were revolting in a woman. Always pinched for money while duchess of Courland, she wallowed in the luxury that the Russian imperial revenue could provide her. During the reign the court expenses rose to five times their level under Peter the Great.

The empress brought with her from Courland a train of favorites and lovers, most of them German, who with Anne's approval dipped into the public treasury and quickly acquired fortunes. The most influential of these was Ernst Biren, who became a count and then, at Russian dictation, received the duchy of Courland, which was a fief of the Polish crown. As Anne's chief favorite, Biren effectively controlled the administration. Under him two other Germans who had long served tsardom, Ostermann and Count Münnich, directed civil and military affairs respectively. To provide places for the many other Germans who had come with her and to counterbalance the influence of the Preobrazhensky and Semenovsky Guards, Anne created two new Guards regiments, the Izmailovsky and the Horse Guards, whose officer ranks were reserved for Baltic Germans.

To take the place of the Supreme Secret Council Biren set up a "Cabinet" made up of Ostermann and two native Russians, which he dominated but on which he disdained to serve. Its chief function was to keep the revenue flowing to the imperial treasury. The Senate, always a stronghold of conservatism but a symbol of Russian nationalism in this rotten period of German bureaucracy, declined to insignificance. Taxes were wrung mercilessly from the serfs, and those landlords who could not collect them were fined or imprisoned. Regular military expeditions marched through the countryside trying to force taxes from the people and imposing mass tortures, mass floggings, and mass deportations to Siberia upon those who could not pay. Those who complained were tortured by the "Secret Chancery," the new name for the security police. Biren's name became a synonym for the system of spying, informing, banishing, and slaughter which he perfected. Many members of the old princely families, notably the Dolgorukys and the Golitsyns, suffered death or Siberian exile. The situation became so unbearable that even some of the Germans—Ostermann and Field Marshal Münnich, at least—complained. Even the empress herself finally objected. Russians, commoners as well as princes, never overcame the hatred for things German brought on by the brutality of Anne's officials.

Through the years after the death of Peter the Great the government lost sight of Peter's insistence that every last Russian must render service to the state. Neither Catherine I nor Peter II nor Anne cared whether the gentry fulfilled their service obligations; they were content as long as the peasants paid taxes. Even before Anne's accession two-thirds of the gentry were on permanent leave from their regiments. Biren relaxed the military obligation of the gentry, cutting the period of service to twenty-five years and excusing second sons, who, however, were required to obtain enough education to allow them to render civil service.

During Anne's reign Baron Ostermann directed Russia's foreign relations. He concluded an alliance with Austria—a logical arrangement for Russia for two reasons: both countries were natural enemies of the Ottoman Empire; and France, Austria's foe for centuries, steadily resisted Russian policy toward Poland, Sweden, and Turkey.

France and Russia had been at odds during the reign of Peter the Great over who should occupy the Polish throne, and the Russian candidate,

Augustus II, the Strong, had won out with Russian support. In 1733 Augustus died and, while St. Petersburg promoted the candidacy of his son to be Augustus III, France supported the perennial anti-Russian candidate, Stanislas Leszczynski, who was the father-in-law of Louis XV. When the Polish gentry elected Stanislas, a Russian army marched into Poland to redress what St. Petersburg chose to regard as a threat to Russian interests. Stanislas ran away when Russian troops approached Warsaw, and the Polish gentry meekly held another election to raise Augustus III to the Polish throne. In this War of the Polish Succession Russian troops succored an Austrian army which was threatened by the French. The Russians even marched toward the Rhine and threatened to invade France.

Turkish objections to Russian interference in the Polish election, added to Ostermann's determination to put a stop to Tatar raids, provided sufficient excuse for another Russo-Turkish war in 1735. St. Petersburg was convinced that the Turkish Empire was on the point of collapse and expected the appearance of Russian troops across the Pruth to spark a rising of Balkan Christians. Constantinople remembered the ease with which Peter the Great had been halted in 1711 and continued to hold Russian troops in contempt. In 1735 Russia, Austria, and Persia—the latter having been bribed by a return of the Caspian shore which Peter I had won— declared war on Turkey.

The Russians were everywhere successful. Marshal Münnich overran the Crimea, the Tatar stronghold that so long had proved impregnable. Another Russian force captured Azov, while a third defeated the Turks on the lower Dnieper. In 1739 Münnich crossed the Pruth into Moldavia and was greeted with an offer of the gentry to make the Russian empress the ruler of the principality. There were setbacks mingled with the impressive victories, however. Russia's ally, Austria, fared poorly in the field and was forced out of the war. While the men in the ranks fought commendably, Russia's armies were poorly supplied, as usual, and her generals argued over strategy. The gains from the costly war were modest enough. The Peace of Belgrade in 1739 allowed Anne to keep Azov and the land around it, but Russia had to promise not to launch a fleet on the Black Sea.

Anne's dissolute life undermined her health, and she died in 1740 after naming an infant as her successor and appointing Biren, now the duke of Courland, as regent. There was still no end in sight to the rule of German favorites.

IVAN VI

The farcical parade of successors to Peter I now brought to the Russian throne Ivan VI (1740–1741), a two-month-old baby who was the great-grandson of Peter the Great's half-witted half brother Ivan V. Biren's contemptuous and domineering manner provoked the hatred and jealousy of the influential Ostermann and Münnich, who had their own following. When the regent considered disbanding the Guards regiments Münnich led a company of the Preobrazhensky Guards to take him prisoner, and Biren was overthrown and banished to Siberia just three weeks after the opening of the new reign. The infant emperor's mother, Princess Anne of Brunswick, assumed the regency.

The regent spent her time lounging about the palace in a dressing gown quarreling with her husband and gossiping with her German lover and her German lady in waiting. Münnich, who had become a sort of chief minister after Biren's exile, quit in disgust to be succeeded by Ostermann, who encouraged the regent's worthless husband to seize control of the government.

Russians finally lost all patience with the German comedy that had dragged on for sixteen years. Their mounting hatred of Germans and Balts, and their disgust at the spectacle of foreigners quarreling over who should rule the land, led them to center their hopes for an end to German domination upon a *coup d'état* by Peter the Great's younger daughter Elizabeth. The initiative, however, came not from Russians but from the Swedish government. Stockholm announced magnanimously that Russia must be freed from foreign rulers. The French ambassador in St. Petersburg encouraged Elizabeth and paid for drinks for officers of the Guards who promised to support her. A Swedish army entered Russia on the pretense of restoring the government to the Russians but with every hope of winning back some of the territory conquered by Peter I.

The regency attempted to thwart the coup by ordering the Guards to the Swedish front to get them away from the capital. A delegation of officers pleaded with Elizabeth to throw out the Germans and mount the throne. On a November night in 1741 Elizabeth, cross in hand, appeared before the cheering Preobrazhensky regiment. At the head of a company of Guards she entered the regent's bedchamber and announced, "Time to get up, sister." Ivan VI, now fifteen months old, was sent to a dungeon, where he grew to manhood only to be murdered to thwart a plot to restore him. His mother and father were also imprisoned and Ostermann and Münnich were exiled to Siberia.

THE EMPRESS ELIZABETH

A woman of striking beauty, Elizabeth (1741–1761) was thirty-two years old at the time of her accession. She never married, although her father had tried to affiance her to the French king and later she had been betrothed to the Lutheran bishop of Lübeck, who died before they could be married. Elizabeth consoled herself for the rest of her life with a succession of paramours, being partial to Cossacks and officers of the Guards. She spent enormous sums on her wardrobe until it contained fifteen thousand dresses. She loved to lead court promenades in striking clothes but was content to live in apartments that were slovenly kept. Thoroughly Russian, she enjoyed the company of peasant women and common soldiers. Charming, friendly, and carefree, Elizabeth was little bothered by official papers and reports. Important documents might wait months to be signed while the empress dallied with her favorites.

Elizabeth immediately announced that she would rule in the spirit of her father. While she did not emulate Peter in his attention to the details of government, she did revive the administrative machinery her father had created. She restored the Senate, whose sessions she occasionally attended, to its role of coordinating the work of the colleges, and reactivated the office of procurator-general of the Senate which had hardly been filled or used for nearly a generation. She dissolved the Cabinet which Anne had established and replaced it with "Her Majesty's Chancery" to manage and finance court functions. After Russia's entry into the Seven Years' War, she regularly met with the new "Ministerial Conference" to hear the advice of chief government officials on foreign affairs. The most welcome move to many of her subjects was the reappearance of Russian names—Razumovsky, Trubetskoy, Cherkasov, Vorontsov, Shuvalov—among those close to the throne.

There was a modest rise of French influence at the Russian court, in part the result of French support for Elizabeth's accession and in part a sympathy for French culture and French learning as a reaction to the German stuffiness of recent years. Russian interest in European civilization focused not upon the techniques and skills which had fascinated Peter the Great but upon literature, art, and thought. The founding of the University of Moscow in 1755 reflected the new cultural interest in Western Europe, although the standards of the first Russian university remained incomparably low for many years. But the fact that the reign could produce the first important Russian poet, Michael Lomonosov, who imitated French forms while he dealt with Russian subject matter, was a respectable achievement.

During Elizabeth's reign the increase in war and court costs combined with a steady shrinkage of revenue to enlarge the government deficits which had been commonplace since the death of Peter I. Occasionally, government officials and the church were asked for a contribution to relieve the pressure, and in one year officials were paid in commodities manufactured in government plants because there was no money in the treasury. The empress' Paris milliner even denied her further credit.

Elizabeth's chief minister, Count Peter Shuvalov, warned her that the tax burden upon the peasants was intolerable, and the soul tax was reduced during the latter half of the reign. To make up for the loss of revenue Shuvalov debased the coinage and raised the prices of salt and vodka, which were sold through state monopoly. The government attempted without success to float a foreign loan, and Elizabeth even considered selling some of her gowns and pawning her diamonds. The government fell back upon what amounted to a domestic loan by issuing paper money called "assignational rubles." The peasants ran away by the thousands to the Caucasus and beyond the Urals, and even sought sanctuary on the estates of Polish nobles. To relieve the depression among the gentry the government established a Nobles' Bank which lent money to needy landowners at low interest rates.

The government tightened the hold of the gentry over their serfs, who lost whatever rights they had had after the legalization of bondage. No serf could marry anyone from another estate without his owner's consent. The serf was formally forbidden to buy land without his master's permission. Since the peasant could not enter the army without his owner's approval, the masses had no legal escape from bondage. There were always the illegal ways, however, of flight and revolt. The reign of Elizabeth was filled with peasant uprisings and with mass flights to the frontier.

The Swedish attack upon Russia in 1741 opened the way for Russian victories which only demonstrated the decline of Sweden as a military power. Russian armies overran Finland meeting with little opposition; Helsinki and Abo, the then Finnish capital, were captured. By the Peace of Abo in 1743 the Russian frontier edged farther to the west along the north shore of the Gulf of Finland.

The Swedish war made it momentarily impossible for Russia to assist her ally Austria in the War of the Austrian Succession, which had broken out during the short reign of Ivan VI. French support for the coup which enthroned Elizabeth had aimed at keeping Russia out of the war or even of bringing her into it on the side of France and Prussia. St. Petersburg managed to stay out of the war, but during its course Russia was torn between French intrigue and the Prussian inclinations of Elizabeth's nephew and heir presumptive on the one hand, and English pressure and the pro-Austrian sympathies of the chancellor, Alexis Bestuzhev, on the other. Finally, the French sympathizers were driven from court, not so much from Russian affection for Austria as from a growing concern over the waxing strength of Prussia.

In 1756 Russia sided with Sweden, Saxony, France, and Austria in the

Seven Years' War against Prussia and England. A Russian army overran and devastated East Prussia, which was lost to the Prussian King Frederick II for the duration of the war. In the summer of 1758 the Russians met Frederick in person at the bloody battle of Zorndorf, which ended in a draw—something of an achievement against such a military genius as the Prussian king. A year later the Russians soundly whipped Frederick at Künersdorf and scattered his army in disorder after inflicting three times as many casualties as they suffered. Frederick admitted that all but three thousand of his fifty thousand men had been lost and despaired of his country's ability to survive. But Künersdorf, like the other battles which Frederick lost to the Russians, was a tribute to the fighting quality of the men in the ranks rather than to any intelligence among the Russian commanders. Time and again they threw away the fruits of victory by failing to follow up a tactical gain with vigorous pursuit. Costly as the war was to Prussia, Frederick was permitted time after time to get away and recover his strength. Only in the last year or two of the war did young, aggressive, talented generals—Peter Rumiantsev and Zakhary Chernyshev —provide Russian troops the leadership they deserved.

In the fall of 1760 a Russian cavalry squadron occupied Berlin, ransacked the shops, and laid the city under tribute. Had the occupation been carried out effectively and resolutely, Prussia might have been forced to sue for peace. But Frederick II bribed the Russian commander to withdraw and the advantage was lost. The Prussian king years later admitted that he still had nightmares at the thought of the Cossacks in Berlin.

Empress Elizabeth was determined that the Prussian king should be demoted in rank to elector and his territory so reduced in size as to make him impotent. She expected to retain East Prussia, which had been in Russian hands since the second year of the war. Had she lived no one could have prevented it. With the later absorption of Courland, the entire south coast of the Baltic would have come under Russian control and Russia's western frontier would have rested on the Oder.

Frederick the Great and Prussia were saved by the sudden death of Elizabeth on the day of the Russian Christmas, 1761. Peter III, her nephew whom she had considered ruling out of the succession, was so enamored of things Prussian that he often kissed the bust of Frederick II. He immediately ordered an armistice and invited the Prussian king to draft his own peace terms. Russia gave up everything she had won. Then Peter ordered the Russian army to switch to the other side and join Prussia against Austria. France had already settled her differences with England and the war soon came to an end. Except for the gain of considerable military prestige, Russia might as well not have entered the war which had cost her so many lives and so much money.

PETER III

Soon after her accession Empress Elizabeth called to St. Petersburg her nephew Peter, the thirteen-year-old son of the duke and duchess of Holstein, whose parents had died years earlier. His tutors, and later his advisers, had difficulty keeping him sober long enough to eat his meals, much less tend to state business; Peter was already a drunkard at the age of eleven. Born a Lutheran, he was converted to Orthodoxy, although it was no secret that he thoroughly hated the Russian church. He was made a Russian grand duke and proclaimed heir to the throne. In 1745, at the empress' orders and on the suggestion of Frederick II of Prussia, the youth married Princess Sophia Augusta of Anhalt-Zerbst, who took the name Catherine and the rank of grand duchess. She, too, was received into the Russian Orthodox church and embraced it fervently.

Relations between the bride and groom were cool from the very beginning. Peter much preferred the company of his mistresses and encouraged Catherine to find lovers of her own. Nine years after her marriage Catherine bore a son, the Grand Duke Paul, whose father Catherine candidly admitted was not Peter but Count Sergei Saltykov. Those who insist that the child was legitimate like to point out that both Peter and Paul were ugly and of debatable sanity. Whatever the child's parentage, Paul was taken from his parents at birth and raised by Elizabeth, who wanted to direct his education as a possible heir. She quickly became disgusted with her nephew and admitted that he was not fit for the throne.

Although the view has recently been challenged, most historians agree that Peter was a scoundrel of no character whose intellectual growth stopped at a childish level. He enjoyed playing with dolls, particularly with toy wax or wooden soldiers at which, dressed in Prussian uniform, he shouted military commands. A rat which devoured two of his "sentries" was caught, court-martialled, and hanged from the ceiling. He idolized Frederick II, whom he called "the king, my master," and knelt before his portrait. Peter made no secret of his detestation of things Russian and his fondness for his native Holstein and for Prussia. He detested Orthodoxy and attended church only to ridicule the services, pace up and down talking at the top of his voice, stick out his tongue at the priest or burst out in insane laughter when the congregation knelt in prayer, and then run cackling from the building. He issued orders for the removal of the holy icons from the churches and for priests to shave and dress like Lutheran pastors. He loved to scrape vigorously and tunelessly on his violin to the annoyance of all who could not escape his entertainment. He took keen delight in insulting Catherine at court functions, in parading his mistresses in public, and in loudly questioning the paternity of Catherine's children.

Peter III occupied the throne a bare six months (1761–1762), but in that short time his policy was constructive and mild. He abolished the "Secret Chancery"—the security police force which Anne had created—put an end to the system of informing which had sent many innocent men into exile, and refused to permit men to be tried for their political sympathies. He freed those of his predecessors' victims who were still alive.

The gentry profited most from the so-called reforms of Peter III. They were freed from the responsibility of state service and allowed to travel abroad. The estates of the church were secularized and placed under the control of an "Economic College." The clergy in effect were put on salaries, while the revenue from church lands went to the state. Peter "reformed" the army by adopting the uniform and the "ballet dance" drill of the Prussian Army. He threatened to reduce the Guards to line regiments and replace them with his new Holstein Guards, which were officered, according to a spiteful critic, by "sons of German cobblers." He humiliated old retired officers by ordering them into uniform and personally drilling them for long hours like common soldiers. When he threatened to involve Russia in a war with Denmark so that his native Holstein might recover Schleswig, a war that would have taken the Guards out of the capital and forced them to march to the Elbe, his wife's supporters decided they had had enough of Peter III. His threat to send Catherine to a convent and marry his mistress Elizabeth Vorontsov, added to his alienation of the Guards who had decided so many successions since 1725, brought his downfall.

Catherine admitted in her memoirs that from the moment of her marriage the ambition grew upon her to become empress of Russia. She carefully cultivated the friendship of Empress Elizabeth. She made a great display of her respect for Russian customs, particularly for her newly-donned Orthodox faith. She sought out the friendship of leading officials who resented Peter's insults. She won over officers of the Guards, one of whom, Gregory Orlov, was her lover.

On a midsummer night in 1762 Orlov and his four brothers led Catherine to the quarters of the Izmailovsky and Semenovsky Guards, who escorted her to the Winter Palace to announce that Peter III was no longer tsar. The Senate and the Holy Synod, carefully assembled beforehand, enthusiastically acclaimed Catherine as empress, thus ignoring the claims of her son Paul and the forgotten Ivan VI. Then, in the uniform of the Preobrazhensky Guards, Catherine led the joyous troops to Peter's residence in the suburbs to inform her husband that he no longer ruled. Peter raised little objection but begged to be allowed to keep his violin, his dog, and his mistress. A week later he was killed at his country estate by a band of courtiers led by one of the Orlov brothers. The woman who had no blood right whatever to the throne now ruled as Catherine II.

SUGGESTED READING

Bain, R. N., *Daughter of Peter the Great* (New York, Dutton, 1900).
———, *Peter III, Emperor of Russia* (London, Constable, 1902).
———, *Pupils of Peter the Great* (London, Constable, 1897).
Cambridge Modern History, Vol. VI (New York, Macmillan, 1909).
Kliuchevsky, V. O., *History of Russia,* Vol. IV (London, Dent, 1926).
Maroger, D. (ed.), *The Memoirs of Catherine the Great* (New York, Macmillan, 1955).
Walsh, W. B., *Readings in Russian History* (Syracuse, Syracuse University Press, 1950).

15

Catherine the Great

CATHERINE II (1762–1796), WHOSE fawning admirers called her the Great, considered herself the heir and executor of the reforms of Peter the Great. Unlike Peter, however, whose reforms were thoroughly practical if seldom thought through, Catherine was doctrinaire in the reforms which she conceived. They were planned in the spirit of enlightened despotism of which Catherine was a devotee and a classic example.

Soon after her accession Catherine convened a Legislative Commission charged to draft the principles upon which a new law code should be written. To guide the delegates in their deliberations she wrote out a *Nakaz*, or set of instructions, dripping with all the liberal sentiment of the time. The *Nakaz* itself was more memorable than the commission which it was designed to guide, for the commission came to no conclusions or recommendations and the law code was not revised.

Catherine instituted a number of reforms in government which were designed to decentralize the administration and encourage local responsibility. She abolished most of the colleges, turning their functions over to local agencies responsible to the Senate. She raised the number of provinces to fifty and divided each into districts. The gentry in each province and district chose delegates to a local assembly which dealt with local problems and elected a provincial and also a district marshal of the nobility. However, so many local administrators were appointed rather than elected, thus being responsible to the procurator-general in St. Petersburg, that the effect of the reshuffling was to make local agencies responsible to the capital rather than to a local electorate.

The empress reissued and extended Peter III's Charter to the Nobility, freeing them from all responsibility for state service. New legislation perfected the control of the gentry over their serfs, whose plight became worse under Catherine than ever before. A Charter to the Towns professed to encourage municipal self-government but left the government of each city in the hands of a few of the wealthiest citizens.

The foundation was laid for a national system of elementary education. Catherine invited colonists, particularly Germans, to settle in Russia to set her people an example of improved farming. She founded libraries, orphanages, and hospitals and encouraged interest in public health. Perhaps she did most to raise the educational level of Russians by the example she set them of interest in Western liberal thought.

The crystallization of the institution of serfdom brought widespread revolt in the provinces. The worst was that led by Emelian Pugachev, who gathered together discontented Cossacks, Old Believers, and serfs, ravaged the Volga basin, and vowed to overthrow the empress. The social upheaval was directed primarily at landowners and was an avowed effort to put an end to serfdom. Loyal armies put down the rebellion but left the gentry and the court forever after with a dread of another peasant rising.

Catherine's greatest achievements were in adding territory to the state and in reducing or eliminating the threat to Russian security posed by neighbors to the west and south. Two successful wars against Turkey carried the Russian border to the Black Sea and west to the Dniester river. Most ominous for the future peace of the Ottoman Empire and for Europe, Russia obtained the right, vaguely stated, to interfere in the domestic affairs of Turkey on behalf of Christians living under the sultan's rule. Catherine planned, but failed, to rid the European continent of Turkish power and even to revive the Byzantine Empire as a sort of Russian protectorate.

The growing debility of the Polish kingdom, which Russian rulers promoted and of which they took every advantage, led to the complete disappearance of the state whose king had once hoped to rule in Moscow. In three partitions of Poland the sovereigns of Russia, Austria, and Prussia calmly pared away shares for themselves until, in 1795, Poland was erased from the map.

Catherine's successor, her son Paul, had waited so long for his inheritance that his sanity was debatable by the year 1796 when he finally came into his own. He sought to undo his mother's work but was assassinated after four years before he could throw the nation irretrievably into chaos. He threatened the rights of the gentry, even restoring their service obligations, and so aroused the resentment which led to his murder. He involved Russia in war—after complaining that the nation had known no peace in his mother's time—first against revolutionary France and then in alliance with her. Even his own son finally concluded that his father must be set aside.

YOUTH AND CHARACTER

Catherine grew up in the atmosphere of the stuffy little German principality of Anhalt-Zerbst. Her father, a general in the Prussian army, was thrifty and sober, while her mother was a woman of extravagant taste. As a grown woman Catherine showed both characteristics. The child received a modest education but acquired a good knowledge of French from her Huguenot tutor. She early developed a passion for reading which relieved many boring moments for her after her marriage to Peter III.

Catherine admitted in her memoirs to being a very ugly child but insisted that the ugliness rapidly disappeared after she was ten. Her native intelligence, her acquaintance with writers of the day, her bearing, and her vivacity made her an attractive woman. But her awareness that she was never beautiful may have stimulated her vanity, for she took advantage of her position at the Russian court to surround herself with young and handsome men. The older she grew the younger were her favorites, until the last of them was twenty-two when Catherine was seventy. Her disappointing marriage led her unashamedly to welcome liaisons, and one statistician credits her with fifty-five lovers. However, like Peter I, she did not abandon herself to sensuality as had some of her immediate predecessors. She worked hard and conscientiously at the job of governing Russia personally, not through favorites, and went to her lovers almost by way of seeking relaxation from strenuous toil. She began the day at six, an unheard-of hour for Russian officials in any age, lit her own fire, spent little time before the mirror, and worked twelve or fifteen hours a day. Like Peter the Great, who considered himself the first servant of the state, Catherine labored more diligently than any other person in the government.

The extent of her knowledge and her appetite for reading made her one of the best-read women in Europe and the most unusual and outstanding woman in Elizabethan Russia. For that reason, among others, she much preferred the companionship of men and prided herself on her ability to converse and correspond, as an equal in many cases, with the best minds of her day. Voltaire, whose sincerity is hardly open to question in spite of the fact that he received generous gifts from her, was one of her most uncritical admirers. Diderot was her pensioner and visited Russia to become a keen admirer of her remarkable gifts both as a woman and as an intellectual. She corresponded at great length with Frederick II, Joseph II, Gustavus II, and with D'Alembert, Falconnet, Grimm, and others of the encyclopedists, of whom both she and they considered her one. She read Plato, Tacitus, Blackstone, Buffon, Montesquieu, Rousseau, Bayle, and Beccaria, as well as the

Encyclopédie which fascinated her. She was an author of perseverance if not of much merit, turning out in French and Russian comedies, tragedies, essays, and even an ambitious history of Russia in addition to a great volume of letters which certainly show more literary polish than any of her other works.

Catherine was extremely ambitious. Even at the time of her marriage at sixteen she looked forward to becoming the ruler of Russia. With her husband out of the way she was still ambitious—to add to the glory of her reign, to acquire territory, to win recognition abroad for herself and her empire, and even, as her care in the raising of her grandson would indicate, to have her policies perpetuated after her death.

THE *NAKAZ* AND THE LEGISLATIVE COMMISSION

Steeped in Western liberal thought, determined not to dilute her autocratic power but to use it for the benefit of her subjects, Catherine conceived an ambitious plan to provide the nation with a new law code which would reflect Western humanitarian principles. There had been no revision of the Russian code since 1649. There were at least ten thousand laws on the books, many of them contradictory or obscure or hopelessly out of date. The chaotic state of the law made it impossible for officials or subjects to interpret and administer or even to know the law. Peter the Great had been fully aware of the need for a revision, but the press of practical matters and day-to-day problems left him no time to deal with something that could be put off. The spate of legislation for which he was responsible made the situation still more hopelessly confused. Both Anne and Elizabeth had called assemblies of elected nobles and merchants to draft a new law code, but nothing had come of their labors. In the last year of her reign Elizabeth had complained of the inefficiency of her administration and noted that the laws were neither observed nor enforced. Catherine had heard Elizabeth bemoan the corruptibility and selfishness of officials, the callousness of the courts, and the distrust and skepticism with which all Russians viewed their government. Now Catherine, who greatly admired Peter the Great and considered herself the heir and executor of his reforms, hoped to correct a situation which her predecessors had done nothing to relieve.

Catherine decided to convoke a great national commission of elected delegates to work out the principles upon which a new law code could be based. To give direction to their deliberations the empress herself worked for two years on a *Nakaz,* or set of instructions. Finally the remarkable volume was published, not only in Russia to guide those who would sit on the commission, but abroad as well, where its daring acceptance of liberal principles delighted reformers and shocked conservatives. Louis XV forbade its distribution in France, but Frederick II expressed his approval by making the empress a member of the Berlin Academy. Voltaire compared her to Solon.

Catherine's *Nakaz,* written with her own hand but considerably modified by her advisers, contained twenty chapters and over five hundred paragraphs suggesting principles to which the enlightened state should adhere in politics, economics, social welfare, culture, and religion. More than half of the statements were taken straight out of Montesquieu's *Spirit of the Laws* or Beccaria's *Crime and Punishment;* the empress quickly admitted as much. But there was something of Catherine in it, too—of her ignorance of Russian society, of her naïve assumption that principles worked out tortuously over centuries in other countries could be transplanted, of her supreme confidence in absolutism. The final draft was stripped, at the prompting of serf-owning advisers, of suggestions that the lot of Russian serfs should be improved. Catherine gave way—spinelessly, her critics charge—before the insistence of court nobles that there be no hint of emancipation or even of the right of a serf to buy his freedom. Her apologists point out that she had no right to the throne, that she owed her accession to the support of the nobles who might easily unseat her by withdrawing that support.

Even with all the editing Catherine meekly accepted, the "Instructions" retained much Western liberal thought that was far in advance of most governments of the time. The *Nakaz* declared that all subjects should be equal before the law; all should obey the law; the state should aim less at the punishment than at the prevention of crime; torture should be abolished and capital punishment resorted to only rarely; serfdom could be justified only if it served the state, but to sweep away bondage at a stroke would be rash and dangerous; all men should be free to do whatever the law does not specifically proscribe; religious dissent ought to be tolerated; the right to own land should be widely encouraged. No nation in Europe practiced or even accepted the validity of all these ideas, and few on the continent practiced any of them.

Catherine unquestionably believed the propositions put forward in the *Nakaz.* But Catherine was a true benevolent despot. There was no hint that these high-minded principles should operate through a representative assembly. Rather, they should guide the sovereign, who would retain in his own hands the full power of absolute monarchy, the only sensible type of government for a land as sprawling as Russia. "The ruler is the source of all civil and political power," according to the *Nakaz.* But that power must be used wisely and justly with the welfare of the people in view. The *Nakaz* also laid down the principle that "the people do not exist for the ruler but the ruler for the people."

The instructions were scattered widely over Russia, and six months later Catherine called for the election of delegates to a "Legislative Commission" whose assignment was to draft a new law code. In the summer of 1767 over five hundred elected representatives gathered in the Kremlin in Moscow. There was a delegate from each of two hundred towns, eighty chosen by the Crown peasants, fifty from the Cossacks, twenty-eight high officials, a hundred and sixty from the gentry, and thirty-four to represent "foreign" peoples in the empire—including Bashkirs, Kalmyks, and Samoyeds, at the very mention of whose unfamiliar names disbelieving Europeans laughed. There were no representatives from the landowners' serfs who made up more than half of the peasants and nearly half the nation's entire population. No one spoke for the clergy as a class, for churchmen voted with merchants in the election of town delegates. Each delegate came with one or more statements of grievances or recommendations drawn up by individuals or groups of those who had chosen him. The statements the delegates brought with them were filled with petty, picayune complaints, while Catherine's *Nakaz* had proposed that the Commission concern itself with such lofty ideals as the rights of man.

Meetings and committee sessions went on to the end of the year, when the sittings were transferred to St. Petersburg to go on for another year. In December, 1768, just after the opening of the first of Catherine II's wars with Turkey, the plenary sessions were adjourned and most of the delegates went home. Committees continued, however, to meet for another six years.

The Legislative Commission held over two hundred sessions and innumerable committee meetings. Many of the speeches were less constructive than complaining. Some of the nobles from old families resented the intrusion into their class of those who became gentry through Peter's Table of Ranks. The merchants resented the loss of their trade monopoly and the growing threat of competition from serf-manned factories on landowners' estates. Commoners resented the gentry's monopoly of the right to own serfs, and merchants and Cossacks appealed for the same right.

There were a few constructive suggestions along with the selfish demands. Dmitry Golitsyn's plea at the time of Anne's succession for a legislative assembly and constitutional restrictions on the autocratic power was revived. Several enlightened nobles appealed for a reduction of the landowner's authority over his serfs or at least for a definition of serf rights so that abuses might be punished. Such men were jeered for betraying their own class.

The accomplishments of the Legislative Commission were disappointing. Not even a beginning was made on a new code. The meetings adjourned without even completing the reading of the fifteen hundred statements of grievances brought by the delegates. The debates, however, were a source of information to the empress. Some of the things she learned there helped her in defining some of the later reforms.

THE REFORMS OF CATHERINE II

From the moment of her accession Catherine felt a responsibility to carry on the reforming work of Peter the Great. Within a month of her husband's death she was busy annulling his edict secularizing church estates. There was no sense or reason behind her action; perhaps she assumed the secularization to be somehow wrong because Peter III had ordered it. Early in 1764, however, she changed her mind and again confiscated the lands of the church, putting their administration under the Economic College as her predecessor had done. The clergy and the few monasteries not closed received their income from the state.

There were a few minor alterations in the machinery of the central government. During her first Turkish war Catherine created an Imperial Council to advise her on war policy and foreign affairs. The council continued to function, always under the strong hand of the empress, to the end of the century. She abolished most of the colleges and turned their functions over to new local agencies which were responsible, for a while at least, to the Senate. The Admiralty, the Army and the Department of Foreign Affairs were the only colleges to survive. The functions of colleges which had dealt with collection of revenue and the administration of justice were assumed by the procurator-general, who was removed from his earlier contact with the Senate and made a separate and powerful official. This abolition of some offices and transfer of duties from one agency to another was so confusing that when Alexander I later asked the senators what their duties were they were not sure of the answer.

Catherine's reforms in the area of local government were more impressive. Peter the Great had despaired of developing much governmental initiative on the local level when he found there were not enough capable and intelligent men to staff local administrative offices. That such was the case was primarily due to the obligation of every member of the gentry to serve in the armed forces, leaving no one in the provinces to accept civil assignment. The situation altered quickly after Peter's death, however, when most of the gentry shirked their service responsibilities with impunity and returned to their estates. Then Peter III freed the gentry entirely from their obligations.

By a succession of orders between 1764 and 1785 Catherine refined the system of local government which Peter had barely begun. The number of provinces was increased to fifty, each supposed to contain three or four hundred thousand inhabitants. Each province was divided into districts of from twenty to thirty thousand inhabitants each. A governor named by the crown was responsible to the Senate for the administration of each province. However, a number of administrative functions—finance, police, and social welfare—were assigned to provincial boards who were responsible not to the governor but in most cases to the procurator-general's office in St. Petersburg. Civil and criminal courts in the provinces were also accountable to the procurator-general. All these provincial officials were appointed, the governor typically from a well-to-do and influential noble family, the others from the lesser and poorer gentry. The effect of this reorganization of local government was not to promote self-government but to improve the machinery for carrying out the will of the sovereign. Whether this was Catherine's intention may be argued, but that this was the consequence is beyond question.

The gentry of each district and each province received the privilege of electing delegates to a district or provincial assembly which met every three years. The assembly, within certain limits, voted assessments for local needs and elected a "marshal of the nobility," the district assembly on the district level and the province on the provincial level. The provincial or district marshal had to be a person of some influence and dignity, for it was he who had to plead the needs of the nobles before the provincial governor or the appropriate official, sometimes even the tsar, in St. Petersburg.

The provincial and district plan of local organization was established eventually in the Baltic provinces, Russian Finland, and the Ukraine. Serfdom was extended to the border areas where it had not already appeared, and the peasants were required to pay the Russian soul tax. The Cossacks lost what little independence was left to them—the office of hetman was abolished, the circle or assembly broken up, and the Cossack lands divided among the three provinces which were carved out of the Ukraine.

The gentry received complete freedom from irritating restraints and from all obligations to the state in Catherine's Charter of the Nobility, proclaimed in 1785. The rights granted by Peter III's emancipation of the gentry were not only repeated but considerably increased. The charter relieved the nobles of all responsibility to enter the military or civil service of the state. They could not be subjected to corporal punishment and were exempted from payment of direct taxes. The life, estates, or title of a noble could not be taken from him except by the verdict of his peers, and he could not be stripped of his title even by court sentence without the approval of the ruler. If, by court sentence, he were deprived of his estates, they went to one of his heirs and could not be seized by the state. None but the gentry could own serf-populated lands, and none but they were free to travel abroad. They could maintain factories on their estates and sell the products, thus sharing the trade rights of the merchants without having to pay the merchants' fees.

By the terms of *ukazes* issued at various times during the century and by unwritten privileges tacitly admitted by the sovereign, the gentry won almost unlimited control over their serfs. They could sell or give away their bondsmen singly or in families, with or without land. They could move serfs out of the village and off the land into their manor houses at will. They could send any serf to the army for the twenty-five-year enlistment period, which the masses looked upon as a life sentence to penal servitude, or exile him to Siberia, which one out of four never reached because so many died along the way. The landowner could subject his serf to unlimited floggings; while he could not condemn his serf to death he could order as many strokes of the lash as he pleased, and he went unpunished if the man or woman died of the beating. Peter the Great had held the gentry accountable—even to the loss of their estates—for abusing their serfs, but this restraint was not enforced after his death. In Peter's time serfs might petition the tsar against mistreatment by their owners, but such complaints were forbidden by Catherine.

The privately-owned serf had no enforceable rights whatever. Had the law recognized any rights, the courts, manned by members of the gentry, would never have enforced them against the landowners. The gentry-owned serfs, who made up over half the nation's population, could not own property, real or even personal. The very rags they wore and the miserable huts they lived in were legally the property of the noble who owned them. Their labor and their earnings were at the disposal of the estate owner.

Villagers living on farming estates customarily owed the landlord three days of work each week, called *barshchina,* on that part of the arable land which the estate owner cultivated for his own use. Ideally, half of the arable land was assigned to the serfs, whose village elders allotted in each field strips on which a serf family could raise its own food. But many a landowner, particularly in the rich black-soil area, forced his serfs to work in the fields five or six days a week, adding the villagers' fields to his own and doling out to them whatever food was necessary to keep them alive. In the gray-soil area of central Russia a landlord might take his fields out of cultivation and work his serfs in factories on the estate. Or he might let his bondsmen farm the land on their own in return for their paying him an annual *obrok,* a money payment in lieu of labor. Or he might let them work in a nearby town and pay the *obrok* out of whatever wages they received. Where the *barshchina* serfs worked under the lash in the landlord's fields and suffered constant interference in their daily lives from the bailiff of the estate, the *obrok*-payers were left free to govern themselves and to use their time as they chose as long as the village saw that each serf paid his *obrok.*

While Catherine did nothing to help landowners' serfs, she certainly improved the lot of state-owned serfs by making them all *obrok*-payers instead of *barshchina* serfs. Left to govern themselves in their own village assemblies, and enjoying generous land allotments, they were much better off than privately-owned serfs and were commonly known as peasants rather than serfs. Whatever rights they enjoyed, however, they possessed only by sufferance of the state, which was a milder, or perhaps merely less efficient and less grasping, landlord than were many nobles. Some state peasants suffered during Catherine's reign, however, for the empress gave away hundreds of thousands of them to her favorites. The reign is commonly looked upon as a period when the lot of the peasants reached its lowest point, for the control of the landowners over their serfs was refined in full detail and whatever rights the privately-owned serfs had previously retained were legally swept away. And millions more peasants were depressed into serfdom as bondage was extended to the Baltic provinces, the Ukraine, and to that part of the Polish-Lithuanian lands which Catherine acquired where serfdom did not already exist.

Peter's efforts to establish municipal government had met with little success beyond the capital. In a 1785 Charter to the Towns Catherine announced a new basis for self-government in the nation's cities. Each city's population was grouped in six categories—owners of real estate, native merchants, foreign merchants, craftsmen, unskilled workers, and "eminent citizens," a catch-all group containing bankers, officials, and university graduates. The city elected a mayor and a duma, or council, which would meet every three years, presumably to decide broad policy matters. In the intervals between its meetings a committee of six, one from each of the corporate groups into which the citizens were divided, was supposed to sit regularly to guide the city administration and to levy taxes. The mayor was responsible to the provincial governor for his administration, as was the head of the local police, who was an appointed, not an elected, official. For most Russian cities, however, Catherine's proposed municipal self-government never went beyond the paper stage. A confusion of appointed officials maintained order and collected taxes until the last half of the nineteenth century. Town inhabitants were exempted from payment of the soul tax which was the exclusive privilege of the "souls" living on state-owned or private estates.

Some new towns came into existence during Catherine's reign. The government claimed to have built nearly a hundred and fifty of them, scattered the breadth of the land from the Arctic to the Black Sea. In 1787, accompanied by a following of Western ambassadors and, most notably, by the Austrian Emperor Joseph II, Catherine went "on progress" down the Dnieper and into the Crimea to view the accomplishments of her government in the land so recently under Turkish rule. Her former lover, Prince Gregory Potemkin, now governor of the area, carefully planned the itinerary and built a number of cities along the way in which the empress was greeted with happy, dancing townsmen in holiday dress. But, in some instances at least, there really were no towns, only false fronts of buildings hastily thrown up like stage settings to impress Catherine and her party. The "Potemkin villages" may have pleased the empress at the time, for she was not privy to the deception, but word of their nature soon leaked out and brought the derision of all Europe.

Catherine encouraged foreigners to settle in the thinly populated lands of the empire, allowing them tax exemptions and freedom to practice their religion in the hope that they would set Russians an example of industry and improved farming methods. Over a hundred colonies of Germans settled in the lower Volga and the Ukraine, jealously clinging to their language and customs until the middle of the twentieth century.

There was a modest approach to *laissez-faire* principles in the economic policies of the government under Catherine. The monopolies which Peter the Great had granted to encourage Russia's infant industries were removed. Tariffs were scaled down to encourage competition. Foreigners were invited into the country to establish factories under preferred conditions, even enjoying the privilege of buying serfs to man their plants, a right which Russian merchants were no longer allowed. The elimination of the monopoly privileges of Russian merchants, however, was a blessing primarily to the gentry, who obtained the right to build factories on their estates and even to sell their products.

In spite of the steady rise in prices brought about by large issues of paper rubles, Russia's foreign trade volume increased markedly during the reign. The government arranged commercial treaties with Western nations, stimulated imports by moderate tariffs, and built or expanded seaports through which the goods could flow. Odessa was founded shortly before Catherine's death, and the empress had visions of a thriving Black Sea trade through the Bosporus, which she hoped Russia might some day control. But not until the latter part of the nineteenth century would the traffic through the southern sea exceed that through the Baltic ports which Peter had done so much to promote.

Catherine made a beginning on a national system of lay schools. Two-year elementary schools were proposed for every district in every province, although many of them never opened and a few closed for want of teachers, students, or funds. Four-year "high" schools were operating in most of the important cities of European Russia by the end of the reign. The government established a teachers' college to produce the teachers with which to staff its new schools. By 1790 sixteen thousand students were enrolled in lay and church schools out of a population of twenty-six million—a pitifully small percentage, but still a beginning. Most of the students came from middle-class homes, for serfs had no time for such frills and the gentry employed private tutors. There were still no schools of any kind in the villages, which meant that at least half the nation's population had no educational facilities.

The empress founded a school for orphans in St. Petersburg and another in Moscow, and she opened the Smolny Institute in the capital as a finishing school for daughters of the gentry. Most sons of the gentry obtained their education either at the officers' schools founded by Peter or from French tutors. They learned to read the works of the French radicals of the time whose writings were popular at court and influential among the nobility throughout this reign and that of Catherine's grandson, Alexander I.

Catherine organized a college of medicine at the University of Moscow. It had graduated only one student by the end of the century, for most Russian medical students sought their education abroad. She set her people an example of confidence in new medical practices by being the first to be vaccinated against smallpox, the scourge of the villages. And she encouraged the health authorities to use quarantine and to forbid the kissing of icons when the plague swept over South Russia during the Turkish war. She ordered the building of a public library in St. Petersburg. She organized the Free Economic Society to stimulate interest in Russian agricultural development. In its first year the society offered a prize to the citizen of any country who should submit the best essay on the problem of serfdom. The winner, a resident of Aix-la-Chapelle, suggested abolition of serfdom. He received the prize, but the society, most of whose members were nobles, refused to publish his essay. They were willing to discuss social theories among themselves, but refused to broadcast this concrete proposal for the alteration of the social order from which they drew so much profit.

 The Catherinian reforms differed from those of Peter the Great in one fundamental way. Peter did not pretend that his reforms were carefully thought out or that they were based upon any philosophical precepts. Often they came at the spur of the moment with little regard for their consequences. Almost invariably Peter's reforms were of the practical sort, unadorned with philosophical falderal to lend them dignity. On the other hand, Catherine's reforms, which with few exceptions were much less substantial and much less enduring than Peter's, were conceived and justified in the spirit of enlightenment which was the fad of the age. The empress was proud, if not vain, of her correspondence with other enlightened despots and philosophers and was most anxious to be known abroad as one of such people. She did her best to cultivate among Westerners the belief that Russia was a Western, a European nation and, beyond that, that Russia was particularly prosperous and contented under Catherine's rule. Catherine was always concerned with what people thought of her and Russia. Peter cared little about what others thought as long as he could whip the nation to a level of achievement which would satisfy him and, more important, satisfy Russia's own needs. But it was Catherine, and not Peter, who set the intellectual tone of modern Russia. If Russian merchants and industrialists looked westward in Peter's time, it was the Russian intellectual who looked westward from Catherine's time onward.

PUGACHEV'S RISING

Catherine's reign was filled with outbursts of popular resentment against the bondage system which reached its worst condition in the last half of the eighteenth century. In keeping with a long tradition of pretenders to the throne, there was a succession of peasant leaders claiming to be Peter III or Ivan VI, whom Catherine had ordered slain. Each such claimant won a following among the masses, who had sufficient cause to welcome a change of rulers. At other times, when there was no leader of glamorous name to follow, the peasants fled the settled districts in an endless stream toward the frontier—to the lower Volga and beyond into Central Asia, to the southern steppes, and frequently to Poland to seek the supposedly gentler treatment of a Polish landlord.

The Russian government had long since grown used to such discontent and had even come to take armed risings with a certain unconcern, as though it almost welcomed such opportunities to give its troops experience in the field. In 1773, however, a wave of revolt swept over South Russia that frightened the government and the privileged classes out of all complacency. The leader was a Don Cossack, Emelian Pugachev, who had served in the army but who had been severely punished several times for desertion and had just escaped from prison. Pugachev claimed to be Peter III, the sixth or seventh rebel in a decade to do so, and called his mistress—he had left his wife and children in a Cossack village on the Don—the empress.

In the spring of 1773 Pugachev gathered about him a motley band of followers. There were Cossacks from the valley of the Yaik, as the Ural River then was called, and other Cossacks from the Don and the Dnieper. There were Old Believers who cheered the leader's promise to restore the old faith. There were four thousand criminals released from the prisons of Kazan. There were swarms of peasants, bitter at the exactions of the taxgatherers and the recruiting of their sons, who resented the emancipation of the gentry from service and hoped to force their own. There were Bashkirs who had risen under Peter I and Tatars and Kirghiz and Chuvash and Votiaks who resented the seizure of their lands by the Russian government.

The rebellion met with alarming success through the autumn of 1773 and the following spring. There were only handfuls of soldiers in the sparsely populated lands between the Volga and the Urals, and local authorities were little respected. The government was busy with the Turkish war, and for the moment there were no troops to spare. Pugachev's following sprawled over the countryside in pillaging columns, growing to thirty thousand. Lacking in discipline and having no leaders with command experience, the rebels behaved less like an army than a horde. Still, they took Saratov and Kazan, looting wherever they went and taking particular delight in burning manor houses of the gentry and torturing officials and Orthodox priests. Pugachev encouraged such actions, swearing to rid Russia of landowning gentry and to abolish the laws against beards. After taking Kazan he threatened to march on Moscow, and the governor of the old capital prepared to defend his province. Pugachev vowed to pack Catherine off to a convent and enthrone her son Paul.

For some time Catherine persisted, at least in the front she kept up in her correspondence with foreigners, in believing that this was just another Cossack disturbance which would quickly be suppressed. But when an army sent to capture Pugachev failed to bring him in, Catherine admitted the seriousness of the challenge and sent her best commanders against the outlaw. With the end of the Turkish War troops were available to turn against the rebellion. After nearly two years of maintaining his own "court" and leading a class war that swept aside all government authority over a wide stretch of territory, Pugachev was seized and taken to Moscow, where he was beheaded. The Yaik Cossacks were reorganized and renamed the Ural Cossacks, and the Yaik River became the Ural in an attempt to efface the name of Pugachev's most loyal supporters.

Pugachev's rising was the last organized and widespread outbreak against the government and the institution of serfdom. From that time on resentment smoldered in the countryside and occasional *Jacqueries* brought destruction and death to scattered estates. One of her generals had told Catherine, "It is not Pugachev that matters, but the general indignation." The name Pugachev went down in the language as a synonym for peasant fury against the landlord as a symbol of oppression. And the gentry never quite got over their fear of another *Pugachevshchina*, or wave of "Pugachevism." From that time on, the government stationed garrisons of troops among its own people to move sternly against any threat of revolt.

CATHERINE'S WARS WITH TURKEY

Catherine, whose forte was certainly diplomacy and who confessed as much, was successful in disposing of the remaining enemies along Russia's western frontier. Peter the Great had settled with Sweden and had so reduced her military potential as to commit her to the rank of a second-rate power. He had contributed much to the decline of Poland, already rushing toward her own destruction, by interfering in Polish elections to prevent a foreigner under hostile influence from ruling in Warsaw. With Turkey, however, Peter had managed only momentary success and final ignominy.

In the year after her own accession Catherine interfered in the election of a new Polish king, and Russian troops and officials moved into Poland, ostensibly to remain. The intervention inspired a belated Polish effort to halt the nation's decline and recover its independence. The pursuit of Polish nationalists by Russian armies near the Turkish border provoked the Porte, urged on by Western diplomats, to demand that Russian Cossacks evacuate Poland. Meanwhile, the Crimean Tatars, always sensitive to Russo-Polish tension, threatened another of their perennial raids into Russian territory and thus provided Catherine with an excuse for war against their overlord, the sultan. The empress spurned the Turkish demand that she pull her Cossacks out of Poland, and the Crimean Tatars opened the war in 1768 with a drive north through the Isthmus of Perekop.

Catherine was always her own foreign minister. Through most of her reign she left vacant the chancellorship, as the foreign ministry was called, letting insignificant vice-chancellors do her bidding. But in foreign affairs, as in most matters, she was subject to informal pressures and influences by the favorites with whom she adorned her court. At the opening of the Turkish War, Gregory Orlov, her lover at the time, suggested a program for Russian action in the Near East upon which Catherine proceeded to act. Orlov proposed to incite the Greeks and the Balkan Slavs to rise against their Turkish masters and support Russian arms in hurling the Turk off the European continent. Peter the Great's effort to do the same thing had been ignominiously checked. The Crimea was to become "independent," which was a nice way of saying that the peninsula should become a Russian protectorate, and Moldavia and Wallachia—the provinces which eventually became Romania—would be similarly liberated. All this was to be accomplished by Russian naval victories over Turkey in the Black Sea and the Mediterranean timed to coincide with the drive of Russian armies down the Balkan Peninsula to Constantinople.

Early in 1769 the Crimean Tatars broke out of their peninsula to raid South Russia, the last time they were ever to do so. Their weak attack did not even have nuisance value, for the Russians were not distracted from their two-pronged drive toward the Balkans and against Azov. Turkish territory around the mouth of the Don was quickly overrun, and men were set to work building ships on the shores of the Sea of Azov. As Gregory Orlov had proposed, Russian launched a naval attack against Turkish power in the Caucasus and at the same time moved to cut off Constantinople from relief by sea. In that same summer of 1769 another Russian fleet left the mouth of the Neva for the long voyage around Europe into the Mediterranean to advance against Turkish power from the west. Meanwhile a Russian army under Count Peter Rumiantsev crossed the Dniester and then the Pruth, captured Jassy, overran Moldavia and Wallachia, seized Bucharest, and drove the Turkish armies across the Danube. The year 1769 was a glorious one for Russian arms everywhere.

In the following spring the Russian Baltic fleet under Alexis Orlov arrived in the eastern Mediterranean. However, its landings in Greece were feebly manned, and the general rising of Christians in the Balkans did not materialize. Then in July, 1770, Orlov and his English squadron commanders completely destroyed the Turkish fleet at Chesme in the Aegean, winning the most convincing victory in the annals of the Russian Navy. Instead of following up his triumph by passing the Dardanelles and bombarding Constantinople, Orlov wasted his time by occupying some Aegean islands. Again Russian land forces were victorious, usually against odds of ten or more to one.

During the following year, 1771, Russian armies in the lower Danube accomplished little. However, Prince Vasily Dolgoruky crashed through the Isthmus of Perekop, overran the Crimean peninsula, and replaced the sultan's vassal with a Tatar khan of Russia's own choosing. The Porte was ready to discuss peace terms, and an armistice quieted the fighting through 1772. Other Christian capitals were growing concerned over Russian successes. They were even alarmed lest too much Turkish territory fall to Russia. Western Europe's fear of a great Slav state which would bring the Balkan Christians under Russian rule, a fear that plagued Russia's relations with the West through the nineteenth and twentieth centuries, was born during Catherine's first war with the Ottoman Empire. Now Frederick II of Prussia thought to appease Russia's appetite for Slavic lands by suggesting that he and Catherine partition Poland. With the duplicity of which he was a master he prompted Austria to oppose Russian seizure of Moldavia and Wallachia and at the same time urged Catherine, whose friend he professed to be, to deal gently with the sultan.

The peace talks in 1772 accomplished nothing, and the Russians advanced again the following summer. This time the victories went chiefly to Alexander Suvorov, a junior commander who had distinguished himself in the fighting in Poland. Suvorov, the greatest of all Russian generals, had served for years as a common soldier and was able to get more out of his men than any Russian commander before or since his time. The courage of his men in bayonet charges and in fighting off Turkish forces of vastly superior numbers distinguished the campaign of 1773 even beyond those of the earlier years of the war. Suvorov drove across the Danube and might, with better support and supply, have pressed on to the Turkish capital. But the Turks had had enough, and at Kuchuk-Kainardji in 1774 they accepted the Russian peace terms. The Pugachev rising made Catherine as willing as the sultan to see an end to the war.

Catherine's gains by the treaty of Kuchuk-Kainardji were modest enough. In return for an indemnity Turkey recovered Bessarabia, Moldavia, Wallachia, and the Aegean islands which Russia had overrun and might, over the objection of the other powers, have retained. Except for the tip of the

Kerch peninsula, which went to Russia, the Crimea became independent. The land between the Bug and the Dnieper rivers also went to Russia, thus returning her to the coast of the Black Sea for the first time since the days of Kiev. And the mouth of the Kuban was ceded to Russia, whose territory now completely surrounded the Crimea, which soon would be ripe for plucking. Russian merchant vessels were to enjoy free use of the Black Sea and entry and exit through the straits. In return for Russia's evacuation of the Turkish provinces on the Danube, the sultan promised to allow the Balkan Christians the free practice of their faith. The Russian government was given a vaguely worded right to protect Christians in the Ottoman Empire and to address the sultan in their behalf. Nineteenth-century tsars interpreted this clause as recognizing Russia's right to intervene in Turkish affairs on behalf of all Christians living under Ottoman rule.

Catherine could not long be satisfied with the Treaty of Kuchuk-Kainardji, for she planned nothing less than the complete expulsion of Turkey from Europe. To make this possible Russia needed the support of Austria, not so much for the military as for the diplomatic value of that support. England, France, Sweden, and Prussia, whose king was wholly unreliable from Catherine's standpoint, might be expected to oppose further aggrandizement by Russia at the expense of Turkey. But Austria might, for a price, welcome the partition of the Ottoman Empire which had cost her so much blood. So Catherine dropped the alliance with Prussia which had lasted for the first eighteen years of her reign and shifted her favor to Austria.

At Catherine's invitation the Austrian Emperor Joseph II visited Russia in 1780, and the two discussed the partition of the European portion of the Turkish Empire. Nothing definite was concluded, and the two corresponded over the partition for the next three years. Basic to Catherine's proposed solution was her famous "Greek project," which was conceived by her chief adviser and lover of the moment, Gregory Potemkin. The project aimed at the revival of the Byzantine Empire, for which Catherine condescended to provide an emperor in the person of her infant grandson, whom she significantly named Constantine. Moldavia and Wallachia were to become independent under an Orthodox ruler; Catherine and Potemkin had Potemkin in mind for the post. The Russian frontier was to be moved west from the Bug River to the Dniester.

Joseph II had some thoughts of his own on this matter of carving up the Turkish Empire. He wanted to push his own borders down both sides of the Danube beyond Belgrade and insisted on the Turkish provinces at the north end of the Adriatic. He also wanted the Dalmatian coast, which belonged to Venice. Cyprus, Crete, and the tip of the Greek peninsula might go to Venice in compensation for her loss of Dalmatia to Austria. Joseph's suggestions were not at all to Catherine's liking, and the two came to no agreement on the disposition of the spoils. They did agree, however, to join forces when the time seemed right to attack Turkey.

Catherine proceeded on her own to nibble away at the Ottoman Empire. In 1783 the Russian-appointed khan of the Crimea resigned and turned over his principality to Catherine. South of the Caucasus Georgia became a Russian protectorate in the same year. Four years later the Russian and Austrian rulers paraded down the Dnieper and into the Crimea, stopping at Sevastopol to review Catherine's new Black Sea fleet. The English, French, and Prussian ambassadors to the Porte screwed up the sultan's courage to protest this obvious threat to Turkey by imprisoning the Russian ambassador. In the Second Turkish War that followed, Austria and Russia fought as allies.

Catherine's second war with the Ottoman Empire saw no such parade of Russian victories as had her first. The new fleet won some unimpressive victories over the Turks but lost a costly number of ships to a Black Sea storm. Russian troops crossed the Dniester but found hard going against a Turkish army that had been reorganized and noticeably stiffened. Suvorov covered himself with glory, but Rumiantsev and Potemkin accomplished little. The revamped Turkish army defeated the Austrians whenever Suvorov was not near enough to help them. Catherine lost her ally when Joseph II died in 1790 and his successor withdrew from the war.

Meanwhile, Sweden, encouraged by England and Prussia, attacked Russia in the hope of recovering some of the territory lost to Peter the Great. This made it impossible to send the Russian fleet from the Baltic into the Mediterranean, and the Swedes even threatened St. Petersburg. The antagonists traded victories, but the Russians managed successfully to resist Swedish pressure in the north without weakening their attack against Turkey. Without support from those who had pushed her into the war, Sweden was forced to withdraw before she gained or lost anything.

Catherine persisted in the face of British and Prussian threats in her determination to weaken Turkey further. Russian victories in 1791 forced the sultan to sue for peace. By the Treaty of Jassy in 1792 Turkey surrendered to Russia the land between the Bug and the Dniester and admitted Catherine's absorption of the Crimea. The terms of the Treaty of Kuchuk-Kainardji, which the sultan had repudiated, were confirmed.

The end of her Second Turkish War brought Catherine far less than she had hoped for. But the empress was not yet finished with the sultan. Early in 1795 she arranged a treaty with the new Austrian emperor, Francis II, who agreed to press once more for the expulsion of the Turks from the continent. Europe's growing involvement in the French Revolution and Catherine's death in 1796 put a temporary end to Russia's ambitious drive toward the Dardanelles. Her grandson would return to the attack after the turn of the century.

THE PARTITIONS OF POLAND

Of all Catherine's triumphs in diplomacy the most shady and unscrupulous, in the minds of Western moralists, was her participation in the destruction of the Polish kingdom. The heinous crime of the Polish partition has continued through the centuries to shock those who persist in ignoring the setting in which it took place. Catherine has borne the odium of the partition almost alone, although the idea was not hers and the partition was certainly not in Russia's interest. Had Russia swallowed all of Poland, as Catherine would have preferred, the outcry would not have been so loud as it was over the division of Poland among her three neighbors. By some obscure reasoning this was held to be a more monstrous crime.

Suggestions to partition some country or other were popular in the seventeenth and eighteenth centuries. At various times since the closing years of the sixteenth century there had been proposals, sometimes lengthy discussions, and frequently overt attempts to partition Spain, Sweden, Prussia, Poland, Turkey, Austria, and Russia. At the accession of Maria Theresa the Prussian King Frederick II had led the powers to a vulture's feast on the Austrian woman's inheritance. Catherine discussed with Joseph II the partition of the Ottoman Empire and Voltaire encouraged her. Presumably, to carve up the dominions of the infidel Turk would have been not a crime but a commendable deed worthy of the praise of all Christian rulers. Prussian kings for generations had been suggesting the partition of Poland, and Frederick II urged it again in 1771 as a way of saving Turkey, whose support Frederick might some day need against Austria and Russia.

Poland's supine weakness was attributable to many factors—her vulnerable geographic position without defendable frontiers, the voracity of her powerful neighbors, the adventuresome character of some of her kings, and the running sores of religious strife and class hatred and rivalries of noble families among her own people. The most obvious factor contributing to Poland's decline was the selfishness of the gentry and their willingness to sacrifice the nation's strength to further their own interests. Successive kings, elected by the assembly or Diet of nobles, had so bargained away their authority in return for their election that they retained no power whatever over the nation whose throne they occupied. If they went to war, they did so at their own expense and had to provide their own armies. They could not recruit soldiers or levy taxes upon their Polish subjects. The *liberum veto,* the right of any member of the Diet to block legislation by his single vote, made the enactment and execution of national laws impossible. There was no order in the land. Civil war was a normal state of affairs as powerful families, around which the lesser gentry clustered, contested for power; they

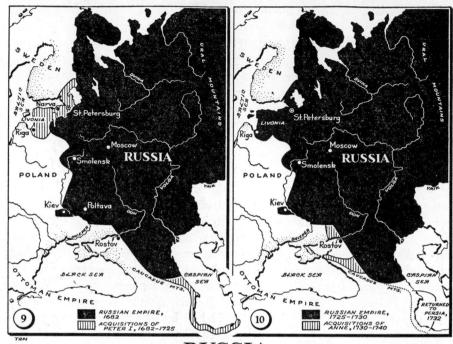

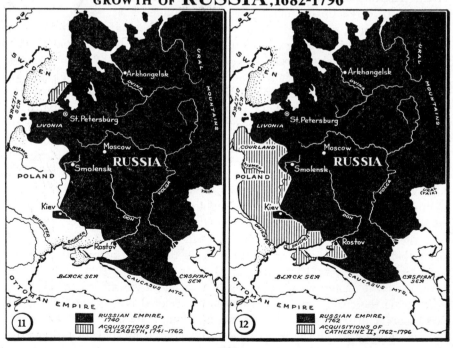

GROWTH OF **RUSSIA**, 1682-1796

did not hesitate to call in Swedes, Russians, Cossacks, and Turks to help them. The mass of the people were serfs, as badly used as were those in Russia. A sizeable minority of Protestants in western Poland and another of Greek Orthodox in eastern Poland were sorely persecuted by Catholic landowners as bigoted as their Jesuit confessors.

The death of Augustus III in 1763 prompted the usual scramble among Polish factions. Powerful neighbors, along with France, whose dabbling in Polish affairs was inspired by her effort to keep Warsaw hostile to France's Habsburg enemy, began to influence the succession. The Russian candidate for the Polish throne was Stanislas Poniatowski, a native Pole and one of Catherine's discarded lovers. Catherine and Frederick II of Prussia agreed to back his candidacy with troops if need be, to fight together if the intercession brought war with Austria or France, to force the Poles to grant toleration to Orthodox and Protestants, and to "defend" the Polish constitution by preventing any revival or strengthening of the power of the Polish government. The noble faction led by the Czartoryski family supported the Russian candidate, and Russian troops in Warsaw helped the Diet to make up its mind in favor of Poniatowski as the new king of Poland.

Once elected, Poniatowski set to work to make his kingship hereditary and to recover something of royal power. This brought a Russian army into the country, ostensibly to defend the Orthodox minority from persecution. A confederation of Polish nobles dedicated to resist Russian domination had little success against Suvorov, who distinguished himself for the first time against a Polish opposition that was divided over the question of abolishing the monarchy. When Russian troops overran the country and drove the Polish patriots to the Turkish border in 1768, the sultan declared war.

The succession of Russian victories over the Turks disturbed most European capitals and prompted Frederick the Great to intercede with Russia, posing as Catherine's friend. He warned her of Austrian vengeance if Russia were to seize Moldavia and Wallachia, and suggested that Catherine take Polish rather than Turkish territory. Austrian resistance could also be bought off with some Polish land, and, of course, Frederick himself should receive a reward for thinking up the happy solution. Catherine went along with the plan, even suggesting that Frederick might find in his archives some legal claim to justify his acquisition. Frederick was an old hand at finding such legal loopholes in the property titles of other rulers. Certainly Catherine had some claim on historic and ethnic grounds to the land she proposed to take.

Austria, Russia, and Prussia agreed in a series of treaties in 1772 on the so-called First Partition of Poland. The Austrian Empress Maria Theresa professed to abhor the partition, but Frederick II observed that "the more she wept the more she took." Catherine suffered a diplomatic defeat in sharing Poland with the others, but with the Turkish war, the Pugachev rising, a terrible plague in Moscow, Austrian indignation, Prussian pressure, and the threat of war with Sweden on her hands, there was little else she could do.

A year after the signing of the treaties the Polish Diet was bribed and cowed into approving the partition. The kingdom lost over a fourth of its territory and almost a third of its inhabitants. Catherine's share was thirty-five thousand square miles of territory—the Russian and White Russian lands around Polotsk, Vitebsk, and Mogilev—and nearly two million people who were predominantly Russian and overwhelmingly Orthodox in religion. Austria took nearly as large a bite in Galicia and Frederick II received the smaller but richer basin of the lower Vistula, except for Danzig.

Russian troops stayed on in what was left of Poland after the partition, presumably to prevent the overthrow of the king who had accepted the loss of his territory. Cautiously, the king, with the support of some of the gentry who discovered a belated sense of loyalty to the nation, recovered some of the royal power which had been bargained away over the centuries. There was growing resentment against the presence of the Russian Army in the land and to the contemptuous treatment of Poles by the Russian ambassador.

In the midst of Catherine's second war with Turkey the Polish government concluded an alliance with Prussia aimed against Russia. Supposing the Prussians to be trustworthy, the Polish king and the noble faction which supported him won over the Diet to a new constitution which made the kingship hereditary, swept away the *liberum veto,* and strengthened the powers of the king. Under threat of war with Prussia and Poland the Russian troops went home, and Catherine temporarily surrendered her position as guarantor of the old Polish constitution.

When her war with Sweden and Turkey came to an end Catherine sent an army of a hundred thousand men to the Vistula to punish the Poles for their arrogant behavior. Russia received the support of a faction of Polish nobles embittered at the loss of their influence. Prussia's new King Frederick William II reneged on his pledge to help the Poles, and the Russians overran the country with little opposition. The Polish king was forced to scrap the constitution which the Diet had adopted the year before and to consent to the restoration of "Polish liberties"—the elective kingship and the *liberum veto.* Fearful that Russia might confiscate all of Poland, the Prussian king demanded compensation for recent losses in his war with revolutionary France and for his consent that Catherine should pare away another slice of Poland.

By the terms of the Second Partition of 1793, Poland lost half of her remaining territory and population. Prussia received the port of Danzig and the rich districts of Poznan and Torun with a million inhabitants. Catherine took three million people and ninety thousand square miles of territory, including most of Lithuania and the western Ukraine from the Dnieper to the Dniester rivers. Again the Diet was prompted by the presence of Russian troops in Warsaw to approve the seizure. Austria did not share in the second partition.

A national revival and a war in 1794 to rid the land of Russians came too late to save Poland. Guerilla bands slaughtered many Russian soldiers and a revolutionary government was set up in Warsaw. But the cause was hopeless. A Prussian army advanced against the Poles and Catherine sent Suvorov to retake Warsaw. The fighting was all over in six months. By the terms of the Third Partition of Poland, Russia received the rest of Lithuania and the Ukraine and took formal title to the duchy of Courland, which she had controlled for over thirty years as a protectorate. Austria received the Cracow region, and Prussia was awarded the remainder of Poland, including the city of Warsaw. The kingdom of Poland was erased from the map of Europe.

The territory gained by Russia in the partitions of Poland brought with it some complications. A large Jewish minority became part of the population of the Russian Empire for the first time, as most of the Jews who, in medieval times, had fled from western Europe had settled in the eastern Polish provinces which Russia now acquired. The Uniats—members of the Orthodox faith who had accepted the jurisdiction of the Pope—also were absorbed. Both Jews and Uniats suffered persecution under Russian rule.

Russia's diplomatic position was altered by the fact that now Russia had a common frontier with two powerful potential enemies. A weak Poland had provided something like a cushion protecting Russia from Central Europe. On the other hand, the three partners in the crime against Poland were to some extent drawn together by their suppression of Polish nationalism. The submerged, hostile peoples came to feel a greater loyalty to their language, their customs, and their cultural heritage than they had ever felt before the death of the Polish state.

CATHERINE AND THE FRENCH REVOLUTION

Catherine's correspondence with French men of letters and her sympathy for the ideas of the enlightenment did not prevent her turning violently against the French Revolution. The excesses of the Paris mob sickened her. She ordered home the sons of Russian nobles who had been living in France and exiled to their estates those who had become infected with French radicalism. She looked upon the Polish patriot Thaddeus Kosciuszko and his followers as "eastern Jacobins" for their promise to emancipate the Polish serfs in 1794.

Catherine moved sternly against her own "Jacobins." In 1790 Alexander

Radishchev published his *Journey from St. Petersburg to Moscow,* which bitterly condemned the institution of serfdom and attacked the corrupt rule of Russian officials. The empress had Radishchev tried and condemned to death for his radical views, although she herself had encouraged such views in the early years of her reign. Eventually Radishchev was let off with exile to Siberia.

As long as the revolutionary government in France kept its attention upon western Europe, Catherine was content to fulminate against it. But when General Bonaparte defeated the Austrians in North Italy and threatened to move on to Vienna, Catherine could no longer afford to ignore the French danger. France under the Bourbons had long opposed Russian interests in Poland, Sweden, and Turkey. Russia could not allow a more aggressive republican France to dominate Austria as well. In the autumn of 1796 Catherine made plans to march Suvorov, now a marshal, with sixty thousand men to the relief of the Austrians in North Italy. But before Suvorov could leave Russia the old empress died, and her son Paul cancelled the expedition. Without the help of Russian troops Austria was forced to accept the costly Peace of Campo Formio.

THE SIGNIFICANCE OF CATHERINE'S REIGN

In many ways Russia seemed to be a part of European civilization for the first time in Catherine's reign. Educated Russian nobles could travel abroad and show themselves to be perfectly at home in the salons of Paris. They spoke the languages of Western Europe, particularly French, and some even disdained to use their own Russian language because it was the language of the unwashed masses. They imitated the manners of the West so faithfully that when they returned home some of them were ridiculed as mincing fops. They steeped themselves in the thought, particularly the liberal thought, of the West, and some few of them were stricken by a sense of shame for their own Russian society. This fascination for things Western was a result of the example set by the court, for Catherine deliberately patterned court society after Versailles.

Polite society became "civilized" in Catherine's reign, in contrast to the "barbarous" time of Peter I. All Russian nobles now wore Western dress and were quite indistinguishable from Western Europeans. Peter had been ashamed of his Russian companions in the salons he visited in 1697. The coarseness of manners in Peter's time—the filthy language, the crude jokes, the lewd dances, the drinking bouts, the fights and brawls—gave way to a gentility in Catherine's time that put the two reigns ages apart. Peter's savage tortures and mass executions were a thing of the past. Even Pugachev was not tortured, and his beheading was almost the only political execution in Catherine's thirty-four years.

By the end of the eighteenth century Russia was respected and even feared as a great power. Her armies, when well led, were the equal of any in Europe. Her naval power was formidable. Her diplomats were well received and her sovereign treated with the same flattery that was showered upon any Western ruler. Other nations sought alliances with her and Frederick II acclaimed Catherine as the arbiter of German affairs.

If, by Catherine's time, the nation had taken on a veneer of Western manners and had developed an outward strength that commanded respect, internally Russia was not sound. The condition of the serfs was worse than ever before. The gentry completely dominated Russian society. The central government was in a state of chaos. What there was of local government was managed by and in the interest of the serf-owning landlords. But Pugachev's *Jacqueries* gave awful warning that there was a limit to the patience of the masses. Catherine's successors would not long be able to ignore the demand that the worst abuses must be corrected.

THE EMPEROR PAUL

Catherine II had seriously considered passing over her son, as she had every right to do under Peter the Great's succession law, and settling the throne upon her grandson Alexander. She was well aware of Paul's serious limitations—of his pettiness, his vicious temper, his strange quirks, his resentment, and particularly his hatred of everything she had sought to accomplish. So she had carefully prepared Alexander for the succession and directed his education in the philosophy of the enlightenment. The empress's intention was well known, but Alexander insisted when the time came on letting his father have his turn as emperor. Paul, the senior claimant after his father's assassination, had been kept off the throne for thirty-four years by his ambitious mother, who had had no legal title to the throne whatsoever.

Paul (1796–1801) was reared by his grandmother Elizabeth and saw little of his mother during his childhood. Through the long years of waiting to succeed Catherine he developed an insane hatred for her. His resentment at being kept off the throne was intensified because many of the gentry, in 1762, had expressed a preference for Paul as emperor, with his mother to act merely as regent. As soon as Catherine died the new emperor lashed out at his mother's memory, spitefully repealing much of her legislation and seeking to undo everything his mother had done. He took grim delight in exhuming the body of Peter III, which Catherine had refused to bury among former sovereigns, and laying it alongside the wife who had been privy to her husband's murder.

At the time of his accession Paul seemed sane enough, although he was subject to violent fits of temper that threw him into a rage. He was extremely eccentric, however, and many of his actions in the latter part of his reign were those of a man not quite sane. Perhaps it was only to demonstrate his power that he forced everyone along the street or highway to kneel at the approach of the royal carriage and to remain on his knees until the tsar had passed. Those who tried to hide or run away were seized and imprisoned or sent to Siberia. There was a rigid formality to court ritual, and neglect or violation of it was sternly punished.

During Catherine's reign Paul and his second wife—the first had died while giving birth to a child by one of Paul's friends—had lived on the estate of Gatchina near St. Petersburg. The "little court" was the center of discontent and intrigue occasionally involving foreign ambassadors. Catherine's impatience with the meddling and the scheming is hardly surprising. She thought to keep her strange son amused by assigning to Gatchina a battalion of troops for him to command. But Paul took the assignment seriously and spent long hours every day parading, drilling, and inspecting his soldiers. Enamored of the Prussian dress and drill, he ordered his troops into the stiff, uncomfortable Prussian uniform and forced them to wear pigtails and to lard and powder their hair with flour or brick dust. He adopted the ballet-type marching and posturing so typical of the Prussian parade ground, and gave the orders himself for the endless drills. But he most enjoyed inspections, when he took a martinet's delight in finding a button missing or a uniform soiled and ordering the culprit to be knouted. After his accession he "reformed" the army by extending to all units the discipline and stupid formality of the Gatchina battalion. The Guards regiments were threatened with being removed from the capital and the Gatchina battalion was made their equal.

There was little design or intelligent thought behind Paul's governmental alterations other than his peevish determination to change his mother's pattern of doing things. Where Catherine had attempted to decentralize the administration, Paul sought to centralize it. He attempted to bring back into his own hands powers that his mother had encouraged subordinates to accept. He restored some of the colleges which Catherine had abolished but gave them no power. He revived the office of procurator-general but every few months dismissed the man appointed to fill it, as though he feared that long tenure might increase the appointee's influence. He abolished many elective posts in provincial or district government or made them appointive. He annulled Catherine's Charter to the Towns and filled town offices with his own nominees. Paul's political philosophy was simple and clear. "The only man in Russia who is important is the one to whom I happen to be speaking," he is supposed to have said, "and he is important only while I am speaking to him."

The reign began and continued on a note of reduced privileges for the gentry. Paul ordered the serfs as well as other classes to take the oath of allegiance to him, thus implying that the serf owed his loyalty first to the tsar and only second to the landlord. Merchants again received the right to own serfs as factory laborers, thus ending the monopoly of the gentry and encouraging the competition of the merchant class against the estate industries of the landowners. In effect, the Charter to the Nobles was repealed. Direct taxes were levied upon the gentry, and the tsar forced the nobles back into military service. Those found guilty of a crime might be flogged, a humiliating disregard for one of the fundamental exemptions of the gentry since Catherine's time. The provincial assemblies were discontinued, the marshals of the nobility were appointed, and the gentry lost their right to petition the throne. Paul's insulting treatment of the nobles, his abrogation of their privileges, his capricious dismissal of nobles from office, and his imprisonment of many of them made them sympathetic to his assassination.

The serfs fared no better at Paul's hands than did the gentry. The tsar's announcement that the serfs must take the oath of allegiance led them to suppose that they had been freed. Many of them refused to go back to their work. Widespread rebellion at the time of the coronation had to be put down by regular military expeditions. A half million state-owned peasants were given away to favorites during the four years of Paul's reign, while his mother had given away only eight hundred thousand in thirty-four years. He allowed peasants to petition the sovereign but made the right meaningless by insisting that they do so individually and not by groups. He forbade the gentry to work their serfs on Sunday but made no effort to see that the rule was enforced. He ordered landowners to exact no more than three days' *barshchina* from their serfs but provided no system of inspection to insure their obedience. The effect of the order was to increase by half the amount of *barshchina* for the serfs in Little Russia, where the peasants customarily had worked only two days in the landlord's fields.

Autocrat that he was determined to be, Paul had only the most intense hatred for the French Revolution. He forbade Russians to travel abroad but welcomed French *émigrés* and provided the future Louis XVIII with a pension and an estate in Courland. He banned the wearing of revolutionary dress—top boots, frock coats, and round hats—and personally stripped such clothes off anyone he found wearing them. He proscribed the importation of Western books, and even music, lest they spread revolutionary ideas.

Paul followed a foreign policy as erratic as that in domestic affairs. He opened his reign with a pledge to remain at peace and criticized his mother for keeping the nation at war for forty years. He cancelled Catherine's order to Suvorov to lead a Russian army to the assistance of Austrian troops in North Italy. But his loathing for the French Revolution and his irritation at Bonaparte's rumored project to revive Poland soon made Paul forget his promise of peace.

Catherine II had tried to enlist the support of the Knights of Malta in her wars with Turkey, and individual knights had served in the Russian armed forces. In 1797 a delegation from Malta prevailed upon Paul to accept the title of protector and later that of Grand Master of the order. Napoleon's seizure of the island on his way to Egypt in 1798 was taken by Paul as a personal challenge and insult. Consequently, Russia joined England, Austria, and Turkey in a war against France.

The Russian Black Sea fleet cooperated with a Turkish squadron to recover the Ionian Islands from the French. The Baltic fleet joined British warships in landing Russian and Allied troops in Holland. But the most brilliant, if fruitless, action of the war was Suvorov's campaign in Italy and Switzerland in 1798. Paul had driven the old marshal into retirement, but the Allies requested the tsar to allow the Russians, with other troops, to serve under the supreme command of Suvorov. One French general after another was defeated time and again by Suvorov in the summer of 1798, and the marshal announced his intention to drive on to Paris. His men's march over the St. Gothard pass in a driving blizzard to relieve the Allied force in Switzerland, and their victories over the French after their arrival, made an epic story of heroism in spite of privation and poor equipment.

In 1800 Paul deserted the coalition and shifted to the French side. He was irritated at the Austrians for their lukewarm support of Suvorov; he blamed the British for the defeat and capture of the Russian force in Holland; and he lost his temper completely when the British recovered Malta from the French but refused to turn it over to the Russian fleet. First he joined Denmark, Sweden, and Prussia in the "League of Armed Neutrality" to maintain the freedom of the seas against the British. He closed Russian ports to British shipping and even imprisoned English sailors stranded in Russia.

Napoleon, by then first consul of France, carefully cultivated Paul's friendship. He freed Russian prisoners of war and sent them home loaded with presents and decorations. He offered to turn Malta over to Russia, knowing very well that he could not do so as long as the British controlled it. He let Paul believe that the two should divide up the Turkish Empire. As a result, the tsar annexed Georgia and dreamed of acquiring Constantinople and the entire eastern half of the Balkan Peninsula. To help his ally Napoleon undermine British strength, Paul early in 1801 dispatched an army of twenty thousand Cossacks to conquer India.

Paul's Assassination

There had been talk of Paul's assassination within two years of his accession. Several nobles close to the emperor worked out the plot, which was joined by officers of the Guards under the leadership of Count Peter Pahlen, then military governor of St. Petersburg. Paul's oldest son Alexander was a party to the plot, although he may not have given his consent to have his father actually murdered. Apparently Alexander, naïvely to be sure, thought it would be possible simply to remove the emperor and put the government in the hands of a regency.

One night in March, 1801, the conspirators broke into Paul's bedroom and strangled him. Alexander, who was waiting in another wing of the palace, was notified of his father's death. Almost in a state of collapse, he had to be carried to the balcony overlooking the courtyard where troops had already been assembled to cheer his accession.

Of all the acts of Paul's reign, perhaps the most constructive was the repeal of the law of succession to the throne which had permitted such chaos since the death of Peter I. Paul's new law settled the succession in the Romanov family, a pointed insult to his mother, and ordered the throne to pass from father to oldest living son.

Fortunately for Russia, the reign of Paul did not last long enough to leave any permanent scars. The trend of developments after the accession of Peter the Great, and particularly after the accession of Catherine, who also called herself Great, was only momentarily interrupted. Alexander quickly reverted to the policies of his grandmother.

SUGGESTED READING

Anthony, K., *Catherine the Great* (Garden City, N.Y., Garden City Publishing Co., 1925).

———— (ed.), *The Memoirs of Catherine II* (New York, Knopf, 1927).

Blease, W. L., *Suvorof* (London, Constable, 1920).

Cambridge Modern History, Vol. VI (New York, Macmillan, 1909).

Lobanov-Rostovsky, A. A., *Russia and Europe, 1789–1825* (Durham, Duke University Press, 1947).

Lord, R. H., *The Second Partition of Poland* (Cambridge, Harvard University Press, 1915).

Maroger, D. (ed.), *The Memoirs of Catherine the Great* (New York, Macmillan, 1955).

Reddaway, W. F. (ed.), *The Documents of Catherine the Great* (New York, Cambridge University Press, 1931).

Soloveytchik, G., *Potemkin* (New York, Norton, 1947).

Thomson, G. S., *Catherine the Great and the Expansion of Russia* (London, English Universities Press, 1947).

Waliszewski, K., *The Romance of an Empress* (New York, Appleton, 1929).

————, *Paul the First of Russia* (Philadelphia, Lippincott, 1913).

16

A Royal Enigma

IN THE OPENING YEAR OF THE NINE-
teenth century Alexander I (1801–1825) came to the Russian throne—a
ruler so full of contradictions in character and in action that he has
fascinated scores of biographers. Arguments still rage over such questions
as whether he was actually the son of the Emperor Paul, the extent of his
involvement in his father's assassination, the degree of his moral degeneracy,
whether he was the dupe of Napoleon and later of Metternich, what was
really his purpose in setting up the Holy Alliance and, most violent of all
such arguments, whether he actually died in 1825 or simply disappeared
to live on for another forty years as a religious recluse in Siberia.

The reign may profitably be divided into three periods to reflect the
changes in problems which faced the nation and to reveal shifts in the
tsar's temperament and outlook. The first period, from Alexander's accession to the Peace of Tilsit (1801–1807), opens with the promulgation of
several minor reforms and consideration of the need for fundamental political
and social reorganization. This is a time when confidence that Russia's
despotism may be softened is inspired by the tsar's leadership toward, or
at least interest in, a better society. The period closes in a war with France,
during which all thought of reform necessarily is put aside. The second
period, from the Peace of Tilsit to the Congress of Vienna (1807–1815),
begins with a return of the tsar's interest in reform—an interest that wanes
as relations with France again become strained—and closes in a crusade
against Napoleon. This is a time when the nation's every energy is bent
toward the war effort and when the struggle for survival leaves no time
for thought of social change. Alexander dons the mantle of the savior of
Europe, divinely appointed to deliver the world from the forces of darkness

epitomized by Napoleon. The third period, from the Congress of Vienna to the end of the reign (1815–1825), is one of disillusionment and unrest for the Russian people. Contact with Western thought during the war has made all the more pressing and obvious the need for thoroughgoing reform of Russian government and society. But the tsar, perhaps overwhelmed and confused by the problems which burden him, turns finally away from reality and toward religious mysticism. His energy is directed toward the maintenance of the peace settlement of Vienna which he has done so much to make possible. The reign which began so benignly and which promised greater relief for the Russian people than any other in history ends in tragic frustration and revolt.

ALEXANDER'S EDUCATION AND CHARACTER

Soon after his birth Alexander was taken from his mother by Empress Catherine, who carefully directed his life from then until his marriage. The grandmother named the child, designed his clothes, played with him, taught him the alphabet, wrote a book of maxims for him, and gave him a globe which inspired in him an interest in geography which he never lost. To toughen the future tsar to the sound of cannon Catherine installed him in a room of the Winter Palace overlooking the parade ground, but the salvos from the salute guns deafened him in one ear, a weakness of which he was conscious throughout his life.

At the age of seven the boy's formal education began under a staff of carefully selected tutors. The most formative of the influences to which Alexander was subjected for the next seven years was that of Frederick La Harpe, a Swiss liberal of avowed republican sentiment. The youthful grand duke studied Demosthenes, Plato, Montesquieu, Locke, and Rousseau, while the teacher added his own strong views on the evils of tyranny, the ugliness of serfdom, and the merits of liberty, equality, and justice. The head of "the little twelve-year-old politician-philosopher" was filled with the democratic theories of the most advanced classical and modern thinkers; and by drawing vividly upon the lives of Genghis Khan, the Borgias, and Philip II, La Harpe inspired in his pupil a hatred of despotism and a fondness for liberty. On many later occasions Alexander insisted that hereditary monarchy was an inexcusable and insufferable institution. At Tilsit the tsar and the French emperor indulged in a friendly discussion of the subject. "He argued that hereditary right was an abuse," Napoleon reported, "and I had to use all my eloquence and logic for a full hour to prove that hereditary right guarantees the peace and happiness of nations."

Before Alexander's sixteenth birthday his grandmother decided that the grand duke had had enough of formal education. In an effort to prove to the Russian people that this youth who she hoped might succeed her was now a grown man, Catherine arranged his marriage to a German princess who took the name of Elizabeth. The coldness of the fifteen-year-old bride, at least to her husband, turned Alexander to the companionship of a Polish countess whose beauty wore much better than did that of his wife, who was fat and pimply before she was thirty.

While Empress Catherine was alive her son Paul was excluded from the capital and maintained his own court at Gatchina. It was part of the schedule to which Catherine kept Alexander that he and his brother Constantine spent every week end with their father. Paul, already nearing insanity, passed his time in endlessly drilling the few troops allowed him, and his sons were forced to join the maneuvers when they visited him. Alexander developed an intense passion for armies and parades despite having had to witness Paul's disgusting fits of temper and the brutal punishments he imposed for the slightest deviation from the strict Prussian drill. On one occasion, when the son was kneeling before the father to beg pardon for a soldier guilty of a minor infraction, Paul kicked the grand duke in the face. Perhaps, too, Alexander's later reputation for diplomacy and charm and ability to please owed much to the necessity for quickly changing his manner as he shuttled between the brilliant, profligate court at St. Petersburg and the harsh discipline of Gatchina.

In a land where all political power rests with the ruler the sovereign's character may be a determinative influence in shaping national development. Throughout the nineteenth century Russia's progress toward needed reform or her descent into reaction was decided by the tsar's moods and whims. Certainly it is true that bureaucrats often formulated policies and administered them intelligently or punitively, but it must be remembered that such officials were responsible only to the tsar, appointed and dismissed at his will.

The character of Alexander I is more elusive than that of any other Russian monarch, with the possible exception of his grandmother, Catherine II. While many will debate the details of his character, few will deny that the tsar's nature in general was extremely complex and puzzling. And so it seemed to his contemporaries. "Of great loftiness of character," Napoleon admitted, "he possesses both intellect and charm and is highly accomplished; easily led astray, one cannot trust his ingratiating manners; he is lacking in frankness, a true Byzantine." "Alexander's character," remarked Metternich, "represents a strange blending of the qualities of a man and the weaknesses of a woman." "It would be difficult to have more intelligence than the Emperor Alexander," Napoleon mused, "but I find there is something lacking in him, and I have never managed to discover what it is." Napoleon named him "The Talma of the North" after the most accomplished actor in the Paris theater at the time. The last ambassador of Napoleonic

France to the Russian court confessed to his superior that "the character of the Emperor Alexander becomes daily more of an enigma to me." To his intimate friend, Prince Adam Czartoryski, the tsar was no such puzzle. The prince declared Alexander to be "lacking in profound and definite convictions."

Alexander was thoroughly spoiled as a child by the pampering of Empress Catherine. Her boastful letters to the philosopher Grimm insist upon the child's unusual promise. "When you speak of Alexander you touch a weak spot in me. I have told you of his health and strength, and he is now beginning to show a remarkable intelligence for a child of his age. I dote upon him, and I intend, if possible, to have him always with me." When the child is a year old his grandmother writes: "He is as beautiful as a little god of love. Everybody is fond of him, I more than others, and I can do anything I like with him. He can walk alone now, and even when his teeth are giving him pain he is just as good-tempered as ever, and laughs and frolics while he makes us understand he is suffering. He understands everything that is said to him, and has a wonderful language of his own of signs and sounds." A year later she reports: "He writes me letters from his own room, sends for me if he is ill, and really seems to get better as soon as I appear. Those who do not watch him as closely as I do not know how much understanding or what quick instincts he has; he is as advanced in all ways as a child of four or five. He comes to me whenever he wants anything explained, and he does not consider he knows a thing properly unless he has learned it from me." And yet she insists that "he gets spoiled when away from me!"

The grand duke's education in the high-flown principles of democracy and justice left him with a theoretical approach to government that was to prove completely unrealistic when he ascended the throne. He often showed little understanding of the practicalities of government, and particularly of the need to temper his ideals with reason. Sometimes he seemed to mock the ideals he proclaimed by the actions he felt honestly impelled to take. "I shall always be a republican," he insisted, but at the same time he refused to permit the creation of a representative assembly to share his legislative power. He professed to hate despotism, but was irritated at the pressures brought upon him to assist the Greeks in ridding themselves of the tyrannous oppression of the sultan.

That his father's assassination had been planned with his knowledge and carried through with his tacit consent left Alexander with a growing sense of guilt. Late in life his guilt overwhelmed him and turned him into a religious fanatic who spent so many hours kneeling in repentance on the stone floors of Russian churches that he developed large callouses on his knees. "His grief and the remorse which he was continually reviving in his heart were inexpressibly deep and touching," wrote his intimate friend

Czartoryski. "He continually saw in his imagination the mutilated body of his father, and his mental tortures never ceased." His efforts to escape from this feeling of guilt in the closing years of the reign drove him to feverish journeys from one end of the country to the other, leading his critics to grumble that "Russia was being governed from the seat of a post-chaise." It may have been the effort to avoid being left with his own thoughts that made him seek the comforts of love which his wife was unable or unwilling to provide him. Women fell easily under his charm, and the cynics insist that his life was a parade of conquests.

Brave as he surely was on the field of battle, Alexander was often weak and vacillating in defending his own views. Napoleon respected his tenacity, but interpreted it as stubbornness rather than conviction. Lacking in self-confidence, a dreamer to the core, he never faced reality. Time and again, both before and during his reign, he threatened to retire to a cottage retreat on the Rhine and give up the responsibilities he had inherited. He leaned heavily upon advisers, but chose them without discrimination. Of the men enjoying his confidence on the eve of the French invasion, Speransky was perhaps the finest statesman that Russia has produced, and Arakcheyev was one of the most sadistic brutes that ever counselled a ruler.

Alexander was alternately enthusiastic and depressed, ambitious and discouraged, simple and devious, logical and obscure, moralistic and depraved, winsome and retiring, impulsive and hesitant, energetic and slothful, communicative and suspicious. He blew hot and cold on almost every serious problem that faced him. His subjects reacted to him in similar extremes, greeting him with overtures of joy at his accession and plotting to assassinate him at the close of the reign.

ALEXANDER'S ACCESSION AND PROMISE

The death of Paul, which was officially announced as the result of apoplexy, brought a sense of welcome relief to all segments of Russian society. People wept for joy and embraced in the streets on hearing that the pall of sorrow which had hung over the nation for five dragging years had been lifted. That a new era had dawned in Russia was patent to all who saw Alexander walking unguarded through the streets of the capital, speaking and smiling in the manner of one who considered his subjects his peers. The new sovereign, steeped in the egalitarianism of the French Revolution, eagerly sought the love and confidence of his people by appearing to be one of them. The ecstasy which greeted the tsar continued for years, and often the appearance of his coach in the streets of a provincial town was the signal for his cheering subjects to remove the horses and draw the carriage themselves. His accession was taken throughout Europe to herald a new Russian policy of opposition to tyranny and oppression. Men remembered the liberal education to which Catherine had subjected her grandson. They forgot her abhorrence of revolution, an abhorrence which Alexander later came to share.

The imperial manifesto by which Alexander announced his succession promised that he would "rule over the people committed to our care according to the laws and the benevolence of our grandmother, Catherine the Great, whose memory will forever be dear to us and to the whole nation." After the nightmarish cruelties of Paul's reign, men were inclined to forget Catherine's shortcomings and to look upon her rule as progressive and gentle. While it is perhaps debatable whether Alexander was ever the liberal he loudly professed to be, it is clear that at this moment the twenty-four-year-old monarch was sincere in his determination to follow Catherine's lead in bringing much-needed reform to the nation.

On the very night of his father's murder Alexander ordered the recall of a Cossack force sent out by Paul to conquer India. Even if it had not consumed its provender and exhausted its horses, the expedition had been doomed to failure because it had not been provided with maps of the unknown territory through which it was travelling. Paul was charged with deliberately planning its extermination because of the democratic sentiments which the Cossacks were presumed to hold. Peace was restored with England and commercial relations between the two countries re-established. At the same time the tsar signed an agreement of peace with France, and friendly gestures were advanced to Sweden and Persia. "The tsar of peace," his subjects dubbed him.

A number of other measures taken at the moment of his accession seemed to confirm Alexander's resolution to mitigate the evils which Russia suffered. Twelve thousand political prisoners locked up by Paul were ordered released. The secret police and the tribunal before which political prisoners had been tried and forced to confess were abolished, and the tsar promised that accused persons would thenceforth be tried and punished according to law. Torture was forbidden. Thousands of officials dismissed by Paul for trifling offenses were restored to their jobs. The proscription against foreign books was lifted, and private publishing houses were allowed to reopen. Russians once more were permitted to travel abroad. The charters of liberty granted to the nobles and townsmen by Catherine, which had been repealed by Paul, were reissued. Advertisements for sale of serfs without soil were forbidden in capital newspapers. For the most part, these orders, issued within the first week of the new reign, simply removed the most obvious offenses of the mad Paul. Fundamental reorganization and reform could not be undertaken until weeks of study and consideration were devoted to the needs of the state.

THE UNOFFICIAL COMMITTEE

To discuss national conditions and help him work out a plan of reforms Alexander selected a committee of four intimate friends who began, within three months of his accession, to meet with the tsar over coffee. The choice of these advisers indicates the liberal temperament of the tsar at the time. Prince Adam Czartoryski was an uncompromising Polish nationalist who had been indoctrinated with the philosophy of the French Revolution but whose chief concern was the restoration of an independent Poland. The revival of Poland was itself a reform measure loudly urged by every liberal in Europe. He frankly warned Alexander, who named him deputy foreign minister of Russia, that when Russian interests conflicted with those of his native Poland he would defend the welfare of his own country. Count Paul Stroganov, the wealthiest nobleman in Russia, had lived in Paris during the Revolution and had there joined the Jacobin club and served as its librarian. Romm, his companion at the time, later became a member and temporary president of the Convention. The most radical of the unofficial committee, Stroganov retained his democratic sympathies long after Catherine recalled him from revolutionary France, but he had lost some of his Jacobin ardor before joining Alexander's committee. He praised the tsar's good intentions but considered him lazy and weak. Count Nicholas Novosiltsev, Stroganov's cousin, was the oldest of the group, being ten years older than the tsar, and was inclined to be cautious and less zealous than the others. Count Victor Kochubey, a brilliant diplomat reared in England and much more familiar with that country than with his own, was less liberal than Stroganov but more so than Novosiltsev. All of the brain-trusters were in their twenties or early thirties.

The committee first set itself the task of discovering what conditions actually obtained in Russian government and society, for none of them, least of all the tsar, possessed more than a superficial knowledge of Russia. After thus taking stock of the situation the committee hoped to move on to a reorganization of the governmental machinery and a reform of society; and to assure that such reorganization and reform would continue they planned to draft a constitution. Finally, Alexander expressed the desire to cap the new edifice with a formal declaration of human rights. He corresponded with Thomas Jefferson on the problem of constitutional reform, and the American president sent him commentaries on the Constitution of the United States. The committee went off on tangents, considering various aspects of national policy as they came into view, and kept to no central theme in its deliberations. One particular point of discussion is noteworthy for its revelation of the tsar's naïveté and impetuous nature. When foreign policy was being considered Alexander, who had just concluded a treaty of amity with England, voiced his sentiment for a European coalition against England. Kochubey pointed out that England was Russia's best trade customer and natural ally against an aggressive France; Alexander, to his credit, readily admitted to being wrong.

The tsar expressed the hope of reorganizing the Senate to make it a representative legislative assembly, but the nobles who testified before the committee wanted to limit the right to vote to Russians of their own class. The members of the committee were inclined to the view that the welfare of the people would be better served by leaving the legislative power in the hands of the sovereign than by permitting it to be exercised by the usually selfish nobles. The need for limiting the autocratic power, consequently, was not to be met for another century. All agreed that a limited monarchy or constitutional order of some sort was desirable, but felt that it could not be established in a Russia where better than half the population lived in bondage. Education of the people would have to precede any such move, and in the meantime the administrative machinery of government should be overhauled and brought to a high standard of efficiency. Only then could government control be shared with representatives of the Russian people. Such was the sentiment of the committee, and it must be admitted that there was logic in their stand.

When the problem of what to do about serfdom came before the committee, the members revealed their caution and their concern not to be tarred as Jacobins by their fellow nobles. One of the most liberal nobles to appear before the group argued that the government had no right to interfere with the ownership of private property, which included serfs, but he believed that serf labor would ultimately prove uneconomical and serfdom would naturally disappear. Another proposal considered by the committee was to prohibit the ownership of house serfs, the present ones to be freed and their owners compensated by the government. To all such recommendations the members were opposed in varying degrees. Novosiltsev noted that the government had no money with which to purchase the freedom of house serfs and questioned the advisability of forcing freedom upon irresponsible wretches who might not be able to support themselves. He was most insistent that care should be exerted to avoid irritating the nobility, but Stroganov was scornful of this point. Kochubey cautioned against freeing some of the serfs and so making the others restless. Stroganov, consistently liberal, reminded the tsar that the loyalty of the serfs had been withdrawn from the ruler in Catherine's time and might be withdrawn again if their hopes for emancipation were shattered. La Harpe, whose opinion was solicited, expressed a fear of abolishing serfdom until the masses were educated, but noted the danger of educating the people before they were free. The committee agreed that serfdom was an evil institution, but it did no more than express the pious hope that some day it might disappear.

EARLY REFORMS

At Czartoryski's suggestion, concurred in by the entire committee, Alexander abolished the colleges, or boards, which headed the administrative branches of the government and replaced them with ministries each headed by a single appointee responsible to the tsar. Under the collegiate system no individual was accountable for the operation of a department, and the resultant shifting of responsibility had made efficient administration impossible. Ministries of foreign affairs, war, navy, interior, finance, education, justice, and commerce were established, and the ministers were ordered to submit annual reports to the Senate. The ministers, together with a number of other appointive officials, were to make up the Council of Ministers with power to recommend to the tsar but with no power to determine policy. Alexander retained the final legislative, executive, and judicial authority unshackled by any restrictive limitation whatever.

The Unofficial Committee asked the Senate to investigate and describe its own powers and duties, for no one, including the senators, really understood them. Now the position of the Senate was clearly defined. As the supreme administrative and judicial agency of government its powers were declared to be limited only by the will of the tsar. Its *ukazes,* or decrees, were to enjoy the same force as did those of the ruler who alone could countermand them. It would receive annual reports from the ministers, call them to account, and recommend their dismissal. Only the tsar could review its judicial judgments. The Senate might even question an imperial *ukaz* if it seemed to contradict existing law. A few months after this definition of senatorial powers received the royal sanction the Senate unanimously protested an imperial order to the tsar's face. Alexander colored, but agreed to reconsider his action. Later he pronounced that the Senate had misinterpreted the definition of its authority. It was free to question pronouncements of his predecessors, but those of the present ruler must be accepted without question.

It has been maintained, with considerable justification, that the greatest accomplishment of the Unofficial Committee was to provide Alexander with a knowledge of conditions in Russia and of the workings of the machinery of government which he had not acquired and could not possibly have learned so quickly in any other way. The committee's deliberations may also have had the effect of making clear to Alexander the practical difficulties of providing theoretical solutions to the problems which he had assumed could be solved simply. And, unquestionably, the reorganization of the executive agencies was an important achievement. Thereafter there was less "oriental disorder" in the administration, and responsibility for executive action could be maintained. The chaos which characterized the collegiate system was considerably reduced.

From his consultations with the Unofficial Committee Alexander became convinced that the nation needed a well-run and well-financed school system more than it needed a constitution. In this opening period of the reign he provided more for education than did any other ruler of Russia, allocating nearly four times as much money for its support as had Catherine, who was renowned for her organization and endowment of schools. Alexander ordered the erection of a university in each educational district, the establishment of a *gymnasium*, or secondary school, in every provincial capital, and the maintenance of primary schools in all counties. Attendance at the schools was not to be limited to sons of the gentry but to be free to all classes of society. By the end of the reign nearly fifty secondary schools were serving an average of over a hundred students each, and over three hundred primary schools could boast nearly the same average attendance. An institution to train teachers was set up in St. Petersburg, and six universities, four of them new, were in operation by the end of the reign. An *ukaz* in 1804 promised academic freedom and permitted the universities to govern themselves, although such liberties were curtailed later in the reign and withdrawn entirely by Nicholas I.

A number of liberal magazines, some of them subsidized by the state, began publication in the early years of the century. Articles critical of serfdom and arguing for constitutional government were passed by the official censor, who was ordered to be lenient. Books on economics, politics, and philosophy appeared in volume, among them translations of liberal writings from Western Europe. The government paid for the translation of Adam Smith's *Wealth of Nations,* the whole tenor of which was an indictment of non-free elements in the economy, thus providing Russians with scientific arguments in favor of the abolition of serfdom.

While the Unofficial Committee drew back from any proposal to abolish serfdom as an institution, Alexander himself ordered several measures which constituted a first step in the direction of total emancipation. It will be recalled that the tsar, during his first week on the throne, had forbidden notices of sale of serfs to be printed in capital newspapers. While the command has been derided as a sop to the sensibilities of foreign residents in St. Petersburg, it had the effect of serving notice that serfdom did not enjoy royal approval.

Furthermore, in the first year of the reign another edict granted to any free person the right to own land. While landowners' serfs were not affected by this, the order did put an end to the monopoly of land ownership by the gentry. It immediately prompted a number of liberal nobles to submit to the government for approval contracts by which their serfs would be freed with land in return for a schedule of cash payments over a period of years. After a number of such cases the tsar issued a law regularizing the procedure, empowering nobles to free whole serf villages, but only with land, or individual serf families without land, provided the arrangement regarding financial settlement was approved by the government. The leading historian of the time, the conservative Karamzin, belittled the move, saying that serfs belonging to humane landowners would not want their freedom and those belonging to bad ones were too poor to buy it. Only fifty thousand serfs, called "free farmers," purchased their freedom under the act before it was repealed to make way for general emancipation in the latter half of the century.

In 1804 the government liberalized conditions among the serfs of the Baltic provinces, strictly limiting the dues collectible by the landowners, forbidding the sale of serfs without land, and granting the peasants the right of self-government. Alexander's own attitude toward serfdom was apparent from the severity with which he punished serf-owners found guilty of abusing their serfs, often denying them the right to manage their own estates. And the tsar made and kept the promise not to transfer any more state serfs to private landowners.

WAR WITH NAPOLEON

After three years of sincere effort to find solutions to the internal problems of Russia, Alexander turned his attention abruptly to the field of foreign affairs. From what is known of his character it seems less likely that international problems forced the tsar to give up his concern for domestic reform than that he was unable any longer to maintain interest in the prosaic problems that faced him at home. He was never able to concentrate upon one matter for long, nor was he often courageous in sustaining the attack upon difficult issues. His flair for the dramatic and his fascination for the glitter of international politics had already become evident. Alexander now fancied himself a diplomat. And it is not impossible that he was coming to consider himself the savior of Europe, just as he had been called the savior of Russia after the crushing despotism of Paul's reign.

By 1804 Alexander came around to Pitt's view that unless the nations of Europe stood together against the insatiable ambition of Napoleon they would go down one by one. The Corsican's disturbance of the power balance in Europe constituted a deadly threat to every free state. In March, 1804, the *émigré* French nobleman, the Duc d'Enghien, was seized in Baden by French troops who crossed the border in crass violation of Baden's sovereignty. A drumhead court-martial convicted the duke of plotting to assassinate Napoleon, and he was shot. The Russian court at St. Petersburg wore mourning in open expression of disapproval of the execution, feeling the action to be particularly insulting to Russia since the Empress Elizabeth was a princess of Baden. When the tsar voiced his indignation that the territory of a sovereign state had been violated, Napoleon crudely asked him whether Russian troops would not have crossed the border in pursuit of the assassins of the Emperor Paul had they been known. This indelicate reminder that Alexander's complicity in his father's death was widely suspected only infuriated the tsar. By the end of the year Napoleon took upon himself the title "Emperor of the French," an affront in itself to the crowned heads of Europe, who considered the Corsican a parvenu.

Alexander's awakening to the threat of Napoleonic imperialism began when, early in 1804, Napoleon spurned the tsar's naïve proposal that France satisfy herself with her natural boundaries and withdraw from all territory beyond the Rhine and the Alps. Alexander recalled his ambassador to France, after flauntingly decorating him with Russia's highest order. The tsar then sent his friend Novosiltsev to England, which was then fighting alone against Napoleon, to explore the possibility of a European crusade against France. Novosiltsev's instructions were to propose a coalition to drive the French out of Germany and Italy and Napoleon out of France. The peoples of Europe should be guaranteed the right to constitutional government. When peace should come it should rest upon recognized principles of international law. Disputes among nations or threats to legitimate governments should be settled by mediation.

The British prime minister had little sympathy for Alexander's lofty ideals. It may be that the practical Pitt suspected that the tsar's visionary proposal to call Europe to a crusade for freedom was not entirely unselfish. The memoirs of Czartoryski, the Russian foreign minister, reveal that in Alexander's view of postwar Europe Russia was to receive the Danubian principalities of Moldavia and Wallachia, Constantinople and the Straits, and Prussian and Austrian as well as Russian Poland—a program of "slight border rectification" to which England could never agree. However, Pitt was willing to subsidize the march of a Russian army against Napoleon, and from the Anglo-Russian agreement and the Austro-Russian treaty signed earlier was born the Third Coalition against France. The signatories agreed that France must be pushed back to her pre-Revolutionary boundaries. The French emperor managed to keep Prussia out of the alliance against him by dangling the prospect of giving Hanover to her. For Prussia and her king, Napoleon always showed the greatest contempt, saying that "the Prussian eagle is half vulture." He distracted the Prussian jackal now by tossing him "a bone to gnaw."

The Allied plan was that Russia should move her army into central Europe to join that of Austria and catch Napoleon before he could concentrate his forces, then poised at Boulogne for an invasion of England, against them. But Bonaparte, in one of his finest displays of strategical genius, brought his troops from the English Channel to South Germany so quickly that the main Austrian army was surrounded at Ulm and forced to capitulate almost without a struggle before the Russians could come up. "Our Emperor conquers the enemy with our legs," the French troops remarked after Ulm.

The Russian commander, General Kutuzov, whom Napoleon called "the old fox of the North," managed to escape temporarily, but was forced, with the Austrian remnant, to challenge the French at Austerlitz. The Russian tsar, who now fancied himself a man of military talent, overruled Kutuzov and made the decision to stand against Napoleon instead of falling back to draw out still further the long French lines of communication. Alexander, who later showed some real military ability, took a bitter lesson from the master. On the first anniversary of his coronation as emperor, Napoleon won the most brilliant victory of his career. The Allied army was cut in two, and one half was annihilated while the other was badly mauled. The Russians fought heroically but to no purpose under leaders who were completely fooled and outmaneuvered in what has been called the first great battle of modern times. Allied losses totalled 25,000 men, nearly a third of those engaged, while the French suffered 10,000 casualties, about 8 per cent of their force. Nearly all of the Russian guns were captured, and they could be less easily spared than could the soldiers. Alexander, who barely escaped capture, was found after the battle sitting on the ground weeping bitterly. The coalition was broken and its armies destroyed or routed. The tsar was granted an armistice by the terms of which he had to withdraw his armies behind the Vistula. Austria lost her Italian territories to the Napoleonic kingdom of Italy and sanctioned the reorganization of Germany which the French emperor had carried through. The Holy Roman Empire was laid to rest, and the Habsburg ruler henceforth was to be known as the emperor of Austria. Prussia was confirmed in her acquisition of Hanover.

The king of Prussia, who had already lost his Rhenish provinces and was stripped of influence in Germany by the creation of the Confederation of the Rhine as a French satellite, now had to face the prospect that Napoleon would take Hanover from him and offer to return it to England in exchange for peace with the island kingdom. A spirit of nationalism was beginning to surge in Prussia, and the king was driven by the importunities of the war party led by his chauvinistic wife to mobilize for war. A month before Austerlitz the Prussian king and the Russian tsar had sworn eternal friendship at a midnight meeting at the tomb of Frederick the Great. Now, although badly beaten at Austerlitz, Alexander spurned the treaty of peace which Napoleon offered and won over Prussia to a new coalition against France aimed, among other things, at recovering the Prussian territories on the Rhine. Having made up his mind to go to war, the Prussian ruler rashly moved his troops into the field before his Russian allies could come up to support him. At the battles of Jena and Auerstädt, fought on the same day, the Prussian army was completely destroyed. The Prussian forts fell one after another and the country was completely overrun. Napoleon marched into Berlin and the Prussian king was driven for safety to his most distant stronghold, the fortress of Königsberg on the Russian border. Rarely has a nation been so thoroughly humbled as was Prussia in 1806.

Alexander returned to Russia after the Austerlitz disaster more determined than ever to destroy "the enemy of peace." Through the Holy Synod he ordered a proclamation to be read in every church in the land pronouncing anathema upon Napoleon as an atheist, a usurper, and a consorter with Jews—the latter an apparent reference to the fact that French Jews officially condoned Bonaparte's rule. The regiments decimated at Austerlitz were recruited to full strength, wagons and horses were requisitioned, and an enormous militia force, untrained and poorly equipped, was marshalled to defend the frontier against the expected French invasion.

The Russian troops under General Bennigsen, a Hanoverian by birth, moved into Poland to meet the French. Napoleon paraded through Warsaw, greeted enthusiastically by the Poles, who placed in him their hope that Polish independence might be restored. Alexander had foolishly ignored Czartoryski's advice to liberate the Poles, and was to suffer now and later for his shortsightedness. As usual, Bonaparte's force outnumbered that of his opponent, for a sizeable Russian army had been dispatched into the Balkans to meet the Turks who, at French urging, had recently declared war against Russia. But even with the good fortune of having fine weather, Polish support, and superior numbers, Napoleon faced more serious obstacles in this campaign than in the earlier contests with Austria and Prussia. The Russian army had been hastily but effectively reorganized since Austerlitz under Alexander's painstaking supervision, and the cavalry, particularly, had been strengthened. Bennigsen, an able strategist and, at his best, a competent tactician, learned quickly from Napoleon's campaigns and applied the lessons to the best of his ability. Bonaparte's earlier successes were in some measure due to the fact that his Austrian and Prussian opponents persisted in fighting in the manner of the eighteenth century. Finally, Napoleon found foraging a continual problem in the poor Polish countryside, quite different from the lush and heavily populated lands of central Europe.

Napoleon was defeated in minor engagements, and the French, exhausted by long marches, scanty supplies, and chill nights, went into winter quarters. The year ended without Bonaparte's being able, as in earlier campaigns, to force a great battle which would wind up the affair. The Russian withdrawal, always in good order, must have been particularly frustrating to the French emperor.

A momentary break in winter weather led Bennigsen to hope for an early spring, and he moved to the attack in February, 1807. At Eylau the two

forces, of about equal strength, collided in the bloodiest battle since Mal-
plaquet a century before. During part of the day a blinding snowstorm
turned the fight into a hand-to-hand melee that ended in frightful slaughter.
The best French troops were roughly handled, both armies lost heavily in
officers, and Napoleon himself was nearly captured. Each side lost twenty
thousand men, half of them killed. "What a massacre," the French Marshal
Ney observed, "and without any result." Both armies bivouacked on the
field. Napoleon was strangely quiet, not boastful as usual, when he and his
generals gathered around the campfire. But during the night French reinforcements arrived and Bennigsen withdrew. At daybreak Napoleon was
relieved to find the Russians gone. He claimed the victory, but his frightful
losses and the exhaustion of his men made pursuit impossible. The Russian
troops, many of them veterans of Austerlitz, had stood bravely and stubbornly, and won the respect of the French man in the ranks. "These Russians fight like bulls," French soldiers admitted.

Soon after Eylau Napoleon offered Prussia an alliance, but Alexander
succeeded in keeping the Prussian ruler in his own camp. Bonaparte, as
fascinated as ever with the Middle East, then hurried an envoy to the Shah
of Persia to urge a back-door attack upon Russia. And, ever mindful that
his first enemy was still England, Napoleon suggested a combined Franco-
Persian attack upon India.

When the combatants returned to the fight four months after Eylau,
Napoleon took another defeat before being handed the opportunity to win
the great victory that would end the war. Bennigsen, in a rare lapse of his
usual skill, chose to defend an impossible position at Friedland. Again the
fighting was vicious and the losses staggering. Again the Russian troops
acquitted themselves with such valor that even Napoleon praised them. But
Bennigsen's errors combined with Napoleon's skill to produce a Russian
defeat sufficiently costly to decide the tsar to ask for peace. Russia was
winning one war against Turkey, where the prospect of gain was much more
promising, and facing another with Persia. Alexander may suddenly have
awakened to the fact that he was fighting practically alone on the continent
in defense of the interest of all Europe; he may have concluded that the
game was not worth the candle. He did not hide his impatience with England
for not providing him with greater subsidies, and he could not continue the
financial burden alone.

THE PEACE OF TILSIT, 1807

Ten days after Friedland the Russian and French armies were drawn up
on opposite banks of the river Niemen at Tilsit. As the troops cheered and
the artillery fired salutes the two emperors left their respective shores and

were rowed to a canopied raft anchored in the middle of the stream. Napoleon arrived first and greeted Alexander effusively. The tsar is reported to have said, "I hate the British as much as you do," to which Napoleon replied, "In that case, peace is made." The story is probably a fabrication, but the words attributed to Alexander do express his probable resentment at England's shabby support. Little more than pleasantries were exchanged in this dramatic setting, and the tsar was invited to be Napoleon's guest in Tilsit while the two arranged the settlement. The Prussian king remained ashore during the meeting, riding his horse back and forth impatiently along the Russian bank, now and again wading his mount into the stream and cocking his head as though trying to overhear the conversations which might be deciding his fate.

For two weeks the negotiations went on between the emperors while their subordinates drafted the formal document. Each did his best to charm the other and both succeeded, if their statements at the time can be believed. Napoleon wrote home to his wife that the tsar "is a very handsome, good young emperor, and has more intelligence than is generally believed," high praise indeed from the vain Corsican. In turn, Alexander flattered Napoleon by saying to him, "Why could we not have met before?" After the two had parted the tsar wrote to his sister, "Napoleon thinks I am a fool, but he laughs best who laughs last." Bonaparte probably thought the same thing. Both certainly were insincere in their profession of friendship, but both gained so much from the settlement that they could afford to appear generous.

The most serious obstacle to cordial relations between the eastern and western emperors was removed when Alexander accepted the realignment of territories in Germany and Italy which Napoleon had accomplished prior to the present war. But the tsar held out doggedly against French plans for destroying Prussia. Napoleon, so contemptuous of the Prussian king that he saw no justification for continuing his political existence, would have torn away the rich Prussian province of Silesia. Alexander successfully parried that disaster, but was forced to agree to the loss of all Prussian territory west of the Elbe, leaving that river, sixty miles from Berlin, as the western frontier of Prussia. Prussian Poland was reconstituted as the grand duchy of Warsaw, to be ruled by the king of Saxony, whom Napoleon considered trustworthy. The tsar swallowed his indignation at this partial revival of Poland as a French puppet and military outpost on the shores of the Vistula. Prussia was saddled with an indemnity so impossibly heavy that French occupation forces, who were to be settled in the kingdom until its payment, could look forward to a long residence. The Prussian king was allowed to retain about half his former territory. Napoleon intended the Prussian sacrifices to be irreparably crippling, but he let it be known that Prussia owed her existence to "special deference to His Majesty, the Emperor of

All the Russias." He dismissed the protests of the Prussian minister with the reminder: "Your king owes everything to the chivalrous support of the Emperor Alexander. Without him your dynasty would have lost its throne and I should have given Prussia to my brother, Jerome. Your king may look upon it as a favor from me that I leave anything at all in his possession."

Russia agreed to attempt to compose the differences between France and England and to go to war against England if she should refuse a settlement. France consented to act in a similar way to end the Russo-Turkish war. Indeed, if Turkey did not agree to peace with Russia, Napoleon agreed to assist the tsar in "liberating" all the Balkans, except for Constantinople and its environs, from Turkish rule. Alexander pleaded for the inclusion of Constantinople, asking "would you deny me the key to my house?" But Napoleon would not hear of the suggestion that Russia should control the Straits. Russian ports were to be closed to British shipping as Napoleon's new ally joined his "Continental system." Russia surrendered to France the large islands off the Greek coast—Corfu, Cephalonia, Zante, and Ithaca —which Paul had captured; they were important to Napoleon's ambitions in the Near East. As compensation Russia received from Prussia the Polish district of Bialystok, which Napoleon was confident would stir Prussian enmity against Russia. Alexander seems to have given Napoleon a free hand in dealing with the Pope's territories in return for encouragement to seize Finland. The emperors concluded a mutual defense agreement against all aggressors, even working out the military commitments in case either were attacked.

In informal conversations prophetic of the Nazi-Soviet pact of 1939 Napoleon offered to divide Europe with Alexander, the Vistula to form the boundary between the two empires. England, of course, did not figure in the plan, for Napoleon was confident that "the nation of shopkeepers" could be brought to her knees by destroying her trade with the Continent. To him it must have seemed a concession to agree to share the rule of the world with one partner; he would not abide another. "I have often slept two in a bed," he quipped to the tsar, "but never three." He might have added that he much preferred to sleep alone.

With the conclusion of peace at Tilsit Alexander was free to return to Russia to take up once more the internal problems which he had escaped only momentarily by leaving the country. He might have congratulated himself upon dealing so successfully with a victor who had never granted a soft peace. The loss of the war had won Alexander some territory and the assurance of much more to come. The erection of a French satellite state at Warsaw was an irritation, but the threat would have been much more serious had Silesia been added to the grand duchy, an eventuality which the tsar had managed to prevent. The sidewalk diplomats in the Paris cafes wondered whether Napoleon's new alliance with "the Talma of the North" had not been bought at too high a price. That defeated Russia had not been punished was something for Frenchmen to ponder. Might they not have to fight her again? Napoleon himself admitted that the maintenance of the peace of Europe depended upon the Russian tsar.

SUGGESTED READING

Bruun, G., *Europe and the French Imperium* (New York, Harper's, 1938).

Cambridge Modern History, Vol. IX (New York, Macmillan, 1934).

Choiseul-Gouffier, Comtesse de, *Historical Memoirs of the Emperor Alexander I and the Court of Russia* (A. C. McClurg, 1901).

Czartoryski, A., *Memoirs of Prince Adam Czartoryski and His Correspondence with Alexander I* (Remington, 1888).

Caulaincourt, A. A. L., *Memoirs of General Caulaincourt* (Cassell, 1938).

Hodgetts, E. A. B., *The Court of Russia in the Nineteenth Century* (New York, Scribner's, 1908).

Kornilov, A., *Modern Russian History* (New York, Knopf, 1943).

Lobanov-Rostovsky, A. A., *Russia and Europe, 1789–1825* (Durham, Duke University Press, 1947).

Paleologue, M., *The Enigmatic Tsar: the Life of Alexander I of Russia* (Hammish-Hamilton, 1938).

Rappoport, A. S., *The Curse of the Romanovs* (Chatto & Winders, 1907).

Strakhovsky, L. I., *Alexander I of Russia* (New York, Norton, 1947).

17

Truce, Reform, and War

THE PEACE OF TILSIT GAVE RUSSIA temporary respite from the contest with France. That the truce would prove uneasy and that there would be a renewal of the conflict was inherent in the settlement, for it left control of Europe divided between two giants suspicious of each other. The lesser powers and England had not been destroyed, however, and they were left to carry on the struggle until Russia could sufficiently recover her breath for another test of strength. "At least I shall gain time," the tsar had sighed after Tilsit. He had assured Prussia that she would some day recover everything she had lost.

Alexander had not given up hope that fundamental reform of the political and social structure of the nation might be effected, and he was ready to apply himself once more to that task, although foreign affairs continued to demand attention. Nothing more was done to curb the ruler's autocratic power or to relieve the mass of his subjects from the blight of serfdom. Alexander continued to admit and to consider the problems, but he shied away from any serious effort to solve them. After five years of peace Russia was invaded by France, and once again all thought of reform had to be given up while the nation and the tsar bent every energy toward defending the homeland. Alexander was not content simply to drive the invader from Russian soil but pursued him across Europe and entered his capital in full triumph. The peace which came with Napoleon's exile was in no small measure the result of Russian sacrifices and entitled the people to expect that long-delayed reforms should now be their reward.

POPULAR OPPOSITION TO THE FRENCH ALLIANCE

It has been maintained that Napoleon fought Russia between 1805 and 1807 not to humble her but to win her friendship in the interest of extending the Continental system, his only effective weapon against his most implacable foe, England. If this thesis is accepted it must be admitted that his attempt to secure Russian good will failed completely. He did not even succeed in winning the tsar's friendship, for Alexander looked upon Tilsit as no more than a way to buy time. Napoleon could not have been so naïve as to suppose that he could win Russian favor by reviving the Polish state.

Alexander hurried home after Tilsit to quiet the popular grumbling at the loss of the war. He must have expected to find opposition, for there had been frequent indications of discontent after Austerlitz. Most Russians had felt little sympathy for a war in which the nation seemed to have no interest, a war which seemed to them to concern only Western Europe. Now that the defeat had been confirmed by a treaty with the godless Napoleon, expressions of dissatisfaction were hardly restrained. The bitterness of the tsar's mother was particularly keen, and those who gathered around her even hinted at conspiracy to overthrow the emperor. Alexander must have suspected that some courtiers were recalling the circumstances of his father's death in a tone that intimated that the drama might be repeated. The liberal friends of his youth left the capital—Stroganov to enter the army, Czartoryski to settle in Poland, and Kochubey and Novosiltsev to go abroad—as though in protest against the alliance which few Russians could abide. The tsar could not protest that he was misunderstood and that he had accepted the peace only to buy time, nor could he announce the fact that he had been given a free hand in Finland without revealing the secret clauses of the recent treaty and so forewarning Sweden. The sensitive ruler was stung by the criticism that was implicit in the manner of those near him, but there was nothing he could do but bear it. Disillusioned, he never recovered his buoyant enthusiasm for improving conditions in Russia, and when he returned to consideration of domestic reform he did so halfheartedly.

Napoleon sent Savary to St. Petersburg, ostensibly as envoy but actually to estimate the value of the new alliance and to gauge sentiment in the northern capital. St. Petersburg took the appointment as an insult, since Savary had been a party to the seizure and execution of the Duc d'Enghien which had so inflamed Russian society. The French diplomat reported to his master that he was snubbed and ignored in the Russian capital. Alexander insisted that Savary be treated with courtesy, but during his entire stay court circles displayed only grudging civility toward the unwelcome guest. Plays in capital theaters which contained anti-French sentiments performed to packed houses and met with enthusiastic applause. Magazines that printed articles declaring that the Peace of Tilsit could be no more than a truce between campaigns came under royal censure, but, significantly, only after Savary complained to the tsar. Made painfully aware that the alliance with France was thoroughly unpopular, Alexander did his best to maintain correct relations with his partner. But Napoleon soon came to suspect that the tsar was only keeping up appearances.

FRANCO-RUSSIAN RELATIONS AFTER TILSIT

Had St. Petersburg society realized the high stakes at issue between their ruler and the French emperor, its distaste for the strange alliance might have been tempered with some patience. For three years following the Peace of Tilsit Alexander maintained pressure upon France in a diplomatic chess game in which he showed himself to be Napoleon's peer.

Carrying out the letter of his commitment at Tilsit, Alexander proferred to the British government an offer to mediate its differences with France. When the offer was declined, Russia declared war upon England. The five-year war was militarily painless, however, since Russia took no other action than to close her ports to British commerce, and England satisfied herself with seizing a few Russian sloops.

Since Sweden refused to join the Continental system, Alexander attacked her through Finland and marched an army over the ice of the Gulf of Bothnia to within sixty miles of Stockholm. By resisting the invasion with scorched earth, the Finns won from Alexander the assurance of autonomy under Russian rule. The treaty ending the war gave Finland and the Aland Islands to Russia, while Sweden agreed to end all trade relations with Britain.

Alexander had fulfilled his obligations to France by engaging in two wars, one of which had cost him nothing and one of which had added a territory larger than Russian Poland to his empire. Now it was Napoleon's turn to carry out the promises he had made at Tilsit. In return for Russian pressure upon England and Sweden, the French emperor had agreed to mediate the war between Russia and Turkey. French influence, always strong at the Porte, produced a Turkish peace offer on the basis of withdrawal of Russian troops from Moldavia and Wallachia. Alexander was furious at Napoleon's failure to back up his promise at Tilsit that the Danubian Principalities should go to Russia, and ordered his armies to stand on the Danube. He further let it be known that Russian troops would not pull out of Turkey until the French forces occupying Prussia, some of them stationed on the Russian frontier, were also withdrawn. Napoleon now suggested that Russia might be given Moldavia and Wallachia if Alexander agreed to the addition of Prussian Silesia to the grand duchy of Warsaw. But the tsar was keen enough to appreciate the fact that any such strengthening of the grand duchy at the expense of Prussia would only weaken his potential ally and buttress the French outpost on the Vistula.

Disturbed at the possibility of alienating Russia, whose friendship seemed to promise the defeat of England, Napoleon embarked upon one of his dreamiest flights of fancy by proposing that France and Russia share in the partition of Turkey. In return for satisfying Russian ambition in the Balkans Napoleon asked for a combined Russian-French conquest of India to bring England to terms. The Russian foreign minister who discussed the matter with the French ambassador in St. Petersburg enumerated the Turkish territories which Russia would demand in any such partition—Moldavia, Wallachia, Bulgaria, Thrace, Constantinople, the Bosporus, and the Dardanelles. He was willing for France to have Albania, Greece, Macedonia, western Rumelia, and Crete, and would throw in Egypt and Syria if Russia might add Serbia to her list. The French ambassador complained that the Straits alone were more valuable than all the provinces France would receive under the proposal, and countered with an offer to Russia of the Danubian Principalities and Bulgaria while France would take Thrace, the Straits, Anatolia, Syria, and Egypt. The conversations broke down when Alexander refused to budge on Russian control of the Straits and Napoleon insisted upon having them for France if Turkey were to be partitioned. Both powers henceforth stood for the integrity of Turkey, which was simply a way to insure that neither would benefit at the expense of the other. War against Austria the following year and the deepening involvement in Spain kept Napoleon from following up his dream of attacking India through the Near East with Russian support.

The Franco-Russian conversations reveal Alexander at his hardheaded best in diplomatic intrigue. He saw Russian interests at the Straits with an understanding as clear as that of any Russian ruler. Many of his predecessors and all of his successors revealed an obsession for domination of the Straits, but none stood forth more ambitiously or more uncompromisingly than did Alexander I.

A year after Tilsit the French and Russian emperors met again at Erfurt to discuss points at issue between them, especially to agree, if possible, over Turkey. Napoleon's foreign minister, Talleyrand, already putting out feelers to protect himself should Napoleon fall, urged Alexander to undertake the salvation of Europe and France, assuring the tsar that the French people would welcome deliverance from the usurper. The two emperors could come to no understanding on the partition of Turkey, although Napoleon did approve Russian annexation of Moldavia and Wallachia. France and Russia agreed to a common defense should either be attacked by Austria. Both powers guaranteed Turkish integrity. Napoleon's tantrums at Erfurt, calculated to break down Alexander's resistance to French proposals, were of no avail. "Your Emperor is as stubborn as a mule," fumed Napoleon, "deaf to what he does not wish to hear."

To many who watched as the emperors fenced at Erfurt there seemed a possibility that the Franco-Russian alliance might dissolve, although the surface cordiality between the sovereigns continued throughout the conference. Concerned to establish a dynasty of his own and to give it an air of respectability by marrying into one of the ancient ruling houses, Napoleon proposed a marriage with the tsar's sister. Alexander stalled for time by pleading that only his mother could dispose of the girl, but soon after his return to St. Petersburg his sister's marriage to a German prince was arranged in obvious haste. Napoleon was enraged but found consolation in marriage with the Habsburg Marie Louise.

In the months after Erfurt Napoleon contemplated another war with Austria, and besought his Russian ally for support. Alexander put him off with vague assurances of friendship, and at the same time let it be known in Vienna that his sympathies lay with Austria. Long after the war opened a Russian army moved slowly toward the Austrian frontier, but it showed more interest in preventing a Polish uprising than in fighting the Austrians. People in the streets of St. Petersburg cheered news of Austrian successes against the armies of the French "ally." With the end of the war Alexander refused to be a party to the punishment of Austria and took no part in the peace conference. Galicia, which Austria had received in the partition of Poland, was added to the grand duchy of Warsaw. News of this strengthening of the French satellite on the Russian frontier was received with alarm in St. Petersburg; nor was the misgiving reduced by the award of the Polish district of Tarnopol to Russia. Napoleon later admitted that he assigned Tarnopol to Russia in the hope that it would embitter the Austrians against Russia. When Napoleon shipped rifles into the grand duchy and strengthened the defenses of the city of Warsaw all pretense of continued friendship between France and Russia disappeared. An end to the uneasy alliance was assured the moment the two powers were prepared to renew hostilities.

RETURN TO REFORM

When the Peace of Tilsit relieved Russia of the strain of war with France, Alexander determined to take up once more the internal needs of his country. While the conflicts with England, Sweden, Turkey, Persia, and Austria sapped Russian strength and distracted the tsar, they did not require the concentration of nation and ruler as had the war with Napoleon. The tsar was deeply disappointed upon returning home from Tilsit to find his people enraged at the French alliance, but he hoped to recover his popularity by tackling the political and social problems which grieved the nation.

The man who now became the tsar's confidant was Michael Speransky. A commoner, son of a village priest, Speransky began his career as professor of mathematics and physics at the St. Petersburg Seminary, from which he had graduated with high honor. A state councillor at the age of twenty-five, he rose rapidly in every position he filled because of his integrity, his rare perspicacity, his fondness for hard work, and his unusual talent in oral and written composition. He possessed probably the finest intellect of any of the advisers to the tsars from the seventeenth century to the end of the monarchy. When the new ministries were organized early in the nineteenth century he was taken under the wing of Kochubey, the minister of interior. Most of the important enactments of the early years of Alexander's reign were drafted by Speransky. The tsar took him along to Erfurt as an observer, and later asked him what he thought of Western nations as compared to his own. "They have better institutions than we, but we have better men," he answered.

Alexander and his new adviser discussed the possibility of establishing a constitutional monarchy for Russia. A year after Tilsit Speransky completed the draft of a plan for the tsar's consideration, a plan which the self-effacing commoner insisted was the product of his sovereign's own devising. If the ideas were those of the tsar, their orderly arrangement into a workable form must be credited to Speransky. The completed document examined the weaknesses of the political and social structure of Russia and detailed the corrective measures which Speransky considered necessary.

The social order the plan envisaged was one in which free people were governed by a constitutional monarch assisted by elected representatives. Russian society, the document pointed out, was made up essentially of two classes—landowners and their serfs. The gentry were slaves of the absolute sovereign, while the peasants were slaves of the gentry. All Russians, then, except the mendicants who escaped it, were in bondage. Reform, said Speransky, must begin with emancipation of the serfs. He did not suggest that they be given land by breaking up the estates of the gentry, and so would have made of them a landless peasantry working for wages or renting or purchasing their own plots as they found the means. The freed men would not at first take part in the political direction of the state, for that privilege would be reserved to the gentry. However, the civil rights of all classes—aristocracy, middle class, and urban and rural workers—would be guaranteed. Courts would be set up by the government to adjudicate disputes between serfs and gentry as the former emerged from bondage.

The plan provided a duma, or assembly, to meet once every three years in every *volost,* or township, to consist of all landowners and of representatives of free peasants, one delegate for each five hundred of the latter. The duma would select a board of its members to receive and dispense *volost* revenue, manage affairs of purely local interest, and elect delegates to the district or county duma. The latter, made up of delegates from the *volost* dumas, would choose its administrative board to govern the district when the duma was not in session, levy and spend revenue for district needs, hear petitions from the *volost* dumas, and elect delegates to the provincial duma. The latter was to operate on the provincial level in the same manner as did the *volost* and district dumas on lower levels, and it would send delegates to an Imperial Duma which would meet annually in St. Petersburg. The national legislature, or Imperial Duma, was not to have the right to initiate legislation, but its approval was to be necessary to the adoption of any law. Ministers of state were to be subject to censure by the Imperial Duma for conduct of their departments, and the Duma was to have the right to petition the throne for redress of grievances. The indirect representation suggested here by Speransky was adopted in the early constitutions of the Soviet regime.

Alongside the dumas in *volost*, district, and province there was to be a hierarchy of courts, served by juries under elected judges. The Senate, henceforth to consist of men nominated by the provincial dumas and confirmed by the tsar, was to serve as the supreme judiciary, hearing appeals from the lesser courts whose operations it was to supervise. The administrative and advisory functions which had been allowed to the Senate in 1802 were to be transferred to the Council of State.

At the pinnacle of the governmental edifice which Speransky proposed was to be the Council of State, its members to be named by the emperor, who would preside over its meetings. The group would render advice on important administrative matters when called upon by the tsar, and would draft such legislative proposals as the sovereign chose to introduce in the Imperial Duma. An Imperial Chancery, headed by an imperial secretary, would serve the Council of State as reference bureau and secretariat.

Alexander pondered and discussed the plan with Speransky but, fearful of moving too rapidly in altering the machinery of state and so inviting chaos, decided to adopt it piecemeal. He inaugurated the consultative Council of State and honored the plan's author by naming Speransky imperial secretary. But he never went beyond this timid step. Since Speransky himself had recognized that to adopt his full plan would be to overturn the entire social order, it is not surprising that Alexander drew back from going so far. Over a half century later the local dumas suggested by Speransky were established by Alexander II, but the Imperial Duma was not brought into being until the twentieth century.

In spite of the fact that his proposal to provide the nation with representative institutions was shelved for so long, Speransky's recommendations are remarkable. Had they been adopted Russia would have enjoyed the nearest approach to democratic government to be found in any great continental European power. Speransky conceived a plan which dominated political reforms in Russia until long after the tsars had disappeared, a plan that was dusted off and applied in some part by Alexander II, Nicholas II, and finally by Lenin. While Alexander I drew back from allowing representative bodies, he did create the Council of State which was to continue into the twentieth century to act essentially as Speransky recommended. For nearly a century the council controlled the ministry, appointed officials and held them to account, planned state finances, distributed favors, and drafted laws and decrees—always, it need hardly be noted, at the will of the tsar. While the creation of the ministries in the early years of the reign had done much to settle responsibility for departmental operation, the Council of State gave Russia a central coordinating agency whose job it was to oversee the ministers and all other state officials. Never had there been such order in affairs of state. From now on "there was a right and a wrong way of conducting government business in Russia," for "Speransky gave the bureaucracy a conscience, and henceforward it knew when it was not following it" (Pares).

As imperial secretary and the tsar's chief adviser, Speransky carried through a number of reforms designed to improve the administration. State councillors and other high government officials were required to be university graduates and to pass examinations. Those holding titles of nobility by other than hereditary right had to perform some government service or lose their privileges as nobles. The internal administration of the ministries was made more efficient by being subdivided into orderly, intelligible departments. Prophetic of later stern measures, a ministry of police was established to tighten internal security.

In an effort to improve the financial plight of the government, which had been steadily worsening since Elizabeth's reign, Speransky inaugurated a number of reforms which were helpful, if not popular. The issue of paper money, which had reached alarming proportions and which had destroyed public confidence, was halted, the amount in circulation funded as a public debt, and a gradual retirement of the almost worthless paper was assured by levying a new tax on the gentry whose proceeds were to be devoted entirely to the purpose. Government expenses were to be drastically curtailed, even to reducing expenditures for some of the tsar's pet projects such as expanding educational facilities. Approved methods of accounting in government agencies were imposed. To provide some immediate relief a tax on every serf, to be levied against the serf owner, was to be collected for one year. To correct Russia's unfavorable trade situation the importation of luxuries was forbidden, a measure which struck particularly at French goods.

Speransky's plans and achievements stirred up so much bitter opposition from the nobles that Alexander was forced to dismiss him. His proposal to abolish serfdom found little favor among the rank and file of the gentry. His suggestion that only university graduates be admitted to high office struck at the class privileges of the nobles. His tax program played no favorites, and his restrictions upon foreign trade were aimed at the wealthy. His constitutional blueprint was scorned by the conservative historian Karamzin, who insisted to the tsar that good government for Russia could come only from a good autocrat and not from revolutionary changes in organization. Karamzin was undoubtedly sincere in believing that the autocracy had made Russia great and powerful and should not be tampered with. Speransky's opponents blamed him for the depression, which was in fact due to Russia's participation in the Continental system; they finally invented the charge that he was dealing with France. Seeing the need for unity as the nation faced another war, Alexander sent his faithful and hardworking minister into exile just three months before Napoleon invaded Russia.

THE DRIFT TOWARD WAR WITH FRANCE

The animus in court circles that had greeted Alexander on his return from Tilsit continued unabated through the five years of truce that followed. Capital society delighted in parading its hatred for things French and in applauding things English, Austrian, and particularly Russian. If anything, the hatred for the alliance mounted, for Russia's partnership in the Continental system threw the nation into a depression that grew daily more severe. Russian landowners lost the foreign market for their grain, hemp, timber, and flax when the nation's ports were closed to British shipping. Wheat exports, for example, fell by 1810 to a sixth of their volume before Tilsit. Internal trade suffered from the decline in foreign commerce, and the price of goods commonly brought in by the British became prohibitive. Sugar sold for nearly three rubles (a dollar and a half) a pound in St. Petersburg a year after Russia joined the Continental system. Speransky finally reminded the tsar that the system was supposed to harm England but was actually destroying Russia. Government deficits rose as Alexander built up the army, and taxes increased as Speransky sought vainly to bridge the gap between revenue and expenditures. Francophobes correctly blamed Russia's sorry economic plight upon the French alliance, although it is only fair to recognize that the Turkish, Swedish, and Persian wars were costly. When in 1810 Alexander, on Speransky's advice, opened Russian ports to British vessels flying neutral flags and to American ships carrying British goods, levied a tax on French wines, and forbade the importation of the luxury goods that came from France, Napoleon received the news as though it announced a declaration of war. The tariff of 1810 probably saved Russia from economic collapse. Foreign commerce quickly revived, and agriculture and internal trade responded to the stimulus.

From the French point of view war became inevitable the moment Alexander curtailed trade with France and abrogated the Tilsit agreement by deserting the Continental system, the only weapon Napoleon could effectively use against Great Britain. From the Russian point of view war became necessary when the French emperor restored and then strengthened the Polish state, backed down on his promise to mediate the Russo-Turkish conflict, and insulted Alexander personally by confiscating the territory of his uncle, the duke of Oldenburg. The war fever against France that never waned in Russian court circles only strengthened the tsar's hand. Probably from the moment of Tilsit, and certainly after Erfurt, Alexander considered himself destined to deliver Europe from the insatiate Napoleon. Indeed, at Erfurt the Machiavellian Talleyrand had urged the tsar to assume the mantle of liberator.

By 1810, two years after Erfurt and two years before the French invasion, Alexander was busily seeking allies against the enemy he knew he would soon have to fight. He offered to compensate Sweden for the loss of Finland by supporting her acquisition of Norway from Denmark, a staunch friend of Bonaparte. Just before the French attack upon Russia the Swedes accepted the offer, but promised support only in a war outside Russian territory. In 1811 special Russian envoys sought to win over Austria, even promising Moldavia and Wallachia in exchange for an alliance. But the Russophobe Metternich managed to hold his sovereign to the French alliance. In the same year Prussia offered to join with a hundred thousand men against Napoleon, provided the Russian armies crossed the Vistula to fight the war in central Europe. Alexander, however, chose to fight a defensive war, and Prussia later had no alternative but to join Napoleon against Russia. At the same time the tsar's offer to restore Poland to her borders before partition and to revive her as an independent nation was turned down. The Poles persisted to the very end in their confidence that their best assurance of revival lay with Napoleon.

Russia entered the war with Napoleon with all Europe arrayed against her except Turkey, Sweden, and Portugal. The French emperor endeavored to buy Turkish support by promising the sultan the Crimea and the north coast of the Black Sea. But Turkey had had enough of war with Russia. That war, which Turkey had begun at French prodding, came to an end less than a month before the French invasion. Russia satisfied herself with the acquisition of Bessarabia and returned the Danubian Principalities to Turkey in order that the army on that front might hurry north to defend the homeland. The war with England that had been going on for five years was not terminated until a month after Napoleon crossed the Niemen.

Alexander succeeded diplomatically, then, in putting himself in the best possible posture to face the French attack. By neutralizing Turkey and Sweden he avoided attacks on both flanks that might have proved disastrous. Prussian support of Napoleon was unavoidable, but it was certain to be given grudgingly. And, shortly before the war opened, the Austrian emperor assured Alexander that he had no intention of assisting France with any enthusiasm, thus repaying Russia for her benevolent attitude in 1809.

In the spring of 1812 Napoleon offered Alexander peace in exchange for Russian compliance with the Continental system and a favorable trade treaty with France. The tsar countered with the proposal that France evacuate Prussian territory, after which the two might discuss other matters, but he warned that Russia would not again close her ports to English shipping. Caulaincourt, who had served as French ambassador in St. Petersburg, was convinced that the only serious irritant to Franco-Russian relations was the existence of the grand duchy of Warsaw. Napoleon could abandon it and have peace, he insisted, or keep it and have war. Certainly Poland was important, but it was only indicative of Napoleon's realization that he could not completely dominate Europe until he had conquered Russia, and he must conquer Russia in order to destroy British commerce. The conquest would accomplish the elimination of the last remaining powers who blocked his scheme of world domination.

THE FRENCH INVASION, 1812

Over 600,000 men, not including reserves of nearly that number who had been left in central Europe, made up Napoleon's Grand Army. Even after dropping strong detachments to defend communications with his base at Danzig, Napoleon crossed the Niemen on June 24 with upward of half a million troops. "The army of twenty nations" the Russian people called it. Over half were French, but Italians, Dutch, Belgians, Swiss, Germans, Danes, Austrians, Magyars, Spaniards, Poles, and Illyrian Slavs marched with them. Napoleon hoped for an early decisive battle that would destroy the Russian army and force the tsar to sue for peace, as had been the case after Friedland in 1807. Failing that, he frankly faced the possibility that he would have to occupy one of the Russian capitals, either St. Petersburg or Moscow, in order to bring Alexander to terms. But the tsar had told the French ambassador a year earlier that, if Russia were invaded, he would retreat to Kamchatka rather than sue for peace.

Because there was no indication of which direction the invasion might take, the Russians had only vague plans for meeting it. Russian action would unquestionably have to be entirely defensive, for the three armies which gathered to meet the French numbered only 180,000 men. The main army of about 100,000 assembled at Vilna under the war minister, Barclay de Tolly, a Scot whose forbears had emigrated to Russia. Barclay, cautious but realistic, understood that any but defensive tactics were out of the question. The second or southern army of perhaps 35,000 gathered east of Bialystok under Bagration, who had served under Suvorov. Suspicious of Barclay and impetuous by nature, Bagration favored an advance westward across the frontier to attack Napoleon's supply line. A third Russian army of 40,000 guarded the southwestern border against a possible attack by Napoleon's ally, Austria. Alexander retained the supreme command, knowing that his generals bitterly disagreed and that Barclay enjoyed little confidence among officers or men.

Soon after the enemy crossed the frontier Alexander sent an envoy to Napoleon to offer peace on the terms proposed earlier in the year. Napoleon dismissed the offer with scant patience. When the envoy let it be known that Alexander would have peace on no other terms, Napoleon asked him what was the best road to Moscow. "Charles XII took the road by Poltava," was the Russian's answer. When the tsar learned of Napoleon's determination that the war should go on, he renewed his earlier pledge that he would make no peace as long as a single French soldier remained on Russian soil.

Four days after ferrying the Niemen the French occupied Vilna. Here in the ancient Lithuanian capital the French emperor established a provisional capital and arranged for conscription of horses and supplies, but he turned a deaf ear to all entreaties that Poland-Lithuania be revived as an independent state. A sizable French force was dispatched to the south to destroy Bagration's army, or at least to prevent it from joining Barclay. For three precious weeks Napoleon stayed in Vilna, awaiting word that Bagration had been put out of action. In all that time he accomplished nothing more than making enemies of the Lithuanians, who had accepted him at first as a deliverer. When Lithuanian landowners asked for help against their serfs, who were rising against them, French troops put down the rebellions with a ferocity that convinced the peasants they had more to gain from defending Russia than from joining the invader. And the Lithuanian nobles grumbled to no avail at the oppressive tribute levied upon them.

Bagration's southern army successfully fell back to the northeast before the French army sent to destroy it, and Barclay withdrew to the east hoping to effect a junction with Bagration at Vitebsk. But the French drove the southern army farther east and the two Russian forces joined only at Smolensk, a meeting which Napoleon had hoped to prevent. Indeed, Bagration's success in escaping to join Barclay was a masterful accomplishment, as Napoleon himself grudgingly admitted, calling Bagration the best general in the Russian army. Now, Bonaparte consoled himself, the combined forces might be destroyed, for none knew better than he that the object of war is to knock out the enemy's armies and not simply to take territory. But Barclay fought only a rear-guard action at Smolensk and withdrew still further into the Russian interior.

A month before Smolensk Alexander left the army. His advisers, remembering his costly interference at Austerlitz, insisted that his presence was necessary in Moscow to inspire the people to greater sacrifices and to steel them against further adversity. It is probable that those near him were "far less concerned with where the tsar should go than with his departure from the army" (Tarle). There, in the true capital of Russia, Alexander's presence worked wonders. Nobles came forward to volunteer their serfs for a militia force, and over a hundred thousand of these recruits were quickly mustered. But there were no rifles for them and they were armed with almost harmless pikes. The merchants of Moscow answered the tsar's call for money with ten million rubles. Moscow nobles added another three million. The war became a people's war—the "Patriotic War," the Russians have always called it—as every class in society forgot its grievances for the moment and strained its greatest efforts to save the nation.

The Russian gentry were fearful from the beginning that Napoleon might announce emancipation of the serfs and so precipitate a social revolution which, combined with invasion, would have been more frightful than Pugachev's uprising. But the Great Russian serfs remained intensely loyal. Uprisings in some of the militia regiments were prompted by impatience to see battle action rather than by a desire to bring about social change. It is probable that the peasants were confident that their freedom would come more quickly from the tsar than from the foreigner who pillaged and plundered and massacred as he advanced. It is also true that peasants who joined the army in 1812 commonly believed that the act of enlistment freed them from bondage.

When Barclay pulled out of Smolensk with no more than token resistance Alexander gave in to the clamor of the people and the army for a new commander. Kutuzov, fresh from the successful Turkish war, was named to supreme command. Although the tsar personally disliked and later distrusted him, Kutuzov was popular in the army as well as with the nobles, who hoped that he would stop the French advance and with it the threat that Napoleon might free the serfs. Then sixty-seven years old and so fat that he had to be moved about in a carriage, his personal bravery had long since won him the respect of the men in the ranks. He had been twice critically wounded and had lost an eye in the Turkish wars in Catherine's time. "Endowed with much native cunning, he felt confidence in his ability to conquer the great man, by guile if not by battle" (Stschepkin, *Cambridge Modern History*). But Kutuzov knew that all Russia insisted he fight one great battle in defense of Moscow. He chose his position at Borodino, seventy miles west of the city.

The six hundred miles that the Grand Army had marched since entering Russian territory had cost the French frightfully. The heat was intense in that summer of 1812, and thousands had dropped exhausted along the way. Dysentery and typhus had taken heavy toll. By the time Napoleon reached Vitebsk, at the western edge of Great Russia, he had lost over a hundred thousand men. Some of these, sick or wounded, would return to their regiments, but most had deserted or died or soon would die. Discipline was unusually poor and there was much straggling. While the French army had been well provisioned, the baggage train was often far in the rear. The Russians swept the land clean as they pulled back, and French forage parties returned empty-handed or did not return at all. The horses died from want of provender or from glutting themselves on unripe grain; those which were left were too weak to draw the wagons and artillery, so that many guns had to be abandoned. A French cavalry general, criticized because his charges lacked their earlier dash, remarked cynically, "My horses are not patriotic. The soldiers will fight without bread, but the horses insist on oats."

The Russian armies, poorly served by their own commissary, lived off the country. The peasants willingly turned over their food and grain to the troops and then burned what they could not carry away. Village after village was left deserted and in flames before the invader. Even Smolensk was half burned before the French could put out the fire and loot what remained, and all but a thousand of its fifteen thousand inhabitants moved off with the Russian army. Napoleon soon came to realize that "people who destroyed not only their villages but even their large cities were not likely to seek an early peace" (Tarle). Between the people and the troops, the Russian land was deliberately and systematically devastated. The Cossacks stripped the farm land clean for miles on both sides of the road of retreat, and the scorched earth gave up nothing to the invading horde. The peasants picked off French foraging parties and then fled to the woods to creep out noiselessly at night for hit-and-run raids. The foreigner grew desperate as he plodded on into the unknown, hostile, deserted land, the horizon aflame in every direction from burning cottages and haystacks. The French, aroused to ferocity by the desolation around them, were fiendishly cruel to the few peasants they captured. But their cruelty prompted a surge of anger among the peasants, who dealt all the more savagely with the enemy. Napoleon sent an officer to Kutuzov to offer peace and at the same time complain of the barbarous behavior of the Russian peasants toward the invading troops. Kutuzov retorted that he "could not civilize a nation in three months who regard the enemy as worse than a marauding force of Tatars under Genghis Khan." To the Frenchman's protest that "there is at least some difference," Kutuzov granted, "there may be, but none in the eyes of the people."

The opposing armies at Borodino were nearly equal in strength. Napoleon had 130,000 men, Kutuzov slightly fewer. The Russian artillery was heavier and more numerous than the French, a number of cannon having been brought in from England. Kutuzov disposed his troops in prepared positions, then left the conduct of the battle to his division commanders while he waited the outcome in a village far to the rear. Unable to see the entire battle ground, Napoleon also had to rely upon the judgment of his subordinates. The contest developed into several almost independent battles among which there was little coordination. The slaughter was frightful on both sides, the artillery fire being heavier and more destructive than in any of Napoleon's battles. Few compare with Borodino in bloodshed, in the truculence of assault and counterassault, in the stubbornness of the defense, and in the resolute determination of the attack. "The most terrible of all my battles," Napoleon considered it. Forty generals, including Bagration, fell on the field. The Russians lost fifty-eight thousand men, or about half of those engaged, while the French suffered fifty thousand casualties, or 40 per cent of their effectives. But Napoleon's Guard Corps, composed of French veterans and probably the finest fighting force of its size in the world at the time, was still intact. Napoleon had refused to use it in the battle, not wanting to risk it so far from France. He had thereby lost the possibility of destroying the Russian army completely.

After remaining on the field of Borodino the day after the battle, Kutuzov gave up all thought of renewing the fight and took up once more the withdrawal toward Moscow. Just west of the city the old general called a council of war, where opinion was divided over whether to defend the capital. There was no loss of confidence among men or officers in the Russian commander, but Kutuzov decided against risking the complete rout of his shattered army and chose to retire beyond Moscow, saying that the army was more important than any Russian city. As French cavalry edged into the western suburbs the Russian rear guard retired through the southeast gate, taking with them all but ten thousand of the two hundred thousand residents. Only foreigners, vagabonds, and criminals released from the jails at the last moment remained behind. The city was ominously still—no welcoming delegation of citizens, no one on the streets, the shutters drawn and shop fronts locked. No other European capital, and Napoleon had been in most of them, had prepared such a reception.

As Napoleon looked down upon "Mother Moscow" from the Sparrow Hills on September 14 he expected to receive Alexander's offer of peace at any moment. But no word came, nor was there any answer to the proposals which Napoleon himself sent the tsar from Moscow. The French emperor moved into the city and took up residence in the Kremlin.

That evening fires broke out all over the metropolis and soon were raging out of control. Some were set by French looters, others by patriotic citizens determined to burn the capital as other Russian cities had been fired to prevent anything of value from falling to the hated enemy. Two hundred townsmen were executed for starting the conflagration, but new fires continued to break out. Since the mayor had withdrawn all fire-fighting equipment during the evacuation, the fires spread unchecked. Napoleon had to leave the Kremlin when smoke and sparks made it unbearable, but he returned through the charred ruins after the fire had burned itself out. For six days the holocaust continued until over three-fourths of the city was consumed. Of its fifty thousand houses, less than a thousand escaped completely. Of its sixteen hundred churches, eight hundred were destroyed and seven hundred others damaged. So complete was the devastation that Russians divide the history of Moscow into a "pre-French" and a "post-French" period.

The invaders marched into Moscow fully confident that they would find not only staples but abundant riches and luxury and that they could rest there in comfort until the tsar offered peace. But there was no store of provisions to sate the hunger of troops who had been living on horseflesh since before Borodino. The French soon emptied the wine cellars of what had not been carried away, and drunkenness and looting became unmanageable. The vandal fury of the conquerors knew no bounds as they saw themselves cheated of the food and luxury they had toiled so far to enjoy. The houses not destroyed by fire were stripped of furniture, and pieces too bulky to remove were smashed or used to kindle campfires. Cavalry stabled their horses in the churches and used the altars for dining tables. One church became a butcher's shop; a convent was turned into a slaughterhouse. Knowledge of such depredation only stung the Russians to greater wrath when the opportunity came for revenge. Foraging parties sent into the countryside found nothing, and small detachments were wiped out by the Cossacks. Napoleon found himself unwilling to leave but unable to remain because of the desperate food situation.

For five weeks the Corsican paced restlessly in his Kremlin palace waiting for an answer to his peace proposals. By mid-October the emperor awoke from the lethargy into which he had fallen and ordered the evacuation of Moscow. In a fit of spite he ordered the Kremlin blown up by the rear guard. With reinforcements that had arrived and stragglers that had come in the French force numbered 110,000 men. The army filed out of the city accompanied by thousands of foreigners—men, women, and children who feared the vengeance of returning Muscovites—and encumbered by a huge baggage train containing the furs, art treasures, furniture, and other spoil the looters had accumulated.

After withdrawing beyond Moscow Kutuzov had taken a position south and slightly west of the city near Kaluga, which he had turned into a supply depot to re-equip his troops. Napoleon now advanced toward Kaluga, but found his way blocked by Kutuzov's rested army. After another typically vicious battle Napoleon had no choice but to return to the invasion route and try to escape over the same scorched earth by which he had advanced to Moscow. He had ordered supplies to be gathered at Smolensk, where a strong detachment had been left to hold the city. But Smolensk was two hundred miles to the west.

In the retreat from Moscow the French army was plagued every step of the way by vigorous pressure from the Russian regulars, by flank attacks of the Cossacks, and by hit-and-run raids of guerilla and partisan bands. Napoleon was fighting not an army but a nation. Troops of peasants, varying in number from a score to several hundred, sometimes gathered around a local leader, sometimes organized by army officers, hung close to the retreating Grand Army, picking off stragglers, knifing pickets and even invading camps at night. Women, armed only with pitchfork or scythe, fought as fiercely as their men. The partisans took no prisoners, and were shot without trial when captured.

The French dragged on, eating only the flesh of their horses and such dogs as they could catch. Marshal Murat was breakfasting on cat one morning when the Cossacks surprised him. Only the weather favored the retreating army, for the winter was late in coming and the October days were pleasantly mild. In early November, however, the nights turned cold. Snow covered the road and made it slippery by the sixth of that month. Three days later fifty thousand, less than half those who had left Moscow, staggered into Smolensk. There a disappointingly small stock of provisions awaited the Grand Army, and only the Guard Corps fared well.

By late November the temperature had dropped to fifteen degrees below zero and the wind drove like needles against friend and foe alike. Napoleon approached the Berezina river still with fifty thousand men, for the places of the thousands who had fallen since Smolensk had been filled as the Grand Army gathered in its flank detachments. Under heavy Cossack pressure and artillery bombardment the rush for the crossings became a panic. One bridge collapsed, carrying soldiers and refugees into the icy water. Ten thousand civilian men, women, and children drowned or died of exposure at the crossing. After the most dependable troops had crossed, the French burned the bridges, leaving fully half of the army to be taken prisoner.

Russian cavalry pressed the pursuit after the crossing of the Berezina, and within three days the Grand Army numbered no more than nine thousand. Many froze to death in the bitter cold, while others saved themselves at night by piling stiffened bodies into a shield against the biting wind. A week later only four thousand remained, and when the French staggered back over the Niemen out of Russia only a thousand of the Guards maintained any semblance of order. Small groups of stragglers kept coming back for days afterward, and a small Polish army managed to escape. The two wings, far to the north and south, fared better. But as for the core of the

French force, Ney almost literally spoke the truth when he announced after crossing the Niemen, "I am the rear guard of the Grand Army."

Kutuzov's army, well supplied, operating in friendly territory, growing rapidly in size and with fine morale, might conceivably have cut off the retreat, captured Napoleon, and thus spared Europe and Russia another thirty months of war. But the old general refused to risk a pitched battle, in spite of the impatience of his subordinates and the shouts of "Moscow! Moscow!" from the ranks; he confessed his willingness simply to usher Napoleon out of Russia. He was satisfied that he could substitute space and scorched earth for the lives of his men. Even after heavy reinforcements came up from the southwest border, where the Austrians had made only a pretext of assisting Napoleon, Kutuzov allowed only advance elements of his army to press the attack. The tsar was sure, as military historians have been, that the French emperor was allowed to escape by Kutuzov's indifference to all considerations except defense of his homeland. Nationalist to the core, he cared not a whit for the welfare of non-Russians and candidly admitted to the belief that only England would profit from the downfall of Napoleon.

The campaign of 1812 cost the Russians 200,000 casualties, of whom perhaps half were killed. But it cost Napoleon upward of a half million men, fully half of whom had died in Russia. Of the remainder, over a hundred thousand were taken prisoner and the rest deserted or were returned to France badly wounded. The French emperor left the army soon after the disastrous river crossing, bidding his marshals farewell with the comment, "From the sublime to the ridiculous is but a step." He admitted the loss, blaming it upon the early Russian winter. But the weather had become severe only after Smolensk. The Grand Army was wiped out by starvation, by savage battle action, and, particularly, by Cossack and partisan raids. It might almost be said that, except for Borodino, the invader had been destroyed without a battle. It is more accurate to say that there was one continuous battle from the time the Grand Army entered Russia until a miserable remnant was driven back across the Niemen.

Napoleon objected, after Waterloo, to being sent to St. Helena. The British admiral to whom he complained suggested that "surely St. Helena is preferable to a smaller space in England, or being sent to France, or perhaps to Russia." "Russia!" Napoleon repeated. "God preserve me from it!"

THE DOWNFALL OF NAPOLEON

Alexander rejoined his army at Vilna and crossed the Niemen in mid-January, 1813. Russian opinion was divided about the desirability of delivering the rest of Europe from Bonaparte. Many Russians considered the war at an end when the last foreigner had been driven back across the frontier, and Kutuzov was bitterly opposed to continuing the fight. But the old man died soon after the close of the Russian campaign, and Alexander considered himself destined to free Europe from oppression. The Prussians greeted the tsar as a deliverer, and their king was swept along by the national revival to join Alexander in a pledge to drive the French beyond the Rhine.

Napoleon had hurried back to Paris after the crossing of the Berezina to raise another army. The raw young levies he gathered in France and the surly troops from the subject nations he still controlled were not the equal of his earlier armies. However, Napoleon himself had lost none of his genius, and the Allies were beaten in hard-fought battles. The British foreign minister Castlereagh was ready for peace, but not Alexander. "I cannot be coming twelve hundred miles every day to your relief. There can be no peace as long as Napoleon is on the throne." When Austria joined the coalition the odds against the French were overwhelming. In the three-day battle of Leipzig Napoleon's new army was routed as the large Saxon and Bavarian contingents deserted to join the Allies. At Alexander's urging, the Allied armies moved into France after agreeing on the general terms which they would accept and vowing to continue the alliance for twenty years. On the last day of March, 1814, flanked by an Austrian general and the Prussian king, Alexander rode into the French capital at the head of his troops.

The conduct of the Russian soldiers during the stay in Paris was exemplary. Even the Cossacks were on their best behavior, for the tsar refused to permit any vengeance for Moscow. While he was convinced that there could be no compromise with Napoleon, he was satisfied with his deposition and exile to Elba. Alexander was extremely doubtful of the wisdom of returning Louis XVIII to the French throne, and consented to it only at the assurance of the scheming Talleyrand that France desired it. At the tsar's insistence, the Bourbons granted the people a constitution. That France was allowed to keep the boundaries she had held in 1792 was also largely the tsar's doing.

After the signing of the First Treaty of Paris in 1814 Alexander visited England, where his handsome figure and his position as the leader of the coalition which had defeated Napoleon won him wide popular acclaim. He was hardly discreet, however, in currying favor with the Whig minority in Parliament, for by so doing he assured himself of opposition from Tory leaders at the later peace conference. Stopping off at Vilna on his way back to Russia, he greeted an assembly of Poles with the promise to consider their problems as soon as there was time for it. St. Petersburg welcomed him effusively, but he refused the title of "the Blessed" which the Senate pressed him to accept. In September he left Russia once more, this time for the Austrian capital where the powers assembled to redraw the map of Europe.

Map 13: RUSSIAN EMPIRE, 1796 ACQUISITIONS OF PAUL, 1796-1801

TRM

Map 14: RUSSIAN EMPIRE, 1801 ACQUISITIONS OF ALEXANDER I, 1801-1825

NAPOLEON'S ROUTE IN 1812

GROWTH OF RUSSIA, 1796-1881

Map 15: RUSSIAN EMPIRE, 1825 ACQUISITIONS OF NICHOLAS I, 1825-1855

Map 16: RUSSIAN EMPIRE, 1855 ACQUISITIONS OF ALEXANDER II, 1855-1881

THE CONGRESS OF VIENNA, 1815

The Austrian emperor played host to a glittering array of emperors, kings, minor princes, diplomats, and fortune hunters, most of whom spent the nine months of conference in an endless round of reviews, balls, and receptions. Alexander was assisted by a corps of advisers which included the Germans Stein and Nesselrode, the Swiss La Harpe, the Greek Capodistrias, the Corsican Pozzo di Borgo, and the Pole Czartoryski. The tsar's determination to restore the Polish kingdom with himself as king nearly caused war among the powers, and Alexander even challenged Metternich to a duel. Prussia promised to surrender Prussian Poland if, in return, she received Saxony, which had been Napoleon's staunch ally. But neither England nor Austria would consent to the movement of the Russian frontier so far into central Europe. The unscrupulous Talleyrand inspired a secret agreement, signed by Austria, France, and England, to go to war with Russia should Alexander refuse to budge from his determination to reunite Poland. When sober counsel prevailed, however, the powers realized that Europe was sick of war, and a compromise was agreed upon. Austria retained the Polish territories she still held in 1815. Prussia recovered most of the land she had gained in the three partitions, except for Warsaw, in addition to receiving about two-fifths, instead of all, of Saxony. The remainder of Poland, which was thus repartitioned for the fourth time, became a kingdom with the tsar of Russia as king. The existence of Talleyrand's secret agreement was not revealed until two months after its conception, when Napoleon, escaped from Elba to gather another army, sent the French copy to Alexander in an effort to divide his foes. The tsar confronted Metternich with the paper and then destroyed it, saying, "As long as we live we must never speak of this affair." Nothing, Alexander felt, must interfere with allied unity until Napoleon had been put down once and for all.

Bonaparte's Hundred Days ended at Waterloo before Russian armies could participate in his defeat. But Alexander was hailed by Parisians as deliverer when he returned with his troops to find Blücher and the Prussians levying heavy tribute and preparing to blow up the bridge named for Napoleon's victory at Jena. Napoleon was exiled to St. Helena, the French border was reduced to that of 1790, an indemnity was imposed and Allied troops were to be quartered in France until it was paid. A Quadruple Alliance was organized among the victorious allies to maintain the peace settlement, and the powers agreed to meet again within three years to review matters of common interest and to assure continued peace.

While the negotiations for the Second Treaty of Paris were under way, the rulers of Austria, Prussia, and Russia signed a pronouncement called the Holy Alliance, by which the signatories declared themselves to be "members of one and the same Christian nation" and swore to act thenceforth toward each other as brothers and toward their subjects as fathers of families. Letters to other princes invited them to join this "union founded on the sacred principles of the Christian religion." The Pope and the sultan of Turkey were not invited to join the alliance, but the other European rulers, with the exception of the prince regent of England who pleaded lack of authority, subscribed to the pious document.

That Alexander should have conceived the idea of the Holy Alliance is not really surprising. While his education had inclined him toward agnosticism, the burning of Moscow seems to have stirred in him a profound sense of religious values. He became fascinated not so much with the teachings of any particular sect as with the basic precepts of Christianity. He took to studying the Bible daily and to discussing meaningful passages with friends. A Russian Bible Society, under royal patronage, began in 1812 to disseminate tracts and to promote reading of the Scriptures. Many of those close to the tsar, including Speransky and Prince Golitsyn, the minister of education, were devotees of the various brands of mysticism and pietism so popular in Europe at the time. Alexander may have been a Freemason, as were many of the Russian nobles. The tsar outgrew his fondness for dalliance and came to lead a virtuous life. In his journey from Vienna to Paris in 1815 he granted long audiences with various mystics with which battle-torn Germany abounded. During his stay in the French capital he often met with the Baroness Juliana de Krüdener, estranged wife of a Russian diplomat, who had forsaken a sinful life for one of pietistic evangelism and prophecy. The baroness convinced Alexander, who probably needed little convincing, that he had been divinely appointed to bring peace to Europe and to lead mankind back along the paths of virtue. When in England, the tsar met with Quaker leaders and assured them of his love of peace. That he honestly felt an abiding horror of war is beyond question. Finally, it must be remembered that Alexander never quite overcame his sense of remorse for the murder of his father.

But the Holy Alliance grew out of something more than the "sublime mysticism and nonsense" which Castlereagh scorned. Behind it lay the tsar's sincere conviction that only an acceptance of Christian principles could bring an end to war and all its misery. "If men were vital Christians there could be no wars," he told a Quaker leader. "I am sure that the spirit of Christianity is decisive against war." Pitt had spurned his suggestion of a political federation of Europe back in 1805. Now the tsar put forward the idea of a Christian federation of the continent to accomplish the same purpose—an end to war. But nineteenth-century rulers had no more patience with the idea of governing by Christian principles than twentieth-century politicians felt for the outlawing of war. "High-sounding nothing," Metternich termed it, and agreed to it only to please the tsar, as the men at Paris a century later agreed to the League of Nations to please Wilson.

With peace apparently assured Alexander returned to St. Petersburg ready to take up once more the problems of internal reform that had been laid aside three years earlier. Those who had travelled with him in Western Europe had come to know a civilization far in advance of that in Russia and had observed and discussed institutions and ideas quite foreign to the Russian experience. That such men would be impatient for reform of their homeland no one knew better than the tsar. Tired as he surely was, Alexander left Paris with the determination to free Russian society from its feudal bondage. "With God's help," he swore, "serfdom will be abolished before my reign ends."

SUGGESTED READING

Artz, F. B., *Reaction and Revolution, 1814–1832* (New York, Harper's, 1934).

Bruun, G., *Europe and the French Imperium* (New York, Harper's, 1938).

Caulaincourt, A., *No Peace with Napoleon* (New York, Morrow, 1936).

———, *With Napoleon in Russia* (New York, Morrow, 1935).

Clausewitz, Karl von, *On War* (New York, Modern Library, 1943).

Knapton, E. J., *The Lady of the Holy Alliance, the Life of Julie de Krüdener* (New York, Columbia University Press, 1939).

Lobanov-Rostovsky, A. A., *Russia and Europe, 1789–1825* (Durham, Duke University Press, 1947).

Schenk, H. G., *The Aftermath of the Napoleonic Wars* (New York, Oxford University Press, 1947).

Tarle, E., *Napoleon's Invasion of Russia, 1812* (New York, Oxford University Press, 1942).

Tolstoy, L., *War and Peace*.

Webster, C. K., *The Congress of Vienna* (London, Bell, 1934).

Wilson, Sir Robert, *Narrative of Events During the Invasion of Russia by Napoleon Bonaparte, 1812* (London, J. Murray, 1860).

18

The Tired Reformer

ALEXANDER RETURNED TO RUSSIA DEtermined to pursue the course of social reform which had been halted by the recent war. He adopted a constitution for Poland and later set advisers to work to draft one for Russia. In 1816 he freed the serfs of Esthonia without land, and some liberals urged him to do the same in Russia proper. He established the hated Military Colonies, which were designed to soften the burden of army service for the peasants but developed into the worst agency of oppression.

The tsar was most concerned after 1815, however, with the need to maintain the peace of Europe. He feared the revolutions which followed the Vienna settlement as the greatest threat to that peace, and cooperated with Prussia and Austria to support legitimate governments no matter how reactionary in the hope of preventing another war. Impatient demands by his own countrymen for fundamental reform roused in him a dread of revolt in Russia. While he talked of abdicating he succumbed to the influence of reactionaries at home and abroad. In the closing years of the reign secret societies gathered support for a movement to overthrow the autocracy and establish constitutional government. The tsar knew of their existence and membership and of plans to assassinate him, but could not bring himself to punish others for ideas he had supported in his youth. His death precipitated a revolution aimed at bringing about the changes which he had long favored but which he had lacked either the ability or the courage to institute.

THE KINGDOM OF POLAND

Czartoryski's dream that his native Poland might be restored to her pre-partition borders was made impossible by the fact that the Vienna settlement left Prussia with the provinces of Posen and West Prussia, Austria with Galicia, and Russia with the non-Polish White Russian and Lithuanian districts. "Congress Poland," as the remainder was called, became a kingdom with the tsar of Russia as king.

A commission made up entirely of Poles drafted a constitution more liberal than the one granted to the French people, and Alexander took an oath of allegiance to it in 1815. The document provided freedom of the press and freedom from arbitrary arrest, recognized Polish as the official language, limited the holding of office to Polish subjects, gave the kingdom an army of its own, and granted suffrage to males over thirty with a moderate property qualification. The Diet consisted of an upper house where sat the Catholic bishops and great landowners and a lower house composed of representatives of the lesser gentry and town dwellers. At its biennial meeting the Diet considered but could not initiate legislation presented by the ministry, which was vaguely responsible to it. The tsar's brother, the irascible Grand Duke Constantine, was appointed to command the Polish army, while a Polish republican general who had served with Napoleon was named viceroy rather than Czartoryski, who might have been a better choice. Alexander hinted at restoring the White Russian and Lithuanian provinces to the kingdom, but word of it provoked sharp hostility among both conservative and liberal Russians.

WAR DAMAGE AND RECONSTRUCTION

The awful devastation which the war of 1812 had wrought in Russia took years to remove. Property destruction in the neighborhood of Moscow alone approached three hundred million rubles, and every district along the invasion route suffered proportionally. Hundreds of landowners had been bankrupted by the burning of buildings and the killing of livestock, while the nobles generally had contributed most or all of their funds to the war effort. Peasants lost their huts, carts, tools, animals, and poultry, and seed for the spring planting was very scarce. The population in the war-ravaged provinces was so impoverished that payment of taxes in western Russia had practically stopped by 1815. A hundred thousand corpses lay still unburied west of Smolensk in the spring of 1813, and the consequent epidemics carried away many who had survived the war. In place of the normal population increase of six hundred thousand, that year there was actually a decrease.

The nation set about to repair the war damage, and to all outward appearance the recovery was complete in a remarkably short time. With the aid of government subsidies, but primarily by private effort, Moscow and the other burned cities quickly rose again. Farm areas came back more slowly, for decimated herds needed years to build up, and broken and lost tools could be replaced only when the farmer found money or credit to buy them. Factories in the Moscow area had been ruined or forced to evacuate to other locations, but industry in general had grown rapidly under the protection of the Continental system and suffered relatively little from the war. The cost of living remained insufferably high for years, in part due to heavy government issue of paper money during the war, in part the result of widespread property loss.

The government took several steps to ease conditions brought on by the invasion. Unpaid taxes were forgiven, further issue of paper money was halted, and the government debt was reduced in an effort to revive public confidence. Roads were restored and improved to make possible relief from crop failures. The tariff was liberalized by removing prohibitions upon foreign trade and by drastically cutting duties on raw material imports in an effort to encourage rapid industrial recovery. However, manufacturers convinced the government that finished goods must be protected, and the nation returned to a protectionist policy toward the close of the reign.

REFORM EFFORTS

The tsar's acceptance of the Polish constitution raised the hope of liberals that a similar step would soon follow in Russia. At the tsar's order Novosiltsev drafted a "Constitutional Charter of the Empire" which envisaged a federal system similar to that of the United States, whose constitution Alexander had studied. The plan was adopted in part in the fading years of the reign when a governor-general was appointed to administer each Russian province with an executive council to advise him. With the variation in political institutions to be found in the western border areas, Novosiltsev's suggestion of federation was sensible. Alexander was sympathetic to the idea and might have applied it in full had his death not terminated all consideration of reform. But his successors refused to permit even the publication of so liberal a plan.

When Alexander formally opened the first session of the Polish Diet in 1818 he urged the Poles to show the world that "free institutions whose sacred principles some confuse with destructive teachings are not a dangerous dream, that on the contrary such institutions are in perfect accord with social order and confirm the well-being of nations." But conditions in Russia were not the same as in Poland. The latter had long enjoyed a constitutional regime before the partition. Indeed, Poland had suffered from too much constitutional freedom, for the *liberum veto* had made effective government of the kingdom impossible. The memory of limited monarchy was still fresh in Polish minds. But Russians had long since forgotten the time over a century earlier when the last curb on autocratic power had been swept away. Alexander went to the heart of the matter when he told the Polish Diet: "The former existence of this constitutional order in your country has enabled me to grant you at once that which has not ceased to be the object of my cares, and the beneficial influence of this free institution I hope to expand to all countries entrusted to my care. Thus you have given me a means to demonstrate to my own country that which I have long been preparing for it, and which it will enjoy as soon as the foundations for such an important matter reach the necessary ripeness."

A constitution, the tsar felt with honest conviction and with considerable justification, could not successfully be promulgated in Russia at one stroke. Too many obstacles to a constitutional regime had first to be cleared away. Bondage must come to an end, for only free people could operate free institutions. Illiteracy must be reduced. Honest and efficient public servants must be found. Shortly after his return from Vienna Alexander undertook to fill the thousands of official positions over the nation with reliable and qualified personnel. The task seemed hopeless. "I know that the majority of the administrative officials should be dismissed," he admitted, "and that the evil comes both from the higher officials and from the poor selection of lower officials. But where can you get them? I am unable to find fifty governors, and I need thousands of other officials. The army, the civil administration, everything is not as I would have it, but what can you do? You cannot do everything at once."

While the tsar had not lost hope that a constitutional regime might in the near future be established, it is worth noting that Kochubey, one of the members of the Unofficial Committee, had come around to the view that the nation could best be governed under unlimited monarchy. "The Russian Empire is an autocratic state," Kochubey declared. "Whether we consider its dimensions or its geographic position, the degree of its education and many other circumstances, we must admit that this form of government is the only one that will be proper for Russia for many years to come."

The problem of serfdom was perhaps less difficult of solution than was that of inaugurating a constitutional regime in Russia. It must not be supposed, however, that the tsar was entirely a free agent who might move without fear of interruption to put an end to bondage. Palace revolutions had plagued the monarchy since the last quarter of the seventeenth century, and both Alexander's father and grandfather had been struck down by assassins. The Romanovs stayed on the throne by tolerance of the nobility and, with few exceptions, they chose to tread softly in dealing with them. It will be remembered that Catherine II, a much more imperious ruler than was Alexander, chose not to abolish the serfdom which she recognized as evil for fear of antagonizing the nobles to whom she owed her throne. Alexander himself had heard whispered warnings after Tilsit that what had happened to his father might happen again. But if he sometimes lacked courage, he was always a man of deep conscience. His desire to abdicate, which was common knowledge after Vienna, must have grown in part from a feeling that he was helpless to provide Russia with decent institutions. It must be borne in mind that the United States found the same problem of bondage not easy to solve. It is true that American slaves differed from the Russian in color and in numbers, but abolitionists in the two countries expressed in their correspondence the conviction that the problem was the same.

There was some indication in Alexander's Russia, as in the United States at the time, that serfdom might gradually disappear because it was uneconomical. Some who testified before the Unofficial Committee in 1802 had expressed the belief that serfdom could not last. In 1816 the nobles of the Baltic province of Esthonia successfully appealed to the tsar to free the serfs without land. The industry of the province, which was controlled by the gentry, was far ahead of that in Great Russia, and the owners had come to realize that free labor was less costly than serf labor. The following year the serfs of Courland were freed for the same reason, and in 1819 bondage ended in Livonia. The result of emancipation was to stimulate industry in the Baltic provinces by providing a free landless labor force. Some of the gentry of Great Russia urged the tsar to extend emancipation without land to the rest of his dominions, but the vast majority of nobles opposed it.

In 1818 Alexander ordered his chief adviser, Arakcheyev, to draft a plan for the emancipation of the Great Russian peasants with land, but he realistically cautioned that the gentry's interests must be protected if the plan were to be acceptable. Arakcheyev faithfully proposed that the government spend five million rubles a year to purchase the serfs of landowners willing to sell, along with five acres of land for each peasant. The laudable suggestion was doomed partly by the fact that there was no room in the state budget for any such expenditure, but chiefly by the unwillingness of most of the gentry to surrender their serfs without government pressure.

THE MILITARY COLONIES

Alexander was convinced after Vienna that Russia needed an army equal to those of Austria and Prussia combined. The cost of the recent war, however, made a reduction in government expenditures imperative. And the burden of enlistments imposed an excessive hardship on the villages at a time when every man was needed to restore the land.

In a sincere effort to ease the burden of military service by permitting the soldiers to train at home, and in a grim determination to establish model communities, Alexander in 1817 organized the first so-called military colony in an area near Novgorod where land and serfs were owned by the crown. Each village in the district became a military camp. All male peasants between eighteen and forty-five became soldiers in the new regiment, which was staffed and instructed by a cadre brought in from the regular army. Unmarried soldiers were quartered in the homes of the married, where they were expected to labor as farm workers. Married soldiers and "master colonists," or peasants over fifty, were given a new brick cottage and cattle, poultry, and tools. Even the children from the age of seven dressed in uniform and were trained in preparation to take their place in the ranks. Marriages were permissible only with the consent of the military authorities, for the lives of the colonists were thoroughly regimented, even to rising, dining, and retiring to bugle calls. Discipline was extremely harsh, for the inhabitants were subject to flogging for infractions of military rules. By the end of the reign a third of the Russian army, two hundred thousand men, was stationed in the military colonies in the Novgorod-St. Petersburg area and in Little Russia. Exemption from national and local taxes could not compensate for the goose-stepping life in uniform, and revolts swept through the colonies from the very year of their founding. The colonists pleaded to be returned to their former status, saying they preferred to have a son taken from every household as in earlier times to having the entire family drafted.

The program was administered by Count Alexei Arakcheyev, a martinet trained in Paul's regiment at Gatchina, who was renowned for the brutality with which he treated the serfs on his own estates. Peasant wives who failed to have a child each year, or whose child was stillborn, or who bore a girl instead of a boy, were subjected to a regular scale of fines. He found a sadistic delight in condemning those who broke the colonies' rules to running the gauntlet between two five-hundred-man rows of soldiers armed with birch rods and rifle butts, after which Arakcheyev "regretted to report" that some of them died. When Alexander came to inspect the colonies the same roast pig was smuggled from house to house ahead of the tsar to convince him that the inhabitants lived well. "Backs covered with sores from frequent beatings were concealed under neat military uniforms, and Alexander usually left well pleased with the condition of the colonies" (Mazour). The failure of the experiment was assured from the fact that too much time was consumed in drill to permit adequate attention to be given to farming. In the minds of the peasants the military colonies came to symbolize oppression, and "Arakcheyevism" became a synonym for brutality.

REACTION

Alexander seemed unable after 1815 to recover the enthusiasm for reform which had marked his early years. Some have held that his mysticism and religious groping turned him away from worldly interests. Others maintain that he spent so much time travelling about Russia and attending international conferences that he had little left for internal problems. Cynics insist that he had never been sincere in his profession of liberal views and that now he simply revealed his true character.

Whatever the reason, after returning home from the Congress of Vienna the tsar seemed more willing than in earlier years to leave the administration to others. His reliance upon Arakcheyev may be attributable to the fact that the "corporal of Gatchina," as Arakcheyev was styled, was impeccably honest and as faithful as a dog. He had no other ambition than to please his master, and his grovelling obedience may have blinded Alexander to his bestiality. So fully did the tsar trust his loyal slave that all business passed through his hands, and Arakcheyev, anxious to relieve his master of worry and care, intercepted complaints addressed to the throne. If Arakcheyev needed any prompting in his determination to put the nation into a strait jacket, he had it from his confessor, Photius Spassky, a fanatical monk who spent his nights wrestling with the devil.

The reaction which Arakcheyev led and Photius inspired first appeared in the field of education. Prince Alexander Golitsyn, a former liberal and intimate of the tsar, added the ministry of education to his position as procurator-general of the Holy Synod. Alexander himself contributed to the drift toward church domination of education with the pronouncement in the spirit of the Holy Alliance that "Christian piety should always be the foundation of all true education." Golitsyn investigated the University of Kazan and found "dangerous" ideas being disseminated. Several professors were dismissed and the rest were warned that henceforth their teaching, whether in science, social science, or humanities, must conform to Biblical principles. In geometry the triangle should be shown to represent the Trinity. Copernicus and Newton must not be mentioned in physics classes, for their laws were contrary to the Bible. Dissection by medical students was forbidden as being disrespectful to the dead. Economics professors must uphold serfdom. The director of the university was advised that the government's purpose in educating students was "the bringing up of true sons of the Orthodox Church, loyal subjects of the state, and good and useful citizens of the fatherland." The other universities were subjected to the same sort of purge. Foreign professors were discharged and Russians who had studied in foreign universities were denied appointments. Again as in Paul's time, Russian students were forbidden to study abroad. Even Golitsyn was too liberal for Photius and was forced to resign as minister of education. His place was taken by Admiral Shishkov, who believed that increasing literacy might prove disastrous. "To teach rhetoric to the son of a peasant would make him a bad and useless subject, if not a really dangerous one." However, he agreed that every member of society should receive instruction in the "rules and principles of Christian conduct and good morals."

Censorship restrictions upon all publications tightened after 1815. Double censorship by the ministry of education and by the police made sure that nothing in the least questionable got into print, for the police might confiscate publications that had been passed by the ministry of education. No criticism of public officials was allowed, and the restrictions reached the ridiculous point of forbidding unfavorable comment upon actors who performed before the tsar.

Alexander had accepted the Finnish constitution already in force when he conquered the duchy in 1809, and he had guaranteed complete autonomy except in foreign affairs. In the closing years of his reign, however, he deliberately violated the Finnish laws which he had sworn to uphold. Orthodox Russians were appointed to many government posts for which only Lutheran Finns were by law eligible. The Diet was not convened, and the finances of the duchy were managed .arbitrarily from St. Petersburg in violation of the constitutional power of the Diet to approve the budget. Imperial *ukazes* issued from the Russian capital in spite of the fact that all laws should have had the Diet's approval. Even Russian censorship regulations were extended to Finland, whose laws forbade censorship.

The guarantees provided in the Polish constitution fared similarly after the honeymoon of the first few years. Press censorship was extended to the kingdom in violation of the constitutional sanction of freedom of the press. Freedom from arbitrary arrest went glimmering in 1819, when the viceroy was given power to limit personal liberty in the interest of internal peace. Complaints of such violations of the constitution were brought forward in the Diet of 1820, but they met from Alexander, now fearful of the revolutions which were breaking out all over Europe, only the stern warning that Poland's continued survival depended upon a docile Diet. For five years the Diet was not convened, although the constitution provided for biennial sessions. The Russian government interfered in the elections for the Polish

Diet in 1825, and troops surrounded the palace where the Diet held its meetings. The Poles took the hint and restrained themselves so well during the session that Alexander seemed well satisfied. "How nobly gave he back to Poles their Diet, then told pugnacious Poland to be quiet" wrote the poet Byron.

In 1820, while Alexander was abroad attending an international congress, he received word of a mutiny in the Semenovsky Regiment which the tsar himself had once led. Earlier in the year the regiment had received a new commanding officer, the martinet Colonel Schwarz. In his zeal to bring the troops back to "discipline" and good order, by which he meant Prussian formalism, he flogged several soldiers who had been awarded the Order of St. George. By law, recipients of the order were expressly exempted from corporal punishment. The troops complained in a body and petitioned the colonel to observe their privileges, whereupon the entire regiment was imprisoned. The affair could hardly be called a mutiny, and certainly the men had been unduly provoked. But Metternich made the most of the matter when he relayed the news to Alexander, as though to remind him of the danger of courting liberal ideas. The tsar was badly shaken by the news, convinced that revolution threatened his empire. No matter how sincere he had been in his early profession of democratic principles, Alexander never had any patience with revolution, which to him meant chaos and war. Liberal institutions were desirable, he felt, but must be the gift of a benevolent monarch. He always looked upon any popular pressure for reform as evidence of ingratitude.

THE TSAR ABROAD

The great powers agreed at Vienna to convene periodically, and in 1818 the tsar was off to the first meeting at Aix-la-Chapelle. The Quadruple Alliance was renewed as a safeguard against France, the birthplace of revolution. However, at Alexander's behest France, whose government seemed stable enough, was admitted to membership in what now became the Quintuple Alliance. The tsar recommended a mutual reduction of armaments and the creation of an international army to discourage aggression, but without success. His proposal that the powers bind themselves to suppress revolution wherever it appeared provoked fear in the British Parliament that Cossacks might be quartered in Hyde Park to quiet the House of Commons. The ridiculous charge ignored the constructive nature of the tsar's recommendation. He wanted to require all legitimate governments to grant their people liberal constitutions; only then would they be maintained against revolt. Metternich was horrified at the suggestion, as was the Englishman Castlereagh.

A plot to assassinate the members of the British cabinet, the murder of the French king's nephew, and the outbreak of revolutions in Spain and in Naples in 1820 indicated to Alexander the need for another conference. The meeting at Troppau dealt only with the Neapolitan uprising, for Britain would not countenance interference in Spanish affairs lest Spain's American colonies, where England's trade interests were vital, should be prevented from obtaining their independence. It was at Troppau that Alexander received word of the Semenovsky mutiny in St. Petersburg. Convinced that this was but a phase in an international conspiracy, the tsar assured Metternich of his impatience with popular uprisings. Now Austria, Prussia, and Russia formally agreed to suppress revolution by joint action wherever it appeared. Then the powers adjourned to Laibach near the Adriatic to hear testimony from the king of Naples on the uprising in his dominions.

At Laibach Austria received Russian and Prussian approval to march into South Italy to suppress the revolution in Naples. Alexander volunteered a Russian contingent for the expedition, but Metternich successfully parried the offer. No agreement was reached on intervention in Spain. Meantime, the conferees learned of rebellion in Greece against Turkish rule, but agreed to postpone action until a later meeting.

By the time the powers convened at Verona in 1822 the sultan seemed to have the Greek situation momentarily in hand, but the Spanish revolutionists had imprisoned their king and established a government of their own. Again the tsar offered an army to restore order, but the powers assigned the task to France. Restoration of Spanish rule in the Americas was precluded when President Monroe, assured of British backing, announced that European intervention in the Western Hemisphere would not be tolerated.

The Greek war for independence which broke out in 1821 first came to the attention of the great powers at the Congress of Laibach. Because of the romantic appeal of the Greek cause the fact is often ignored that the rebellion was only a part of the whole Near Eastern question, the crux of which was "the ability of the inherently weak Ottoman Empire to survive" (Puryear). Persia attacked Turkey in the very year of the Greek revolt. Egypt, whose ruler was militarily stronger than the sultan, was considering secession. The Barbary pirates roamed at will over the Mediterranean, a constant embarrassment to the sultan, who would make no effort to control them for fear of losing the entire north coast of Africa. Serbia and the Danubian Principalities had won local autonomy under Russian protection. Russia was the recognized defender of Orthodox Christians throughout the Ottoman Empire and had been nibbling at the Turkish border for half a century.

The Turkish problem was more immediately of concern to Russia than to any other power. Odessa, the south Russian port with a Greek name, had been since Catherine's time the residence of many Greek traders. In 1814 they organized a secret society named the Hetairia for the purpose of reviving the Greek Empire at Constantinople. Six years later the Greek Prince Ypsilanti, who had served with the Russian forces during the Napoleonic wars, became leader of the society and began laying plans for a rising of Greeks all over the Ottoman Empire. Ypsilanti was convinced that he would have Russian support, for the sympathy of Orthodox Russians for their coreligionists in the Balkans was scarcely veiled. Many Russian nobles joined Ypsilanti's force when it crossed the Pruth river in 1821.

Turkey had not carried out the terms of the Treaty of Bucharest which, in 1812, had ended the last of the Russo-Turkish wars. The autonomy promised Serbia and the Danubian Principalities, for which Russia stood guarantor, had been violated, and Russian commerce through the Straits had been subjected to unpredictable levies and downright interruption. The price of wheat in the port of Odessa, which handled a third of Russian exports, slumped under the threat that grain ships might be denied exit from the Black Sea. The questions at issue were long under discussion, but negotiations ended abruptly and the Russian minister left Constantinople in 1821 after a Russian war vessel had been detained and searched in the Turkish capital. None of the great powers questioned the justice of the Russian complaints, for they all suffered from whimsical Turkish treatment of foreign commerce; but England and Austria sided with Turkey for fear that her collapse would give Russia control of the Straits. So fearful was the British government lest Russia attack Turkey that she brought the two disputants back into correspondence. The British ambassador in Constantinople warned the sultan against his "unreasonable" obstinacy and won Turkish compliance, at least for the moment, with most of the Russian claims. All points at issue were settled definitively soon after Alexander's death, but the settlement lasted less than two years.

The Greek revolt, then, was only an irritant to relations between Russia and Turkey that had long been strained. As for the Greeks themselves, Alexander considered them far too barbaric to merit or appreciate independence. Aside from the fact that he could not with good grace have supported revolution in Greece while opposing it elsewhere, he seems to have been motivated by a high-minded determination to keep the peace at almost any cost. His restraint in dealing with the Porte won high praise from the British foreign minister Canning who admitted that "Russia can conquer Turkey and Greece when she pleases." But "to critics who failed to understand an idealist approach to politics, the tsar's attitude seemed rather foolish" (Schenk). Only with the consent of the other great powers would he consider intervention, for that was the policy he had sponsored and continued to support at every international conference. When two years after his death Russia did take a hand in the Greek struggle and in the greater Turkish problem, it was only by agreement with her allies.

THE DECEMBRISTS

Within a few months of the end of the Napoleonic wars a small group of young army officers in St. Petersburg organized a society called the "Union of Salvation" to discuss the need for reform. All were high-ranking members of the nobility whose service in Western Europe had stirred in them shame and deep resentment at Russia's backwardness. All were well educated, steeped in the philosophy of the enlightenment and the French Revolution. While the members differed in aims and methods, all were agreed on the need to abolish serfdom and to win constitutional government.

Other young nobles joined the group, among them Colonel Paul Pestel, who became the fiery leader of the society. While some members were inclined to caution and urged a policy of cooperation with the government, Pestel insisted that the society must be secret. From the very beginning he assumed that the aim of the society was revolution to establish a constitutional regime. If the goal were not achieved in Alexander's lifetime, the oath of allegiance must be withheld from his successor until he granted a constitution. The members, he believed, should work for abolition of serfdom, public trial, equality before the law, termination of the military colonies, and shorter terms of military service.

Later the society changed its name to "Union of Welfare," established branches in the provincial capitals, and adopted a constitution. Pestel was away from the capital when the document was drafted, and the program approved was much milder than Pestel believed satisfactory. The members were urged to treat their serfs humanely, build schools, support hospitals and orphanages, agitate for prison reform, oppose government corruption and bribery of officials, encourage the founding of insurance companies, and work for the economic development of Russia. So conservative and harmless was the document that one of the members, General Orlov, chided the group with being "more German idealists than French Jacobins." Pestel agreed to accept it only as a front to hide his revolutionary aims and to facilitate the enlistment of new members.

The St. Petersburg group lost interest in the movement for want of vigorous leadership when Colonel Pestel was transferred to a post in southern Russia. Here at Tulchin near the Romanian border he established another branch which from the beginning reflected his own radical views. On a visit to the capital in 1819 Pestel succeeded in revitalizing the society in the north and even won the members over to his conviction that Russia should become a republic like the United States. The majority of his northern friends balked, however, at his insistence upon assassinating the emperor to make way for a republic.

Many of the officers of the Semenovsky Regiment were members of the Union of Welfare. After the mutiny the regiment was broken up and its officers scattered among other units. The effect was to spread the infection over the empire and to make possible the organization of new cells or branches wherever the men were stationed. Not all the members of the society, however, had been officers in the Semenovsky Regiment. Enough remained in the capital to carry on the work. Soon after the mutiny the tsar organized a corps of secret military police to watch subversives, and the organization decided to disband. In its place there arose two groups, the Northern Society with headquarters in the capital and the Southern Society located at Tulchin.

The leader of the Northern Society, the twenty-six-year-old Nikita Muravev, drew up a constitutional blueprint for the new Russia he envisaged. Serfdom was to disappear, freedom of speech, press, and religion were guaranteed, and trial by jury was provided. Russia was to be divided into thirteen states with limited autonomy, suggestive of the American system. A bicameral legislature, consisting of a Supreme Council representing the states and a House of Representatives chosen in electoral districts, would ratify treaties, confirm appointments, impeach officials, and share in passing laws. The House of Representatives would control tax measures and initiate all bills. The executive was to be the hereditary emperor with powers comparable to those of the American president. The right to vote and to hold office was limited to property owners on such a restrictive basis as to exclude all but the gentry and merchant class. The former serfs, who were to receive five acres at the time of emancipation, would have no political status. It was to this provision, which "legalized a terrible aristocracy of wealth," that Pestel most objected.

The detailed plan of the Southern Society—*Russkaia Pravda*, or Russian justice, as it was titled—was drawn up by Pestel. Russia was to become a republic by assassinating all members of the royal family to eliminate all claimants to the throne. To Muravev's federal principle Pestel opposed a highly centralized state with Great Russian the only language and Russian Orthodoxy the only religion allowed. The church would function as a branch of the government, with the clergy as state employees. Mahommedanism was to be proscribed, and the Jews were all to be packed off to Palestine. Local institutions and customs were to be disallowed except among the Poles, to whom Pestel conceded a small measure of autonomy in order to win support of Polish revolutionaries. Territories bordering on Russia which Pestel deemed vital to national security—Mongolia for example—would be conquered.

The society which Pestel proposed was a strange mixture of capitalism and communism. Class would disappear as serfdom was abolished and all social distinctions eliminated. All land was to be nationalized and divided into two categories. Part was to be reserved for state use to provide revenue and to permit creation of large experimental farms. The rest of the land was to be divided among the peasants, each family to have a plot sufficient for its support. Such plots could not be alienated, however, for title would lie with the state. Pestel would have promoted industry by encouraging individual enterprise and by freeing trade and production from restrictive tariffs, taxes, and regulations.

Pestel believed that during the transition from the old to the new society Russia would have to be governed by a dictatorship or "Directory" of five members. The period of dictatorship he supposed would last no longer than ten years, during which all Russians would enjoy freedom of speech, press, and religion and the right to vote. Incidentally, no societies, open or secret, would be tolerated. After the passing of the period of tutelage the nation would be governed in much the same way as Speransky had proposed earlier. Each county would elect an administrative board and a duma to handle local problems; its duma would choose representatives to the district duma, which in turn would send delegates to a provincial duma which would elect members to sit in a national Duma. A "Directory" of five would serve as a national executive. Pestel left the details of governmental powers to be worked out later, for he was most concerned with overthrowing the monarchy and abolishing serfdom. He expected to work out fine points of the system afterwards.

In the programs of the Northern and Southern Societies are to be found the two extremes which liberal thought in Russia was to pursue to and beyond the end of the monarchy: constitutional monarchy *versus* republicanism; evolution *versus* revolution; federalism *versus* centralism; tolerance *versus* intolerance. By some, Pestel has been termed the first Socialist, by others, the first Communist, long before there were either Socialists or Communists. The similarities between his *Russkaia Pravda* and Bolshevik practice are striking. Muravev, on the other hand, represents the position taken by moderate reformers in the early twentieth century.

While the Northern and Southern Societies were at odds on aims and methods, they were completely in accord in insisting that the new Russia must be created under the leadership of a few. All members feared mass uprising; consequently, no effort was made to enlist widespread support. Membership in the two societies never exceeded a few hundred. This lack of faith in the masses was typical of Russian revolutionary movements until near the close of the nineteenth century.

Alexander knew not only of the existence of the secret societies but of their programs and membership, for the secret police kept careful watch over their activities. He refused, however, to punish them for liberal views which he himself had done so much to encourage. Shortly before his death he learned that they were plotting his assassination, but still he made no move against them. Plans for the "first Russian Revolution" went forward without interruption from the throne it aimed to overturn.

END OF THE REIGN

Alexander seemed to tire of the cares of government after 1815, and he grew increasingly restless under the frustration of problems at home and abroad that he could not solve. After the Semenovsky mutiny he reluctantly turned away from the liberal views of his youth. The cynicism which greeted his efforts to keep peace among the nations on a high moral plane and the ingratitude which many Russians showed for his well-meaning but admittedly ineffective attempts to improve domestic conditions indicated to the tired reformer that his life had been a failure. He came to regard such catastrophic events as the death of his natural daughter, of whom he was sentimentally fond, and the terrible St. Petersburg flood of 1824 as divine punishment for his sins.

As early as 1812, and again in 1819, Alexander informed his brother Nicholas of his intention to abdicate and retire. Peter's succession law providing that the emperor might name his successor had been set aside by Paul, who pronounced in favor of strict heredity. Since Alexander had no sons, his next older brother Constantine would by Paul's law succeed to the throne. But Constantine had disqualified himself by divorcing his wife and contracting a morganatic marriage; he formally renounced the throne in 1822. Thereupon Alexander declared Nicholas the successor and drew up a statement to that effect which he kept secret, probably because of his determination to retire at some future time. The original was hidden in the altar of the Cathedral of the Assumption in Moscow, and sealed copies were deposited with the State Council, the Senate, and the Holy Synod. The act was known to the tsar's mother, to Constantine and Nicholas, to the metropolitan, and to Golitsyn, then procurator-general of the Holy Synod. But the secrecy which surrounded the matter was to lead to awkwardness and nearly to disaster at the opening of the new reign.

In the autumn of 1825 Alexander left St. Petersburg for Taganrog on the Sea of Azov. The Empress Elizabeth was in poor health and physicians prescribed a mild climate for the winter. A short time later the emperor himself fell ill and died there in December, 1825. He refused to take medicine, as though he were impatient to have done with a life that had lost interest for him. The suddenness of his death gave rise to a rumor that he did not die until 1864, that he lived on as Fedor Kuzmich, a saintly recluse who had settled in Siberia about 1825. Even members of the royal family in the nineteenth century credited the tale, and Alexander's latest biographer, Strakhovsky, makes a convincing case for it.

The many who have dealt with the life of Alexander I have differed sharply in their estimation of him. Liberal writers generally have been critical, and recent Russian historians particularly so, because he did not abolish serfdom. But it is only fair to recall that feudalism in Western Europe was swept away only by the French Revolution and Napoleon. That the problem should prove more formidable in Russia, backward and completely agricultural as she was, was only to be expected. Indeed, not all medieval trappings disappeared from Russian society until the twentieth century, and then only at a bloody cost.

SUGGESTED READING

Artz, F. B., *Reaction and Revolution, 1814–1832* (New York, Harper's, 1934).
Cambridge Modern History, Vol. X (New York, Macmillan, 1934).
Johnson, W. H. E., *Russia's Educational Heritage* (Pittsburgh, Carnegie Press, 1950).
Laserson, M. M., *The American Impact on Russia* (New York, Macmillan, 1950).
Masaryk, T. G., *The Spirit of Russia* (New York, Macmillan, 1919).
Mazour, A. G., *The First Russian Revolution, 1825* (Berkeley, University of California Press, 1937).
Puryear, V. J., *France and the Levant* (Berkeley, University of California Press, 1941).
Schenk, H. G., *The Aftermath of the Napoleonic Wars* (New York, Oxford University Press, 1947).
Strakhovsky, L. I., *Alexander I of Russia* (New York, Norton, 1947).
Thomas, B. P., *Russo-American Relations, 1815–1867* (Baltimore, Johns Hopkins Press, 1930).

19

Nicholas I, a Royal Gendarme

NICHOLAS I (1825–1855) SUCCEEDED his brother Alexander only after a pitifully weak effort by secret societies to alter the succession and bring to Russia some sort of constitutional government. The revolt was put down and the conspirators punished with a bloody vengeance that cast a pall over the new reign. Nicholas assumed the mantle of defender of the *status quo* in Russia and throughout Europe, for he was convinced that revolution anywhere was a threat to his own throne. At home he carried through a number of mild reforms aimed at strengthening the bureaucracy and the autocracy in which he placed his faith. Abroad he supported reactionary governments and offered assistance to any legitimate ruler whose throne was imperilled by democratic pressures. He snuffed out the kingdom of Poland and incorporated its territory into the Russian Empire.

Frightened by the revolutions of 1830 and 1848 in the West, he leaned upon advisers who were thoroughly reactionary. Education suffered the blight of clerical domination, the border was sealed to prevent travel abroad, religious sects were cruelly persecuted, the press was strangled by censorship, and the secret police kept busy rounding up those who whispered criticism of the regime. The serfs grew increasingly restless and the mounting number and severity of *Jacqueries* made it apparent even to the tsar that the bondage system could not endure. Because of, as much as in spite of, the repression, Russian literature enjoyed the opening of a brilliant era. Writers found ingenious ways of circumventing the censorship and attacking the Augean stables of the administration, poking fun at the stupidity and cupidity of officialdom or crying out against the tyranny of serfdom or

379

subtly suggesting the need for a revolution that would rid Russia of oppression.

THE DECEMBRIST UPRISING

One week after Alexander's death, when the news reached St. Petersburg, royal officials and Nicholas swore allegiance to Constantine. Pictures of "Constantine I, Emperor and Autocrat of All the Russias" appeared in the streets of the capital. When Constantine heard of it in Warsaw he repeated his disavowal of any interest in the succession, and in turn took the oath of allegiance to Nicholas. There followed three weeks of correspondence between the brothers, Nicholas pressing Constantine to come to St. Petersburg and formally renounce the throne if he did not want it, Constantine repeating that he had renounced his rights and finally threatening to flee abroad if he were further pestered. Although he well knew that he was heartily disliked among the Guards regiments and feared they might not accept him without Constantine's personal appearance and renunciation, Nicholas decided at last to proclaim himself emperor.

Meanwhile the Northern Society, meeting daily at the home of the poet Ryleyev, learned of the confusion in court circles and decided to refuse the oath of allegiance to Nicholas. The members spread word through the streets that this was all a trick to exclude Constantine from the succession. Although Constantine was the most stupid of the brothers and notorious in the army for his brutality and "paradomania," some of the members of the Northern Society seem to have credited him with liberal tendencies. The very reverse was true. Metternich preferred Constantine to Nicholas as the new tsar.

Troops in the capital were paraded on the morning of December 14 to take the oath of allegiance. Forewarned of the activities of the secret societies and of their plan to exploit the occasion, Nicholas so arranged the troops in the Senate Square that he could call upon those of unquestioned loyalty should the need arise. When the soldiers were ordered to take the oath, many shouted for "Constantine and Constitution." Nicholas sent General Miloradovich, a hero of the Napoleonic Wars, to convert the men, but he was shot dead. Michael, the youngest of the grand dukes, went out to reason with the men, but he withdrew when a shot barely missed him. One of the generals near Nicholas said to him bluntly, "Either abdicate or let us clear the square with gunfire." "You ask me to shed the blood of my subjects on the first day of my reign?" Nicholas parried. When told that there was no other way, he ordered up artillery with the comment, "What a happy beginning for my reign!" The cannister tore gaps in the ranks of the mutinous regiments, and many civilian bystanders died as well. As the crowd fled across the frozen Neva cannon balls broke the ice and scores were drowned. Bloodstains on the pavement were quickly scrubbed away and the dead were stuffed under the ice of the river to get them out of sight. It was charged that in their haste to clean up the mess the police threw a number of wounded into the river. The "Decembrist Uprising" had failed. The throne was secure.

All the members of the Northern Society were seized, for the government had a full membership list. Prince Sergei Trubetskoy, descended from the ancient ruling family of Lithuania and a colonel of the Guards, was taken in the Austrian Embassy where he had sought sanctuary. Although he had been chosen to serve as dictator if the throne should be overturned, he took no part in the street scene. Few others were so cowardly. Prince Odoyevsky set out for the Senate Square exulting, "We shall die, but oh how gloriously we shall die!" Ryleyev expected defeat but believed that "it would awaken Russia."

Pestel was arrested in the south the day before the uprising in the capital. But the rest of the Southern Society went ahead with its own revolution. Several companies of troops marched hither and yon in the neighborhood of Kiev, capturing a number of small towns. They were joined by the Society of the United Slavs, a secret revolutionary group of Poles and Russian army officers whose prime hope was to unite all Slavic peoples in one republic. After four days of campaigning the rebels were defeated in a bloody battle with loyal troops, and the leaders were carted off to St. Petersburg to stand trial.

The government moved quickly to round up not only the known leaders but everyone suspected or accused of any association with members of the secret societies. The tsar presided over a committee which interrogated every suspect, and Nicholas himself decided whether each prisoner in turn was to be jailed, chained, dismissed under surveillance, or freed. The treatment to which the men were subjected revealed "the bestial vengeance of this gifted gendarme in the purple robe" (Mazour). Uncooperative prisoners spent weeks chained to the walls of damp dungeons with only black bread and water to sustain them. The tsar performed with artistic skill in the role of the grand inquisitor. Promising pardon to some, cajoling or threatening others, now abusing, now pleading, Nicholas put on a new mask for each Decembrist dragged before him. He was disappointed, outraged, hurt, insulted, or disillusioned according to the temper of the suspect. Priests visited the cells as though administering to condemned men, and the confessions they heard immediately went to the tsar. Many who held firm under the foul conditions of the jails broke under gruelling night-long interrogations. Speransky and the poets Pushkin and Griboyedov were mentioned as being accomplices, but there was nothing more to implicate them than the desperate testimony of witnesses broken by mental torture.

After five months of gathering evidence the investigating committee submitted its findings and recommendations to a special court. The presiding justice was completely deaf, and the prosecutor was one whose intelligence even Nicholas questioned. The accused never appeared in court but were called upon in prison to verify the signatures to their confessions. The court, which sat only a week, tried nearly six hundred, of whom about half were acquitted. Half of those convicted were given light sentences, while a hundred and twenty-one were held to be most culpable. Five leaders were condemned to be quartered, thirty-one to be beheaded, and the rest banished to Siberia at hard labor. But Nicholas had seen enough bloodshed. The five leaders, including Pestel and Ryleyev, were hanged, thirty-one were condemned to hard labor for life in Siberia, and the rest given various terms in Siberian mines. The tsar's pose of clemency did not reduce amazement at the severity of the penalties. That five men should die in a nation where the death sentence had been illegal since Elizabeth's time shocked the world. Rain fell the night before the hanging, and the executioner bungled the job with the wet ropes. Three of the five had to be hanged twice and one, whose legs were broken when the stool was pulled from under him, lamented, "Poor Russia! She cannot even hang decently."

Nicholas never relented in his bitter hatred of the Decembrists. A year after his death and thirty years after the trial his successor pardoned the twenty exiles still alive. Most of them chose to remain in the communities where they had found friends. One remarked that the grave would be no warmer in European Russia than in Siberia.

THE TSAR'S YOUTH AND CHARACTER

Born in the year of Catherine's death and nineteen years younger than Alexander, Nicholas spent a childhood much different from that of his oldest brother. His education was directed by his mother, the domineering Empress Marie. He was trained as a possible heir to the throne, but his schooling was along very conservative lines. He early revealed a proclivity for military affairs, but showed little interest in anything else. He himself admitted that he usually yawned and dozed through lectures on history, economics, and government. As a child he was arrogant, domineering, and rude, and the thrashings administered by his tutor did not break him of pugnacity and stubbornness. He was always a poor pupil, and at fifteen his formal education ended. He accompanied Alexander to Paris in 1814, where he satisfied his taste for military show by watching the endless parades. He took a whirlwind journey through Russia and Western Europe soon after the war. English society was impressed by his handsomeness and military bearing. While he enjoyed the social life of London, he felt only disgust for the endless debates in Parliament. When he returned home at the age of twenty he was raised to the rank of general of a brigade of Guards, and soon found his forte in restoring the discipline that had slipped with the end of war.

Nicholas received no practical experience in administration before his succession, for Alexander never invited him to attend council sessions or introduced him to the work of any governmental agency. He learned nothing of conditions in Russia until he heard the testimony of Pestel and others.

ADMINISTRATIVE ALTERATIONS

As he questioned the Decembrists Nicholas was less moved to fear than to disbelief that anyone should presume to question the autocracy. He moved at once to correct the slackness in his brother's administration that had made the uprising possible. The new tsar's abiding faith in authority never wavered; especially after the uprisings, he had full confidence that what was needed was a strengthening of the autocracy, not a relaxation of it.

Before his accession the agency known as the Imperial Chancery had dealt primarily under the tsar's personal direction with matters affecting the royal household. Nicholas added to its duties, organizing new sections or departments to deal with specific tasks. The First Section retained the functions of the former chancery. The Second Section, under Speransky, was assigned to publish a new law code. The infamous Third Section directed the political police force whose responsibility it was to discover unrest and track down subversives and agitators. The Fourth Section handled royal charities and administered the schools and hospitals financed by them. The Fifth Section, created later, managed the state-owned serfs. Nicholas would have preferred to run every government department himself, but confessing his inability to do so he kept in personal touch with important agencies by making the section heads accountable personally to him.

Impressed with the Decembrists' animosity toward influential officials in the closing days of Alexander's reign, Nicholas dismissed those who had been running the government. Arakcheyev's resignation was accepted, Photius was returned to his monastery, and the obscurantist heads of the universities were retired. The emperor chose for advisers men who were conservative but not reactionary. Speransky returned to the capital, and Kochubey, a member of Alexander's Unofficial Committee, won the tsar's confidence. But Kochubey had forsaken his liberal views of 1801 and now was convinced that Russia could only be governed by autocracy. Speransky, whose loyalty to conservative principles Nicholas had tested by naming him to the committee which had investigated the Decembrists, had done penance for his earlier liberalism by approving the vicious sentences. Kankrin and Kiselev, both sympathetic to mild peasant reforms, were carried over from the previous reign. No matter who occupied government posts, however, the emperor never lost firm control of the administration, unlike Alexander in the waning years of his reign.

Nicholas hoped that Russia's ills might disappear under a disciplined, military-like bureaucracy. He considered himself the nation's commander-in-chief, and referred to his bureau heads as chiefs of staff. The peace and quiet of the countryside he held to be the responsibility of the landowning, serf-owning gentry, whom he looked upon as a corps of unpaid policemen. But Nicholas really trusted no one. The government became a quagmire of regulations, reports, investigations, recommendations, and orders. No official could take any action without filling out a mass of documents. In one case, papers reporting evidence of fraud in a government contract filled ten carts, but papers, carts, horses and all were lost on the way to the capital. Half-way through the reign the Ministry of Justice reported a backlog of over three million cases pending in its courts; all the other ministries were equally far behind. The primary concern of government agencies came to be not the conduct of business but "evacuation of paper" (Kliuchevsky). When the administration threatened to break down under the weight of paper Nicholas appointed a committee to investigate the possibility of reducing the volume of official correspondence. As the reign drew to a close it became apparent to all that the officialdom was so bogged down in bureaucratic nonsense that it was unable to govern the nation.

REFORM MEASURES

Nicholas set himself determinedly to resist progress. He never wavered from that course. He was willing, however, to consider any measure which would make autocracy more efficient. It is from that point of view that his interest in what he termed "just reform" must be considered. "I shall always distinguish," he pronounced, "those who desire just reforms and expect them to emanate from the legal authority, from those who want to undertake them by themselves, employing God knows what means." At his coronation the tsar warned that faults in government could be corrected, "not by impertinent, destructive dreams," but only by act of the sovereign.

Under the leadership of Speransky, the Second Section of the Imperial Chancery gathered together in an orderly collection all the laws that had been issued since the publication of the *Ulozhenie* in the time of Alexis. The codification had been sorely needed for generations, and both Catherine and Alexander had admitted as much. Before 1832, when the code appeared, judges and lawyers had had no way of knowing what the law was. Justice had been haphazard if not impossible. The codification which made the law understandable now revealed many abuses that had crept into relations between serfs and their owners. For example, the law, long forgotten, required landlords to feed their serfs in time of crop failures and subjected to fine those who permitted their serfs to beg. Men discovered how serfdom had developed—that it had once seemed excusable as a way of making possible the gentry's service contribution to the state. Now that the upper classes had been freed from that obligation the institution of serfdom was seen to be without justification.

When the last of the Decembrists had been dragged off to Siberia Nicholas appointed the first of his "secret committees" to consider the nation's problems. Headed by Kochubey, the committee included Speransky, Alexander's Minister of Education Golitsyn, and three generals. The group was asked to learn what plans for reform Alexander was considering at the time of his death, what problems existed, and what should be done about them. Nicholas became concerned about conditions among the serfs, for the first of a continuing wave of peasant revolts flared in 1826. As Speransky reviewed the history of serfdom the conservative committee was forced to recognize that many of the evils which plagued society had grown illegally. The group mildly suggested that the state peasant communities be governed in an exemplary fashion in the hope that private landowners would follow the lead. Even the tsar was disgusted with the committee's lack of ardor.

Five other secret committees sat during the reign to consider reform needs, particularly the problem of serfdom. But since the emperor chose not to reorganize Russian society administratively as well as socially, there was only tinkering with the system. The ownership of land and serfs made the landowner the local administrator. He was responsible for the collection of taxes which only the serfs paid, and yet he owned the land which made the payment possible. The serfs could not be freed without land, for to do so would deprive them of the means for payment of taxes. The landowner also was responsible for drafting men into the army, and if the serfs were freed to roam at will recruiting might be seriously complicated. Yet to free the serfs with land without compensating the owner would be to punish the very class which most consistently supported the autocracy. And only by autocracy, Nicholas was sure, could Russia be governed.

A few ameliorative measures were adopted during the reign, but their effect was pitifully negligible. A number of gentry found guilty of abusing their serfs had their lands and chattels seized by the government, and a few were exiled to Siberia. Alexander's *ukaz* permitting landowners and their serfs to agree on terms by which the serfs would purchase their freedom along with land had produced a trifling number of emancipations. Kiselev, Nicholas's "Chief of Staff for Peasant Affairs," now permitted serfs to be freed by their owners and be given land to use but not to possess, in return for which the freed men paid in labor or produce for a specified period. In the thirteen years the law operated only three landowners worked out such agreements with their peasants. Serf owners were forbidden to sell peasants apart from their families, but the fact that the *ukaz* had to be reissued suggests that it was ineffective. By another order the gentry were forbidden to transfer ownership of their serfs in payment of debt without first giving the serfs opportunity to buy their freedom. But such peasants had only thirty days to raise the money, and there were no financial institutions from which they could borrow. Nicholas granted the serfs the right to purchase immovable property with their owner's consent. But as soon as a serf asked for the consent he revealed that he had laid by some savings, which could then be confiscated by the noble. In such a case the serf could appeal to the government for redress, but the appeal went to an official who was a member of the same class as the one against whom the appeal was made and so would be lost or ignored. Serf owners were forbidden to sell land unless their estates were large enough to provide eleven acres for each peasant, but this enactment was unaccountably omitted from the law code when its revision was published. What the Imperial Chancery gave to the peasants, government underlings or serf owners took away.

The tsar's puny efforts at reform had more than a palliative effect. They implied that the serfs were not private property but subjects of the state. And they made the peasants impatient for freedom. Revolts became increasingly common and severe. A month before he died Nicholas had a stern warning that the peasants would no longer be put off. With the Crimean War going badly for Russia, the tsar issued a call for volunteers to serve in the militia. The rumor swept the countryside that any serf who enlisted would be freed with his family. Peasants swarmed into the towns of South Russia to volunteer, but insisted first that the officials read "the tsar's manifesto which promises us freedom in return." When told that there was no such document the serfs were convinced that the local gentry were dissembling, and the violence they threatened was only averted by armed force.

Industrial development during the thirties and forties did much to condemn serfdom to an early end. The number of factory workers, most of them serfs, grew from slightly over two hundred thousand at Alexander's death to a half million before the Crimean War. Some factories, particularly those producing munitions, paper, and cloth, had been erected by the government and leased or sold to middle-class entrepreneurs, often to foreigners exempted from taxes as an inducement to bring their skills into Russia. Such plants were staffed with state serfs assigned to the manufacturer, with free peasants, or with *obrok* serfs whose owners approved their working for wages in order to exact from them higher dues. Other factories were built by landowners who manned them with their own *barshchina* serfs. Such workers, however, were inclined to soldier on the job, and a few nobles preferred to free their peasants and hire them for wages. Also, those who worked in estate factories in the winter and returned to village agriculture in the summer took with them a knowledge of the skills they learned in the factories.

They set up looms in their cottages, and the sale of the cloth they wove there added appreciably to their income. The gentry did not object to this, for it permitted them to charge a higher *obrok* or sell freedom to the serfs at a high price.

Conditions in possessional factories—those leased or sold by the government to professional manufacturers—were even worse than in Western Europe and America at the time. The sixteen-hour day was typical. Punishments ranged from flogging, sometimes to death, to exile to Siberia, or enrollment in the army. Serfs were paid half the wage of free men with whom they worked. Poor food, filthy quarters, and hazardous machinery made the life of the factory serf more intolerable than life in the village. Strikes, although illegal, were frequent and costly. Kankrin, the finance minister responsible for regulation of the possessional factories, drew up Russia's first factory act in 1835. Its requirement that employers keep accurate account of wages paid meant nothing since there was no government inspection. Another act a decade later which forbade night work by those under twelve was not enforced. Such regulations, ineffective as they were, did not even apply to estate factories.

The rapid growth of cottage industry—in 1850 there were eighteen thousand looms in manufacturing plants in the province of Vladimir and eighty thousand in the villages—prompted manufacturers to protest to the government. But the administration would not interfere with a trend that improved the finances of the gentry by permitting them to reap higher *obrok*. Manufacturers quite naturally supported emancipation of the serfs, and without land, in order to tap the country's great potential labor supply.

Kankrin encouraged Russian industrial growth by maintaining a protective tariff, but kept the duties sufficiently low to force entrepreneurs to keep abreast of technical improvements abroad under the threat of competition. Spinning and weaving machines were imported tariff-free from England, and the production of cotton, linen, and wool cloth rapidly expanded. The possessional factories were freed from the limitation which forced them to sell their output to the government for uniforms, but there was little promise of a profitable domestic market as long as serfdom continued.

The government's financial plight eased noticeably under Kankrin's leadership. The paper money without backing, which had flowed from government printing presses in ever-increasing volume since Elizabeth's time, fluctuated widely in value and so hampered trade. Now the government retired the almost worthless paper rubles and replaced them with paper money redeemable in gold or silver. This long-needed reform restored public confidence and did much to stimulate commerce. The Bourse, or commodities-and-securities-exchange building, in St. Petersburg was erected by Kankrin, who also promoted interest in economic progress by organizing Russia's first industrial exhibits. He founded the forestry and mining institutes, which soon won world-wide respect. Although Kankrin was skeptical of railroads, Russia's first lines, from St. Petersburg to the royal village at Tsarskoe Selo and from St. Petersburg to Moscow were completed during his long ministry.

THE END OF THE POLISH KINGDOM

Nicholas felt himself obligated to govern Poland according to her constitution, although he followed Alexander's precedent of convening the Diet at irregular intervals. From the very beginning he chafed under the restrictions which the Polish constitution imposed upon his government there. Poles involved in the Decembrist uprising had to be tried by Polish law in Polish courts which handed down insultingly mild sentences. A new Polish underground organization appeared almost immediately. In 1829 Nicholas condescended to be crowned king of Poland in Warsaw, but significantly he was crowned with a Russian crown, not the Polish one. The Diet flaunted its independence by refusing to pass measures sponsored by the Russian viceroy. The Poles kept up their clamor for the return of the Lithuanian and White Russian provinces which, although not inhabited by Poles, had been ruled by Poland before the first partition. While Alexander had encouraged such hopes, Nicholas quickly dashed them by refusing to consider the transfer of lands populated by Russians.

The year 1830 was one of many revolutions in Europe, and the fever spread to Poland. In November of that year a band of students and army officers broke into the viceregal palace in Warsaw and killed a number of the guards, although the Grand Duke Constantine whom they were seeking escaped to the protection of Russian troops stationed outside the capital. The Diet deposed Nicholas, established a provisional government, and took over command of the Polish national army. The revolutionaries issued a call for Lithuania and Volhynia to join them, but met with cool indifference. Many Polish army officers refused to support the revolt, the peasants in general were suspicious of the upper-class movement, and the leaders quarreled among themselves over how radical the change should be. General Paskievich at the head of a hundred and fifty thousand Russian troops brushed aside the Polish army and advanced to the suburbs of Warsaw. Russian artillery was trained on the capital, and the rebels had no choice but to surrender.

The Polish constitution was rescinded, the Diet and the separate army abolished, and Poland became part of the Russian Empire. While a separate administration was supposed to govern the country, actually Poland was thenceforth ruled from St. Petersburg. Russian became the official language and the only one taught in the schools. The universities of Warsaw and

Vilna were closed and Poles forbidden to go abroad. Many of them managed to escape to Western Europe, where they kept up a hymn of hate against Russia from that day forward. Russian censorship proscribed the writings of Polish scholars, and the study of Polish history was not allowed. The Roman Catholic church in Poland was needled and embarrassed. The tsars followed a policy of Russification in an effort to break Polish nationalism, but the greater the pressure applied, the more stubbornly did the Poles cling to their nationalistic spirit and aspirations.

CENSORSHIP AND REPRESSION

Nicholas I could never be reminded of the Decembrist revolt without trembling at the thought of it. Subversive ideas, he believed, were unnatural and foreign to Russia and must not be allowed to enter the country. Students must not be allowed to study abroad, for that would be to expose them to infection. No Russian was permitted to cross the border except on official business. Two Jews from Odessa were condemned to death for trying to escape an epidemic by fleeing abroad. But the tsar softened the sentence to running a gauntlet of a thousand men twelve times. "God be thanked, with us the death penalty has been abolished, and I will not reintroduce it," he said.

Nicholas took a keen interest in education, not as a way of stimulating independent thought, but as a means of inculcating loyalty and obedience. Count Sergei Uvarov, the most infamous of all Russian ministers of education, declared "Orthodoxy, autocracy, and nationalism" to be the principles upon which education must be based. Schools once more catered to particular classes, as they had before Alexander's reforms. Peasant children attended the village schools, sons of merchants the district schools, and nobles the *gymnasia* and universities. Teaching of the nonprivileged classes aimed at making the people content with their lot and providing them with skills which would be of service to the state. Uvarov admitted that he would die happy only if he could "retard the development of the country by fifty years," and looked upon the schools as the agency by which he might accomplish this end. The University of Moscow, which the tsar termed "the wolf's den," lost its chair of philosophy. The teaching of higher mathematics, which might encourage speculation, was banned in all universities. Logic could be taught only by theologians. Courses in comparative law and constitutional history were thrown out. History professors were required to glorify Russian history and could not mention such topics as the Reformation. As for the humanities, Uvarov "expressed a strong desire that Russian literature should cease to exist" (Masaryk). But even Uvarov seemed dangerous to Nicholas when he used the word progress in an official report. "Progress? What progress?" Nicholas wrote in the margin. "This word must be deleted from official terminology."

Censorship was tightened early in the reign in an attempt to gag Russia intellectually. Texts on physiology could not contain anything which might "offend the instinct of decency." Musical scores could not enter Russia from Germany, for the notes might constitute seditious messages in code. Newspapers were suppressed for mentioning the names of seditious writers. So many agencies operated the censorship that a supervisory committee was established, but even it was subjected to censorship by another committee. Nicholas himself took a hand personally in such work, suggesting to Pushkin that he write more like Sir Walter Scott.

Nicholas had no patience with religious sectarianism, for conformity to the state religion was a distinguishing mark of loyalty. The Dukhobors, or "Spirit Worshippers," were driven from their villages into Siberian exile for their refusal to render military service. The Molokane, who showed their opposition to the state church by drinking milk during Lent, which Orthodoxy forbade, were similarly persecuted, although they and the Dukhobors had enjoyed protection under Alexander I. The Raskolniks, or Old Believers who refused to accept the church reforms of the seventeenth century, were particularly suspect because their religious dissent was known to mask political unrest. A government commission set out to ascertain the number of sectarians, which was presumed to be less than a million, and discovered that there were probably eight million of them. Since the church in Russia was simply a branch of government after Peter's time, the dissenters were guilty of treason, and most of them proudly flaunted it by omitting the sovereign's name from their prayers. The number of trials and persecutions of dissidents mounted as the reign dragged on, but the sects continued to flourish and even to prosper until the end of the monarchy.

THE GOLDEN AGE OF RUSSIAN LITERATURE

Under the pall of censorship which marked the reign of Nicholas I Russia produced her first great crop of literary giants. Owing much to the revolutionary heritage of Western Europe, and yet intensely nationalistic as a result of the French invasion of 1812, Russian authors sought and won recognition not by an effort to please the senses but by challenging the political, social, and moral corruption which tsardom epitomized. Poets, novelists, dramatists, essayists, and literary critics all found release for their genius in attacking the evils which the nation suffered. Pushkin, the Russian Byron, was suspected of Decembrist sympathies, and the poet Ryleyev was a leader of the uprising. Griboyedov's *The Misfortune of Being Clever* was a thinly veiled protest at Nicholas's preference for foreign, particularly German, advisers. Gogol levelled a scathing attack upon serfdom in his *Dead Souls,* and he scorned stupid Russian officialdom with such effective sarcasm in *The Government Inspector* that even the tsar laughed at it.

After 1830 Russian writers, while in agreement on the need for reform, disagreed violently in their attitudes toward the direction in which Russia should move. To some, the Slavophiles, the nation needed to return to the purity and simplicity of early Russian society. Russia's ills, they believed, were caused by foreign influence and by the government's importation of Western institutions. The Slavophiles had little patience with bureaucratic stupidity and autocracy, but they sought relief in primitive Slavic democracy and Christian brotherhood. To the Westernizers, on the other hand, Western Europe stood for enlightenment and freedom and Russia stood for obscurantism and slavery. Russia suffered, they argued, not from too much Western influence but from entirely too little. The West to them meant democratic government, economic progress, intellectual freedom, and moral dignity.

Because of censorship restrictions the works of Russian writers often circulated in manuscript. In some cases long passages were committed to memory, as was Bielinsky's famous letter to Gogol. Bielinsky, Russia's greatest literary critic, excoriated the author of *Dead Souls* for turning conservative and excusing the autocracy. Sometimes works were published abroad or printed on hidden presses. Occasionally authors gave up the struggle against social injustice and succumbed to the threats or rewards of the government. In such cases they condemned themselves to obscurity, for when they stopped crusading they lost their following. Some suffered cruelly from the Third Section. Dostoevsky, for example, was condemned to death and reprieved on the scaffold to serve ten years in Siberia. The police were on their way to arrest Bielinsky when he died.

The importance of the literary fecundity of the reign lies not in the success with which it overcame the obstacle of censorship, but rather in the fact that the writers of the time set the course of Russian literature for a century to come. Thenceforth every Russian writer worth his salt took a stand on the social issues of his day, whether his medium were the essay, the novel, the short story, drama, or poetry. And from that day forward the struggle between the Slavophiles and the Westernizers went on, not only in the field of literary production but in social, economic, and political thinking as well. Even after 1917 there frequently was evidence in the highest circles of the Communist Party that Slavophilism and Westernization still found their devotees. Lenin and Trotsky were steeped in Western radicalism. Litvinov symbolized Russia's cooperation with the democratic West against fascism. Stalin and Molotov, on the other hand, frequently reflected typical Slavophile suspicion of the West.

THE FAILURE OF NICHOLAS'S SYSTEM

The year 1848 had hardly opened before a mounting wave of revolutions broke out all over Europe. Only the Romanov throne was not threatened that year, for revolutionary movements in Russia had been effectively deprived of leadership for a generation when the Decembrists were disposed of. Lest there be any misunderstanding of his implacable opposition to "impertinent, destructive dreams," Nicholas issued a manifesto warning Western rebels against trying to import their subversive ideas into Holy Russia.

While Nicholas had no need to fear for his throne in 1848, he was alarmed to find that his repressive measures had produced only modest success. In spite of the gagging censorship writers managed to get into print with their ridicule of the regime, and some, like Bakunin and Herzen, wrote freely in exile. Uvarov's trinity—Orthodoxy, autocracy, nationalism—had become the guide to governmental policy under Nicholas, but it had failed. Persecution of the sects only multiplied their numbers. The longer serfdom continued, the more numerous became the peasant revolts against it, and autocracy could not provide efficient government when it had to depend upon a host of unscrupulous and dishonest subordinates. Russification in Poland only provoked the Poles to cling to their language and culture with greater determination, and the Westernizers argued convincingly against the policy of nationalism.

Even before 1848 there were modest beginnings of protest against the repression. Groups of progressive young men gathered in private homes to comment upon works of Russian writers and to discuss political and social problems. Such meetings were common in provincial capitals, but perhaps the most famous was that which met in the St. Petersburg home of Michael Petrashevsky, a young noble. Some of the group were moderately socialist in their thinking, but there were no such brave plans for uprising as the Decembrists had laid some twenty years earlier. When Nicholas learned of the meetings, Petrashevsky and a dozen of his fellows were seized and sentenced to hang, among them the brilliant Dostoevsky. Their lives were spared, however, and the men packed off to Siberia. Another group at the University of Kiev, called the "Brotherhood of Saints Cyril and Methodius," discussed the need to end autocracy and centralism and supported a federation of Slavic states each of which would enjoy cultural and political autonomy. Harmless though the organization was, it was broken up and its members imprisoned or exiled.

The tsar's faith in his system was rudely shaken in the Crimean War. Russian land was invaded again, but this time there was no patriotic surge to repel the attack. Official corruption hamstrung the prosecution of the war. Peasants showed enthusiasm for the war only because they expected to be freed when they enlisted, and they revolted when informed that there had been no order for emancipation. Army equipment had not kept pace with improvements since the Napoleonic war, and the leaders with few exceptions were stupid and unimaginative.

Nicholas died as much of disappointment at the failure of the system in which he so confidently believed as of the cold he contracted in the spring of 1855. Rumors persisted that he committed suicide. On his deathbed he admitted to his son, "I am not turning over the command to you in good order." It is possible that he warned his successor that unless serfdom were abolished from above it would be destroyed from below by a revolution which might overturn the monarchy. It is less possible that Nicholas seriously considered or could have faced up to carrying through the reforms which he must have realized could no longer be postponed. Hated as he was, he could not have counted upon popular cooperation. A group of courtiers playing cards when the tsar's death was announced did not even look up from their game.

SUGGESTED READING

Cambridge Modern History, Vol. X (New York, Macmillan, 1934).

Conybeare, F. C., *Russian Dissenters* (Cambridge, Harvard University Press, 1921).

de Grunwald, C., *Nicholas I* (New York, Macmillan, 1954).

Herzen, A., *My Past and Thoughts; the Memoirs of Alexander Herzen* (New York, Knopf, 1928).

Johnson, W. H. E., *Russia's Educational Heritage* (Pittsburgh, Carnegie Press, 1950).

Karpovich, M., *Imperial Russia, 1801–1917* (New York, Holt, 1932).

Kliuchevsky, V. O., *A History of Russia*, vol. V (London, Dent, 1931).

Kohn, H., *The Mind of Modern Russia* (New Brunswick, Rutgers University Press, 1955).

Kornilov, A., *Modern Russian History* (New York, Knopf, 1943).

Leary, D. B., *Education and Autocracy in Russia from the Origins to the Bolsheviks* (Buffalo, University of Buffalo Press, 1919).

Masaryk, T. G., *The Spirit of Russia* (New York, Macmillan, 1919).

Mavor, J., *An Economic History of Russia* (New York, Dutton, 1925).

Miliukov, P. N., *Outlines of Russian Culture* (Philadelphia, University of Pennsylvania Press, 1948).

Nechkina, M. V., *Russia in the Nineteenth Century* (London, Macmillan, 1952).

20

Nicholas, Europe, and the Near East

Nicholas I showed himself just as determined as his brother to play a leading role among the powers of the world. Where Alexander I was inclined to finesse and patience, however, Nicholas was frank and brusque. He sought a clear solution of Russia's outstanding issues with Turkey by attacking the Porte during the Greek War for Independence, and brought Turkey for a number of years under Russian domination. His efforts to win international recognition of Russia's vital interests at the Straits broke down, and he found himself involved in the Crimean War against a coalition of powers determined to end the Russian threat to Turkish independence and integrity. Throughout the reign Nicholas accepted a personal responsibility to defend the monarchs of Europe against the threat of revolution. He supported reaction abroad as well as at home in the conviction that a threat to legitimate government anywhere was a challenge to his own throne. When the system of international security which he had promoted broke down in the Crimean War Nicholas died of disappointment, unwilling or unable to sacrifice his system in the interest of moderation and compromise.

WAR WITH TURKEY

Alexander I bequeathed to his brother Nicholas an urgent need for settling the problems that had irritated relations between Russia and the Porte since the Treaty of Bucharest in 1812. The Turks never could be held to their commitments without force, and Alexander had hesitated to use it. The situation was complicated by the Greek war for independence which had been dragging on since 1821. Unable to put down the uprising himself, the sultan called upon his vassal Mehemet Ali, the pasha of Egypt, to send an expedition to Greece. The pasha's son with a well-trained army quickly overran the Peloponnesos in 1825 and alarmed all Christendom with the threat of merciless punishment of the Greeks. Just before his death Alexander called for a conference of the powers in St. Petersburg to consider steps to be taken to ease the pressure upon the Greeks.

Soon after the new reign opened England and Russia agreed to push for Turkish recognition of Greek autonomy. France joined the other two in an ultimatum to Turkey calling for an end of hostilities, but the sultan ignored the request. Thereupon naval squadrons of the three allies moved into Navarino Bay to tie up the sultan's fleet and prevent landing of additional forces in the Greek peninsula. In the battle that followed, the Turco-Egyptian fleet was blown out of the water. The sultan was so incensed at the Allied action that he stepped up his pressure upon the Greeks and, in violation of treaty obligations, closed the Straits to commercial shipping. When all Christians were driven out of Constantinople Russia, acting in her recognized role as protector of Christians in the Turkish Empire, declared war.

In the summer of 1828 Russian armies drove the Turks out of Moldavia and Wallachia, which the sultan had occupied after Ypsilanti's uprising seven years earlier, and passed the Danube. A year later they crossed the Balkan Mountains, seized Adrianople, and threatened the Turkish capital. The Russian Black Sea fleet entered the Bosporus and sailed to within sight of the sultan's palace. Meanwhile a Russian force crossed the Caucasus, drove deep into eastern Turkey, and carried the forts of Kars and Erzurum. England and France moved their fleets to the Dardanelles, ostensibly to protect foreigners in the Turkish capital from mob violence but in reality to prevent Russian seizure of the Straits. The collapse of the Turkish Empire was accepted as almost a certainty in the capitals of Europe. The Egyptian pasha was bargaining for French assistance to conquer Syria. The Barbary States were threatening secession. Greece was lost. The Danubian Principalities and Serbia already enjoyed Russian protection. Bosnia and Bulgaria hoped for independence. One Russian army was well inside Asiatic Turkey, while another was camped within a day's march of Constantinople.

The great powers toyed with various schemes for the partition of Turkey, and particularly with the notion of setting up a new Christian state to control the Straits. Nicholas I, however, was not sympathetic to the appearance of a state which almost surely would come under Western domination. Nor did he relish the thought of partitioning Turkey among the powers even though he might receive the Straits, for Russia's position there would be difficult to defend against an alliance of hostile powers with bases or vassal states nearby. For that reason Nicholas preferred that Turkey survive and come under Russian protection. He agreed with his advisers that "the advantages of the maintenance of the Ottoman Empire are superior to the inconveniences which they present; its fall therefore would be contrary to the true interests of Russia." Consequently, the terms he offered the sultan were surprisingly mild. By the Treaty of Adrianople in 1829 Russia took no territory, although her earlier annexations from Persia south of the Caucasus were recognized and Turkey gave up all claim to Georgia. The autonomy of Serbia and the Danubian Principalities was confirmed, and Greek independence conceded. Turkey guaranteed freedom of commerce through the Straits to all nations and promised to abide by her earlier treaties with Russia.

The guarantee that Russian commercial access to the Straits should not be interrupted was calculated to underwrite the prosperity of Russian Black Sea ports and particularly of the Russian landowners whose wheat was exported either in Russian or British vessels. The economic potential of South Russia could not be developed without free use of the Straits. Within fifteen years more than twice as much grain was shipped from Black Sea points as from all other Russian ports combined, and Odessa by 1843 was handling 10 per cent of all Russian commerce.

"THE SICK MAN OF EUROPE"

The Russian decision in 1829 to maintain Turkish integrity was not, of course, publicly announced. But all the powers recognized that the sultan continued to rule only by Russian sufferance. The new Russian policy was soon tested. Within two years of the tsar's decision Mehemet Ali, the sultan's troublesome governor of Egypt, invaded Syria and marched toward Constantinople. The sultan called for Russian help, and a Russian fleet sailed to the Bosporus. A Russian envoy went to Alexandria to warn the pasha against unreasonable demands, and soon afterward Mehemet Ali and the sultan came to terms.

Two months after the settlement of the Egyptian crisis Nicholas signed a mutual-defense pact with Turkey. By this treaty of Unkiar-Iskelessi of 1833 the two nations promised to join forces in case either was attacked. Russia agreed, however, that in case of war Turkey need not assist Russia with troops but could fulfill her obligation simply by closing the Dardanelles to the warships of all other nations. The arrangement was to last for eight years and would then be renewable. With the signing of the agreement Russia satisfied her need for closing the breach in her southern defenses; at that moment she enjoyed the strongest position at the Straits ever attained by a Russian government. Metternich approved of Russia's maintenance of Turkish integrity with the proviso that Austria should share the spoils with Russia if Turkey fell apart of her own internal weakness.

Since the pasha of Egypt was only temporarily appeased, the prospect of having to fulfill her obligations under Unkiar-Iskelessi faced Russia continually after 1833. The Russian fleet was expanded until it became the second most powerful in Europe. Odessa and Sevastopol became important naval bases, and the Black Sea fleet rapidly grew to respectable proportions. The threat posed by Russian naval strength in the Black Sea seemed to statesmen in London to be aimed at Great Britain. If Russia's domination of Turkey and her overshadowing influence in Persia should be turned to aggression, England's position in India might be seriously impaired—so reasoned Palmerston and his Conservative friends in Parliament.

When Mehemet Ali with French support rebelled against the sultan in 1839 and again threatened Constantinople, Nicholas decided that Turkey could only be maintained by common action among the powers. Austria, Russia, Prussia, and England agreed to defend the Turkish capital against Mehemet Ali, whose ardor was dampened by being offered the hereditary governorship of Egypt and control over Syria for the rest of his life. The Porte agreed to close the Dardanelles and Bosporus to warships of all nations when Turkey was at peace, a simple restatement of ancient Turkish policy. Russia's adherence to this "Pacification of the Levant" in 1840 constituted a resignation of her position as sole protector of the Ottoman Empire won at Unkiar-Iskelessi. The tsar's willingness to back down was the result, first, of his determination to uphold Turkish independence at all costs and, second, of his eagerness to dispel British suspicions and so to reduce the possibility of a Franco-British alliance against Russia at the Straits. France avoided permanent isolation by joining with the other powers the following year in the so-called Straits Convention by which the signatories agreed to respect the long-time Turkish practice of closing the Dardanelles to foreign warships except when Turkey herself was at war.

Nicholas was convinced by this time that Turkey, "the sick man of Europe," was dying and that plans should be made for disposing of "the remains." He considered the possibility of creating a Christian state under international guarantee to control the Straits. "I do not want Constantinople, but I do not want it to become either a French or British dependency," he declared. In 1844 he visited Queen Victoria in London and suggested that Austrian and Russian armies and a British fleet should assemble at the Straits to preside over the demise of the Ottoman Empire. While British diplomats listened wide-eyed at such candor, Nicholas bluntly announced: "Turkey must fall to pieces. We cannot preserve its existence no matter how hard we try. I do not want a single inch of Turkish soil, but never shall I permit Constantinople to fall into the hands of England or France. If the English, French or any others wish to take Constantinople, I will expel them. Once in Constantinople I shall never leave!" The diplomats of Europe never forgot the closing sentence. What the tsar meant was that he would occupy the Turkish capital if necessary to prevent its seizure by any other power potentially hostile to Russia. Actually, Nicholas expressed the conviction that Austria should succeed to Turkish territory in Europe, for on Austrian friendship he was cocksure he could depend.

The Liberal ministry which governed England at the time accepted a secret agreement with Nicholas whereby the two powers agreed to cooperate to defend Turkish integrity and come to an understanding on partition if and when Turkey could no longer be kept alive. Since Russia and Austria had similarly agreed to confer on partition in case "the sick man" should die, France again was excluded from any future settlement of the Turkish problem. In return for the oral accord with England, Nicholas promised military action against France should the latter attempt to seize Belgium as she was threatening to do, a matter upon which Britons were extremely sensitive. Nicholas' conversations with British diplomats were differently understood in London and in St. Petersburg. The tsar was convinced that England would back him unreservedly at the Straits, while the British believed that they had succeeded in bridling Russia and preventing unilateral disposition of the Turkish issue. And when Anglo-Russian relations became strained nine years later, the friendly Liberals were no longer in control of British policy. The Crimean War was the result.

NICHOLAS, THE POLICEMAN OF EUROPE

From the moment of his accession Nicholas lived in constant fear of revolution. As the self-appointed champion of the *status quo* he determined not only to suppress liberalism at home but to defend conservatism abroad. Liberal ideas were infectious, he knew, and he was particularly suspicious of England and France as the birthplace of such notions. The German states, too, showed themselves alarmingly productive of radical thoughts, and their princes must be encouraged not to surrender to popular pressure for reform.

The seals had hardly set on the Treaty of Adrianople when a revolution in Paris drove the French king into retirement. The duke of Orleans, of the younger branch of the Bourbons, became "King of the French People" and accepted a liberalization of the constitution. Nicholas was furious at this violation of the principle of legitimacy which had guided the settlement at Vienna in 1815. Louis Philippe, the new French ruler, was a dangerous character in the eyes of Nicholas, for he had expressed sympathy for republican ideas and for the American constitution. Time and again after 1830 the tsar publicly displayed his detestation for the French king.

The Paris outbreak was the signal for risings all over Europe. The Belgians rose against their Dutch masters and declared their independence. Several German states won constitutions from their rulers, one of whom was deposed. Italians rose against their princes but were overborne by Austrian intervention. Revolutions broke out in Portugal and Spain. Riots developed all over England against the refusal of the government to reform the House of Commons. The spirit carried even to the Vistula, but the Polish rising failed miserably before the threat of Russian guns.

Nicholas took the initiative in bringing together the governments of Austria, Prussia, and Russia in a reaffirmation of the Holy Alliance. The three invited any sovereign threatened by revolt to call upon them for assistance in suppressing it. In 1846 the three acted together to wipe out the Republic of Cracow, set up by the Congress of Vienna, which had become a haven for Polish exiles from the eastern monarchies.

The revolutions in Central Europe in 1830 were doomed to failure by the inability of France to support them in the face of warnings from Austria, Russia, and Prussia. But the movements did not die out. "Young Italy," an organization which aimed to unite Italy under a republic, numbered thousands in its membership. German liberal thought continued to thrive in spite of persecution. Slav and Magyar minorities dreamed of independence from the Habsburgs. Nationalistic fervor continued to mount in the Balkans.

Early in 1848 the monarchy in France was replaced by a republic, and again the epidemic spread over Europe. Metternich slipped out of Vienna in disguise to avoid rough handling by a mob. Bohemia demanded autonomy, and Hungary set up a liberal government. All Italy was in revolt, and the Sardinian king was forced to grant a constitution. Liberals from all the German states gathered at Frankfort to work for a united Germany, and rioters in Berlin frightened the king of Prussia into accepting a constitution. Thousands marched in London to point up the need for further reform of Parliament.

Nicholas accepted these disturbances as a personal challenge which he met with more bravado than good sense. When he received news of the Paris revolution he strode in riding boots into the palace where his son was giving a ball and called to the dancing nobles, "Saddle your horses, gentlemen. France has just proclaimed a republic." While he rejoiced at the ill fortune of Louis Philippe, whom he heartily detested, he insisted that Russia must march an army to the Rhine to contain the radicalism in France. When informed that the treasury would not stand such a campaign and that he must therefore give up the thought, Nicholas contented himself by broadcasting a warning to all revolutionaries. "Take heed, ye peoples, and submit, for God is with us." The "us" of course referred to legitimate rulers everywhere.

On the Austrian front Nicholas could take a hand against the forces of revolution without marching his troops so far and at such expense. The

Austrian emperor called for Russian assistance to put down a Hungarian
revolt which had declared the end of Habsburg rule. A Russian army crossed
the Carpathians and took the surrender of the rebel forces. This broke the
back of revolutionary movements elsewhere in Austrian dominions, and
the youthful Emperor Francis Joseph quickly recovered control of his inheritance.

Nicholas warned the Prussian king to reject the offer of the crown of a
united Germany from the Frankfort parliament. Even had the Hohenzollern
been so inclined, such an act would have precipitated a war with Austria
and thereby disrupted the union of the eastern monarchies which was the
bulwark of the tsar's policy. But Frederick William had no desire for a
crown bought at the price of a constitution imposed upon him. He did, however, grant his own Prussian people a constitution and refused to go back
on his word in spite of the irritation of his uncle, the tsar.

The failure of the revolutionary movement in Central Europe in 1848 was
in no small measure due to the support and encouragement rendered by
Nicholas to the conservative cause. The tsar firmly backed Metternich in
his policy of dominating Germany and dousing every spark of liberalism
as soon as it appeared. He patched up disagreements between Austria and
Prussia over leadership of the German Confederation. It was primarily
through his efforts that the three monarchs of the east stood squarely
against the tide of liberalism that threatened to engulf all Europe. Not until
his death could Europe rest easy that the Holy Alliance had come to an end.

THE CRIMEAN WAR

The French Republic established in 1848 was short-lived. Four years after
its birth the president, Louis Napoleon, nephew of Napoleon I, tore up the
constitution and proclaimed himself emperor. A drab character, this Napoleon III contrived to catch the fancy of the French people by embarking
upon a bold foreign policy. In an effort to gain Catholic support in France
he insisted that the sultan grant to Catholic clergymen the right to maintain and protect the holy places in Palestine. As defender of Greek Orthodox
Christians in the Turkish Empire, Nicholas protested and marched his
armies into Moldavia, which was Turkish territory under Russian protection.
Being assured by the British ambassador, acting entirely on his own, of the
support of the British fleet, the sultan declared war against Russia in 1853.
When the tsar rejected an ultimatum to evacuate the Danubian Principalities, England and France joined Turkey against Russia. Months earlier,
before the Turkish declaration of war, British and French fleets had passed
the Dardanelles, thus violating the Straits Convention of 1841.

Actually, of course, the Crimean War was not fought over control of

Christian sanctuaries in Palestine. England was not willing to allow Russian domination of Turkish domestic policy, which seemed to be the aim of Nicholas' impatience with the sultan's surrender to French demands. On the other hand Nicholas accepted the Porte's concession to France as an indication that the time had come to partition Turkey. Its government could not be trusted and had not the strength to maintain itself honorably. Nicholas conferred with the Austrian emperor on "putting an end to the filthy housekeeping on the Bosporus and to the oppression of impoverished Christians by the Turkish dogs" (Puryear). But Francis Joseph had little sympathy for the tsar's suggestion that the Balkans be placed under a joint Austro-Russian protectorate and Constantinople made a free city under international guarantee. Just before the war Nicholas warned the British ambassador in St. Petersburg that Turkey "seems to be falling to pieces, and it is very important that England and Russia should come to an understanding" over the pieces. He suggested that England take Egypt and Crete, that Serbia and Bulgaria be completely free, and that Russia continue her protection of the Danubian Principalities. Presumably, Constantinople would be free under international protection; he repeated that he did not want the city but that England must not have it.

British statesmen refused to believe that Nicholas might not seize Constantinople and hold it, thus precipitating the demise of the Ottoman Empire. England could not afford to see that happen, for she profited much more from trade with the sprawling Turkish domain than she could expect to do if the territory were broken up into economically nationalistic free states or came under the sway of protectionist Austria or Russia. Nicholas, on the other hand, convinced that the Turkish Empire was breaking up, was as determined to prevent England from gaining control of the Straits as were the British to keep Russia from seizing them. Austria, too, preferred to keep "the sick man" alive, for she might be strangled commercially if the mouth of the Danube came permanently under Russian control. France seems to have bludgeoned England into supporting her strong stand at the Porte by threatening to attack Belgium. Indeed, England's attitude toward Russia was much more cautious than was that of Napoleon III, who hurried his fleet to Turkish waters in an obvious attempt to goad the sultan into rejecting Russia's offer to negotiate the squabble over the holy places. In the diplomatic seesaw preceding the war England seems to have been convinced of the tsar's decision to preside over the partition of the Ottoman Empire and to have determined to prevent the partition which French diplomats warned would be the signal for France to seek territorial compensation in Western Europe—that is, in Belgium.

Hardly had the war begun when Austria joined the Western powers in diplomatic pressure aimed at restoring peace. In fact, Austria threatened to attack Russia unless the latter accepted the terms, which prompted Nicholas to deprecate the duplicity of the nation to whom he "had given a tribute of blood" in 1849. The powers demanded that Russia agree to give up her protectorate over Serbia and the Danubian Principalities; surrender the partial control of the mouth of the Danube which had been awarded Russia by the Treaty of Adrianople; consent to a revision of the Straits Convention of 1841 looking toward reduction of Russian power in the Black Sea; and renounce her protectorate over Greek Orthodox Christians in the Turkish Empire. The second point was insisted upon by Austria, whose grain shipments Nicholas had shortsightedly refused passage of the Danube. The fourth point was of no great importance to any power but was designed to avoid future international complications such as had precipitated the present war. The first point would redound to Austrian benefit by keeping Russian forces away from the Danube. It was apparent that the terms offered Russia were calculated to bring Austria into the war should Nicholas refuse to accept them, thus making possible a flank attack across the Pruth and a military victory which the Allies seemed otherwise unable to accomplish. That Nicholas was not stubbornly unreasonable is apparent from the fact that he readily accepted these three of the four points at issue.

British diplomats purposely left the third point, the only one of concern to England, vague in the hope that Russia would reject it and Austria might thus be forced to join the coalition. England would be satisfied with nothing less than the destruction of Russian naval power in the Black Sea, for she regarded that power as the means by which Russia could continue to dominate Turkey and so threaten India through Persia. Unless Russian warships were driven from the Black Sea the tsar might continue to control Turkish policy by the very ease with which he could seize Constantinople. Once the war was on, Britain determined not to end it until this Russian menace was removed.

In Vienna the representatives of Great Britain, France, Austria, and Russia discussed the terms of a peace settlement for nearly a year. Since only the problem of the Straits and the Black Sea remained at issue, Prussia should have been invited to the conference, for she was a party along with the others to the Straits Convention of 1841. In fact, the Western powers had threatened Prussia with a severance of diplomatic relations unless she joined in pressure upon the tsar. As soon as the diplomatic wrangling began British war aims became clear—Russia must not be allowed to maintain a naval base on the Black Sea and must limit her warships there to four. Austria refused to go to war for four ships more or less, and pointed out the insult to the tsar's pride in asking him to demolish Sevastopol, which was still holding out against the Allies. Austria veered toward supporting Russia against British intransigeance, and French public opinion cooled toward a war that produced no brilliant victories.

The war touched scattered points from one end of the Russian Empire to the other. British naval forces attacked Russian outposts in the Baltic, the White Sea, and Kamchatka, and bombarded Odessa on Good Friday, whereupon Nicholas stormed that Russians were slaughtered while in the very act of worshipping the Prince of Peace. The naval raid on eastern Siberia convinced the Russian government that Alaska was indefensible, and soon after the war the territory was sold to the United States. Russian troops entered Moldavia but withdrew at Austrian insistence, and the principalities were occupied by Austria as a precaution against a Russian drive to the Danube. This act of "malevolent neutrality" may possibly have cost Russia the victory. It had been commonly believed in Western Europe for a generation that Russia could take Constantinople by land whenever she cared to, and by seizing the shore batteries on the Dardanelles could easily bottle up any warships caught in the Straits or the Black Sea. Considering the weak and backward state of the Russian army at the time, however, this is pure conjecture. The only Russian success came in Asia Minor, where Kars was captured in the closing days of the war.

The Allies threw their main effort against the Crimea, where they could use both their modern steam-driven warships and their armies. In the fall of 1854 the British, French, and Turks landed sixty thousand men in the peninsula and attacked the naval base at Sevastopol, after quarreling long enough over policy to allow the Russian commander, Todleben, to prepare a stout defense. The Russians sank their wooden Black Sea fleet in the neck of the harbor at Sevastopol to prevent close-in bombardment by enemy warships and sallied out occasionally to attack the allied base at Balaklava. The British counterattack produced the gallant "Charge of the Light Brigade," on which a French witness commented, "It is magnificent, but it is not war." The troops on both sides suffered unspeakably from winter cold, shortage of provisions, cholera, and foul medical care. Florence Nightingale improved British hospital service during the campaign and succeeded in overcoming prejudice against the appearance of feminine nurses with the army. Her Russian counterpart, Darya Sevastopolskaya, did what she could to relieve suffering among the defenders. With the approach of another winter Todleben decided to withdraw. After a year's siege the great base was relinquished to the Allies, and the war quickly ended. Nicholas had died six months earlier, and his successor expressed a willingness to meet honorable terms.

The conduct of the war did not redound to the credit of either side, but the Russians outdid their opponents in mismanagement. The campaign cost the Allies a hundred thousand casualties, the Russians three times as many. Nicholas mobilized a million men, but most of them saw no action. The Russian supply system broke down completely, and England serviced her troops less ineffectively from London than the tsar could do in his own land. The Russian army had not kept up with technical improvements and fought with the same weapons as at Borodino. The unbelievable corruption and stupidity which characterized the conduct of Russian officialdom destroyed even Nicholas' confidence in the bureaucratic system he had perfected. Popular disinterest in this invasion of Russian territory must have dispelled any illusions the tsar may have had about what his subjects thought of him.

Nicholas died of a severe cold which he showed no interest in checking. Stunned at what he considered English perfidy in refusing to cooperate over the Turkish question, shocked at the betrayal of Austria, saddened at the poor showing of his troops, amazed at the corruption which sapped the nation's strength, and disturbed at the peasant resistance to recruiting, the tsar was unable to face the future. Rumor soon had it that Nicholas took poison. The Russians seemed unwilling to believe that a tsar could die a natural death.

THE TREATY OF PARIS, 1856

His nation exhausted, his treasury empty, and faced with an overpowering alliance against him which now included Sardinia, Alexander II had no excuse to continue the war after the fall of Sevastopol. But the Allies, too, were tiring of the conflict. Austria was supporting Russia diplomatically. France had lost interest. When the peace conference finally opened in Paris, Napoleon III refused to go along with extreme British demands and let it be known that unless Russia were offered a compromise Britain would have to carry on the war alone.

Territory seized by both sides was restored, Russia returning Kars to Turkey and the Allies returning the Crimean forts to Russia. In order to safeguard shipping down the Danube Russia surrendered the southern tip of Bessarabia to Moldavia, and the river came under international guarantee. All the powers undertook the protection of Christians in the Ottoman Empire, and all guaranteed the autonomy of Serbia and the Danubian Principalities. The Black Sea was neutralized: commercial vessels had free access to it, but it was forbidden to the warships of all nations. Once more the Straits were declared closed against the warships of all powers when Turkey was not at war, which simply meant that any future enemy of Russia must drag Turkey into a war in order to use the Straits. England, France, and Austria bound themselves in a separate agreement to defend the independence and integrity of the sultan's empire against any aggressor, but the contingency that the empire might explode from internal pressure was not anticipated. All the powers swore to abolish privateering, to respect ships flying neutral flags in time of war unless carrying contraband, and agreed that blockades to be binding must be effective.

Alexander II was not happy with the terms of the treaty, but he was in no position to refuse them. All the diplomats were skeptical about how long the settlement could last. Palmerston hoped that the Russians would suffer the restrictions for ten years and openly warned the Turks that Russia would be at war with them again within a decade. Actually, the limitations upon Russian use of the Black Sea lasted fifteen years, and the Russo-Turkish truce for twenty.

Nicholas I's suggestion to Great Britain in 1855 for a disposition of the Ottoman Empire proved to be prophetic. By 1923 independent Christian states had replaced the Turkish dominions in Europe, the Straits were internationalized, and Britain controlled not Egypt and Crete but Egypt and Cyprus. But the successor states in the Balkans proved to be anything but friendly to Russia.

The Crimean War was the first conflict among the great powers since the Napoleonic period. Its outbreak signaled an end to the Concert of Europe by which the powers had managed for forty years to settle differences by negotiation. For Russia the war was decisive in that it made imperative a radical overhaul of society. Nicholas had sought to maintain internal pacification and external security, which, as he believed, went hand in hand. When the one dissolved, the other came to an end, and the new ruler was faced with the dual problem of domestic and diplomatic readjustment.

SUGGESTED READING

Binkley, R. C., *Realism and Nationalism* (New York, Harper's, 1935).

Cambridge Modern History, Vols. X and XI (New York, Macmillan, 1934).

Florinsky, M. T., *Russia: A History and an Interpretation* (New York, Macmillan, 1953).

Mitchell, M., *The Maritime History of Russia, 848–1948* (London, Sidgwick & Jackson, 1949).

Mosely, P. E., *Russian Diplomacy and the Opening of the Eastern Question in 1838* and *1839* (Cambridge, Harvard University Press, 1934).

Puryear, V. J., *England, Russia and the Straits Question, 1844–1856* (Berkeley, University of California Press, 1931).

Rodkey, F. S., *The Turco-Egyptian Question in the Relations of England, France and Russia, 1832–1841* (Urbana, University of Illinois Press, 1923).

Skrine, F. H., *The Expansion of Russia* (New York, Cambridge University Press, 1915).

Taylor, A. J. P., *The Struggle for Mastery in Europe, 1848–1918* (Oxford, Clarendon, 1954).

Tolstoy, L., *Tales of Sevastopol.*

21

The Great Reforms

Russia's defeat in the Crimean war indicated to all classes and even to the tsar that fundamental political and social change could wait no longer. Even though Russian soil was occupied, the mass of the people remained apathetic toward the war. Bungling administration reduced the effectiveness of even the feeble effort the nation managed to put forth. Troops in the field were badly disorganized, poorly led for the most part, and miserably serviced.

With the return to peace the new tsar, Nicholas's son Alexander II (1855–1881), called for consultations among the gentry to suggest ways of emancipating the serfs. The time had passed for pondering the question of whether there should be freedom for the mass of the Russian people. The problem now was how that freedom should come about. After postponing the judgment day as long as possible the committee assigned the task brought in a proposal for emancipation which the government could accept, and bondage in Russia came to an end. Emancipation brought with it the need for administrative change; judicial, military, educational, economic, and financial reforms and alterations in the machinery of local government all followed.

By nature at least as conservative as his father, Alexander II granted the reforms because he saw them as necessary to the continuation of the monarchy. But what the tsar gave with one hand he took away with the other. While he could not revoke the changes he had made, he could and did strip most of them of their effectiveness by curtailing through punitive administration the privileges that the reforms at their face value were designed to provide. Yet, however strong the determination of Alexander II and his successors to compromise the great reforms, there could be no turning back. The administrative and social changes of the reign began a new period in the history of modern Russia.

THE TSAR LIBERATOR

There was much in the new sovereign's background to encourage the view that the "gentry era" would continue without interruption. Alexander's youth had passed under the stern direction of his father, who had thrashed the tsarevich on occasion with his own hand. The conservative court poet Zhukovsky had done his plodding best to inspire the heir with a love of letters, but his pupil had shown more interest in the parade ground than in his books. Speransky had taught Alexander something of law, and other officials had added a smattering of finance, diplomacy, and military tactics. Travels at whirlwind speed from one end of the empire to the other had given the tsarevich a fleeting view of his land, but reviews and formal welcomes at every stop had sheltered him from disturbing insights into the wretched condition of his people. At twenty-one he had visited the capitals of Europe, but fêtes and balls had left him little time for the educational aspects of the tour. Upon his return Nicholas had appointed him to the State Council, to a succession of military commands, and to the Council of Ministers. While such contacts had exposed the heir only to conservative influences, at least they gave him more of an introduction to affairs of state than his father had had.

By temperament as well as by training the new tsar seemed disposed to resist reform. Subjected by his father to rigid discipline in his daily life, Alexander had little patience with those who disobeyed orders. Irritable and short of temper, he was often callous and cruel. Haughty and indifferent, he had none of the warmth and charm of his uncle, the first Alexander. Inclined to take the easy way, he was not a leader. He must have seemed flabby and colorless to those who compared him with his predecessors. Alexander placed his trust not in his own judgment and actions, as did Nicholas, but in the autocracy and in the exercise of the autocratic power by the bureaucracy, in whose hands he felt the empire safe. Seldom sure of himself, he inspired little confidence. Indeed, the conservative nobles soon discovered that it was not from the gentry but from the bureaucrats that the tsar would take his cues. Finally, he felt an unshakable confidence in God to the point where he showed an amazing indifference to the many attempts to assassinate him.

PREPARATION FOR EMANCIPATION

Proponents of reform greeted news of the death of Nicholas with a sigh of relief that the strongest bulwark of the rotten social order had been removed. The wildest rumors sped through the villages that the new sovereign would call an end to serfdom, and "once it was told about that upon the top of a mountain at the Crimean Isthmus the Tsar of All the Russias was sitting in his golden cap dispensing freedom to all who came promptly to his royal throne" (Robinson). The *Jacqueries* mounted in number and severity, and the flames of burning manor houses and the pitchfork murders of landowners brought regular military expeditions into the countryside.

The smell of smoke awakened Alexander to the realization that fundamental reform could no longer be postponed. "Better to abolish bondage from above than to wait for the time when it will abolish itself from below," he told the nobles of Moscow province a fortnight after proclaiming the end of the Crimean War. The tsar urged the nobles to "think over how this could be accomplished," for he preferred that the initiative should come from the gentry if possible rather than from the throne. But the serf owners responded slowly, and not until nineteen months later did a petition from the nobles of Lithuania ask permission to free their serfs without land. Meanwhile, early in 1857, Alexander named a secret committee to consider ways of abolishing serfdom.

The committee, following time-worn practice in such matters, moved cautiously. Among its members only the minister of interior, Lanskoy, came round to favor emancipation after opposing it at the opening of the reign. The hated words "freedom" and "emancipation" were never used in the deliberations of the committee, and the press was forbidden to discuss the fact that the end of bondage was being considered. Alexander was urged by his aunt, the Grand Duchess Helen, and by his brother, the Grand Duke Constantine, to spur the committee to action, and Constantine took over the chairmanship in an attempt to speed the work.

Toward the end of 1857 the committee sent to all provincial governors and marshals of the nobility a set of suggestions to guide discussion of the serf problem, together with the emperor's approval should the nobles decide to set up provincial committees of their own. This action and the fact that abolition of serfdom was being considered were now publicized in the press, thereby committing the government for the first time to a course of action from which there could be no turning back. In the next eighteen months committees appeared in every province, composed of elected representatives of the gentry and of nobles appointed to represent the interests of the serfs. Within six months the provincial committees sent their recommendations to the Central Committee, as the former secret committee was now called. In every case it was apparent that the gentry were resigned in the face of imperial determination to the fact that bondage must go, but had "determined to sell the liberation of the serfs at the highest possible price" (Florinsky). Nobles from the rich but overpopulated black-soil provinces were not unwilling to free their serfs but demurred at giving up much land. Those from the poor gray-soil central provinces were inclined to be generous on the question of giving land to the peasants, but pressed for substantial reimbursement for the *obrok* which they would lose if the serfs were freed.

The reports of the provincial committees were turned over to an "editing commission," made up chiefly of bureaucrats, and this body submitted to the Central Committee a tentative draft of the emancipation manifesto. The State Council finally went over the legislation, the tsar gave his approval, and on February 19, 1861, bondage came to an end for over twenty million peasants.

THE LAW OF FEBRUARY 19

The emancipation law, comprising a score of chapters each containing over a hundred articles, was bulky, involved, and in places obscure. A general act freed the landowners' peasants from personal bondage, and special acts, necessitated by peculiar local conditions, dealt with house serfs, serfs working in factories, serfs in Lithuania, in Little Russia, in the Caucasus, in Bessarabia, in western Siberia, and in Great Russia, White Russia, and New Russia. A special act set up machinery for redemption of land by the peasants, and another provided that appointed nobles called "mediators" should supervise the conversion and arbitrate disputes between landowners and peasants over the land settlement.

All landowners' serfs were immediately freed from personal bondage to their former owners and could now own property, marry at will, and sue and be sued at law. No longer were they subject to sale like cattle, or liable to be transferred from field work to stable duty or house service at the master's whim, or "sent for a soldier" or packed off to Siberia for insolence or insubordination. Now at last they were human beings in a legal sense, and this was the most important aspect of the emancipation.

Those who drafted the law of February 19 decided that the serfs must be freed with land and so provided the wherewithal to maintain themselves. To have freed twenty million people without land in a nation so overwhelmingly agricultural and so lacking in industry to absorb them would have caused chaos and misery. By the terms of the law the peasants might work out with the landlord an agreement to purchase the allotments or plots which they had cultivated for their own use under bondage. Because the amount of land available to the former serfs for their sustenance may have been in dispute or deemed inadequate, the government required that the allotments be at least of a certain size, roughly three to ten acres per male peasant, varying from district to district according to fertility of the soil and other factors.

When peasants and former master agreed, under the eye of the mediator, on the amount, kind, and location of the land to be transferred, the government advanced four-fifths of the price to the estate owner. The peasants were supposed to pay the other fifth, but the owner frequently had to forego that 20 per cent because of the poverty of his people. The landlord received not cash but government bonds, the price of which soon fell to three-fourths of par as the nobles flooded the market with the securities. The peasants must pay the government the amount advanced to the former master, plus interest, over a period of forty-nine years. The allotments, however, were turned over not to the individual peasant but to the village community which in its corporate capacity held the land in trust, collected money from the villagers to meet the annual installments, and was responsible for the payment of the annual redemption dues to the government. Only when the last of the forty-nine payments had been made to the state was the land to be finally redeemed, at which time the individual peasant might claim his share of the village land to own and to dispose of as he saw fit.

The peasant was given the privilege of accepting only a quarter of the allotment to which he otherwise would have been entitled, thereby being exempted from the schedule of redemption payments which other villagers must pay. Since the amount of land in these "poverty lots" was nowhere near sufficient to provide for himself and family, the peasant who chose this settlement usually sold it or left it to the village and went to the city to find work. The house serfs—those who had been taken from the villages to serve as domestics in the manor house—were freed without land. A few returned to their families in the village, some stayed on with the estate owner as hired hands, and others moved into the cities.

Not until a redemption agreement was worked out with the landlord was the peasant rid of the money payment—*obrok*—or labor service—*barshchina* —which had been required of him under bondage. Many villagers refused to believe that the law required the continuation of the hated services and had to be whipped back to work under "temporary obligation"—that is, until a redemption agreement could be worked out with the estate owner. Indeed, the full statement of the emancipation law was heard in an air of skepticism as the landlord read out the provisions to the village assembly. In the days of bondage the serfs had come to believe that the land belonged to those who tilled it. "We are yours but the land is ours," they had maintained to the gentry. How could it be that the tsar now ordered them to be given only their allotments, roughly half the arable land on the estate? And furthermore, who could believe that they would actually have to pay for what was rightly theirs? The common reaction was to dismiss the law's provisions as a trick of the nobility. When it became clear that the enactment of February 19 had been correctly explained to them, the peasants commonly looked forward to a second act of emancipation which would turn over to them all the land and call an end to the payments and services which the first had required.

In some districts the villagers were slow to seek redemption agreements with the gentry. Some may have held back in the conviction that a second act of emancipation was forthcoming and that it would be better to wait for more favorable terms. Many put off a settlement with the landlord, however, because the burden of redemption payments, added to taxes, contributions for village services, and payments in kind or in money to the landlord for the fifth of the redemption price they could not borrow from the government, was actually a greater burden than the people had borne under serfdom. The price at which the village could redeem its allotments averaged considerably above the going market price for the land, the difference being the amount by which the nobleman was compensated for loss of the serf's labor. It is surprising that there were as many redemptions as there were. In 1881 the government ordered the completion of redemption agreements for all former serfs, of whom 15 per cent still had not accepted a settlement.

The annual payments to the government were so high, based as they were upon an inflated valuation of the land, that the peasant communities frequently defaulted. Arrearages mounted until they had to be cancelled, only to have the villages fall again into arrears. In 1896 a new schedule of moderate payments was announced by the government which would have stretched the installments beyond 1950. During the revolution of 1905, however, all further payments were forgiven.

The amount and character of land transferred to the village community varied widely over Russia. In general, the grants tended to be parsimonious in the black-soil areas of the south and liberal in the central and northeast districts of the country. Roughly half of the plow land on the former estate remained with the landlord, while the remainder went to the village. The latter, however, commonly received a disproportionately small share of the woods, pasture, and meadow land. Since the peasants received at best only that amount of land which they had tilled for their own use under bondage, a task which had required their attention only three days a week while they worked the other half week for the landlord as *barshchina,* the land assigned them under the redemption program was sufficient only to occupy half their time. What was more important, the grant was not generous enough to provide them sustenance and a surplus with which to meet taxes, make redemption payments, and purchase necessary equipment. In many cases individual peasants rented land from their former master; in others the village community rented a block of land to be worked as a corporate enterprise. In the black-soil provinces, where allotments were grossly inadequate, competitive bidding for the additional acres so necessary to permit the peasants to make ends meet drove rentals sharply upward, but the land hunger in South Russia was never satisfied.

For generations past the gentry had farmed their portion of the estate as a production unit of one, two, or three large fields. On the other hand, that part of the estate assigned to the village often had been scattered in small fields over the estate, some of them miles distant from the village. In each of these village fields the land had been divided into a crazy-quilt pattern of strips, typically a few yards wide; and several of such strips in each field had been assigned to each peasant household. In some villages the strips were held by the serf in heredity. In others the village assembly periodically voted to reassign strips among heads of families, thus permitting equitable treatment by providing that all must share the good and the poor land to be found in every field, and making possible adjustments in size of allotments to allow for changes in size of families. Each village field, cut as it was into ribbons of individual holdings, necessarily was tilled as a unit—the same crop planted at the same time and harvested at the same time so that the village cattle could be turned in to gather what the gleaners had missed. Until long after emancipation one-third of the arable land lay fallow to recover its fertility, for there was a chronic shortage of animal fertilizer and frequent redistribution discouraged the peasant from investing commercial fertilizer in plots that might not be his to work next year.

If the peasant achieved the dignity of a human being in a strictly legal sense by the law of February 19, in an economic sense he was hardly more free than before. He had exchanged the landlord for a new master, the *mir*, a master perhaps less cruel but often more exacting. The village assembly reassigned plots in the open fields, assessed and collected taxes levied by the national, provincial, or district government, and dispensed justice among its members as it had always done. After emancipation the community was responsible for the police functions which the gentry had fulfilled under the old regime. Since the corporate village had to account to the government for the annual redemption payment, it was understandably merciless in wringing his share of the burden from each family head. Default was punishable at the will of the community by flogging, forced labor, seizure of property, or assignment to military service, and the peasants who managed to scrape together their share of the payment were not inclined to deal softly with one who tried to escape his lot. It was almost impossible to withdraw from the community; travel beyond the village was illegal without a passport endorsed by the village elder. Emancipation had little meaning for the average *muzhik*, or peasant, at least in an economic sense. The act of February 19 brought him "limited rights and little land, but abundant obligations" (Robinson).

By 1866 the thirteen million state-owned serfs had won their freedom under conditions substantially better than those applying to landowners' serfs. Land allotments were more generous and redemption dues were lower, although it is true that for the most part the state peasants were located in north, central and east Russia where the quality of land was far below that in southern Russian where lived most of the privately-owned *barshchina* serfs. The terms of the emancipation of the state peasants were carried out through the agency of the village or *mir,* as was true in the case of the landowners' serfs.

REFORM OF LOCAL GOVERNMENT

The termination of bondage, and with it the administrative authority of the estate owner over his "souls," forced a revision of local government machinery. The reforms that were promulgated seemed designed to bring a measure of self-government to Russia. In practice, the reforms were emasculated and institutions of self-government were nearly paralyzed by interference from bureaucratic officialdom.

Many police and administrative functions formerly performed by the gentry were transferred by the Emancipation Act to the village community. From then on the landowner was a stranger in the midst of the peasants, "though still living among them with all the memories of his past authority" (Pares). By the act of February 19 several neighboring villages were combined into a township, or *volost.* Heads of families in the township, acting as the *volost* assembly, chose a *volost* elder, an executive council, and a court to deal with minor civil and criminal offenses. But the *volost* assembly rarely met, and its elder, together with the elders of the villages which made up the township, managed peasant affairs and passed sentence upon wrongdoers. Since the elders were responsible for the maintenance of order to police officials appointed by the central government to control each district, there was little of real self-government in the villages.

Early in 1864 the imperial government announced the second great act of reform, the Zemstvo Law, which put into operation the local government suggestions offered by Speransky in 1809. Agencies of local self-government, called zemstvos, were established in the county and province. The zemstvo of each county was to consist of an elected assembly, presided over by the marshal of the county nobility, and an executive zemstvo board. Delegates to the assembly were to be chosen by three classes of electors: private landowners, village communities, and townspeople in the county. Each three thousand allotments in the villages sent one delegate to the assembly, and one or a group of landowners owning approximately the same amount of land also chose one delegate. An equivalent amount of town property was similarly represented, the right of townsmen to vote being limited to those owning real estate worth three thousand rubles or operating a business having a turnover of twice that amount. The delegates, chosen for three years, selected from among their number an executive board of five or more members. The assembly itself might number as few as fourteen or as many as a hundred, depending upon the amount of property and size of allotments in the county. The county assembly elected delegates to the provincial assembly, which chose its own zemstvo board.

The county zemstvo assembly met annually to vote the county budget, levy taxes to meet the expenses to which the zemstvo committed itself, and approve projects to be carried out by the zemstvo board. Maintenance of county roads and bridges; construction and support of hospitals, asylums, prisons, churches, and schools; the extension of medical and veterinary services; stimulation of industry and trade; instruction in improved farming methods; poor relief; public health needs—to such problems did the zemstvo devote its attention, the county zemstvo on the county level and the provincial zemstvo on the provincial level.

The new institutions of self-government suffered from the beginning from financial embarrassment. While the zemstvos might tax real estate and commerce, the extent to which they might do so was definitely restricted by the imperial government. Furthermore, part of what monies they did take in went at government order for expenses from which the county or province drew no benefit—meeting the costs of drafts for military service and providing subsistence for various government officials. Several provinces were not allowed zemstvo organization, and where such institutions did exist they came increasingly under bureaucratic suspicion and restraint. Even so, the zemstvos did yeoman service for rural Russia in relieving suffering, reducing ignorance, and improving generally the miserable conditions which blighted agricultural life. And the deliberations of the zemstvo assemblies provided political schooling for many men who later became leaders in national affairs. Those who participated in zemstvo politics were almost without exception men of honor and conscience, men whose enthusiasm for the welfare of the lower classes made them suspect in official circles.

Self-government of Russian cities had been granted by Catherine II, withdrawn by Paul, and granted again by Alexander I; but the institutions designed to implement the royal grants had never been set up, not even in the capitals. In 1870 Alexander II ordered the cities to establish governmental machinery similar to the rural zemstvos. Each city was allowed a legislative council, or duma, and an executive board headed by a mayor. The right to vote for delegates to the duma was limited to taxpayers, who were divided into three classes: those few citizens who paid one third of city taxes chose one third of the delegates; those who paid the second third of taxes elected another third of the delegates; and the many small taxpayers who paid the final third of city levies were also represented by one third of the members of the duma. Control of the city council, then, rested with the relatively few large taxpayers, a fact deliberately intended to make the dumas conservative. As in the zemstvos, the duma chose its executive board and mayor. The city councils were to concern themselves with the same sort of problems with which the zemstvos were allowed to deal; their tax resources were similarly limited, and they came under the same suspicion and restriction from which their country cousins suffered as the government grew increasingly reactionary.

JUDICIAL REFORM

Pre-reform Russia had known only a travesty of justice, for an equitable court system catering to the needs of all classes without discrimination did not exist before 1864. Judges, appointed and retained at the pleasure of the bureaucracy, were notorious for their immorality, ignorance, and downright illiteracy, for the cruel sentences they imposed, for their readiness to wink at the law for a bribe, for their tenderness with the well-born and their heartlessness with those who came before them empty-handed. But the faults of Russian justice lay not entirely with the judges. Normally, years and often decades passed before cases were adjudicated, for the judicial process—called by the people *volokita,* which means dragging or procrastination—was extremely complex. The secret police employed torture on witnesses and principals in inquisitorial sessions before the trial. Court sessions were secret; defendants were not allowed counsel; decisions were handed down without argument or cross-examination. "My blood chills and my hair stands on end," Ivan Aksakov shuddered at the very memory of Russian legal action before the reform of the law courts.

While one committee after another through the first half of the nineteenth century had managed to postpone court reform, the end of bondage created a judicial void which had to be filled without further delay. In 1864 the tsar affixed his signature to the Judiciary Act, which applied to the Russian court system various elements borrowed from Western Europe. Justice was to be available to all without discrimination. The judiciary was to be freed from bureaucratic meddling, and judges were to enjoy tenure without fear of removal except for malfeasance. Trial by jury was introduced for all criminal and some civil cases. The judicial process was simplified and speeded up, and all trials were to be open to the public. Preliminary investigation was removed from the "unclean hands" of the police, and the accused was to enjoy the right to be represented by counsel and to appeal the judgment to a higher court. Cruel punishments, such as flogging, branding, and the bastinado, were forbidden. Regulations concerning costs and fees aimed to prevent the venality which had made a mockery of justice in the old courts.

A justice of the peace, chosen by the county zemstvo, heard minor cases on the local level, but his judgment might be appealed to a monthly session of all the county justices of the peace sitting in the county capital. More serious cases—civil actions involving more than five hundred rubles or charges of crime where the punishment was a fine of three hundred rubles or one year in prison—were heard in district court, final appeal lying with the Imperial Senate which acted as supreme court. Judges of the district court were chosen by the imperial minister of justice from a list of qualified candidates drawn up by the bar association.

The court system was established slowly and piecemeal over the nation, not reaching Kiev, for instance, until 1881. Neither jury trial nor justice of the peace was ever introduced into the Polish and Lithuanian provinces. Jury service was limited to those owning two hundred and seventy acres of land or other property worth five thousand rubles. Many types of cases did not come within the purview of the new courts: church courts retained control over the clergy and over divorce cases among the laiety; administrative tribunals punished wayward officials; courts-martial dealt with crimes against public safety; violations of publishing laws were tried in special courts; the police still handled disturbances of the peace; and crimes against the state could be decided without reference to any court.

While the law suffered from serious limitations at the time of its enactment and was subjected to further mutilation under the later reaction, the reform of the judiciary was in principle the most radical of all the great reforms. European liberals generally hailed it more than any of the other reforms as qualifying Russia for admission into the family of civilized nations. The law profession thenceforth attracted men of high purpose and integrity who fought stubbornly and desperately for the principle that legal justice should not be made subject to the whims of an arbitrary bureaucracy. To the dying days of the monarchy men trained in the law marched in the vanguard of those who battled against tyranny and oppression.

REFORM OF THE ARMY

The military establishment, particularly, stood indicted by the humiliating defeat in the Crimean War. At the end of hostilities the army contained over two million men, less than a fourth of whom had seen front-line service. Bungling mismanagement of supply, training, recruitment, and troop movement kept the rest lying idle in camps when they might better have been left in the villages to do the spring ploughing. With the return to peace, the war minister Dmitry Miliutin was encouraged by the tsar to reform the many abuses from which the army suffered.

Since the time of Peter the Great Russia had maintained an enormous standing army in which the enlisted ranks served a term of twenty-five years. Each landowner annually received a draft call for so many recruits, based upon army needs at the time and the number of male serfs he owned. Some of the gentry left the choice of recruits to the villages, while others sent up the names of insolent or lazy peasants. Condemnation to military service was a common form of punishment, and those whose life was ruined by being sent away for twenty-five years looked upon the sentence as no better than penal servitude. It was in part to lighten the burden of army service that Alexander I had established the military colonies. Once in the army, the individual led a miserable life. Army contractors made fortunes from providing poor food, shoddy clothing, and drafty quarters. Breaches of discipline were punished by flogging or being condemned to run the gauntlet between files of men armed with birch rods or rifle butts. In combat the troops were trained to carry enemy positions with the bayonet rather than to rely upon their firearms, which were poor in comparison to those of Western armies. Worst of all, the burden of conscription fell only upon the villages. The nobility and merchants were exempt from military service, and freemen subject to the draft evaded it by hiring substitutes to take their place.

Reforms in the army were spread over two decades. The hated military colonies, symbols of abject slavery against which there were perennial revolts, were abolished in 1857. The infantry was equipped with rifles to replace the smooth-bores in use during the Crimean War. The medical and supply services were reorganized along Western lines. The humiliating punishments characteristic of the old army were forbidden. Military law was humanized by removing many irksome restrictions from the list of offenses for which the soldier might be punished. Court-martial procedure was liberalized by providing that an accused soldier should be allowed defense counsel. The more manageable division replaced the unwieldy corps as the unit of organization. Schools for officers were modernized and the curriculum liberalized to produce intelligent men as well as martinets. Provision was made to teach enlisted men to read and write, and the army became a significant adjunct to the nation's educational system.

In 1874 the emperor approved a new draft law reducing the term of active service from twenty-five to six years, after which the discharged soldier was enrolled for nine years in the reserve, when he was called only for summer maneuvers. Finally, he spent five years in the militia, which was called up only in time of national emergency. Every man regardless of class was liable for military service, substitution being prohibited, and the one man drafted out of four or five eligible was chosen by lot. Only sons and breadwinners were exempt, university students had to serve only six months, high school graduates for two years, those who had finished primary school for four years, and all students might volunteer and cut their required service by half.

Of all the great reforms, only those in the army continued undiluted in later years, for Miliutin stayed on as minister of war to the end of the reign. The democratizing effect of subjecting all classes to service, of teaching the peasant soldier to read and write, and of abolishing the bestial treatment of the men, created in the minds of conservative Russians a fear that the army might prove unreliable when called upon to defend the state. Liberals, however, welcomed this end of military bondage with the claim that now the Russian soldier could look upon his service as fair and honorable.

REFORMS IN EDUCATION AND CENSORSHIP

All levels of education suffered from the benighted policy of Nicholas I, but it was upon the universities that the sternest regulations were imposed. To make it easy for police to spot them in a crowd, students were ordered into uniform and required to wear their hair in a peculiar trim. A government official, the inspector of morals, kept strict check upon student conduct in and out of school. The minister of education must approve texts and suggested readings for every course. Professors had to submit advance copies of their lectures to the Ministry of Education, and deans were held responsible for seeing that the professors delivered their lectures precisely as they had written them. Only professors of Greek Orthodox theology could teach philosophy or psychology, and logic and metaphysics were stricken from the curriculum. The number of students allowed to enroll in every Russian university was reduced and fees were sharply increased in an effort to ensure that only sons of the safely conservative wealthy should attend institutions of higher learning. Serfs were forbidden by law to attend a university. Less than four thousand students were enrolled in the six Russian universities in 1855, of whom 70 per cent were sons of nobles, officials, or clergymen; half the rest came from the merchant class, and the remainder were sons of craftsmen or state peasants.

Students at all Russian universities grew restless after the accession of Alexander II, and there were many demonstrations calculated to stampede the government into granting educational reforms. But only a few months after the emancipation of the serfs the tsar appointed as minister of education the uncompromising reactionary Count E. V. Putiatin, "who had been an admiral in the navy and was supposed to know how to deal with recalcitrant youth" (Johnson). Putiatin issued a new code of university regulations outlawing all student organizations and forbidding students to gather for any purpose without the consent of university officials. The new code was met by further demonstrations which ended in street fights between students and police or soldiers. Three hundred students at the University of St. Petersburg were arrested and many expelled, while in Moscow the police incited the mob to violence by spreading the rumor that the students were dispossessed landowners demanding the return of serfdom. But the more the *nagaika,* or Cossack whip, "danced on their backs," the more determined the students became to put an end to their own bondage. The tsar finally realized that repression would accomplish nothing and replaced Putiatin with A. V. Golovnin, who was well known for his liberal views.

In 1863 Golovnin issued a new code of regulations which restored to Russian universities the autonomy they had been allowed only momentarily under the regulations of 1804. Each faculty received the right to elect the officials who would govern the university, a privilege still not enjoyed by many American colleges a century later. Responsibility for disciplinary action against students was taken from the former government inspector of morals and assigned to a court of three professors. A faculty council was to control instruction, requirements for graduation, and approval of university publications. Courses proscribed in the preceding reign returned to the curriculum. Limitation on enrollment was abolished, fees were reduced and were waived for those too poor to pay. The universities were still not open to women, who customarily went abroad for their education, nor did the students recover the privilege of organizing their own associations.

A new regulatory code issued in 1864 reorganized the secondary school system, providing for two types of high schools. The curriculum of the "classical *gymnasium,*" emphasizing the Greek and Latin languages and the humanities, was designed for the student who would enter the university. That of the *"real gymnasium"* or *realschule,* which omitted the classics and concentrated upon the sciences, was intended to prepare the graduate for advanced study in technical or professional institutions or for immediate entry into commerce or industry. The *realschule* graduate was not eligible for admission into the university. Girls were not admitted to either type of high school, although a number of private schools catered to daughters of the gentry. The class character of the school system, which directed sons of nobles and wealthy merchants into the universities and those of the middle and lower classes into trade schools, was clearly intentional. The secondary schools were maintained and completely controlled by the minister of education, whose temperament and outlook determined the method, curriculum, course content, point of view, and personnel for every high school in the land.

The weakest link in the Russian educational chain at the middle of the nineteenth century was in the area of primary education. Official records boasted that in the last year of the reign of Nicholas there were 7,500 primary schools with a total enrollment of 216,000 in a population of over seventy million. Official estimates were notoriously inaccurate, however, and many schools were known to exist only on paper. Of the schools in operation, approximately half were maintained by the Holy Synod and half by the Ministry of State Domains in communities of state-owned peasants. With the rare exception of an occasional school maintained by an enlightened noble for his peasants, the serfs of the gentry enjoyed no educational facilities whatsoever.

In 1864 Alexander II signed a law approving a system of primary education. Schools were to be built and maintained by the communities which they served, and attendance was to be open to all who could afford the tuition set by the local authorities. In each county a board made up of zemstvo representatives, a clerical appointee, the chief of the district police, and an inspector supervised the primary schools, employed teachers, and fired those who were politically unreliable. In practice, the inspector, who had the time to travel about the county, controlled the system, and he in turn was controlled by the Ministry of Education. The law proclaimed the duty of primary teachers to be the inculcation of religious and moral principles and the dissemination of "useful elementary knowledge." Since zemstvo budgets were pitifully small and had to meet many local needs, primary school facilities came only slowly into existence. By 1914, however, the zemstvos were spending well over a hundred million rubles a year, or nearly a third of their budgets, on primary education.

Reactionary ministers of education did their best in later years to cripple the educational system born in the 1860's. Teachers were constantly under suspicion and subject to discharge without hearing on an unsupported accusation. Textbooks and lectures were censored, curricula dictated, the morals of teachers and students spied upon and their personal associations reported. But the more rigid the censorship imposed upon the educational system, the more determined the fight against the censorship and against the bureaucracy which decreed it. Many a Russian student reacted to the flogging, expulsion, or exile with which he was constantly threatened by joining a secret organization whose avowed aim it was to put an end to the autocracy from which all society suffered.

The closing years of the reign of Nicholas had witnessed a respectable increase in the number of Russian newspapers and periodicals, although the press had been effectively gagged by the law requiring all copy to be submitted to official censors and approved before publication. With the accession of Alexander II the government vacillated between relaxing the censorship laws and forbidding discussion of social problems, notably the question of emancipation. In the spirit of relief that swept the country upon the death of Nicholas there was a flurry of journalistic optimism which evidenced itself in the appearance of a number of new periodicals and newspapers. By 1859 the press was permitted to discuss the problem of serfdom. The tsar even went so far as to express his disapproval of oppressive censorship, provided the journalists revealed no "evil tendencies."

A new censorship law, referred to as "temporary regulations," was announced in 1865 and remained in operation for forty years. Books of more than ten pages were freed from preliminary censorship, a provision aimed to keep pamphlet literature and political broadsides under control. The government, of course, could confiscate all copies of a book discovered after publication to be subversive. The minister of interior was given power to decide whether newspapers and journals should be submitted to preliminary or to punitive censorship. In the latter case the editor was not required to submit copy to the censor before publication, but might be warned, fined, or forced to suspend publication if he criticized the government or discussed forbidden matters—foreign affairs, during one period—or showed himself otherwise indiscreet. By decision of the minister of interior only St. Petersburg and Moscow editors were privileged to publish under punitive censorship, thus leaving all provincial publications still suffering from the deadening effect of preliminary censorship. The list of punishable offenses lengthened after 1865, and soon the Russian press had slipped back into the mire of bureaucratic oppression from which it had escaped momentarily in the first decade of the reign. One vigorously liberal periodical, *The Bell*, managed to escape the official muzzle. Copies of the journal, published in London by the Westernizer Herzen, were smuggled into Russia and occasional issues even turned up mysteriously on the tsar's breakfast table.

ECONOMIC AND FINANCIAL REFORM

The years immediately following the accession of Alexander II were years of economic growth. Talk of emancipation of the serfs inspired the business community to dream of a free labor market and a consequent fall in production costs. The government legalized the limited liability of corporations, and the sum of private capital invested in corporate organizations jumped over 400 per cent between 1856 and 1859. By 1879 some 560 limited-liability enterprises were in operation with a capital of three quarters of a billion rubles, most of it subscribed by Russians. The individual state-owned banks functioning before 1860 were abolished after the government had destroyed public confidence in them by heavy borrowings during the Crimean War; they were replaced by a central state bank designed to stimulate commerce and stabilize the currency. The financial minister, Count Michael Reutern, was most anxious, however, that private interests rather than the government should lead the way in developing the economy. Private banks, savings and loan associations, and mortgage companies appeared for the first time in the 1860's, and their numbers and volume of business rose steadily through the reign.

By the death of Alexander II Russia possessed 15,000 miles of railway, constructed in part by foreign syndicates but chiefly by Russian companies with domestic capital. As in other countries, government subsidies, unsound speculation, and unreasonably high cost characterized the early period of construction. Fifty thousand miles of telegraph lines were built during the reign, and the telegraph service as well as the postal service were operated by the government. Foreign trade more than doubled between 1860 and 1880, although Russia's share of expanding world commerce remained the same, partly because of the increasingly protectionist nature of government trade policy as the century wore on.

While private capital and management undoubtedly profited from the post-emancipation boom, the lot of the workers failed to improve. Unsanitary and unsafe working conditions, overcrowded housing, and a working day of from twelve to eighteen hours typified industry as the coming of the Industrial Revolution brought to Russia the same hardships Western Europe had endured earlier. Factory management ordinarily paid wages quarterly or semiannually, and fines for absenteeism or damaging equipment or material ran as high as one-fourth of the annual wage. The substitution of machine- for hand-methods of production, and the flow of population from rural to urban areas in an attempt to escape the growing poverty of the village, produced an expanded labor force and a competition for employment that drove real wages down approximately 25 per cent in the generation after 1860.

The dawn of industrial capitalism broke slowly in Russia for various reasons. Certainly the politico-economic climate was less favorable here than in the West, where a governmental policy of *laissez-faire* had freed business growth from interference. A shortage of investment capital at home and the reluctance of foreign capital to enter a nation so frequently torn or threatened by rebellion hampered economic progress. The drift of many factory workers back to the village during the slack season of production slowed the appearance of an industrial labor force skilled in modern manufacturing techniques. The encouragement given to immigration of foreign organizers and technicians suggests a shortage of the management skills so necessary to industrial development. Perhaps "the lack of cultural tradition and civilized habits" (Florinsky) among the mass of the people accounts more than any other factor for the halting pace at which the nation approached industrial maturity.

THE SIGNIFICANCE OF THE GREAT REFORMS

Whatever dates one accepts for the bracketing of modern Russia, the era falls clearly into two periods separated by the reforms of Alexander II. The "Tsar Liberator" and his successors may have done their stubborn best to emasculate the reforms, but there could be no return to the old feudal society. Bondage once swept away could not be reimposed. The voice of local governmental institutions might be hushed, but it could never be stilled. The Western system of justice might be perverted, but its ideal could never be effaced. Economic reform made Russia a member of the capitalistic system of the West, and even the cataclysmic upheaval of 1917 could not relieve the nation of the interdependence of modern states upon one another.

Russian society accepted the changes of the sixties and called for still further reform. The repression that followed those changes could not for long be successful, and had rather the reverse effect of calling into existence a succession of popular movements whose aim was to speed up national progress toward the new social milieu envisaged by the great reforms.

SUGGESTED READING

Florinsky, M. T., *Russia: A History and an Interpretation* (New York, Macmillan, 1953).

Graham, S., *Tsar of Freedom* (New Haven, Yale University Press, 1935).

Hans, N. A., *History of Russian Educational Policy, 1701–1917* (London, King, 1931).

Johnson, W. H. E., *Russia's Educational Heritage* (Pittsburgh, Carnegie Press, 1950).

Karpovich, M., *Imperial Russia, 1801–1917* (New York, Holt, 1932).

Kornilov, A., *Modern Russian History* (New York, Knopf, 1948).

Kovalevsky, M. M., *Russian Political Institutions* (Chicago, University of Chicago Press, 1902).

Langer, W. L., *European Alliances and Alignments, 1871–1890* (New York, Knopf, 1950).

Lyaschenko, P. I., *History of the National Economy of Russia to the 1917 Revolution* (New York, Macmillan, 1949).

Mavor, J., *An Economic History of Russia* (New York, Dutton, 1914).

Maynard, J., *Russia in Flux* (New York, Macmillan, 1948).

Robinson, G. T., *Rural Russia Under the Old Regime* (New York, Macmillan, 1949).

Seton-Watson, H., *The Decline of Imperial Russia, 1855–1914* (New York, Praeger, 1952).

22

Internal Unrest and Expansion

THE HALF-EMANCIPATION OF THE SERFS began a socio-economic revolution which Alexander II and his successors tried desperately to check. Popular demand for further reform, particularly for relaxing the autocracy and granting the people a voice in national government, was given expression by the intelligentsia. As in the Decembrist movement early in the century, those who clamored for reform diverged into two streams: those who followed the Fabian way of peaceful pressure and even cooperation with the government, and those who were convinced that necessary reform could come only after the Romanovs had been turned out and an entirely new society brought to birth. The reign degenerated into a struggle between the government, fighting for its very existence, and a succession of progressive and revolutionary parties whose attention came increasingly to concentrate upon the assassination of the emperor and the replacement of the autocracy by some sort of liberal regime—constitutional monarchy or republic or socialist state. The extremists triumphed over the moderates and perpetrated the murder of the tsar.

Poland, too, became a center of unrest. The halting steps toward reform in the kingdom taken by the new ruler only made the Poles impatient for complete independence. An uprising in 1863 was brutally put down, the kingdom of Poland ceased to exist, and the land became simply the "Vistula Provinces" of the Russian Empire. Alexander thenceforth followed a policy of Russification in an attempt to destroy every evidence of Polish nationalism.

Empire-builders pushed back the frontier in southeastern Siberia and in Central Asia to incorporate vast new lands under the double eagle. Russia led a war of liberation against Turkey and succeeded in freeing much of the

Balkans from the sultan's rule. The victory was tempered, however, by the refusal of the great powers to accept Russia's plans for redrawing the map of the Balkan Peninsula. To the indignation of the Slavophiles Russia was forced at the Congress of Berlin to accept a revision of the terms she had imposed upon the Porte.

THE POLISH RISING

The oppressive reign of Nicholas I was no more successful among Poles than among Russians in halting the rumblings of discontent. An *émigré* center established in Paris under Prince Adam Czartoryski clamored for an independent nation under the liberal constitution of 1791. Another agency, the Polish Democratic Society with headquarters in London, demanded not only an end to Russian rule but a radical political and land reform program. Both groups maintained contact with Poles at home, and both hoped to enlist the support of Western European states in the struggle for independence.

The accession of Alexander II brought hope that the new tsar would lift the pall of oppression that had settled over Poland after the 1830 rising. While the new sovereign's address to Polish nobles in Warsaw soon after the end of the Crimean War offered little promise of a gentler policy, there were several moves toward moderation. Prince Michael Gorchakov, the new viceroy, listened patiently to Polish pleas for reform. An amnesty was proclaimed for those who had languished in Siberian prison camps and for others who had fled abroad. St. Petersburg permitted the opening of a medical college in the Polish capital and hinted at the revival of the University of Warsaw. With the tsar's approval the Poles organized an agricultural society whose members soon passed beyond a consideration of land reform to a discussion of the restoration of Polish liberty. In 1861 Alexander named a Council of State to receive petitions or complaints from Poles, and charged a newly-appointed committee on education and religion to restore the use of the Polish language in the schools and to establish a university. Councils of self-government were established for town, district, and province. The Jews were emancipated. A Polish committee was allowed to grant modest land reforms which, however, left the peasant with even less land than his Russian brother received at the same time. Grand Duke Constantine, credited with liberal views after his service as chairman of the committee that drew up the Emancipation Act of February 19, replaced Gorchakov as viceroy in a further attempt to assuage Polish opposition to Russian rule.

These modest measures succeeded only in provoking further unrest, for the Poles would be satisfied with nothing less than independence. The few who had cooperated with the tsar in carrying through the reforms were stigmatized as traitors to the cause of Polish nationalism. Attempted assassination of Grand Duke Constantine and of Poles who had collaborated with him miscarried, and in retaliation an order went out for widespread drafting of Polish young men into the Russian army. This was met by the creation of a left-wing revolutionary committee in Warsaw which called for a national rising and proclaimed Polish independence. A conservative committee of landowners appeared at the same time in an attempt to prevent the movement from becoming a radical social and economic revolution, and the two groups working at cross purposes caused the peasantry to become suspicious and indifferent to the revolt. A pitifully small and poorly-equipped Polish army scattered at the appearance of a Russian force many times its size, but guerrillas carried on sporadic fighting for more than a year. The revolution in Russia which Polish nationalists hoped would catch fire from the spark in their own country did not materialize, and the nations of Western Europe limited their intervention to feeble protests which St. Petersburg met with firm rejection, if not with open contempt. Prussia's Bismarck supported Russia throughout the crisis, partly in fear that a revived Poland would demand a return of the territory annexed by Prussia during the partitions, and partly in the hope of winning Russia's benevolent neutrality in the coming Austro-Prussian conflict.

The rising of 1863 had been gentry-inspired and gentry-led. For the most part, the peasantry had stood aloof. After the rebellion was quelled the Russian government sought, by introducing certain reforms, to make permanent the split between the upper and lower classes and so to reduce the likelihood of united Polish action in the future. The great estates were broken up and the peasants assigned allotments considerably more generous than those provided by the earlier emancipation act in Russia. The Polish peasants paid no redemption dues but contributed through taxes, as did all landowners, noble and non-noble, to the fund from which the gentry were reimbursed for loss of their land. By a reform of local government, township assemblies included gentry and peasants on equal terms, a provision which tended to submerge gentry influence under a sea of peasant votes.

By a policy of stern repression and Russification St. Petersburg sought to stamp out every vestige of Polish nationalism after 1864. Russians replaced Poles in official positions. The University of Warsaw became a Russian, instead of a Polish, university. Use of the Polish language was forbidden, first in administrative circles, then in secondary schools, and finally in primary schools. The Roman Catholic church, whose priests generally had sided with the insurgents, suffered increasing restrictions, and Uniats were forced back into the Russian Orthodox church. The Poles must be sternly punished for their failure to appreciate the earlier mild measures of their Russian master.

REVOLUTIONARY THOUGHT AND ACTION

The intellectual leaders of Russia, disappointed at the halfway measures of reform promulgated by Alexander II, kept up a literary attack against the regime throughout the reign and inspired others to carry on civil and political attack. Alexander Herzen, from his safe retreat in London, called for rebellion against the anemic emancipation act in his publication *The Bell*.

Nicholas Chernyshevsky, heir to the tradition established by Bielinsky in the preceding reign, bitterly attacked the belletristic and aesthetic approach to art, insisting that art, whatever its medium, must concern itself with the social problems of the day. When he raised the banner of revolutionary socialism in his publication *The Contemporary,* he was imprisoned and later exiled to Siberia for twenty years. He anticipated later Bolshevik thought, as Lenin admitted, in urging collectivization of all land and in believing that Russia could vault from communal ownership in the *mir* to socialism and communism without passing through the stage of capitalism.

Dmitry Pisarev, who did most of his writing in prison, called upon students to pay their debt to society by serving as intellectual leaders of the people along the path of reform. Effective leadership, he held, required an acceptance of the social implications of modern science and a rejection of the past with its emphasis upon humanistic studies. His plea to accept nothing of the old Russia led the novelist Turgenev to brand his philosophy "nihilism," a term later applied to all bomb-throwing revolutionaries.

Peter Tkachev looked forward to peasant revolt but warned that such a revolution could only be successful if led by a small, disciplined party. Lenin later agreed with him. Peter Lavrov saw the need for a "civilizing minority" of dedicated men who should exemplify intellectual development and moral character. This core of leadership must work for the overturn of the rotten social order and for the creation of a new society based upon principles of "truth and justice." Only socialism could promise the ideal, but Lavrov could see its arrival only after a long period of education of the masses by his "civilizing minority."

Such men as Herzen, Chernyshevsky, Pisarev, and Lavrov had little to offer in the way of a detailed, constructive program for the inauguration of the new society which they agreed must come about. Nor were they anything but vague in suggesting the form the new society should take.

The first to suggest in detail a type of new society was Michael Bakunin, the founder of modern anarchism. To him truth and justice could come to society only through abolition of the state, the agency which by its compulsive and punitive nature denied men freedom and contributed to the exploitation of the many by the few. He would do away with private property, turning over the land to peasant communes and the factories to organizations of workers. The family, like the state an agency which tended to perpetuate the old regime, must disappear. Women freed from the toils of marriage would enjoy equal rights with men, while all children would be reared and educated as public charges. Religion would be proscribed as all men professed atheism. Bakunin and Karl Marx agreed on many points, but on the fundamental issue of the position of the state in the new society they were poles apart. Marx would take over the machinery of the state and use it to carry out his program. Bakunin would eliminate the state.

Sergei Niechaiev, a primary teacher in his early twenties, emphasized revolutionary technique and organization. He did not concern himself with the nature of future society, but focused his attention upon assassinating the tsar and overturning the regime. "To build is not our task, but that of those who follow us," he believed. Niechaiev planned to blanket the country with five-man cells which would stir up and lead the revolution on the local level. To protect the entire organization against police discovery, each local five would know only its own members. A district five would control the local units and in turn come under the direction of a provincial cell, the whole organization to be led by a national committee which Niechaiev would dominate. Members must sacrifice all honor and moral scruple to the welfare of the organization, spying on each other and killing and robbing on order without question. The movement would devote its energy entirely to assassination and terrorism, which Niechaiev naïvely believed would sweep the monarchy from power. When the members of a Moscow cell on order from Niechaiev murdered one of their number suspected of being an informer, the police broke up the entire organization. Scores were imprisoned or exiled and Niechaiev, who had escaped to Switzerland, was brought back to live out his life in a dungeon. Dostoevsky's novel *The Possessed* immortalized the affair. The ruthlessness of the movement and the callous murder of the Moscow member turned even hardened revolutionaries against such Jesuitism and cast disrepute upon all reform movements. Later the Bolsheviks applied the methods and organization first tried out by Niechaiev.

Barely had the Tsar's signature dried on the act of February 19 when student protests and demonstrations against its modest provisions broke out at the University of St. Petersburg. Cossacks rode down the students, many of whom were imprisoned; hundreds of others were expelled. Incensed at such treatment, Herzen in London addressed the students in *The Bell*. What should become of these young men whose education the government had cut short? Where should they go? "To the people (*V Narod*)," he answered, although he did not make clear whether he expected these "exiles from knowledge" to organize a rising or simply to educate and propagandize among the people. From his challenge, *"V Narod,"* accepted as a call to action by liberals and radicals alike, the reformers of the sixties and seventies, moderate or extreme, have been lumped together under the name of *Narodniks* or Populists or those who went "to the people."

In the early seventies young reformers who disapproved of the Jacobinism of Niechaiev gathered around Nicholas Chaikovsky, who was convinced that a long period of education and preparation of the people must precede the revolution. Members of the "Chaikovsky Circle" organized meetings of factory workers to discuss recent books on social and economic problems, particularly Marx's *Das Kapital*. Others went into the villages to work among the peasants, young women serving as midwives and practical nurses, the men as blacksmiths, veterinaries, teachers, or simple laborers. In living a peasant life and dressing in peasant garb Chaikovsky's followers hoped to win the peasant's confidence and to educate him to the need to overthrow the regime. To waste the people's energy in strikes and local rebellions was only to invite recrimination. The strength of the masses must be conserved for the day when the nation would rise in invincible unity and burst its chains. But Chaikovsky met only frustration. The peasants, concerned only about the land shortage from which every village suffered, showed little interest in a recasting of all society. The uncalloused hands and the uncommon speech of the city-bred reformers made the peasants suspicious that they were *agents-provocateurs*, and some were handed over to the police. The movement collapsed when the government moved in to seize the presses on which the organization was printing subversive pamphlets and to bring to trial many of the leaders.

Men of the Chaikovsky Circle who escaped prison sentence or exile now organized a new society with the intriguing title "Land and Freedom." The very name promised concrete things—land to the hungry village, to the *muzhik* freedom from the oppression of the *mir*, and to all society freedom from the autocracy. More carefully organized than earlier movements, Land and Freedom sought to utilize the talents of all, liberal and radical, who volunteered to fight tsardom. Some were to propagandize peaceably among students and laborers or establish contacts with dissident groups such as the Old Believers. Others were to organize riots and strikes or urge people to refuse payment of taxes or avoid military service. Still others specialized in counterfeiting passports. Those with no patience for such prosaic work joined the "disorganizing" section, whose assignment it was to work the assassination of government officials. The chief of the secret police and the governor-general of Kharkov were murdered; the military governor of St. Petersburg was seriously wounded; and attempts on the tsar's life barely missed. Every arrest, every trial, every execution of a revolutionary was countered by a new act of terror.

There were squeamish men in the Land and Freedom movement, however, who had no stomach for blood-letting, and the organization split into two factions. One, calling itself "Land Partition," aimed at working openly and without force for the distribution of public lands and great estates among the peasants. Ineffective in winning support, it soon evaporated. The other, "The People's Will," carried on the relentless war against officialdom but came quickly to concentrate its attention upon the assassination of the tsar. After a half dozen failures the group succeeded, and Alexander fell badly mangled by a home-made bomb.

The reform and revolutionary movements in the reign of Alexander II continued to reflect the two extremes which had appeared among the Decembrists in the time of the first Alexander. One segment of Russian thought and action, Fabian in its approach, sought by education and peaceful propaganda to win popular support for continued reform and hoped to convert the government to such a policy. Men of such conviction were inclined to place their confidence in the peasants and to concentrate upon the problem of land reform to the exclusion of all others. Opposed to these moderates were the radicals, who despaired both of government sincerity in carrying through fundamental reforms and of peasant support for the revolution which alone could rid the nation of its Asiatic wretchedness and oppression. Such men and women came round to the view that only among the working class in the cities could they find appreciation of the need for thoroughgoing social revolution. And these radicals were naïvely confident that terror and assassination could sweep away the old regime.

RUSSIA IN THE FAR EAST

The boundary between Russia and China had been fixed by the Treaty of Nerchinsk in 1689 along the peak of the Stanovoi Mountains, from north of the Amur River to their approach to the Sea of Okhotsk. Further Russian pressure in eastern Asia had thus been channeled toward the northeast corner of the continent. The Kamchatka peninsula was soon occupied and the port of Petropavlovsk opened near its tip. By the middle of the following century Russian merchants had landed in the Aleutians and Alaska in search of the rich furs which the area offered. The Russian-American Company, chartered in 1798, was granted a monopoly of trade in Alaska, and an ambitious director extended the company's influence as far south as California, building a trading post just forty miles north of San Francisco.

Russia made no serious attempt to encroach upon Chinese territory until 1847, when Nicholas Muravev was named governor-general of eastern Siberia. Accepting his appointment as a challenge to expand Russian influence in the area, he sent parties into the forbidden Amur Valley and others to land in Sakhalin and the Kuriles. Only three years after landing in eastern Siberia he established the port town of Nikolaievsk at the mouth of the

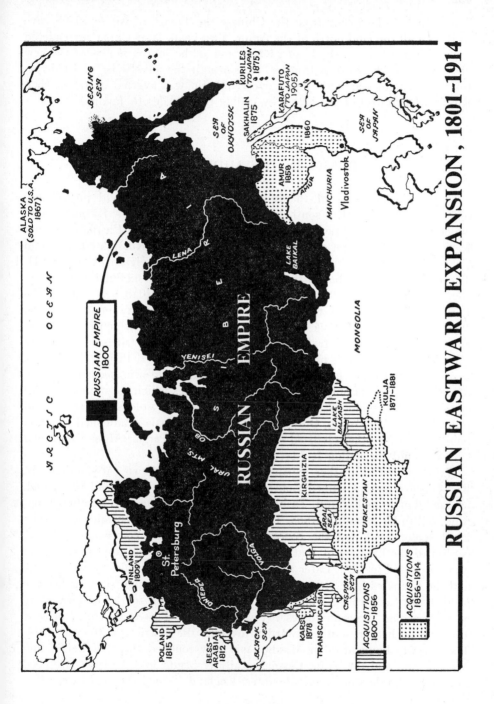

RUSSIAN EASTWARD EXPANSION, 1801–1914

ARCTIC OCEAN

BERING SEA

ALASKA (SOLD TO U.S.A. 1867)

RUSSIAN EMPIRE 1800

LENA

YENISEI

OB

URAL MTS.

RUSSIAN EMPIRE

LAKE BAIKAL

SEA OF OKHOTSK

KURILES (TO JAPAN 1875)

KARAFUTO (TO JAPAN 1905)

SAKHALIN 1875

AMUR 1858

AMUR

1860

MANCHURIA

Vladivostok

SEA OF JAPAN

MONGOLIA

KULJA 1871–1881

LAKE BALKASH

KIRGHIZIA

ARAL SEA

TURKESTAN

St. Petersburg

VOLGA

DNIEPER

FINLAND 1809

POLAND 1815

BESS- ARABIA 1812

BLACK SEA

KARS 1878

TRANSCAUCASIA

CASPIAN SEA

ACQUISITIONS 1800–1856

ACQUISITIONS 1856–1914

431

Amur. In 1858 he wrung from the Chinese the Treaty of Aigun which gave to Russia all the land north of the Amur. Two years later China surrendered the entire east bank of the Ussuri River, and at the southern edge of the new province, near the Korean frontier, Russia built the naval base of Vladivostok. A threat of war with Japan over Sakhalin was averted in 1875, when Russia won control of the island by ceding the Kuriles to Japan.

RUSSIA IN THE MIDDLE EAST

In the closing years of the reign of Nicholas Russia had pushed her Siberian frontier farther south by conquering the nomadic Kazakh tribes which roamed the steppe between the northern end of the Caspian Sea and Lake Balkash. This first step set off a chain reaction of Russian conquests in Central Asia which continued through and beyond the reign of Alexander II. The wild mountain tribes of the eastern Caucasus were subdued as the Russian boundary moved down the west coast of the Caspian Sea to meet the Persian border. East of that sea the Russian frontier lay up against the Moslem khanates of Khiva, Bokhara, and Kokand, from which raiders were wont to seize Russian traders or attack the Kazakh tribesmen recently brought under the tsar's protection. The foreign minister, Prince Gorchakov, insisted to the other great powers that Russia could win security on the Middle Asian border only by subduing the khanates which constantly pressed against it; he reminded the powers that their own colonial histories had followed a similar course. Only, he argued, when Russia established common boundaries with other civilized states in the area—Persia, Afghanistan, and China—could the nation feel secure.

Having justified further expansion, at least to its own satisfaction, the Russian government named General Michael Cherniaev to lead the attack on the khanate of Kokand. Tashkent, with a population of a hundred thousand, fell to his assault in 1865. Three years later the ancient city of Samarkand surrendered and the conquest of Kokand was complete. Bokhara, capital of the khanate of that name, was stormed in the same year. Khiva was conquered in 1873. Later revolts in the area were ruthlessly suppressed, and the khanates were either incorporated into the Russian state or became protectorates controlled from St. Petersburg. Turning to the eastern shore of the Caspian, Russian forces overwhelmed the Turcoman tribes of that area and pushed on southeastward to overrun the district of Merv in 1884. The Russian boundaries in Middle Asia now touched those of Persia and Afghanistan, and the Trans-Caspian Railway begun in 1879 soon stretched to the very borders of those two states. England seemed justified in her fear that Russia was threatening India.

RUSSIA AND THE GREAT POWERS

The Crimean War and the humiliating peace which terminated it forced Alexander II to reconsider Russia's relations with the European powers. England, whom Nicholas I had hoped to make his ally, had been most responsible for pushing Turkey into the war and had held out at its close for the most punitive terms against Russia. Austria, whose dynasty Nicholas had defended against revolution in 1849, had maintained a malevolent neutrality throughout the war and had threatened an invasion of South Russia unless the tsar accepted the Allied peace terms. France, which Nicholas hated as a breeding ground of revolution and whose ruler he held in contempt, had been most friendly to Russia at the conference table and had threatened to sign a separate peace unless Britain agreed to compromise. Prussia, ruled by a brother-in-law of Nicholas I, had stood aside from the conflict but had shown such sympathy for the Russian cause that she was invited to participate in the peace conference only after all the debatable points had been settled.

Prince Alexander Gorchakov, charged with the conduct of Russian foreign relations after 1856, worked hard to bring about cordial relations with France. The two nations agreed on the union of Moldavia and Wallachia in the principality of Romania, a move opposed by England and Austria on the ground that the new principality might become a Russian satellite. A palace revolution in Serbia which brought a pro-Russian dynasty to the throne received France's blessing. France and Russia cooperated in abetting a Montenegrin attack upon Turkey. When France went to war against Austria in support of Sardinia's bid to unify Italy, Alexander II hamstrung the Austrian war effort by posting a threatening force on the Austro-Russian frontier. The tsar was never really happy with the friendship of France, however. To countenance the upstart Napoleon III was almost too much for the legitimist Alexander II to carry off with good grace. The tsarina would have nothing to do with the French empress when their husbands met for conversations in Stuttgart in 1857. Any illusion that Franco-Russian understanding could last long was dispelled when Napoleon tried to arrange an international conference to intercede for Poland in the uprising of 1863. The tsar would brook no interference in what he considered a domestic problem.

Prussia's relations with Russia, consistently cordial throughout the reign of Nicholas I, improved steadily after the Crimean War. Otto von Bismarck, Prussian ambassador in St. Petersburg from 1859 to 1862, did his best to steer Russia away from a close tie with France and to capitalize on the good will that existed between the tsar and his uncle, William I of Prussia. When nearly every state in Europe joined France in pleading the Polish cause in

1863 Bismarck, as Prussian chancellor, not only refused to criticize Russia but offered to permit the passage of Russian troops through Prussia if necessary to put down the Polish rebellion. That Prussia could hardly condone an uprising that might spread to her own Polish provinces did not lessen the tsar's gratitude for his uncle's support. When Prussia and Austria seized the Danish duchies of Schleswig and Holstein in 1864, Russia raised no objection and even threatened to mass troops on the Swedish frontier if Sweden should offer to support Denmark. Prussia and Austria fought over the division of the spoils and after the Prussian victory both duchies were added to Prussia. Again St. Petersburg did not protest, although many in the Russian capital questioned the wisdom of permitting the growth of a strong Germany. When in 1870 Bismarck was planning a war with France to complete the unification of Germany, Alexander II gave his word of neutrality in the coming conflict and promised to mobilize against Austria should the latter offer aid to France.

In the midst of the Franco-German War Russia notified the other great powers that the Black Sea clauses of the Treaty of Paris of 1856 would no longer operate. Since Germany backed Russia in the abrogation, there was nothing the other powers could do but acquiesce. Henceforth Russia as well as Turkey was to be free to station war vessels on the Black Sea and to provide on its shores the naval establishments necessary to maintain them.

Bismarck had worked persistently to prevent Russia's alignment with either France or Austria. The latter possibility was remote, considering the display of Habsburg ingratitude during the Crimean War, and a Franco-Russian alliance was much less likely than the German chancellor feared. After the defeat of France in 1871, however, and the French clamor for revenge that followed, Bismarck sought to insure Germany's gains at the Peace of Frankfort by diplomatically isolating France. In 1872 the emperors of Russia, Austria, and Germany drew together in an entente, and a year later Russia and Germany signed a mutual-defense pact committing each to assist the other in the event of an attack by a third power. The agreement of the three emperors to work together toward the solution of common problems was soon brought to the test in the Near East.

PAN-SLAVISM

Ever since the Treaty of Kuchuk-Kainardji in 1774 Russian rulers had assumed the right to protect Christians in the Ottoman Empire, particularly in the Balkan Peninsula. The Porte and the Western powers, however, insisted that the right extended only over the Serbs and the Romanians. Nicholas I had held to the broader view and had gone to the assistance of the Greeks in part because of their Orthodoxy.

After the disappointment of the Crimean War many Slavophiles began to think of compensating for the Russian defeat by extending Russian influence over all other Slavic peoples, of freeing those peoples from subservience to Turkey and the Western powers. To such Pan-Slavs, the incorporation of all Slavs into the Russian Empire was necessary to Holy Russia's defense against the West, not only in a politico-military sense, but even more in a cultural sense. Narrower Pan-Slavs, like Ivan Aksakov, clung to the Slavophile tenet that Orthodoxy was the only true Christianity and that Russia should spread her mantle only over Orthodox Slavs. Another problem which divided the Pan-Slavs was whether the Slavic nationalities should band together in a federation allowing local autonomy or be welded into a single strong power under Russian domination. To those who held the latter view, Pan-Slavism was simply Russian imperialism in the Near East. Tsardom must extend its boundaries to the Straits, to the Aegean, and to the Adriatic.

Pan-Slavs of all persuasions were extremely sensitive to disturbances in the Balkans. Some would rush to the assistance of oppressed peoples in the peninsula simply or primarily to relieve their coreligionists or support their cousin Slavs. Others not so high-minded would use any unrest in the area as an excuse to push Russian influence or control nearer the strategically important seas. The reason for Pan-Slav interest in the Near East is less important than the fact that Pan-Slavs of one stripe or another were influential at court, in the army, and in the press from the mid-nineteenth century to the end of the monarchy. The tsar's occasional opposition to their ideas did not prevent such individuals from stirring up incidents which embarrassed, even if they did not overtly involve, the administration.

A RUSSO-TURKISH WAR

Uprisings in Bosnia and Herzegovina in 1875 threatened to spread among all the Balkan Christians languishing under the sultan's misrule. Since the powers signatory to the Treaty of Paris a generation earlier had guaranteed the integrity of Turkey, the revolt called forth prompt action. The Russian, Austrian, and German governments, with French and Italian support, called upon the sultan to ease the tax burden upon the rebels, to assure equal treatment of Christians and Moslems before the law, to clean up the rotten police administration in the area, and to provide representation of both groups in local government. The sultan, cocksure of British support against the other powers, spurned the advice, whereupon Serbia and Montenegro declared war upon Turkey. The Bulgars joined their fellow Christians and mounted a pitifully weak attack, only to be butchered with a savagery that stirred the world to protest.

Pan-Slav circles in Russia pledged their services and their purses to the support of their Orthodox brothers in the Balkans at the very moment when the tsar's government was acting with admirable restraint in full co-operation with Berlin and Vienna. In defiance of the tsar's orders a hot-headed Pan-Slav Russian general, Cherniaev, accepted command of the Serbian Army. When the Serbs were defeated and the small nation threat-ened with annihilation, the Russian government stepped in and forced an armistice. During the lull in the fighting the great powers—Russia, Austria, Germany, Great Britain, France, and Italy—called upon Turkey to grant autonomy to Bulgaria and Bosnia and Herzegovina under Christian gov-ernors. Confident that Britain, suspicious of Russia, would support him in a showdown, the sultan rejected the proposal. Russia obtained Romanian con-sent for the passage of troops through her neighbor's territory in return for a promise to respect Romanian integrity, and in June, 1877, the Russian armies passed the Danube. Austria had earlier consented to the Russian attack upon Turkey on condition that no large independent Slavic state be created in the peninsula. Romania, Serbia, and Montenegro soon joined in the holy war against the forces of Islam.

The Russian General Gurko crossed the Bulgarian plain, seized Shipka Pass in the Balkan Mountains, and threatened to drive on to Constantinople. Then the Russian advance collapsed in the face of pressure on its flank from the fortress of Plevna under the command of Osman Pasha. Repeated Russian efforts to storm the stronghold were hurled back. Plevna was finally starved into submission by a strangling siege which the Turkish general, outnumbered three to one, was unable to break. In biting cold temperatures and blinding blizzards the Russians crossed the Balkan Mountains in Jan-uary, 1878, and pressed on to the shores of the Sea of Marmara. The British fleet, standing off the Dardanelles since the early days of the war, threatened to steam to the Bosporus if the Turkish capital were occupied. The com-batants agreed to an armistice, and a month later, in March, 1878, they signed the abortive Treaty of San Stefano.

The corruption and mismanagement in the Russian army and govern-ment were exceeded only by the corruption and mismanagement which marked the Turkish defense. The orders of the Russian military leaders were debated and countermanded by the tsar's brothers, who nominally commanded, and the tsar's presence at headquarters only increased the confusion. Bickering and petulance among the grand dukes and their toadies hampered the faulty leadership of the generals, whose military prowess was put to shame by that of their Turkish counterparts. Medical service was pitifully inadequate. Russian rifles and cannon were obsolete and the troops, short of ammunition as supply broke down, moved against prepared defenses with the bayonet. "In the end the Russian colossus demoralized and crushed its opponent by sheer weight and pressure (Langer)."

By the terms of the Treaty of San Stefano Turkey recognized the complete independence of Serbia, Romania, and Montenegro; ceded sizable blocks of territory to Serbia and Montenegro; surrendered to Russia—in addition to the Asian towns of Ardahan, Kars, and Batum—the Dobrudja south of the Danube, which Russia arranged to exchange with Romania for southern Bessarabia; promised reforms in the government of Bosnia and Herzegovina; and agreed to pay Russia a cash indemnity. Most alarming to the great powers was the creation of an autonomous Bulgaria with an elected Christian prince who would vaguely acknowledge Turkish suzerainty, the new state to extend from the Danube River south to the Aegean, east to the Black Sea, and west to the Serbian and Albanian frontiers. Turkey would be nearly squeezed off the European continent, retaining only Thrace, Salonika, and Albania. Fifty thousand Russian troops would occupy Bulgaria for two years, ostensibly to help the new state to its feet.

THE CONGRESS OF BERLIN

While the borders of the new principality quite accurately approximated Bulgarian ethnic limits, the other powers, particularly Great Britain and Austria-Hungary, refused to accept the creation of this extensive Slav state which might reasonably be expected to become a Russian satellite. British troops were hurried from India to Malta, and the Austrian army prepared to march to prevent the execution of the Russo-Turkish treaty. Bismarck, insisting that Germany was impartial and disinterested in the threatening tension, proffered his services as "an honest broker," and invited the powers to Berlin to consider revision of the treaty.

At Berlin the powers scrapped the Treaty of San Stefano and replaced it with a document both punitive and humiliating to Russia. Great Britain and Austria insisted that the greater Bulgaria sketched out at San Stefano be carved up. The principality was trimmed to one-third its former size, filling roughly the area between the Danube and the Balkan Mountains. Another third of the former Bulgaria, now called Eastern Rumelia, was given autonomy under a Christian prince appointed by the sultan and responsible to him. The final third of Bulgarian territory was returned to Turkey. Bosnia and Herzegovina were to be occupied and administered "temporarily" by Austria, although theoretically they still belonged to Turkey. Thirty years later the temporary occupation came to an end and these two Serbian districts were annexed outright to Austria. The rich province of Southern Bessarabia, inhabited largely by Romanians, went to Russia, a disposition which long embittered Russo-Romanian relations. Romania was compensated with the miserably poor land of Dobrudja south and east of the Danube. Romania, Serbia, and Montenegro were recognized as independent. Disraeli pocketed Cyprus for England.

The Russians had gone to Berlin fully confident that, in return for their support of Prussia in 1871, they could count upon Germany's support. However, Bismarck and Gorchakov, the head of the Russian delegation, were bitter personal enemies, and the German chancellor threw his influence behind England and Austria at every turn. The Russians left the congress feeling wronged and cheated, and blamed Bismarck and Germany for their diplomatic defeat. Slavophiles at home spoke out bitterly against the tsar for accepting such terms, for San Stefano had been cheered as a victory of Greek Orthodoxy over the infidel and of Slavdom over the hated Turk.

THE REVIVAL OF THE AUSTRO-RUSSO-GERMAN ENTENTE

On his return to St. Petersburg the Russian foreign minister, Gorchakov, announced his opinion that German perfidy at Berlin had brought to an end the understanding among the three eastern empires which had existed since 1872. The Slavophile press joined him in heaping vituperation upon Austria and Germany, and particularly upon Bismarck. Alexander II wrote his uncle, the kaiser, charging him with ingratitude. Many urged that Russia go her way alone, avoiding alliances that were not dependable.

Soon after the Congress of Berlin the aging Gorchakov went into retirement, and the direction of foreign affairs fell to his assistant, Nicholas Giers. Whereas Gorchakov's handling of foreign relations was always colored by his personal feelings, Giers handled the Foreign Office with a cold detachment that served Russian interests better than had his predecessor's heat. The new minister understood that Russia's real enemy was not Germany but Great Britain, who stood unswervingly athwart Russian advances in the Balkans, in Turkey, and in the Middle East. Giers won the tsar's consent to press for a Russo-German alliance. Since Germany had recently signed a defensive agreement with Austria, Bismarck suggested a league of the emperors of Austria, Germany, and Russia. Alexander II agreed to such an alliance, but the formal treaty was not concluded until after his death.

ASSASSINATION OF THE TSAR

Alexander II had carried the nation into war against Turkey with the enthusiastic support of the vast majority of his people. But once victorious war had ended in ignominious peace he quickly lost that support. And while the Bulgars received a constitution at the hands of their liberator, the Russian tsar, there was no letup in the police-state rule which that same tsar imposed upon his own people.

The revolutionary movement flared anew. "The People's Will," under its brilliant organizer Alexander Mikhailov, returned to the attack upon officialdom. The chief of the infamous Third Section, the security police, was shot in broad daylight, and the assassin escaped abroad to boast of his achievement. The chief's successor died similarly. The governor of Kharkov province was struck down. Vera Zasulich, daughter of a noble, fired point-blank at General Trepov, the military governor of St. Petersburg. One high official after another fell under an assassin's bullets, and the government's ruthless persecutions only called forth new acts of violence.

During the last two years of the reign the revolutionaries concentrated their efforts upon the life of the tsar, and his death sentence was blatantly published for all to see. Mines were laid under bridges over which the imperial coach should pass, but either the mines failed to explode or the emperor's carriage took another route. Railroad tracks over which the tsar was scheduled to move were blown up, but Alexander miraculously escaped. A worker smuggled dynamite into the imperial palace and detonated it at the moment the tsar was to sit down to dinner with a foreign guest. But the visitor's train was late and Alexander was not in the dining room when the explosion occurred. The tsar had become a fugitive, not only in his own empire, but even in his own palace.

The revolutionaries, growing more desperate the more they were disappointed, met frequently to practice throwing bombs, and organized small groups to line routes the tsar might take when he ventured abroad. On a Sunday early in March, 1881, Alexander's carriage passed along one of the prepared routes. Sophia Perovsky, a nobleman's daughter, signaled with her handkerchief for her friend Rysakov to hurl his bomb. The explosion wounded some Cossacks riding in attendance, and the tsar alighted to express his sympathy, thanking God that he was not hurt. "It is too early to thank God," shouted another of the revolutionaries, and hurled his bomb at the tsar's feet. Alexander, horribly mangled, was carried back to the palace to die.

The leaders of "The People's Will" were captured and six of them, including Sophia Perovsky, died on the gallows. "The most striking feature of the whole story seems the fact that a few dozen brave and ruthless people were able to defy the largest police force in the world and to kill the most powerful and best-guarded autocrat" (Seton-Watson).

LORIS-MELIKOV'S PLAN

The extremists were not alone in opposing the benighted reaction of the government. While the dedicated assassins in "The People's Will" looked to the tsar's murder as the spark which would ignite a general rising, less violent men hoped that reform could be brought about by an urgent appeal to the ruler. When the government called upon the people to have done with lawlessness, several zemstvo assemblies in effect answered that the government had been as guilty of lawlessness as had the revolutionaries. Conference after conference of zemstvo men asked the tsar to revive the reforms of the sixties, to replace the courts-martial with civil courts, and to grant freedom of speech and press and assembly. The answer to the revolutionaries was not further repression, they reasoned, but an extension to the people of the means by which they might freely and in full legality plead the cause of reform. But the government paid no heed to these sincere liberals. The arrests, the floggings, and the executions went on.

After the bombing of the imperial dining room in February, 1880, Alexander established a Supreme Commission under the chairmanship of General Loris-Melikov to deal with the mounting danger of revolution. With one hand the general tightened police controls, but with the other he offered some concessions to zemstvo opinion. The brutal Third Section was abolished, and internal security became the task of the minister of interior. The reactionary minister of education, Dmitry Tolstoy, was sent into retirement, and there was some relaxation in press censorship. These modest gestures pleased neither the conservatives, who considered them dangerously liberal, nor the radicals, who aimed at a thoroughgoing revamping of society. "The People's Will" sought to assassinate Loris-Melikov, but without success. The Supreme Commission sat only a few months, but its chairman stayed on as minister of interior.

More constructive than the mild measures initiated by the Supreme Commission was the plan Loris-Melikov proposed for bringing elected representatives of the people into consultation with government to suggest ways of completing and clarifying the great reforms. He suggested that zemstvos and town councils choose delegates to sit with appointed officials in a national commission to advise the Council of State on administrative and financial reform. He was not suggesting a legislature, nor was he proposing anything like a constitution. The step, had it been taken, would have been a significant one, nevertheless. That elected representatives of the Russian people should have even a consultative, advisory voice in national matters would have been a radical departure from current governmental practice.

A few hours before his assassination Alexander II signed his approval of Loris-Melikov's plan. Whether his wish would be carried out would depend upon the will of the new tsar. To withdraw the plan might imply the son's disrespect for his father. On the other hand, to allow its promulgation might seem to condone the radical pressures which had forced Alexander II to appoint Loris-Melikov. Not to reject the plan might be interpreted by the revolutionaries themselves as a sign of weakness which they would surely exploit.

SUGGESTED READING

Berdyaev, N., *The Origins of Russian Communism* (New York, Scribner's, 1937).

Cambridge History of Poland (New York, Macmillan, 1941).

Carr, E. H., *Michael Bakunin* (New York, Macmillan, 1937).

Dallin, D. J., *The Rise of Russia in Asia* (New Haven, Yale University Press, 1949).

Footman, D., *Red Prelude* (New Haven, Yale University Press, 1944).

Kennan, G., *Siberia and the Exile System* (New York, Century, 1891).

Kohn, H., *Pan-Slavism* (Notre Dame, University of Notre Dame Press, 1953).

Kropotkin, P. A., *Memoirs of a Revolutionist* (New York, Houghton-Mifflin, 1930).

Kucharzewski, J., *The Origins of Modern Russia* (New York, Polish Institute of Arts and Sciences, 1948).

Langer, W. L., *European Alliances and Alignments* (New York, Knopf, 1931).

Lobanov-Rostovsky, A. A., *Russia and Asia,* rev. ed. (Ann Arbor, George Wahr, 1951).

Lossky, N. O., *History of Russian Philosophy* (New York, International Universities Press, 1951).

Maynard, J., *Russia in Flux* (New York, Mamcillan, 1948).

Seton-Watson, H., *The Decline of Imperial Russia, 1855–1914* (New York, Praeger, 1952).

Seton-Watson, R. W., *The Rise of Nationality in the Balkans* (London, Constable, 1917).

Sumner, B. H., *Russia and the Balkans, 1870–1880* (New York, Oxford University Press, 1937).

Taylor, A. J. P., *The Struggle for Mastery in Europe* (Oxford, Clarendon, 1954).

Zenkovsky, V. V., *History of Russian Philosophy* (New York, Columbia University Press, 1953).

23

The Tsar of Peace

ALEXANDER III (1881–1894) TORN BE-
tween loyalty to his father and hatred for the radicalism that had been
responsible for his father's murder, decided against executing the Loris-
Melikov plan which Alexander II had signed on the morning of his assassination. Setting himself firmly against any action that might suggest appease-
ment of those who called for reform, the new tsar immediately announced
his complete confidence in the autocracy and his determination to defend
it.

Taking his cues from archconservatives and particularly from his tutor,
Constantine Pobiedonostsev, the emperor proceeded further to emasculate
the reforms of the sixties. The form of local political institutions was allowed to continue, but the substance was so altered as to make a mockery
of them. The bureaucrats tightened the censorship of the press, swept
away whatever of self-government the universities had enjoyed for a generation, restricted admission to secondary schools, and even brought primary
education under strict government surveillance. Vicious persecution of dissenters and a studied policy of anti-Semitism were aimed at forcing religious
conformity upon the nation.

Agricultural distress became acute as the shortage of land in rural Russia
grew steadily more alarming. New areas came under cultivation and Siberia
offered some opportunity to those who could leave the settled areas, but
population grew more rapidly than did the outlets to relieve the pressure.
New industries rose in the towns and old ones grew in size. Foreign capital
came slowly into Russia, and the government invested heavily in railroad
construction and mining development. But the nation remained far behind

Central and Western Europe, not only in the volume of her industrial output, but in the growth of production techniques and skills.

The government sought to stimulate capitalist enterprise by subsidy, by protective tariffs, and by curbing the restlessness of city labor. The first factory reforms sought mildly to improve conditions of work. But to strike was illegal, for the government had a horror of resistance to authority lest it lead to political action against itself.

Russia joined with Germany and Austria in the League of the Three Emperors, and so escaped the isolation which she had felt keenly after the Russo-Turkish War. Continued friendly relations with Austria proved impossible, however, as the two came to friction in the Balkans. A Russian attempt to turn the recently-freed Bulgaria into a satellite failed utterly, and Pan-Slav intrigue in the Balkans made enemies rather than friends. With the breakdown of the alliance with Germany and Austria, and with the failure to remain closely bound with Germany alone, Russia once more faced isolation. The Franco-Russian alliance cemented a strange friendship that would last to the end of the dynasty. The reign spans the longest period in Russian history to know no serious war.

THE PAN-SLAV AUTOCRAT

Alexander III, his father's second son, was thirty-six years old at the time of his accession. A man of giant stature and powerful physique, he was proud of his ability to tie an iron poker in knots or straighten horseshoes with his bare hands. His obstinacy and violent temper, coupled with his fabulous strength, made him a dangerous man to those near him when he flew into a rage. Awkward, shy, and reticent, he was uncomfortable in court society and preferred the informal intimacy of his family circle, where he played the bassoon in the family orchestra. His morals were above reproach, at least after his marriage—something of a novelty among the Romanovs. He was honest and industrious to the point of insisting upon reading every document he signed. His early training had not aimed at preparing him for the throne, for his older brother lived until Alexander was twenty. To his tutors he must have seemed as impervious to education as his grandfather, Nicholas I, whom he resembled in so many ways. A man of no imagination and extremely modest intellect, he lacked the mind to deal with the problems which faced the nation. But at least he recognized his limitations and left many decisions to his ministers.

Alexander's chief tutor, Constantine Pobiedonostsev, sometime professor of law at the University of Moscow, had helped to draft the judicial reforms of 1864. Since then he had lost all sympathy for reform and had grown steadily more conservative. As procurator-general of the Holy Synod from

1880 to 1905, he became the symbol throughout this reign and into the succeeding one of stubborn, blind reaction. As chief adviser, he dominated the mind and the actions of Alexander III. An uncompromising foe of Western liberalism, he held up to derisive scorn freedom of press and religion and jury trial, and referred to parliamentary government as "the great lie of our time." Russia's salvation, he swore, lay in clinging to her native Slavic institutions, to be safeguarded by autocracy, Orthodoxy, and nationalism.

From Pobiedonostsev and his friend Michael Katkov, the rabid Slavophile editor of the *Moscow Gazette,* Alexander III took his cues. Suspicious of liberalism of any sort, he had fought the softer touch of Loris-Melikov in the closing months of his father's reign and looked upon the assassination as proof of the fallacy of such a policy. An enthusiastic communicant in the Russian Orthodox church—he kept strict account of the number of church services he attended each year—he could not be expected to ameliorate the persecution of the sects. Anti-Austrian, anti-British, anti-French, anti-German—his Danish wife was the first non-German consort of a Russian ruler since Peter the Great—the tsar was by his own inclination an ardent nationalist. He was sympathetic toward Pan-Slavism, which amounted to the extension of Slavophilism into the field of foreign affairs, although it contained some tenets to which he could not subscribe. He would look with favor upon the freeing of South or West Slav peoples from German, Hungarian, or Turkish rule. But he frowned upon the democratic tendencies of some of the Balkan Slavs. And he was suspicious of all non-Orthodox Slavs. Pan-Slavism to him, as to Pobiedonostsev and Katkov and Count Nicholas Ignatiev, who had dictated the Treaty of San Stefano, meant that all Slav states should follow the Russian lead in autocracy, Orthodoxy, and nationalism.

COUNTER-REFORM MEASURES

One week after his father's murder Alexander III called together his ministers and Pobiedonostsev to decide the fate of Loris-Melikov's proposal that representatives of the people should be asked to advise the government on financial and administrative reform. Loris-Melikov and Miliutin, the liberal war minister, urged that the proposal be adopted but were forced to defend it as in no way introducing a constitutional regime. Pobiedonostsev attacked the scheme as a subtle way of bringing on parliamentary limitation of the autocracy; he thundered that this would mean the end of Russia. As usual, the tutor had his way with his royal pupil, and Alexander decided against accepting the proposal which his father had signed. The liberal ministers immediately resigned to be replaced by men nominated by Pobiedonostsev.

The procurator-general of the Holy Synod was then given the job of drafting the imperial manifesto which would announce to the nation the course which the new emperor would follow. In it Alexander avowed his "complete faith in the strength and truth of the autocracy," and swore that "for the good of the people" he would "maintain and defend the autocratic power against attack."

The new minister of interior, Count Ignatiev, opened his brief term of office by cracking down on the liberal press and preparing a law allowing the government to declare a state of emergency—in effect, martial law— to deal with local unrest in any designated district. Administrators of any locality assigned emergency status had the authority arbitrarily to fine, imprison, seize property, remove officials, close schools, curtail publications, or transfer cases from civil to military courts. Announced as a temporary measure, the vicious law remained in operation until 1917.

Ignatiev next appointed a committee of experts to submit recommendations on the reorganization of local government, reform of the police system, and reduction of peasant dues. Several zemstvo assemblies protested that the committee should include elected representatives of the people, but the protest went unheeded.

Like many Slavophiles, Ignatiev had little confidence in the bureaucracy, which seemed to constitute a barrier between the tsar and his people. He and his Slavophile friend Aksakov conceived the idea of reviving the *Zemskii Sobor* of the sixteenth and seventeenth centuries. This assembly would consist of some three thousand delegates elected to represent the various classes in society including the peasants. It would have no right to initiate or even to pass upon legislation, but would gather at odd times to be lectured by the tsar or his ministers. The bureaucracy, product of Western influence introduced by Peter the Great and strengthened through the eighteenth and nineteenth centuries, would be bypassed; the contact between the ruler and his faithful subjects would be restored in the *Zemskii Sobor*. The growing clamor for representation in government would be stilled and the danger avoided that the parliamentarianism of the radical West might creep into Holy Russia.

But the scheme of the Slavophiles Ignatiev and Aksakov ran into the bitter opposition of the Slavophiles Katkov and Pobiedonostsev. The latter warned the emperor that this was but another attempt to lead the nation into a constitutional regime. Upon Pobiedonostsev's advice Alexander dismissed Ignatiev and replaced him with the safely conservative Dmitry Tolstoy, minister of education in the preceding reign. As minister of interior Tolstoy followed a policy of uncompromising reaction until his death in 1889, and his successor, Durnovo, followed the same policy.

Tolstoy drafted three statutes to reorganize local government, the aim of which was to undo or to cripple the reforms of the sixties. An 1889 act abolished the justice of the peace and placed the peasant township under a new official, the land captain, who served as both judge and administrator of the township. He had to be a member of the landowning nobility, chosen by the minister of interior, to whom he was responsible, from a list drawn up by the provincial governor and marshals of the nobility. Township elders, formerly elected by the township assembly, were now appointed by the land captain, who could discharge peasant officials at will, fine and arrest peasants without trial, and abrogate enactments of the township assembly. "A sham self-government was preserved, yet peasant Russia was actually ruled by petty officials drawn from the midst of the landed nobility and controlled by the minister of the interior" (Florinsky).

The Zemstvo Act of 1890 amended the Act of 1864 by arranging those entitled to vote for members of county zemstvo assemblies into three classes: nobles, peasants, and all others. Township meetings nominated candidates from which the provincial governor selected men to represent the peasants in the county assembly. The right to vote in non-peasant categories was limited to real estate owners, and Jews were denied the vote entirely. Fifty-seven per cent of the seats in county and provincial assemblies went to the nobility; 30 per cent to the peasants; the remainder to "the others." The provincial governor could veto, suspend, or amend enactments of the zemstvo assembly at will and approved all officials, even teachers and doctors, named by the zemstvo.

The Municipal Act of 1892 retained the machinery of the Act of 1870, but tightened property qualifications and so reduced the electorate in most cases to a third or less its size under the earlier act. Jews were disfranchised except in the Pale, where they were allowed only 10 per cent of the membership of the municipal council. City officials were responsible to the minister of interior, and matters handled by city governments were sternly curtailed. Those few citizens who could share in city government showed an increasing lack of interest in civic improvement. At the opening of the twentieth century there were many municipalities in Russia with a population running into thousands or tens of thousands which had no hospital or primary school financed from city funds.

During the decade of the eighties the court system inaugurated under the Act of 1864 came under a number of restrictions. Ignatiev's law of 1881 permitting the creation of emergency districts to deal with unrest or sedition placed such a district completely outside the court system during the period of the emergency and left the administration of justice in the area under the arbitrary control of the local administrator. In 1885 the powers of the minister of justice over judges was extended to include the right of the minister to demand an explanation of a decision handed down. Jews could be admitted to the bar only with the explicit consent of the minister of justice; only one was admitted during the first decade when this restriction was applied. The right of trial by jury was withdrawn from those who attempted to assassinate public officials, such cases coming under the jurisdiction of special courts. Justice for the peasants after 1889 came under the control of the land captain, always a member of the local landowning nobility. Curiously enough, Alexander did not abolish the jury system when urged to do so by the Slavophiles. Perhaps he felt that the care used to appoint only safe judges—or rather, deputy judges who by law enjoyed no judicial tenure—would assure that the court system would not become a threat to the autocracy.

Minister of Interior Tolstoy steadily increased restrictions on the press. After three warnings that its publication policy was contrary to the government's interest a newspaper or periodical had to submit all copy for official censorship before publication. A committee headed by the procurator-general of the Holy Synod could suspend or permanently close down any publication, and even forbid its editors to continue with any other journal.

The University Code of 1863 was repeatedly amended by bureaucratic action during the reign of the third Alexander. Under a revised code issued in 1884, university officials and professors owed their position to appointment by the minister of education rather than to election by their colleagues as under the earlier reform. Student organizations were proscribed. The enrollment of women was first curtailed and then forbidden. Admission to members of the lower classes was effectively blocked by limiting entry into the *gynmasia* to children of the gentry or government officials or wealthy merchants. Secondary school or university enrollment of Jews was limited to 10 per cent of the student body in schools in the Jewish Pale, to 5 per cent outside the Pale, and to 3 per cent in St. Petersburg and Moscow.

Even primary schools came under official scrutiny. Private schools operated by Roman Catholics or Protestants were placed under the Ministry of Education. In Poland and in the Baltic provinces instruction in even the primary grades had to be conducted in Russian, even though the language of the home in those areas might be Lithuanian, Yiddish, Polish, or German.

Religious persecution went hand in hand with the tightening of controls in other areas. Baltic Lutherans, Ukrainian Uniats, Polish Catholics, and even the Moslem tribes of Siberia were under constant pressure to give up their religion. The Dukhobors and Stundists, or Russian Baptists, particularly felt the wrath of the government because of their pacifism and resistance to military service. Regular military expeditions marched against their colonies, and their leaders were packed off to Siberia. Toward the end of the century the Dukhobors emigrated to Canada.

A rabid anti-Semite, Alexander III allowed organized pogroms against the Jews—popular uprisings often led or instigated by police officials.

"Temporary" regulations, announced in 1882 and continuing in operation to the end of the dynasty, forbade Jews to acquire rural property and closed their shops on Sunday. Jews were kept out of government office and could elect only 10 per cent of the delegates to their own city dumas. Subject to military draft, they could not obtain commissions. In effect, they were denied the practice of law. A Jew could always get around the law by bribery, and petty officials levied regular tribute from the Jewish community in return for softening the regulations against them. But Pobiedonostsev expressed the hope that a third of them would become Christian, another third emigrate, and the rest die of hunger.

Under the leadership of the hated Pobiedonostsev the government followed a policy of unmitigated persecution of religious dissenters and Russification of ethnic minorities, who were officially classed as aliens. Even the Russian Orthodox church, of which Pobiedonostsev was lay leader, suffered from the punitive policies of this archpriest of reaction. Clergymen who showed any disposition to criticize the government were required to have their sermons approved by a church censor before being allowed to deliver them. Parish priests were expected to report to the police the names of parishioners whom they suspected of subversive conduct.

AGRICULTURAL DISTRESS

The most pressing problem in rural Russia in the decades after emancipation was that of a shortage of arable land, a situation that grew progressively worse as the century wore on. The acreage of allotment land available for distribution by the village to its peasant families increased very slowly, perhaps by 10 per cent by 1905. However, the peasant population of European Russia grew by 60 per cent between 1860 and 1897. The average size of allotments per family diminished from thirty-five acres in 1877 to twenty-eight acres in 1905.

From his shrinking plot the peasant must feed and clothe his family, meet his annual redemption dues, contribute his share to village expenses, and pay taxes to the zemstvos and the national government. Added to this array was a heavy burden of indirect taxes on such items as vodka, sugar, tobacco, kerosene, and matches, and tariffs on such imports as tea, cotton, and iron. Over 90 per cent of government revenue in the reign of Alexander III came from direct and indirect taxes which fell primarily upon the peasants. The burden became simply unbearable. Often there was no money to pay taxes. Taxgatherers might go into the countryside and literally flog whole villages in an effort to wring collections from the penniless peasants. Something had to give way. The chief financial burden which the peasant could dodge or postpone was the redemption dues, and these fell steadily deeper into arrears. The government could not ignore the problem, and in 1881 and again three years later the redemption debt of former landowners' serfs was reduced. The soul tax was abolished in 1886. Such measures provided only temporary relief, however, and arrearages continued to mount. The only possible solution was a drastic reduction and finally the elimination of redemption payments, a step to which the government eventually was driven under political pressure after 1905.

Certainly, the plight of the average peasant was bad enough. But land distribution in rural Russia was extremely uneven. While the few most fortunate—one-fifth of one per cent of the peasants—belonged to villages whose allotments averaged 275 acres, nearly 30 per cent of peasant families were members of villages whose average allotment was thirteen acres, and 2 per cent lived in communities where the allotment averaged only two and a half acres.

The average allotment of all Russian peasants, thirty-five acres, was nearly four times the size of peasant holdings in Western Europe. But the peasant's yield per acre in no way compared with that of other grain farmers over the world. His wheat crop produced about nine bushels to the acre, one-fourth as much as in England and only two-thirds as much as in the United States, where farmers were notoriously profligate and wasteful of their land. Shallow ploughing and lack of fertilizer, both imposed by lack of capital, brought him little return for his labor. Even had he possessed the money for fertilizer he would have been discouraged from using it by the practice of periodic redistribution of the allotments which might pass next year to another the plot which this year he had enriched with fertilizer. Rotation of crops was impossible where his strips were intermingled with those of many others in a huge field which must be sown and harvested at the same time; furthermore, it was not practicable in view of his reliance upon one cash crop, wheat, which must provide him the wherewithal to meet his many obligations. In central Russia the land was cropped for years on end and then left fallow for several years to recover its fertility. In the black-soil provinces, where the three-field system was common practice, one-third of the arable land always lay fallow. Over much of Russia, allotment land did not provide enough grain and potatoes to feed the family and leave seed for the coming year.

Many found relief from this sorry plight in renting additional acres from the landowner, but this drove rents up sharply, leaving the tenant little profit from his enterprise. Some few managed to buy land, and a Peasants' Land Bank was established by the government in 1883 to assist in such purchases. By 1905 the peasants had bought or were buying sixty-five million acres, about one-sixth the amount they were cultivating. But competitive buying drove land prices unreasonably high, and as they rose the average peasant was squeezed out of the market for the land he needed so urgently.

Many contracted to buy land they could not pay for and so lost the part payment they had managed to make. Grain prices, determined in a world market, fell off in the 1880's and remained low through the rest of the century. But the cost of commodities the peasant needed to buy remained artificially high, for Russian manufacturers enjoyed the protection of high tariffs. The peasant was forced to sell wheat and buy rye with which he made the coarse black bread which was his staple food. The declining number of draft animals reflected the growing poverty of the countryside; in the last year of the reign of Alexander III a third of Russian farm households had no horses, while nearly another third had only one. The peasant and his wife became beasts of burden.

Some found relief from low income by hiring out to others, but wages were wretchedly low. Forty kopeks (twenty cents) a day was an average rate for work in harvest time, when wages were unusually high. Thirty rubles (fifteen dollars) a year plus subsistence, less than the American farm laborer received in a month, was normal for the worker who hired out for the year. Others trooped to the cities when work was slack in the villages, there to bid against each other for jobs in industry and consequently to depress the wage rate not only for themselves but for the city workers as well. But as industry mechanized and insisted upon year-round operation, the transient worker had to make his choice either to take his chances in the city or return to the hungry village. A worker might move his family to the factory town or send money home to his family who continued to till the land.

One avenue of escape lay open to the sturdy peasant who could break away from the village community. Some few obtained the consent of the elders to move eastward through the steppe and into Siberia. Many more left without permission. Construction of the Trans-Siberian Railway encouraged the movement, and the government even came round to lending money to those who moved to the eastern frontier. By the end of the reign of Alexander III perhaps 80,000 peasants were moving into Siberia every year, a pitifully small number from a total Russian population of 120,000,000. The rural population of European Russia was increasing at a rate fourteen times the number who emigrated.

Those who were tied to the village were never far from starvation. The terrible famine of 1891, followed by a severe cholera epidemic, affected thirty million peasants, killing them off by thousands and leaving scores of villages without a single soul. But the 1891 famine stands out only because it was more severe than those which preceded and those which followed it. Indeed, famine was endemic in the Russian countryside.

In a puny effort to reduce the threat of peasant revolt Alexander III adopted a number of relief measures. In 1881 the government ordered the completion of redemption agreements by those former serfs who had not yet worked out a solution with their landlords. Fifteen per cent of the former landowners' serfs were thus affected. In the same year blocks of state-owned lands were opened to lease by village communities, but not by individual peasants. An enactment of 1893 forbade villages to sell village land without official sanction. At the same time the redistribution of allotment land by the village came under the scrutiny of the land captain. Such mild measures were of little avail in mitigating the agricultural distress which the nation suffered. When conditions passed human endurance the peasants rose in vicious attack upon the system which held them captive. In the first seven years of the reign of Alexander III there were over three hundred uprisings of sufficient magnitude to require organized military expeditions to suppress them. Countless others were put down by local authorities. Government officials comforted themselves with the conviction that disorders had reached a stable figure, that the average number would not go beyond fifty a year, and prayed that there would be no general rising, or *Pugachevshchina*.

INDUSTRIAL PROGRESS

Emancipation of the serfs produced a decline of industries operated with serf labor and a rapid growth of those which depended upon free labor. Production in the home also fell off in favor of manufacture in mushrooming factories. The most remarkable shift from hut to factory came in the field of cotton textiles. St. Petersburg, the Moscow area, and Lodz in Poland, the most important textile-manufacturing centers, grew rapidly in population. Villagers flocked to the cities to work seasonally in a desperate effort to eke out a living that the land could not provide. Ivanovo-Voznesensk, a textile suburb of Moscow, grew from a village of slightly over a thousand people to a city thirty times that size between emancipation and the end of the century. Expansion of cotton textile production during the time of Alexander III is indicated in part by a trebling of raw cotton imports, most of which came from the United States, to a total of three hundred thousand tons. Add to this the steady growth in the production of home-grown cotton in the Trans-Caspian area, a source which fed the Moscow center particularly. Protected by a high tariff, the industry enjoyed a monopoly of the domestic market and managed to export some cotton prints to the Middle East, especially to Persia, where they competed with British textiles.

Output of the mining industry rose sharply during the same period. Russia produced one and a third million tons of coal in 1880, near five million in 1895, and more than doubled the latter figure again in the next five years. Her iron mines yielded nearly a million tons of ore in 1880, almost three times that quantity fifteen years later. More than half her output of coal and iron came from the Don-Donets basin in the south, fields developed under the direction of the Englishman, John Hughes. By 1895 the nation was producing a million tons of steel each year and over six million tons of oil, the latter entirely from the Baku fields. Her oil wells, brought in with French and British capital, outproduced those of any other nation in the world before 1900.

The construction of railroads, begun so dramatically by Nicholas I with the Moscow-St. Petersburg line, went on apace during the last decades of the nineteenth century. At the death of Nicholas the nation had boasted only a thousand *versts*, or 670 miles of track. At the accession of Alexander III the figure had risen to 14,000 miles, and during his reign another 8,000 were added. A fourth of the railway net was owned by the government, the rest by a host of small companies who fought each other for business with such cutthroat methods that the government had to step in to regulate rates, force consolidation, and buy out the weakest lines. By the turn of the century two-thirds of Russia's 35,000 miles of railroad were government-owned. A most remarkable achievement was the construction of the Trans-Siberian line, over four thousand miles in length, begun in 1891 and financed by French loans. With its completion in 1900, the vast Siberian frontier could receive a flood of immigrants from the overcrowded provinces of European Russia.

Industrial expansion was marked here, as elsewhere, by the growth of big business. By Alexander III's last year three-fourths of Russian textile workers were employed in factories whose labor force numbered over one hundred. The trend was observable as well in the paper, steel, chemical, and metal-working industries, in mining and in oil. Small operators continued, by and large, to run sugar and vodka plants, the food-processing industry, and the making of samovars, bast shoes, coarse linen, carts, and the like. But capitalistic techniques crept into even such industries as these, as craftsmen sold their products to a merchant who wholesaled the goods to retailers. At the time of the great reforms there was hardly a corporation in Russia; by the end of the century there were over seventeen hundred.

GOVERNMENT ECONOMIC POLICY

As the Industrial Revolution crept slowly into Russia it brought with it the cycle of business fluctuations which the Western world had known for a long time. The early years of the reign of Alexander III were depression years. Many factories closed down or curtailed production, and the rate of business expansion, which had been steady since emancipation, fell off sharply.

The government nurtured the nation's infant industrial plant and sought to shield it from the effects of the business cycle in a number of ways. The extension of the railway net under government ownership or subsidy freed the coal and iron interests and steel manufacturers from the vagaries of the world market. Government purchases of iron and steel for railway construction at twice the market price drove the cost of railroad building beyond all reason but guaranteed good profits to the favored firms. The tariff of 1891, fixing import duties at the highest level in the nation's history, sought to preserve the domestic market of consumers' goods as well as raw materials for Russian producers. "The Russian consumer was forced to pay for poorly made goods of domestic origin two to four times as much as similar products of a higher quality cost in Western Europe" (Lyashchenko). Taxes on the business community were kept at such low levels as to produce only one-fifteenth of the national revenue, while the peasants and town laborers in contrast probably returned four-fifths of the government's yearly income. The presence of members of the merchant class in official positions and investment of members of the gentry class in business enterprise guaranteed that government would deal softly with management.

By 1890 the industrial labor force numbered two million. Of these one fourth worked in textile mills, another fourth in metal-processing plants, and another fourth on the railroads, leaving only a half million workers in all other types of industry. As the century drew to its close the tie between urban worker and the agricultural village was dissolving. The labor force was rapidly becoming permanently committed to city dwelling, as its members gave up their allotments in the *mir* and took their chances on industrial employment.

Conditions of work in Russian factories were not standardized by law but were left to the whim of the employer. Women and children, even three-year-olds, worked along with men and slept with them in the same straw-carpeted barracks provided by the factory owner, or on the floor of the shop where they worked. Hours of work, not yet fixed by law, ran normally to fourteen a day and frequently to sixteen or eighteen for women and children as well as men. The accident rate was high as exhausted workers fell into unguarded machines and were maimed. Wages were paid annually or at irregular intervals. Men received seven dollars a month on the average, women five, and children three. Even this pittance was reduced by fines for breakage or non-appearance for work and by deductions for the worker's purchase of all provisions at the company store.

The end of the Russo-Turkish War brought an end to government orders for cotton and woolen goods, and the mill owners, particularly in the St. Petersburg area, cut wages sharply. In protest the workers went out on strike, the first important walkout in Russian history. Other strikes followed in the early 1880's, almost exclusively among textile workers asking for better pay, shorter hours, and better working conditions.

Alexander's finance minister, Nicholas Bunge, promulgated a number of factory reforms designed to meet the chief complaints of the workers. This succession of regulations forbade the employment of children under twelve; set an eight-hour maximum on the work of persons between twelve and fifteen; prohibited night work for women and youths; ordered that boys employed in factories be allowed time to attend school; defined legitimate causes for dismissal; required regular payment of wages; and made strikes illegal and encouragement to strike a grave crime. Factory inspectors responsible to the finance minister had the power to arbitrate disputes, limit fines, regulate housing of workers, inspect factories, and enforce the conditions imposed by the new regulations.

However radical Bunge's reforms may have seemed to the mill-owners, they were not inspired by any humanitarian sympathy for the plight of the workers. Officialdom hoped by meeting the worker halfway to prevent him from moving in desperation from economic to political rebellion. After 1900 such tactics reached the point where the government deliberately organized and led trade unions in the hope of controlling the labor movement. Whatever the inspiration behind the factory legislation of the 1880's, an influential segment of the business community hounded Bunge from office, and his successor, Vyshnegradsky, allowed the new laws to become practically inoperative.

Bunge carried through a number of other reforms designed to improve Russian finances and to ease the nation's transition into modern capitalism. A Peasants' Land Bank, founded in 1883, proposed to lend money, occasionally to individuals but ordinarily to village communities or cooperative groups, for the purchase of land. By 1905 nearly a third of the land retained by the gentry at the time of emancipation had been purchased by the peasants, most of it with the aid of the land bank. But the bank did nothing to relieve the land hunger of the poor peasant. Only the well-to-do peasant, the *kulak,* who already owned an extensive acreage for collateral or who could pay down a fifth of the purchase price, was likely to have his loan approved. A Nobles' Land Bank was also established to advance loans to the gentry, one-third of whose lands by 1905 were mortgaged and the payments far in arrears.

While the nation was at peace Bunge found it possible to curtail the issue of paper currency and even to begin the accumulation of a gold reserve which would some day permit Russia to go on the gold standard. Bunge juggled the state revenues by abolishing the soul tax and reducing the redemption dues, attempting to offset these losses by tightening the collection of revenue, raising the tariff, and levying a modest inheritance tax. He even considered, but did not adopt, an income tax. His successor made the sale of liquor a government monopoly, a move which brought the government one of its chief sources of income. By opening the gin shops as soon as church was out on Sunday and keeping them open on holidays the government stimulated its tax receipts by trading upon the moral debasement of the mass of the Russian people.

The economic policy of the government, like its social and political policies, was deliberately aimed at favoring the merchants and the gentry, those classes from which it drew its chief support. To the extent that any favors fell to the lower classes, they were granted only in an effort to deter the masses from political action.

The reign of Alexander III saw Russia move slowly but surely away from the feudal agrarian economy of the days of serfdom in the direction of modern capitalism. Industrially and technologically the nation would remain backward for years to come. Indeed, to the end of tsardom and beyond she would lag far behind Western Europe, intermingling even in the twentieth century much that was medieval with much that was modern. Her greatest enterprise, agriculture, retained many archaic features long after the passing of serfdom. Her industry, born and nurtured under the stifling control of bureaucratic government, would never rid itself of that paternalistic blight. But by the end of the reign there could be no turning back from the choice the nation had made to seek the position of a modern industrial power.

FOREIGN RELATIONS

The renewal of the League of the Three Emperors, allying the empires of Germany, Austria, and Russia, had been arranged before the death of Alexander II and was approved shortly thereafter. By its terms the powers agreed to remain benevolently neutral should one of them go to war with an outsider. They promised to seek agreement among themselves before sanctioning any revision of Turkey's frontiers, and each swore to consult the others on peace terms before going to war with Turkey. The three vowed to maintain the principle of closure of the Straits, a provision that assured Russia there would not be another Crimean War. Austria won the right to annex Bosnia and Herzegovina at a time of her own choosing. The three agreed not to oppose the union of Eastern Rumelia with Bulgaria if that should come about. Russia promised Germany neutrality in the event of a French attack and agreed not to disturb the *status quo* in the Balkans. The three-year agreement, whose terms were successfully kept secret until after World War I, was renewed but was allowed to lapse in 1887.

Two substantial advantages accrued to Russia by her membership in the League of the Three Emperors. The complete isolation which she had suffered immediately after the Russo-Turkish War was broken, and she won German and Austrian guarantees to maintain the closure of the Dardanelles. But improved relations with Germany and, particularly, with perfidious

Austria did not please the Pan-Slavs. Their suspicion that the government
had surrendered its freedom of action in the Balkans prompted vituperative
fulminations against the Austria that had so recently proved ungrateful and
the Germany that had wrought Russia's humiliation at the Congress of
Berlin.

The government of Bulgaria, whose autonomy was recognized by the
Treaty of Berlin, was organized under Russian guidance. The Russian-
drawn constitution established a national legislature which, at Russian
prompting, elected Alexander II's favorite nephew, Alexander of Battenberg, to rule the new principality. The "Battenberger" was assigned two
Russian generals as intimate advisers; the principality's high civil administrators were all Russians; Russian officers staffed the new Bulgarian
army; and Russian capital came in to construct the first railway. It seemed
patently clear that Bulgaria was marked for the position of a Russian
satellite, a steppingstone in Russia's projected march down the Balkan
Peninsula to the Straits.

Alexander of Battenberg was so piqued at the cavalier treatment he
received at the hands of his Russian advisers that he packed them off
home. Now the tsar's enthusiasm for the union of Eastern Rumelia with
Bulgaria waned, and when the two joined in spite of his protest he called
home the Russian officers in the Bulgarian army, leaving it stripped of all
personnel above the rank of lieutenant. Serbia, encouraged by Austria to
protest against the expansion of Bulgaria, threw an army across the Bulgarian frontier. The Bulgars surprised everyone by hurling back the Serbs
and threatening an invasion of Serbia, but were warned off by Austrian
threats.

A Russian-inspired *coup d'état* unseated the Battenberger, and the Bulgarians elected another German prince to succeed him, this time a Roman
Catholic, whose election the tsar declared to be illegal. Not until 1896, when
the new Bulgar prince embraced Greek Orthodoxy, did the Russian government recognize him. Meanwhile, Russian influence in Bulgaria had rapidly
disappeared and Russian prestige in the Balkans had suffered a serious
setback. The Slavophile press heaped opprobrium upon Foreign Minister
Nicholas Giers for having allowed the nation's influence in the Balkans
to deteriorate and, particularly, for his known friendliness to the German
powers.

Soon after the Bulgarian fiasco the alliance of the three emperors expired.
Giers worked for its renewal but the tsar overruled him. Austria's support
of the Russophobe ruler of Serbia and her role in the recent Serbo-Bulgar
affair were not to be condoned. Giers did succeed, however, in winning the
emperor's approval of a "Reinsurance Treaty" with Germany which was
signed in 1887. By its terms each power promised to remain neutral if the
other went to war with a third power; this provision would not apply,

however, if Russia attacked Turkey or Germany attacked France. Germany admitted Russia's "historic rights" in the Balkans, particularly her primary interest in Bulgaria. The two agreed that there should be no alterations in the Balkan map without their mutual consent, and Germany endorsed the dismissal of Alexander of Battenberg. Once again Germany promised to cooperate in enforcing the closure of the Straits. Bismarck had won the assurance of Russian neutrality in the event of a French attack upon Germany. Giers had won German recognition of Russia's preponderant influence in the eastern Balkans.

Assurances of German sympathy for Russia's interests in the Balkans, however, were of little value. Bismarck frankly told Giers that Germany was first and irrevocably allied with Austria, the implication being clear that if Russia and Austria should tangle anywhere Germany must side with the latter. Even before the signing of the Reinsurance Treaty England, Austria, and Italy had agreed to maintain the *status quo* in the Mediterranean, Adriatic, Aegean, and Black seas. Russia failed in her efforts to get the powers to join her in dictating the election of a new Bulgarian prince. England and Italy allied to defend the *status quo* in the Near East. These developments served notice upon Russia that further pressure into the Balkan Peninsula would not be countenanced. The Foreign Office and even the tsar admitted that the nation was checked in the area. Russian interest quickly shifted to the Far East, not to return actively to southeastern Europe for a generation.

The great accomplishment of the reign of Alexander III in the field of foreign affairs was the conclusion of a defensive alliance with France. The Reinsurance Treaty between Germany and Russia was allowed to lapse in 1890, partly because of tensions between the two countries arising out of a tariff war, partly because Bismarck, with his fear of a Franco-German war and his concern to propitiate Russia, had gone into retirement. Once more Russia was isolated, and once more Giers moved to end the fearful isolation. Since relations with England over Russian pressure in the Middle East were anything but cordial, and since Italy was allied with Austria and Germany in the Triple Alliance, France was the only possible alternative. A wedding between republican France, birthplace of revolution, and autocratic Russia, symbol of reaction, seemed fantastic; yet many Frenchmen advocated such an alliance to permit a war of revenge against Germany for the wrong done in 1871, and many Russians, particularly the Slavophiles, had long protested that the nation should ally herself against the Teuton, not with him. In 1892 the two parties exchanged vows that would not be broken until 1917.

By the terms of the alliance Russia would support France if the latter were attacked by Germany or by Italy and Germany together, while France would join Russia if the latter were attacked by Germany or by Austria and Germany together. The number of troops each would move against Germany was carefully specified, and the two agreed to staff talks to plan common action. Each swore not to accept peace without the other when and if war should come. Soon French loans poured into Russia and French rifles came in to arm the Russian soldier. Thus, within two years of Bismarck's passing an alliance directed against Germany had come to birth. Russia had been driven into opposition and France had found a friend.

The reign of Alexander III stands out as an era of peace. While there were border incidents and minor engagements in Central Asia as the glacier of Russian expansion moved slowly southward, there had never in Russian history been such a span of years without a major war. Alexander III is known to Russian historians as the "Tsar of Peace."

REVOLUTIONARY AND COUNTER-REVOLUTIONARY MOVEMENTS

The assassination of Alexander II accomplished nothing, for it displaced one reactionary only to make way for another. Indeed, it served only to alarm liberals and conservatives alike. Many liberals, shocked at the regicide, deserted reform movements that would go to such extremes. Conservatives organized a group calling itself the Holy Host which swore to defeat terror with terror against the revolutionaries. Led by a high palace official its followers cooperated with the police, organized pogroms against the Jews, and attacked radicals wherever it found them. It soon withered away, finding its work amply carried out by officialdom.

The People's Will party which had carried off the murder of Alexander II offered to stop terrorism if his successor would consent to pardon the regicides and call a representative national assembly. But the tsar would not bargain with his father's assassins. Four men and two women were hanged, some managed to escape abroad, others lived out their lives in dungeons. The party languished, ineffective, into the next reign and finally disappeared as its remaining members joined new movements. Only one serious attempt was made to assassinate Alexander III and that miscarried. For plotting it five university students, among them Lenin's brother, Alexander Ulianov, went to the gallows. On one occasion the imperial train was wrecked while trying to make too much speed on the faulty roadbed. The tsar's daughter clutched her father about the neck and sobbed, "Oh! papa dear! Now they will come and murder us all!" Even the royal children lived in constant fear of assassination.

The assassination of Alexander II and its consequences indicated to some leaders a need for reorganization and reorientation of the entire reform movement. The peasants, who would profit as much as anyone from the overthrow of the regime, took little notice of the tsar's murder. "Rural

Russia remained sullen, still and apparently unmoved" (Florinsky). Terror and assassination brought only brutal revenge.

Some of the reform leaders turned to the teachings of Karl Marx, foregoing for the time being any resort to terrorism and giving up all hope that the peasants would support any political movement. George Plekhanov, long active in the Land and Freedom movement of the seventies, fled to Switzerland and there in 1883 established the first Russian Marxist party, called the Emancipation of Labor. The new organization, expecting that Russia must first become capitalist before it could become socialist, placed its confidence in the city worker, not in the peasant as earlier movements had done. A few disciples gathered round Plekhanov in Geneva, and others more daring organized small Marxist groups among students and intellectuals in Russia. Such groups met only to discuss the writings of Marx and Engels and took no part in the labor disturbances which broke out during the eighties and early nineties. In the next reign the Russian Social Democratic party and its offshoot, the Bolshevik party, would burgeon from Plekhanov's party of Emancipation of Labor.

THE LEGACY OF THE TSAR OF PEACE

The death of Alexander III in the autumn of 1894, from overindulgence and a weak heart, left to his successor an array of problems which a ruler of far greater ability than Nicholas II would have found formidable. While the nation had known peace for nearly a generation, Russia must tread her way warily in the field of foreign relations. Tension ran high in Central Asia and was mounting in the Far East. The strain in the Balkans had eased only momentarily, and the reasons for that strain had not disappeared. The nation, no longer isolated, had found a new friend in France, but a friend whose interests might bring Russia disaster.

In the domestic area the problems which faced the new tsar were much more obvious and far more difficult to solve. How long could the autocracy endure? How long would the people abide the inefficient, corrupt and heartless bureaucracy? How long could the clamor for a national assembly be ignored? How long could the demands of labor for better pay and working conditions be refused? How long could the peasants' hunger for land go unsatisfied? In the absence of answers to these questions the fundamental question would follow: how long could the revolution be postponed? The anomaly of a nation still politically feudal advancing rapidly toward modern capitalism could not long continue. Time was running out. The new tsar must find solutions to these problems or face violent social and political upheaval.

SUGGESTED READING

Cambridge Modern History, Vol. XII, "The Latest Age" (New York, Macmillan, 1934).

Florinsky, M. T., *Russia: A History and an Interpretation* (New York, Macmillan, 1953).

Karpovich, M., *Imperial Russia, 1801–1917* (New York, Holt, 1932).

Kohn, H., *Pan-Slavism* (Notre Dame, University of Notre Dame Press, 1953).

Kornilov, A., *Modern Russian History* (New York, Knopf, 1917).

Langer, W. L., *European Alliances and Alignments, 1871–1890* (New York, Knopf, 1931).

———, *The Franco-Russian Alliance, 1890–1894* (New York, Knopf, 1929).

Lowe, C., *Alexander III of Russia* (London, Heinemann, 1895).

Lyashchenko, P. I., *History of the National Economy of Russia to the 1917 Revolution* (New York, Macmillan, 1949).

Mavor, J., *An Economic History of Russia* (New York, Dutton, 1925).

Maynard, J., *Russia in Flux* (New York, Macmillan, 1948).

Pokrovsky, M. N., *Brief History of Russia* (London, Martin Lawrence, 1933).

Riasanovsky, N. V., *Russia and the West in the Teachings of the Slavophiles* (Cambridge, Harvard University Press, 1953).

Robinson, G. T., *Rural Russia Under the Old Regime* (New York, Macmillan, 1949).

Seton-Watson, H., *The Decline of Imperial Russia, 1855–1914* (New York, Praeger, 1952).

Wallace, D. M., *Russia* (New York, Cassell, 1912).

Walsh, W. B., *Readings in Russian History* (Syracuse, Syracuse University Press, 1950).

24

The Last of the Romanovs

An autocrat only in name, Nicholas II (1894–1917) was by far the weakest of the nineteenth-century tsars. Dominated by his tutors and by his imperious if well-meaning wife, the decisions he made were as unfortunate as was the choice of advisers who influenced him. An appeal by moderate liberals to set aside rule by bureaucratic whim and let Russia know a rule of law was dismissed at the moment of his accession as "senseless dreams." Stupid censorship and persecution and Russification of ethnic minorities went on as during the preceding reign.

Russian industry enjoyed a short but significant period of prosperity during the new tsar's early years. Foreign capital poured into the country, production and employment figures showed a phenomenal rise, and foreign trade expanded far beyond previous records. The nation became an industrial power, although she continued to be primarily an exporter of raw materials and an importer of manufactures. Working conditions in factory and mine were far behind those of the West and wages remained pitifully inadequate. Strikes, though illegal, occurred with growing frequency and severity in an effort to win decent standards of work. City labor was rapidly losing its tie with the agricultural village and so becoming a permanent proletariat. Urban workers began to develop political consciousness, and the strikes of the early twentieth century frequently were inspired by political as well as by economic aims. The administration sought unsuccessfully to divert labor from its social and political goals by fostering labor unions, led by government officials, which would demand only better pay and better hours. Soon after 1900 Russia followed the rest of the world into depression.

461

The first decade of the reign witnessed the birth of new revolutionary movements. The Social Democrats, owing much to earlier extremist thought going back to Pestel, sought to understand and apply the teachings of Karl Marx. They based their hopes primarily upon the urban proletariat, which they proposed to lead in the overthrow of autocracy. The group split over methods into Bolsheviks, who would sweep away capitalism along with monarchy and move immediately toward a socialist milieu, and Mensheviks, who would cooperate with capitalists in turning out the Romanovs, after which Russia would pass slowly through a capitalist regime into a distant socialism. Another group, the Socialist Revolutionaries, based their tenets partly upon Marx but aimed primarily at land reform and sought support chiefly among the peasants. They achieved particular notoriety for terrorism and assassination of public officials. Moderate reform elements, lumped together loosely as the Liberals, hoped for a republic or constitutional monarchy patterned on Western lines. To the extent that they felt the need for economic reform, they would free Russian capitalism from state controls and redistribute land. The agitation of both reform and revolutionary factions prodded the nation along the road to the abortive uprising of 1905.

NICHOLAS AND ALIX

The new tsar, twenty-six years old when his father died, had grown up, in the usual way of heirs to the Russian throne, with little training for the office he would some day fill. From the age of fourteen his head tutor was Michael Katkov, the Slavophile editor of the *Moscow Gazette,* who imbued his pupil with the principles of nationalism and autocracy. Pobiedonostsev, the "evil genius of Russia," assisted in the grand duke's education, but admitted that, since he could not question his pupil, he had no way of measuring his success. Narrow-minded and weak-willed as an adult, disliking responsibility, lacking in self-confidence, Nicholas's opinion was usually that of the last man he talked to. To one who pressed advice upon him the tsar protested, "I have my own opinion and my own will." He rarely showed it. His saving graces were a gentle kindliness, a winning charm, and a real unwillingness to hurt anyone.

The tsar's political credo, from which he never graduated, was childishly simple. His unfailing confidence in the autocracy stemmed from the teachings of Pobiedonostsev and Katkov, the convictions of his father, and the preachments of Prince Vladimir Meshchersky, the reactionary editor of *The Citizen,* the emperor's favorite newspaper. Like many Slavophiles, Nicholas was skeptical of bureaucracy and hoped to establish a close communion between the ruler and the people. This would come about, however, not through representative institutions, of which the tsar was suspicious, but in some vague, mystical way or perhaps through the impotent *Zemskii Sobor,* whose revival Ignatiev had urged upon Alexander III. Nicholas never honestly accepted the Duma which the Revolution of 1905 forced upon him; he looked upon that modest compromise of his authority as a personal affront and a violation of the sacred trust reposed in him.

Puny and nervous as a child, Nicholas was encouraged to seek relaxation in play and continued his enthusiasm for childish games and pranks far into adulthood. At the age of twenty-five he enjoyed playing hide-and-seek with others his own age. A year later he and his friends chased each other about hurling chestnuts or pine cones, the chase beginning on the palace grounds and ending on the roof. Perhaps the remarkable thing is that Nicholas should confide to paper the details of these frivolities and the childish satisfaction they gave him. In his remarkable diary, which he kept to the end of his life, he entered notes about the weather, picnics, frolics with his dogs, visits with his relatives, games with his children, reviews of his troops, walking, riding and hunting excursions, and the number of cats and crows he shot in the palace grounds, but seldom a word about the grave problems of state from which he was never free and the important decisions he was forced to make.

As a young man the heir enjoyed a liaison with a Polish dancer who bore him several children. Nicholas took the affair so seriously that he wanted to marry the girl, but the tsar, a strict father, separated the two and put an end to the matter. The grand duke's sulking was to no avail. He was sent on a tour around the world, coming back to Russia through the Far East and Siberia. While in Japan he was nearly killed by a fanatic, an event which confirmed his fear of radicalism.

When the emperor persuaded Nicholas that he must marry, the tsarevich chose the Princess Alice of Hesse-Darmstadt, granddaughter of Queen Victoria. Alix, as her friends and husband called her, had grown up in London and preferred English to any other language. Nicholas courted her in England, pressing his suit while boating on the Thames and picnicking on its banks, and succeeded in breaking down her aversion to joining the Russian Orthodox church. Alexander III insisted she come to Russia, where she arrived in time to march in his funeral procession. A month later she married Nicholas, cementing what all agree was a sentimental and fond love that endured to the end of their lives.

Empress Alix embraced Orthodoxy with all the fervor of the convert, accepting it not only as a comforting faith but as a bulwark of the autocracy which she and her husband revered. Her abiding hatred of democratic institutions and her concern that her husband should rule as a benevolent despot and hand down the autocratic power to his son undiluted grew in large measure from her borrowed religious convictions. But even Orthodoxy could not satisfy her religious craving completely. She enthusiastically fell in with the fad of mysticism so popular in court circles at the turn of the century, attending seances and consorting with quacks and charlatans and wandering fanatics. Rasputin was only the last and the most sinister of such influences.

The tsarina bore her husband four beautiful daughters, and as each came along the concern for the succession grew deeper, particularly in the coterie surrounding the dowager empress, who hated and constantly nagged her son's wife. Emotionally unstable and failing in health, Alix grew desperate at the thought that the tsar might not have an heir. The assurances of a quack French doctor that she was *enciente* and would bear a son proved unreliable and embarrassing. In 1904, however, an heir was born. Before he was out of his cradle he was discovered to be a victim of hemophilia, an incurable disease characterized by frequent and uncontrollable bleeding which was hereditary in his mother's family. The slightest accident—a bump or a fall— might start the bleeding which the best physicians in Europe had trouble halting. Every attack threatened to be fatal. The empress, despairing of saving the child by medical care, besought her God to send her a savior. "The savior appeared in the uncomely guise of Gregory Rasputin, a half-literate peasant from the wilderness of Siberia" (Florinsky), who wandered into the capital when the eighteen-month-old tsarevich was suffering an attack. Highly recommended by grand duchesses and ladies-in-waiting no more stable than the tsarina, Rasputin was hurried to the palace and introduced to the royal family as a miracle-worker. The bleeding boy recovered as he listened spellbound to the endless yarns about frontier Siberia spun by this "man of God." As Rasputin left the palace he warned the royal parents that the destiny not only of the child but of the dynasty was irrevocably linked with his own life. The tsarina believed him, and for the next decade the influence of this "holy devil" over the empress, and her influence in turn over the tsar, determined high matters of state.

Gregory Rasputin, who had left a wife and family in Tobolsk in western Siberia, was one of those wandering holy men so familiar to imperial Russia. Straying aimlessly to and fro over the land, filthy and in rags, living off the bounty of simple peasants, healing and working miracles, and preying upon the credulous, such men stirred the imagination of humble folk much more than could the clergy of the state church. From the practices of the strange sect of the *Khlysty,* whose meetings Rasputin attended, the "mad monk" came to believe and to preach that one was nearest to God when he was filled with a spirit of contrition and that the surest way to reach that spirit of contrition was to indulge one's appetite for sin. The sessions which he led always ended up in feverish dances and sexual orgies, after which the communicants were presumably overwhelmed with a desire for forgiveness. Many women at court joined his following, and thousands sought his favor

EXTRA! EXTRA!

BIG SAVINGS ON TIP!!

Order TIP from April 15 - June 14, and Southern Bell will waive the service connection charge ($9.00 - Residence, $12.50 - Single-Line Business).

ORDER NOW AND SAVE!!

See TIP insert for details

Southern Bell
A **BELL**SOUTH Company
April 1986

as his power over the royal family gave him authority to override bureaucratic decisions.

Rasputin's influence at court and the disturbing rumors that were current in the capital came up for questioning in the Imperial Duma. The empress never forgave the man who raised the question, and in effect told the tsar that democratic institutions always led to such meddling. During World War I army commanders were appointed and dismissed at the nod of Rasputin, who had not the slightest knowledge of military matters. The tsarina influenced the tsar to dismiss officials of cabinet rank by telling him that "Our Friend" wanted this man or that relieved of office. Rasputin was poisoned, shot, and drowned in 1916 by a group of patriots that included the tsar's nephew in a desperate, but belated, effort to save the nation.

THE EARLY YEARS

The accession of Nicholas II was welcomed as bringing to an end the militant conservatism of the late tsar. There was nothing in the son's education or character to justify such a view. But many, particularly the liberal zemstvo leaders, hoped that there would be a return to the Loris-Melikov plan which Alexander II had signed on the morning of his assassination. These hopes were quickly dashed as the new ruler made unmistakably clear his determination to rule in the spirit of his father.

Among the delegations which came to the palace to congratulate Nicholas on his accession and marriage was one from the zemstvo assembly of the province of Tver, an assembly which consistently led liberal thinking in the closing years of the monarchy. The address carried up by the delegation expressed gratitude for the tsar's earlier pronouncement that he would devote himself to the happiness and welfare of the nation, and voiced the popular confidence that the welfare of the Russian people would advance under the new tsar's leadership. It went on, however, to express the hope that the law would henceforth be observed not only by the emperor's subjects but also by the bureaucrats, whose whimsical administration encouraged disrespect for the law. A plea for protection of the rights of individuals according to law was followed by a request that zemstvo delegations in the future might once again know the right to petition the throne, as they had been empowered to do by the reform of the sixties.

Nicholas answered with a curt speech prepared by Pobiedonostsev, who had guessed the general nature of the Tver petition: "It has come to my knowledge that during recent months there have been heard in some zemstvos the voices of those who have indulged in senseless dreams that the zemstvos might participate in the direction of the internal affairs of the state. Let all know that I shall devote my energy to the service of the people, but that I shall maintain the principle of autocracy as firmly and unflinchingly as did my father."

Thenceforth there could be no misunderstanding about how Nicholas looked upon "senseless dreams." Some of the intelligentsia considered the speech as the tsar's declaration of war upon his people. No longer would those outside the law include only revolutionaries and assassins. Now they were joined by any zemstvo leader or moderate liberal who dared to protest vocally against a hated order of things.

During the coronation festivities held in Moscow the common people were herded into a field to receive token gifts. Pressed back by mounted police, the crowd stampeded. Over a thousand were trampled to death and other thousands were injured. That night the imperial couple attended a ball given by the French ambassador, an act that made the tsar seem cruelly indifferent to the sufferings of his people.

Out of respect, Nicholas II kept around him the same advisers who had served his father—Durnovo as minister of interior, the vicious Delianov as minister of education, Witte as minister of finance, and Pobiedonostsev as procurator-general of the Holy Synod. Beyond these he chose his ministers with little thought or care and dismissed them whenever the whim struck him or some backstairs influence-peddler whispered calumny in his ear. His apologists point to his kindness in usually informing an official of his dismissal by mail, perhaps only a few hours after a friendly conversation. Where Alexander III would have told an official frankly and bluntly to his face that he was no longer welcome, the autocracy now had no autocrat. But dismissal by any means must often have come as a relief. No official, even of ministerial rank, knew when his directives would be countermanded by the tsar, not by working through the official but by going behind his back. Occasionally he followed the advice of the Council of State, the agency established by Alexander I to investigate problems and recommend solutions. More often he did not, and frequently he did not even consult it.

During these early years the policy of the government continued to be that of Alexander III. Repression of all semblance of educational freedom simply provoked university students to rebel. But student strikes were broken up by Cossacks and the strikers inducted into the army or imprisoned. Thirteen thousand Moscow and Petersburg students struck in 1899 and all were expelled or ordered into the army. One student who had twice suffered expulsion shot and killed the minister of education in 1901.

Persecution of ethnic and religious minorities went on uninterrupted. Finland, autonomous since the time of its acquisition by Alexander I, lost its constitutional rights and became simply a Russian province. Nicholas, who had sworn at his coronation to uphold the grand duchy's constitution, appointed a military governor-general to rule over it, to subject the men to military draft, to fill government offices with Russians, to order official use of the

Russian language and finally, when the people threatened rebellion, to enforce martial law. In 1904 the heretofore docile Finns assassinated the governor-general. Georgia and Armenia underwent similar dragonnades and similarly reacted by sprouting revolutionary movements.

DEVELOPMENTS IN INDUSTRY

The Russian economy, both in agriculture and in industry, had suffered the doldrums through the eighties and early nineties, the depression reaching its depth in the famine and cholera epidemic of 1891–1893. During the preceding decade Russian industry had progressed, it is true, but at a much slower rate than had the economies of Western and Central Europe.

With the accession of Nicholas II, but in no way growing out of it, Russian industry began to recover and expand at a steady and rapid pace. By 1897 the number of industrial enterprises had increased by nearly a third over the number a decade earlier, the labor force had grown by more than half, and the value of factory output had more than doubled. Forty thousand factories were employing over two million workers and producing nearly three billion rubles worth of goods. Furthermore, Russian industrial production came increasingly to be characterized by large-scale enterprise. Indeed, the rate of concentration, stepped up by business casualties during the depression of the eighties, far exceeded that of Germany with all her cartels.

If Russia's rate of industrial growth fell below that of Western Europe in the eighties, it far surpassed that of the West in the nineties. During the latter decade the smelting of iron grew in England by 18 per cent, in the United States by 50, in Germany by 72 and in Russia by nearly 200 per cent. By the turn of the century Russia stood fourth in the world in iron smelting, in which she had ranked sixth a decade earlier. Coal and iron ore production and the number of spindles turning out cotton thread show similar advances. Of course, "the high percentage of increase was due entirely to the low initial level of production" (Lyashchenko). And it must not be overlooked that Russia jumped into the middle of the Industrial Revolution. She did not have to plod through the slow and costly period of invention and experimentation in which England, particularly, had led the way.

Railroad building went on at a phenomenal rate in the closing years of the century. In 1895, 32,000 miles of railroads were operating, but half as many more were laid down during the following decade. This included the dramatic achievements of completing the Trans-Siberian Railway connecting the Baltic with the Pacific over a stretch of six thousand miles and a Central Asian line connecting Tashkent with the European railway net. These were respectable accomplishments, certainly, but they gave Russia a mileage of less than one-fifth that of the United States, comparable in many ways but much smaller in area. Some of the capital for railway construction came from abroad, but most of it was provided by Russian investors, and particularly by the government, which raised the money by borrowing from the savings banks, spending the income from the vodka monopoly, and levying high excise taxes. Construction companies made huge profits, as was generally true in other countries. A British offer to deliver rails for the Trans-Siberian at a third the price quoted by Russian manufacturers was turned down and the order went to domestic firms.

The inflow of foreign capital reached sizable proportions as the new century drew near. One-third of the corporation capital in the country in 1890 was foreign, a decade later nearly half. The adoption of the gold standard in 1897 did much to encourage foreign investors to take their risks in Russian enterprise. By the turn of the century 70 per cent of the mining industry and 40 per cent of metallurgy were foreign-owned. On the other hand, the manufacture of textiles and the processing of food were entirely native-owned. French, Belgian, and British capital dominated foreign investments in Russia, while Germany, which had provided most of the funds in the seventies and eighties, fell far behind.

The increase in Russian production during the reign of Nicholas II was primarily an increase in raw-material production, and much of that went abroad. For example, the average Russian was consuming an eighth of a ton of coal a year while the Briton used over four tons and the American and German two and a half. Per capita consumption of pig iron was only one-seventh that of the American or English figure and a fifth that of the German. Much of her wheat and sugar went abroad; her flax was exported as raw material and returned as finished cloth. Russia's economic relations with the industrial giants to her west, both in regard to foreign investments and the nature of her foreign trade, were essentially those of a colonial area.

THE LABOR FORCE

The concentration of production in large-scale units tended also to concentrate the labor force in relatively large bodies. By the early twentieth century half the factory workers in Russia were employed by only 4 per cent of the firms. The fact is usually ignored that this concentration promoted the rapid growth of the economic and political consciousness of the Russian worker. It made him more receptive to agitation, more anxious to organize, more attentive to appeals for political reform. Add to this the fact that he had constantly before him the example of the growing power of labor in foreign lands.

The factory worker in Russia was rapidly becoming a permanent, city-dwelling proletarian. While there was a steady rise in the number who walked to town for seasonal employment and trudged back to the village as business fell off, there was also a rapid growth in the number of those who did not return to the village but dwelt in the city the year round and took their chances of finding sufficient work to keep them alive. By 1900 half the industrial labor force of Russia were sons whose fathers before them had been factory workers. Practically all those employed in metal-processing plants were permanent, city-dwelling laborers, as were 90 per cent of the workers in the Petersburg area, politically the most tender spot of the nation. Many a peasant cast adrift from his village no longer could accept whatever wages were tossed his way to add to his basic income from the land. Now he and his family must live, or try to, entirely on his factory earnings, for he had given up his rights in the village and lost his allotment land. There were still many others, however, as late as the turn of the century who lived in town and sent home part of their wages to the family who stayed on in the village and who themselves returned to the village in time of sickness or unemployment or old age.

Bunge's factory reforms of the eighties, aimed at reducing the worst abuses in the employment of women and children but doing little for adult males, fell largely into disuse during the last half of the reign of Alexander III. The normal workday ran to twelve hours, often stretching to sixteen with overtime. Wage rises came slowly and were more than offset by rising prices. The walkout of thirty thousand spinners and weavers in the St. Petersburg area set off a wave of strikes that swept all over Russia and Poland. The government was prodded into announcing a new set of factory laws. The workday for adult male workers was limited to eleven and a half hours, and Sundays and holidays were set aside as rest days. Children under fifteen could not work more than nine hours, and those under seventeen ten hours. The regulations applied only to shops hiring twenty or more workers, thus leaving conditions in small enterprises untouched. The inspection system was ineffective, and presumably the factory inspectors were no more above taking bribes than was the rest of Russian officialdom.

The advances made by the Russian economy in the nineties were largely the work of the minister of finance, Sergei Witte. Rising from the position of railway stationmaster to that of head of the southwestern group of railroads, he filled the office of minister of communications until appointed minister of finance, a position he occupied for eleven years. In 1903 he became prime minister. His energy was behind the rapid expansion of the railway net in the eighties and nineties, and the Trans-Siberian was begun under his direction. It was he who put Russia on the gold standard, thus winning the confidence of foreign capital which theretofore had hesitated to enter Russia because of the unpredictability of currency values. It was Witte who created the state monopoly on the sale of vodka, ostensibly to reduce liquor consumption, and it was his office that harvested the revenue as liquor sales mounted to alarming proportions. Strongly sympathetic to the business community and particularly to big business, Witte carried through only such modest factory reforms in 1897 as were necessary to quiet labor unrest. He used a high protective tariff more intelligently than it had ever been used before, practically excluding items which he felt Russia could and should produce and admitting at nominal rates such things as machinery and agricultural equipment which the nation did not manufacture. Under his leadership private business was stimulated by stepped-up government enterprise in such basic industries as railroad construction, banking, and development of state-owned mines and timber resources as well as tariff protection and subsidy and favorable government contracts. The state budget doubled to two billion rubles during his ministry, and the national debt rose by 40 per cent to nearly seven billions. Indirect taxes, of which the peasant paid the greatest share, brought in most of the revenue. Witte's influence showed itself in every phase of economic activity in which the government interested itself. Among ministers of finance and particularly among prime ministers he stands pre-eminent.

DEPRESSION

National economies the world over reached a crisis at the close of the century, and Russia had become so intertwined with other nations economically that she tumbled into depression along with all the rest. The money panic abroad was soon felt in Russia, and both the foreign and the domestic demand dried up. Between 1900 and 1902, when the falling market stabilized, prices of the raw materials which were the nation's chief exports dropped by nearly half. Production declined markedly and again, as in the eighties, thousands of weaker firms sold out to stronger ones or simply went out of business, leaving the shrunken market to those who were able to weather the storm.

As employers cut wages and laid off workers the number of strikes mounted. Walkouts spread from St. Petersburg and Moscow to as far away as the Lena gold fields, the Baku oil wells, Tiflis, Novgorod, Kiev, Astrakhan and Batum, where the revolutionary Stalin led the way. The infection spread to rural Russia, particularly to the Volga and Ukraine. Land hunger, the chronic cause of discontent, and the grinding poverty that grew out of it drove the peasants in the black-soil provinces to desperation. Allotment land in some of the rebellious villages amounted to no more than an acre per male peasant, and many families were without a single cow. As usual, the risings witnessed the seizures of timber and grain, the firing of manor houses, and the callous murder of landowners. Peasant and urban defiance reached a climax in the Revolution of 1905, which had both political and economic goals.

Early in 1902, when labor unrest and the peasant risings were at a peak, the minister of interior Plehve received a daring plan for counter-action from the head of the Moscow security police, Sergei Zubatov. Under the plan the government would encourage and indeed organize and participate in pseudo-labor unions, which would be encouraged to put forward economic demands but to steer clear of political action. The "Society for the Mutual Help of Workers in the Engineering Industry" included not only the workers in Moscow metalworking factories but also plant foremen, policemen, and clergymen. The chief of police of Moscow took over as treasurer and named the members of the society's executive council. But Plehve thought the movement potentially dangerous when the first meeting brought out fifty thousand workers, even though the session opened with solemn prayers before the monument to Alexander II. Professors from the University of Moscow, momentarily duped into thinking the movement bona fide, addressed the audience upon the need for higher wages and improved working conditions, while policemen circulated through the crowd. On later occasions officialdom supported strikes and even paid strike benefits.

This "police socialism," which the government was willing to promote in all industries to insure that the working-class movement would not adopt a political program, made little appeal to factory owners. The French ambassador protested when the Zubatov organization struck a French-owned plant; other foreigners were equally disturbed. Moscow textile manufacturers raised bitter objections to "Zubatovism." The movement collapsed in the Moscow area when Zubatov was driven from office, but it appeared later in St. Petersburg under the leadership of the Orthodox priest Father Gapon.

SOCIAL DEMOCRATS

The government failed to still the cry of protests against the nation's economic and political evils either by shooting the strikers or by trying to capture their organizations. This was largely because Russia, rural and urban, was being educated by a variety of parties and platforms. Some were moderate, some extreme. Some urged political, some economic, pressure, and some urged a combination of both. Some sought their support among peasants, some among city workers, some among intellectuals.

George Plekhanov's Emancipation of Labor movement won many converts among the Russian intelligentsia after its founding in 1883. It aimed immediately at winning constitutional government and the basic freedoms of press, speech, and association by means of which the working class could be educated ultimately to take political and economic action. From its office in Geneva the organization fed a stream of Marxist writings to small discussion groups of Russian students and intellectuals. In spite of its title, the Emancipation of Labor never became a serious working-class movement. It had no contact with the strikes of the eighties and early nineties which aimed not at political but at economic goals. At that time the Emancipation of Labor groups were concerning themselves only with violent arguments over the meaning and application of Marx's theories.

In 1895 Vladimir Lenin and Julius Martov led a number of these discussion groups into a new organization to be called the Fighting Union for the Liberation of the Working Class. Branches appeared in Moscow and elsewhere. Lenin and Martov determined to carry their cause into the ranks of labor, which they hoped to inspire with Marxist sympathies and organize for revolutionary as well as economic purposes. Printing presses working in hidden basements turned out a spate of Marxist pamphlets; other tracts were smuggled in from abroad. A magazine which managed to keep within the censorship laws carried subtle preachments by Lenin, Plekhanov, and other Marxists. Members of the organization took some part in stirring up the strikes of the mid-nineties.

The Fighting Union lasted only three years. In 1898 nine delegates from its five branches and from the Jewish Social-Democratic Bund assembled in Minsk and organized the Russian Social Democratic Labor party. This congress chose a Central Executive Committee to direct party activity at home and abroad. But from its very birth the new party was torn with bitter disagreement over tactics and refinements of Marxist doctrine. The columns of its first newspaper, *Iskra* (the *Spark*) carried the arguments and recriminations of Lenin, Martov, Plekhanov, and the girl, Vera Zasulich, who back in 1878 had shot the military governor of St. Petersburg and escaped.

BOLSHEVIKS AND MENSHEVIKS

The second congress of the Russian Social Democratic party convened in Brussels in 1903 but moved on to London at the invitation of the Belgian police. Before the forty delegates split in violent disagreement over the election of leaders they managed to agree on a maximal and a minimal platform. The maximal or long-run goals were the prosecution of a socialist revolution, the overthrow of capitalism, and the creation of a dictatorship of the proletariat. The minimal or short-run aims included the replacement of the autocracy with a republican government, an eight-hour day for city workers, and expropriation of the gentry's estates and their allocation to the peasants. A later amendment called for the socialization of land—the ownership and control of all agricultural land not by individuals but by local communities.

These remained the party's aims down to 1918, although the members could not agree on how the program should be carried out nor on who should lead them.

The contest to fill the chief offices of the party—membership on the Central Executive Committee and the editorial board of the party organ, *Iskra* —produced such bitterness that the new-born party split into two sections. Those who followed Lenin won the elections and hence came to be called Bolsheviks, or men of the majority. Those who followed Plekhanov—the Mensheviks, or men of the minority—refused representation on the governing boards since they could not control them. The wound never healed. In 1905 the Bolsheviks met again in London, the Mensheviks in Geneva; the two met in Prague and Vienna respectively six years later, by which time the Mensheviks found a new supporter, the lone wolf Marxist, Leon Trotsky.

The divorce of Bolshevik from Menshevik was in some measure inevitable because of a clash of personalities. The suave, professorial Plekhanov considered himself the dean of Russian Marxists and resented the intrusions of the upstart Lenin. The latter had none of Plekhanov's mildness either of manner or of aims. The rest of the party divided its loyalty between the two leaders, shifting from one side to the other as expediency or conscience dictated.

But underneath the rivalry of prima donnas lay a fundamental difference in approach to the socialist revolution to which both groups looked forward. After the overturn of the autocracy the Mensheviks expected Russia to be governed by a democratic republic which would be succeeded only in some vague, distant future by a socialist state. Consequently, they would work with non-Marxist liberals in achieving the overthrow of the Romanovs and continue that cooperation as long as the republic survived. The Bolsheviks, however, would have nothing to do with this Fabianism. They would replace the monarchy with a dictatorship of the proletariat which would immediately overthrow capitalism and develop the socialist state. Lenin played no favorites between monarchists and capitalists, but would sweep away both at once. As for party organization, Lenin demanded an unquestioning obedience to the intellectual discipline of the majority, and would have its program and tactics dictated by the party leadership. Among the democratic-minded Mensheviks, on the other hand, all would share in the drafting of policies and the approval of tactics.

SOCIALIST REVOLUTIONARIES

The Socialist Revolutionary party, founded in Kharkov in 1900, brought under its banner the sort of revolutionary who had supported the People's Will party back in the seventies. Its distinguishing mark was its confidence in terrorism and the assassination of public officials, a type of action which the Bolsheviks and Mensheviks disapproved in their own followers but applauded when carried out by the S.R.'s, so-called to distinguish them from the S.D.'s or Social Democrats. Along with their practice of terrorism, the Socialist Revolutionaries had a platform based in part upon Marxist principles. They worked for the overthrow of tsarism, but expected it to be followed immediately by a socialistic society whose birth the weak Russian capitalism would be unable to prevent. Making their appeal primarily although not exclusively to the peasants, they would abolish private ownership of land and turn its control over to the peasant village. Among the leaders of the S.R.'s were Catherine Breshkovskaya, "the little grandmother of the revolution," and the party's brilliant theoretician Victor Chernov, who would lead the party through the 1917 revolutions.

An important section of the Socialist Revolutionary party was its Terroristic Organization, created a year after the party's birth. This element specialized in the murder of public officials and in armed robberies of banks and government agencies. Plans to assassinate the tsar miscarried, but an S.R. bomb-thrower managed to kill Minister of Interior Plehve in 1904.

The leader of the Terroristic Organization who ordered Plehve's murder was Yevno Azev, who at the same time was an agent of the *Okhrana,* or secret political police, the descendant of the Third Section of the Imperial Chancery of Nicholas I. He attained high office in the S.R.'s and became their leading terrorist organizer. The government gave him complete freedom to instigate the murder of officials and then turn over to the police the names of those implicated in the crime. He organized the assassination of the Grand Duke Sergei, the Minister of Interior Plehve, and a number of army colonels, provincial governors, and other officials, in addition to attempting many assassinations which did not come off, including those of the Grand Dukes Vladimir and Nicholas. By the terms of his arrangement with the *Okhrana* he promised not to touch the royal family but, carried away with his work, he organized three attempts on the life of the tsar. After each enterprise Azev carried to the secret police the names of those who took part in the project and thus was responsible for sending hundreds of revolutionaries to their death. The revelation that he was both a revolutionary leader and a police spy undermined the confidence of many S.R.'s in their own movement. From that time on, political terrorism fell into disrepute.

The sensational acts carried out by the Socialist Revolutionaries gave them an importance far beyond the size of their membership. Even the Bolsheviks, hardly less numerous, boasted only eight thousand members by 1905. The strength of both movements, however, could not be measured by the number of "card-carrying" members nor even by the hundreds of thousands of pamphlets distributed each year. It lay, rather, in the widespread discontent and resentment which infected the entire countryside and which made the peasants attentive to revolutionary propaganda.

LIBERALS

Political liberalism in late nineteenth-century Russia traced its origin to the moderate wing of the Decembrist movement led by Muravev. In the forties it found comfort in the Petrashevsky circles. But it burgeoned to respectable proportions in the sixties as a consequence of the creation of the zemstvos. Moderate liberals in the zemstvo assemblies called for continued reform, hoping to see a national duma, with consultative if not with legislative power, to "cap the edifice" of local institutions of self-government. With the emasculation of the reforms of the sixties many conscience-stricken nobles joined the *Narodnik* group led by Chaikovsky. When that movement collapsed these modest social reformers found vent for their energy in promoting the erection of schools and hospitals to serve the rural communities and in financing the activities of veterinarians and agricultural agents to teach the peasant improved methods of farming. During the awful famine of 1891 the zemstvoists worked wonders in relieving widespread misery, and in doing so gained a sense of importance and a realization of the need for more effective organization. The zemstvos of the provinces of Moscow and Tver led the others in their concern to ameliorate conditions of life in rural Russia; they were also the most insistent in pressing their liberal political views upon the government.

The Zemstvo Act of 1890 had aimed at curbing the liberal tendencies apparent in some provincial assemblies by drastically reducing the electorate. But liberal and even radical thought continued to grow in the zemstvos, to some extent in the assemblies but most considerably among the doctors, nurses, veterinarians, teachers, engineers, accountants, and clerks who served under the zemstvo boards. Many were Socialist Revolutionaries, a few were Social Democrats, probably most were simply liberal in point of view.

One of the most substantial accomplishments of the zemstvo movement was the production of a number of leaders of liberal thought and action. Ivan Petrunkevich, of the province of Chernigov, had suffered exile for daring to suggest to Alexander II that the only way to relieve revolutionary pressure was for the government to grant freedom of press and speech. Fedor Rodichev, a brilliant lawyer of Tver, had helped to draft the appeal to the throne at the time of Nicholas's accession. Dmitry Shipov, who would have been satisfied with a national assembly having only consultative authority, had his re-election as president of the zemstvo board of Moscow province cancelled by Plehve.

When the zemstvo leaders gathered in Moscow to attend the coronation of Nicholas II, they agreed thenceforth to hold annual congresses. After the first meeting that same year, however, the men were told that such congresses could not continue since they were "unconstitutional." Forbidden to organize among themselves, the zemstvoists connived at the organization of the professional men who served under them. There sprang up unions of doctors, lawyers, teachers, and engineers which soon became nation-wide in scope. The Union of Unions, which embraced all the individual professional organizations and which some labor unions later joined, gave liberal opinion a strong voice in the Revolution of 1905. By this time such outspoken opponents of the autocracy as the eminent historian Professor Paul Miliukov and the political economist Professor Peter Struve, a former Marxist, had come into the liberal movement and were urging their students to leave school and join in the struggle against the regime. But some students found work to do without withdrawing. When all student organizations were proscribed some leaders, including the future S.R. leader Victor Chernov, turned the orchestra and chorus at the University of Moscow into propaganda agencies. Students at the University of St. Petersburg went out on strike and the movement spread to all universities and high schools, forcing them to close down for want of attendants.

The Liberals could no more agree upon a program than could the Social Democrats, but where the latter split into two factions the former splintered into many. They were in general agreement that the autocracy must go, but they were at odds on what should replace it. Some preferred a constitutional monarchy like that of England, the bulk of governmental power to reside in a bicameral legislature. Some would place executive power in a responsible ministry. Others would leave to the emperor a modified executive authority, possibly making the ministers responsible to him. Still others would make the national assembly purely consultative. Most could agree that the civil rights of speech, assembly, press, and conscience should be guaranteed. Many were suspicious of the masses, rural or urban or both, and would have preferred a limited suffrage.

By 1900 liberal leaders from all over Russia, representing the various professions and conservative labor unions, were meeting quietly to exchange views. Later they formed the Union of Liberation and agreed to press for a constitution. Meetings continued in hiding, for even this mild action was proscribed. Their newspaper, *Liberation,* was printed abroad and smuggled into Russia, where it was read as avidly as were the pamphlets of the revolutionaries.

Liberals probably much more than revolutionaries helped, perhaps without meaning to, to give Russia a bad name abroad. During their frequent visits to the spas and resorts of Europe and in their tours as visiting professors at American universities the Russian intellectuals of liberal political

views constantly criticized their native land for its ignorance, its superstition, its poverty, its autocracy. The strides that had been made in recent decades these travellers chose to ignore or play down. In their obvious
love of things Western and in the ease with which they moved in polite
society they won friends not for Russia but for themselves. They, together
with the Polish *émigrés*, may have contributed to the weakening of Russian
credit abroad, and certainly they made all the more difficult the work of
honest, sincere, hard-working diplomats. And they must bear some responsibility for the fact that the new revolutionary Russia, which was not to
their liking, has seldom received a fair hearing.

Witte, who earlier had warned Nicholas that the zemstvos must be
abolished unless he cared to face the prospect that they would grow into
a national assembly, began to curry the favor of zemstvo-men as part of
the struggle for power between his Ministry of Finance and Plehve's
Ministry of Interior. Some zemstvos had recently shown the audacity to
complain of the government's scorn of civil rights and the limitations which
burdened their own activities. Some had called for the right of the zemstvos
to discuss all laws applicable to local problems before their enactment and
even the right to help write such legislation. Witte now permitted the
zemstvos to consider the needs of agriculture, but Plehve warned them
against taking a stand. The great majority of such meetings came out
strongly not only for agricultural reform but for correction of bureaucratic
abuses, recognition of civil rights, and the convening of a national assembly.
These requests pointed squarely at Plehve, who as minister of interior was
responsible for vicious police action and suppression of civil rights. Plehve
won the tsar's support over Witte, who was dismissed as finance minister
and temporarily given a purely honorary position. Plehve, now the tsar's
chief minister, closed down the zemstvo discussions and stepped up his
program of repression. Witte warned him that such methods would lead
to his assassination. Plehve answered that the approaching revolution
could be prevented by "a little victorious war." The war, with Japan, was
perhaps little but hardly victorious and succeeded only in precipitating the
revolution which Plehve had hoped to avoid. Soon after the Japanese attack
Plehve fell before an assassin's bomb.

THE RUNNING SORES OF EMPIRE

Had Nicholas II faced only the problems raised by his own Great Russian
people, he would still have had to deal with an array of difficulties for which
his feeble abilities ill prepared him. But still other problems, some which
he inherited and some of his own making, pressed in upon him. The Poles,
both abroad and at home, never let up in their relentless attack upon tsardom.

The Finns, loyal for a century, rebelled at the Russification to which they, too, were now subjected. A strong nationalist movement in Little Russia urged separation and the creation of an independent Ukraine. Jews who could not leave for America joined revolutionary bands or subscribed funds for the restoration of the Jewish homeland in Palestine. Georgians and Armenians, proud of their own long history, chafed under the Russian yoke. Esthonians and Latvians hated their Baltic masters who had so long enjoyed the favor of the Romanovs. German colonists brought into Russia by Catherine II still kept to their native customs and language, despising the Russians and their inefficient ways of doing things.

Witte is supposed to have remarked that foreigners should not be surprised that Russia had a government far from perfect but, rather, that she had any government at all. Thoughtful Russians might well have asked themselves what held the empire together. The answer lay, at least in part, in a neutralizing balance of hatreds deliberately encouraged by the bureaucracy. Not only did the administration do nothing to soften the hatred of Pole for Russian, of Ukrainian for Pole, of Latvian for Balt, of Uniat and Catholic for Orthodox, of Moslem and Jew for Christian, but Pobiedonostsev consciously stimulated such bitterness. Not only did the administration do nothing to soften the hatred of peasant for landlord and of both for the merchant, of worker for employer, of student for Cossack, of civilian for bureaucrat. Plehve and others like him felt that such mutual animosities would insure against a revolution.

But if there was one thing upon which the vast majority of the peoples of the empire could agree it was in their contempt for the symbols of authority. Even to the faithful Orthodox, the priest was a man to be despised. Even to the gentry and merchants who profited most from the regime, the bureaucrat was a man of no principle. And in one respect, at least, there was little loyalty even to the throne. More of the Romanovs died by assassination than was true of any other ruling family in history.

SUGGESTED READING

Alexander, Grand Duke, *Once a Grand Duke* (New York, Farrar, 1932).

Alexinsky, G., *Modern Russia* (New York, Scribner's, 1913).

Breshkovskaya, E., *Hidden Springs of the Russian Revolution* (Stanford, Stanford University Press, 1931).

Dillon, E. J., *The Eclipse of Russia* (London, Dent, 1918).

Florinsky, M. T., *Russia: A History and an Interpretation* (New York, Macmillan, 1953).

Gurko, V. I., *Features and Figures of the Past: Government and Opinion in the Reign of Nicholas II* (Stanford, Stanford University Press, 1939).

Karpovich, M., *Imperial Russia, 1801–1917* (New York, Holt, 1932).

Kornilov, A., *Modern Russian History* (New York, Knopf, 1917).

Lyashchenko, P. I., *History of the National Economy of Russia to the 1917 Revolution* (New York, Macmillan, 1949).

Mavor, J., *An Economic History of Russia* (New York, Dutton, 1914).

Miliukov, P., *Russia and Its Crisis* (Chicago, University of Chicago Press, 1905).

Pares, B., *Russia and Reform* (London, Constable, 1907).

Pobednostsev, C., *Reflections of a Russian Statesman* (London, Richards, 1898).

Seton-Watson, H., *The Decline of Imperial Russia, 1855–1914* (New York, Praeger, 1952).

Treadgold, D. W., *Lenin and His Rivals: The Struggle for Russia's Future, 1896–1906* (New York, Praeger, 1955).

Yarmolinsky, A., *The Memoirs of Count Witte* (New York, Doubleday, 1921).

25

The Revolution That Failed

AFTER THE COLLAPSE OF RUSSIAN pressure in the Balkans in the mid-eighties the empire's interest shifted to Asia and particularly to the Far East. The Trans-Siberian Railway spanned the continent to the Pacific, and a short cut branch line across Manchuria provided a back-door entry for Russian expansionists inside the Chinese Empire. Some imperialist-minded schemers plotted to extend Russian influence and control over all of Asia. In pushing into north China, Russia ran athwart Japanese ambition on the mainland, and the two powers, Russia the most backward of the Europeans and Japan the most modern of the Asiatics, went to war in 1904. Some circles in St. Petersburg welcomed what they hoped would be a "little victorious war" as a way of avoiding revolution at home. But governmental bungling, poor leadership in the field, and national indifference gave Japan the victory.

There was famine in the Russian countryside in the early years of the century, and the number of peasant risings mounted alarmingly. At the same time there was growing urban unrest as the expanding labor force clamored for satisfactory working conditions and a living wage. The Social Democrats were active among city workers and the Socialist Revolutionaries encouraged the peasants to rise up against the government. The latter party carried off the assassination of a number of public officials. Liberals in zemstvo circles organized a new party and appealed to the government to grant political reforms.

As each bit of news from the Manchurian front brought word of further disaster the nation grew increasingly restless. A parade of workers marched to the Winter Palace to plead for reform, but many were shot down. This "Bloody Sunday" opened the Revolution of 1905. In the fall of that year general strikes in the capitals paralyzed industry, and *Jacqueries* spread a trail of fire and blood over the countryside. For a while the St. Petersburg Soviet, or Council of Workers' Deputies, exercised more political power than the government itself. The administration had no alternative but to grant concessions, end the war, and get the troops back home to put down the rebellion. In the October Manifesto the tsar granted civil liberties and established a Duma, popularly elected, which he promised should enjoy full legislative responsibility and control over appointed officials. But he quickly forgot the promise and so circumscribed the powers of the new legislature as to remove all possibility that it could reduce the autocracy.

The first Duma demanded full legislative power, ministerial responsibility, and land reform. It accomplished nothing and was dismissed; scores of its members were arrested. The second Duma fared no better. Before calling the third the tsar so reduced the electorate as to assure a majority of conservative members, and this Duma and the fourth managed to avoid early dissolution. Thenceforth the members had to content themselves with mere existence, with continuing as a body only remotely similar to Western parliaments, with developing the Duma as a platform for the expression, however cautious, of resistance to autocracy.

In an attempt to reduce the ominous and continuing unrest in rural Russia, Prime Minister Peter Stolypin put through a series of land reforms in 1906 designed to put an end to the *mir,* which he and others saw as a nest of socialism and agitation. He made it possible for individual peasants to withdraw from the village commune and receive their allotment lands in hereditary property right, and for each to demand that his strips be consolidated into a single farm. This revolution in land tenure was making slow but definite progress when the nation went to war in 1914.

THE RUSSIAN ADVANCE IN ASIA

The reign of Alexander III saw continuing Russian pressure southward into Central Asia. In 1884 the district of Merv fell to the tsar, and now the Russian border lay up against the frontiers of Persia and Afghanistan. The Trans-Caspian Railway pushed east to Bokhara and Samarkand and then on to Tashkent, bringing Russian political and military power dangerously close to the Indian border. In 1891 a Russian force moved into the Pamir mountain country, almost within sight of India. Following the check in the Balkans some imperialists clamored for further advances in the east; some looked toward India and urged that British power should be forced back to the Indus River; others argued that Russia should accept a civilizing responsibility in the Far East by way of winning domination over China and eventually over all of Asia.

The shift of Russian interest to Asia and particularly to the Far East under Nicholas II grew out of many stimuli. Nicholas's journey through Asia while heir to the throne and his driving the first spike on the eastern terminus of the Trans-Siberian focused the ruler's attention on the area. The completion of the railway made easy the migration of thousands upon thousands of Russian peasants into Siberia, a movement not only condoned but encouraged by the new tsar. Russian influence at the court of China had been strong for centuries, and Russian trade with her eastern neighbor had flourished since medieval times. The growing pressure into East Asia of England, France, and the United States and recently of Japan and Germany could only encourage Russia to join in the struggle for position in an area in which she had long been interested. The stalemate in the Near East forced the nation to turn her back upon the Balkans. The tsar's cousin, Wilhelm II of Germany, constantly reminded Nicholas of Russia's destiny in the Far East and excited his fancy by calling him "Admiral of the Pacific." The Slavophile press never tired of calling upon the nation to have done with Europe and its dangerous radical philosophies and to exercise its leadership in the East, where autocracy was the rule. Witte, who had far more influence in guiding foreign policy than did the foreign ministers— Lobanov-Rostovsky, Muravev, and Lamsdorf all came and went almost unnoticed—championed the peaceful penetration of Russia into the Far East over the Trans-Siberian Railway which he had built. A Buriat-Mongol quack, Dr. Badmaiev, developed a scheme to instigate the Tibetans and Mongols of north China to rise against their overlords and join the Russian Empire. Witte sent Badmaiev's plan to the tsar with the comment that success in the venture would allow Russia to dominate not only Asia but Europe as well. Badmaiev milked the treasury for a huge sum to finance the trading company which would veil his political scheme, but the project never came off.

The Sino-Japanese War brought quick and decisive victory in 1895 to the new Japan over feudal China. The victor seized Formosa and the Liaotung Peninsula in southern Manchuria and forced the Chinese to recognize the independence of Korea. The provisions of the treaty, perhaps "even more distasteful to Russia than to China" (Lobanov-Rostovsky), threatened to block the ambition of Russian expansionists to obtain an ice-free port in south Manchuria. Before the treaty could be ratified Russia, joined by France and Germany, sternly warned Japan to give up all thought of demanding the Liaotung Peninsula. Japan backed down in return for a huge indemnity, which China paid with money borrowed from the Russian government, which in turn had borrowed it from French bankers.

The grateful Chinese government signed a mutual-defense pact with Russia against future Japanese aggression and allowed Russia the privilege of extending the Trans-Siberian Railway straight across Manchuria to

Vladivostok, a short cut which reduced the length of the railway by six hundred miles. The so-called Chinese Eastern Railway was to be built by a Russo-Chinese Bank, presumably to prevent the Russian government from controlling the railroad, but St. Petersburg got around this by having the minister of finance buy up a controlling share of the bank stock. Russia received the right to move troops over the road even in peacetime, and was to control the right-of-way and telegraph lines. From the names of the foreign ministers—Li Hung-chang of China and Prince Lobanov-Rostovsky of Russia—the arrangement is called the Li-Lobanov Treaty. Witte, however, deserves the credit for its terms.

The Japanese triumph broke the back of Chinese resistance to foreign encroachment upon her soil. Over the next few years the great powers carved China into spheres of influence, forcing the dying empire to grant them concessions to build railways and generally exploit their spheres economically. Great Britain took the Yangtze Valley, France southwest China, Japan the mainland opposite Formosa. The United States took the high-sounding "moral" position of the Open Door, insisting that all powers should have free access without discrimination to all of China. Germany won a ninety-nine-year lease over Kiaochow and all rights to mining and railway development in the neighboring province of Shantung. England moved in to seize Wei-Hai-Wei.

Russia joined in the scramble for bits of the Chinese Empire, securing a twenty-five-year lease on the tip of the Liaotung Peninsula and gaining the right to build a commercial port at Dalny on the peninsula and a naval base at nearby Port Arthur, both of which were ice-free the year round. That Russia should now seize Port Arthur, which she had forced Japan to surrender after the recent war, was an insult to Japanese sensibilities. Russia also won the right to connect these south Manchurian ports by rail with the Chinese Eastern, thus obtaining military as well as commercial access to all Manchuria, south, east, and west. The Chinese foreign minister Li Hung-chang advised Russia against this march through Manchuria, but he, according to Witte, looked the other way after taking a bribe of a half million rubles. Finally, Russia received the right to develop China north of the Great Wall as an economic sphere of interest and exchanged with Britain a mutual respect for each other's spheres in the Manchu Empire.

Witte was opposed to some of the pressure into north China, but his influence in foreign affairs was dwindling. Nicholas came under the sway of adventurers who did not scruple to involve the nation in serious conflict to further their own pocket-lining schemes or wild imperialist ventures. Alexander Bezobrazov, whom Witte opposed and Plehve supported, led the group in urging the tsar to permit Russian political and economic pressure not only in Manchuria but in independent Korea as well. Admiral Alexeyev was named viceroy of the Far Eastern provinces, being responsible not to the foreign office but directly to his friend Bezobrazov and the tsar. Russian troops poured into Manchuria; Harbin, Port Arthur, and Dalny became thoroughly Russian cities. The province became a base of political and military operations and intrigue in Korea, the "independent" kingdom where Japanese influence also was being pressed. The Bezobrazov clique organized a company in which the tsar himself invested to exploit the timber resources on the Yalu River in northern Korea.

An awakening nationalism in China produced the so-called Boxer Rebellion, which aimed to throw the foreign "devils" out of the empire. When the Boxers rose in Manchuria and destroyed a section of the Chinese Eastern Railway, a Russian force moved in to restore order. When the rebels attacked the foreign legations in Peking, Russian troops marched to the capital to save European lives. At this show of strength the Chinese agreed to withdraw their troops from Manchuria and to surrender all military depots in the province. An appointee of the Russian Foreign Office settled in Mukden to supervise the administration of Manchuria, and to all intents the country became a Russian province.

After forcing China to recognize Korean independence at the close of the Sino-Japanese war Japan moved quickly to extend political as well as economic domination over the Hermit Kingdom. But aggressive Japanese agents provoked anti-Japanese feeling in Korea, particularly after the country's queen was killed by a Japanese assassin. The king sought sanctuary in the Russian legation and from his refuge announced a program of Russian-dictated reforms. Japan and Russia came to an agreement to share in the stabilization and development of Korea, but Russian advisers to the king and a military mission threatened to relegate the Japanese to second place in the condominium. When the railroads under construction in Korea turned out to be the Russian broad gauge, and therefore simply a spur of the Trans-Siberian and the Chinese Eastern, the Japanese had reason for alarm. Korea under Russian control would become a "dagger poised at the heart of Japan."

By the Anglo-Japanese Alliance of 1902 the two nations promised neutrality if either's interests in Korea or China were threatened by an outside power, but each agreed to assist the other if the aggressor were joined by another. If her differences with Russia could not be settled, Japan could now face Russia without fear of intervention by a third power friendly to the tsar. When Bezobrazov's timber company moved into north Korea, bringing with it Russian soldiers disguised as laborers, Japan broke off the dragging negotiations for settlement and attacked Port Arthur. The diplomatic world was amazed that Japan, which had emerged from isolation only forty years earlier, should show the audacity to challenge the Russian colossus. Few realized the extent to which Russia's internal weakness had sapped her military strength.

THE RUSSO-JAPANESE WAR

This "little victorious war," which some of the tsar's advisers welcomed as a way of shifting the nation's attention away from its domestic grievances, of "dispelling the revolutionary fumes," turned out to be fatal to the autocracy. Indeed, "no more disastrous and badly conducted war could be found in the whole of Russia's history" (Lobanov-Rostovsky). The war minister assured Nicholas that the Japanese were unprepared and untrained and that they had not mastered the military tactics which they had studied in Russian and German academies. On the other hand, he argued, Russia was completely ready and could throw into Korea in a fortnight's time three times as many troops as would be necessary to defeat the contemptible Asiatics. The campaign, he promised, would be a simple military parade. In fact, it turned out to be a parade of defeats, for the Russians won not a single victory.

Early in 1904 the Japanese attacked the Russian base at Port Arthur without a declaration of war. Russian troops were driven north across the Yalu and fell back upon Mukden. When the army under Kuropatkin, the Russian war minister, advanced to relieve Port Arthur it was soundly beaten and the great naval base was forced to surrender. The victory, however, was costly to the Japanese, who counted a hundred thousand casualties against a fourth as many for the Russians. An eight-day battle at Mukden between a half million men on both sides ended in another Russian withdrawal. The Baltic fleet steamed half way around the world to Asiatic waters, en route firing upon English fishing boats in the North Sea which it mistook for Japanese warships. When the fleet arrived in the Tsushima Strait "most of its ships fought their way to the bottom of the ocean" (Robinson), only two capital ships managing to limp away to Vladivostok. The Japanese seized Sakhalin Island and landed a force at the mouth of the Amur River to threaten the Russian rear. The war was characterized on the Russian side by gross mismanagement, disagreement and rivalry in the high command, contradictory orders, personal jealousies, and stupid judgments bordering on treason. As usual the men in the ranks fought bravely but purposelessly under army commanders who were either overly cautious, inexperienced, or downright incompetent. The government kept its best troops in Europe, sending to Manchuria chiefly reservists, men near forty who had not campaigned for years. Some of the men were equipped with new magazine rifles which they did not know how to operate, and the artillery had had no time for training with the new rapid-fire field piece issued as the troops left for the front. The service of supply was at its worst, although it must be admitted that the nation faced an almost insuperable logistical problem in having to depend solely upon the partially-completed single-track Trans-Siberian Railway, a supply line over four thousand miles long.

By the summer of 1905 the Japanese, nearing military and financial exhaustion, were ready to accept a peace offer. The Russian government, while growing in military strength, was facing a crisis at home and also was anxious for peace. The American President Theodore Roosevelt invited the two to send peace delegations to Portsmouth, New Hampshire. Theretofore strongly pro-Japanese, Roosevelt began to be uneasy about continued Japanese successes which might lead to a serious disturbance of the balance of power in the Far East. Witte, who led the Russian delegation, had orders not to surrender any territory and not to agree to an indemnity.

By the terms of the Treaty of Portsmouth Russia recognized Japan's special interests in Korea, ceded the southern half of Sakhalin Island to Japan, extended to her the right to fish in the Sea of Okhotsk and the Bering Strait, and turned over to the Japanese the lease on the Liaotung Peninsula together with all installations. Both powers agreed to withdraw from Manchuria, leaving it to Chinese rule. Witte successfully parried Japan's effort to force the payment of an indemnity. In gratitude that Russia had lost no more than she did, the tsar awarded his chief delegate the title of Count Witte.

RURAL UNREST

The hope of Alexander III's advisers that serious peasant disturbances would level off at around fifty a year were dashed in the early years of the twentieth century. In 1902 the figure reached well over three hundred, and there were nearly half as many the following year. The uprisings were most severe in the rich black-soil provinces of Poltava and Kharkov, where the villagers broke into the landowners' barns to secure grain for themselves and their cattle. The peasants, up in arms almost to a man, destroyed some eighty mansions. In Kharkov the authorities were unable to quell the outbreaks, which ended only when the rioters tired of their looting and burning. But in Poltava the police worked a brutal vengeance. Innocent and guilty alike—the authorities did not trouble to sort them out—were flogged into insensibility. After two hundred lashes from the birch rod some spent two months in hospital; others were dragged off to prison instead of to the hospital. One was taken to his home unconscious after two hundred strokes, but the police followed him home and horsewhipped him until he was half dead.

The government made a serious effort to determine the cause of the outbreaks by questioning village elders. One of them answered that his village had too little land, no grain, no hay, and no pasture. The village was perennially short of food, the crop each year carrying them only into December. When asked whether the propaganda pamphlets of the Socialist Revolutionaries had stirred up the people, he answered, "It is not the little books that are dangerous, but that there is nothing for us to eat." Indifferent to such pleas, the authorities imprisoned eight hundred peasants and forced the villagers to pay the landowners a quarter million rubles in damages.

It is true that the Socialist Revolutionaries distributed thousands of leaflets in the villages of South Russia, that the Social Democrats were not idle in the countryside, and that teachers and doctors and veterinarians not only sympathized with the misery they could hardly relieve but urged the peasants on to revolt. But what moved the peasant most of all was the sight day after day of the great, rich fields of some neighboring landowner lying just across the fence from his own stingy plot. "The poorest peasant, who did not need to be told that he was hungry, hardly needed an agitator to tell him that if he could plow these neighboring lands, and keep the crop, there would be more loaves of black bread in his stove on baking-day, and perhaps leather boots in place of laced-bark slippers between him and the snow" (Robinson).

Official half-measures to reduce tension in the villages began in 1903, when the *mir's* collective responsibility for payment of taxes and redemption dues was abolished in most, but not all, of the provinces. The government may have hoped that by breaking up the group in this way it would promote individual selfishness and so set villager against villager, *kulak* or rich peasant against poor. The desired effect followed, but the vast majority remained poor and grew still poorer and more desperate. Then, caught losing a war abroad and threatened with a determined revolution at home, tsardom was forced to make substantial concessions.

URBAN UNREST

Witte observed in 1895 that Russia had no working class in the same sense as did the countries of the West. He congratulated himself that the nation consequently had no labor problem. Within two years the minister of interior was bemoaning the fact that not only had a working class appeared but that it was becoming revolutionary in outlook and keenly aware of the need for organization. The event that had disturbed the official slumber was a determined but orderly strike of thirty thousand spinners and weavers in the Petersburg area.

In the late fall of 1902 the workmen walked out of the railway shops in Rostov in protest against long hours and low wages. Soon they were joined by employees in the ironworks and other factories and even bakeries and tobacco shops. The Social Democrats moved in to organize daily meetings attended by thirty thousand people of all classes, haranguing the crowds with demands for higher wages and better conditions of work, denouncing capitalism and the autocracy. Police and Cossacks fired upon the crowd and galloped away, leaving several dead and wounded. But the meetings went on for three weeks, after which the strikers gave in and returned to work. While the strike failed to accomplish any of its aims, it was a huge success in the support it commanded.

During the spring and summer of 1903 all South Russia was in ferment. There were meetings again in Rostov, a strike of the employees in the oil fields of Baku joined by every laborer in the city, and general strikes in Batum and Kiev and Kerch and Odessa, the number of strikers running well over two hundred thousand. All shops closed, transportation halted, streets were dark, goods went undelivered, and food shortages developed. Industrial life came to an end. Tension mounted as workers paraded singing in the streets and throngs gathered to hear speeches and police and troops sullenly waited for someone to cast the first stone which would justify the swinging of clubs and whips and sabers. In every city the demands of the striking workers were the same—substantial pay raises, a minimum wage, an eight-hour day, an end to fines, the legalization of unions, recognition of the right to strike. All these were part of the program of the Social Democrats, but to these usual trade-union requests the S.D.'s added a call for the freedoms of speech, press, conscience, and association, an end to arbitrary arrest, and the convening of a national assembly. By 1904 nearly two thousand strikes had flared over South Russia.

The most significant development in labor circles in the early twentieth century was the growing political consciousness of the workers. The Social Democrats, who contributed the great majority of agitators and speakers, did much to further the political education of the proletariat, cleverly intertwining economic with political goals. It can hardly be denied, however, that the two went hand in hand. Without civil rights there could be no agitation for or hope for purely economic gains. Indeed, the strikers seemed to sense this, or were led by the S.D.'s to understand it, for they often lost sight of their trade-union demands in their hatred for the government. This growing political consciousness brought the laborers out of the workshops into the streets, there to mingle with other workers, students, clerks, and small shopkeepers to hear the harangues of the revolutionary firebrands. Their meetings were attacked by the police and Cossacks until "the right of public meeting was vindicated by the simple process of meeting in such numbers that dispersal was impossible" (Mavor). The strikers and revolutionary leaders tore the initiative from the government and simply seized and exercised the rights of free speech, assembly, and press which they were denied in quiet times. Occasionally barricades appeared in the streets, a sure indication of a growing determination to put an end to a regime no longer tolerable. The only solution to the mounting pressure which suggested itself to tsardom was Plehve's "little victorious war."

ASSASSINATIONS

Through the years when peasant *Jacqueries* were increasing in fury and strikes were paralyzing the industries of South Russia, the terroristic organization of the Socialist Revolutionaries was scoring frequently against government officials. In February, 1901, an expelled university student shot Bogolepov, the minister of education, and became the hero of student demonstrations in St. Petersburg and Moscow. An attempt upon the life of Pobiedonostsev a month later barely missed. In 1902 a student shot and killed the interior minister Sipiagin, who was succeeded by Plehve. An effort to kill one provincial governor failed; another succeeded. The governor-general of Finland fell to an assassin's bullet. The Grand Duke Sergei, uncle and son-in-law of the tsar, was murdered, as was the military governor of Moscow. Plehve himself was removed by a bomb thrown on the orders of Azev, the police agent who was at the same time head of the terroristic organization of the S.R.'s.

The liberals, too, grew bold in their distaste for autocracy. Forbidden to meet openly, zemstvo leaders held regular private conferences from 1901 onward and smuggled into Russia the periodical *Liberation,* published in Germany. The Liberal party, organized politically in 1904 as the Union of Liberation, mild though its program was, had to meet as clandestinely as the most uncompromising revolutionary societies. Plehve ordered the zemstvo of Tver disbanded because he thought it subversive, and refused to allow the re-election of the conservative Shipov as chairman of the zemstvo of Moscow. When the Liberals called a halt to pressure upon the government while the war with Japan was in progress they established a society for war relief, but Plehve did his best to prevent this harmless enterprise from functioning. Even the Liberals were left no choice but to believe that the country's real enemy was not Japan but the government.

THE ELEVEN POINTS

Plehve had so convinced the emperor that only he could deal with the flowing tide of revolution that when an assassin's bomb dispatched him the interior ministry stood vacant for over a month. The tsar finally filled the post with Prince Sviatopolk-Mirsky, a known liberal. During "the spring," as Mirsky's brief tenure of office is called, there was some relaxation in the severity of bureaucratic controls; a few political exiles were pardoned; press censorship was softened, and the cry for constitutional government went unpunished.

A convention of Russian liberal and radical organizations met in Paris in the early fall of 1904. The S.D.'s boycotted the meeting, but the S.R.'s were there along with Professors Struve and Miliukov for the Union of Liberation and representatives of Finnish, Polish, and other socialist or nationalist groups representing minorities. The delegates agreed that each attending group should work in its own way for the end of absolutism and the birth of constitutional government in Russia.

A month after the Paris meeting the Union of Liberation announced its own call to action: it urged the zemstvos to demand a national constitution; it arranged a series of banquets, ostensibly to commemorate the anniversary of the court reforms of the sixties, which would propagandize for a constitution; it stimulated the organization of unions of professional men, which soon joined in a Union of Unions.

Prince Mirsky permitted a congress of zemstvo men to gather in St. Petersburg in November, 1904. The president, Shipov, was unable to curb the liberals when the assembly drafted an eleven-point program. The famous "Eleven Points," which came to be the program for all liberal and many radical thinkers from that moment to the end of the monarchy, demanded freedom of speech, press, association, and conscience; freedom from arbitrary arrest; a broadened franchise for local elections; equality of all classes and nationalities before the law; an end to martial law in peacetime; amnesty for political prisoners; and the creation of a representative legislature. On the question of whether the assembly should possess legislative or only consultative power, the liberals overwhelmed Shipov and his conservative fellows three to one.

In the succeeding months one banquet after another and one zemstvo after another passed resolutions approving the eleven points. "Impertinent and tactless," the tsar called such resolutions. An imperial *ukaz* repeated earlier vague assurances of social and economic reforms. Nicholas spurned Prince Mirsky's suggestion that the State Council should be enlarged by bringing in members elected by the zemstvos. Blaming the liberals for the popular unrest that was sweeping the nation, he ordered them to leave off dabbling in matters that were none of their concern.

BLOODY SUNDAY

A Russian Orthodox priest, George Gapon, Zubatov's agent of the "police socialism" movement in the capital, organized in 1903 the "Assembly of Russian Factory and Mill Workers of St. Petersburg." The constitution of this police-sponsored organization announced its aims to be "the sober and rational passing of leisure time by the members" in search of "spiritual and moral" values and the stimulation of "prudent views upon the duties and rights of workers." Local units or "clubs," where drinking and gambling would be forbidden, would meet weekly to join in religious singing or for concerts or to read "useful" publications or to debate religious and moral issues. Its most dangerous activity would be the accumulation of a fund to dole out sickness and unemployment benefits, but no payments were to go to men on strike. The first gathering in 1904 heard the reading of the constitution, approved by Plehve on the promise that the group would stick to nonpolitical subjects, and broke up after joyfully singing "God Save the Tsar." Later Sunday meetings provided tea, dancing, or lectures on Russian history, literature, geology, and economic problems.

In less than a year's time the membership numbered, according to one account, perhaps nine thousand workers, but many thousands more were attending the weekly meetings. By now many socialists had joined the movement, not because the S.D.'s and S.R.'s deliberately sought to capture the organization or were ever anything but suspicious of it, but because the two socialist parties had won many sympathizers who joined Father Gapon's "clubs."

The feeling was widespread among the workers of the time that Russia's sorry plight was not the work of the tsar but of the bureaucrats who surrounded him. If that bureaucratic curtain could be brushed aside, the tsar surely would receive a petition from the hands of his loyal subjects and would correct all the abuses of society. Over Gapon's objection the central committee of the organization drafted a petition and proposed to march with it to the Winter Palace. The petition began: "We working men and inhabitants of St. Petersburg of various classes, our wives and our children and our helpless old parents, come to thee to seek for truth and defense. We have become beggars; we have been oppressed; we are burdened by toil beyond our powers; we are scoffed at; we are not recognized as human beings; we are treated as slaves who must suffer their bitter fate and who must keep silent. We are choked by despotism and irresponsibility, and we are breathless." There followed a description of their fruitless efforts to win from their employers better pay and better working conditions.

The central theme of the petition, however, was the blame they heaped upon officialdom for their beast-like lives. "In us as in all Russian people there is not recognized any human right. We have been enslaved under the auspices of thy officials, with their assistance. All the people—working men as well as peasants—are handed over to the discretion of the officials of the government, who are thieves of the property of the State—robbers who not only take no care of the interests of the people, but who trample these interests beneath their feet. The government officials have brought the country to complete destruction, have involved it in a detestable war, and have further and further led it to ruin."

Then came an enumeration of measures the group thought indispensable to its own and the nation's salvation, including the "eleven points," termination of the war, and end to redemption payments, substitution of an income tax for excise taxes, cheap credit, legalization of trade unions and separation of church and state. "Here, Sire," the petition closed, "are our principal necessities with which we come to thee. Order and take an oath to comply with these requests and thou wilt make Russia happy and famous and thou wilt impress thy name in our hearts and in the hearts of our posterity to all eternity. If thou wilt not order and wilt not answer our prayer, we shall die here before thy palace."

On the bitter cold, snowy morning of Sunday, January 9, 1905, columns of workers, totalling perhaps two hundred thousand, converged from the outskirts of St. Petersburg upon the Winter Palace. The tsar's uncle, Grand Duke Vladimir, commanded the city's security forces, which had been augmented the day before when the police agents belonging to the organization had notified the authorities. Some columns were stopped at the city's gates, others managed to reach the Nevsky Prospect—St. Petersburg's main boulevard—and Kazan Cathedral and the Winter Palace. Everywhere the troops fired into the crowds, killing hundreds and wounding thousands more. Such was Bloody Sunday, or "Vladimir's Day."

Father Gapon fled abroad, whence he addressed an open letter to the tsar warning that he had invited a bloody revolution by his refusal to receive the petitioners. "Let all blood which has to be shed fall upon thee, hangman, and thy kindred." However, he returned to Russia and again joined up with the political police. The terroristic organization of the S.R.'s, under Azev, ran him down in Finland and hanged him.

In a naïve attempt to prove to the world that the march under Father Gapon was not typical of Russian working-class temper, the police chief of St. Petersburg, General Trepov, rounded up a dozen "loyal and decently-dressed workmen" and sent them in imperial carriages to an audience with the emperor. After the interview, which the delegates spent bent over in the "Russian bow," they found their way in third-class coaches back to the factories whence they had come, there to be ostracized by their fellow workers.

Bloody Sunday opened the Revolution of 1905. The reception prepared for the marchers destroyed all popular faith in the tsar; henceforth he and his bureaucrats were lumped together in responsibility for the nation's ills. The demonstration revealed to the workers of the capital that they could muster in sizable and formidable numbers. Moscow and South Russia had learned the lesson years earlier, but few had thought it possible that such an assembly could gather in St. Petersburg. Barricades had appeared during the recent march. Workers over the rest of Russia were quick to take heart from the bold action of their fellows in the capital. Four hundred thousand struck during this month of January, 1905, more than the total number who went out on strike during the entire preceding decade. The government had reason to grow fearful.

THE TSAR GRANTS CONCESSIONS

The lengthening list of assassinations and the growing determination of the masses, rural and urban, prompted Nicholas to order some slight relaxation of autocratic rule. When Sviatopolk-Mirsky resigned after Bloody Sunday his successor as interior minister, Alexander Bulygin, received an imperial order expressing the tsar's willingness "to summon the worthiest men elected by the people to participate in the drafting and consideration of legislation." Nicholas was consenting in this so-called "Bulygin constitution" to a consultative assembly or Duma only. In a directive to the Senate he restored the right of his subjects to appeal directly to the throne. A third measure repealed the laws against dissenters and extended religious toleration to all sects. How these orders would be carried out would depend, of course, upon local police, against whose actions all complaints would be looked upon as subversive.

These halting steps came too late to satisfy even the moderates. The Union of Liberation demanded universal suffrage and a direct secret ballot to elect an assembly empowered to give Russia a constitution. The Zemstvo Congress drew up, to serve as a basis for discussion, a constitutional proposal incorporating Western democratic practices, and announced that it would work closely with "the broad masses of the people" in carrying through political reform. The newly formed Peasant Union met in Moscow to press its demand for distribution of gentry land without compensation to the landlords.

The revolutionaries kept up their assassinations of officials, the peasants their attacks upon landlords' estates. The Union of Unions meeting in Moscow passed a resolution in which it referred to the Romanovs and the bureaucrats who surrounded them as a "gang of robbers." Even the armed forces showed a disposition to defy authority. Some officers were shot by their own men at Mukden. A mutiny developed aboard the newest and most powerful battleship in the Black Sea fleet, the "Potemkin," whose crew hoisted the red flag, bombarded Odessa, and finally was interned in Romania when the ship docked. Sixty crewmen were shot or packed off to penal servitude from another battleship on which an attempted mutiny failed.

Early in June, 1905, a delegation of zemstvo men, headed by Prince Sergei Trubetskoy, detailed to the tsar the growing restlessness that was sweeping the country, begged him to draw away the bureaucratic curtain that separated him from his people, urged him to call the Duma he had promised, and asked that it represent all classes fairly. Telling the delegation to dismiss its doubts, Nicholas pontificated: "Let there be established, as of old, union between the tsar and all Russia, which shall form the foundation of an order corresponding to ancient Russian principles." He was clearly referring to a *Zemskii Sobor* and not to a modern legislature.

Prodded into further action the government announced the conditions under which the promised Duma would assemble. Delegates would be chosen by indirect election—voters would elect representatives who in turn would elect those who would sit in the Duma. The right to vote heavily favored the peasants, assumed for some reason to be safely conservative, and the mass of urban workers together with most of the intelligentsia were disfranchised by a high property qualification for city voters. Prince Trubetskoy's pleas were ignored. The government's terms pleased neither extreme: reactionaries opposed any Duma at all, while the revolutionaries determined to boycott the rigged elections. Perhaps in an effort to provide an escape valve, the authorities returned to the universities the right to govern themselves and to arrange meetings without interference by the police. Classrooms immediately were thrown open to public meetings and the professors sympathetically stepped down to allow popular speakers to address the growing crowds of workers, soldiers, shopkeepers, and students. And in this atmosphere the pent-up hatreds of the masses spewed forth in bitter venom from the mouths of the revolutionaries who rose to speak.

THE OCTOBER MANIFESTO

In early fall the bakers and printers of Moscow walked out on strike and workers in St. Petersburg struck in sympathy. No sooner had this problem been settled than the illegal but active railway union called a strike in Moscow. The movement quickly spread to the ends of the empire and all transportation and telegraph service halted. The strikers demanded an eight-hour day as well as such political concessions as a general amnesty, full civil rights, and a constitutional convention. Other workers joined in, closing down shops, food stores, schools, banks, public utilities, government offices, and even the ballet theatre. Crowds milled in the streets shouting revolutionary slogans and singing the *Marseillaise*. Shortages of food and fuel threatened to become critical. The nation was paralyzed. Some cities were completely shut off from outside contact. Barricades went up in the streets of Kharkov and Odessa, and civilians fought back the troops with sticks and stones instead of running away.

In mid-October there was organized the St. Petersburg Soviet, or Council of Workers' Deputies, consisting of perhaps forty representatives of various labor forces in the capital. Within a month it had grown to over five hundred delegates, two-thirds of whom came from metallurgical plants, others from textile factories and printing firms. Organized simply as a council of strike committees, the Soviet assumed political functions, sending workers' demands to the city duma and to the police. Its executive committee consisted of twenty-two labor delegates and three each from the Bolshevik, Menshevik, and Socialist Revolutionary parties. The Mensheviks George Khrustalev-Nosar and Leon Trotsky served as chairman and vice-chairman respectively of the executive committee. The only printing press operating in the capital turned out the Soviet's official newspaper *Izvestiia*. Soviets appeared in towns all over Russia.

The government seemed likely to collapse. The tsar sent Pobiedonostsev into retirement and called in Count Witte as his chief adviser. But political power lay for the moment in the hands of the St. Petersburg Soviet, to whom soviets in the provinces sent calls for aid and requests for orders. Witte dealt with Khrustalev as though he and not Witte were Russia's chief minister. Nicholas, utterly bewildered and frightened, asked Witte what to do. The Count could offer him only two choices—either grant a constitution or restore order by establishing a military dictatorship. When the tsar offered his uncle, Grand Duke Nicholas, the post of dictator, the grand duke threatened to shoot himself on the spot. Left no alternative, the emperor signed the constitutional manifesto drafted by Witte.

The manifesto of October 17, 1905, granted freedom of speech, press, association, and conscience and freedom from arbitrary arrest; vaguely promised the right to vote to those segments of the population denied that right under the "Bulygin constitution"; guaranteed that no enactment should become law without the consent of the national Duma; and gave the Duma the power of controlling administration officials. Russia finally had her constitution. Whether the government which granted it would respect it was another matter.

Miliukov's recently-organized party of Constitutional Democrats, or Cadets as they came to be called, welcomed the October Manifesto as a victory for moderation over extremes of right and left. The Soviet, spurred on by the show of strength of the working class, continued the general strike and demanded a constituent assembly, a democratic republic, and eventually a socialist state. But the people had had enough of unemployment and shortages. The Soviet was forced to call off the strike.

Reactionaries among bureaucrats, service officers, gentry, and priests organized a "Union of the Russian People" to counteract the forces of liberalism and radicalism. The grand dukes and even the tsar and his son became members. Other extreme counterrevolutionary groups, known as Black Hundreds, operated with full knowledge of the police to stamp out left-wing action or sentiment wherever they saw or imagined it. They beat up students and professors and arranged hundreds of pogroms against the Jews beginning the very day after the issuance of the October Manifesto. Beatings, lootings, burnings, and mutilations were common sights all over the Jewish Pale. In Odessa Black Hundred hooliganism went on for four days while the police stood quietly by or joined in the fun. Thousands were killed and other thousands injured and scarred. Reactionary hoodlums murdered two members of the first Duma and sought twice unsuccessfully to assassinate Witte.

At the very moment the tsar was signing the October Manifesto peasants all over South Russia were attacking the estates of the gentry. Over two thousand manor houses were burned or torn down in a fortnight's time. Mutiny broke out among the sailors at the Baltic naval base at Cronstadt and later at Sevastopol and Vladivostok. Troops in Siberia and Manchuria became rebellious. Meetings all over Poland demanded autonomy. A general strike in Finland aimed at restoring the duchy's ancient freedoms. The government gave in to the Finns, but imposed martial law upon Poland and broke the mutinies in the armed forces with loyal troops. Expeditionary forces marched into the provinces to quell the peasant revolts; then, to pacify the peasants, the redemption payments were cut by half for 1906 and abolished for 1907 and after.

The spectacle of the government issuing the October Manifesto and then lashing out at the elements which had forced it prompted the St. Petersburg Soviet to thunder that Russia did not want "a Cossack whip wrapped up in a constitution." In early November the Soviet ordered a second general strike demanding an end to death sentences and to martial law. But no other city supported the walkout, and even in the capital the strike was a failure. Nor did the armed forces respond this time to the call for action. Witte appealed to the workers for patience and moderation. The city had had enough of work stoppages and shortages. The Soviet was forced to call off the strike after only three days.

Prime Minister Witte now moved cautiously to recover control of the nation. Khrustalev, president of the St. Petersburg Soviet, was arrested, as were the members of the executive committee of the Peasant Union meeting in Moscow. The capital was put under martial law; strikes and public meetings were outlawed.

The Soviet came out with a manifesto of its own, demanding the overthrow of tsardom and the calling of a constituent assembly; it urged the people to refuse to pay taxes, to withdraw all savings from the banks, and to hoard gold in an attempt to drive the government into bankruptcy. Newspapers which published the manifesto were closed down, but the citizens of the capital responded by withdrawing a hundred million rubles from the banks. Witte had the entire Soviet seized and thrown into prison. The members were tried later, and Trotsky, among others, was exiled to Siberia for life. A new Soviet was quickly elected and called another general strike, the third in seven weeks.

The third strike call was practically ignored in St. Petersburg, but a companion call from the Moscow Soviet was more successful. For ten days the Moscow strikers fought off loyal troops and artillery brought in from St. Petersburg. The rebellion was finally crushed with savage cruelty as the commander of the Guards regiments ordered his men not to bother with prisoners. Perhaps a thousand men, women, and children were killed on the rebel side. The Revolution of 1905 burned itself out in the futile rising in Moscow, although unrest continued to smoulder in the countryside for another year.

The peasants were no more satisfied than were urban workers with the political concessions granted by the tsar in October. Nor were they bought off by the cancellation of redemption payments. An All-Russian Congress of Peasants called by the Peasants' Union met in Moscow in November to provide vocal leadership for the action the peasants were taking all over Russia. Some speakers condoned the expropriations that continued spontaneously, expressing doubt that the Duma when it met would sanction the work. Others urged the congress to follow the lead of the Socialist Revolutionaries, who encouraged the people to seize the land and to defend themselves against any who would take it back. Some argued for the convening of a constituent assembly, renouncing as traitors those who supported the elections to the Duma. But it was the land question which drew most fire. There was general support for the socialization of agricultural land, its use to be allowed only to those who worked it without the aid of hired labor.

It was not the All-Russian Congress of Peasants which provided leadership for the peasants, however, but rather the other way round. "The peasants were already smoking out the landlords" (Robinson), turning them out into the road and warning them not to return, driving away livestock, tearing off iron roofing to patch their own leaky huts, carting off furniture and food and equipment, and burning what could not be carried away. Some villagers seized a neighboring estate and fenced it off in plots and seeded it to their own crop. Others turned their cattle into the landowner's pasture. It was the worst rising since the days of Pugachev and much more widespread.

There was no decline in the extent or intensity of the *Jacqueries* after the October Manifesto. Indeed, they increased in number and determination in the following year. The peasants went on seizing land while voting for their delegates to the Duma which they hoped would approve the expropriations they had carried through on their own initiative. Many of the gentry took for granted that these seizures of land would be permanent, that the peasants would not give up what they had already taken. General Dmitry Trepov, the governor-general of St. Petersburg who was hated for his vicious use of troops against strikers, told Witte that he would gladly surrender half his estate without remuneration, for he was convinced that only by doing so might he be allowed to keep the other half.

Troops marched off into the countryside as though to war. Some peasants gave in at the sight of armed forces; others threw stones and so invited attack. After the peasants surrendered, whole villages would be flogged, huts would be burned, and leaders summarily shot. Minister of Interior Peter Durnovo ordered the risings put down at all costs: "It is a useful thing to wipe the rebellious villages off the face of the earth, and to exterminate the rebels themselves without mercy." The government could not forgive the nation for forcing it to make concessions and seemed to take sadistic delight in torturing its own people. Officialdom admitted to carrying out thirty-five hundred executions between 1906 and 1908. It did not bother to tot up the number killed and wounded in street fighting or in campaigns against the villages.

THE FIRST DUMA

The Duma was elected, under rules laid down by Witte, by a suffrage so broad that the royal family never forgave him for his "radicalism." All who paid real estate or business taxes had the right to vote, as did most urban renters. Rural voters were divided into great landowners, small landowners, and peasants, each group voting separately for electors who in turn chose the representatives to sit in the Duma. The city vote was similarly divided into those who paid high taxes and "the others," each group choosing electors who selected the Duma delegates. This indirect method of voting characterized Russian elections down to 1936. The representation was heavily weighted in favor of the rural segment of the population, in the confidence that landowners and peasants were more likely to be conservative than were townsmen.

Meanwhile the tsar had in effect emasculated the October Manifesto by creating a second legislative chamber with power equal to that of the Duma. The State Council was expanded to become an upper house, half of its members to be appointed by the tsar, the other half to be elected by the clergy, provincial zemstvos, the nobility, business management, the universities, and the academy of sciences.

Before the first Duma convened the government issued the "fundamental laws" which detailed the powers of the legislature. Bills to become law must pass both houses and be signed by the tsar, who had an absolute veto. Ministers were responsible to the emperor who appointed them. Many budgetary items were not to be questioned by the Duma; currency and loans

Nicholas **II** and his family

Rasputin   Kerensky

Lenin

Trotsky as an exile

A collective farm, showing individual plots

were controlled by the finance minister; the army and navy, along with their budgets, were beyond the jurisdiction of the legislature; if the two houses approved different budget figures, the tsar could accept either; if the legislature passed no budget, the government could continue the figures of the previous year. The Duma could not even discuss its own powers. The tsar's control over foreign affairs, appointments, censorship, police, armed forces, and even summoning and dismissing the Duma was confirmed. When the duma was not in session the emperor might govern by "decrees," which were supposed to be submitted for confirmation within a month after the reconvention of the Duma. The government managed to get around this provision by simply ignoring it. The fundamental laws reaffirmed that "the supreme autocratic power belongs to the Emperor of All the Russias" and warned that obedience to the royal will was "ordained by God Himself."

When the fundamental laws had been drafted Witte was no longer needed and was rudely dismissed. His place was taken by Ivan Goremykin, a confirmed reactionary who soundly detested the very idea of a Duma. The new finance minister, Vladimir Kokovtsev, was thoroughly competent in the long tradition of capable men in that ministry; the new minister of interior, Peter Stolypin, had been unusually successful as a provincial governor in handling the peasant revolts of 1905 with a minimum of bloodshed.

Before 1905 political parties in Russia had existed only outside the law. Now the October Manifesto legalized all parties, even the revolutionary groups which spurned the cloak of respectability. Two parties, newly organized for the occasion, now stepped forward to lead the parliamentary movement. The Cadets, or Constitutional Democrats, led by the historian Paul Miliukov would have preferred the calling of a constituent assembly to replace the monarchy with a republic. But seeing no immediate prospect of this they were willing to support the Duma, which they hoped would draft a constitution turning the autocracy into something like the English constitutional monarchy. They promised the voters to work for full civil rights, for universal and equal suffrage, for distribution of land belonging to the state, the church and, "when necessary," individual proprietors who should be paid for giving up their land. The other new party, called the Octobrists, succeeded to the position of the conservative element in the Zemstvo Congress. Its aim was to hold the line with the October Manifesto, to support the government in resisting popular pressure, to parry the effort of Cadets and others to carry through extensive land reform. The Zemstvo Congress and the Union of Unions ceased to be political agencies as their members lined up with the new parties.

The Duma which convened on April 27, 1906, included an array of forty parties and national groups—for example, the thirty-member Polish Circle, whose primary interest was autonomy for Poland. By far the largest parties were the Cadets, who won a hundred and eighty of the five hundred and twenty seats, and the leftist but not socialist Laborites, who marshalled over a hundred. There were a dozen Octobrists, a hundred unattached peasant members who usually voted with the left, and a few Social Democrats, mostly Mensheviks, for the Bolsheviks had boycotted the elections until the last minute.

After listening to a flabby and pointless speech by the tsar the Duma unanimously passed an address to the throne demanding amnesty for the seventy-five thousand political prisoners who crowded the nation's jails, universal suffrage, an end to indirect elections, dissolution of the State Council as a legislative upper house, ministerial responsibility, and expropriation of large estates to be divided among the peasants. The government introduced its first bill—a measure to provide a laundry at the University of Dorpat. Then Goremykin came down to tell the house that its demands could not be considered and that it was not even free to discuss such things as ministerial responsibility and the existence of the upper chamber. Obviously, Nicholas wanted a German Reichstag, the members a British Parliament.

The Duma was allowed to sit for another two months, during which time it clamored for land reform; demanded an end to capital punishment which, indeed, had been illegal since Elizabeth's time; insisted that civil rights be respected; and censured the government for allowing the pogroms to continue. The tsar, meanwhile, considered firing his ministers and replacing them with Cadets in an attempt to buy off the opposition. Miliukov refused to compromise, although other Cadets were less obdurate. Nicholas gave up the idea at the urging of Stolypin and others and ordered the Duma dissolved. The palace where it met was surrounded by troops, and Russia's first modern legislative session closed. Only one measure had passed both houses and received the tsar's signature—a bill providing famine relief for the lower Volga.

Two hundred deputies, most of them Cadets, crossed the border into Finland where they drew up the famous "Viborg Manifesto." The members reviewed their labors in behalf of civil rights, responsible government, and land reform, and took the stand that the government had acted illegally in dissolving the Duma. They insisted that the government had no right to gather taxes and draft men for military service without the consent of the Duma, a claim which had, of course, no legal foundation. They called upon the people to refuse payment of taxes and military conscription, and warned that no loan contracted by the government without the consent of the Duma would be considered valid. All who signed the manifesto were placed on trial and given a three-months prison sentence, which marked them as criminals and therefore ineligible for re-election to the Duma which the administration promised to convene in seven months. The voice of opposition had been stilled, the tsar's advisers supposed.

THE SECOND DUMA

Stolypin took over as prime minister after the dissolution of the first Duma and set about to insure that the next one would be more amenable to royal will. Thousands were robbed of the vote by legal technicalities; "undesirable" candidates were eliminated; Black Hundred gangs broke up assemblies of leftist groups; and priests urged their parishioners to vote for safe candidates. The Cadets had been effectively disposed of as a serious political force by the arrest of their leaders after Viborg. While the party did campaign in the new elections, its program was attacked by the Bolsheviks as ineffective and police scattered its meetings as dangerous to the public peace.

Stolypin's efforts to assure a conservative Duma brought disappointing results. Social Democrats and Socialist Revolutionaries together commanded a hundred votes, Laborites another hundred, and the Cadets a few less. This leftist block outnumbered government supporters more than three to one. Nearly half the members of the Duma had at one time or another been imprisoned or exiled or suffered some indignity from the government.

The session accomplished nothing. Radicals sought without success to bring the government to account for the brutal acts of the police and troops against peasant uprisings, but Stolypin announced arrogantly that there would be "first pacification, then reform." Leftists and rightists hurled recriminations at each other, while the Cadets worked to save the Duma as a public platform and agency of political education. The government trumped up a charge that the Social Democratic party was plotting the murder of the tsar and mutiny in the army and demanded that the Duma hand over its S.D. members for trial. The Duma refused and was dissolved after sitting just a hundred days.

THE THIRD AND FOURTH DUMAS

On the very day of dissolution the emperor signed an *ukaz* declaring that the composition of the first two Dumas had not been satisfactory and pronouncing new electoral regulations. The membership of the house was reduced by eighty; the nationalities of Central Asia, now held to be "foreigners," were disfranchised, and others—peoples of the Caucasus, Poland, and eastern Siberia—had their representation cut by two-thirds. The number of electors, who in turn chose the delegates to the Duma, were so juggled as to leave the landowning gentry with over half, peasants—of whose conservatism the government was no longer confident—with a fifth, property-owning townsmen with a fourth, and urban workers with two per cent. As a consequence, the third Duma, the only one of four to live out its legal life, contained a substantial majority of Octobrists and other rightists and a pitiful sprinkling of Cadets, Laborites, and Social Democrats. The third Duma was regarded as so satisfactory in composition that the government did not tinker with the law by which it was elected. The fourth and last Duma showed the same complexion and about the same men as the third, and yet found occasion to voice opposition to the bungling conduct of the war. Docile as the last two were, the administration occasionally ran up against an adverse vote. To overcome it the emperor simply recessed the Duma for three days, issued the bill in question as an "emergency decree," and forced the Duma when it reconvened to acquiesce in the accomplished fact.

While the nation was disillusioned at the collapse of the revolution and the official policy of repression that followed it, the Duma sought by patience and persistence to become a true parliament. The Cadets, steeped in the British tradition, acted with restraint in their role of opposition, while the Octobrists, at least for a while, supported the government. Stolypin, considered far too liberal by the reactionaries at court, leaned upon the Duma and actively sought its backing. The Octobrist leader Alexander Guchkov much preferred to try to work with the prime minister than see him replaced by someone far more conservative. As a merchant, Guchkov sincerely believed in the emphasis Stolypin placed upon individual enterprise. And so the Duma majority gave its support to Stolypin's land reforms, won the government's consent to expand educational facilities, constructively criticized and gained some improvement in budget procedures, and debated military expenditures with the view to seeing that the government got its money's worth. When the Duma assumed cognizance of military budget estimates in 1908 Guchkov dared to criticize the prosecution of the Russo-Japanese War, attacking not the army but the administration and so putting the Duma in the position of being more patriotic than the government itself.

With the election of the fourth Duma in 1912 only the most reactionary would argue whether the institution had come to stay. In its questioning of ministers, in its promotion of such sound government practices as scientific budgeting and use of statistical services, in its being even more liberal than the administration in assigning funds to the armed forces when it saw the need, in its sharpening its own methods by careful attention to creation and composition of committees, in the determination of Guchkov and the other Octobrists not to accept cabinet appointment until the tsar should grant ministerial responsibility, in all these things the Duma worked conscientiously if cautiously for improved government. The nation came to respect it. The Duma in turn served the nation as its only effective sounding board. With the coming of the war the members did not hesitate to protest vigorously against corruption and inefficiency. As the tsar and his advisers persisted in going their own way regardless of legislative counsel, the Duma became an almost unanimous body of loyal opposition.

THE STOLYPIN REGIME

With the dissolution of the first Duma Stolypin began a carrot-and-stick policy of bludgeoning rebels into submission and at the same time offering concessions intended to reduce the opposition. He set up field courts-martial, which came to be known as "Stolypin's neckties," to deal with public disturbances. These military tribunals were ordered to complete their work on each case in four days: investigate a crime in one day, try the accused in secret in not more than two days, and carry out the execution—usually the death sentence—on the fourth. At the same time peasants were granted the privilege of leaving the *mir* without having family heads or village elders sign their passports. The land captain could no longer sentence villagers to petty fines or imprisonment, although he might still impose such penalties upon officials elected by them. Peasants could now be elected to zemstvo assemblies; in fact, all government offices were opened to that class. The Peasants' Bank was ordered to step up its purchase of land from the gentry for resale to the peasants. The bank bought up more land in 1906 than in the preceding thirteen years, paying the nobles an exhorbitant price for it. But the peasants were loath to buy the land, even at the bank's favorable terms, expecting that revolution would bring them the land without payment.

By far the most significant of the so-called Stolypin reforms, the program for which was announced in November, 1906, had to do with land tenure. The peasant received the right to claim his allotment land in freehold tenure and to demand that the strips into which his allotment typically was divided be consolidated in one piece. State-employed surveyors and local committees were to work out the details between the individual and the commune. The government proposed three steps in the operation. By the first, the individual would apply for and must be given full title to his strips and at the same time freedom from the authority of the *mir*. By the second, he would apply for consolidation of the numerous strips into a single plot. If he stopped here he would retain his hut and vegetable garden in the village. If he proceeded to the third stage he would exchange his hut and vegetable garden in the village for a new home site on his own consolidated land; he and his land and his house would be completely separated from the *mir* in an isolated farmstead similar to that which typifies the American and English scenes. Of the thirteen million allotment holdings existing in 1906 only 3 per cent, or 400,000, had passed through the third stage by the 1917 revolution. Another 6 per cent, or 800,000, had passed through the second.

The plan to break up the village commune and promote individual proprietorship was approved by the vast majority of the nobility and vigorously supported by Witte, although it was opposed by conservative, liberal, and radical parties alike. The idea behind it was to deflect the peasant's interest in expropriation by making him a landlord who in guarding his own property rights would learn to respect those of others. Landowning peasants, officialdom reasoned, would be conservative peasants. Well-to-do farmers—*kulaks,* as they came to be called—would oppose expropriation by which they might lose their own lands to the poor peasants. And the *kulaks* must necessarily support the government which defended their property. Stolypin was candid about it when he reviewed the program for the duma: "The government has placed its wager, not on the needy and the drunken," by which he meant the poor peasants, "but on the sturdy and the strong—on the sturdy individual proprietor who is called upon to play a part in the reconstruction of our tsardom on strong monarchical foundations."

Stolypin pushed his land reform with a ruthlessness prophetic of the socialization of land which the Bolsheviks engineered twenty years later. In fact the "liquidation of the *kulaks*" during the first Five Year Plan was Stolypin's reform in reverse. But tsarist bureaucracy was less efficient than Bolshevik. Only a third of the five million peasants who applied for consolidation of their strips saw the process completed between 1906 and 1913. By 1917, when the revolution put an end to the program, two and a half million peasants had completed consolidation proceedings. Half of these had reached the second and third stages—the consolidated acreage with the owner's house remaining in the village, and the isolated farm. The others were groupings of many strips into a few plots, say fifty strips into ten acreages—in other words, partial consolidations.

The "sturdy and the strong" steadily added to their holdings once they had broken away from the commune. Individuals, most of them peasants who already owned a hundred acres or more, bought nearly twenty-five million acres of farm land from or through the Peasants' Bank by 1917. Individuals bought another twenty-five million acres of land directly from the gentry without going through the bank. While some peasants were adding to their holdings, the nobility as a class were rapidly losing theirs. In the forty years prior to World War I the lands of the gentry shrank by over eight hundred million acres, nearly half the amount they had owned in 1877. Finally, some peasants sold out their holdings in the village and trekked east to find free land in Siberia. The flow across the Urals counted seven hundred thousand colonists in 1908 and again the following year, although 15 per cent returned to European Russia disappointed. In the twenty years preceding the outbreak of World War I well over three million peasants moved into

Siberia, but that same generation saw the rural population of Russia increase by nine times that number.

The government undertook a revolution of its own in inaugurating the land reform program, but a revolution that barely got under way before the war of 1914 slowed it down, and the overturn of the monarchy in 1917 brought it to a halt. In breaking up the *mir* it dissolved the last of the social ties that had bound rural society since the sixteenth century. In encouraging individual initiative in agriculture, in substituting capitalism for feudalism in the countryside, it sought an end to the collectivism that had contributed to the retardation of farming for generations.

THE LAST YEARS OF PEACE

There were slow gains in Russian agricultural production in the years immediately following the inauguration of the Stolypin program. The growth of the cooperative movement—in credit, production, consumption, and marketing—made possible an appreciable rise in peasant farm income. Well-to-do peasants showed an interest in improving breeds of livestock and careful selection of seed. Farm machinery, whose use was impossible in the days of the strips, became increasingly popular, although there were still only a hundred and sixty tractors in all Russia in 1914.

Living conditions of the peasant masses continued to be desperately low by European and American standards. Three-fifths to three-fourths of the average family budget went for food alone and most of the rest for clothing, fuel, and repairs to the hut. In Tula province, a hundred miles south of Moscow, a committee appointed to look into the needs of agriculture described peasant life in 1902: "The dwelling of a Tula peasant is usually a cottage of eighteen by twenty-one feet and seven feet high. Cottages having no chimneys are still very common, the smoke being let out through a hole in the roof. Almost all cottages have thatched roofs which often leak, and in the winter the walls are generally covered with dung to keep the place warm. Earth floors are the rule because in cold weather lambs, calves, pigs, and even cows are brought into the cottage. In localities that have no forests the peasants use straw for fuel, and in the years of poor harvest even dung, thus depriving their fields of much-needed manure. Bath-houses are practically non-existent. The peasants almost never use soap. Meat, meal, lard and vegetable oil appear on the family table only on rare occasions, perhaps two or three times a year. The normal fare consists of bread, kvass and often cabbage and onions. In brief, the poverty of the peasant establishment is astounding (Florinsky)."

Industry was prospering mightily in the years after 1910, if not its workers at least its owners. Production figures rose sharply although Russia continued to occupy about the same position relative to the production of other nations. Consolidation of production units into giant enterprises continued; by 1914 well over half the nation's workers were employed by plants whose labor force exceeded five hundred. Foreign capital continued to flow into the country, chiefly from the Entente powers. France alone controlled three-fourths of Russia's iron and coal output.

Labor unions were recognized in 1906 but were forbidden to strike. Denied the right to use their most effective weapon, the membership of most unions dwindled from the peak of a quarter million to practically nothing by 1914. There were strikes aplenty, however, although they were not organized by trade unions. Seven hundred thousand were out on strike during 1912 and twice that many in the first six months of 1914. They practically disappeared, however, immediately after the outbreak of war. The standard of living of the workers continued far below that of Western workers: eleven dollars a month was the average industrial wage in 1913, a year of relatively high prices. Man-hour productivity of the Russian worker was less than a fifth that of the English worker, a reflection of much heavier capital investment in the British Isles.

Soon after its election the third Duma drew up a program intended to provide and require at least four years of free primary education for all Russian children. Over the next six years the number of primary schools increased by 50 per cent to a hundred and fifty thousand. The plan was to have every child of school age in school by 1922. In 1914, however, only half the eligible children could find or take advantage of the facilities. The nation still had a long way to go to overcome illiteracy.

The government sufficiently relaxed press censorship after the 1905 revolution to permit a phenomenal increase in the number of Russian periodicals and, curiously, a wide spread in their political views. Over two thousand journals were appearing in 1912, running the gamut from extreme reaction to the Bolshevik daily newspaper *Pravda*.

Stolypin, whose supposed liberalism made him more and more suspect at court, was shot in 1911 by a police agent who was a Socialist Revolutionary. Many suspected that reactionaries near the court hatched the plot for his assassination. He was succeeded by Kokovtsev, whose feeling toward the Duma was expressed in his remark, "Thank God, we still have no parliament." From then on there was no strong man to set the course, and the government was content to drift. Rasputin became the dominating influence, especially successful in naming his favorites to high office. Guchkov attacked him in the Duma but to no avail. Goremykin returned to the office of prime minister early in 1914 and headed the government through two years of war. By the end of his term it made little difference who was prime minister. The nation was on the brink of revolution.

SUGGESTED READING

Baring, M., *A Year in Russia* (London, Methuen, 1908).

Cambridge Modern History, Vol. XII (New York, Macmillan, 1934).

Dillon, E. J., *The Eclipse of Russia* (London, Dent, 1918).

Gronsky, P. and N. Astrov, *The War and the Russian Government* (New Haven, Yale University Press, 1929).

Karpovich, M., *Imperial Russia, 1801–1917* (New York, Holt, 1932).

Kokovtsev, V. N., *Out of My Past* (Stanford, Stanford University Press, 1935).

Kornilov, A., *Modern Russian History* (New York, Knopf, 1917).

Levin, A., *The Second Duma* (New Haven, Yale University Press, 1940).

Lobanov-Rostovsky, A., *Russia and Asia* (Ann Arbor, Wahr, 1951).

Maynard, Sir J., *Russia in Flux, Before October* (New York, Macmillan, 1946).

Miller, M. S., *The Economic Development of Russia, 1905–1914* (London, King, 1926).

Nikolaevskii, B. I., *Azeff, the Spy* (New York, Doubleday, 1934).

Owen, L. A., *The Russian Peasant Movement, 1906–1917* (London, King, 1937).

Pares, B., *Russia and Reform* (London, Constable, 1907).

Pavlovsky, G., *Agricultural Russia on the Eve of the Revolution* (London, Routledge, 1930).

Polner, T. J., *The Zemstvos and the All-Russian Union of Zemstvos* (New Haven, Yale University Press, 1930).

Robinson, G. T., *Rural Russia Under the Old Regime* (New York, Macmillan, 1949).

Romanov, B. A., *Russia in Manchuria, 1892–1906* (Ann Arbor, J. W. Edwards, 1953).

Seton-Watson, H., *The Decline of Imperial Russia, 1855–1914* (New York, Praeger, 1952).

Witte, S., *Memoirs* (New York, Doubleday, 1921).

Wolfe, B. D., *Three Who Made a Revolution* (New York, Dial, 1949).

26

End of an Era

IN THE DECADE PRIOR TO THE OUT-
break of World War I Russia's relations with Germany and Austria-Hungary
steadily deteriorated. The alliance with France, cemented by continued
loans, drew Russia into friendship with Great Britain, whose growing concern over German ambition made her willing to press for settlement of her
colonial rivalries with both France and Russia. The Anglo-Russian Convention of 1907 put an end to the strain that had existed between the two since
prior to the Crimean War. And Russia quickly composed her differences
with Japan. The Bosnian crisis brought Russia to the brink of war with
Austria in 1908, but unpreparedness forced the Foreign Office to accept a
diplomatic rather than a military defeat. The Balkan Wars of 1912 broke
up the Balkan League which Russia had organized to discourage an Austro-
German drive to the Straits and union with Turkey. Growing German influence at Constantinople threatened to deny Russia contact with her western allies through the Dardanelles in the event of war. The assassination of
the heir to the Habsburg throne and the Austrian threat to Serbian existence
led to Russia's involvement with her allies—France, Great Britain, Serbia,
and Japan—against the Central Powers.

The nation went to war, as it had done so many times, ill prepared. Industry was incapable of equipping the military machine, and enemy control
of the water approaches prevented the Allies from shipping in supplies. The
army was half trained, ill equipped, and poorly led, and casualties ran higher
than on any other front. Initial success was followed by months and years
of defeat and withdrawal, a monotonous story occasionally relieved by
momentary gains that could not be held.

The mobilization of fifteen million men proved disastrous to the national economy. Both industrial and agricultural production fell to small fractions of prewar output. The transportation system collapsed as equipment was not maintained. The cities particularly felt the pinch of falling production, growing shortages, and climbing prices. Strikes increased in number and in fury, and the strikers came more and more to blame the government for the cold and hunger which the war brought to their homes.

The Duma met only for brief moments during the early months of the war. Allowed to sit longer in 1915, liberal and conservative members joined in a Progressive Bloc to demand political and social reform in the hope that the people might recover their enthusiasm to defend the nation. But the tsar's solution to declining civilian morale and threat of military disaster was to assume command of the army. When he left the capital he surrendered control of the administration to his wife, who would listen only to the advice of the illiterate religious quack Rasputin. The two so destroyed the confidence even of conservatives and monarchists that there was serious talk of a *coup d'état*. In desperation, three archconservatives murdered Rasputin, but the deed came too late to save the dynasty.

The revolution opened with bread riots in the capital on March 8, 1917. Strikers poured into the streets demanding higher pay. Troops called out to suppress the movement joined the strikers. A committee of the Duma called upon Nicholas to turn out the bungling ministers who were held responsible for the nation's ills. When the tsar did nothing he was asked to abdicate. He gave up the throne with obvious relief, asking if he might live on his Livadia estate in the Crimea, adding plaintively, "I love flowers."

Delegates from factories and army units in the capital organized the Petrograd Soviet of Workers' and Soldiers' Deputies, reviving the experience of the Revolution of 1905. Members of the Duma proclaimed a Provisional Government to govern until a constituent assembly could gather. The Soviet, socialist in point of view, represented the proletariat, while the Provisional Government, liberal in point of view, represented the middle class. The birth of the two groups who would contest for power in the coming months marked the end of an era.

FOREIGN AFFAIRS TO 1914

The center upon which Russian foreign policy focused after 1894 was the alliance with France. While the western democracy and the eastern autocracy seemed poles apart politically, there were many in both countries who sympathized with the arrangement, wholly apart from the security it promised both vis-à-vis Germany and the fact that both were relatively isolated among the nations before the alliance came into existence. Russian liberals drew comfort from the arrangement and hoped that closer ties with France would in some way lead to the achievement of parliamentary democracy in Russia. French liberals who consorted with their eastern friends thought it more likely that Russia might become Westernized and democratic than that Hohenzollern Germany or Habsburg Austria would ever do so. Nicholas II seems to have felt uncomfortable about the French alliance because of the encouragement it gave to the liberal movement at home, and was inclined to embrace Germany as a bulwark against the French radicalism which he feared.

Liberal and nationalist circles in Russia tended to blame the Japanese victory upon Germany, whose kaiser had so encouraged the tsar to turn eastward into Asia. They were all the more incensed when Germany took advantage of Russian embarrassment during the war to impose a tariff treaty most unfavorable to Russia, a treaty which Witte agreed to only when the tsar ordered it. Russian liberals felt that the nation's best interests lay in closer association with Europe, while Pan-Slavs regretted that Russia had turned her back upon the Near East, where lay her "historic mission," even for a moment. The war had been extremely unpopular with all classes and all shades of political opinion except among the reactionaries like Bezobrazov and Plehve.

The wounds of the Russo-Japanese War healed quickly. The two powers in 1907 signed an agreement to respect each other's territory and to support the "open door" principle in Manuchuria. However, in a secret codicil Russia agreed not to interfere in Japanese action in Korea; Japan reciprocated by leaving Russia a free hand in Outer Mongolia. Manchuria was sliced into a northern sphere of Russian influence and a southern sphere of Japanese influence with a neutral zone separating the two. Russia came off with complete control of the territory through which passed the Chinese Eastern Railway, while Japan immediately began the construction of a rail line connecting south Manchuria with Korea. Three years later Japan ended the fiction of Korean independence and annexed the kingdom, while the following year saw Outer Mongolia declare its independence and then become a Russian protectorate. In 1912 Inner Mongolia was divided into spheres of influence, Russia taking the western half, Japan the eastern. The two former enemies got along so well in East Asia partly because of common fear of penetration by American capitalists. A syndicate of American magnates, including J. P. Morgan and E. H. Harriman, aimed at sinking heavy investments in Manchuria, lending money to China in return for concessions in north China, and even obtaining financial control of the Chinese Eastern Railway.

Having mended her fences in the Far East, Russia considered a settlement of her differences with Japan's ally, Great Britain. France and Great Britain had come to an understanding even before the Russo-Japanese War. Now that Russia had patched up her outstanding differences with Japan, and since Britain was now a friend of Russia's own friend France, a Russo-British agreement recommended itself, particularly in view of the waxing ambition of Germany and Austria-Hungary.

By the terms of the Convention of 1907 Russia received northern Persia including the capital Teheran as a sphere of influence, while southern Persia became a British sphere, the two being separated by a neutral zone. Russia received by far the larger and richer portion, England getting only the southern Persian desert. In return, Russia promised to stay out of Afghanistan and to deal with that country only through its protector, Great Britain. Russia also promised not to push her influence in Tibet, and so relieved Britain's anxiety over India.

The Anglo-Russian Convention settled between the signatories the issues in the Middle East as the Russo-Japanese Convention of the same year had settled Russia's problems in the Far East. Russia had joined with Japan to block American penetration into that part of East Asia where Russian and Japanese interests were vital. Now Russia joined with Great Britain in an attempt to block German and Austrian encroachment in the Near and Middle East, areas where Russian and British interests were also vital. The 1907 conventions would determine in part the alignment of the powers in the coming World War. The Triple Entente—Great Britain, France, and Russia—would stand against the Central Powers—Germany, Austria-Hungary, and Turkey.

Turkish massacres of Armenians in the autumn of 1896 raised once more the question of great-power intervention in the Ottoman Empire. British and French foreign ministers broached the question with Nicholas II when he visited London and Paris that autumn. The tsar, however, was cool to the idea of international cooperation at the Straits, preferring the sultan's control there to seeing Western battle fleets in Turkish waters. But on his return home Nicholas listened attentively to a plan put forward by Nelidov, his ambassador to Turkey. If British ships should move to the Dardanelles, Nelidov proposed that Russia should seize the Bosporus. The tsar approved and troops were gathered in preparation for the assault. An inquiry in Paris, however, brought the unequivocal reply that France would not be a party to the venture, and Witte insisted that the plan must not go through without French support. He was satisfied that the Straits were closed and would not risk the loss of French loans. And the British Foreign Office seems to have outgrown its determination to defend Constantinople. In 1897 the Near East was put "on ice" by an Austro-Russian agreement that neither would disturb the *status quo* in the Balkans and that the two would cooperate to prevent anyone else's doing so. An Austrian hint that she and Russia parcel out the Balkans some time in the future, giving Bosnia and Herzegovina to Austria, was turned down by the tsar.

During the Russo-Japanese War, which had come about in some small part at least because of Wilhelm's urging his cousin Nicholas to take up Russia's civilizing mission in the Far East, the kaiser attempted to draw Russia into an anti-British alliance. While the two emperors were cruising in the Baltic Wilhelm pulled from his pocket a defensive agreement against attack by any European power. The tsar signed the treaty, but later had to withdraw when it was pointed out to him that it endangered the alliance with France and the loans she seemed so willing to advance. This so-called Treaty of Björkö is important only in revealing the tsar's naïveté and his willingness to deal behind the back of the officials charged with the conduct of foreign policy. Count Lamsdorf, the foreign minister, knew nothing of the tsar's conversations with the kaiser.

Russia and Austria had agreed in 1897 and again five years later to maintain the *status quo* in the Balkans. In 1906, however, there entered the foreign offices of the two powers men who were not satisfied to leave the Balkans "on ice." Both Alexander Izvolsky in St. Petersburg and Baron von Aehrenthal in Vienna jockeyed for advantage in the Near East. Izvolsky's first concern was to remove the restrictions, recognized in treaty after treaty since 1841, upon the use of the Straits by Russian warships. The Black Sea fleet could neither succor other naval units operating beyond the Bosporus nor be rescued by Russian vessels based in other seas. Proposals to Britain for support of Russia's use of the Straits always met counterproposals that the matter could only be settled by opening the Dardanelles to war vessels of all nations. This was enough to prompt Russia to seek elsewhere for understanding of her position at the Straits.

Meanwhile, Aehrenthal proposed to construct a rail line from Austria through Bosnia and on southeast to Salonika. Taking this announcement as a breach of Austria's commitment to maintain the *status quo* in the Balkans, Izvolsky in a cabinet meeting urged that Russia, working closely with Great Britain, should raise vigorous protest to Vienna. The foreign minister was prevented from doing so by a warning from the rest of the cabinet that the army was in no way ready to back up his threats.

When the Young Turk revolution in 1908 seemed to indicate a weakening of the Ottoman Empire both Aehrenthal and Izvolsky saw an opportunity to gain advantage. The two agreed in private conversations that Austria should annex Bosnia and Herzegovina, the provinces which had been Austrian protectorates since the Congress of Berlin, while Vienna would not oppose the forcible opening of the Straits to Russian warships. The Russian foreign minister supposed that the two actions would be taken simultaneously and only with the approval of the powers signatory to the Berlin treaty. But the announcement of the annexation of the two provinces came while Izvolsky was on his way to Paris; he first read of it in French newspapers. Pan-Slav circles in Russia were furious. Serbia challenged the annexation and prepared for war, fully expecting Russian support. Since the Russian army was not ready for war, and since St. Petersburg was notified that Austria had Germany's backing in the matter, there was nothing for the Slav powers to do but to back down and take a major diplomatic defeat. Germany demanded that Russia recognize the annexation, and when Izvolsky sought to evade the issue Berlin demanded a simple yes or no. Russia had no recourse but to accept the annexation. Serbia halted her preparations for war, agreed to the loss of the provinces, and promised to conduct herself as a good neighbor toward Austria. Bitter hatred for Austria and particularly for Germany characterized Russian opinion from the moment of the humiliation.

Soon after the Bosnian crisis Izvolsky left the Foreign Office to be succeeded by Stolypin's brother-in-law, Sergei Sazonov, who stayed on until 1916. Sazonov was a relatively mild Pan-Slav who wanted to push Russia's interests at the Straits and support the Balkan powers in their encroachment upon Turkish territory but who would stop short of war in pursuit of such policies. However, his known sympathy for the cause of Slavdom in the Near East gave tacit support to Russian diplomats in the Balkans who, far less cautious than the foreign minister, urged the Balkan powers to aggressive action toward both Turkey and Austria. These diplomats promoted the birth of the Balkan League in which Serbia, Greece, Montenegro, and Bulgaria banded together to attack Turkey at the moment of her weakness after losing a war with Italy.

In the first Balkan War the Allies were everywhere victorious over Turkish armies. By the Treaty of London in May, 1913, the sultan surrendered the island of Crete and all his European territory except a strip of land along the Straits. Then the Allies fell to quarreling over the division of the spoils. When Austria refused to allow Serbia to take former Turkish territory on the Aegean, Serbia demanded compensation from Bulgaria who refused to grant it. The second Balkan War found Bulgaria fighting alone against her former allies and Romania and Turkey. The peace settlement deprived Bulgaria of much of her earlier gains and even regained for Turkey a bit of what she had lost; Greece, Romania, and Serbia won sizable additions. Ethnic boundaries were violated in nearly every exchange of territory under the two treaties. Bulgaria, embittered at her losses, would side with the Central Powers when the war between Slav and Teuton broke out a year later.

Sazonov was unsuccessful in his efforts to prevent the collapse of the Balkan League, which he expected would support Russia in the event of a major war. Both Russia and Austria courted the favor of most of the Balkan states, although Austria was consistently anti-Serb and Russia was less consistently pro-Serb. Sazonov worked honestly to keep the wars from spreading, handicapped though he was by Pan-Slav demonstrations in St. Petersburg, by the clamor of Duma leaders that Russia should take over the Straits, and by the tsar's inclination to go along with chauvinists in court circles.

Since the turn of the century Russia had grown increasingly nervous over German ambition in the Near East. In 1902 Turkey gave Germany the right to build a railway connecting Baghdad and the Persian Gulf with the Anatolian line which Germany already controlled. Construction went ahead for two years until vigorous protests by Russia and Great Britain brought further extension to a halt. In 1911, however, the tsar agreed, without consulting his Entente friends, not to oppose the building of the Baghdad line in return for a German promise not to press for concessions in the Russian sphere of Persia. Again Nicholas was acting in contradiction to the wishes of his own Foreign Office.

Turkey's proposal in 1911 to extend her railway net along the Georgian border and her announced intention at the same time to expand her navy, coupled with Germany's determination to extend the Baghdad Railway, prompted the foreign minister to seek once more the opening of the Straits to Russian warships. While expansionists and particularly naval leaders would be satisfied with nothing less than Russia's seizure of the heights of the Bosporus, the Foreign Office preferred to see Turkey continue in control of the Straits provided passage was available to the Black Sea fleet or to ships coming to its rescue. Russia's hope to open the Dardanelles was dashed, however, by German and British opposition and French indifference.

After the poor showing of her troops in the Balkan Wars, Turkey brought in General Liman von Sanders with a staff of German officers to enliven the Turkish army. At the same time the general was placed in command of the military garrison at Constantinople, a position which made foreign embassies rely upon him for their safety. That the Russian ambassador should be dependent upon a German general was intolerable to St. Petersburg. With French and British support Sazonov demanded that von Sanders be withdrawn. The German government backed down to the extent of promoting von Sanders in rank and so forcing his resignation as commanding general of the Turkish army corps in Constantinople, but it left him in charge of the mission whose assignment it was to restore vitality to the Turkish army. Sazonov could find little comfort in this slender triumph. The Liman von Sanders mission announced to the world that German influence at the Porte was predominant. Turco-German solidarity would block Russia at the Straits and in the coming war would make Anglo-French-Russian cooperation through the Straits difficult, if not impossible. The German kaiser realized what had happened when he admitted, "Russo-Prussian relations are dead once and for all! We have become enemies!"

In the early months of 1914 Sazonov put before the cabinet the seriousness of the situation at the Straits. It was decided to build up the Black Sea fleet and to push forward with army reform and reorganization. Such measures had hardly got under way beyond the cabinet's recommendation, however, when the nation went to war. Russia's inability to command the entrance to the Black Sea would be a crippling handicap.

Those who prayed for peace among the great powers in this fateful year of 1914 could find much to comfort them. While there had been many small fires there had been no great conflagration among the leading powers in nearly a century. While there had been many points of friction in colonial areas, in the past generation particularly, the tension had never brought conflict. A succession of crises in the Near East had been settled peaceably. Even the Balkan Wars had not embroiled the great powers.

In the clarity of hindsight, however, it is obvious that there was little cause for optimism. Austria and Russia might easily come to blows in the Balkans and drag their allies with them into a major conflict. The primary cause for concern lay in the ambitions of the South Slavs, particularly Serbia, and the increasing restlessness of Slavic peoples within the Austro-Hungarian Empire. Austrian statesmen knew full well that Serbia must be dealt with sooner or later, that her overweening hopes of reaching the Adriatic and of gathering in the Serbs and Croats under Habsburg rule must be squelched. Serbian incitement to Pan-Serb sentiment among Bosnians and Herzegovinans could not be tolerated much longer. Serbia had been humiliated in 1909. If she caused trouble again she must be put in her place once and for all, even if it meant a European war. The very existence of the Austro-Hungarian Empire was at stake. If she gave in to Serbian demands she would be faced immediately with the demands of Czechs, Slovaks, Ruthenians, Slovenes, Poles, Romanians, and Italians. On the other hand, no foreign office in Europe expected that Russia would stand idly by and see Serbia destroyed. The next crisis would show to what extent Germany would back up her ally Austria and France would support her ally Russia, and whether the other nations, joined in the one camp or the other, would be drawn into the struggle.

THE COMING OF THE WAR

On June 28, 1914, a Pan-Serb Bosnian student assassinated the heir apparent to the Austrian throne, the Archduke Francis Ferdinand. Convinced of the complicity of the Serbian government and determined to put an end to this perpetual menace to her own tranquility, Austria, with assurances of German support, delivered an ultimatum to Serbia. The Austrian foreign minister, who drew up the ultimatum, deliberately made its terms so severe that, in the words of an official in the Austrian Foreign Office, "no state possessing the smallest amount of national pride or dignity would accept them" (Sazonov). Belgrade, however, agreed to everything except the stipulation that Austrian officials be allowed to join in the Serbian search for the archduke's murderers and in the suppression of anti-Austrian propaganda. Even the German kaiser was so satisfied with the Serbian reply that he believed it removed "every reason for war." Vienna felt otherwise, however, and called home her ambassador from Belgrade. Three days later Austria declared war and shelled the Serbian capital.

Meanwhile, Sazonov had cautioned the Serbian government to use "extreme moderation" in answering the Austrian ultimatum. He advised Belgrade to put up no resistance but to appeal to the great powers to mediate the dispute. Austria, however, spurned the Serbian offer to put the case before the international tribunal at The Hague. Sazonov proposed to the Austrian ambassador to Russia that the terms demanded of Serbia be reconsidered; the Austrian put off answering Sazonov until after his government had declared war upon Serbia and then pleaded that it was too late. The Austrian action was taken in spite of German insistence that her ally negotiate with Russia. Great Britain, France, Italy, Germany, and Russia all exerted pressure upon Austria and Serbia to prevent war but to no avail.

From the moment of the Austrian declaration of war upon Serbia the initiative rapidly slipped from the hands of the diplomats into those of the military leaders. Sazonov announced that the next day Russia would begin partial mobilization, against Austria but not against Germany. But the chief of the general staff protested that there were no plans for partial mobilization and that such a program was unworkable. The tsar gave in to the pressure of his generals and ordered full mobilization on July 30. Two days later France and Germany mobilized, Russia refused a German demand that she halt mobilization, and on the first of August Germany declared war upon Russia. France, Great Britain, Belgium, and Japan soon joined Russia and Serbia, and Turkey lined up with the German powers. All were convinced that the conflict could not last long because of the cost of modern war. But the fighting would go on for Russia, through this war and into a civil war and beyond that through a war with Poland, for more than six long years.

PREPARATION FOR WAR

Russia, like the other combatants, made no financial or industrial preparation for a long war; the government did not expect, nor did it understand, the problems of economic warfare or "total war." While the nation's industries might be expected to satisfy the needs of the army for a short while, there was no plan to mobilize economically—to convert peacetime industry to the production of war material, direct the consumption of strategic materials, assure a supply of skilled labor to war plants, organize transportation to avoid congestion, ration consumer goods. There was a shortage of railroad equipment and a dangerous concentration of railway lines in the western districts whose seizure by the enemy would cripple the transportation system. For the most part the lines ran perpendicular to the front rather than parallel to it, complicating the problem of shifting men and equipment from one section of the front to the other. With the closing of the Baltic and the Black Sea to Allied shipping, the nation had to rely upon the Trans-Siberian and upon a line running south from Archangelsk, ice-bound most of the year, whose narrow gauge would not handle most railway equipment. The warm-water port of Murmansk was of little use until the war was nearly over.

Army reforms since the Japanese war had aimed to improve training and the quality of equipment. But the reforms had been halfheartedly carried out and the Russian army was more poorly trained and equipped than any other major army with the exception of the Austrian. The existing shortage of officers became really alarming after the costliness of the early campaigns. The commander-in-chief, the Grand Duke Nicholas who was well liked by the men if not by the officers, knew his own shortcomings and wept at the news of his appointment "because he did not know how to approach his new duties" (Florinsky). But the situation grew worse in 1915, when the tsar took over as commander-in-chief. Medical service was pitifully ineffective. The supply of equipment and munitions was inadequate from the outbreak of the war. Shortage of artillery and shells was responsible for higher casualties on the Russian front than on any other. Morale held up surprisingly well through the first year, but the men in the ranks had little understanding of why they were fighting. The peasant soldier did not know where Constantinople was, much less why it was worth such sacrifice.

THE OPENING CAMPAIGNS

Russian war plans envisaged two offensives, the weaker into East Prussia to relieve German pressure upon France, the stronger against Austria to succor Serbia and prevent an invasion of Poland. Generals Rennenkampf and Samsonov, who were bitter personal enemies, advanced into East Prussia, the former from the east, the latter moving north from Warsaw. Rennenkampf moved cautiously, Samsonov too rapidly through unfamiliar woods and swamps, neither knowing of the other's whereabouts, toward an undetermined rendezvous in the rear of the German defenders. But the German commander, von Hindenburg, boldly attacked Samsonov at Tannenberg and killed or captured so much of his army that Samsonov shot himself. Then Hindenburg turned upon Rennenkampf and drove him back out of Prussia. Russia lost upward of a quarter of a million men and six hundred guns. The disaster gave some comfort to the Allies, however—the advance into East Prussia had brought German troops hurrying from the western front, thus helping to make possible the Allied victory over Germany at the Marne. The German plan to "lunch in Paris and dine in St. Petersburg" had been thwarted.

Meanwhile, the Russians, enjoying better success against Austria, drove to the Carpathian Mountains, captured the Galician capital Lemberg, and besieged the key fortress of Przemysl. The campaign cost Austria more casualties than Russia had suffered in East Prussia. Russian leadership on the Austrian front was greatly superior to that against the Germans; the opposition was much inferior; and the Slav units in the Austro-Hungarian army were for the most part indifferent or hostile to the cause they served. The Russian advance was stopped when Hindenburg shifted his attack to southwestern Poland, forcing the Russians to move armies to meet it and so relieving the pressure on the Austrians. German troops were within sight of Warsaw before the Russians regrouped and stabilized the front as winter set in.

THE GREAT RETREAT

The spring of 1915 opened favorably on the eastern front. British and French troops landed at the Dardanelles in an effort to pry open the Straits to Allied shipping and so feed a stream of supplies into the Black Sea. Italy joined the Entente powers and provided some relief for Russia by a back-door attack upon Austria-Hungary. Russian armies resumed the advance in Galicia and took Przemysl with over a hundred thousand men and nearly a thousand pieces of artillery. The Russians threatened to seize the passes of the Carpathians and debouch upon the Hungarian plain. The Dual Monarchy faced imminent destruction.

Hindenburg, now commanding in the east, received several divisions from the western front and massed artillery and planes for a drive to relieve the Russian pressure upon Austria. On the first of May the Germans opened a vigorous attack in western Galicia and drove the surprised Russians back in confusion. Never had the Russians seen such artillery preparation. Hindenburg stepped up the pressure all along the thousand-mile front from the Carpathians to the Baltic, so that the defenders could not shift forces from one sector to another. The Germans took a hundred and fifty thousand prisoners before the month was out. The Russians fell back beyond Przemysl and then beyond Lemberg, and by early July were retreating through Poland. Warsaw fell in early August, and the forts behind it gave up without a struggle as the psychology of retreat infected the defenders. Most of Galicia and all of Poland, Courland, and Lithuania and part of

White Russia were surrendered to the invader. As these western provinces fell to the Germans Russia lost the most vital and the most efficient portion of her railway net. Thenceforth adequate supply of her retreating front became almost impossible.

At Tannenberg Russia had lost so many guns that every battery in the army had been cut from six guns to four. Neither home industry nor Allied aid managed to make up the shortage. And Russia had practically no heavy artillery. The Germans advanced eastward in the summer of 1915 confident that they would run into no heavy fire. The Third Russian Army, for example, had only four heavy guns to the two hundred the Germans used against it. And because of the shortage of ammunition the Russian field pieces were limited to fewer shells a day than the Germans were firing per minute. Waves of infantrymen walked into battle without rifles, hoping to arm themselves with the weapons of comrades shot down in front of them. Machine guns and cartridges for them were in short supply. "This is not war; it is slaughter," a Russian soldier protested. "The Germans expend metal; we expend life," one general observed. Food and clothing were scarce and of poor quality. Soldiers even went without bread for as much as five days at a stretch. Grand Duke Nicholas complained at one point that his men could not advance because of the shortage of boots. Apparently they could retreat without them.

As was to be expected, the morale of the troops ebbed rapidly. Men took the attitude that there was no use in their fighting, since they were always beaten. Many played sick, thousands ran away to their homes, and other thousands surrendered to the enemy. During the summer of 1915 the killed and wounded alone numbered nearly a million and a half while the loss in prisoners ran to nearly a million, over three times the average on all fronts for the entire war. Those who deserted communicated to the civilian population in the rear their sense of hopelessness and their suspicion that treason in high circles was responsible for the shortages of equipment and arms.

During the great retreat the civilians behind the front fled in panic to the east. "Refugees move in a solid mass; they tread down the fields, destroy the meadows and woods. They leave almost a desert behind them, as if a swarm of locusts or the hordes of Tamerlane had swept the country" (Golovine). What the refugees did not trample the army high command ordered deliberately destroyed. But the scorched-earth policy that had succeeded so well in 1812 was disastrous now. Where Napoleon had advanced into Russia along a narrow road, Hindenburg was driving forward along a front hundreds of miles long. The entire Polish and White Russian countryside was devastated; the villagers were forcibly removed if they had not already fled. The Germans were saved the trouble of caring for a conquered population and had no need to fear sabotage of their supply lines by guerillas.

In late summer, as the withdrawal into Russia went monotonously on, Grand Duke Nicholas was removed to the Caucasian front and the emperor took over the leadership against the Germans. The news of the shift came "as a final and a stunning blow." What little morale remained in the army was owing to the immense popularity of the grand duke among the rank and file. Cabinet ministers begged the tsar not to take the step, and warned of grave consequences to Russia and to the dynasty. But the emperor spurned the advice of all except Rasputin and the empress, who urged the move.

"What were Russia's allies doing?" the man in the ranks asked during this awful summer of 1915. Twice as many German troops were thrown against Russia as occupied the trenches in France. The Serbian army collapsed and the Balkans were overrun by the Central Powers. The Allied effort at the Dardanelles failed miserably; French and British troops pulled out and left the approaches to the Black Sea in Turkish hands.

By late fall in 1915 the Germans had advanced as far into Russia as they cared to. The line stabilized just west of Riga, then southeast to Dvinsk, and thence south to Czernowitz on the Romanian border. The new war minister, the able General Polivanov who joined the Bolsheviks during the revolution, worked frantically to heal the wounds of the great retreat. Production and importation of rifles, artillery, and ammunition increased to a point approximating the needs of the army. The training of recruits was considerably improved and they were better equipped. Units were brought up to full strength to make good the awful attrition of the recent campaign. The army was ready for another offensive, and the Russian government promised its western allies to return to the attack in mid-1916.

THE BRUSILOV OFFENSIVE

Three months before Russia was pledged to open the 1916 campaign the western Allies came forth with their perennial cry for help, this time to ease the pressure of the German assault on Verdun. Soon the Italians chimed in with a frantic plea for a Russian drive into Galicia to draw Austrian troops away from their attack in the Trentino. The Russian high command came to the rescue once more, and sent General Brusilov, commanding in the southwest, in a two-pronged attack around the Austrian flanks designed to knock the Dual Monarchy out of the war. For the first time, the Russian troops were adequately supported by artillery. Through the summer of 1916 Brusilov advanced into Galicia, overrunning 10,000 square miles of territory —an amount which Russia's allies could not match in three years of fighting—and capturing over 400,000 prisoners and 600 guns. Meanwhile Russian forces attacked the German lines south of Vilna, gaining no ground but running up long casualty lists. The pressure, however, pinned down German divisions which otherwise might have gone south to be used against

Brusilov. Ludendorff, Hindenburg's chief of staff, admitted that for a while the situation was almost critical for Germany on the eastern front.

The summer's work cost the nation over two million dead and wounded and a third of a million prisoners. Little wonder that most Russians looked upon the war as senseless butchery. But the French obtained some relief at Verdun, as the Germans were forced to speed eighteen divisions from the western front to stiffen their ally's defense. The Italian army was saved as Austria had to interrupt her attack in the Trentino to stop the Russian advance in Galicia. Romania entered the war against the Central Powers but was quickly overrun, thus weakening the Russian front by extending it to German and Austrian pressure from Moldavia.

In the early months of 1917 the Allied generals gathered in Petrograd, as the capital had been renamed, to plan the campaigns for the coming spring. The Russian staff once more committed itself to a share in the attack. But the government which made the pledge did not live to fulfill it. Hardly had the visiting staffs left Petrograd when revolution toppled the dynasty.

RUSSIA IN THE ECONOMIC WAR

Six and a half million men were drafted into the armed forces by the end of 1914 and over five million more the following year. By March, 1917, Russia had mobilized some fifteen million for military service. Of the nation's manpower of working age, 15 per cent was thus withdrawn from civilian production in 1914, 25 per cent in 1915, 36 per cent in 1916 and 1917. The effect upon the economy was disastrous.

At the very moment when there was critical need for a rapidly expanding labor force Russian industry lost vast numbers, many of them key workers, to the army. Prisoners of war, refugees, children, and women—by 1917 over half the industrial workers were women—made poor and inefficient substitutes. Increasing the length of the working day could not make up for declining productivity; by 1917 man-day output of the average worker had fallen to two-thirds or less the prewar output. The coal and iron mines and the sugar, textile, and machine plants of Poland and Lithuania were lost to the Russian economy as the front moved eastward. The manufacture of ironware and steel, agricultural equipment, textiles, and leather goods fell off sharply, and industrial output, what there was of it, went chiefly to the army. Russia's economy, particularly her industrial plant, was simply incapable of satisfying both military and civilian needs.

Railway transportation broke down early in the war. The great retreat surrendered to the invaders that part of the nation most adequately served by the railway net. French investment in Russian railways had been aimed at gridding Poland and White Russia with a system that could quickly mobilize and serve the eastern ally against the common enemy. Now that network was captured. But even for the remainder of the nation rail service declined sharply. Equipment was not maintained and fell rapidly into disrepair. By 1917 over half the prewar locomotives were standing idle for want of repairs, only a third of freight cars were still in use, and rail output had fallen to barely a fourth the prewar figure. What was left was commandeered to serve the army, and manufacturing output slowed down for want of raw materials.

Agricultural production declined sharply. The huge block of farm land, eight million acres, pared away by the German advance cut grain output but did not commensurately reduce the number of mouths to feed as many of the peasants fled eastward. The conscription of agricultural workers into the armed forces left owners of great estates, whose output went almost wholly to market, helpless to carry on production. The peasant communities as well felt the pinch of conscription. It was "getting empty in the villages," noted one who had lost three brothers and inherited their families to care for. The loss of horses drafted for the army affected the great landowners far more than peasant operators. Cereal acreage on the great estates fell during the war to 30 per cent of the 1913 acreage. In addition to Poland, all of whose farm land fell to the Germans, the arable land of Russia shrank by 10 per cent during the war. The mounting food shortages grew rapidly more severe with the collapse of the transportation system. As industry turned out fewer goods for civilian consumption the peasant grew ever more reluctant to produce more than he could eat. Indeed, with the loss of the foreign market the peasants fared better than they had in peacetime. The nation consumed more of its produce than ever before, although the sharing was far from equitable.

The cities, particularly the urban working class, suffered most when the army took the bulk of the marketed produce and the transportation system could not adequately distribute the rest. Bread, flour, vegetables, and dairy products flowed in a dwindling stream from the farms, and yet the urban demand for them rose considerably because of the population growth of industrial centers. Wages on the average doubled during the war. But the worker's living costs by 1917 had climbed to three or four times the 1913 level. The government came round slowly to ration food and fix prices, but a flourishing black market hampered the feeble efforts at control. There were food riots as early as 1915, and the revolution opened two years later to the shouts of angry mobs before the bakers' shops of Petrograd.

During the first six months of 1914 there were nearly twice as many strikes and strikers as during the entire preceding year. Then, with the coming of the war all political parties except the Bolsheviks urged a moratorium on political and economic demands for the duration. Strikes all but disappeared during the first few months of war. But with the military collapse and economic chaos that set in the following year morale rapidly waned. The year 1915 saw over a half million workers marching in a thousand strikes. In 1916 there were half again as many strikes and twice as many strikers. During the last two months of the old regime nearly seven hundred thousand workers were in the streets. Most ominous was the fact that as the war progressed the demands of the strikers became increasingly political. City workers were blaming the government for their deepening misery.

The rural population, too, became increasingly restless as the war dragged on. As prices of the manufactured goods he needed rose more rapidly than the prices he could claim for his produce, the peasant consumed more of the food he raised and did not bother to plant as many acres as formerly. When the government forbade the sale of liquor during wartime the peasant took up making his own from the grain he harvested, grain whose sale to the government at fixed prices would in any event bring him little reward for his labor. There was mounting resistance to conscription, especially during and after the 1915 retreat. The authorities were unable to cope with the growing number of peasants who fled into the woods to escape the draft. Deserters and refugees brought back to every village a grim tale of shortages at the front and military disaster and frightful casualties.

The war cost the Russian government nearly forty billion rubles. Over half of this was borrowed, eight billions from abroad; the rest was made up by printing additional currency. From a billion and a half rubles in mid-1914 the amount of money in circulation rose to nearly twenty billions by the fall of 1917. The effect of such an increase was to drive prices precipitately upward and to concentrate property in the hands of those who had the wherewithal to buy from those who were forced in desperation to sell. The government made no serious effort to finance the war by taxation. The nation as a whole, of course, paid for the war as it went along in the capital destroyed, in the civilian goods not produced, in the seven million casualties, half of them killed and wounded. A fifth of the cost of the war was shifted to foreign governments whose loans to Russia were never repaid.

THE WAR AND THE RUSSIAN GOVERNMENT

It has been pointed out that Russia in 1914 was a curious "blend of medievalism and Western democracy" (Florinsky), and that these two contradictory forces both were strengthened by the war. Nicholas II gave in only grudgingly and never completely to the limitation of the autocracy which the 1905 settlement imposed upon him. Now the war gave him an opportunity to recover personal command of the government. On the other hand, the war contributed to the dignity if not to the power of the Duma, and opened the way for participation by zemstvos and municipalities, by representatives of business and labor, in the conduct of the war. As these autocratic and democratic tendencies gathered strength the clash between them became inevitable. Thus did the war contribute to the rapid collapse of the old regime, a collapse toward which the nation had been drifting for generations.

One week after the nation went to war the members of the Duma gathered for a one-day session to assure the government of their support. Laborites and Mensheviks refused to vote war appropriations; so did the Bolsheviks, who voiced their condemnation of the war and the socio-economic system that produced it. When the five Bolshevik members urged the view that the enemy of the workers of all nations was not the hostile army but the capitalistic system and the government that maintained it, they were declared guilty of subversion and packed off to Siberia. The rest of the Duma members joined in "sacred union," agreeing to postpone political differences until "Europe and Slavdom are delivered from German domination." Within the month the nation's municipalities formed an All-Russian Union of Cities and provincial and district zemstvos joined in an All-Russian Union of Zemstvos to care for wounded and sick soldiers and establish military hospitals.

After the brief opening session the Duma adjourned and did not sit again formally for six months. Many of its members remained in the capital, however, and met frequently to discuss the conduct of the war and to agree on common policy when the Duma should reconvene. When the members were called back into session early in 1915, the aging Prime Minister Goremykin hardly bothered to veil his contempt for the Duma and his impatience to dismiss it, while the grossly corrupt and inefficient war minister, Sukhomlinov, gave his smiling assurance that all was well at the front. Members pressed for permanent or at least a protracted session of the Duma and demanded that the bungling and unpopular cabinet be replaced by men "enjoying the nation's confidence," by which was meant men whom the Duma could trust. The Duma was hastily adjourned.

In June, 1915, when Russian armies were pulling back all along the front, the tsar called the nation to greater effort in prosecuting the war, summoned the Duma to meet again a month later, and dismissed several of the most objectionable ministers including the contemptible Sukhomlinov. Goremykin, however, stayed on for another six months as prime minister in the face of unanimous opposition from the Duma.

When the Duma met in mid-July, 1915, its six leading parties, conservative as well as liberal and representing the preponderance of membership, joined in a Progressive Bloc which adopted a program of modest reform. The members, disturbed at the administration's handling of the war and alarmed at the steady advance of the enemy, hoped to stiffen the nation and encourage it to greater effort. The Bloc's platform called for a ministry in which the nation could have confidence and one with which the Duma could work for a more effective prosecution of the war. It sought an amnesty for political prisoners, religious toleration, abolition of the Jewish Pale and the granting of civil rights to the Jews, an end to persecution of ethnic minorities, restoration of autonomy to Finland and Poland, legalization of labor unions, removal of restrictions upon agencies of local government, and equality of all classes before the law. It aimed at freeing wide areas behind the front from the dictatorship of military commanders by which civilians hundreds of miles from the front came under martial law.

Several cabinet members sympathized with the proposals of the Progressive Bloc, but Goremykin considered them a challenge to the crown. With the tsarina's support he obtained the emperor's consent to prorogue the Duma. The Union of Zemstvos, the Union of Cities, the Russian Red Cross, and other agencies took up the program of the Progressive Bloc and some went beyond it and called for the convocation of an assembly to draft a constitution.

Immediately after the dismissal of the Duma the tsar assumed the position of commander-in-chief of the armies in the field. All but two of the cabinet ministers begged Nicholas not to take the step, and the president of the Duma, Michael Rodzianko, warned Nicholas that if the current military reverses could not be halted the emperor himself would be saddled with the blame. But the warning went unheeded. The tsar preferred the advice of his wife, who was bitterly jealous of the popularity of Grand Duke Nicholas.

From the moment the emperor left the capital to assume command of the army the government, or what passed for government, came under the direction of the tsarina. Nicholas encouraged Alexandra to pick up the reins of administration, writing from the front, "Wifey, dear, don't you think you should help hubby while he is away?" "Wifey" took up her new assignment with the greatest enthusiasm, firmly convinced that she could and must guide the nation safely through to victory.

One of the tasks the empress set herself was the strengthening of her husband's will against the advice of those she considered pernicious. In the steady flow of correspondence she kept moving to headquarters she constantly urged Nicholas to be "more autocratic," "remember that you are the emperor," "use the whip," "crush them all," "teach them to fear you" "for Baby's sake." She harped, as she had since the day of her marriage, on the tsar's obligation to pass the autocratic power on to their son undiluted. "Never forget that you are and must remain an autocratic emperor," she admonished him. "Be Peter the Great, Ivan the Terrible, the Emperor Paul; smash them all," she wrote when Duma leaders questioned the administration. She called the ministers "rotten" and asked if it were not possible to hang "that fat Rodzianko" and exile Duma leaders and the

Grand Duke Nicholas to Siberia. The tsar thanked his wife for her scolding
letters and confessed himself "your poor little weak-willed hubby."

. In her position as head of the civilian administration Alexandra looked
for direction to her "man of God," Rasputin. The influence of the "holy
devil" upon the empress had grown steadily since his first appearance at
court in 1905. Down to 1915, however, he had interfered in political matters
only rarely. He had suggested the appointment of an occasional minister,
notably Goremykin for the premiership in 1914. But with the tsar's departure from the capital Rasputin came quickly to exercise near-dominant
influence in the making of military as well as civilian policy and in the
naming of men to political office. The tsarina who now decided so many
matters turned constantly to "Our Friend," as she called Rasputin, for
advice. "We must pay more attention to what He says," Nicholas was told.
Campaign plans were brought to the holy man to be blessed. He who had
no military knowledge whatever called for an advance near Riga in the
winter of 1915, giving as reason only that "it is necessary." Six months
later he advised that "we should not yet strongly advance" in the same
area.

When Nicholas left for the front the government was led momentarily
by a cabinet of exceptionally honest and, aside from Goremykin, liberal
men. But during the next few months Rasputin and the empress changed
all that. Few would have mourned the passing of Goremykin except for
the fact that he was succeeded by Boris Sturmer, "an even more contemptible
specimen of the St. Petersburg bureaucracy than his predecessor" (Florinsky). Sturmer, who was known to be sympathetic to Germany, also assumed
the office of foreign minister when the pro-English Sazonov was dismissed
in spite of the plea of the Allied governments that he stay on. The exemplary
Samarin gave way to one of Rasputin's lackeys as procurator-general of the
Holy Synod. The highly-respected Alexander Krivoshein, who commented
bitterly that "the government is no longer a government," was driven from
the Ministry of Agriculture. The capable minister of interior, Nicholas
Shcherbatov, was replaced by the craven and nearly insane Alexander
Protopopov, who continued in office at the insistence of the empress when
even the tsar had had enough of him. Nicholas faintly protested that so
many dismissals and appointments "make my head go round." The reactionary Duma leader Vladimir Purishkevich referred to the comings and
goings of shadowy cabinet members as "ministerial leapfrog" and later
joined the plot to assassinate Rasputin.

During the nine-month premiership of Sturmer the government simply
let matters drift. Strikes increased ominously in Petrograd. Bare living
became nearly impossible for many as prices quadrupled while wages only
doubled. The food situation was approaching a crisis. The transportation
system was breaking down. Financial scandals came to light in which

Sturmer, surrounded by petty, scheming toadies, was implicated. With continued military reverses a mood of defeatism spread over the capital. Criticism in the Duma reached the point where Sturmer shrank from appearing there. In November, 1916, Professor Miliukov rose in the Duma to call attention to the "dark forces" at work in government circles and to charge the empress and Rasputin with leading the nation into chaos. He reviewed the story, point by point, of ineptitude and bungling and corruption in officialdom, asking after each point, "Is this stupidity or is it treason?" Purishkevich, the most zealous monarchist in the lower house, repeated the reference to the "dark forces" that were ruling Russia. He bitterly assailed Sturmer, Protopopov, and the loathsome Rasputin and called for an end to this treacherous leadership.

Sturmer was forced from office by these biting attacks, leaving the management of affairs to the despicable Protopopov and to Rasputin and the empress who pulled the strings. The new prime minister, Alexander Trepov, offered Rasputin a bribe of two hundred thousand rubles if he would consent to the dismissal of Protopopov, but Rasputin spurned the offer. Protopopov stayed on and Trepov went the way of all others who tried to clean out the Augean stables. There was no other recourse but violence. In December, 1916, Rasputin was poisoned and shot and his body stuffed under the ice of the Neva by Purishkevich, the Grand Duke Dmitry, and Prince Felix Yusupov, husband to the tsar's niece, who announced, "I have killed Rasputin, the enemy of Russia and the tsar."

On the eve of Rasputin's murder Nicholas prorogued the Duma for a month. Trepov, hated by the empress because he had never catered to "Our Friend," was replaced by the formless nonentity Prince Nicholas Golitsyn. The insane Protopopov and the hysterical empress remained as the shadow of government. The Duma was not allowed to meet again at the appointed time. The tsar postponed the promised session until late February, 1917, thereby adding one more to the causes for popular resentment against this caricature of a government. Certainly there were many to prophesy where such a course would lead. The tsar's brother-in-law, the Grand Duke Alexander, warned: "Disaffection is spreading very fast. Strange as it may seem, it is the government which is preparing the revolution." General Krymov reported to Duma leaders that the army would welcome a *coup d'état*. And Rodzianko told Nicholas to his face that for twenty-two years the tsar had been pursuing a wrong course.

THE FALL OF THE MONARCHY

In late February, 1917, the Duma convened at last, its members resolved not to accept another prorogation. Discontent was showing itself in every segment of Russian society. Aristocrats bent on saving the monarchy were considering the possibility of replacing Nicholas II with another Romanov. Business leaders, in spite of the enormous profits they were making, were dissatisfied with arbitrary government and interference by army leaders in the administration of areas as far from the front as Petrograd itself. Soldiers, interested only in an end to the war, were deserting in droves and infecting the communities to which they returned with the spirit of hopelessness that pervaded the front. Peasants, who had never supported the war and whose fathers and sons made up the long casualty lists, wanted peace; failing to get it, they vented their wrath against a neighboring landlord, the symbol of the authority they hated. Strikes spread to every industrial center. The populace of the capital was growing surly over the severe hardships brought about by the shortage or maldistribution of food and fuel and the strangling effect of rising prices. All Russia was sick of war. Even those few who wanted to see it through to victory complained that the government was crippling the nation's war potential.

On March 8 bread riots broke out in Petrograd. Housewives clamoring for their lean ration at the meagerly-stocked food shops were joined by thousands of workers who walked out in protest against their falling real wages. Banners reading "down with autocracy" appeared in the crowds and there were clashes with the police. The giant Putilov plant locked its gates rather than give in to the demand of its well-organized metal workers for higher pay, and fifty other factories closed down.

The next day the number of strikers had swelled to two hundred thousand. The Petrograd garrison was called out but showed little disposition to attack the crowds. Even Cossacks were seen to wink at the strikers as they moved gently against them. The action was significant. The Cossacks had always been the most reliable strikebreakers and now they were going soft. Three days later most of the troops had joined the mob. Now the insurgents had rifles and machine guns, and soldiers and civilians joined in attacking public buildings, opening the jails, hunting down policemen, and breaking into the arsenal to arm those who came into the streets empty-handed.

The Duma was ordered to disperse on March 12 but decided to remain in session. It chose a provisional committee, under the chairmanship of the Duma president Rodzianko to assume leadership in the growing chaos. Alexander Kerensky, leader of the radical but non-Marxist Labor party, and the socialist Nicholas Chkheidze joined with Miliukov, Guchkov, and others of the Progressive Bloc to form the provisional committee. Rodzianko telegraphed the tsar at army headquarters pleading with him to save the situation by appointing a cabinet in whom the nation could feel confidence. There was no reply. A few days later the committee, supported by the army's leading generals, demanded that the tsar abdicate. Nicholas thought at first to leave the throne to his son, but fearful for the boy's health he abdicated on March 15 in favor of his brother, the Grand Duke Michael. Members of the Soviet protested: "No more Romanovs! We want a republic!" The grand duke refused to accept the crown and threw his support to the Provisional Committee. After three centuries of occupying it, the Romanovs gave up the throne almost without a protest. In the very midst of the abdication crisis Nicholas wrote of the future, "I shall take up dominoes again in my spare time."

Meanwhile, on March 14, some two hundred and fifty delegates elected from factories and army units in Petrograd gathered to organize the Soviet of Workers' and Soldiers' Deputies. The *soviet,* or council, was developed as a revolutionary institution during the 1905 rising; many who sat in the Petrograd Soviet in 1917 had attended the sessions twelve years earlier. Remembering the 1905 disappointments and failures and swearing to avoid them now, the delegates determined to seize the initiative and hold it. Non-socialist parties, branded as capitalist or "bourgeois," were denied seats in the Soviet. The executive committee of the Soviet assumed various governmental functions: it set up a commission to control the supply of food in Petrograd; it established a militia of workers to succeed the police who had been shot or driven into hiding; it allowed only a few left-wing newspapers to continue publication; and it named the terms upon which it would consent to cooperate with the provisional committee of the Duma. On the day of the tsar's abdication the provisional committee of the Duma and the executive committee of the Petrograd Soviet agreed on the creation of a Provisional Government.

The president of the new government was Prince George Lvov, a mild-mannered Cadet who had won respect and admiration as chairman of the Russian Red Cross and president of the Union of Zemstvos. The brilliant if obstinate Miliukov, the Cadet leader who would have preferred a constitutional monarchy on the British model to the republic he now served, became foreign minister. The old Octobrist Guchkov, also a monarchist in sympathy, headed the War and Navy Ministry. The brilliant thirty-six-year-old lawyer Kerensky, an emotional and flamboyant orator and soon to emerge as the dynamic spirit of the new cabinet, became minister of justice. As vice-chairman of the executive committee of the Soviet and member of the Provisional Government, Kerensky was the only link between the two agencies which fenced for power through the spring and summer of 1917. With the exception of Kerensky, the cabinet consisted of moderate liberals of such renowned respectability as to win cordial approval abroad if not at home. The United States extended recognition to the new government within a week of the tsar's abdication, and Great Britain, France, and Italy quickly followed suit.

The Provisional Government announced the program, approved and in fact drawn up by the Soviet, upon which it proposed to act. There was to be an immediate amnesty for all political prisoners. Freedom of speech, press, and assembly was guaranteed, and labor was to enjoy the right to organize and to strike. Restrictions upon individual freedom because of class, creed, or ethnic origin were removed. Soldiers when not on duty were to enjoy the same privileges as civilians. Troops which had taken part in the overthrow of the monarchy were not to be disarmed or removed from Petrograd. The death penalty was abolished. Finally, the government would begin preparations for convening a national assembly chosen by secret and universal suffrage to draft a constitution. The Provisional Government next appointed one committee to draw up a program of land reform to submit to the Constituent Assembly and another to suggest a democratic reorganization of local government. The peasants undertook their own land reform, however, and local soviets appeared all over Russia to tear away the power from provincial governors and zemstvos.

The Petrograd Soviet rapidly gathered strength both in numbers and influence. Fifteen hundred delegates attended the second day's meeting, and there were twice that number a week later. Many who represented nobody just wandered in off the streets to hear and, especially, to be heard. In an effort to bring order to the representations the Soviet decreed that each delegate should be chosen by two thousand factory workers or soldiers dwelling or stationed in the capital. Soviets soon appeared in Moscow and other cities and also in army units at the front.

While most leaders of the Bolsheviks and Socialist Revolutionaries were abroad or in Siberian exile, the Soviet was dominated by socialists and made its appeal to and was supported by the proletariat. On the other hand, the Duma and the Provisional Government were led by business and professional men and reflected liberal, middle-class interests and attitudes. The March Revolution developed into a contest for power between the radical, socialist, proletarian-oriented Petrograd Soviet and the liberal, democratic, bourgeoisie-oriented Duma men who predominated in the Provisional Government. It was inevitable that the two groups should look upon each other with suspicion and distrust.

Although the Soviet was overwhelmingly socialist in spirit, there was sharp disagreement over what role the organization should play at this stage of the revolution. On the left the Bolsheviks, who had not yet come round to the view that the soviets should put themselves forward as agencies of political power, wanted a revolutionary government to assume control only until the election of the Constituent Assembly. On the right the conservative minority urged full cooperation between the Petrograd Soviet and the liberal bourgeoisie in the Provisional Government. Between these extremes lay the mass of delegates, who accepted the revolution as middle-class in character with which it would not be seemly for socialists to associate, but who

"The Attack on the Winter Palace in 1917," a painting by the Soviet artist, Kuznetsov.

A parade in Red Square in Moscow. St. Basil's Cathedral is at upper left. Lenin's tomb is partly obscured at center.

believed with the Bolsheviks that the Soviet itself should not overturn the Provisional Government. This was in keeping with the conviction of many Marxists, Mensheviks particularly, that Russia must become a mature capitalist society before it could graduate to socialism. The Bolsheviks, a small minority, were many times outnumbered by the Mensheviks and Socialist Revolutionaries who made up the great bulk of delegates to the Soviet. Indeed, total Bolshevik strength in Russia was surprisingly small. The party may have had thirty thousand members at the time of the revolution and only forty thousand a month later.

At the insistence of the Soviet the imperial family was placed under house arrest at the palace of Tsarkoe Selo. When Miliukov put out feelers to obtain asylum for the royal family in England, the Soviet demanded that the tsar be imprisoned. This proved unnecessary when the Provisional Government promised that "Citizen Romanov" and "Alexandra the German," as some revolutionaries delighted in calling them, would not be allowed to leave Russia without the consent of the executive committee of the Soviet. In mid-summer the family was moved to Tobolsk east of the Urals and in the following spring to Ekaterinburg. There the local soviet ordered their execution and on July 16, 1918, Nicholas and his wife and children were shot and the bodies destroyed. Several of the grand dukes, including the tsar's brother Michael, met a similar fate.

The ease with which the dynasty was overturned must have come as a surprise to those who pondered the bloody vengeance wrought upon revolutionaries in the eighteenth and nineteenth centuries. Only two days before the fall of tsardom Kerensky had declared the overthrow of the regime to be impossible at the moment. The revolution broke out spontaneously, with no planning and without leadership. Those who joined the bread riots and strikes, those who won over the troops, those who brought round the sailors in the naval base at Cronstadt, those who led the mobs to fire the public buildings and seize the arsenal and break open the prisons—they were all nameless. Only later did revolutionary leaders catch up with the movement and attempt to set its course.

The March Revolution was accomplished with surprisingly low cost in human life. Those in Petrograd who were killed or wounded numbered only thirteen hundred. Many naval officers were murdered at Cronstadt. Elsewhere the revolution was accomplished "by telegraph" as soldiers and officials deserted the old regime at the first command to surrender. Over the entire nation "the change was accepted too easily and too generally to involve serious bloodshed" (Chamberlin). But from the moment of its birth the government which replaced tsardom lived a turbulent and precarious existence.

SUGGESTED READING

Carr, E. H., *The Bolshevik Revolution, 1917–1923* (New York, Macmillan, 1952).

Chamberlin, W. H., *The Russian Revolution* (New York, Macmillan, 1935).

Churchill, W. S., *The Unknown War: the Eastern Front* (New York, Scribner's, 1931).

Curtiss, J. S., *Church and State in Russia: the Last Years of the Empire, 1900–1917* (New York, Columbia University Press, 1940).

Deutscher, I., *The Prophet Armed* (New York, Praeger, 1954).

Florinsky, M. T., *The End of the Russian Empire* (New York, Macmillan, 1931).

Golder, F. A., *Documents of Russian History, 1914–1917* (New York, Century, 1927).

Golovine, N. N., *The Russian Army in the World War* (New Haven, Yale University Press, 1931).

Gronsky, P. P., and N. J. Astrov, *The War and the Russian Government* (New Haven, Yale University Press, 1929).

Knox, A., *With the Russian Army, 1914–1917* (London, Hutchinson, 1921).

Kohn, S., and A. F. Meyendorff, *The Cost of the War to Russia* (New Haven, Yale University Press, 1932).

Letters of the Tsaritsa to the Tsar, 1914–1916 (London, Duckworth, 1923).

Letters of the Tsar to the Tsaritsa, 1914–1917 (New York, Dodd, Mead, 1929).

Lobanov-Rostovsky, A., *Russia and Asia* (Ann Arbor, Wahr, 1951).

Lockhart, R. H. B., *British Agent* (New York, Putnam's, 1933).

Miliukov, P., *Russia and Its Crisis* (Chicago, University of Chicago Press, 1905).

Miller M. S., *The Economic Development of Russia, 1905–1914* (London, King, 1926).

Nolde, B. E., *Russia in the Economic War* (New Haven, Yale University Press, 1928).

Paleologue, M., *An Ambassador's Memoirs* (London, Hutchinson, 1925).

Pares, B., *The Fall of the Russian Monarchy* (New York, Knopf, 1939).

Sazonov, S., *Fateful Years* (London, Cape, 1928).

Shub, D., *Lenin* (New York, Doubleday, 1948).

Taylor, A. J. P., *Struggle for Mastery in Europe* (Oxford, Clarendon, 1954).

Trotsky, L., *History of the Russian Revolution* (New York, Simon and Schuster, 1936).

———, *My Life* (New York, Scribner's, 1930).

Vassilyev, A. T., *The Ochrana* (Philadelphia, Lippincott, 1930).

27

Troublous Times

THE TSAR'S ABDICATION WAS FOLLOWED by a contest for power between the Provisional Government and the Petrograd Soviet, which spoke for the industrial workers. Socialist leaders returned from exile and prison to raise their voices in Soviet meetings for social reform, sequestration of great estates, and an end to the war. Kerensky, prime minister and in effect dictator during the summer and fall of 1917, tried to balance himself between political extremes—the conservatives on one hand, who hoped for a Western-type parliamentary democracy and continued participation in the war, and the Bolsheviks on the other, who demanded peace and a thoroughgoing social revolution. His refusal to end the war forced him to rely increasingly upon right-wing elements who threatened to engulf him and set in his place a military dictator. The attempted coup of General Kornilov frightened the masses into shifting their support to the Bolsheviks in order to save the revolution.

Meanwhile the revolution deepened. Soldiers mutinied or deserted; peasants seized and parcelled out among themselves the estates of the gentry; and city workers struck against high prices and the scarcity of food. The government pleaded for patience and promised early convocation of a national assembly to write a constitution and deal with the problems facing the country. But the revolution went on of itself, and the masses sternly and vengefully settled their own problems.

Kerensky finally ordered the arrest of the Bolshevik leaders who were calling for his overthrow. But hardly anyone would support him. The troops and workers in the capital joined the Bolsheviks in turning Kerensky out. Lenin became President of the Council of People's Commissars, as the Communist government called its cabinet.

The new rulers nationalized land, banking, railroads, shipping, and housing; bridled the Church; organized a secret police force; moved the capital to Moscow; and substituted the *soviet* system for the old territorial pattern in local government. They signed the costly Treaty of Brest-Litovsk ending the war with Germany in order to obtain a "breathing space" to consolidate the administration. They tried vainly to keep factories running and workers on the job, and confiscated grain surpluses to feed the desperate cities.

After Brest-Litovsk Russia's former allies intervened with men and money to overthrow the Bolshevik regime, equipping and financing native counterrevolutionary forces which at one time or another controlled all Russian ports, Siberia, Ukraine, the Caucasus, and the Baltic provinces. The nation was squeezed back into its fifteenth-century frontiers. To defend itself the infant government organized the new Red Army, inaugurated a reign of terror to wipe out sabotage, and brought the productive forces of the nation tightly under state control. Strengthened by these measures and fighting for its life, the new Russia beat back every White and foreign challenge. Then Poland attacked her eastern neighbor, hoping to return to her 1772 frontier by incorporating Belo-Russia and the Ukraine. The Red Army drove the Poles back to Warsaw but in turn was pushed back into its own territory. The two welcomed an end to hostilities and accepted a compromise frontier that satisfied neither. By 1922 Communist Russia had defeated the last of her internal and foreign foes and could turn to the work of reconstruction.

DUAL POWER

No sooner had the tsar abdicated than it became apparent that those who had cooperated to bring about the revolution had done so for contradictory reasons. The middle-class and professional men had supported the revolution in the belief that a new administration would more energetically prosecute the war and in the real fear that Nicholas might even seek peace with the Central Powers, whom he regarded as sympathetic to the autocracy so dear to his heart. The masses, on the other hand, tired of the war to the limit of their endurance, had supported the revolution in the determination that it must bring peace. The liberal element never had its roots among the people and failed utterly to understand their longing to end the war. The leaders of the Provisional Government aimed at establishing Western political liberalism, while the masses wanted socialism. The socialists did not trust the Provisional Government and supported the system of soviets as a counterbalance and check upon it. The liberals had little sympathy for social revolution. The masses would insist upon it.

From the moment of its creation the Provisional Government enjoyed little power and saw its orders carried out only when they were approved by the Petrograd Soviet, acting through its executive committee which was dominated by socialists. While the Bolshevik members were few in number and not influential, the Mensheviks controlled the Soviet; their leader, Chkheidze, presided as chairman of the executive committee. Chkheidze refused a cabinet post in the Provisional Government, but Kerensky, who deserted the Labor party for the Socialist Revolutionary, accepted the Ministry of Justice while retaining his position as vice-chairman of the Soviet and member of its executive committee.

The first split between the Provisional Government and the Petrograd Soviet developed over control of the army. On the eve of the creation of the Provisional Government, Duma and Soviet leaders had agreed that soldiers should have full civil rights and that the Petrograd garrison was neither to be disarmed nor sent outside the capital. But before the announcement could be published the Soviet newspaper *Izvestiia* proclaimed the famous Army Order Number One, which called for the election of regimental delegates to the Soviet; ordered the organization of company committees to maintain "discipline," punish "rudeness" of officers to men, arbitrate differences between them, and assume control of the issue of arms and prevent their falling into the hands of officers; abolished the salute; and forbade troops to carry out orders of the government unless they were approved by the Soviet. Several days later the executive committee of the Soviet announced that it had not intended that enlisted men should elect their own officers, as some had been doing, and that Order Number One was meant to apply only to the Petrograd garrison. The harm had already been done, however. Discipline in the entire army melted rapidly away. Army and navy unit committees or soviets, whose election the Provisional Government could do nothing to halt, looked to the Petrograd Soviet for direction. Troops debated and voted on every order to advance. When the government thus lost control of the armed forces, Minister of War Guchkov resigned in disgust to be replaced by Kerensky.

The Petrograd Soviet and the Provisional Government were soon at odds over foreign policy. Miliukov, the foreign minister and dominant figure in the cabinet, failed or refused to understand the revolution as a protest against further participation in the war. He insisted that Russia must abide by her commitments to the Allies and that the war must go on to victory. Derisively he was named "Miliukov Dardanellesky" for his stubborn position that the nation must continue fighting to gain the spoils—Constantinople, among others—promised her by the Allies in the secret Treaty of London in 1915. His defiance of Prime Minister Lvov, who was willing at least to discuss with the Western powers the possibility of peace without annexations, led to Miliukov's withdrawal from the cabinet just two months after joining it.

Soviet leaders were not of one mind on the question of war or peace.

The right wings of the Menshevik and Socialist Revolutionary parties professed their opposition to offensive war but pledged themselves to defend the nation. The left wings of the two parties urged an early "peace without annexations or indemnities on the basis of the self-determination of peoples." Socialists of all parties agreed in supposing that the March Revolution in Russia would quickly spread to other countries. *Izvestiia* called upon the peoples of the world to reject the war aims, the expansionist programs, of their governments and to take upon themselves the power and the will to end hostilities.

With Guchkov and Miliukov gone Prince Lvov reorganized the cabinet in an effort to strengthen the Provisional Government. Six of the fifteen portfolios were assigned to socialists, including Kerensky as minister of war and Chernov as minister of agriculture. From then on Kerensky was the outstanding figure in the government. Left out of the cabinet, the Bolsheviks refused to support it and waited for the moment when they would have the strength to turn out both the liberals and the moderate socialists whom they regarded as enemies of the revolution.

RETURN OF THE EXILES

On the morrow of its birth the Provisional Government granted an amnesty to political leaders who had been imprisoned or exiled under the old regime. Prince Kropotkin, Martov, the novelist Gorky, and Plekhanov, "the grand old man of Russian Marxism" (Schuman), came back from Western Europe. Nicholas Bukharin and Leon Trotsky, who for a year had published a socialist newspaper in New York, returned from America. The Polish revolutionary Felix Dzerzhinsky, soon to head up the secret police, was released from a Moscow prison. Kamenev, Molotov, and Stalin came out of Siberia. Zinoviev, Radek, and Lenin returned from exile in Switzerland, having been granted passage across Germany in a sealed coach by a German government hopeful that their appearance in Petrograd would weaken the Russian war effort. This led to the ridiculous charge that Lenin and the Bolsheviks were German agents.

In mid-April Lenin stepped from the train at the Finland station in Petrograd to receive a tremendous welcome. Two days later he presented his views, the so-called "April Theses," to Bolsheviks assembled from all over Russia. He declared that the revolution was only in its first, or bourgeois, stage and branded the Provisional Government as capitalist in sympathy, imperialist in aim, and incapable of or unwilling to bring peace. The revolution soon must move into its second stage, where power would be transferred from the Provisional Government to the soviets, the truly revolutionary form of government. The Bolsheviks did not yet control the soviets, but Lenin expected that they would soon win control because of the party's superior discipline over that of the other two socialist parties, both of which were torn by dissension. The second stage of the revolution would not yet introduce socialism but would pave the way for it: agricultural land would be nationalized and parcelled out under soviet control to the peasants; banks would be consolidated into one national institution under soviet management; some great estates would be operated by the soviets as model farms. Soviets, in other words, would direct and control production and distribution. The "bourgeois" army, police, and administration would be swept away, their places taken by a people's militia and officials chosen by and responsible to the soviets of elected delegates of the workers, soldiers, and peasants. The Bolsheviks, he urged, must assemble a national party congress to adopt the new revolutionary program and work out the tactics for its being carried into operation. Since the Second Socialist International had broken up over support of the war, a new Third International, which would admit only "real revolutionaries," must be organized to turn the "imperialist" war into a civil war against capitalism in every country. To make clear the distinction between uncompromising revolutionary socialism and the moderate socialism of the Mensheviks, it was time for the Bolsheviks to drop the name "Social Democrats" and adopt the more proper name "Communists." Then the party must lead the revolution into its second stage by winning control of the soviets. Once that control had been won the Bolsheviks would raise the cry "All Power to the Soviets" and advance to the overthrow of the Provisional Government.

Lenin's proposals were derided as "delirium" and "the raving of a lunatic" by Menshevik leaders, and even the Bolshevik Kamenev wrote them off as unacceptable. But the rank and file of the party and in growing numbers the masses of the people caught up the cry for peace and land which Lenin had voiced in the "April Theses." The national conference of Bolsheviks which met in the capital in early May adopted Lenin's program by an overwhelming majority. From that moment Lenin's leadership and command over the party, while frequently questioned, were never seriously challenged. His driving energy, his refusal to compromise, his sharp, biting sarcasm, his genius for cutting through theoretical verbiage to express in catch phrases the demands of the people made him tower above all others, with the possible exception of Trotsky, in popular appeal.

THE GOVERNMENT CHALLENGED

In mid-May, 1917, an All-Russian Congress of Peasants' Deputies gathered in Petrograd. A majority of the delegates were Socialist Revolutionaries, most of the rest not members of any party. The gathering voted to back the

Provisional Government and to support the continuation of the war. It disapproved Lenin's demand for nationalization of land immediately, calling for socialization only with the sanction of the Constituent Assembly whose meeting the government had scheduled for early fall.

The First All-Russian Congress of Soviets assembled in the capital in mid-June. Of the nine hundred delegates over half were S.R.'s and Mensheviks; the Bolsheviks could muster only a scant hundred. When the Bolsheviks let it be known that they were going to organize mass demonstrations against the war and the "capitalist ministers," the congress forbade the move and denounced Lenin for seeking to overthrow the government. The Soviet Congress then announced its own demonstration in support of the Provisional Government, but the Bolsheviks joined the parade in overwhelming numbers, carrying banners denouncing the government and shouting out their demand for peace and land. The administration stood helplessly by while some of the marchers cheered it mildly and others jeered it boisterously.

The Provisional Government had promised the western Allies another offensive to ease German pressure in France. Kerensky, the war minister, attached to each army unit commissars whose task it was to mediate differences between the soldiers' committees and the officers and to try to restore morale among the troops. Kerensky visited the front, seeking by the power of his colorful oratory to inspire the men to great deeds, but he won for himself only the derisive title, "persuader-in-chief." On July 1 the Russians advanced to the attack in Galicia. The assault was momentarily successful against Austrian troops, but when German reinforcements appeared the Russians fled to the rear in disorder. The awful attrition of three years of war, the effect of Order Number One, the success of Bolshevik peace propaganda among the troops, and the fraternization of the soldiers with the enemy had completely demoralized the Russian army.

The troops in Petrograd, strongly sympathetic to Bolshevism, heard the rumor that they were to be sent to the front, and they called upon the Bolshevik leaders to order an armed demonstration against the government. Lenin, believing the time not yet ripe, refused. However, the next day, July 17, the streets filled with workers, soldiers, and sailors proclaiming a new revolution and demanding the arrest of the ministers. Kerensky fled the city in the nick of time and Chernov was rescued from a mob lynching by Trotsky, who had just joined the Bolsheviks. Some members of the party were for seizing the initiative and overturning the government. Lenin, however, counselled caution and insisted that the party should accept leadership of the demonstration only to end it. The time had not yet arrived, Lenin felt, for a Bolshevik seizure of power. While the party leaders argued among themselves over a course of action the ardor of the mob cooled. The next morning a government-inspired press story charged Lenin with being a German agent. Some of the troops accepted the lie without question and threw their support to the Provisional Government. Loyal police smashed the presses of the Bolshevik newspaper *Pravda* and rounded up Trotsky and other Bolshevik leaders. Lenin escaped by crossing into Finland. The party was not banned, however, and its members continued to serve in the soviets.

With the failure of the unplanned July uprising the first period of the revolution, a period that has been called "the deepening of the revolution," came to an end. The four months after the fall of tsardom witnessed the collapse of discipline and morale in the army; the widespread seizure of land by the peasants; the impatient clamor of the proletariat for higher wages and their steadily growing demand for worker control over production and distribution; the growth of separatist movements in the borderlands of Finland, Ukraine, Poland, and Asia; and the mounting insistence of the vast majority on an end to the war. These hopes of the masses were voiced in simple language by a Bolshevik manifesto: "The peasants want land, the workers want bread, and they both want peace." "Peace, land, and bread" became a rallying slogan calculated to catch the fancy of the masses.

SWING TO THE RIGHT

The second period of the revolution, the two months following the suppression of the July rising, witnessed Kerensky's juggling efforts to balance the revolution between extremes of left and right.

The "July Days," which Lenin viewed as "something more than a demonstration and less than a revolution," constituted a test of strength between the Bolsheviks and the government. The ineffective Prince Lvov gave up the premiership to Kerensky, who vowed to save the nation from Bolshevism. The Provisional Government had apparently won out when it had locked up some of the Bolshevik leaders, driven others into hiding, and smashed the party press. But it had lost its own struggle for liberal government. Kerensky drifted into the position of dictator, forced more and more to rely upon the backing of the old officer class in the army, a backing that to many exemplified reaction and restoration of the monarchy.

In an effort to provide himself wider support than just the Petrograd Soviet, limited as it was to socialists, Kerensky revamped the administration. While a majority of the new cabinet were socialists, they were all of the mild, anti-Bolshevik variety, and four Cadets were prevailed upon to serve. The executive committee of the Petrograd Soviet agreed to support the new cabinet, but only if the government promised to carry out land reform, convoke a constitutional convention in not more than two months, and ask the other Allies for a conference on war aims. Kerensky did convene a temporary assembly, but one which had only advisory power. To the so-called Moscow State Conference came former Duma members, generals, industrialists, delegates from cooperatives and trade and professional unions, representatives of ethnic minorities and soviet leaders. All political points of view were represented except the Bolsheviks, who were forbidden to send delegates. Kerensky pleaded in his usual flamboyant style for unity. General Kornilov, the newly-appointed commander-in-chief of the army, demanded a return to order and discipline both at the front and in the rear. After three days of fruitless debating the Moscow State Conference adjourned. Meanwhile, the Bolsheviks had sought to embarrass the government by calling a general strike in Moscow.

In response to pressure from the generals, Kerensky named the war hero Kornilov, son of a Siberian Cossack peasant, as commander-in-chief. Kornilov, who "wished to see an army where the soldiers would obey orders instead of debating them" (Chamberlin), accepted the nomination only on condition that he be given a free hand in operations, in naming subordinates, and in restoring discipline. The general, reputed to have "the heart of a lion and the brain of a lamb," was politically illiterate and saw no difference between Bolsheviks and right-wing socialists who opposed Lenin as much as he. Kerensky and Kornilov were suspicious of each other, the former of the general's ambition, the latter of Kerensky's willingness to cooperate with socialists.

Rightists of every hue—conservative constitutionalists like Miliukov and Rodzianko, industrialists who feared the seizure of their plants by the workers, landlords who saw their estates being expropriated by land-hungry peasants, officers who deplored the waning strength of the Russian Army, Cossacks who dreaded the social revolution that might spread to their own lands, churchmen who regretted their loss of influence, monarchists who hoped to bring back the Romanovs—came to look upon Kornilov as a possible savior of the land from further turmoil and anarchy.

Even before the meeting of the Moscow State Conference Kornilov had voiced his decision that the Petrograd Soviet must be swept aside and the Bolsheviks all hanged. A fortnight later, in early September, he gave the orders for troops loyal to him to march on Petrograd, ostensibly to "save" the Provisional Government from the Bolsheviks and from German armies that were driving toward the capital. Kerensky cashiered him but Kornilov refused to give up his command. But his contemplated coup quickly evaporated. Railway workers sided with the government and refused to move the trains loaded with his troops. Telegraph workers refused to dispatch orders to his subordinates. Soldiers loyal to the government mingled with Kornilov's Cossacks, urging them not to fire upon their brothers. Generals on other fronts could not support Kornilov, for their own men refused to move against the government.

Alarmed at the threat to the capital, the masses forgot their differences of

July. Mensheviks and Socialist Revolutionaries asked the Bolsheviks to cooperate in defending Petrograd. Trotsky and the other Bolshevik leaders arrested in July were released. A Committee to Fight Counterrevolution which included Bolshevik members was organized and called for the creation of similar committees all over Russia. It legalized the so-called Red Guard, or Bolshevik militia, twenty-five thousand strong and well armed with rifles and machine guns. But the attack never came. Kornilov's troops deserted to the Provisional Government. He and the generals who had supported him were arrested, a move that probably saved them from mob lynching. After the November Revolution they all escaped to organize the resistance movement in South Russia.

The Kornilov mutiny, which closed the second period of the revolution, proved the utter futility of attempting to restore the old regime. The fiasco had one important consequence—it freed the Bolsheviks and restored them to a position of influence, permitted the rearming of their fighting force, and paved the way for their eventual seizure of power.

ON THE EVE

In the final period of the March Revolution, through the eight weeks following the Kornilov rising, pressure upon the government steadily increased. Having survived a threat from the left in July and another from the right in September, Kerensky now maneuvered desperately to avoid further crisis. He reshuffled the cabinet, retaining a few non-socialists but relying chiefly upon moderate socialists and retaining in his own hands the chief executive power. He declared Russia a republic, implying that the government was no longer "provisional," and by this mild step called down the criticism of liberals generally, who accused him of arrogating to himself authority which only a national body should possess. He arrested Guchkov and outlawed the reactionary Officers' Union which had backed the September mutiny. Kornilov's plan to bring discipline back to the armed forces, chiefly by restoring the death penalty at the front, was cancelled. Kerensky announced that elections of delegates to the Constituent Assembly would take place in November. Finally, to win broad support for his new coalition cabinet, he gathered about him in Petrograd the so-called Democratic Conference, made up of fourteen hundred representatives of rural and city governments, soviets, trade and professional unions. Its membership included all shades of political opinion. Even the Bolsheviks took part. Like the Moscow State Conference before it, this Democratic Conference debated endlessly and meaninglessly and made itself ridiculous in the things it could agree upon. For example, it voted to support a coalition cabinet, then agreed to exclude Cadets, and finally defeated a motion to approve a cabinet without Cadets. Little wonder that the Petrograd Soviet scoffed at the performance and promised that the coming Second All-Russian Congress of Soviets would give Russia "a truly revolutionary government."

When the Democratic Conference broke up it established the Council of the Republic, five hundred of the nation's keenest minds, who unfortunately represented only themselves, to sit regularly as a consultative body until the Constituent Assembly could gather in late autumn. Much to Lenin's disgust the Bolsheviks voted to elect delegates to the new body. The Council of the Republic met and did nothing from the time of its creation to the moment when Bolshevik bayonets scattered it in November. Trotsky rose in the first session of the council to accuse it and the government of treason to the revolution and of seeking to drag out the war. Then he and the other Bolsheviks dramatized their contempt for the council by resigning from it and walking out of the session. Three weeks later it passed unnoticed and unmourned into the limbo of pre-Bolshevik institutions.

SOCIAL UPHEAVAL

In the eight months during which the Provisional Government managed uneasily to cling to power Russia was undergoing a social revolution far more fundamental and significant than the relatively mild political disturbances that were going on in Petrograd. The real revolution swept into the countryside and the industrial centers and through the army. The most radical leaders in the capital often could not keep up with the radical thoughts and demands of those they professed to represent. In their resolution to divide up the land, the peasants of many districts were far ahead of the Socialist Revolutionaries who spoke for them. In their impatience to seize control of industry, the workers of Petrograd and Moscow moved too rapidly even for Lenin. In their determinatin to end the war quickly, vast numbers of soldiers were far out in front of most of the Bolshevik leaders.

At the beginning of 1917 there were nearly seven million Russians under arms. In the next eight months a million of them "demobilized themselves" and went home. Those who remained, poorly armed, shabbily clothed, and miserably fed, had lost all stomach for the war. Men at the front, their morale riddled by socialist propaganda, passed the time in listening to speeches of revolutionaries from the capital, debating social and political questions, electing new officers and demoting old ones so that "cooks became colonels and colonels cooks," choosing standing committees to arbitrate disputes with officers and special committees to investigate the food situation, sending off delegations to Petrograd to ask "Comrade" Kerensky if he had really ordered an advance as their officers insisted, hounding the doctors to give them medical discharges, trading their arms to the Germans for tobacco, and querying every arriving batch of replacements as to whether conditions at home were as bad as rumor made them. Resistance to authority showed itself in refusal to obey commands, unwillingness to drill, beating and killing of officers and even commissars sent out by the government or the Petrograd Soviet, restraining the artillery from firing at the enemy lest it bring reprisal, feigning sickness, and deserting. Peasant soldiers disappeared into the night in droves to hurry back to their villages to share in the expropriation of land. As Lenin put it, "the army voted for peace with its legs."

The army chief-of-staff in the summer of 1917 pondered how to restore discipline—the death sentence, but that would mean hanging whole divisions; court-martial, but that would put half the army in Siberia; imprisonment, but many would welcome it—and concluded that the elected committee in every unit provided for in Order Number One was the only means left of checking the drift toward complete disintegration. Other generals believed that the committee system contributed more than anything else to the collapse of morale. Defeat, war-weariness, poor equipment, propaganda, and the committee system all contributed to such demoralization in the old army that when the November Revolution broke out the Provisional Government could muster to its defense only military students, women, some companies of soldiers, and a few hundred Cossacks of the millions in uniform at the time. And the Bolsheviks later had to organize an entirely new fighting force. The old Russian Army simply evaporated in the summer and autumn of 1917.

In some sections of the navy the situation was even worse than among the land forces. The garrison at Cronstadt was strongly Bolshevik in sympathy. The sailors of the Baltic fleet, while not all Bolshevik, were hostile to the Provisional Government from the very beginning. Admiral Kolchak kept the Black Sea fleet in line for a while, but by June, 1917, the sailors were hurling their officers overboard and electing new ones. Kolchak resigned in indignation and later led the anti-Bolshevik movement in Siberia.

Over four-fifths of the population of Russia in 1917 were peasants. Never reconciled to the land settlement of the sixties, they were obsessed with the belief that the land should belong to those who tilled it. The peasants begrudged the absentee landlord, the royal family, the state, and the church their rich acres. Traditionally much of the land was cultivated communally, and "the sacred right of private property, so passionately defended since the Bolshevik Revolution by Russian opponents of socialism, was, until 1906, very nearly an empty sound for the masses of the Russian people" (Florinsky). Even after the Stolypin reform the amount of land that came under private ownership was almost insignificant.

Very few Russian peasants were as comfortably situated as were those of Germany and France. The great majority were miserably poor, and both their numbers and their plight were growing worse in the twentieth century. Although many districts of South Russia were heavily overpopulated, it is true, the problem was less one of land shortage than of backward methods. The peasant persisted, however, in attributing his sorry condition to the size of the small plot he tilled and the high rent he had to pay the neighboring squire for leasing an additional acre or two. He was convinced, and had been for generations, that the only way out of his misery lay in seizing as much of the landlord's fertile estate as his fellows would let him fence off. Government statisticians could show him that the percentage of arable land under peasant proprietorship was steadily rising. But the poor peasant or the "middle" peasant could draw little comfort from the fact that a few *kulaks* were renting or buying hundreds of acres from the nobles. Many could look beyond their own tiny plots upon the broad expanses of a neighboring aristocrat or rich peasant. And the average peasant did not distinguish between the two, the noble or the commoner who had more than his share of land.

The war demanded its heaviest human sacrifice from the rural community. Nearly twelve million of the strongest peasants and two million horses were mustered into the army. Much land went out of cultivation because of the manpower shortage, perhaps 10 per cent in European Russia by 1917 and a fourth in the rich valleys of the north Caucasus. Army purchases made up for the loss of foreign markets, but the government paid for its requisitions in paper money whose value shrank as its volume increased. Peasants grew loath to sell their produce since the factories were turning out so few of the goods they needed and the rubles they were paid would buy so little. The Provisional Government inaugurated a system of requisitions at fixed prices, but the peasant's response was simply to hide his grain.

The overthrow of the monarchy and the rapid disintegration of authority that followed upon it gave the peasant the opportunity to order the land settlement to his own liking. But remembering the government's ferocious vengeance after the 1905 Revolution he now moved cautiously. He sickled a few sacks of grain at night from the neighboring aristocrat's field or raided his forest for firewood. He pastured his cow in the squire's meadow. He and his fellows in the village commune demanded prohibitive wages for their agricultural labor and would not allow prisoners of war to work on the great estates. Gangs raided the barns and granaries of the gentry, carrying off grain and livestock. Growing bolder by the day, the villagers advanced on the manor houses with clubs, axes, and scythes, sometimes ushering the noble families into the road and telling them not to return, sometimes murdering them. Manor houses went up in flames and with them deeds, leases, and mortgages. Great landowners, peasant and noble, all suffered the scourge. They poured into the capital demanding that the Provisional Government save them and their estates. Punitive expeditions marched again as in 1905 into the countryside, but this time the troops refused to fire at the villagers and often joined them. There were nearly six thousand peasant "disturbances" in 1917, the number growing rapidly in the months just prior to the Bolshevik Revolution. Most of the attacks were against the gentry. The *kulaks*, knowing the peasant mind, usually gave in to the demands of the villagers and went along with the movement to save their own lives.

As soviets of workers' and soldiers' deputies sprang up during the March Revolution, soviets of peasants' deputies also began to appear. In mid-May a Congress of Peasants' Deputies convened in Petrograd. A majority of the delegates were not peasants but intellectuals elected by village soviets. There seems little doubt that they were more conservative than those who sent them. Of the eleven hundred deputies, over half were Socialist Revolutionaries and only fourteen were Bolsheviks. Many brought with them instructions from the soviets which had chosen them, and over two hundred had been ordered to support a model land law which would forbid the private ownership of land, allowing only its use by any citizen and limiting the amount any individual might cultivate to what he could work with his own labor. The resolution became the basis for Communist land policy later, but the Congress of Peasants' Deputies now turned it down. The congress condemned the expropriations then going on. It expressed sympathy for the confiscation of state and church lands and great estates, but insisted that the coming Constituent Assembly must approve and direct such confiscation. Such, too, was the policy of the Provisional Government, and so it remained until the November Revolution.

The peasants of Russia refused to allow the government to defer the land question until the meeting of the Constituent Assembly. They took the law into their own hands and divided up the great holdings, so that gentry estates disappeared and even peasant-owned farms of fifty acres were broken up. Over much of European Russia the average holding fell to between five and thirty acres. Before the Bolsheviks came to power the land question had already been settled.

Army mutiny and rural outbreaks would not of themselves have overturned the Provisional Government. The soldier and the peasant were concerned primarily with local or individual problems. Many a village, focusing its attention upon its land shortage and the nearby means of correcting it, lost all interest in the war and even forgot that one was going on. The soldier, the peasant in uniform, was concerned only to get out of the army to get back to the village and claim his share of the neighboring estate. Furthermore, those most anxious to upset the government, namely the

Bolsheviks, had very little and only spotty support among soldiers or peasants. If the government were to be turned out it must be with the help of urban workers, the class upon which the Bolsheviks had long focused their efforts.

The Russian working class constituted only a small percentage of society, but the middle class was even smaller, relatively, than in Western Europe because so many workers were employed in foreign-owned plants. Furthermore, as Lenin clearly foresaw, the urban proletariat could expect at least the tacit support of the mass of the peasants who, having little sense of private property, could be relied upon not to defend the existing regime. When the troops withdrew their support from the government which insisted upon continuing the war, the proletariat became the most influential segment of society in determining the course of the revolution. Their poverty, insecurity, and brutish conditions of work and living gave the workers every incentive to destroy the society which gave them so little. That they would swing far to the left once the bonds of restraint were loosed might easily have been predicted. They had nothing to lose in casting out the old and everything to gain in venturing the new.

The war had brought increased hardships to Russian workers, whose prewar standard of living was far below that of Western labor. Average factory wages in 1913 were twenty-two rubles, or eleven dollars per month. While the ten-hour day was not unusual, the legal limit was eleven and a half and this was often exceeded. Many were housed in barracks where guards kept order with the lash. Money wages rose during the war, but prices climbed even faster and real wages fell by 40 per cent between early 1916 and November, 1917. The poor harvest of 1917 forced down the bread ration from a meager pound a day to a half pound by late autumn. Urban population grew rapidly, bringing overcrowding and squalor. The progressive breakdown in transportation threatened the city workers with starvation in the spring of 1917. Strikes multiplied as the war went on, and one widespread work stoppage followed another during that spring and summer. The strikers demanded higher wages, the eight-hour day, worker control over employment and dismissal. Strikes were answered by lockouts. In many instances the workers forcibly kept the plants open, in many others the factories closed down permanently, adding to the mounting unemployment. Often there was worse violence; brutal foremen and employers were beaten and occasionally killed, although in general city workers were much less bloodthirsty than were the peasants and soldiers. By the fall of 1917 labor had gone beyond the usual trade union demands and was calling for socialization of industry and the surrender of political power to the soviets.

Elected factory and shop committees sprang up in the capital during the March Revolution to speak for the workers in negotiations with employers and dealings with the government. Soon the committees all over the capital and in other industrial centers were demanding that management of Russian factories be controlled by committees of workers. Trade unions, legal since 1906 but harmless and almost nonexistent before the overthrow of the monarchy, expanded quickly thereafter. Membership exceeded a million and a half by June, 1917, when Petrograd was host to an All-Russian Conference of Trade Unions. The trade unions tended to be moderate, the factory committees radical in outlook. The trade unions tended to limit their program to seeking improved wages, hours, and conditions of work. The factory committees added political and social to economic demands. Mensheviks and Socialist Revolutionaries predominated in the trade-union leadership, while the Bolsheviks strove for and won the support of the factory committees. The trade-union leaders supported the Provisional Government; the factory committees early turned against it.

As the government seemed unwilling or unable to satisfy the soldier's hope for peace and the peasant's need for land, so it proved completely ineffective in meeting the worker's problems. Prices continued to rise, real wages to fall, food to grow scarce, factories to close down, unemployment to increase, strikes to spread. The patience of the worker, like that of the soldier and the peasant, was nearing exhaustion.

THE BOLSHEVIK TIDE

In early August, 1917, the Sixth Congress of the Bolshevik Party, the first in a decade, met secretly in Petrograd to appraise the July uprising and plan future action. Lenin, still hiding in Finland, did not attend but spoke through the party leaders Stalin, Molotov, and Sverdlov. The party saw that power was slipping away from the Provisional Government into the hands of militarists and reactionaries and declared that only a Bolshevik-led armed rising of workers and peasants could save the revolution. It was assumed that the Bolshevik Revolution in Russia would touch off similar risings in Western Europe. Some party leaders, with the notable exception of Stalin, insisted that a socialist experiment in Russia must inevitably fail unless capitalism were overthrown in the West. The principle of "democratic centralism" was adopted, providing that differences of opinion were permissible only up to the point where the party "line" or policy was worked out. Thereafter there must be no deviation; members must accept the policy without criticism and must obey all orders and decisions without question. Lenin had insisted on such discipline from the moment of his entry into the socialist movement. Now he had his way. Finally, the party agreed to shelve the demand "all power to the Soviets," since there seemed no immediate prospect of driving the Mensheviks and S.R.'s from control, particularly in the Petrograd Soviet. Party membership now numbered nearly a quarter million, an eightfold increase since the abdication of Nicholas II.

The Kornilov mutiny removed from the Bolsheviks the stigma of official disapproval, for the government needed their help to survive. Now armed and respectable, their influence quickly grew. On the day of Kornilov's arrest a Bolshevik resolution passed the Petrograd Soviet, which thereby deserted its Menshevik and S.R. leaders. Many members of the two parties, the one growing increasingly conservative and the other badly split between right and left wings, joined the Bolsheviks. Soon the latter took over control of the Soviet and Trotsky became its chairman. A week later the Moscow Soviet also turned Bolshevik, and the drift in their favor was apparent in many of the provincial soviets. In the third week of October the Petrograd Soviet chose a Military Revolutionary Committee, with Trotsky as chairman, to organize troops in the capital for a defense against an expected German advance from Riga. The Bolsheviks now had an army, for the soldiers of the Petrograd garrison showed themselves more willing to take orders from the Military Revolutionary Committee than from the Provisional Government.

Through October Lenin poured forth a barrage of letters and pamphlets, trying to win over the other party leaders to his view that the time was at hand for the Bolsheviks to drive "Kerensky and Company" from power. Some urged that the party must wait for the meeting of the Second All-Russian Congress of Soviets, scheduled to assemble in Petrograd on November 7. But Lenin, believing that "the crisis is ripe," that the people had had enough of speeches and resolutions and that Bolshevik influence might decline if the coup were postponed, insisted that "to wait is a crime, a childish play at formality." To those who protested that the Bolsheviks were not sufficiently numerous to seize power and hold it Lenin retorted: "After the Revolution of 1905, 130,000 landlords governed Russia. Cannot 240,000 members of the Bolshevik party govern Russia in the interests of the poor against the rich?"

On October 23 the Central Committee of the Bolshevik party met secretly in the capital to argue out the party's position. After ten hours of heated debate Lenin carried the others with him in concluding that, for a number of reasons, the time for action had arrived. The mutiny in the German fleet and the prospect for socialist risings in Germany and elsewhere, the supposed willingness of Kerensky to surrender Petrograd to the German armies rather than lose it to the Bolsheviks, the threat of another attempted coup by the generals, the crescendo of peasant disturbances, the growth of Bolshevik strength and their victory in the soviets all combined to make this the moment when the party must make its bid for power. A resolution to this effect carried ten votes to two, Kamenev and Zinoviev opposing. To act as the general staff of the revolution the group chose from among its own membersh'p a Political Bureau, or "Politburo," consisting of Lenin, Trotsky,

Stalin, Zinoviev, Kamenev, Sokolnikov, and Bubnov. Zinoviev and Kamenev continued openly to oppose an early rising down to the very moment of the Bolshevik Revolution, a flagrant violation of the party discipline upon which the Sixth Congress had insisted.

That the Bolsheviks were planning to overthrow the government was no secret, but Kerensky seemed to scorn the threat. No military measures were taken, and perhaps none was possible. "The soldiers of the Petrograd garrison were so accustomed to a life of loafing about the streets that they could scarcely be expected to put up a vigorous fight for anything" (Chamberlin). And the troops at the front were hardly more reliable. The government seemed confident that a Bolshevik uprising could be put down as easily as the July demonstration. In fact, just four days before the November Revolution Kerensky voiced the hope that the Bolsheviks would attempt something and expressed confidence that he would crush them once and for all. While he was speaking the workers of a munitions plant, on orders from the Military Revolutionary Committee, were turning over five thousand rifles to the Bolsheviks. And reports were coming in from as far away as the middle Volga and the Caucasus that popular meetings were calling for the overthrow of the Provisional Government. Delegates from nearly all the regiments in the Petrograd garrison promised the Military Revolutionary Committee full support in whatever action it should choose to take.

THE BOLSHEVIK REVOLUTION

On November 4 the Bolshevik-dominated Military Revolutionary Committee issued a proclamation accusing the Provisional Government of serving counterrevolutionary interests and calling upon the Petrograd garrison to disregard all orders except those of the committee. At government headquarters in the Winter Palace the cabinet decided at last to take up the challenge. It was agreed on the night of November 5 that the next morning the Bolshevik newspapers should be suppressed, the party leaders arrested, the Military Revolutionary Committee disbanded, and some supposedly loyal troops brought to the capital. Some printing presses were damaged the next day, but that was as far as Kerensky's orders were carried out. After a few hours' delay the Bolshevik newspapers appeared, the print shops now guarded by soldiers called out by the Military Revolutionary Committee. Meanwhile Kerensky was addressing the sterile Council of the Republic, swearing to put down the uprising and asking for a vote of confidence. Not getting it, he threatened, but only threatened, to resign.

At the Smolny Institute, former convent and girls' school, now headquarters of the Petrograd Soviet, the Bolshevik leaders met on November 6 to analyze the situation. Lenin came out of hiding and now took up residence in the Smolny, from which he directed the revolution. That night soldiers under orders from the Military Revolutionary Committee seized railway stations, strategic bridges over the Neva, the state bank, and the telephone exchange, shutting off all communication between the Ministry in the Winter Palace and the outside. Even the Cossack regiments refused to rescue Kerensky. To his hysterical calls for help they answered repeatedly that they "were getting ready to saddle their horses."

At ten o'clock in the morning of November 7 the Bolsheviks announced that the Provisional Government had fallen. There was no resistance. Kerensky escaped from the city in a car owned by the American Embassy. The entire city was taken over by the Bolsheviks almost without the firing of a shot. The Winter Palace—where the rest of the cabinet was "defended" by the women's battalion, some cadets, and a few stray Cossacks—surrendered after a few artillery shots, most of which missed, and a rush by Red Guards. Six of the attackers were killed but no lives were lost among the defenders. The members of the cabinet were arrested, but soon released. The November Revolution was carried out with far less bloodshed than the March Revolution, which itself had cost remarkably few lives. The Provisional Government could find fewer defenders than the monarchy which it had replaced.

Kerensky reached the front and managed to round up a few hundred soldiers to send back to the capital. But they were halted before they reached the city, and the effort to revive the Provisional Government collapsed. None of the generals at the front would or could move to put Kerensky back in power.

In Moscow the Bolsheviks ran into heavy opposition and managed to win control of the city only after a week of hard fighting. In the industrial centers of central and northern Russia the revolution encountered little resistance. In the Urals and western Siberia the Bolsheviks won easily. But a hostile regime appeared in the Georgian capital of Tiflis, and in Kiev nationalist Ukrainians moved to set up an independent republic. The Don and Kuban Cossacks, who would later support White commanders, successfully resisted the Reds. Fighting went on in most of the provincial capitals, some of which did not surrender to the Bolsheviks until the following spring.

Back in Petrograd the Second All-Russian Congress of Soviets of Workers', Soldiers', and Peasants' Deputies met on November 7, even before the firing had died down. Of the six hundred and fifty delegates, most of them from northern and central European Russia, the Bolsheviks and the left wing of the Socialist Revolutionaries who supported them numbered over five hundred. The Mensheviks and the right-wing Socialist Revolutionaries walked out of the very first session, ridiculed by Trotsky as "so much refuse that will be swept into the garbage can of history."

Lenin put before the Congress of Soviets a proclamation addressed to the peoples and governments of all belligerent powers demanding immediate peace without annexations or indemnities and announcing that Russia annulled and would immediately publish all the secret treaties. The proclamation asked British, French, and German workers to help force an end to the conflict. Put to the vote, the document was approved unanimously. In effect, the new government, only one day old, thereby announced Russia's withdrawal from the war.

Next Lenin presented a decree outlining the government's land policy. It wiped out ownership of great estates without compensation, turning over such estates together with church lands to local land committees and peasant soviets. Private ownership was forbidden and no land could be sold or rented. The Constituent Assembly would finally settle the land question. Meanwhile, anyone could use as much land as he and his family could work, but the hiring of labor was forbidden. In the interest of fairness the arable land would periodically be realloted. The Bolsheviks had borrowed the principles of the decree on land from the Socialist Revolutionaries, who in turn had based their program upon practices operative in the village communes for centuries.

The Congress of Soviets approved a new cabinet to be called the Council of People's Commissars. The slate was made up entirely of Bolsheviks, for the Left Socialist Revolutionaries refused to join a ministry that was not open to all socialists. Lenin became president of the Council, Trotsky commissar for foreign affairs, Rykov commissar for internal affairs, and Stalin commissar for nationalities. Finally, the Congress elected an All-Russian Central Executive Committee, two-thirds of which were Bolsheviks and the rest Left Socialist Revolutionaries, to serve in place of the Congress of Soviets until the latter should convene again. Then the Congress adjourned. The new administration had been organized, the new government launched.

OPPOSITION AND DISCORD

During the first few weeks of the regime the Bolsheviks tolerated an array of oppositional fragments, perhaps because they underestimated their own strength or overestimated their opponents' weakness. They had toppled the Kerensky government with a ragtag army, perhaps twenty thousand strong, made up of Red Guards, civilians, sailors, and disorganized soldiers. But there were millions of troops at the front who, for all the Bolshevik leaders could be sure, might turn against them. Staff headquarters was known to be a center of hostility to Bolshevism as it had been to the Provisional Government.

Fear of the resistance of army headquarters to the November Revolution proved to be unfounded. The Council of People's Commissars ordered the commander-in-chief, General Dukhonin, to begin peace talks with the Germans. When he refused, Nicholas Krylenko, a former army lieutenant and one of the three commissars for war, replaced him as commander-in-chief. Dukhonin gave way without a murmur.

A number of political remnants from earlier regimes kept up for weeks a feeble protest against the coup of November 7. An organization called the Committee for the Salvation of the Country and the Revolution appeared even before the capture of the Winter Palace. Made up of former members of the Petrograd municipal government, delegates to the Council of the Republic, and various Menshevik and S.R. leaders, the Committee for Salvation called upon the populace not to obey the orders of the Bolsheviks. Congresses of non-Bolshevik members of trade unions and factory committees passed resolutions condemning the change of government. Mensheviks and Socialist Revolutionaries held meetings to debate what sort of government they would support. Some spoke for coalition of all parties, others for coalition only of socialist parties, still others for coalition of non-Bolshevik socialists. Cabinet ministers of the Provisional Government, freed from prison, declared themselves still in office and issued orders and gave out press releases for three weeks until the Council of People's Commissars drove them from the capital. The Imperial Senate, the old supreme court, continued its sessions unnoticed until it handed down a decision that the new government was illegal, whereupon it was dissolved. Bureaucrats in government offices continued to function, refusing to recognize the new administration until they were driven from their desks or forced at pistol point to serve the new order.

There was discord, too, among the Bolsheviks themselves. Many members of the party objected to the curtailment of the freedom of the press when some Menshevik newspapers were closed. Others expressed fear that the Constituent Assembly might not be allowed to meet. Still others questioned Lenin's determination to end the war at all costs. Many favored a coalition cabinet that would include other socialists, and several members of the Council of People's Commissars resigned because they believed that a government made up solely of Bolsheviks could maintain itself only by political terror. Some left-wing Socialist Revolutionaries then were named to the council, but they only added to the disagreement and resigned three months later. Lenin, like Lvov and Kerensky, had trouble with his early cabinets.

EARLY LEGISLATION

During the first several weeks of the Soviet regime there was a spate of legislation, much of it of far-reaching importance. By the decree on land which Lenin read to the Congress of Soviets the peasants won the government's sanction of the steps they had already taken to redistribute the land. Now the proletariat received somewhat similar power over private industry by a decree giving workers a determining voice in management, production, and price setting. In addition, railroads, shipping, and all banks were nationalized and foreign trade became a government monopoly. The eight-hour day was established. The debts of earlier governments to foreigners were disallowed. Inheritance of private property was made illegal, all such property to fall to the state when the owner died. All private homes and apartments were to be taken over by municipalities, whose soviets were empowered to remove bourgeois families in favor of workers, the furniture of the former occupants to remain for the use of the new.

While proclaiming freedom of worship, the administration ordered complete separation of church and state, forbidding the church to own property but allowing the churches to be used for religious functions upon application to the government by organizations of laymen. Religious instruction was forbidden in the schools but allowed privately. The recording of births and marriages, heretofore a church function, was assumed by the government. Only civil marriages were now legal. Divorce became possible by a simple declaration of both parties or by application by one of them to a court. The Gregorian calendar, never accepted in Orthodox Russia because a Roman pope had developed it, came into operation, thus ending the thirteen-day difference between the Western and Russian calendars. The complicated Russian alphabet, a plague even to Russian students, was stripped of its superfluous characters.

A decree of the Council of People's Commissars swept away the old institutions of local government and installed in their place a hierarchy of soviets, elected as all soviets were by professional or occupational groups rather than by geographic areas. The old court system was replaced by a system of "People's Courts" whose judges were elected by the people and whose juries were chosen by the soviets. The functions of the tsarist police system, liquidated by the revolution, were brought under the control of local soviets. A security police agency, the infamous Cheka, was created to ferret out counterrevolutionaries and saboteurs. Its first chief, the Polish revolutionary Felix Dzerzhinsky, made it into the most efficient and the most dreaded secret police system the nation had ever known.

Finally, the new government "democratized" the army. Rank, titles, decorations, and epaulettes were outlawed, and all positions of command were to be filled by election. No attempt was made to keep the men at the front and "the old army melted away in a vast torrent of homeward-moving demobilized soldiers" (Chamberlin). Early in 1918 an entirely new force, the Red Army, came into being with the usual military discipline restored.

The effect of these early decrees was to wipe out many vestiges of capi-

talist society as Russia had come so recently to know it. Much of the legislation has continued in operation down to the present time. Some of it, for
example the democratization of the army and the easy divorce laws, sooner
or later was repealed or modified.

THE CONSTITUENT ASSEMBLY

Late in November, 1917, there took place the elections to the Constituent Assembly which had been ordered by the Provisional Government.
Well over half the delegates were right-wing Socialist Revolutionaries, over
two-thirds were definitely anti-Bolshevik, and less than a third were Bolsheviks and their left-wing S.R. friends. Lenin did not forbid its meeting,
as he might have been expected to do, but he published a statement of his
views on its position. Declaring that the soviet system was "a higher form
of democratic organization" than a constituent assembly, he proposed that
the assembly should abdicate its power to the Congress of Soviets. He
threatened in veiled terms that if this were not done the Constituent Assembly would be dissolved.

The assembly met for its first and only session on January 18, 1918. It
rejected Lenin's proposal that it should surrender its authority to the Congress of Soviets and spent the rest of the session in tedious and pointless
debate. At five o'clock the next morning the armed Bolshevik at the door
ordered Chernov, the chairman, to adjourn the meeting since "the guards
are getting tired." During its recess the government dissolved the assembly.
Its passing was little mourned. The people had been indifferent to its election—less than half of those eligible had voted—and none could rightly
claim that it reflected the sentiment of the nation. But with its dissolution
the last freely-elected representative body in modern Russia came to an end.

THE OBSCENE PEACE

One month after the November Revolution Krylenko, the new commander-in-chief of the army, arranged an armistice with the Central Powers
at Brest-Litovsk. In the peace talks which followed the Germans insisted
upon keeping all the Russian territory behind their lines—all of Poland,
most of the Baltic provinces, and part of Belo-Russia. Foreign Commissar
Trotsky, who accompanied the Russian delegation, refused to concede such
a crippling loss and announced to the Germans that there would be "no
war, no peace" on such terms. Back in the capital the Bolshevik leaders
violently disagreed over whether to accept the German offer. The debate
raged for a month with Lenin finally having his way, after threatening to

resign, that it was a matter of life and death for the nation to have a breathing spell at any price if the revolution were to survive. Since the army had already been demobilized, there was really no choice. By a vote of seven to six the party Central Committee agreed to the enemy's terms, which by now were even harsher than those offered earlier. Since Trotsky refused to look upon the Germans again, Sokolnikov signed the treaty. He did so without reading it to emphasize that it was a dictated and not a negotiated peace.

By the Treaty of Brest-Litovsk, dated March 3, 1918, Russia recognized the independence of the Ukraine and Georgia and confirmed the independence of Finland which she had approved two months earlier. She surrendered Poland, Estonia, Latvia, and Lithuania to Germany and Austria-Hungary to do with as they chose. It turned out later that this meant occupation and tribute. In effect, the territory was added to that of the German Empire. Over a hundred thousand tons of grain, eggs, butter, and meat were shipped back to Berlin from the Ukraine alone. Russia also gave up Kars, Ardahan, and Batum to Turkey and later was ordered to pay an indemnity of six billion marks to Germany.

The treaty cost the Russian nation a million and a quarter square miles of territory and sixty-two million people. She lost a third of her farm land, a third of her population, a fourth of her railroad mileage, nearly half of her industrial plant and equipment, four-fifths of her iron, and 90 per cent of her coal production. Russia was deprived of the territorial acquisitions of the last two centuries. The "obscene peace," Lenin named it.

The general peace settlement at Paris in 1919 ostensibly abrogated the Treaty of Brest-Litovsk. But in effect the harsh terms continued to stand. The independence of Finland, Poland, Estonia, Latvia, and Lithuania was recognized by the Allies as was the session of Bessarabia to Romania. Four-fifths of the Ukraine, however, returned to Russia.

THE BORDERLANDS

The Bolsheviks early recognized, in a "Declaration of the Rights of the People of Russia," the full "equality and sovereignty" of all the nationalities that made up the old empire and declared their right to secede and proclaim their independence. The government hoped, however, that the minorities would not claim the right and that they would take their place along with Russia proper as member states in a Communist federation.

The concession of independence to Poland cost the Bolsheviks nothing, since the entire area was back of the German lines. In mid-December the Finnish Diet proclaimed the former duchy's independence, and the Council of People's Commissars approved. An attempt by Finnish pro-Bolshevik

500 MILES

NORWAY

SWEDEN

GERMANY

AUSTRIA
HUNGARY

SERBIA

GREECE

ARCTIC OCEAN

Murmansk

Arkhangelsk

NORTHERN DVINA

URAL MOUNTAINS

FINLAND

BALTIC SEA

ESTONIA

LATVIA
LITHUANIA

Petrograd

TERRITORY
SURRENDERED
BY RUSSIA
AT THE TREATY OF
BREST-LITOVSK
MARCH, 1918

Moscow

VOLGA

Vilna
WHITE
RUSSIA
Minsk

Vitebsk
Smolensk

RUSSIA

Brest-
Litovsk

POLAND

Kiev

UKRAINE

Kharkov

●●●●●●●●●
FARTHEST
ADVANCE OF THE
CENTRAL POWERS
MARCH, 1918

DNIESTER
BESSARABIA
(TO ROMANIA 1918)

DNIEPER

DON

VOLGA

URAL

Rostov

ROMANIA

DANUBE

BULGARIA

BLACK SEA

CAUCASUS MOUNTAINS

CASPIAN
SEA

(TURK.) Constantinople

OTTOMAN

EMPIRE

Tiflis

KARS-
ARDAHAN

·········
TURKISH ADVANCE
JUNE, 1918

RUSSIA AFTER THE TREATY OF BREST-LITOVSK, 1918

TRM

Socialists to seize control was supported by Russian troops but was defeated by Finnish nonsocialists with German support. Bolshevik and anti-Bolshevik forces, encouraged and abetted by Russian and German support, contested for power in Estonia, Latvia, and Lithuania.

Immediately after the abdication of the tsar Ukrainian nationalists set up a thoroughly unrepresentative parliament, or *Rada,* in Kiev. It named a cabinet, organized an army from stragglers drifting back to the villages from the front, and claimed the power to administer the entire Ukraine. A few days after the Bolshevik coup in Petrograd the *Rada* proclaimed the Ukraine a "people's republic" and announced elections for an Ukrainian Constituent Assembly. It arranged its own peace with Germany, exchanging foodstuffs for a promise of German support against the Bolsheviks. Ukrainian Bolsheviks fought the separatist movement and joined Russian troops in driving the nationalists out of Kiev in February, 1918. Their success was only temporary, however, for the Ukraine was to be a battleground between Reds and Whites through years of civil war.

THE BREATHING SPACE

The costly Treaty of Brest-Litovsk had seemed to Lenin necessary if the soviet regime were to endure. But the breathing space, cut short three months later by armed rebellion, provided no relief from the economic crisis which the war and the revolution had brought on. The food situation in the cities had grown steadily worse through the summer of 1917 and the harvest that autumn was far short of normal. With the loss of the Ukraine and the Caucasus the situation became critical. The "bony hand of hunger" threatened to throttle the people of Petrograd in the spring of 1918. Bread riots broke out in cities all over European Russia, and Soviet officials were beaten to death because they had no food to distribute. The administration banned private trading in grain and ordered all grain not needed to feed the peasant's family to be sold to the government at fixed prices. "Committees of the Poor" were organized in the villages to force the rich peasants to turn over their surplus. Armed squads of city workers joined the poor peasants in smelling out hidden stores and seizing livestock before the rich peasants could kill and eat it. The Committees of the Poor were disbanded that autumn, but the village soviets, made up chiefly of poor peasants, continued the raids. This policy of confiscation did bring enough food into the cities to prevent widespread starvation, but only at the cost of stirring uprisings among the well-to-do peasants which had to be put down by military force.

Industrial production nearly collapsed completely in the spring of 1918. War industries closed down, their output no longer needed. Fuel and raw material dwindled away, forcing many firms out of business. Factories that managed to keep running saw their output curtailed by constant interference of workers' committees in management. Three-fourths of the laboring population of Petrograd was thrown out of work, many of whom returned to their villages to get something to eat.

The only solution to the food shortage, aside from the ruthless policy of grain confiscation which the administration adopted, lay in producing enough industrial goods to encourage the peasants to trade their produce for the output of urban factories. This proved impossible, partly because of the collapse of labor discipline, partly because of the complete disruption of the transportation system, which was either worn out or in enemy hands, partly because of the loss of the Ukraine and with it nearly three-fourths of the nation's iron and steel output and 90 per cent of its sugar production.

The food crisis and industrial stagnation contributed to a growing anarchy in the spring of 1918. As unemployed workers deserted the cities in quest of food, the very class whose support had brought Lenin to power melted away. Socialist Revolutionaries and Mensheviks won control in many soviets, although in the chief cities the Bolsheviks managed to retain slim majorities. Anti-Bolshevik forces met covertly to plot the overthrow of the regime. Armed bands of anarchists and criminals roamed the streets at night, plundering and murdering almost at will. Red Guards often deserted and joined such parties. Many who had helped to turn Kerensky out of office now rebelled at the government's efforts to restore discipline in the factories and on the railroads. There were many uprisings in cities large and small, particularly along the middle and lower Volga, but they were put down one after another because there was as yet no effort to coordinate them. The political police force, the Cheka, had its hands full trying to restore order and obedience in that spring of 1918 and many a Cheka agent lost his life in the struggle.

THE CZECH ODYSSEY AND ALLIED INTERVENTION

The government's battle to establish discipline and maintain control over the nation was soon complicated by open war with the famous Czech Legion. Czechoslovak prisoners and deserters from the Austrian army had been freed by the Provisional Government and armed thirty-five thousand strong for use on the eastern front. After Russia's withdrawal from the war the Czechs received permission to join the western Allies and started over the Trans-Siberian Railway toward Vladivostok on their journey round the world to the western front in France. To prevent the Czechs from supporting an anti-Bolshevik movement in Siberia Trotsky ordered local soviets to disarm the legion, whose units were scattered from the Volga to the Pacific. The Czechs, however, could not be disarmed by the feeble Soviet forces sent against them and town after town from one end of the railroad to the other, from Samara on the Volga to Vladivostok, fell under their authority. Local anti-Bolsheviks from stranded army officers to Socialist Revolutionary peasant leaders joined the legionnaires in driving the Bolsheviks from power throughout Siberia. The Allied aim of moving the Czech corps to the western front was soon forgotten as the Western powers saw an opportunity to overthrow the government that had deserted them in the war.

After Brest-Litovsk the Western powers looked to anti-Bolshevik Russians to remove Lenin and restore the eastern front against Germany, while the opponents of the new regime looked to the Allies for support in their war against Bolshevism. Many Western statesmen and military leaders recommended that their governments aid resistance groups, but little was done until the Czech corps offered a nucleus of strength. French, British, and American troops landed at Murmansk in the spring of 1918, ostensibly to prevent military supplies stored there for Russian use from falling into German hands. Other Allied detachments landed at Vladivostok to join hands with the Czechs who were to maintain control of the Trans-Siberian and support anti-Bolshevik movements all over Siberia. The United States landed seven thousand men at Vladivostok, Japan ten times that number, and there were smaller British, French, and Italian contingents. The Allied powers had openly committed themselves to the overthrow of the Communist government.

THE OUTBREAK OF CIVIL WAR

The Czech defiance and the decision of the Western powers to intervene against Lenin's government was followed immediately by the desertion of the left Socialist Revolutionaries from their uneasy coalition with the Bolsheviks. The Fifth Congress of Soviets met in early July, 1918, in Moscow, which three months earlier had replaced Petrograd as the capital of Communist Russia. The S.R.'s refused to accept the Peace of Brest-Litovsk and favored reopening the war against Germany. They also opposed the government's policy of inciting class war in the villages by turning poor peasants against the well-to-do. When their stand was voted down by the Bolshevik majority the S.R.'s resorted to armed resistance. Their attempt to seize Moscow was defeated by a whiff of grapeshot, but they embarrassed the government by assassinating the German ambassador, Count Mirbach, in the avowed hope that Germany would reopen the war and Russia would be forced back into the alliance with the Entente powers. The Germans, however, were too busy on the western front to afford another war in the east. The government rounded up and shot some of the S.R. leaders, while others escaped into hiding. Now the Bolsheviks were left alone to rule Russia. All other parties—Socialist Revolutionaries, Mensheviks, Cadets, and monarchists—were dedicated to the overthrow of Bolshevism and were in effect outlawed.

During that summer of 1918 the Whites, as the counterrevolutionaries came to be called, organized on various fronts and received encouragement and support from foreign governments. A combined British and American force landed at Arkhangelsk and established a counterrevolutionary government with the aid of local anti-Bolsheviks. At Samara, the present-day Kuibyshev, Chernov and other S.R. members of the Constituent Assembly announced the birth of a "democratic" government and organized their own "People's Army." They proposed to link up with the Allied forces at Murmansk and Arkhangelsk and drive on to Moscow. General Krasnov, hetman of the Don Cossacks, organized the Don valley as a White fortress and hoped to join hands with the Czech Legion and the Samara government. General Denikin, sometime chief of staff under the Provisional Government, gathered a "Volunteer Army" of former officers and Kuban and Terek Cossacks, won control of the northern Caucasus, and captured the Black Sea port of Novorossisk, thus assuring himself of Western support and supplies. In the southwest General Petlura commanded the army of the Ukrainian Republic, which enjoyed the backing of the Central Powers. The democratic-minded Samara government gave way to a dictatorship under the former commander of the imperial Black Sea fleet, Admiral Kolchak, who extended his authority over all the land from the Volga east to Lake Baikal. The ruthless Cossack leader Semenov, backed by the Japanese, ruled Siberia east of Lake Baikal. The former tsarist general Horvath controlled the Chinese Eastern Railway and much of Manchuria. The so-called Northern Corps, later commanded by General Yudenich, advanced toward Petrograd from the Baltic provinces.

Although Kolchak called himself "Supreme Ruler" and was so acknowledged by Denikin, Yudenich, and the western Allies, there was little cooperation among these several challenges to Soviet authority. They were similar in many ways, disparate in others. Some like Semenov and Horvath were no better than bandits, while others like Denikin and his successor Baron Wrangel were men of high principle who tried desperately to curb the violence their motley armies wrought. Some were avowed monarchists, while others, notably Denikin and perhaps Kolchak, were liberal or conservative moderates. The moderate element among the Whites steadily lost ground, however, and the entire movement came to be suspected of wanting to restore the Romanovs and the great landlords. For this reason, the White armies never won the confidence of the peasants; they endured only so long as they retained the support of foreign governments and the Cossack hosts. All the White leaders received money and equipment from abroad, Horvath and Semenov from the Japanese, the others from France, Britain, United States, Italy, Serbia, Finland, Germany, Austria-Hungary, and Turkey. And the population in all the pockets of White control was subjected to unspeakable atrocities. Pogroms against the Jews were worse than under the tsars, and peasants who resisted the restoration of the great estates were tortured and flogged without mercy. The White terror was at least as cruel, and certainly more widespread, than the Red Terror of which foreigners heard so much.

THE REVOLUTION DEFENDS ITSELF

Lenin recognized by mid-summer of 1918 that the most critical moment of the revolution had arrived, that there was serious question whether the new government could survive. The food crisis was at its worst just before the harvest; the people were literally at each other's throats in the fight for the few remaining scraps of nourishment. The White armies of Siberia were in the outskirts of Kazan, barely four hundred miles from Moscow. Ukraine and the Caucasus were lost and counterrevolutionary forces were converging on the capital from Arkhangelsk and from Estonia. The Russian state was squeezed into a territory smaller than that of the principality of Moscow late in the fifteenth century. The government was without an effective administration, since many tsarist bureaucrats had deserted or been purged and those who remained could not always be trusted. There was no army worthy of the name, for the old army had evaporated and the undisciplined Red Guards were unreliable. The disaffected Socialist Revolutionaries went underground and worked sabotage at every opportunity. The chief of the Petrograd Cheka, Uritsky, was assassinated by a former army officer. An S.R., Fanny Kaplan, shot and seriously wounded Lenin.

These attacks upon government leaders prompted the administration to take the most drastic steps to defend itself. The nation's economy was placed under thoroughgoing governmental control in what came to be known as War Communism. The Cheka inaugurated a reign of terror aimed at wiping out every evidence of subversion. And a new Red Army was organized to fight off the attacks of counterrevolutionary forces.

The Bolsheviks had nationalized banks, railroads, shipping, foreign trade, and the land on the morrow of their coming to power. Further than that Lenin had refused to go, realizing that the professional revolutionaries who had assumed leadership had no knowledge of the management skills required to run the nation's factories. During the so-called "breathing space" he had hoped that business leaders would go along with the revolution, as they had with the Provisional Government, if they were allowed to keep their factories. But with the outbreak of civil war and the sharpening of class hatred which it precipitated, Lenin gave up all thought of cooperating with the industrialists, who were anti-Bolshevik to a man. During the summer of 1918 one plant after another was confiscated by the state without compensation to its owner. The government put itself in the business of producing sugar, petroleum, textiles, minerals of all sorts, pottery, cement, and many other commodities. The food commissar had· full authority to confiscate all stocks of food, fuel, and clothing and even to dictate the use of large private dwellings. Private trading became illegal.

State control was extended to every branch of production by a 1920 decree nationalizing all plants using mechanical power which employed more than five workers and all nonmechanized plants which employed more than ten. Labor was subject to conscription for critical work. Military units, when not needed on campaign, were assigned to maintaining roads and railroads. The entire economic life of the nation came under the authority of a Supreme Economic Council. Management of individual plants was at first assigned to committees, but when these produced more talk than work individual managers were named for each enterprise. The commissar for agriculture sought to force the peasants, even at bayonet point, to turn over to the government an ever increasing supply of grain. But the peasant reacted by planting less and less, since he knew that any surplus would be taken from him. All food was strictly rationed, workers receiving two or three times the dole allowed to professional men and unemployed. A year after the introduction of War Communism the highest ration for Petrograd workers consisted of a half pound of bread a day and a pound of sugar, a pound of salt, half a pound of butter, and six pounds of fish a month. Those who had any valuables to sell could buy food at exorbitant prices in the free markets which throve in every city although they were illegal and subject to frequent raids. Peasants raised their own food and so did not feel the pinch of rationing. The government attempted slowly but steadily to abolish money as a medium of exchange, and what goods did change hands ordinarily did so by barter. Decrees at the end of 1920 ordered that all food would be distributed through government stores without charge to holders of ration cards and announced an end to collection of taxes except in kind. Wages were paid in goods and services. Dwellings with water and electricity furnished were assigned rent free. There was no charge for postal service or transportation. The last bank was closed in 1920 as being no longer necessary.

In an effort to insure production during the civil war emergency and avoid the slowdowns which might have been expected if industry were left in private hands, the government tried to become the sole producer and the sole distributor in the nation. Faced with the alternatives of nationalizing production or restoring the profit motive of private ownership and operation, the government, in keeping with the Marxist tenets to which its leaders subscribed, chose to nationalize production and distribution. But as an experiment in production War Communism was a tragic failure. With the removal of all incentive but force individual production fell far below pre-war standards. By 1921 the government admitted the failure and abandoned the experiment. The New Economic Policy adopted in that year was a retreat from the communistic practices of the previous three years. It was a compromise with private enterprise and individual initiative which seemed necessary to restore production to respectable levels.

The second step the administration took to defend the revolution was to liquidate its opponents inside the territory which it ruled. Heretofore the Cheka had acted with surprising moderation in handling cases of defection and sabotage. Now the political police dealt ruthlessly with enemies of the regime. In retaliation for the murder of Uritsky and the attempt on Lenin's life five hundred Petrograd citizens, including four former tsarist ministers, were shot. The Cheka took hostages from among known Socialist Revolutionaries and Cadets, and shot a hundred and fifty of them to settle the account of one Petrograd worker killed from ambush. Women as well as men faced the Bolshevik firing squads. Torture was frequently used to wring confessions or reveal accomplices. Many well-to-do peasants were put to death for resisting grain requisitions. In the towns the terror was directed primarily against tsarist officers and bureaucrats, professional men, clergymen, and the wealthy. All of the Romanovs who did not escape abroad were shot.

The number of victims of the Red Terror during the Civil War has been estimated at fifty thousand. The Cheka had the power to execute without trial, and by Communist admission many innocent people died. But the leaders believed it better that ten innocent ones should suffer than that one guilty man should escape. The terror varied in intensity from time to time, according to the apparent danger its leaders sensed. It was at its height immediately after the wounding of Lenin and was at a low ebb at the end of the civil war. Numbering perhaps thirty thousand agents, the Cheka had branches in every province, its own network of spies, and its own troops. Rumor had it that many agents of the Okhrana, the secret police of tsarist times, found their way into the new organization.

To the Red Terror the Whites opposed a terror of their own as savage and as ruthless as that led by Dzerzhinsky. Each White government maintained its counterespionage agency which vied with the Cheka in indiscriminate slaughter of those suspected of opposing it. Furthermore, in every White district thousands were killed and tortured by sporting soldiers whom their leaders seemed unable to control. Captured Bolshevik troops who would not join the Whites customarily were shot by White commanders. Territory which changed hands was subjected to vicious recrimination now by Whites and then by Reds. Kiev, for example, was taken and lost nineteen times during the course of the Civil War, and each time scores and hundreds paid with their lives for the city's misfortune.

The new leaders took a third step to defend their revolution when they organized the Red Army early in 1918. At first they called for volunteers, but when this produced a scant hundred thousand the government fell back upon universal conscription. Within two years the Red Army numbered five million men, although only a fraction ever saw front-line service. More important than the mere numbers swept into the ranks were the stern discipline imposed upon the men and the reorganization imposed by War Commissar Trotsky. The election of officers was abolished and the army, short of officers it could trust, was staffed by thousands of tsarist officers whose families were held hostage for their good behavior. Political commissars were assigned to every unit to propagandize among the men and to keep under surveillance the old officers whom the government was forced to use. As quickly as trustworthy men in the ranks gained military experience they were appointed officers to replace those whose service in the old army made them suspect. Politically reliable subalterns and noncommissioned officers in the tsarist army rose to high rank in the Red Army. A former lieutenant, Michael Tukhachevsky, eventually became a marshal as did Sergei Budenny, a cavalry sergeant during the first World War, and Voroshilov, a former noncommissioned officer. Another, Michael Frunze, who revealed particular talent as a military organizer, had had no other experience than shooting at tsarist officials. But the man most responsible for whipping the new, green force into a respectable and dedicated army was Trotsky. He dashed restlessly from one front to another in a special train to inspire the men to greater effort, to order traitors shot, and sometimes even to interfere with strategical plans. The contribution of this organizer of victory to the military success of the new government was undoubtedly greater than that of any other man.

THE END OF CIVIL WAR

During the summer of 1918 the White armies advanced far into European Russia and threatened the Communist regime with annihilation. The so-called People's Army drove north from Samara to take Kazan at the bend of the Volga and threatened to join hands with the Allies pressing south from Murmansk. Denikin, at the head of his Volunteer Army, consolidated the Caucasus; his ally Krasnov won control of the lower Don. If the two could capture Tsaritsyn, later renamed Stalingrad, they could link up with the Czechs and the People's Army and so control the entire lower Volga. But the Reds, inspired by Trotsky's fiery exhortations, drove the Whites out of Kazan back into Siberia, and another army led by Voroshilov and spurred on by Stalin refused to surrender Tsaritsyn. The threat that the White armies in north, south, and east might join forces was momentarily beaten off.

With the end of the World War the Allies no longer had the excuse to intervene in Russia to prevent military stores from falling into German hands. Point Six of Woodrow Wilson's Fourteen Points indicated the American President's preference that Russia should work out her own destiny unfettered by foreign interference. The British Prime Minister, Lloyd George, took the same stand. But Clemenceau of France and Winston Churchill of Great Britain pressed for vigorous intervention. The Allies finally agreed on a degree of participation in the Russian Civil War too modest to be of much service to the Whites and yet sufficiently active to embitter East-West relations for decades afterward. The French landed a division in Odessa; the British moved troops to the oil-rich cities of Batum and Baku; both moved supply ships into the Black Sea, the Baltic, and the Arctic Ocean. The armies of Kolchak, Denikin, Yudenich, and Miller at Arkhangelsk were equipped with British, French, Italian, and American weapons and supplies. Finland under the leadership of the reactionary Mannerheim became a base for Allied pressure in the Baltic provinces, her effort financed by a substantial American loan later mistakenly thought of as a part of the Allied war debts to the United States.

In the spring of 1919 Admiral Kolchak, with a British staff and a river fleet of British gunboats, pushed his forces into the Volga valley and again threatened Kazan and Samara. Allied hopes that he could press on to Moscow dimmed quickly, however, for Red troops stopped him before he reached the river. He had lost the support of the Czechs, his troops were poorly disciplined and badly trained, and the peasants behind his lines had turned against him because of his conscripting men and confiscating grain. Trained for the sea, he was thoroughly inept as a land commander. By early July he was driven back across the Urals and retreated steadily into central Siberia. His motley army deserted, and finally he himself was handed over to the Communists, who tried and executed him.

While the Reds were dealing with Kolchak, General Denikin in the south had better success. During the summer of 1919 he drove west out of the Don basin to take Kharkov and then Kiev and finally captured Tsaritsyn, thus consolidating all of South Russia from the Dnieper to the Volga. Then he advanced north, pushing to within two hundred and fifty miles of Moscow by early fall. But the peasants back of his seven-hundred-mile front were bitterly hostile to him because of the savagery of his troops and because they had little to gain from the restoration of the old regime which he, wrongly, and most of his officers, rightly, were suspected of favoring. The Ukrainian nationalist Petlura, who supported Hitler in 1941, preferred cooperating with the Poles to joining Denikin, whose triumph he frankly announced must mean the revival of the old frontiers and the inclusion of border minorities within the new Russia. The anarchist Makhno fought and embarrassed Reds and Whites alike.

Denikin reached Orel by mid-October, 1919, but that was as close to Moscow as he could get. From then on his strength ebbed rapidly. Every engagement cost him casualties which he could not replace. His long front and lengthening communications became increasingly difficult to man. Allied interest cooled and Trotsky observed that "behind Denikin there is nothing but a rear that is hostile to him." On the other hand, Red strength continued steadily to mount. When the Red Army began its counterattack it outnumbered Denikin's force two to one in men, artillery, and machine guns. And the Red cavalry under Budenny surprisingly proved superior to the Cossack horsemen of the Volunteer Army.

Before the year was out Denikin was in demoralized retreat, the morale of his troops broken and his officers' confidence in their leader destroyed. The Reds swarmed over the Ukraine and Denikin was left, in the words of Lloyd George, "occupying a little back yard near the Black Sea." In the spring of 1920 the tattered remnant of the White Army in South Russia escaped aboard British ships to the Crimea. Denikin turned over the command to Baron Peter Wrangel, an avowed monarchist, and went into exile.

Meanwhile, in the autumn of 1919 General Yudenich with British, Finnish, and Baltic-German support was advancing on Petrograd from Estonia at the same time that Denikin was threatening Moscow from Orel. But the Red Army had the great advantage against the Whites of fighting on interior lines and being able to use what was left of the railway net of which Moscow was the hub. By late October Yudenich was within thirty miles of Petrograd and Lenin favored abandoning the city. But Trotsky fired the city's workers to set up barbed wire and barricades in the streets, swearing to contest every block and every house if necessary. Yudenich, with thirty thousand, had too small a force to attempt such a fight in a city still left with a million people. During the closing weeks of the year, while Denikin was being routed in the south, the so-called Northwestern Army retired in good order to Estonia where it disbanded. With the withdrawal of Yudenich there remained only one serious native Russian challenge to the authority of the new government—that presented by Wrangel in the Crimea. But his troops needed rest and new equipment. For the moment he was in no position to renew the attack.

THE POLISH WAR

By 1920 the Western powers had lost hope that the Bolsheviks could be overthrown. Mutinies among Allied troops in Russia forced their recall, and

Western workers even refused to load ships with supplies destined for the White armies. The Allied governments decided to stop sending goods and money, particularly to the succession states on Russia's western frontier; they recommended that such states seek a peaceful settlement with the Bolsheviks. During the year Russia signed treaties of peace with Estonia, Latvia, Lithuania, and Finland recognizing the independence of each and delimiting boundaries. With Poland, however, such a settlement was to come only after another campaign.

The Allies at the Paris Peace Conference of 1919 suggested a boundary between Poland and Russia, the so-called Curzon Line, which was remarkably accurate in setting off Poles to the west and non-Poles to the east of the line. But the new Polish government, not interested in ethnic frontiers, demanded Poland's "historic" boundaries—those of 1772 before the First Partition—and called upon Russia to surrender all land west of the 1772 border. The request was refused and the Polish dictator, Marshal Pilsudski, confident that the Bolsheviks were now exhausted from civil war, launched an attack in the spring of 1920. Poland had held back from joining the White forces earlier because the White leaders, particularly Kolchak and Denikin, had vowed that the new Russia would be "great and undivided," thereby announcing their refusal to admit the self-determination of the border states and pledging to restore the boundaries of Imperial Russia.

Polish troops drove into the Ukraine, reaching the Dnieper and capturing Kiev by early May, 1920. But the Ukrainian separatist movement which they counted on for support fizzled out. Budenny's cavalry relieved Kiev and drove Pilsudski, whom Trotsky dubbed "a third-rate Bonaparte," back into southern Poland. Another Red force under Tukhachevsky, only twenty-seven years old, drove into northern Poland and the two prongs threatened the capture of Warsaw. Moscow now envisaged the possibility of tumbling the Polish government and replacing it with a soviet regime. When Russian armies drew within sight of Warsaw, Britain and France threatened intervention. The Bolsheviks ignored the threat but agreed to talk peace with Polish delegates. Russia offered peace and a frontier more favorable to Poland than the Curzon Line, but only on condition that a soviet republic be proclaimed in Warsaw. The Poles refused and the war went on.

Now Pilsudski, with newly-arrived French equipment and the French general Weygand at his elbow, opened a counterattack against the outnumbered Russians and drove them back deep into their own country. The Poles had had enough, and the Russians wanted a free hand to deal with Baron Wrangel in the Crimea. In mid-October, 1920, the two powers agreed to the terms of the Peace of Riga which was signed six months later. The new frontier was well to the east of the Curzon Line but short of the 1772 boundary which Pilsudski had hoped for. It left four and a half million Belo-Russians and Ukrainians inside Poland, a humiliation which Soviet leaders were quick to wipe out in 1939.

PEACE AT LAST

While the Polish war was going on the Reds were driving Baron Wrangel back into the Crimea, from which he had emerged cautiously in an effort to regain the valley of the lower Don. His disorganized army and a horde of civilian refugees were bottled up in the peninsula in the fall of 1920. Then the Red Army forced the Isthmus of Perekop and literally drove the last White corps into the sea. Nearly a hundred and fifty thousand civilians and soldiers were evacuated aboard French ships to Constantinople, whence they gradually scattered to centers of Russian exile in Europe and America.

With the collapse of White strength in South Russia and the withdrawal of Allied support, the anti-Bolshevik governments in Georgia, Azerbaidzhan, and Armenia were left helpless in the face of Russian pressure. The three surrendered their brief existence and were incorporated into the new Soviet state as socialist republics, ostensibly independent but in fact tributary to Moscow. The Central Asian provinces similarly came back under Russian rule soon after the defeat of Kolchak.

The area east of Lake Baikal proved more difficult for the Reds to recover. There the Cossack Semenov with Japanese backing robbed and sacked and pillaged the peasant communities, while Japan seized the southern half of Sakhalin and ravaged coastal Siberia. To serve as a buffer against these foreign and bandit forces Moscow encouraged the creation of the Far Eastern Republic under liberal local leadership. Its socialist but not communist government provided for an elected parliament and guaranteed the usual democratic civil liberties along with the right to own land. A treaty with Moscow recognized the republic and delimited its boundaries. The new government rid the land of Semenov and his cutthroats and, with strong American backing, prevailed upon the Japanese to go home. With peace and order established and the foreigner gone, the early demise of the Far Eastern Republic was a foregone conclusion. Too small to defend itself against powerful neighbors to east and west, the people were forced to choose between the two. Since they were bitterly anti-Japanese, there could be no question where the choice would lie. Late in 1922 the national assembly of the republic voted to become a part of the new Communist Russia.

After eight long years of war, foreign intervention, and civil strife peace came at last to the Russian land. By far most of the fighting had taken place on Russian soil. Millions had been killed in battle or had suffered cruel death during the Red and the White Terrors or had died of famine or the plagues which followed in the wake of drought. The battered land had been made unproductive for years to come. Much of Russian humanity had been uprooted as men deserted the cities for the countryside in search of food and others fled or were driven from home by the marching armies. The Russian land had never known, perhaps no land had ever known, such bitterness and hatred and torture and suffering. Now the nation faced the staggering task of rebuilding.

SUGGESTED READING

Alexander, Grand Duke, *Once a Grand Duke* (New York, Farrar, 1932).

Allen, W. E. D., *The Ukraine: A History* (New York, Cambridge University Press, 1941).

Buchanan, G., *My Mission to Russia* (New York, Cassell, 1923).

Bunyan, J., *Intervention, Civil War and Communism in Russia, April–December, 1918: Documents and Materials* (Baltimore, Johns Hopkins Press, 1936).

———— and H. H. Fisher, *The Bolshevik Revolution 1917–1918: Documents and Materials* (Stanford, Stanford University Press, 1934).

Carr, E. H., *The Bolshevik Revolution, 1917–1923* (New York, Macmillan, 1953).

Chamberlin, W. H., *The Russian Revolution* (New York, Macmillan, 1935).

Degras, J., *Soviet Documents on Foreign Policy* (New York, Oxford University Press, 1951).

Denikin, A. I., *The Russian Turmoil* (London, Hutchinson, 1922).

Deutscher, I., *The Prophet Armed* (New York, Praeger, 1954).

Fischer, H. H., *The Famine in Soviet Russia, 1919–1923* (New York, Macmillan, 1927).

Graves, W. S., *America's Siberian Adventure* (New York, Cape, 1931).

Hindus, M., *The Russian Peasant and the Revolution* (New York, Holt, 1920).

Kennan, G. F., *Russia Leaves the War* (Princeton, Princeton University Press, 1956).

Radkey, O. H., *The Election to the Russian Constituent Assembly of 1917* (Cambridge, Harvard University Press, 1950).

Reed, J., *Ten Days That Shook the World* (New York, Boni and Liveright, 1919).

Reshetar, J., *The Ukrainian Revolution, 1917–1920* (Princeton, Princeton University Press, 1952).

Schuman, F. L., *Soviet Politics at Home and Abroad* (New York, Knopf, 1946).

Seton-Watson, H., *From Lenin to Malenkov* (New York, Praeger, 1955).

Shub, D., *Lenin* (New York, Doubleday, 1948).

Stewart, G., *The White Armies of Russia* (New York, Macmillan, 1933).

Trotsky, L., *History of the Russian Revolution* (New York, Simon and Schuster, 1936).

————, *My Life* (New York, Scribner's, 1930).

Warth, R. D., *The Allies and the Russian Revolution* (Durham, Duke University, 1954).

Wheeler-Bennett, J. W., *The Forgotten Peace: Brest-Litovsk, March, 1918* (London, Macmillan, 1938).

Wilson, E., *To the Finland Station* (New York, Harcourt Brace, 1940).

28

The Nature of the Soviet State

Building upon the foundation laid by Marx and Engels, Lenin conceived of the socialist state as only a step toward ultimate communism. During this interim period the state, under the dictatorship of the proletariat, would liquidate the capitalist class, do away with private ownership of productive capital, and manage all production and distribution. Other European socialist revolutions would be necessary for the Russian experiment to succeed. Stalin modified Marxist-Leninist theory by insisting that socialism could exist and prosper in one country.

The 1918 Constitution outlined the governmental framework in Russia, providing for a hierarchy of soviets of workers', soldiers', and peasants' deputies, atop which an All-Russian Congress of Soviets would function as a national legislature. A Council of People's Commissars, the socialist cabinet, would serve as the national executive. After the civil war, border areas were incorporated with Russia in a federation of Soviet Socialist Republics. The 1936 Constitution retained the governmental organization of the earlier period but ended the class and group discrimination, indirect elections, and open balloting which had characterized the 1918 document, and added a bill of human rights and duties. Justice was administered through a hierarchy of courts paralleling the soviet structure. The Communist party, with its units lying alongside the city, county, province, and region soviets, dominated local as well as national government. Its Politburo ruled the party and the nation while its general secretary, Stalin through most of this period, kept tight control over the rank and file.

From the moment of its triumph the Communist party has undergone a succession of purges directed by its leaders to weed out disloyal or ineffective members. In Lenin's time the purges were mild and bloodless, but under

Stalin there was widespread, uncontrolled liquidation of party members and citizens of all ranks and professions. The purges were conducted by the political police, which arrested, tried, and condemned millions to execution, imprisonment, exile, or forced labor in camps under its direction.

Between his triumph over Trotsky in the twenties and his death in 1953 Stalin surrounded himself with a clique of slavishly loyal henchmen and turned the relatively mild rule of Lenin into a merciless dictatorship. He deliberately cultivated obeisance and acclaim of himself as a leader who could not make mistakes and whose accomplishments in nearly every field of endeavor had never been matched. He was so universally feared in Russia that widespread credence attached to the rumor that he was murdered.

After Stalin's death there was a succession of changes in the party and government of Russia. Through them all, however, there was repeated insistence that leadership of the nation must be "collegial," that "the cult of the individual" must not be allowed to return. The new leaders castigated Stalin for his many crimes and published Lenin's deathbed warning that the sinister Georgian could not be trusted with power.

THE THEORETICAL FRAMEWORK

In his many writings Karl Marx, the grandfather of modern communism, had analyzed the nature and weaknesses of modern capitalism and had predicted its inevitable collapse. He and his co-worker Friedrich Engels had concerned themselves hardly at all, however, with the detailed nature of the society that should succeed capitalism. While hiding out from the police in the summer of 1917 Lenin drafted *The State and the Revolution,* which elaborated the course which society must follow after the defeat of the bourgeoisie.

According to Marx and Lenin, the state, born of the class struggle between workers and employers, is an instrument of suppression by which the ruling class—the employers, the "exploiters" under capitalism—keeps itself in power. Capitalism, however, contains within itself elements which lead to its deterioration and weakening, and at the right moment it can be overthrown by a movement of the industrial workers, or proletariat, led by a disciplined vanguard, the Bolshevik or Communist party.

Since the state, the theory continues, is an agency by which the exploiting class which owns society's productive property holds in subjugation the exploited class which works with, but does not own, the productive tools, the overthrow of capitalist society and the expropriation of the capitalists or owners will lead eventually to a classless society, communism, where there will be no exploitation; consequently, the existence of the state will no longer be necessary.

The birth of communism, however, will not follow immediately upon the passing of capitalism. There will come a transition stage, socialism, during which the state will continue as a "dictatorship of the proletariat" succeeding the "dictatorship of the capitalist class." The productive machinery of society will be socialized or nationalized under state control and operation. Limited private ownership may continue, but the employment and exploitation of one man by another will not be countenanced. No one will be allowed to enjoy unearned income—profits, rents, or inheritances—for the socialist principle is, "He who does not work shall not eat." All must work to live and all who work will be rewarded according to the quality and quantity of their output—"from each according to his ability, to each according to the quantity and quality of his work." The state will continue, not as a tool by which one class dominates another, but as an agency to protect the limited property rights of individuals and to oversee and distribute production. During the period of socialism the last resistance of the former exploiters will be broken. In Lenin's mind this socialist stage would not take long, although how long he did not say.

Finally, with the arrival of the millennium of communism, classes will disappear; poverty will vanish as profits no longer accumulate to individuals and national output is equitably shared; avarice and jealousy and dishonesty and crime will cease; there will be no need for a bureaucracy or a standing army to restrain one class or one individual against another, and the state must and will "wither away." Then man will enjoy the real and complete freedom that is impossible as long as the oppressive and restrictive agency, the state, continues to exist.

Lenin and his colleagues assumed that socialist revolutions in central and western Europe would follow the Bolshevik seizure of power. Uprisings would be contagious and would produce a world-wide revolution. Indeed, they were convinced that revolution must tumble at least some bourgeois governments for the one in Russia to succeed. And for a moment after the war their hopes seemed justified. There were communist uprisings in Hungary, Germany, Austria, Italy, Finland, and Poland, some of them briefly successful. Quickly, however, the revolutionary fever subsided, leaving Russia alone to carry on the socialist experiment. The question whether socialism could exist in a single country surrounded by hostile capitalist states was long debated between Trotsky and Stalin in their contest for power after Lenin's death in 1924. Trotsky protested that to attempt to make socialism work in one country was to betray the world revolution. Stalin insisted that a nation with Russia's size and resources could go it alone. He was willing to shelve, if not to forget, the open promotion of socialist revolutions abroad, at least until Russia should become strong enough to undertake the risks involved in such a policy.

Stalin contributed other refinements to the Marxist theory of the founding fathers. Lenin insisted that the national minorities which joined the federal Soviet state should have the right to secede. Stalin qualified this by saying that whether a territory would be allowed to secede would depend upon the international situation. The risk that a small area might withdraw from the socialist state and then lose its independence to a capitalist neighbor could not be taken. Nor could the state wither away as long as Russia remained a socialist island in a capitalist sea. He even insisted upon the rank heresy that the state could continue even when the nation had passed beyond socialism into communism as long as capitalism endured. The state, which Lenin saw as inimical to individual freedom, might continue indefinitely.

THE CONSTITUTIONAL STRUCTURE

The Second All-Russian Congress of Soviets was in session in Petrograd at the moment of the Bolshevik Revolution. On the first day of the new era the Congress approved the list of cabinet ministers, called the Council of People's Commissars, with Lenin as president. It then elected a Central Executive Committee of a hundred members to serve in its stead when the Congress was not in session. The Congress of Soviets thus clothed itself with supreme authority in the nation, then delegated legislative power to its Central Executive Committee and administrative power to the Council of Commissars. In operation, the Council of Commissars became both executive and legislature whose enactments were rubber-stamped by the Central Executive Committee and whose conduct of state business was approved without question by the Congress of Soviets which reconvened from time to time.

In July, 1918, the Fifth Congress of Soviets adopted a constitution for Russia which had been prepared by its Central Executive Committee. The Constitution, under which the nation was to be governed for the next eighteen years, proclaimed Russia to be "a republic of soviets of workers', soldiers', and peasants' deputies" and named it the Russian Socialist Federated Soviet Republic, the R.S.F.S.R. The preamble announced the government's aim to build socialism not only in Russia but all over the world, to liquidate the bourgeoisie as a class, and to end the dependence of man upon man. The document went on to proclaim freedom of the press for workers and peasants but not for the bourgeoisie, the right of assembly and organization, the right to a free education and freedom of "religious and antireligious propaganda." It approved the decree on land, the nationalization of industry, and the repudiation of tsarist debts which the Bolsheviks had ordered during the early days of the revolution.

The Constitution then outlined the governmental framework of the new state. The basic political unit was the city and village soviet to which dele-

gates would be elected by show of hands by all men and women over eighteen
except members of the Romanov family, capitalists, former officials, clergymen, lunatics, and criminals. Each local soviet would elect delegates to a
county soviet, which would send delegates to a district soviet, which in turn
would choose representatives to a provincial soviet. The latter would send
on some of its members to attend the national All-Russian Congress of
Soviets. The national Congress would contain one representative for each
twenty-five thousand city dwellers and one for each hundred and twenty-
five thousand rural inhabitants. This weighting of representation in favor
of the cities reflected the Bolsheviks' confidence in industrial workers and
their suspicion of peasants. The Congress would continue to choose the
Central Executive Committee as it had been doing for the past year, and the
Committee in turn would name the Council of People's Commissars, the one
to serve as an interim legislative committee, the other as executive cabinet.

From time to time non-Russian minorities were allowed to form autonomous Soviet Socialist Republics or autonomous regions or national
districts within the R.S.F.S.R., the government of each modelled after that
of Moscow. With the end of the Civil War some arrangement had to be
made for associating the liberated borderlands in the new state. In 1922 the
All-Russian Congress of Soviets sanctioned the creation of the Union of
Soviet Socialist Republics of four ostensibly equal partners. The R.S.F.S.R.
was joined by the Ukrainian Soviet Socialist Republic, the Belo-Russian
S.S.R., and the Transcaucasian S.S.R. In 1925 two more Soviet Socialist
Republics were added, the Turkmen and the Uzbek. The Transcauscasian
S.S.R. was divided into three, the Azerbaidzhan, the Georgian, and the Armenian. The Tadzhik, Kazak, and Kirghiz Republics came in later. By
1929 there were eleven in all. To handle recent acquisitions of territory five
more were added in 1940, the Estonian, Latvian, Lithuanian, Moldavian,
and Finno-Karelian. The government of the constituent republics was patterned after that of the R.S.F.S.R., and each sent delegates to an All-Union
Congress of Soviets.

The first Congress of Soviets of the U.S.S.R. assigned to a special committee the task of drafting a constitution for the new union. Accepted at the
next Congress, this 1924 Constitution outlined the government of the Union
of Soviet Socialist Republics. The hierarchy of soviets already in operation in the R.S.F.S.R. was duplicated in the other member republics, with
the All-Union Congress of Soviets the supreme authority in the nation. The
Congress, whose members numbered over two thousand, was to meet annually, later changed to biennially, and had the sole power to amend the
Constitution. The document created an All-Union Central Executive Committee and a two-house legislature consisting of the Council of the Union,
made up of delegates representing the nation as a whole apportioned on the
basis of population, and the Council of Nationalities, which contained five

representatives of each member republic, five from each autonomous republic, and one from each autonomous region. In both bodies the R.S.F.S.R. occupied a dominant position, naming two-thirds of the members of the Council of the Union and over half the delegates to the Council of Nationalities. The two houses were supposed to convene thrice a year for short sessions, meanwhile turning over their powers to a Presidium of twenty-seven members which they elected. Since the Central Executive Committee met infrequently and irregularly, the legislative authority came to reside in the Presidium. The executive power was exercised by the Council of People's Commissars of the U.S.S.R., the new national cabinet.

The 1918 Constitution of the R.S.F.S.R. and the 1924 Constitution of the U.S.S.R. remained in operation until 1936, when the draft of a new document appeared and was ordered discussed in group meetings all over Russia. A half million meetings attended by thirty-six million citizens proposed a hundred and fifty thousand amendments resulting in forty superficial changes in the original draft. Printed in every foreign language, the Constitution was couched, at least in part, in propaganda terms slanted for consumption abroad as well as at home. For example, Article 2 declared the political foundation of the U.S.S.R. to be "the Soviets of Working People's Deputies, which grew and became strong as a result of the overthrow of the power of the landlords and capitalists and the conquest of the dictatorship of the proletariat."

The U.S.S.R. is defined as a federal state "formed on the basis of a voluntary union" of sixteen "equal" republics. The central government is sovereign in deciding questions of war and peace, directing national defense and internal security, monopolizing foreign trade, planning the national economy, controlling money and credit, determining principles of land tenure and use of natural resources, guiding education, guarding public health, supervising criminal and civil codes, legislating principles regarding marriage, and insuring conformity of constitutions of member republics with that of the U.S.S.R. Beyond these delegated powers each constituent republic "exercises state authority independently." The provision that only the U.S.S.R. could conduct relations with other nations was amended in 1944, when Churchill, Roosevelt, and Stalin were debating the nature of the proposed United Nations, to permit constituent republics to conduct direct relations and sign treaties with other nations. After this hasty amendment of the Constitution, Stalin insisted that Belo-Russia and the Ukraine receive seats in the United Nations Assembly along with the U.S.S.R. The right of any member republic to secede from the union is baldly stated, but men accused of instigating secession movements in the late thirties were held guilty of treason and counterrevolution.

The governmental machinery of the state was only slightly altered by the Constitution of 1936. The legislative branch, the Supreme Soviet, contains two houses elected every four years—the Council of the Union, where sits one delegate from each electoral district of three hundred thousand population, and the Council of Nationalities, where twenty-five deputies represent each constituent republic, eleven sit for each autonomous republic, five for each autonomous province, and one for each national region. The two houses are coequal and bills must pass both to become law. The Supreme Soviet elects a Presidium of thirty-two members and a president, with power to order national elections, issue decrees, interpret law, name ministers and question their actions in certain cases, appoint military commanders, declare war, ratify treaties, and send and receive ambassadors.

The Supreme Soviet chooses the Council of Ministers, the name adopted in 1946 to replace the revolutionary-sounding Council of People's Commissars. With fifty or sixty members, the Council of Ministers is much larger than the typical Western cabinet because the central administration concerns itself with many economic and social problems and activities which in democratic countries are left to private or quasi-public agencies. For example, there are separate ministries to supervise the automobile, aircraft, railway, oil, rubber, coal, chemical, steel, electrical, paper, textile, machine tool, timber, food, fish, moving picture, and meat and dairy industries. Ministries come and go as some are combined, others abolished, and new ones created. Referred to as "the government of the U.S.S.R.," the Council of Ministers is "the highest executive and administrative organ," carrying out all the functions and exercising all the powers in areas in which the U.S.S.R. is sovereign. The chairman of the Council of Ministers, formerly the Council of People's Commissars, is comparable to the premier or prime minister in Western Europe and to the president of the United States. Lenin filled the office from 1917 to his death in 1924, Rykov until 1930, Molotov until 1941, Stalin until his death in 1953, Malenkov for the next two years, and Bulganin after 1955.

The constituent and the autonomous republics have constitutions closely paralleling that of the U.S.S.R., and their governmental structure is almost identical to that of the federal union. Each has its Council of Ministers, its Presidium, and its Supreme Soviet which, however, is unicameral. Each subdivision—province, city, county, and village—is governed by its own soviet, or local legislature, which chooses an executive committee to carry out its will, enforce the law, and handle matters within its particular competence.

All men and women over eighteen, regardless of race, religion, social origin, property status, or "past activities," may vote for delegates to local, district, and national soviets except the insane and those deprived of electoral rights by court sentence. The same qualifications apply to those who stand for elections, except that they must be twenty-three years of age. Elections are direct and voting is by secret ballot. Candidates for election in each district may be nominated only by labor unions, cooperatives, youth groups, cultural societies, or branches of the Communist party. This makes it unconstitutional to organize a political party for the purpose of nominating candidates for office. Indirect elections, open balloting, the weighting of urban against rural votes, and the disfranchisement of capitalists, landowners, former officials, and clergymen—all peculiarities of the earlier constitutions—were abolished.

The judicial structure of the Soviet Union, as the U.S.S.R. came to be called, was provided for partly in the 1936 Constitution and partly in a special law passed by the Supreme Soviet two years later. The nation's chief law-enforcement officer is the procurator-general, who is chosen by the Supreme Soviet for a seven-year term. He is primarily responsible for the observance of the law by every citizen. He names a procurator for every republic, who in turn appoints a procurator for every district, town, and rural area. One of the procurator's chief functions is to keep the judges of his district under observation and to file criminal charges against them when justified.

On the local level the so-called "people's court," whose judges are elected by the people, handles civil cases and such criminal cases as murder, assault, robbery, and official misconduct. Provincial and territorial courts, similarly chosen, hear appeals from the people's courts and exercise original jurisdiction over cases involving counterrevolutionary actions and theft of public property. Each republic has its supreme court and over all is the Supreme Court of the U.S.S.R., whose members are chosen by the Supreme Soviet. It is primarily a court of appeal from lower courts and has no right to question the constitutionality of the laws passed by the Supreme Soviet.

All judges are elected for three or five years, either by the people directly, in the case of the people's courts, or by the appropriate soviet, in the case of the higher courts, and all are subject to recall by the electorate which chose them. Otherwise judges are held to be independent and "subject only to the law." Any Soviet citizen eighteen or older may be elected to a judgeship; there are no educational restrictions. In an effort to improve the quality of Russian justice, the minister of justice in 1938 inaugurated a six-month training program for local judges. But ten years later his successor complained of the ignorance of men on the bench, suggested improvements in legal training, and ordered the indictment of judges found guilty of negligence or "conduct unbecoming a Soviet judge."

Finally, the Constitution of 1936 detailed certain "fundamental rights and duties" of Soviet citizens, including the right to work, the right to "rest and leisure" and paid vacations, the right to maintenance in old age and during sickness or disability, and the right to an education. Freedom of speech, press, assembly, and organization were "guaranteed by law," as was "freedom of religious worship and freedom of antireligious propaganda."

Citizens were guaranteed freedom from arrest, "except by decision of a court or with the sanction of a procurator," and promised inviolability of the home and privacy of correspondence. The citizens' duties included obedience to law, the honest performance of public responsibilities, the maintenance of "labor discipline," protection of public property, and respect for "the rules of socialist intercourse." To defend the nation, not only as a member of the armed forces but as a civilian, was held to be "the sacred duty" of every citizen, and "treason to the motherland" was declared "punishable with all the severity of the law as the most heinous of crimes."

On paper the 1936 Constitution is an extremely liberal document. But Soviet sympathizers in the West who hailed it as such overlooked the many safeguards which insured the continuation of the authoritarian nature of the regime. Freedom of speech, press, assembly, and street demonstrations were hardly "ensured by placing at the disposal of the working people and their organizations printing presses, stocks of paper, public buildings, the streets, communications facilities, and other material requisites for the exercise of these rights." Not just any organization could exist, for the courts would surely condemn any group which might be charged with counterrevolutionary aspirations. Inviolability of person and home could not be expected to extend to those suspected of treasonable intentions. The Constitution tacitly assumed that any other than the Communist party aimed at overthrowing the government. The assurance that all candidates for public office would be nominated by the Communist party or by associations which it could easily dominate made a mockery of the apparently democratic machinery of the government. On the eve of the unanimous vote of the Supreme Soviet adopting the "Stalin" Constitution, Stalin admitted that the document left unchanged "the present leading position of the Communist party." On another occasion he was still more frank when he declared that the dictatorship of the proletariat amounted in essence to the dictatorship of its vanguard, the party. Some Western sympathizers accepted at face value Moscow's boast that it had the most democratic government in the world. But when the men in the Kremlin make that boast, perhaps sincerely, "it is presumably because they identify the policies of the Party leadership with the welfare of the masses" (Fainsod).

THE ROLE OF THE COMMUNIST PARTY

The Communist party pyramid bears close resemblance to the hierarchy of soviets which constitutes the governmental framework of the Soviet Union. While the organization has changed slightly over the years and party organs have been renamed recently, the structure has remained essentially the same since the early days of the regime.

In 1919 the Central Executive Committee of the party organized three new agencies to handle the Committee's work when it was not in session. The Political Bureau, or Politburo for short, which had operated during the Civil War but fallen into disuse, was resurrected to deal with all major policy questions requiring immediate action. Its five members included Lenin, Trotsky, and Stalin. From the beginning the Politburo concerned itself with both important and insignificant matters having to do with every phase of government. Lenin complained that a request by the Moscow Consumers' Cooperative to buy a small order of French canned food came to the Politburo for approval. Every aspect of Soviet life, from federal elections, the national economic plan, foreign affairs, and military matters to efforts to improve motion pictures and radio programs, came under the scrutiny of these top leaders. The Organizational Bureau, or Orgburo, on which Stalin also served, was given supervisional and organizational control over the party membership. The General Secretariat was intended to coordinate the work of the other two. Stalin interested himself primarily in organization and membership of the party, and when he became general secretary in 1922 he took with him his knowledge of and control over the party workers. From then on the Orgburo became unimportant. From then on the Russian people "lived under Stalin's virtual rule, without being aware of the ruler's name" (Deutscher). They would learn it soon enough.

The secretary headed a huge staff, assigned and supervised party personnel, and guided propaganda work. His appointment of regional secretaries to direct and report on activities of local cells and individuals gave him effective control of the rank and file of the party. Within a year Trotsky was complaining that Stalin's methods left the impression among most party workers that all decisions were made by the general secretary. The Secretariat continued to supervise party membership, control most appointments, and see to the carrying out of the propaganda work, and Stalin's position as general secretary was primarily responsible for his success in stilling all opposition to his rule.

In 1952 the Nineteenth Congress of the Communist Party, the first to meet in thirteen years, abolished the Politburo and the Orgburo and substituted the new Presidium of ten members, most of them former members of the Politburo. Ostensibly the Presidium is elected by the party's Central Committee, but in fact, like its predecessors, it is coöptative among the party leaders. Since those who sit in the Presidium are also the nation's chief ministers, it is this small clique which rules the U.S.S.R.

Theoretically the "supreme organ" of the party is the All-Union Congress of the Communist Party, which is supposed to gather at least every four years. The meetings last only a few days and are taken up with leaders' reports which are loudly cheered and unanimously approved. Here new plans and goals are outlined, shifts in party strategy or "line" are indicated, and new appointments made to leading party posts. The Congress also elects a Central Committee, made up of a hundred and twenty-five members and nearly as many "candidates" for membership. National and regional party secretaries, members of the Council of Ministers, important military and police figures, and leading intellectuals and Marxist theorists make up the Central Committee. It is essentially an honorary body, since its meetings are infrequent and its work is done for it by the Presidium. In theory, the Central Committee elects the Presidium and the general secretary. While the Secretariat still exists, its work is closely watched by the Presidium, which decides all important matters whether affecting governmental policy or party organization. Certainly, neither Stalin's successor, Malenkov, nor Khrushchev who followed him, exercised any such awful power and influence as did Stalin.

Branches of the Communist party appear in all constituent republics, each holding its own party congress and each choosing its own central committee, administrative bureau, and secretariat, or accepting the choice made for it by Moscow. In each region of each republic party units receive orders from the echelon above and pass them on to units in cities and counties under their jurisdiction. Beneath the city and county organizations are the "primary party units," formerly known as cells. The secretariat on each level is responsible for passing down directives and passing up reports, for naming men to key positions in the party, youth organizations, and labor unions, for providing leadership in pushing economic production, for carrying on propaganda work, and, on the county and city level, for keeping records on every party member showing his personal history, movements from one district to another, education, employment record, punishments, and awards. The multiplicity of assignments borne by city and county party officials and the sheer physical burden of handling them takes such a heavy toll that the rate of turnover of these party hacks is high.

The primary party unit, or cell, of which there are three hundred and fifty thousand, is the basic unit of the Communist party. It is the organization found in the factory, the shop, the collective farm, the army company, or the government office. It may contain hundreds of party members but never less than three; typically it numbers twenty. Its job is to carry on educational and propaganda work among nonparty citizens, to recruit and train new members, to inspire workers to fulfill production quotas, to discover and report mismanagement in factory or farm, and generally to provide leadership in the political, economic, and cultural life of the community. Again there is a local secretary to collect membership dues, keep records, make reports, lead discussion groups, edit or even write the local newspaper, and direct the work of the others in the cell.

To become a member of the Community party a person submits an application giving his life history. He must be sponsored by three party members who have been in the party for at least three years and who have worked with the applicant for at least a year. The candidate is on probation and under scrutiny for a year, after which his application is voted upon by the local unit and forwarded with the endorsement of the unit secretary to the city or district Central Bureau. Once a member of the party, he is expected to lead an exemplary moral life, to set those around him an example of hard work and devotion to the cause of socialism, to attend party meetings and take part in discussions, to be ever watchful for laxity, mismanagement, and sabotage, to explain and support party programs and goals, to urge people to vote and to campaign for party candidates. One who follows such a course and who faithfully carries out the orders he receives is the ideal Bolshevik. Frequent criticism in the Russian press indicates, however, that many fall short of the ideal.

Theoretically, the Communist party operates under the guiding principle of "democratic centralism," which is supposed to mean the election of all executive agencies from the lowest echelon to the highest, their frequent reporting back to the bodies which elected them, the acceptance of majority rule, and the carrying out by lower bodies of decisions handed down from above. In practice, however, executive agencies on the top level are not elected but coöpted, and administrators farther down the hierarchy are appointed by their superiors. Executive bodies do report to those who elect them, but the decisions of the party leaders are subject to neither challenge nor criticism; they can only be endorsed and carried out. That a body anywhere along the line should repudiate its leadership and put forward alternative proposals is inconceivable. Of course there is acceptance of majority rule, for there is no minority. The party speaks with one voice. No open opposition, much less the existence of an organized faction within the party, is tolerated. Those at the top order; those beneath them obey. And yet, leaders often complain of the lack of initiative among local leaders. There is discussion in party gatherings, but it must be constructive. It is permissible to debate how best to implement a plan but not to question the plan itself. There is frequent criticism of officials who hold subordinate positions, and the leadership encourages such attacks upon scapegoats. But through the thirty years of Stalin's rule any questioning of his policy was accounted treason.

Party membership first reached a million in 1929 and passed two million four years later. During the purges of the thirties the membership was pared down drastically. During World War II men and women, particularly in the armed services, were encouraged to join the party. By the end of 1952, when the population of the U.S.S.R. approached two hundred million, there were six million on the party rolls and nearly another million candidates awaiting acceptance. But the leaders were not interested in mere numbers. They urged subordinates to bring in only the best people, those with leadership potential in science, industry, the military, agriculture, and the arts. And they bid particularly for the young. Two-thirds of the party membership after the war were less than thirty-five years of age, and nearly a fifth were under twenty-five. The predominance of young people in the party membership is in part a result of the purges which have fallen most heavily upon old Communists, in part a reflection of the fact that Russia's population is a youthful population, with its numbers concentrated in the young age groups.

Membership in the Communist party is not necessary to hold political office or serve as a delegate to a soviet. The nearer the top of the governmental pyramid, however, the greater the likelihood that the officeholder is a party member. All important national and republican posts are occupied by Communists, as are sensitive spots in industry. At minimum, party sponsorship is absolutely necessary for election to any position. The party or party-dominated organizations such as trade unions and cooperatives nominate candidates, and only one is put forward for each office. During the thirties the leaders made much of their slates of Communists and "non-Party Bolsheviks." There is never any opposition. One may register disapproval of the list of candidates only by not voting or by turning in a blank ballot. Nearly 97 per cent of the eligible voters went to the polls in the federal elections of 1937, and over 98 per cent of them voted for the party candidates. Since the second World War the percentages in both cases have risen.

On the morrow of the November Revolution the Bolsheviks organized the League of Communist Youth, the *Komsomol,* which exemplary young men and women from fourteen to twenty-three years of age might join. The aim was to enlist the nation's youth in support of the goals of the new society, to have the members report counterrevolutionary sympathies in the school or even in the home, help others their own age to understand the principles of socialism, and set before all an example of Communist discipline and youthful enthusiasm for the new society. They were very active and extremely effective in helping put over the collectivization of agriculture, the industrialization program of the First Five-Year Plan, the drive to stamp out illiteracy, and the crusade against religion. On the lower Amur River they built an industrial city, Komsomolsk, whose population rose rapidly to seventy thousand in 1939 and to over two hundred thousand by 1956. There were sixteen million members of the *Komsomol* in 1952 and another nineteen million in the Young Pioneers, a similar organization for youths aged ten to sixteen. Children eight years of age may join the Little Octobrists. No other youth organizations are permitted. Progression from one group to another and so into the parent organization, the Communist party, is now normal. The great majority of party members are graduates of the youth organizations.

THE PURGES

From time to time the nation's leaders have subjected the Communist party membership to scrutiny from the point of view of loyalty to the party, devotion to duty, and personal conduct. Those who do not pass the test are dropped from the rolls and may be punished by exile, imprisonment, or execution. Under Lenin's leadership members of the party were relatively free to disagree with and criticize their leaders and even to attack party plans in the press after their adoption. There was no punishment for those who opposed Lenin so violently for his insistence that there was no alternative to accepting the German terms at Brest-Litovsk. Those who the following year protested against the drift toward overcentralization and the concentration of power in the hands of a few did so with impunity. And the bitter attack upon Lenin and Trotsky for using former officers in the new army brought no recrimination. His patience and his willingness to forgive and welcome back those who strayed away made Lenin the most beloved of all Communists, and many who fled the country under Stalin looked back nostalgically to the free and easy times of his predecessor.

But Lenin was not a man of unlimited patience. In 1920 the so-called "workers' opposition" group demanded that labor unions operate the factories and protested against excessive centralization in the Communist party. Lenin carried a majority of the party congress with him in condemning "syndicalist and anarchist deviation" and threatened those who persisted in factionalism with expulsion from the party. When the warning went unheeded Lenin demanded the expulsion of these "wavering Communists," and a third of the members of the party were expelled. But he never went beyond this mild punishment and resorted to even this "extreme measure" only rarely.

Stalin was not so candid. While Lenin lay paralyzed and unable to work Stalin teamed with the leftists Kamenev and Zinoviev to keep Trotsky from succeeding Lenin. Stalin and Trotsky had violently disagreed years before the revolution, and the Georgian was not one to forgive a hurt. Kamenev, incidentally, was Trotsky's brother-in-law. Now Trotsky's supporters were quietly removed from important positions in government and party and then the little firebrand, left to stand alone, was accused of "petty-bourgeois deviationism." He was not immediately expelled from the party but was dismissed as war commissar. After the triumph over Trotsky Stalin deserted his friends and teamed up with the rightists in the Politburo to destroy Kamenev and Zinoviev. Their supporters were driven from the party and they, together with Trotsky with whom they had become reconciled, were removed from the Politburo.

Through 1927 the contest went on, Trotsky and the others accusing Stalin of suffering defeats in foreign affairs—the Communist failure in China and the rupture of diplomatic relations with Great Britain—and of following a policy of reaction at home. Trotsky arranged secret meetings with his sympathizers, operated an underground press, and even organized street demonstrations against Stalin. The political police trumped up the ridiculous charge that Trotsky was conspiring with Whites to overthrow the regime, and he, Kamenev, and Zinoviev were expelled from the party. Early in 1928 Trotsky was exiled to central Siberia. He was later deported to Turkey and thence to Mexico, where, in 1940, he was killed with a hatchet by a disgruntled admirer. His supporters were deprived of their party membership, although Kamenev and Zinoviev abjectly recanted and eventually returned to the party.

Having overpowered the leftist opposition, Stalin now turned against the right whose support had enabled him to defeat Trotsky. When Rykov, Tomsky, and Premier Bukharin opposed rapid industrialization and the persecution of *kulaks,* Stalin, now in full control of the party and with his appointees filling nearly every important post in the land, drove the three from the Politburo. Stalin's trusted friend Molotov replaced Rykov as premier, or chairman of the Council of Commissars.

Late in 1934 Stalin's reliable henchman and friend Sergei Kirov, party secretary in Leningrad after Zinoviev's disgrace, was assassinated by the husband of his secretary. Insanely furious, Stalin lashed out to right and left, convinced that the deed was the work of a conspiracy led by Zinoviev and financed by foreign capitalists. A hundred former tsarist officials who were nowhere near the scene and could not possibly have been implicated were shot. Through a succession of carefully staged trials during the next four years top party leaders of both left and right who had opposed Stalin at one time or another paraded to the witness stand to confess plotting treason, assassination, sabotage, and conspiring with Poles, Germans, Japanese, and Trotsky to overthrow the regime. A grim nation-wide search directed by Yezhov, the new head of the secret police, swept up hundreds of thousands of suspects in every walk of life—officials, army officers, industrial and labor leaders, teachers, artists, and ordinary citizens. The opportunity to hurl charges or whisper suspicions allowed many to settle personal grievances, and Stalin later admitted that many of the victims were innocent. Bukharin, Zinoviev, Kamenev, Rykov, Yagoda, and many other Old Bolsheviks who had joined the party long before the revolution were executed. Tomsky cheated the executioners by committing suicide. Over three-fourths of the Central Committee of the Communist party were killed or imprisoned. Marshal Tukhachevsky and six other top-ranking army leaders were condemned to death for supposedly betraying military secrets to Germany and conspiring to restore capitalism. Officers of all ranks throughout the army suffered dismissal or worse. Many senior diplomats were purged. "The casualties read like a Communist *Who's Who* of the twenties" (Chamberlin). Stalin finally called a halt to the bloody business, but not before he had "purged the purgers." Yezhov himself was liquidated and his place was taken by Lavrenty Beria. The "Great Purge," or *Yezhov-shchina,* as the Russians call it, sent thousands before firing squads, imprisoned other thousands, and put untold numbers in forced labor camps or in exile in Siberian wastelands. Many thousands got off with expulsion from the party.

By the time the eighteenth party congress met in March, 1939, the purge had come to an end. The Old Bolsheviks and the intellectuals in the Communist party, among them Lenin's followers who had opposed Stalin's "socialism in one country," had been cleared in one way or another from the ranks. What remained was not the Communist party as Russia had known it but Stalin's party. Every Soviet citizen was given to understand that Stalin was the state and that to question his leadership or policies would be to invite the charge of treason.

Immediately after World War II the party underwent a bloodless purge to rid it of politically-illiterate lackeys who had wormed their way into subordinate posts during the conflict. Nine out of ten county secretaries were cut loose in Belo-Russia and half of such officials in the Ukraine. Many of the rank and file who had been admitted without much discrimination in an effort to widen and popularize support for the party were found wanting and were expelled. Between 1948 and 1950 several top party officials disappeared without explanation. Two years later Stalin ordered a number of Ukrainian leaders shot for "counterrevolutionary wrecking." According to later revelations by Khrushchev, Stalin threatened to kill Molotov, Malenkov, and Mikoyan, in fact all the old members of the Politburo, and hinted that he suspected Voroshilov of being a British spy.

In mid-January, 1953, Moscow newspapers announced that nine doctors had been arrested and charged with plotting to assassinate by medical means top Russian officials, particularly military men. They were accused of conspiring with American and British agents. Six of the nine were Jews supposed to be Zionists, and a bloodletting among Jews of every profession followed. Then the attack veered round to the Communist party, particularly in the Ukraine, and to the security police, whose supposed laxity had allowed the plot to develop. The terror of the thirties seemed about to be repeated. "The old man has reached for the bottle again," one American observer told another.

But this particular terror was short-lived. On March 5, 1953, Stalin suddenly died of a cerebral hemorrhage at the age of seventy-three. Many were quick to spread the rumor that he had been assassinated by party leaders fearful for their own lives. Now there was another purge, this time of Stalin's henchmen. The doctors imprisoned a few weeks earlier were freed and the nation was told that they had been falsely accused. Malenkov succeeded as premier, with Beria, head of the security police, threatening to overturn him. Molotov made the third in the triumvirate that now ruled in Stalin's place. Three months later Beria, accused of treacherously promoting discord among Soviet nationalities, was overthrown and shot. The party, especially in Georgia, his birthplace, was purged of his supporters. Army leaders, particularly the popular Marshal Zhukov, had shared the responsibility for his overthrow. With his passing there was evidence that the dreaded security police would not again be allowed to wield its awful power over party and people to the extent it had in the thirties and forties.

In 1955 Malenkov, confessing his failure to restore agricultural production, stepped down to a ministerial post. Again a collegial group came forward to lead the government. Marshal Nicholas Bulganin, an industrial leader who had been given military rank for his work in the Defense Ministry, Nikita Khrushchev, general secretary of the Communist party, and Molotov made up the new triumvirate, the first as premier. Slowly but with determination they carried forward a new purge, this time of Stalin himself. In a program of "de-Stalinization" the mistakes, the cruelty, the vindictiveness, the pettiness, and all the weaknesses and crimes of the former leader were condemned before the public. Even Lenin's "political testament," in which Stalin was criticized as being impulsive, spiteful, capricious, and "too rude," was published in Russia for the first time. The dying Lenin had urged the party to remove Stalin as secretary, warning that he had already gathered enormous power and that he could not be trusted to use it wisely.

There were indications after Stalin's death of a somewhat gentler manner of dealing with those who fell from favor. An amnesty freed prisoners whose only crime had been to incur Stalin's displeasure. Beria, of course, was quickly dispatched, but with the power of the police behind him perhaps there was nothing else to do. As for others, men now could be demoted or dismissed without being executed. In the summer of 1957 Molotov, Malenkov and other high-ranking officials were cashiered and given minor posts in remote areas. And while the party membership continued to show a high rate of turnover, all but a very few of those who left it did so without further punishment. But after thirty years of Stalinist terror Western cynics were slow to believe that a purge could be bloodless and that it might serve constructive ends.

THE STALIN CULT

One consequence of the purges that dot the Stalin era, particularly of the "Great Purge" of 1934–1938, was the demotion or elimination of party workers of middle age or beyond who had grown up with the revolutionary movement. Stalin surrounded himself with men of different temperament and background from those who had gathered round Lenin. The new toadies for the most part were party hacks rather than intellectuals, of whom Stalin, hardly an intellectual himself, was always suspicious. They had risen in the ranks because of their devotion to Stalin and their effectiveness in party work. Members of the Politburo ceased to be Stalin's partners and became simply his henchmen. Thus he compensated for a deep sense of inferiority that ran back into his early life and that grew in the years when Lenin and Trotsky received all the plaudits of the party faithful. The rank and file were made up of young men who knew nothing of the comparative freedom in the party which Lenin had allowed and even encouraged. Many knew little of the Stalin-Trotsky contest, for the history books had been rewritten to strike out every mention of Trotsky's name. These young men could not remember when Stalin was not the ruler in the Russian land. They had learned, for all Russia had been sternly taught, that the party secretary would brook no criticism and not the slightest opposition. Their generation had been subjected to a constant stream of propaganda, through all the media of modern mass communication, which taught them that Stalin was all-knowing and all-wise, that his judgment was infallible, that when things went wrong it was not his fault but that of the "wreckers, spies, saboteurs" sent into the country by hostile capitalist governments. The press constantly attributed to him wisdom and genius in everything, from history, politics, government, military strategy, and economics to science, art, music, and literary criticism. Every textbook was filled with references to the work of "Our Great Leader Stalin." Stalin dictated his own biography, which reeked with fulsome praise of his every thought and deed. He edited the *History of the Communist Party of the Soviet Union,* which attributed to him all the good that had come to Russia. Every public speech was cluttered with glowing tributes to him. Pictures of Stalin, sometimes along with those of Marx and Lenin but often alone, adorned public buildings, and statues of him were erected in town squares. Cities all over the U.S.S.R. were named for him—Stalingrad, Stalinabad, Stalinsk, Stalinir, Stalinogorsk, Stalino— as well as streets, mountains, canals, collective farms, and constitutions. Books and plays and symphonies were dedicated to him. At election time he was nominated and elected to represent dozens of constituencies.

During World War II Stalin took the titles of Marshal and Generalissimo, assumed credit for military strategy that won victories and successfully shouldered upon others the responsibility for defeats. He identified himself with the nation and the people, with guerrilla bands and the Red Army, and, because of the accident of the alliance he shared, with the cause of freedom and democracy. He met with leaders from the West who had long been frank in their denunciation of Communism and elicited their respect and admiration. Many hoped that he and Russia had changed, that through association with the democracies the dictatorship might soften.

But with the end of the war it became apparent that Stalin had not changed. The Stalin cult was carried even further, and the fawning adulation which the aging leader demanded disgusted many. Now he became the godlike hero of the entire Communist world, which had expanded far beyond Russia's borders. His likeness was displayed in the streets of cities all over Eastern Europe, where his wisdom was acclaimed and his words repeated by toadies who ruled in his image. When Yugoslavia's Tito refused to bend the knee to Stalin's orders he was anathematized and all the Communist faithful spurned him. When Stalin died, it is no wonder that party leaders all over the world were confused and found difficulty adjusting to the new line that soon emanated from Moscow. Stalin's henchmen in the satellite nations slowly slipped from power.

Those who succeeded to Stalin's power in Russia deprecated "the cult of the individual" and sought to restore the prestige of the Communist party which Stalin had reduced to the position of servant to his stubborn will. Khrushchev and other party leaders in 1956 publicly accused Stalin of brutality and capriciousness, of fabricating cases against his political opponents, of condoning the use of barbarous tortures, of condemning men without trial, of suppressing retractions of public confessions obtained by threat of "cruel and inhuman" treatment, of slowing down the "march toward socialism" by his mass persecutions, of endangering the nation's survival by liquidating experienced generals and as self-appointed "Generalissimo" countermanding orders of military leaders during World War II, of refusing to heed Churchill's warning that Hitler would attack Russia, of cowardice during the war, of developing a "persecution mania" after the war, of anti-Semitism, of fabricating the "doctors' plot" of 1952. Khrushchev even hinted that Stalin himself was responsible for Kirov's murder in 1934 and implied that it was conceived to give Stalin an excuse to get rid of many of whom he was suspicious. He derided the "loathsome adulation" which Stalin wrote into his own biography and laughed at the Stalin prizes in art and science with the observation, "Not even the tsars created prizes which they named after themselves." The prizes had been discontinued after Stalin's death. In 1956 they were revived and renamed for Lenin. Khrushchev accused Stalin of knowing the country, and particularly agriculture, only from films and insisted that Stalin had not visited a single village in the last twenty-five years of his life. Finally, he ridiculed Stalin for encouraging "the most dissolute flattery," for permitting his biographer to refer to him as "the greatest leader, sublime strategist of all times and nations," for spending huge sums on statues to himself, and for permitting factories and *kolkhozes* and cities to be named for him. One of his listeners asked Khrushchev, "Why didn't you cut his throat?"

THE RULE OF TERROR

The Cheka, created during the early weeks of the revolution to fight sabotage and counterrevolution, was abolished in 1922 and its personnel and functions were assigned to a new agency, the State Political Administration or G.P.U., a branch of the Commissariat for Internal Affairs of the R.S.F.S.R. Its job was to suppress counterrevolution, prevent espionage, and police the frontier. It had unlimited power to search dwellings and arrest suspects but was supposed to bring charges quickly or dismiss its prisoners. With the birth of the U.S.S.R. in 1924 the G.P.U. became the O.G.P.U. with jurisdiction over the entire Soviet Union.

Through its early years the O.G.P.U. concentrated its attention upon former tsarist officials, merchants, clergymen, and members of non-Bolshevik political parties. But with the appearance of the Trotskyite opposition in the mid-twenties the O.G.P.U. extended its activities over a wider range. Now it interested itself in subversion and heresy within the Communist party, watched foreign diplomats whom Trotsky's followers were charged with contacting, carried on espionage abroad and especially among *émigré* settlements, kept army personnel under surveillance, and guarded against sabotage in industry and transportation. Its prisoners when convicted were sent to concentration camps run by the O.G.P.U. With the adoption of the First Five Year Plan the political police took on the task of rounding up *kulaks* and small businessmen, who previously had been let alone. It also arrested non-Communist intellectuals who were suspected of opposing the socialization program. Between 1928 and 1933 many engineers and factory managers were arrested for failure to meet production goals, and perhaps a million *kulak* families who resisted collectivization were rounded up. Some were shot but the vast majority were sent to O.G.P.U. labor camps in northern Russia and Siberia to work in the forests and mines or on roads and public works. At the same time all criminals whose sentences exceeded three years, regardless of the crime they had committed, were thrown into the forced-labor camps operated by the O.G.P.U.

In 1934 the O.G.P.U. was abolished. Its functions were taken over by the *Narodnyi Komissariat Vnutrennikh Del,* the People's Commissariat of Internal Affairs or N.K.V.D., under Henry Yagoda. Now it encompassed not only the political police but the regular police, fire departments, border guards, traffic officers, prison officials, and its own military force of infantry, cavalry, and tanks. Since the earlier agency had tended to grow independent and to operate as it pleased, some restraints were imposed upon the new one. The N.K.V.D. could, on its own authority, sentence prisoners to administrative exile or imprisonment for no more than five years, but it had to turn over to the regular courts all accused persons who, if found guilty, could be sentenced to more than five years. Thousands taken during the First Five-Year Plan were released from prison, and there seemed some likelihood that the power of the police system would be curbed.

All restraints were lifted or ignored, however, after the assassination of Kirov. The N.K.V.D., assisted by a network of informers, arrested literally millions of suspects during the next four years. No one was safe from the knock on the door at night, the days of endless questioning, the threats to family and friends, the brutality of prison life, the deportation to Siberia. In a succession of public trials important officials of the Communist party confessed guilt to fantastic charges of treason and sabotage, but Khrushchev admitted in 1956 that the trials were staged, that the accused were subjected to cruel tortures, and that the confessions which shocked the world were made to obtain relief from further torture. Thousands were shot without trial at Stalin's order. With the arrest of the N.K.V.D. head, Yagoda, and the appointment in 1937 of Nicholas Yezhov, the fury reached its height. Long after every possible threat to Stalin and the regime had been removed, the seizures and sentences went on.

Then suddenly the leaders seemed to realize that, while the purge at first may have saved the nation from treason and sabotage, its continuation was depriving industry, the army, government, and the party of scarce talent and leadership. The terror now turned against those who were making a career of it, and overzealous party workers and members of the N.K.V.D. were arrested and packed off by thousands to the labor camps to be welcomed by those whom they had put there earlier. Stalin now donned the mask of savior of the people from mass terror and publicly condemned those who "suffer from a lack of concern for people" or who showed a "heartless attitude towards people." The purge was over, but the fear which it engendered never disappeared.

After the war the commissariats were renamed ministries, and the N.K.V.D. became the M.V.D. or Ministry of Internal Affairs. Its duties included the maintenance of internal security, reporting the attitude of the people toward the government, stationing observers in every organization, safeguarding the lives of important officials, carrying on espionage abroad, and providing counterespionage at home. Its organization parallels that of the government and the Communist party, with units on every administrative level from city and county to the ministry in Moscow. One special branch guards against sabotage in industry and transportation; another operates in the armed forces; still another sends its agents abroad to keep check on Soviet foreign officers, contact foreign Communists, and feed a stream of vital military and scientific information back to the Soviet leaders.

There are serious hazards involved in creating and permitting the continued existence of the security police. It tends to become independent, and even to menace the government which established it but which can no longer control it. While that never happened under Stalin, those who followed him obviously were afraid that it might; they seemed to expect Beria, with the M.V.D. behind him, to make a bid for power soon after Stalin's funeral. There is also the risk that the suspicion which the agency encourages and the fear which it fosters may destroy initiative and make men hesitate to accept responsibility; and the economy cannot function, the government cannot operate, the army cannot fight unless many take the initiative and shoulder responsibility. Finally, the M.V.D. tends, through the reports it renders to high officials, through the analyses it makes of foreign and domestic conditions, to color the facts, to convince the nation's leaders that there is constant crisis at home and abroad. Thus it insures its continued employment, and Russian bureaucrats are no different from any others in wanting to keep their jobs.

Yet Lenin believed that terror was necessary, and Stalin compared the N.K.V.D. to the Committee of Public Safety with which the French Revolution defended itself. The Soviet regime has never trusted its own citizens to support it.

WHAT HOLDS THE REGIME TOGETHER

Many Russians, some of them officials of middling importance, some of them members of the Communist party, fled the regime and sought sanctuary in the West during and after World War II. All were bitter in their denunciation of the Soviet regime. But there was remarkable agreement among them that there was no hope, no possibility, that the Communist government could or would be overthrown by an internal uprising. Many factors taken together suggest that they are probably correct. The efficiency of the M.V.D. and the dread in which it is held insure against the possibility that any opposition movement could ever be widely enough organized to promise success. The Communist party, in spite of the fact that it frequently has to be cleansed of dross, constitutes an effective agency for welding the people together. Agitation and propaganda, constantly dinned into the people through the press and radio and television and motion pictures and stage, convince the masses that the socialist experiment is accomplishing great things and that the world will some day follow the lead. While people may not like the irritations they suffer, still the vast majority believes in the regime and is loyal to it. After all, for all but a few there is no basis for comparison, since only a few have seen anything else. There is justifiable pride in the victory over the nation's enemies, in the progress made in industry, transportation, power, education, and many other fields. There is a sense of accomplishment and a conviction that better times will come. There is a knowledge that in many ways life has improved over what it was under the tsars—better schools, hospitals, even better food and clothing, at least as far as the masses are concerned, and most of all better job and professional opportunities. Not the least important is the fact that the elite in Soviet society—party men, government officials, teachers, students, scientists, military leaders, artists, industrial managers, and trade-union leaders have a stake in the regime; understandably, they want to see it perpetuated. Finally, the government has managed to capture the senti- mental love of country which Russians feel so deeply. An attack upon the regime is felt to be an attack upon "the motherland." It was not for Com- munism but in defense of Russia that millions died in World War II.

SUGGESTED READING

Barmine, A., *One Who Survived* (New York, Putnam's, 1945).

Beck, F. and W. Godin, *Russian Purge and the Extraction of Confession* (New York, Viking, 1951).

Berman, H. J., *Justice in Russia* (Cambridge, Harvard University Press, 1950).

Carr, E. H., *The Interregnum, 1923–1924* (New York, Macmillan, 1954).

Chamberlin, W. H., *Soviet Russia* (Boston, Little, Brown, 1930).

———, *The Russian Enigma* (New York, Scribner's, 1943).

Dallin, D. and B. Nicolaevsky, *Forced Labor in Soviet Russia* (New Haven, Yale University Press, 1947).

De Huszar, G. B., *Soviet Power and Politics* (New York, Crowell, 1955).

Deutscher, I., *Stalin, a Political Biography* (New York, Oxford University Press, 1949).

Fainsod, M., *How Russia is Ruled* (Cambridge, Harvard University Press, 1953).

Fischer, G., *Soviet Opposition to Stalin* (Cambridge, Harvard University Press, 1952).

Florinsky, M. T., *Toward an Understanding of the U.S.S.R.* (New York, Mac- millan, 1951).

Gruliow, L., *Current Soviet Policies* (New York, Praeger, 1956).

Gsovski, V., *Soviet Civil Law* (Ann Arbor, University of Michigan Press, 1948).

Gurian, W., *The Soviet Union: Background, Ideology, Reality* (Notre Dame, University of Notre Dame Press, 1951).

Harper, S. N., *The Government of the Soviet Union* (New York, Van Nostrand, 1938).

Hazard, J. N., *Law and Change in the U.S.S.R.* (London, Stevens, 1953).

———, *Soviet Legal Philosophy* (Cambridge, Harvard University Press, 1951).

Inkeles, A., *Public Opinion in Soviet Russia, a Study in Mass Persuasion* (Cam- bridge, Harvard University Press, 1950).

Kulski, W. W., *The Soviet Regime* (Syracuse, Syracuse University Press, 1954).

Lenin, V. I., *Selected Works* (New York, International Publishers, 1947).

Meisel, J. H. and E. S. Kosera, *Materials for the Study of the Soviet Union* (Ann Arbor, Wahr, 1953).

Meissner, B., *The Communist Party of the Soviet Union* (New York, Praeger, 1956).

Moore, B., *Soviet Politics—The Dilemma of Power* (Cambridge, Harvard University Press, 1950).

————, *Terror and Progress—U.S.S.R.* (Cambridge, Harvard University Press, 1954).

People's Commissariat of Justice of the U.S.S.R., *Report of the Court Proceedings in the Case of the Anti-Soviet "Bloc of Rights and Trotskyites"* (Moscow, Four Continent Publishing House, 1938).

Rauch, G. von, *A History of Soviet Russia* (New York, Praeger, 1956).

Rostow, W. W., *The Dynamics of Soviet Society* (New York, Norton, 1952).

Salisbury, H. E., *American in Russia* (New York, Harper's, 1955).

Schueller, G. K., *The Politburo* (Stanford, Stanford University Press, 1951).

Timasheff, N., *The Great Retreat; The Growth and Decline of Communism in Russia* (New York, Dutton, 1946).

Towster, J., *Political Power in the U.S.S.R.* (New York, Oxford University Press, 1948).

Vyshinsky, A. Y., *The Law of the Soviet State* (New York, Macmillan, 1948).

Wolfe, B. D., *Khrushchev and Stalin's Ghost* (New York, Praeger, 1956).

29

The Soviet Economy

Wᴀʀ ᴄᴏᴍᴍᴜɴɪsᴍ, ᴡɪᴛʜ ɪᴛs sᴇɪᴢᴜʀᴇ of grain from the peasants and its socialization of industry, brought production to a dangerously low level and met with resistance from both peasants and city dwellers. It was abandoned in 1921 to be replaced by the New Economy Policy. Peasants now had to pay only a fixed tax in kind and could sell their surplus in the market place. The government retained control of the largest factories, banking, and transportation, but allowed private operators once more to run small plants and hire workers to man them. By 1927 both agricultural and industrial output had recovered to prewar levels.

In 1928 the government gave up its New Economic Policy and began the first of its Five-Year Plans. It proposed to put an end to private enterprise in nonagricultural production, expand heavy industry, and begin collectivization of the nation's farms. The second and third plans aimed at carrying on the work begun under the first and slowly increasing output of consumers' goods. Planning continued during the second World War, but civilian needs gave way to military goals. After the war planning in five-year blocks was resumed, production steadily increased and, after Stalin's death in 1953, the people were promised an appreciable expansion of consumer-goods output.

During the First Five-Year Plan the government attacked individual farming, forcing peasants to join collective farms with their land, animals, and tools. The *kulaks* resisted, burning their grain and slaughtering their livestock. Parties of Communists from the cities fought the rich peasants, killing many and throwing many into forced labor camps. But the willful

594

destruction of grain and animals threatened to impoverish the nation. During the Second Five-Year Plan the collectivization of agriculture was completed and farm output slowly returned to and surpassed presocialization figures. But the peasants accepted collectivization only grudgingly and resented the low prices the government paid them for the share of their crops it took. In spite of mechanization, agricultural production did not keep pace with the nation's growing population and expanding needs. The government was unable to devise any satisfactory means of stimulating individual incentive.

Industry was completely nationalized during the First Five-Year Plan. From then on the government directed most of its capital investment into heavy industry to the neglect of consumer-goods production. The output of coal, iron, petroleum, steel, electricity, transportation facilities and the like increased phenomenally between 1928 and 1940, and postwar production figures have gone far beyond those of the thirties. In the early years of planning, foreign equipment and technicians contributed to the industrial expansion, but since the mid-1930's the nation has equipped its factories, trained its technicians, and financed its growth almost entirely from its own resources. After Stalin's death more attention was given to increasing output of consumers' goods, although heavy industry continued to receive the greatest share of capital investment. Transportation facilities—rail, water, highway, and particularly air—have grown enormously.

During the period of the N.E.P. the government halted the runaway inflation and stabilized the currency, tying the ruble to gold in 1950. It ended requisitions and payments in kind and adopted a revenue system which emphasized excise and income taxes. Banking is a government monopoly, as is foreign trade, which is relatively unimportant in the national economy.

The nonagricultural labor force has grown from six million in 1924 to over fifty million in 1957, chiefly through the shift of population from rural to urban areas. The high rate of labor turnover which hampered industry in the 1920's has been reduced by restricting the worker's freedom to move from job to job. Monetary wages have risen sharply since the beginning of the First Five-Year Plan but have not kept pace with rising prices. Real wages were higher in 1928 than twenty-five years later. Man-hour output of labor has increased but still lags far behind that of the Western European or American worker. Labor unions administer social security benefits, carry on educational work among their members, and exert their influence to increase production. They do not bargain with their employer, the state, nor can their members strike.

The standard of living, already low in 1928, declined through the early Five-Year Plans and fell sharply during the second World War. After the war the government showed some interest in satisfying consumers' needs. By the mid-1950's the average Russian probably was enjoying more and better food, clothing, and shelter than at any time since the revolution. And the Sixth Five-Year Plan promised him still better living conditions.

THE FAILURE OF WAR COMMUNISM

The Bolsheviks had moved quickly after assuming power to nationalize land and key industries and to grant control over management to the laborers in each plant. Workers had expected, naïvely, that by appropriating to themselves the profits that had gone to factory owners they would receive bountiful wages and yet work shorter hours. Production fell off sharply and labor discipline disappeared under the workers' committees which directed the operation of each factory. Workmen showed up when they pleased and left the bench whenever it suited them. When equipment wore out it was neither repaired nor replaced. Men walked off with tools and paid themselves with finished goods or raw materials which they traded for food and clothing. Factories closed when machinery broke down or materials were gone. Industrial output had shrunk by 1920 to a fifth the prewar level and there were jobs for only half as many workers. Many drifted back to their native villages to find the living they could not earn in the cities.

Agricultural output declined sharply as some of the most productive areas were fought over by contending armies or fell under White control, as herds of livestock starved or were slaughtered for a last feast, as great estates which had always produced for market were broken up, and as peasants met government confiscation of surpluses by raising only what they could eat. The harvest of industrial crops—flax, cotton, sugar beets, tobacco—fell to less than half the prewar figure. Barely a fourth as much coal was mined in 1920 as in 1913, and city dwellings went unheated through the severe Russian winter unless their occupants could find deserted houses to knock down for fuel. What little there was could not be effectively distributed because of the collapse of the transportation system. The nation in 1920 produced only a seventh as many locomotives and 4 per cent as many freight cars as before the war, and over half those in existence were not in working order. Real wages fell to a third the 1913 figure. The productivity of labor by 1920 was only a fourth as high as in 1913, partly because workers were woefully undernourished. Epidemics of typhus and cholera swept the land. And all through the period of civil war and intervention the nation was completely blockaded, although there was nothing with which to pay for imports had there been any.

The situation in the areas under White rule was even worse than that in Communist Russia. While the Whites controlled the agricultural districts, their confiscations discouraged production and the trampling armies made orderly farming impossible. Industry was concentrated in the provinces under Communist rule, and there was, of course, no trade between the food-producing area that needed the output of factories and the industrial area that was desperately in need of grain. In 1921 the situation was made worse by severe drought. Over thirty million Russians were starving that year and the next, and there were five million victims of famine and its attendant diseases. The American Relief Administration, directed by Herbert Hoover, was feeding ten million Russians during August, 1922, when the famine was at its worst.

By 1920, with victory in the Civil War in sight, the Bolshevik leaders pondered how to rebuild the nation's economy, how to make productive the desert they had conquered. At Trotsky's insistence they decided to apply the principles of War Communism to the problems of reconstruction. The Russian people, or all who were fit to work, became a labor army driven to work under military discipline. Men still in the army and others con-scripted for labor service marched to tasks assigned them—clearing and planting fields, restoring buildings, repairing equipment, reopening mines, gathering raw materials, rebuilding roads, collecting food supplies. Every citizen had to carry a labor book, in effect a passport, indicating his employ-ment record and present place of work. Those who avoided work were treated as deserters; those who shirked were assigned to punishment squads and put on short rations. But men resisted this militarization of labor. Peasant armies charged with weeding fields long unused in areas ravaged by civil war ran away to their own villages where there was plenty of weeding to be done. Town workers resented military discipline in civilian work. Early in 1921 the number of urban strikes and rural revolts mounted. The peasant sailors at the Cronstadt naval base mutinied in protest against the grain requisitions their families had to undergo; they called for freedom of speech and association for workers and peasants and the parties which spoke for them.

The Cronstadt mutiny, which was essentially an expression of peasant dis-content, convinced Lenin that War Communism could not go on. He knew he would have to find another way to stimulate agricultural production, for the cities where his strength lay had to have food. During the chaotic days of the Provisional Government the peasants had broken up the great estates of landlord and church, and now each had a plot of his own larger by a third than before the war. Never in Russian history had the peasant had such a proprietary outlook as he felt now. He hated the collectivization which the Bolsheviks were considering and wanted to farm his own land for all he could get out of it. Lenin realized that the first need was to get as much land sown as possible in this plowing season of 1921 and knew that without tractors and farm machinery collectivization would fail. He could only retreat in the face of peasant determination. Militarization of labor, dictation to the peasants of what they could plant, proscription of trade, abolition of money, free distribution of food, clothing, housing, and services—War Communism in all its phases would have to go. Collectivization of agriculture and socialization of industry could come later. The need now was to feed the nation.

THE NEW ECONOMIC POLICY

The Tenth Communist Party Congress, meeting in Moscow in March, 1921, agreed to Lenin's proposal that the government collect from the peasants a fixed tax in kind and leave them free to dispose of the surplus as they chose. The state would retain control of the "commanding heights"— the largest factories, transportation, banking, and foreign trade—thus preventing these strongholds of capitalist power from slipping into private hands which might seek to restore the old system. Small plants would revert to private ownership. Through a succession of orders the government inaugurated and expanded its New Economic Policy, the N.E.P.

Peasants were required to pay a tax, at first in kind and later in money, amounting to a percentage of the produce they raised beyond their own needs. This crude income tax encouraged the peasant to produce as much as possible, since most of it he could keep or sell. Private retail trading once more became legal, although only the state could buy and sell wholesale or engage in foreign trade. To stimulate farm output still more peasants were allowed to lease land from those who had more than they could handle, and by 1925 they were allowed to hire workers. The peasants responded slowly, perhaps suspiciously, to these enticements, but by 1927 agricultural production had returned to 1913 levels although the size of the nation had been considerably reduced by secession of the western borderlands.

All industrial units with fewer than twenty workers were restored to their former owners or leased to private operators. Larger plants remained under government management; these amounted to less than 10 per cent of industrial units, but they employed 85 per cent of the industrial workers. Plants which the state operated were grouped in combines or trusts in an effort to reduce centralization. Each trust and each production unit operated free of government restriction, seeking a profit, buying materials where it could get them and selling its products to any who would buy. Foreign capital was invited to invest in Russian enterprise, and Western technicians were brought in to teach their skills to Soviet workers.

With the legalization of private trading the government restored the use of money by stabilizing the ruble, issuing new currency with gold backing and calling in old paper money in exchange for the new. A State Bank to head the nation's credit system opened in 1921.

Lenin understood the risk he was taking in allowing this partial return to capitalism, but felt confident of his ability to restrict it. Through the twenties increasing limitations were placed upon "Nepmen," as private traders and small producers were called. By 1923 three-fourths of all retail trade was carried on by private merchants. But thereafter their taxes were steadily increased, the variety of goods they could sell was increasingly limited, and they were eventually denied the use of the railroads for transmission of their wares. Their share of private trade transactions fell from three-fourths of the total in 1923 to one-fourth in 1928 and to less than 6 per cent in 1930, after which they were driven out of existence. Private industrialists felt the same pinch. They accounted for 20 per cent of the nation's industrial output in 1925, but less than 6 per cent by 1930, and they, too, soon disappeared.

It was the government's hope that the New Economic Policy would win back the support of the peasants, who had turned against it during the period of War Communism. Certainly the position of the peasants was much improved by 1922 over what it had been earlier. The prices the peasant received for his produce were high, while the costs of the industrial goods he bought were low. Another year, however, brought declining farm income and rising industrial prices. The growing spread between the low prices the peasant received and the high prices he had to pay for the things he bought was referred to as the "scissors crisis." The government met it by fixing prices of industrial goods and raising the prices it paid the farmers for the grain they shipped to the cities. But the peasants never quite made up the gap. Like the American farmers, they suffered throughout the twenties a disparity in prices that was distinctly to their disadvantage. It was partly in an effort to relieve the plight of poor and "middle" peasants, partly because of the government's increasing difficulty in getting enough grain for the cities, that the leaders later abandoned the New Economic Policy.

By 1927 the Russian economy had recovered to prewar levels, about the same time, incidentally, that Western European nations could boast full recovery. By that year Russian agricultural production had come back to 1913 figures and industrial output had slightly exceeded them. Real wages for city workers had gone above their prewar level and, while farm income was lower than before the "scissors crisis," the peasants certainly were better off than in 1913.

PLANNING THE ECONOMY

The Fifteenth Communist Party Congress which met in December, 1927, came to some momentous decisions. It expelled Trotsky and the other leaders of the opposition from the party, thus blessing the triumph of Stalin over his personal enemies. Of far greater importance, however, it decided to begin an economic revolution aimed at completely socializing production.

Early in 1921 the State Planning Commission, or *Gosplan*, was created to draft an economic plan for the nation. Originally consisting of forty economists, accountants, and engineers, the organization grew steadily until it came to number thousands of experts working in scores of branch offices all over the Soviet Union. Every year from 1925 on the *Gosplan* suggested production figures and analyzed the nation's resources and potentialities. Then the Fifteenth Party Congress ordered the State Planning Commission to prepare a plan for the expansion of the national economy over the next five years.

The first of several such Five-Year Plans was put into operation on October 1, 1928, and the government decided to press for its fulfillment in a little over four years, by the end of 1932. "Minimal" and "optimal" programs were put forward and the party leaders chose the second, the more ambitious of the two. It assumed normal harvests through the period of the plan and also that foreign credits and trade would increase appreciably. Neither assumption proved valid—the 1931 and 1932 harvests were poor, and foreign trade dwindled when depression engulfed the world.

The First Five-Year Plan aimed at putting an end to private enterprise in industry, expanding industrial output and particularly that of basic industries, increasing electric power production six times over, mechanizing agriculture, and collectivizing at least a fourth of the nation's farms. The Second Five-Year Plan, to run through 1937, proposed to complete the collectivization of agriculture, to continue industrial expansion giving increasing attention to consumer-goods industries while carrying on with the development of basic industries, to improve the transportation net, to move strategic industries east of the Urals, and, as in every one of the plans, to continue the improvement and modernization of the armed forces. The third plan, scheduled for completion in 1942, aimed at further growth, at a slower rate, of the nation's basic industries and promised much greater production of consumers' goods, especially clothing and food. The plan was drastically altered in the face of the threatening international situation to meet expanding military needs. During the war there were only annual plans which concentrated upon requirements of the armed forces to the point where over 80 per cent of the nation's productive effort was going for weapons and war materials.

After the war the nation's planners shifted their attention back to peacetime needs while at the same time aiming to maintain a strong military establishment. The Fourth Five-Year Plan, announced in 1946 to be completed in 1950, proposed to clean up war damage, restore the economy, and raise industrial production above the prewar level. The fifth plan would continue industrial expansion of both basic and consumer-goods industries and provide for further investment in the nuclear weapons which had been indicated in the previous plan. The Korean War, in which Russian equipment was made available to both Chinese and North Korean forces, again brought a shift to military production. Stalin's successors modified the plan and promised to pay more attention to consumers' needs. Published in January, 1956, the Sixth Five-Year Plan proposed to increase industrial production by 65 per cent to bring it by 1960 to two-thirds the American figure and to raise agricultural output by half. It scheduled the erection of atomic power stations and the launching of an atom-powered transatlantic passenger liner. It emphasized the training of technicians, promised to double the number of schools, and offered Soviet citizens a better living through increasing home construction and boosting consumer-goods output by 60 per cent.

Each Five-Year Plan, itself filling several volumes, is supplemented by annual, quarterly, and monthly plans, plans for each area and subdivision, and plans for each segment of the economy. These give in detail figures which the national Five-Year Plan outlines only generally and may from time to time alter goals to keep pace with the changing international picture or with unforeseen internal developments such as a drought. Each Five-Year Plan, finally agreed upon by the Council of Ministers and then formally approved by the Communist Party Congress, involves the allocation of all human and material resources of the nation and the assignment of goals of output for every good and service produced. The planners decide how much of the national product may be consumed and how much will be invested; they determine the nature and volume of foreign and domestic trade, arrange the tax structure, and outline expenditures for running the government and providing for the armed forces. The Five-Year Plan aims at nothing less than ordering the economic and social activities and relations of every Soviet citizen and organization.

Planning the economy involves an intricacy of operational detail that seems to the person untrained in socialist economics to be productive only of hopeless confusion. For example, deciding upon the quantity of steel to be produced in a particular year requires coordinating the goals for every projected use of steel—locomotives and rails, automobiles, tractors, airplanes, ships, machine tools, buildings, bridges, guns, tanks, and thousands of smaller items. It poses the question whether to turn out ten million tons of steel in one plant, two, five, or ten and where to locate them. It must be based upon careful prediction of output of coal and iron mines, carrying potential of railroads, capacity of smelters, and convenience of power. It depends upon the availability of management and of labor, some of it possessing scarce skills. In the absence of unemployment, the decision to produce a certain quantity of steel will force the shifting of labor away from other employment. Once the workers are assembled they must be housed, fed, clothed, nursed, and entertained. If anything goes wrong any-where along the line there will be fewer locomotives or tractors or auto-mobiles or bridges; then the planners must choose which shall be sacrificed. Similar problems and many more face those who must plan for scores of crops, hundreds of industries, and thousands of plants. Students in capitalist countries often forget that their own economy must decide precisely the same questions. Under socialism, however, government officials make the decisions that under capitalism normally are made in the market place.

Fulfillment of the goals of the Five-Year Plans always has been uneven. Some goals have been exceeded, others have not been met. While all the plans have fallen down in some respects and achieved outstanding results in others, the first, particularly, turned out to be "a poor forecast of what actually did happen after its adoption" (Schwarz). Production of machinery and electrical equipment exceeded their goals by more than half, and 60 per cent of agricultural holdings were forced into collective farms instead of the 25 per cent the plan envisaged. But consumer-goods output reached only three-fourths the level planned, while production of heavy metallurgy, grain, and steel fell short of their goals by a third.

Sabotage, sloth, indifference to the fulfillment of the plan, absenteeism, ignorance, and difficult living conditions have held down performance. The government tries to counter these deterrents with wage incentives, rewards and punishments, an endless propaganda campaign designed to instill en-thusiasm and patriotism, and the stimulation of "socialist competition" wherein each shift or brigade tries to outdo the others in fulfilling and ex-ceeding its quota. Managers, under police serveillance if they occupy sensi-tive positions, frequently have been held accountable for their plant's failure to meet its goal. But plans have broken down most noticeably and most often in agriculture, where vagaries of weather are still beyond human control and individual sabotage is most difficult to detect.

With the accumulation of experience in planning, with the improvement of statistical techniques, and with the education of the scientists, economists, accountants, engineers, and other specialists necessary to staff the planning agencies, the organization of Russian production has steadily improved. That the bureaucratic confusion which it generates still has not been eliminated, however, has been admitted by Soviet leaders.

SOCIALIZED AGRICULTURE

At the beginning of the First Five-Year Plan four-fifths of Russia's popu-lation was classified as rural. There were twenty-five million peasant house-holds, half again as many as in 1917, for many had carved out small farms for themselves when the great estates were broken up. A very few held their farms all in one piece; the vast majority had several small plots scattered all over the township.

Here, in the conservative countryside, lay the heart of passive resistance to its own and the nation's progress. Imported tractors had been assigned to cooperatives, but they had been little used and left to rust out when they broke down. The peasant preferred to rely upon his horse or upon his own back for the power he needed. State-owned farms, or *sovkhozes*, had been organized on former imperial estates to set the peasants an example of good farming methods, but few had changed their age-old ways of doing things. Ever since the revolution the government had been encouraging peasants to throw their holdings together and pool their capital in a collective farm, or *kolkhoz*, a unit large enough to make practical the use of labor-saving machinery. But only one peasant household in sixty had joined a *kolkhoz* by 1928. The poor and "middle" peasants who made up the overwhelming majority raised five-sixths of the nation's grain, but they ate most of it and marketed only a tenth. The government had to find some way to increase their output.

Well-to-do peasants had grown still more prosperous during the years of the N.E.P., leasing more land and hiring labor as the government allowed them to do. They had some machinery, good buildings, herds of livestock, and enough money to lend to their neighbors at high interest rates. Their large farms produced much more than they could eat, and they sold the surplus not to the state but in the free market or fed it to livestock to reap a greater profit. There were under a million of these *kulak* families, but their relative affluence and their power as moneylenders and as renters of equipment and horses to their poor neighbors made them the object of bitter jealousy in every community.

There were several reasons why the party leaders decided to collectivize agriculture. Industry was largely government operated, and the Five-Year Plan proposed to nationalize the rest of it. To permit individualism in agriculture while pushing toward socialism in the rest of the economy would have been incongruous. The government proposed to abolish class in the cities; it could hardly allow the continued existence of poor, middle, and rich peasants in the villages. Furthermore, individual enterprise as the Russian peasant worked it was wasteful and inefficient. Large farm units using improved methods and modern equipment would produce much more than the small individual plots. Russian farmers in 1928 were marketing only a third as much as before the war. But while the flow of grain to the government was dropping, the urban population, much of which was fed through state-owned outlets, was rising. Finally, collectivization would make more effective use of labor and free thousands to fill the expanding needs of industry.

The government first tried persuasion to entice peasants into collective farms, favoring them with seed, credit, and the use of state-owned machinery. Some poor peasants, each with his ten acres or so, did join, but these timid ventures could hardly relieve the grain shortage. The *kulaks* and many middle peasants went on as before, thus setting themselves in opposition to the government and to the rest of the farm community. Furthermore, they refused to sell their surplus grain to the state at a time when the cities were feeling the pinch of shortages and high prices. Communist squads from the cities were sent into the villages to seize the surpluses of the *kulaks,* and poor peasants were encouraged to report their rich neighbors' hidden stores. Many *kulaks* burned their granaries and fled to the woods to carry on resistance, lynching the poor peasants who reported them and battling the Communist squads who went after them. When taken, they were shot or thrown into forced-labor camps and their goods and lands were confiscated. Through the fall of 1929 and the following spring the vengeful hunt went on. Many gave in to save their families and joined collective farms. But before they did so they killed their livestock and feasted, walking empty-handed like poor peasants into the *kolkhoz.* Between 1929 and 1933 the number of pigs and cattle in Russia fell off by nearly half and sheep and goats by two-thirds. Bitter *kulaks* even killed their horses, thus depriving the collective farm they joined of much-needed power. The poor peasants, on the other hand, joined the *kolkhozes* willingly. Without equipment and with only an animal or two they had everything to gain by doing so.

Enraged at *kulak* resistance, Stalin stepped up the rate of collectivization against the wishes of many party leaders. By the spring of 1930 well over half of all peasant families were living in *kolkhozes.* But industry was not yet turning out farm machinery in sufficient volume to meet the needs of collective farms. And it was suspected that many a resentful *kulak* had come into the *kolkhoz* with the intention of influencing its members to hide their grain and oppose the government. Finally, the peasants had joined the collectives, voluntarily or under duress, in such droves—ten million families in six weeks—that the resulting confusion threatened to disrupt the planting of the spring crop. In a letter to *Pravda* Stalin, who earlier had ordered "the liquidation of the *kulaks* as a class," now criticized what he called "dizziness from success" and blamed overzealous party members for forcing farmers into collective farms. Anyone who chose to leave the *kolkhoz* and take his animals and equipment with him now was free to do so. Within two months eight million families withdrew, leaving only six million families in the collectives.

Now a different kind of pressure was exerted to promote collectivization. Peasants who operated their individual farms were taxed at a higher rate than were collective farmers and were denied the use of state-owned machinery, which the government through its recently-organized machine-tractor stations rented out at low rates to *kolkhozes.* And peasants who joined collective farms were allowed to keep their gardens and garden tools, a cow or two, and a few chickens for their own personal use. This privilege broke the opposition of the middle peasants, and many moved back into the collective farms. By the end of the First Five-Year Plan fourteen million families, over half the peasant population, were members of *kolkhozes*. But Stalin himself admitted that collectivization had cost the Soviet Union ten million lives, a majority of them in Ukraine, where Nikita Khrushchev pushed the program. Another million or two families of *kulaks* and middle peasants had been deported to lumber camps in the Arctic Circle. Meanwhile the destruction of livestock and grain and the poor harvests which followed the disruption of rural life brought famine as severe as that of the early twenties.

By 1936, 90 per cent of the peasants belonged to nearly a quarter million collective farms which cultivated practically all the arable land not belonging to the state farms. During the next two years the number of individual peasant farms fell to a million, and they contained less than one per cent of the cultivated land of Russia. But the nation's leaders were still not satisfied. When punitive taxes did not eliminate individual farmers, the government restricted the amount of land they could farm to an acre or two. Since the average collective farmer had that much in his garden plot, those who continued to go it alone only spited themselves. The victory over peasant individualism had been won, but at a terrible cost. The nation had lost half its livestock, many farm buildings, and much equipment. American tractors had to be imported in 1933 to replace the fourteen million horses slaughtered by the rebellious peasants.

A *kolkhoz* is an association of peasants—averaging about eighty families prior to 1950—who have turned over their equipment, livestock, and land to a cooperative enterprise in which all work and income are shared. According to the government-drafted charter under which each collective farm operates, each member family is entitled to a house and an acre or two for a garden, both of which he must surrender if he leaves the *kolkhoz*. He may also own not more than one cow, two calves, two sows with their litters, ten sheep or goats, twenty beehives, and as much poultry as he can care for. All other livestock, buildings, and equipment belong to the collective.

Each *kolkhoz* operates under an annual plan which is geared to the national Five-Year Plan. While the *kolkhoz* soviet, to which all members belong, theoretically may decide what to grow, in practice the choice is made by the chairman of the soviet, who is responsible to superiors for the delivery to the government of certain crops to meet the national goal. Each member of the collective farm has two types of work to do: the work he does on his own garden plot and with his own animals, the income from which he may dispose of as he pleases; and the *kolkhoz* work he is required to do in the large fields and with the herds belonging to the collective enterprise. For the latter he receives a share of the net profits based upon the type and quantity of work he has done.

A part of the gross annual collective yield goes to the state at fixed low prices as obligatory delivery of produce which the government accepts as rent for the use of its nationalized land. Another fraction of the crop goes to the M.T.S., or machine-tractor station, as payment for the use of the combines and tractors which the *kolkhoz* has rented during the year. A third is set aside as seed and fodder and reserve for poor harvest. What remains, approximately a third, is divided among the members on the basis of the labor contribution each has made to the crop. Part of the annual livestock increase similarly goes to the government; the rest may be sold directly to consumers in the free market and the proceeds shared among the members. Of the crops and livestock, the government takes a fixed quantity, thus leaving the collective farm to shoulder the burden of crop failures and disease.

Collectivization of agriculture has failed to enlist the enthusiastic support of the peasants, and its weaknesses have plagued the state from the moment of its adoption. The low fixed prices which the government pays for the produce it takes have brought the farmer a paltry twenty cents for each working day he labors in the collective fields. As a consequence, the farmer works as few days as possible on collective land and spends his time intensely cultivating his acre or two of garden, whose produce he may sell at relatively high prices in the free market. Work on his own plot is more than twice as rewarding as that on collective land. Many avoided *kolkhoz* work altogether until, in 1939, the government ordered all *kolkhoz* members to work a minimum number of days in the cooperative fields. During the war the minimum was set at a hundred to a hundred and fifty days, varying from one region to another. Those who do not put in this minimum are fined and forced to do *kolkhoz* work for six months. Poor return on collective land has also encouraged farmers to expand their garden plots by edging their fence lines out into the collective fields. In 1951 farmers of Altai province were discovered thus to have "stolen" sixty-five thousand acres of *kolkhoz* land. Some collective farms are well managed and prosperous. One in Uzbekistan earned nine million rubles in money income alone in 1947, at the same time that many in western Siberia were earning twenty-five thousand rubles. In general, farm income is pitifully small and the peasants resent the fact that they have borne more than their share of the cost of the nation's industrialization.

After the second World War, and particularly after Stalin's death, the government took a number of steps to improve the plight of agriculture. The prices the state would pay for the crops it took as rent were raised substantially in 1953. The following year higher prices were announced for industrial crops, most of which the government buys. The new leadership understood that it must give in to the peasant's desire for better living if it expected him to increase his output so that city workers, too, might live better. In 1955 a delegation of Soviet farmers was sent into the American Midwest to observe methods there, especially to learn about the growing of corn and its use as livestock feed.

The most radical development in agricultural policy in the postwar period was the reduction of the number of collective farms by combining on the average three into one. From 250,000 *kolkhozes* in 1950, the number was reduced to less than 100,000. The average collective farm now enclosed over 4,000 acres of cultivated land and perhaps two or three times as much more in woodland and pasture. The members numbered two or three hundred families scattered in several villages several miles apart. It was hoped that fewer farms could be administered at less cost and that labor could be used more economically. The change also may have been intended to strengthen government control over agriculture by assuring the presence of one or more members of the Communist party in each *kolkhoz* soviet. But Khrushchev admitted in 1954 that the results of amalgamation had been disappointing. The difficulty of coordinating the labor of several villages without telephones and with few vehicles may have reduced rather than promoted efficiency.

In 1950, when he announced that amalgamation would begin, the Communist party secretary suggested that later on the nation should build "agrocities" containing five thousand people or more. The inhabitants would live in new apartment houses and enjoy all the cultural advantages of urban life. Each would have a piece of ground in a large community garden and would ride in a truck to work in the collective fields. But when the peasants protested vigorously, perhaps because their garden plots would come under closer supervision, Malenkov criticized Khrushchev for "forcing the pace," thereby implying that the subject might be raised again some time in the future. At least the leaders were testing new ideas in an effort to make farm life more attractive and to stop the drift of the able-bodied young into the urban centers. During World War II the nation's farms were tilled by old men, women, and children; the picture changed little with the coming of peace.

Ninety per cent of the land under cultivation lies in collective farms which produce seven-eighths of the nation's agricultural commodities. The rest of the output, except for that raised on an insignificant number of individual small acreages, comes from the state farms, or *sovkhozes*. Two thousand of these state farms, which run to five thousand acres or more, are operated by the government with hired laborers. The state takes the entire output and pays the workers the daily wage they earn. Fifteen per cent of the milk, meat, and wool which the government receives comes from its own farms. Many of them specialize in dairy cattle or in the growing of sugar beets, cotton, grain, or vegetables. Others serve as model or experimental farms. New state farms have appeared in the Baltic and Polish lands which were incorporated in the Soviet Union in 1939 and 1940.

Since World War II party leaders have criticized the *sovkhozes* for their overspecialization, their high costs of operation, their high labor turnover. Workmen have not been attracted to them because they often are situated in sparsely settled areas, housing conditions have been bad, and schools and hospitals have been poor or nonexistent. A building program designed to remedy some of these weaknesses got under way in 1954. The government's promise that each worker on a state farm would some day have his own home and garden was designed to encourage good workers to stay on the *sovkhozes*. In spite of their disappointing past, there was a possibility that the state farm might eventually replace the collective farm as the typical or even the sole type of agricultural organization.

In the twelve years following the adoption of the First Five-Year Plan Russian agricultural production moved out of the horse-and-wooden-plow stage into the stage of mechanization. In 1940 three-fourths of the nation's arable land was plowed by a half million tractors, twenty times as many as were in use twelve years earlier. Over two hundred thousand trucks and nearly as many combines helped farmers in 1940, while there was none of either in 1928. But most of this gain was lost during the second World War. What equipment was not requisitioned for the army or the Germans did not take away was worn out and not replaced.

Over the span of the first postwar Five-Year Plan, the fourth, Russian farms received about as many tractors and trucks and combines as they had been operating in 1940. By 1954 the number of all such machines had doubled, and many new types unknown to prewar agriculture had come into use. The government was still not satisfied and ordered increased production of machines of all types, particularly for use in harvesting cotton, potatoes, and sugar beets, where hand methods had previously prevailed. A fourth of Russia's collective farms were served by electricity by 1954, six times as many as before the war. The Sixth Five-Year Plan announced in January, 1956, called for doubling the grain output and increasing the production of meat by half and milk by 80 per cent. Much of this increase was to be made possible by expanded farm-implement production and by doubling the generation of electricity.

Crop rotation is universally followed and the use of commercial fertilizers is common, where both were hardly known before the revolution. The planting of trees in shelter belts to reduce wind erosion, begun under the last tsar, has been carried forward, and by 1950 there were four broad bands hundreds of miles long across South Russia. Irrigation projects had reclaimed eleven million acres of desert land by 1950, and projects for irrigating fifty million more were nearing completion or well under way by 1957.

During the First Five-Year Plan agricultural output in the U.S.S.R. fell 25 per cent. By 1940 it had climbed back to 1928 figures, and the bumper crop of 1937 had been still better. Shells and mines and marching armies had hurt the land badly during the war, and several growing seasons had passed before the land was fully reclaimed. Agricultural output has remained surprisingly low. Khrushchev admitted after Stalin's death that the 1952 totals were only 10 per cent above the 1940 output. During that twelve years Russia's population had grown by almost 10 per cent, partly from conquest and partly from natural increase. Yield per acre has risen considerably since 1928, as is to be expected from improved techniques, and the number of acres planted has vastly increased. Much more of the land has been sown to industrial crops, however, than was true of tsarist Russia, leaving the quantity of bread and vegetables available to each citizen not much greater than before World War I. What improvement there has been in food consumption has resulted largely from fairer distribution. This is especially true of meat products. In spite of Russia's territorial growth in the intervening years, the nation possessed fewer cattle, sheep, and goats in 1953 than in 1913, although there were 75 per cent more swine.

Agriculture has been in almost continual crisis since the adoption of the First Five-Year Plan. Whether that is so because of socialization or in spite of it no one could conclusively prove.

ADVANCES IN INDUSTRY

If agricultural production in the U.S.S.R. has been disappointing since 1928, the nation has made spectacular strides in industry. Soviet figures of expansion, based upon unreliable methods of statistical analysis, boast of a thirteenfold increase in industrial output between 1928 and 1950. Conservative Western estimates figure the rate of growth to have been about half that claimed by Russian statisticians. Nevertheless, the pace has been astounding, all the more remarkable in view of the crippling losses incurred during the second World War.

Soviet policy makers, recognizing that the military potential of the great Western powers rested upon heavy industry capable of turning out huge quantities of weapons, have concentrated through all the Five-Year Plans upon the production of capital goods—power installations, transportation facilities, minerals, oil, steel, rubber, chemicals, and the like—to the neglect of consumers' goods. Capital-goods production increased thirty times over in the quarter century following the adoption of the First Five-Year Plan while there was only an eightfold increase in the output of light industry whose products consumers use. Of the investment in plant construction during that period, only 7 per cent went into consumer-goods industry, a little more into agriculture, a fifth into transportation, and two-thirds into heavy industry. Here lies the key to the rapid growth of Russia's military potential and also the key to the fact that the nation's indisputable economic achievements have brought little to consumers. Soviet leaders have decided that such things as clothing factories will not be built, or will be kept to an absolute minimum, until the nation possesses enough steel mills to insure its adequate defense. So unswervingly have they followed this policy that during the early thirties the nation exported huge quantities of grain in exchange for machinery while thousands were dying of starvation.

During the First Five-Year Plan the government made an effort to get foreign investors to build plants in Russia, offering them liberal concessions to do so. Very few accepted the invitation, and the U.S.S.R. resigned itself to financing its own construction program. It did obtain equipment and the services of technicians from the United States, Great Britain, Germany, and France, some of it on short-term credit. By 1938 its foreign debts, which reached a peak of a billion and a half dollars, were paid off. During the second World War the U.S.S.R. received eleven billion dollars worth of war materials from the United States and two billion from Great Britain and Canada. The government received considerable gains in capital goods from Eastern Poland and the Baltic countries when those areas were incorporated into the Soviet Union just before the war. Further quantities of capital were confiscated in Manchuria and Eastern Europe in the closing days of the war. With these exceptions, which proved considerable between 1939 and 1945, the nation has financed its expansion from domestic sources.

In keeping with the party leaders' conviction that the Soviet regime must keep militarily strong to resist the expected capitalist attack, the Russian economy has developed industrial raw materials so that it might not be forced in wartime to depend upon foreign sources that might be cut off. The expansion of cotton growing and the development of the rubber-producing plant kok-saghyz were aimed at making the nation self-sufficient in those strategic items. The accumulation of uranium stockpiles from the output of mines in Soviet-occupied Germany after the war was meant to save Russian deposits of the ore. The geographic decentralization of industry has been inspired by the concern to reduce vulnerability in time of war. In tsarist times, and even as late as 1940, two-thirds or more of the nation's heavy industry was concentrated near Moscow and Leningrad and in the Ukraine. With the German advance in 1941 thirteen hundred plants were moved east of the Urals, although thousands of others could not be evacuated and were destroyed. The great dam in the lower Dnieper, built during the First Five-Year Plan and an achievement in which the nation took particular pride, was blown up by the retreating Russians. After the war the industrial areas of European Russia were restored, but many new plants were built in Siberia. Half the nation's steel, coal, and oil now comes from east of the Volga.

Much of the early construction of Russian industrial plants was carried through in feverish haste, for the party leaders, Stalin more than the others, expected the capitalist powers to unite in an effort to wipe out the socialist experiment. There were many costly mistakes and much work had to be done over. The government shared the German and American enthusiasm for establishing large units even in situations where smaller units would better have served Russian conditions and needs. By 1938, however, the planners realized the merit in fashioning industrial organization to the country's peculiarities. There was bitter criticism of "gigantomania," as the obsession with large units was called, and Trotsky's followers were blamed for the mistake.

The increases in the production of capital goods have been remarkable, and the recovery and progress registered since the end of the fighting in 1945 particularly so. Coal output reached four hundred million tons in 1956 and was scheduled to rise above six hundred million by the end of the Sixth Five-Year Plan in 1960. This would be more than four times the quantity mined in 1940 and over twenty times the amount Russia produced before World War I. Much of it came out of newly-discovered deposits in the Urals and Siberia, whereas the Donets basin provided most of the nation's coal in tsarist days. Petroleum output has grown from the prerevolution output of ten million tons to seventy-five million in 1956, and the Sixth Five-Year Plan proposed to double that figure by 1960. This would be slightly more than a third the volume of American production. The Baku and Grozny fields which the Nobels and Rothschilds developed before 1870 still are heavy producers, but since the second World War new fields have come into production east of the Caspian and on the west slopes of the Urals.

The nation used about a hundred and sixty billion kilowatt hours of electricity in 1956 and was expected to be using twice that amount four years later. This would raise the figure to about half that consumed in the United States in 1956. But the Russians had come a long way from the five billion kilowatt hours they consumed in the inaugural year of the First Five-Year Plan. Most of the electrical power in the U.S.S.R. comes from steam generating plants, although there are several large hydroelectric stations. The most famous of them all was constructed at the rapids in the lower Dnieper during the First Five-Year Plan under the direction of an American engineer, Hugh Cooper. A number of hydroelectric plants were to be built in Siberia during the period of the Sixth Five-Year Plan. A small five-thousand-kilowatt atomic power station was in operation in 1954 and several others of respectable size were projected. Over seven hundred electric plants of one type or another were under construction or being enlarged in that year. A power revolution has altered the nature of industrial and agricultural production since 1928.

Tsarist Russia was producing about four million tons of steel on the eve of World War I. At the depth of the Civil War practically none appeared, and not until 1928 did production recover to the prewar figure. Then output increased tenfold by 1955 and was supposed to reach seventy-four million tons in 1960, which would be about two-thirds the American output in 1956. Important steel works are located at Moscow and Zaporozhe on the Dnieper, but most Russian steel now comes from mills located in the Urals and Siberia. The plants are very large, but "gigantomania" seems to affect steel production everywhere.

During the First Five-Year Plan American, German, and British firms furnished much of the machinery that went into hydroelectric, steel, tractor, automobile, and other plants under construction. American and other engineers and technicians helped plan the enterprises. Russians who stood at the elbows of their foreign tutors learned their lessons well, and by the late thirties the nation was well supplied with its own engineers. During the second World War and for some time after tanks and not tractors were coming off the assembly lines. As late as 1950 Russia was turning out fewer tractors and combines than in the mid-thirties. Then the Fifth Five-Year Plan called for expanded output of farm machinery. In a bid for peasant support and greater agricultural production Stalin's successors ordered the manufacture of a quarter million tractors of various types by the spring of 1957. By the mid-1950's Russia was exporting large quantities of trucks, tractors, and other farm machinery as well as military equipment to Eastern Europe and Asia. This was less an evidence of the glut of Russian farm needs than of an effort to win friends in other Communist countries.

The Soviet government, like that of the other great powers, has allocated much of its budget since World War II to military preparedness and experimentation. In 1949 the first atomic bomb was exploded; a hydrogen bomb followed four years later. Jet fighters and bombers were added in great numbers to the Red Air Force and many were made available to North Korea and Red China after 1950. But not all such improvements were dedicated to war. Giant jet passenger planes were in operation on civilian routes in Russia in 1956, two years before a similar type was scheduled for service in the United States. Atomic bombs were used to move mountains of earth, and research in radioactive materials looked forward to their use in agriculture and medicine.

Soviet planners have shown much less concern for consumers' needs than for capital-goods production. Manufacture of food, clothing, and the like ordinarily has fallen far shorter of quotas than has production of dams, steel plants, and war materials. Much of the clothing and other items of consumer use has been of very shabby quality. Stories had it that Russian girls removed their swimming suits before going in the water lest they shrink and fade, that shoes wore out after a few days of use, and that cotton shirts and dresses shrank when rained upon. What commodities were manufactured were always in short supply. For instance, the shoe industry turned out one pair for every three citizens in 1929 and about the same number in 1945; by 1950 there was one pair, in 1956 there was a pair and a half, and four years later there would be two pairs for every consumer. After Stalin's death the party leaders promised that soon there would be more food and clothing of better quality and that television sets, washing and sewing machines, vacuum cleaners, and refrigerators, which thus far only those with the highest incomes could afford, would become more plentiful and cheaper. With the temporary relaxation of international tension following Stalin's removal, and with the consequent shift of two million men from the army to civilian pursuits, there was more likelihood that such promises could be fulfilled than at any time in two decades.

Russian progress in basic industry, where the planners have concentrated investment, is apparent from the fact that in 1928 the nation ran a poor fifth to the United States, Britain, France, and Germany in the production of coal, steel, and electricity, but in 1956 was producing as much coal, steel, and electricity as Britain, France, and West Germany combined. Even more impressive, the Sixth Five-Year Plan proposed to add to its already high levels of output facilities for producing as much new steel as West Germany was turning out, as much new coal as Britain was mining, and three-fourths as much new oil production as Britain, France, and West Germany combined were managing in 1955. While Soviet industrial output was still less than half the American figure in 1955, the planners promised that in another five years it would reach two-thirds and by 1965 or soon after would equal American production.

Each Soviet industry—coal, oil, chemical, automobile, aviation, electrical, building, food products, and the like—is headed by a minister who sits in the Council of Ministers, where all decisions affecting the entire economy are ultimately made. He oversees all production of the commodity or group with which he is charged, names major officials under him, and directs through others the planning, financing, hiring, manufacturing, and selling which the industry will do. In some cases he may be responsible for housing the industry's workers, maintaining retail outlets through which they purchase consumers' goods, operating technical schools to develop skilled workers, and even for publishing an industry newspaper. He may consult department heads under him; indeed, he has been encouraged to do so in the "collegial" atmosphere promoted since Stalin's death, but his is the final responsibility.

The basic unit in each industry is the enterprise, which may be a horizontal trust, an integrated vertical combination, or an individual plant. It is managed by a director who is responsible to his superiors and ultimately to the minister for the conduct and operation of the enterprise. This firm, which is a corporate entity suable and with the power to sue others in the courts, theoretically owns the buildings and equipment which the government has turned over to it, employs its own staff, maintains its own account in the State Bank and borrows from it when necessary, buys raw materials, sells its products to other enterprises or to retail outlets, and manages its affairs on a strict accounting basis. In very much the same way that a firm in a capitalist country performs, a Soviet enterprise estimates in great detail for each coming month or year the labor force it will require, the fuel, power, material, and equipment it will need, the bank reserves it must have to meet payrolls and other expenses, and even the profit it hopes to make. It predicts sales, arranges business transactions with other enterprises, prepares for plant expansion, and provides for retirement of worn and obsolete equipment. Thus, it operates under its own monthly and annual plans which are designed to mesh with industry-wide and national plans. Should an enterprise fail to meet its ordered output, or should it greatly exceed its goal, the entire national economy may be affected.

Yet the director of a Soviet enterprise is restricted in many areas in which the manager of a capitalist firm is free. The prices the enterprise charges for the goods it manufactures, the prices it may pay for raw materials and fuel, and the wages its workers may earn all are fixed by state authority. The size of his labor force is dictated to him. The plans he submits to his superior are subject to alteration. His supervision of the enterprise is constantly watched by the *Gosplan,* the State Bank, agents of the M.V.D. and the Communist party from the cell in his factory to the Presidium. If his enterprise fails to meet its quota or to satisfy the constant demand to reduce costs, he may be held guilty of "wrecking," sabotage, or even treason. If the enterprise exceeds its quota the director and exemplary workers may be awarded bonuses, decorations, citations, or paid vacations at a Crimean resort.

Producers' cooperatives, especially among disabled war veterans, were employing two million workers and making fifty billion rubles worth of various commodities in 1953. They are most important in the manufacture of furniture, boots, toys, and pottery, and turn out a third of all the ready-to-wear clothing Russians buy. The consumers' cooperatives which formerly operated some city restaurants and retail stores were abolished in 1949 to leave the government-owned trade outlets without competition. Since then the cooperatives have confined their activities to the villages, where they maintain small retail shops.

PROGRESS IN TRANSPORTATION

The effort of the government to modernize industry in the period of the First Five-Year Plan was hobbled by a transportation system out-of-date and nearly worn out during the war and revolution. The greater demands made upon it after 1928 threatened to exhaust the system completely. When the Politburo realized that industrial progress might be hamstrung by the failure of the transportation facilities to carry the burden, it boosted investment in railroads and assigned to one of its members, Lazar Kaganovich, the responsibility for building the nation a modern transportation net. The industrial accomplishments that the nation has witnessed, and indeed the operation of a highly centralized planned economy, would not have been possible had the step not been taken.

By far the most important transportation agency is the railroad system, which still handles over four-fifths of all the freight that moves in the U.S.S.R. Only 4 per cent moves by truck over the dirt highways, 6 per cent by coastal vessels, and 8 per cent by river barge and steamer. In 1956 there were slightly under a hundred thousand miles of railways in Russia, including the mileage in the Baltic States, Eastern Poland, Bessarabia, and East Prussia annexed since 1939. Much of the net was double tracked, notably the Trans-Siberian. During the First Five-Year Plan the Turkestan-Siberian, or "Turk-Sib" line, nine hundred miles long was completed, and a number of other long lines were built prior to 1945 in Siberia, between Moscow and the lower Don, and in the Urals. A "South Siberian" road paralleling the original Trans-Siberian for several hundred miles has been finished since the second World War, and another north of the Trans-Siberian to the Pacific shore may have been completed by 1957. Nearly as important as the extension of trackage are the vast technical improvements that have been adopted—more powerful locomotives, freight cars of greater capacity, automatic brakes, electrification of many lines, improved efficiency of personnel.

Despite the considerable accomplishments in railroad transportation the Soviet press complained in the 1950's of slow speeds, failure to run on time, and slow handling of freight. Passenger traffic is very light compared to that in Western Europe and America despite the fact that there are few private automobiles and only a few bus lines. Outside of officials moving back and forth across the country and workers riding into cities from outlying districts, people ordinarily do little travelling. The Moscow subway system, modelled after that of London but more ostentatious, carries millions of passengers a year.

The movement of people and freight long distances by truck, bus, and passenger automobile must wait upon the further development of hard-surfaced roads. Paved highways connect the main cities in the west, but there are few such roads east of Moscow and very few in Siberia. While local buses carry many to and from work and trucks move freight in the cities, until recently there have been few cross-country runs of either. The lack of service stations along the highways has discouraged long journeys by automobile. In 1951 *Izvestiia* reported that trucks going from Moscow to Kiev and back had to carry with them enough gasoline for the entire trip and that this reduced by a third the volume of freight they could haul. As late as 1939 there were only seven gasoline stations in all Russia. Some of these handicaps are being removed and some roads are being paved. Since 1950 Moscow freight lines have been extending out to nearby cities, and even to Leningrad nearly five hundred miles away. By 1955 upward of two million automobiles were in use in the Soviet Union, and the factories were adding nearly a half million a year, nearly 90 per cent of them trucks.

Some freight, particularly bulky commodities such as coal, oil, lumber, grain, and cement, is shipped on the rivers with which the Russian land is so bountifully provided. Nearly half the freight and a third of the passengers that use river transportation move over the Volga. Canal building, which has gone on intermittently since the time of Peter the Great, has also attracted Soviet officials. The most important canals dug since the revolution are the Baltic–White Sea or Stalin canal, the Moscow-Volga, and the Don-Volga which opened in 1952 and permitted traffic to move from the Caspian into the Black Sea and thence abroad. Soviet officials have frequently complained that the low-cost inland waterways are not sufficiently used and that plant directors persist in speeding their shipments by rail or even by airplane. But water transportation is highly seasonal, the rivers and canals and coastal seas being frozen over for a varying number of months each year.

Comparatively little freight moves by deep-water vessels along the coast, partly because the coastal waters are frozen through the winter but more especially because, with few exceptions, the population is concentrated inland. Only a few ships cross the oceans to other lands, for Russia owns less than one-thirtieth of the world's shipping. A few German vessels were seized as reparations after World War II, and during the war the United States loaned the U.S.S.R. a number of freighters whose return the Soviet government long postponed. The Sixth Five-Year Plan provides for the launching by 1960 of an atom-powered luxury liner to compete in the transatlantic tourist trade.

Travel and shipment of mail and small-package freight by air have always been popular in Soviet Russia. The enormous distances to be covered, the poor roads over most of the country, and the fact that many places are not touched by highway or railroad make flight both convenient and necessary. Contact with isolated spots can be made quickly simply by establishing scheduled air lines, whereas the building of roads or the laying of rails to such places would take years and involve a heavy investment. Regularly scheduled service now links Moscow with every provincial capital and all large cities. There are daily flights between Moscow and Vladivostok and regular service linking the capital with the capitals of all the Communist countries of Eastern Europe and Asia. Since Stalin's death regular flights have been scheduled to Sweden and France to encourage Westerners to visit the Soviet Union.

Of the communications media, all of which the government has extended to make possible the integration which economic planning requires, most use has been made of radio. News and propaganda as well as entertainment have been carried into every city and village over six million receiving sets, perhaps four-fifths of which before 1950 were set up in public places—community houses, offices, and restaurants. Television programs were being produced before the second World War, and the exploitation of this medium has grown rapidly since the war. The government hoped to produce a million sets in 1956, more than twice the number in existence at the beginning of the year. The sets are smaller than those in use in the West, many having five-inch screens. They are so expensive, however, that few individuals can afford them.

SOVIET FINANCE

During revolutionary days and well into the N.E.P. period the value of money dropped steadily and swiftly. Prices in January, 1918, were already twenty times the 1913 level. A year later the price index had gone to 164; a year after that it stood at 2,420; in 1921 the figure was 16,800 and in 1922 288,000. The end of the Civil War brought no relief; by 1923 prices had climbed to twenty-one million times their prewar level. When the inflation reached its peak in March, 1924, Russians had to pay sixty-two billion rubles for something that in 1913 cost one ruble. Soviet leaders at first were not concerned about runaway prices, insisting that the use of money had no place in a socialist economy. They even welcomed the growing use of barter, and requisitioned goods and made payments in kind for services the government required. Then they came to realize that money could serve the same purposes in a socialist as in a capitalist society: its use as a medium of exchange and a standard of value would permit refinements that simple barter could not measure. The currency was devalued in 1922 and again the following year in an effort to bring prices down to measurable and manageable levels. But only by increasing the production of goods and stopping the printing presses by which the government met its deficits could there be a return to financial stability.

A number of monetary reforms running over several years and completed in 1924 finally gave the nation a stable currency. The treasury called in the worthless currency and issued new paper rubles with gold backing, one of the new for fifty billion of the old. Silver and copper coins worth fifty kopeks or a half ruble and less also went into circulation along with a new monetary unit, the *chervonets* or ten-ruble note, issued by the State Bank, or *Gosbank*, in one-, three-, five- and ten-*chervonets* denominations. With the return to financial sanity, money again came into common use.

Rising employment and wage figures and the government's policy of concentrating upon the production of capital goods created consumer pressure and consequently rising prices through the early Five-Year Plans and during the second World War. The government deliberately let prices rise, slowly, to be sure, by comparison with the earlier inflation, to weaken consumer demand for scarce or nonexistent goods. By 1940 the Russian consumer was paying ten or more times as much for his food as in 1928. Food and clothing were rationed from 1930 to 1935 and from the time of Russia's entry into the second World War until the end of 1947. During such times, particularly in wartime, prices of such items obtainable in the free market without ration coupons rose to fantastic heights. As an extreme example, during the war a pound of sugar sold in Moscow ration stores for under two and a half rubles but brought five hundred in the free market.

In 1947 the government carried through a drastic currency reform, the first in over twenty years. It put an end to the two prices, ration price and open-market price, which had existed for many commodities for five years, and abolished rationing. It issued new currency exchangeable for the old in the ratio of one to ten, thus valuing the old rubles at ten kopeks instead of a hundred. New government bonds were exchanged for old at the rate of one ruble to three. Large bank accounts were marked down to lower figures but not at the severe rate the currency was deflated. The object in differentiating between holders of cash and bank depositors was to punish those, mostly peasants, who hoarded money instead of trusting their savings to the government banking system. The effects of the 1947 monetary reform were to redistribute wealth in favor of low-income groups and to reduce the threat of serious inflation. Three years later the government tied the value of its money to gold and reduced from five rubles thirty kopeks to four rubles the exchange rate with the American dollar.

The budget for the federal government of the U.S.S.R. provides revenues for expenditures in operating the central and some aspects of local government. Revenues and expenditures, which have approximately balanced over the years, doubled between 1938 and the war peak in 1944 and then more than doubled again in the next decade. The chief source of income is the so-called turnover tax, a sales or excise tax, which produces 40 per cent but at one time accounted for 60 per cent of federal revenue. It is levied at different rates upon different commodities and even at different rates on the same commodity in different localities. The producer—the food processor or the factory director—pays the tax to the government on each unit of his output and then passes it on to the consumer. The tax is regressive in effect, taking a greater percentage of small incomes than of large ones. For example, about two-thirds of the retail price of beef, butter, and potatoes and three-fourths or more of the price of sugar, cigarettes, and vodka were made up of turnover tax. The several price reductions ordered in the post-Stalin period have been made possible by cutting the turnover tax on consumers' goods.

The federal government also collects profit taxes from industry, assessing each enterprise a percentage of its planned profit whether it materializes or not. Import duties, which are passed on to consumers as in capitalist countries, account for perhaps 2 per cent of the federal budget. Local governments tax houses and business property and livestock kept in cities. The U.S.S.R. levies income taxes on individuals who work for the state, exempting the first two hundred and sixty rubles and applying rates progressively on higher incomes to a maximum of 13 per cent on everything over a thousand rubles a month. Self-employed workers, writers, and the like pay much higher rates reaching to 80 per cent of income over seventy thousand rubles a year. All taxes taken together, Soviet workers turn over to the government about 60 per cent of their income in taxes. On the other hand, the state provides them many services which, in a capitalist economy where tax rates are lower, they would have to purchase from other private individuals. The government balances its deficits in the same way that capitalist governments do—that is, by selling bonds to its citizens, banks, and insurance companies.

The central bank in the U.S.S.R. is the *Gosbank,* or State Bank, which operates branches in every large city. It serves as a bank of issue of all currency, handles the government's accounts and collects its taxes, and extends short-term credit on interest to economic enterprises or social organizations. The government also operates long-term credit institutions, one to handle borrowings by industry, another for farm loans, and a third to lend to trading organizations. There is also a host of savings banks where individuals may earn interest on deposits. In 1947 there were thirty million accounts averaging four hundred rubles, stored up during the war when consumer goods were scarce. Fear of the inflationary pressure which these deposits would create prompted the government in that year to "reform" or devalue bank holdings as well as currency.

FOREIGN TRADE

The economic relations of the U.S.S.R. with other nations are monopolized by the state and directed through its agencies. The minister of foreign trade, subject to limitations imposed by the Council of Ministers, arranges trade agreements with other powers, plans for the import and export of commodities, arranges foreign credits, and directs the settlement of balances. The quantity and type of goods to be bought or sold abroad are specified in the five-year and annual plans which imports and exports are designed to further. State corporations supervise the handling of particular commodities: *Mashinoimport* monopolizes the importation of equipment and machinery; *Intourist* manages the travel of foreigners in the U.S.S.R.; *Eksportkhleb*—*khleb* is Russian for bread—directs both purchase and sale of grain and grain products. Each corporation operates independently, as do industrial enterprises. A branch of the Foreign Trade Ministry functions under the Russian Embassy in each country to represent Soviet export and import corporations in their dealings with foreign buyers and sellers. For example, the *Amtorg,* or American Trading Corporation, arranges trade with American manufacturers and merchants.

Foreign trade is used deliberately as a political force. Investments in allied and satellite countries, export of machinery to them in exchange for raw materials, and the reduction of trade with unfriendly powers have characterized Soviet trade policy since World War II. Before the war, however, foreign trade relations were conducted less for political than for economic gain. The purchase of machinery and technical skill speeded up the industrialization program during the early Five-Year Plans, and such purchases were paid for by export of grain and raw materials. On the eve of war the government's concern to amass reserves of strategic materials influenced foreign trade patterns. Except for the war years, when the Soviet Union obtained huge quantities of both military and nonmilitary goods, Russia's share of world trade has been insignificant—3 or 4 per cent. The leaders have studiously followed a policy of attempting to increase the nation's self-sufficiency so as to free the country from hazardous reliance upon foreign sources that may dry up in time of tension. Russia is no longer dependent upon foreign cotton, for example, since the growing of cotton in southern Siberia was stimulated in the thirties. Reliance upon Western Europe and the United States for machinery and technical knowledge has given way to an ability to provide them to others. Russian delegates to a world conference of communists held in Cairo in 1958 offered loans to noncommunist nations "without strings attached," an unmistakable reference to American policy of granting economic aid in return for commitment to the West.

THE WORKER AND HIS HIRE

One of the most striking aspects of Soviet economic development has been the growth in the size of the nonagricultural labor force. The number of men and women so employed rose from less than six million in 1924 to nine and a half million four years later and to twenty-eight million in 1938. During World War II the number dropped by a third as much of the industrial area fell under enemy control and the manufacture of many consumers' goods was reduced or suspended. By 1945 the size of the nonagricultural labor force had recovered to about what it was in 1938. By 1948 it had risen to thirty-three million, by 1953 to nearly forty-five million, and by 1956 to roughly fifty million, or one out of four in the population. This growth may be accounted for only in part by the rise in population figures from a hundred and forty million in 1924 to two hundred million in 1956. The percentage of the population engaged in nonagricultural industry has risen in that period from slightly over four to twenty-five. Primarily, the increase has been made possible by shifting men and women from farming to industry, trade, transportation, and the services. This could be done as farm areas, always overpopulated, were drained of young people and as the mechanization and collectivization of agriculture released still more workers to the cities. Unemployment offices closed down when the government announced in 1930 that there were no more unemployed. Soon there was a labor shortage, and the government resorted to pressure to force wives and youths to go to work when the rising cost of living was not sufficient inducement to do so. By 1940 women made up a third of the nation's labor force.

The pressing demand of every enterprise for labor, and the ease with which anyone could obtain employment, created in workers an inclination to drift from one job to another in search of better working and living conditions. Directors bid against each other, particularly in the housing they could offer, for the services of workers, particularly the skilled. Ninety per cent of the average plant's labor complement in 1935 had served the enterprise less than a year. Many did not stay long enough to complete training for the job, while others left at the moment they became most useful. The government moved to reduce this labor turnover, forbidding wage increases for any skilled worker who left the job without permission of the plant director and suspending from industrial employment, with its higher wages, those who floated from one job to another. Those who quit their jobs could be evicted from the plant's housing facilities and their ration cards for food and clothing withheld by the plant director. It became illegal to hire anyone who did not have a release from his previous employer. Tardiness and absenteeism without a doctor's consent came to be punished by fines and loss of preferred jobs. After 1938 everyone who worked for a government enterprise, which meant all but a few, was required to carry a labor book showing his employment record, punishments, rewards, and reasons for leaving earlier jobs. For a director to hire anyone not presenting his labor book in good order, to be held by the employer until released, was illegal. By 1940 those who left their jobs without permission, except to attend school or because of health, could be sentenced to several months in prison. Unexcused absence from work was punishable by freezing the worker to the job and fining him a fourth of his wages.

During World War II the government further tightened restrictions upon the worker's freedom to choose his employment. Skilled workers were assigned to plants wherever they were needed without consideration of their preferences. Boys fourteen and girls sixteen years of age were drafted for enrollment in technical schools and after graduation had to work wherever the government sent them; those nineteen or over with physical disabilities were assigned to jobs in mining or industry to take up the slack of army recruitment. Workers in defense industries were frozen in their jobs and were charged with desertion if they left. Before the war was a year old over half the workers in nonagricultural employment were women.

Many of the restrictions upon the worker's freedom of choice of his job continued long after the war. The labor book was still in use in 1955; punishments for absenteeism were still severe; students in technical schools and colleges still were under government orders for years after graduation. In 1956, however, the worker's freedom to leave his job without official permission was restored. In the postwar period the government kept up its pressure to force people to work at something. Adults who were unemployed, including mothers, received smaller ration allowances than did workers. But the continued high cost of living was most effective in prompting married women to add to their husbands' income. The reduction of the armed forces in 1953 and the post-Stalin amnesty had the effect, whether by design or not, of bringing more people into productive employment. There was continued and increased emphasis upon the training of skilled workers and the education of professional people. In 1954 there were fifty-four thousand graduates of engineering schools, about three times the number turned out by similar schools in the United States.

During the early Five-Year Plans the working day in Russia was seven hours and the employee worked four days and rested the fifth, changed later to five days of work and one of rest. By staggering the rest days of his force, a plant director could operate his equipment at full capacity every day in the year, and by hiring three shifts of workers, he could keep his enterprise going day and night. In 1940 the work week was changed to six days, with the seventh, normally Sunday, the rest day. At the same time the eight-hour day was adopted to make the work week forty-eight hours long.

During the war a worker could be forced to work three additional hours a day, receiving half again as much pay for the extra hours, so that the average worker put in sixty hours a week. Children under sixteen could not be worked more than ten hours. Vacations, to which in peacetime employees are entitled at the rate of two weeks a year, were not allowed between 1941 and 1945, and the worker was paid for the vacation he surrendered. The Sixth Five-Year Plan reduced the workday to seven hours and the work week to forty.

Until well into the period of the First Five-Year Plan labor unions worked out job classifications and wage scales in negotiation with plant directors and industry leaders. Since 1930 the government has determined wage rates without consultation with trade-union representatives. Wages are paid either on a piece-rate basis—so much for each unit of output—or by the hour, day, or week, in which case the worker must turn out so many units—his norm. If he exceeds the norm he may receive a bonus; if he does not meet it his wages are reduced by a certain percentage. The average nonagricultural worker received an annual wage of seven hundred rubles in 1928, eight hundred a year later, over fifteen hundred in 1933, three thousand in 1937, four thousand in 1940, six thousand a year after the war, and nine thousand in 1953. But while money wages have risen steadily, they have not kept up with rising prices. Real wages actually were less in the latter year than they were twenty-five years earlier. In terms of food prices in Moscow, the average worker earned half as much in the mid-thirties as in 1928, a little more than a third as much in 1948 as twenty years earlier, and still in 1953 only 90 per cent his 1928 wage.

If the average worker had to pay out a growing percentage of his income for food, the lot of the artist or scientist, the efficient skilled worker, or the person fortunate enough to be employed in some certain favored industry or in government administration steadily improved. Those party leaders who favored progress toward equalization of wages for all jobs were outvoted, and the regime moved more and more in the direction of appealing to the individual's self-interest through differential pay to stimulate production. During the Second Five-Year Plan some workers were already earning nearly thirty times as much as others. Information published on 1949 incomes indicated that, while the average nonagricultural wage was a little over six hundred rubles a month, many received less than three hundred while outstanding workers earned ten thousand or more a month. College teachers earn eight times as much as the average industrial worker, and those few who are members of the Academy of Sciences receive a monthly bonus of five thousand rubles. Successful authors and composers, high government officials, and directors of large enterprises earn still more, while the winner of a Stalin Prize may receive two hundred thousand rubles in one sum, twenty-two times the average worker's annual income.

One day in 1935 Alexei Stakhanov, a coal miner, by improving his own and his helpers' methods, cut over a hundred tons in six hours and earned for the day's work two hundred and twenty-five rubles, more than the average miner's monthly wage. His record was later broken, but he gave his name to those who emulated his speedup methods. Stakhanovites were publicly acclaimed as heroes, but many workers must have cursed them. The government thenceforth frequently raised the norm or standard day's work, not only for coal miners but among all types of workers, reasoning that if Stakhanov could cut a hundred tons the average worker certainly could cut six or eight or ten or more in the same time.

In the most modern and well-managed plants in the U.S.S.R. the efficiency of the worker, the volume of his hourly output, is as high as that of a comparable worker in the United States. The average worker in the average plant, however, lags far behind the average in American, British, or German enterprises. Nevertheless, the productivity of labor has increased several times over since the revolution as equipment, techniques, and skills have steadily improved. Output suffers from the employment of too many men to do a job, from having to employ several at supporting tasks to keep one man at the bench. Twice or thrice as many Russians are needed to turn out the same volume of goods as Americans working in a comparable plant. Soviet leaders have admitted as much and have striven mightily to build up the efficiency of their workers.

During the first decade of the Communist regime trade unions functioned in some ways as they function in a capitalist economy. Their leader, Michael Tomsky, insisted that the unions must be independent, that they must fight for the interests of the workers against industry leaders and bureaucrats just as capitalist unions fought employers. Through the N.E.P. period the Russian unions negotiated wage contracts and worked out with the proper officials the job classifications for each industry. Stalin, however, insisted that unions must be subservient to the state which hired their members, that they must serve state ends, and that in opposing the government and its agents in a socialist state they were opposing their own interests. The victory went to Stalin before the First Five-Year Plan got under way, and Tomsky gave way to Shvernik, who was of Stalin's mind.

Ostensibly, membership in the labor unions is voluntary, and over 90 per cent of those eligible belong. Union members enjoy greater social-insurance benefits and other advantages which nonmembers do not receive. The unions are of the industrial rather than the craft type. The basic unit is the factory or shop union, which belongs to a district organization, and so the pyramid rises through regional and republic associations to the All-Union Trade-Union Congress whose assembly speaks for all organized workers. Communist party influence is strong at all levels. The unions administer the social security programs and distribute payments for disability, old age, blindness, and the like. They maintain rest homes, children's camps, vacation resorts, libraries, clubs, gymnasia, and swimming pools and organize mutual-loan societies for their members. They carry on educational work, seek ways to improve skills, and organize "socialist competition" to increase production. They do not negotiate wage contracts or press for improved working conditions, and only "participate in" settling labor disputes. The right to strike, which is fundamental to free trade unionism, the Russian unions do not enjoy.

Inmates of forced-labor camps also constitute part of the nation's labor force insofar as the products of their work contribute to national output. The camps are under the direction of the Ministry of Interior, the M.V.D., which is responsible for certain types of enterprise. Five per cent of the coal and 40 per cent of the chromium mined, 11 per cent of the lumber produced, and a fifth of the railroad ties fashioned in 1941, the only year for which statistics are available, were turned out in the camps of the M.V.D. Work on the Don-Volga canal, oil production in the Arctic, road construction, and even the manufacture of some consumers' goods were engaged in by the prisoners of the secret police. Political opponents of the government, *kulaks,* prisoners of war, and common criminals make up the work force of the labor camps. The number of prisoners is a closely guarded secret, but Western estimates have varied from two to twenty million. In 1956 American newsmen were told by Soviet officials that the volume of forced labor was rapidly dwindling, but whether it would ever be completely abolished no man could say.

THE STANDARD OF LIVING

The consumer obtains the goods he buys through a network of state-operated retail stores in the cities, at cooperatives in the villages, and from the free town markets where farmers sell their surplus produce. In the chief cities the government maintains large department stores which sell everything imaginable on the order of similar stores in the United States and England. Prices are set by the state for all goods sold in government and cooperative stores, but produce sells in the free market for whatever it may bring.

Prices have risen sharply since the beginning of the First Five-Year Plan. Moscow food prices, for example, doubled during the course of the first plan and then increased four more times over by 1935. On the eve of World War II the same prices were twelve times and by 1948 nearly thirty times those obtaining in 1928. Almost every year thereafter the government reduced prices, preferring, after the earlier experience with inflation, to cut prices rather than raise wages.

Real wages have fallen as prices rose, for money wages have never kept pace with retail prices. The year 1928 was probably the best the Soviet wage earner and consumer have known. In 1948, when prices were nearly thirty times as high as twenty years earlier, wages were less than eleven times as high as in the base year 1928. The average Moscow worker in 1953 had to work twice as long for a pound of bread as did the average New Yorker, five times as long for his beef, six and seven times as long for his milk and eggs, ten times as long for a cotton dress for his wife, and sixteen times as long for a woolen suit for himself. He had to put in thirteen working days to earn enough for a pair of leather shoes and nearly two months for his suit. In that same year he was forced to work nearly twice as long as in 1928 for the same quantity of essential foods.

By 1954 prices had been reduced to the point where they were only fourteen times as high as those in 1928, while the average wage was about thirteen times what it was in 1928. The Soviet worker had nearly but not quite reached the real-wage level he enjoyed at the beginning of the First Five-Year Plan. He had, of course, survived a very costly war and he had paid for an industrial plant that promised much better living in the future.

Most housing is provided for urban residents either by the municipality or by factories whose dwellings are reserved for their employees. There are a few privately-owned homes and some that are owned by cooperatives. If he lives in a government-operated or factory-maintained house the occupant pays a low rent, amounting to 2 or 3 per cent of his income. Living space has always been rationed, for the nation has never overcome a serious housing shortage. Each Five-Year Plan promised extensive construction, but each fell far short of its goal. Cities were flooded with people leaving the farms to work in the rapidly expanding industries. As Moscow's population doubled to over four million between 1926 and 1939, the housing available to them increased by only 70 per cent. The average space allotted to each citizen was only slightly more than half the average available to Muscovites before the first World War. Of course, it was more equitably shared. By 1950, when the city's population had passed five million, the average person had 10 per cent less space than in 1939. Typically, a family of four or five lives in one room, sharing the kitchen and bath with four or five other families.

During World War II over half the city housing and a fourth of farm homes in the war zone were destroyed or damaged and there was little rebuilding or new construction until the fighting was over. Refugees fleeing before the German advance further overcrowded the cities in the unoccupied area until conditions must have been almost intolerable. Each Five-Year Plan after the war made generous provision for new housing, and by 1953 there was about as much space available to the average city dweller as he had known fifteen years earlier. The Sixth Five-Year Plan was most am-

View of the Kremlin from the Moscow river.

The Politburo in 1949, from a painting by the Soviet artist, Nalbandian. From left to right: Molotov, Shvernik (both seated), Bulganin, Mikoyan, Khrushchev, Stalin, Andreyev, Beria (seated), Kosygin, Voroshilov, Malenkov (seated) and Kaganovich.

bitious, proposing to double the amount of urban housing by 1960. Government officials have publicly admitted that the provision of adequate housing for its citizens is one of the most critical problems facing the nation.

Stalin's successors showed much more concern for the welfare of the consumer than had ever been shown before. But, after nearly forty years of Russian socialism, the average citizen still had to content himself with promises of things to come.

SUGGESTED READING

Arakelian, A., *Industrial Management in the U.S.S.R.* (Washington, D.C., Public Affairs Press, 1950).

Baykov, A., *The Development of the Soviet Economic System* (New York, Macmillan, 1946).

Bergson, A., *Soviet Economic Growth: Conditions and Perspectives* (Evanston, Illinois, Row, Peterson, 1953).

Bienstock, G., S. M. Schwarz, and A. Yugow, *Management in Russian Industry and Agriculture* (New York, Oxford University Press, 1944).

Carr, E. H., *The Interregnum, 1923–1924* (New York, Macmillan, 1954).

Chamberlin, W. H., *Russia's Iron Age* (Boston, Little, Brown, 1934).

Deutscher, I., *Soviet Trade Unions; Their Place in Soviet Labor Policy* (London, Royal Institute of International Affairs, 1950).

Dobb, M., *Soviet Economic Development Since 1917* (London, Routledge, 1948).

Grinko, G. T., *The Five-Year Plan of the Soviet Union* (New York, International Publishers, 1930).

Hubbard, L. E., *The Economics of Soviet Agriculture* (New York, Macmillan, 1939).

Jasny, N., *The Socialized Agriculture of the U.S.S.R.* (Stanford, Stanford University Press, 1949).

———, *The Soviet Economy during the Plan Era* (Stanford, Stanford University Press, 1951).

Kulski, W. W., *The Soviet Regime: Communism in Practice* (Syracuse, Syracuse University Press, 1954).

Miller, J., *Soviet Russia* (London, Hutchinson University Library, 1955).

Schwarz, H., *Russia's Soviet Economy* (New York, Prentice-Hall, 1954).

Schwarz, S. M., *Labor in the Soviet Union* (New York, Praeger, 1951).

Simmons, E. J., *USSR: A Concise Handbook* (Ithaca, Cornell University Press, 1947).

Volin, L., *A Survey of Soviet Russian Agriculture* (U.S. Government Printing Office, 1951).

Vucinich, A. S., *Soviet Economic Institutions: The Social Structure of Production Units* (Stanford, Stanford University Press, 1952).

Yugow, A., *Russia's Economic Front for War and Peace: An Appraisal of the Three Five-Year Plans* (New York, Harper's, 1942).

30

Social and Cultural Developments

While tsarist russia was essentially a nation of villages, Soviet Russia is rapidly becoming a nation of cities. Before the first World War barely 15 per cent of the people lived in cities, but in 1956 44 per cent of the nation's two hundred millions did so. The population is comparatively young, nearly two-thirds of it being under thirty years of age in 1939, the year of the last general census. While the nation's leaders boast of having built a classless society, there are wide differences in income and the recognizable strata—peasants, unskilled workers, skilled laborers, managers, and intelligentsia—show signs of crystallizing into hereditary groups.

The government has made admirable progress in educating the minorities which make up about a fourth of the population of the U.S.S.R., practically eliminating illiteracy where it had been nearly universal under the tsars and developing an alphabet among peoples who had known only a spoken language before. It has swept away feudal social customs and encouraged, to a degree, the retention of folkways peculiar to each people. The Jews fared well under the Communists until after World War II, when there was a revival of anti-Semitism.

The state provides comprehensive social security benefits to its workers, while collective farms care similarly for their own members. Government employees are entitled to retirement pay, accident compensation, and health insurance, the amount of the payment depending upon the length of time the insured has been employed. The cost of the program is shared between the government and the enterprise which hires the worker, who himself contributes nothing from his wages. Women are encouraged to work and receive full pay during pregnancy leaves. Many have gone into the professions, while others have accepted heavy physical jobs normally held by men in other lands. The emancipation of woman at first was taken to mean liberalizing marriage and divorce laws. But when, in the eyes of the nation's leaders, the laws were abused the government made divorce less easy to obtain and began to emphasize the importance of the family.

In its dealings with organized religion the Soviet government has progressed from the extreme of trying to destroy the church to the extreme of restoring the Patriarchate which Peter the Great had abolished. The Communists early decreed the separation of church and state, nationalized all church property, forbade religious instruction in the schools, disfranchised the clergy and denied them ration cards. Bishops and priests were shot, exiled, or imprisoned for resistance, overt or suspected. The state carried on a determined propaganda campaign designed to convert the masses away from religion and closed churches or assigned them to nonreligious uses. It preached atheism in the schools, opened anti-God museums to ridicule the church, and organized the League of Militant Atheists to direct the antireligious campaign. During the First Five-Year Plan the government relaxed the pressure upon the church, hoping to reduce the resistance of the peasants to collectivization by slowing down the attack upon their religion. During the early 1930's religion was tolerated, but it again came under attack during the 1937–1938 purge, when many clergymen were arrested and many churches closed. During World War II the various denominations were mildly treated and the Russian Orthodox church recovered something like its official position under the tsars. The Patriarchate was restored and the government forbade any interference with religious practices. By 1956 the churches of Russia were prosperous and well attended, but by old people rather than by young. Presumably the government believed that, with the schools instructing the nation's children against it, religion would eventually die out.

The early efforts of the government to enroll every child and many adults in school were frustrated by shortage of buildings, equipment, and teachers. By 1955 the shortages had been reduced to the point where all city children were required to finish ten years of schooling and all farm children seven. From 1917 on the Soviet leaders carried on a vigorous campaign against the illiteracy which three-fourths of the population suffered; forty years later it had been virtually eliminated. In 1956 one out of four citizens was in school. Soviet education has tended to emphasize science, mathematics, and engineering to free the nation's industry from its early reliance upon foreign technicians.

The state has recruited its literary and artistic talent to contribute to the aims of the new society. Each artist is expected to use whatever medium he works in to educate the people in socialism, to encourage them to greater effort, to keep them looking toward and striving for a brighter future, to humiliate the laggard and the inefficient, to marshal support in defense of the country, and to support whatever at the moment happens to be Communist party policy. To the extent that he succeeds in doing so the artist enjoys material reward and recognition. To the extent that he fails he is ignored or ridiculed and denied access to the state-controlled means of obtaining an audience.

POPULATION TRENDS

The Soviet government twice has taken a general census, in 1926 and again in 1939. Several careful estimates have been made since the last census, the most recent published in June, 1956. The population of the U.S.S.R. in 1926 was 147,028,000, nearly 40 per cent above the total in 1897, the year of the last tsarist census, in a territory shrunken by loss of border areas after the revolution. By 1939 the same area held over 170,000,000. In the year following August, 1939, the state added an estimated twenty-two million in Eastern Poland, the Baltic States, and land acquired from Romania. Two and a half million more came in during and after World War II. Some Western estimates gave the nation as many as 220,000,000 in 1956, but the Soviet government reckoned the population at just over two hundred million in June of that year.

The density of the population varies from a hundred and eighty per square mile in the Ukraine to six in the Kazakh Republic, from densely-packed cities like Leningrad and Moscow to vast uninhabited stretches in Siberia. Only 6 per cent of Soviet citizens occupy two-thirds of the national territory, while nearly half the population lives in 6 per cent of the land.

The steady growth of urban and the relative decline of rural elements in the population have distinguished the years since the inauguration of the First Five-Year Plan. On the eve of the first World War about 15 per cent of all Russians lived in cities. The percentage had grown to 18 by 1926, to about 33 by 1939, to 40 by 1953, and to nearly 44 by 1956. In the latter year eighty-seven million of Russia's two hundred millions were classified as city dwellers. Part of the growth was due to a much higher birth rate in cities than in rural districts, part to the flow of young workers from country to town as job opportunities opened in expanding industries. Eighty Russian cities increased their population ten times over in the thirty years following the revolution. Sixty-seven new cities sprang up during the years of World War II, most of them in the Urals and Siberia. Moscow led all others in 1956 with five and a half million, while Leningrad numbered three and a half million. Kiev, Kharkov, and Gorky had about a million each and Novosibirsk was approaching a million, while around six hundred thousand lived in Omsk, Baku, Odessa, Tashkent, Tiflis, Rostov, Kuibyshev,

Sverdlovsk, Chelyabinsk, Kazan, Saratov, Riga, Dnepropetrovsk, and Kazan.

World War II forced a radical shift of population from western to eastern provinces and from European to Asiatic Russia. Well over a fifth of all Soviet citizens were living east of the Urals in 1956. The percentage must have been much greater during the war, but many returned west on the heels of the retreating Germans. With the threat of atomic war, the government followed a policy of dispersing rather than concentrating its people.

More than any other great power, the U.S.S.R. is a nation of youth. The Civil War, the famines, and the collectivization of agriculture took heavier toll among old than among young people. By 1939 nearly two-thirds of the population were under thirty years of age and almost half of these were under twenty. War deaths fell most heavily among young people, but still more than half the postwar population had been born after the revolution. As medical advances and improved sanitation brought a declining death rate, which fell from thirteen to less than nine per thousand between 1951 and 1953, the median age of Russians rose perceptibly. And the postwar years witnessed a falling birth rate in spite of the government's promotion of large families.

There has been a growing tendency since the mid-1930's toward stratification in Soviet society. Some party leaders through the first decade of the regime had urged equalization of incomes, but the government soon fell back upon piece-rate wages and income differentiation to provide the incentive to greater effort and greater output that the Five-Year Plans demanded. Different levels of income do not necessarily produce different classes, however. Stalin himself was confused over whether classes could exist under socialism. In 1934 he insisted that socialist society meant a classless society. But two years later he changed his mind and announced that there were two classes of Soviet citizens, workers and peasants, but argued that there was no antagonism or conflict of interest between them. He identified a third group or "stratum," the intelligentsia, which was recruited from the workers and peasants.

Incomes vary widely among the peasants, among the workers, and among the intelligentsia which by Soviet definition includes managers of economic enterprises, *kolkhoz* officials, artists, lawyers, engineers, scientists, teachers, government officials, leading party members, army officers, and top members of the political police. But what inclines Western critics to insist that classes already have emerged is the fact that workers, peasants, and intelligentsia show signs of perpetuating themselves. For a laborer to become a plant manager is becoming increasingly difficult. Accumulations of savings and personal property now are passed on to heirs in a volume impossible before World War II. Where progressive estate levies once swept away up to 90 per cent of an inheritance, since 1943 the inheritance tax runs no higher than 10 per cent. The imposition of fees for enrollment in institutions of higher learning has increased the preponderance of sons and daughters of the intelligentsia among university students. In these ways the very class which governs the country, manages its industries, teaches its children, and directs its propaganda agencies tends to assure its continued control. Westerners who wonder whether the army, the secret police, or the Communist party will win out in a particular struggle for power tend to forget that the intelligentsia occupies the positions of leadership in all three.

NATIONALITIES

The 1918 Constitution of the R.S.F.S.R. pronounced "the equality of all citizens, irrespective of their race or nationality." The 1936 Constitution repeated the pronouncement and added that any restriction of this equality or "any advocacy of racial or national exclusiveness or hatred and contempt" should be punished. The earlier document encouraged areas "with distinctive customs and national characteristics" to form "autonomous regional unions" and join the R.S.F.S.R. as federal partners. The commissar for nationalities, Stalin, made it clear, however, that such autonomous status would be allowed only when the region had purged its middle class and deposited power with its workers and peasants, or more properly with their vanguard, the Communist party.

In 1921 the party leaders, over the objection of the extremists who opposed any concession to nationalism, reduced to specific aims the general avowal of national equality they had made three years earlier. They proposed that the state should assist the diverse nationalities to catch up with the Great Russians politically and culturally. They encouraged the minorities to work out their own economic and political institutions, following soviet and socialist principles, of course, but using their native language and staffing such agencies with local people familiar with local customs. They promised to establish a school system which would teach general education and vocational skills in the native language and to provide newspapers in the language of each minority. The Communist party would direct the education of each nationality through the media of the language and culture of the people with whom it worked, but do so with the aim of developing socialism. "Proletarian in content but national in form" was the formula which would guide the administration's nationality policy. This enlightened attitude was new to Russia, where the tsars had attempted to Russify their subject nationalities, but was not new in the world. Some Western colonial powers had long practiced it.

The government had taken enormous strides by 1939 to educate the minorities in their own languages and dialects. Linguistic experts from Moscow developed written alphabets for forty nationalities who had known only a spoken language before the revolution. Many other peoples adopted the Latin or the Russian alphabet in place of the Arabic or Chinese script they had known. Seventy different languages, many of them for the first time written, were in use in Soviet schools; books were printed in over a hundred. Illiteracy did not immediately disappear but it declined rapidly. By 1939, 70 per cent of the people of the Tadzhik Republic could read and write, whereas less than 4 per cent could do so only sixteen years earlier. In tsarist times only 2 per cent of the Yakuts had been literate, but illiteracy had practically disappeared by the outbreak of the second World War. While native languages are spoken and taught in every minority area, the learning of Russian is promoted as a cultural cement to unite the diverse language groups.

Along with the war against illiteracy, the government campaigned against backward social customs which some of the minorities had practiced for centuries. The wearing of the veil by Mohammedan women was denounced and slowly terminated, although many of the first to drop the veil were subjected to mob violence. Moscow forbade child marriages, polygamy, and bride purchase, which had been common practices among many peoples. Tribal feuds long popular were forbidden. The respect for local customs which the government had promised did not extend to such "barbarisms," which were held to be the mark of obscurantism by which exploiters of the masses had held the people in subjection. Socialism could not move forward until such medieval practices had been eradicated.

Up to a point, the government has stimulated respect for the cultural and social heritage of minorities. Down to World War II the various nationalities were encouraged to remember their folklore, practice their folk dances, and resurrect their national heroes. Plays and operas depicting the careers of past leaders were performed in native languages in many republics and even in Moscow. During and after the war, however, the glorification of such pre-Soviet heroes has been frowned upon as incipient nationalism. Since 1940 the heroes who have been remembered in story and song have been Russian heroes—Suvorov, Kutuzov, Peter the Great, Alexander Nevsky, Dmitri Donskoi, and even Ivan the Terrible. But artistic themes that come out of the present must be those that glorify not Russian or Georgian or Armenian or Ukrainian or Tadzhik nationalism but such as will inspire "Soviet nationalism."

For many years the Jews were not treated as a cultural group, and were to be found in cities all over European and Asiatic Russia, as well as in the Pale in White Russia and the Ukraine where the tsars had concentrated them. However, in 1934 the Jewish Autonomous Republic, with Birobidzhan as its capital, was carved out on the Manchurian border in eastern Siberia. It was hoped that the new refuge would become a homeland for Jews from all over the world. As such it proved a miserable failure, and its failure may have enraged Stalin. He who had once scorned anti-Semitism as "a remnant of cannibalism" trumped up a charge that Jewish doctors in 1953 were plotting the assassination of certain Soviet officials. A vicious anti-Semitic campaign was halted by Stalin's death. But American rabbis charged three years later that the valuable Jewish historical and theological collection which had been accumulated in Moscow was being scattered. They reported that the Jews as a religious congregation were tolerated but not encouraged.

SOCIAL SERVICES

The "socialized wage" of the Soviet citizen, as distinct from his individual earnings, includes an array of welfare services, some of which are administered by the trade unions and others by the minister of social security in each republic. The services he receives through the labor unions are lumped together as "social insurance." Their aim is not to provide the individual with security so much as to increase his labor productivity, and the amount he receives or the percentage of his regular wage paid him by way of such benefit is related to whether he is just an average worker or a Stakhanovite.

Under the N.E.P. all workers were entitled to receive full wages during absence from the job because of illness. This unqualified right was progressively curtailed after the adoption of the First Five-Year Plan. Since 1948 a worker must have been employed for eight years or more on his last job to be eligible for full wage payments in time of sickness. If he has worked more than five but less than eight years on his last or current job he receives health-benefit payments equal to 80 per cent of his wages, and only 50 per cent if his present employment has been for less than three years. Workers who are not members of trade unions are entitled to only half the benefits which union members receive. Under the health-insurance program the insured worker receives free medical care during his own illness or that of any member of his family. Theoretically, he is entitled to spend the period of his illness at a sanatorium or convalescent home, although the limited space available in such places is reserved for those whose production record is outstanding.

Permanent disability because of accident or occupational disease is rewarded by a pension equal to the worker's full wages or a percentage, according to the degree of disability and the length of employment. When a worker dies of an industrial accident or disease his survivors receive a funeral allowance and a monthly percentage of his wages if they are unable to work. In the absence of physical handicap, this is taken to mean parents or wives over sixty and children under eighteen years of age. Retirement benefits as a percentage of the last wage received accrue to men over sixty and women over fifty-five who have been employed for at least twenty-five years. Those in hazardous occupations may retire earlier and after only twenty years of employment. The fact that old-age benefits amount to about half the worker's last wage provides an incentive to continue working as long as possible, and such continued employment does not interfere with the receipt of a pension.

Working women continue during pregnancy leaves to receive payments up to five hundred rubles for approximately a month before and six weeks after the birth of a child. In addition, they receive a hundred rubles or so for baby clothes and a fraction of their pay as a "nursing benefit" during the first nine months of the baby's life. During World War II the government encouraged large families by paying bonuses for additional children. A third child brought its mother a four-hundred-ruble bonus, a fourth, thirteen hundred rubles and eighty rubles a month until the child was five years old. The birth of every child beyond the tenth entitled the mother to a bonus of five thousand rubles and a monthly allowance of three hundred. Unmarried mothers received monthly allowances but no bonus for each child. Mothers of five or six children were entitled to wear the "Medal of Motherhood"; those with seven, eight, or nine could wear the order "Glory of Motherhood"; and those who had reared ten or more bore the title "Heroine Mother." After the war these rewards for large families were reduced as the cost of living fell.

The Ministry of Social Security in each republic handles retirement pensions of those who do not continue to work and payments to nonworking survivors of victims of industrial disease or accident. It also pays veteran's disability allowances, which consist of a percentage of the soldier's prewar wages according to the degree of his service-connected disability.

The Soviet citizen does not contribute to the cost of maintaining the social welfare program. Each enterprise bears a share of the cost for its workers and the state pays the rest. Only employees of the state are entitled to benefits. Members of collective farms do not come under social security. Each *kolkhoz* cares for its own disabled members. *Sovkhoz* workers are handled under the state program, as are all state employees.

WOMEN AND MARRIAGE

Women have outnumbered men quite significantly in Russia ever since the revolution. In 1926 there were 7 per cent more women than men, a situation that was to be expected after seven years of war and intervention. But in 1939, the year of the last census, the predominance of women over men in the population had risen to 9 per cent. By the end of World War II women outnumbered men five to four in the age group twenty to forty-five years, which produces the nation's children.

The numerical preponderance of women, the perennial labor shortage, and the high cost of living have drawn more women into employment than is true in Western Europe and even America. Many perform the most menial tasks. Western travellers have been amazed at the women who carry heavy materials on building projects or clean the streets of Moscow. And they work as hard as the men on the collective farms. During World War II over 70 per cent of the industrial labor force was composed of women. But professional opportunities also are open to them in a volume far exceeding that in Western nations. At the time of the last census over half the country's physicians, nearly a third of the scientific personnel, and not far from half the university students were women. However, they have taken less part in government than their numbers would justify. They made up slightly more than a third of the deputies to local soviets in 1939 and less than a tenth of the delegates to the Communist Party Congress held that year.

The Bolshevik Revolution was hardly a month old when the government liberalized marriage and divorce laws, thus bringing an equality and a freedom to the sexes that earlier religious conventions had made impossible. While couples were free to marry in a religious ceremony if they chose, such a marriage now had no legal standing. A legal marriage consisted of registering the union in the office of the government bureau which handled "civil acts." Divorce could be obtained by mutual consent of husband and wife simply by appearing in the bureau office, or one party could obtain it by going to court. When the courts were flooded with such cases, the government transferred divorce to the Registrar of Civil Acts, who after 1927 could grant divorce to one party without the appearance of the other and notify the partner by postcard of the dissolution of the marriage. For a year or two there were nearly as many divorces as marriages in Moscow, although nation-wide there were only half again as many divorces per thousand marriages as in the United States. The law recognized what English-speaking peoples know as common-law marriage as well as legal or "registered" marriage, and parties to such a union enjoyed the same property rights and responsibility for children as did those married in a registry office.

During the years of civil war marriage came to be looked upon lightly and entered into casually, and many preferred to avoid it altogether. While the law fixed responsibility for children born out of wedlock, the law was not easily enforced during those troublous times. Women insisted upon and obtained in 1920 the right of legal abortion to avoid having children they alone would have to care for. But the government warned that abortion was a social evil and could not long remain legal.

With the growing international tension and the threat of war, the Soviet government in 1936 revised the marriage and divorce laws. Abortion became illegal. Men and women could no longer divorce their spouses by postcard, and both parties had to appear before the proper official. The fee to obtain a divorce was raised to fifty rubles for the first, a hundred and fifty for the second, and three hundred for the third divorce. The date of each divorce was entered in the passport which each individual carried wherever he went. During World War II the divorce fees were raised again, so that either or both parties might be assessed from five hundred to two thousand rubles for the action. Courts were required to look into the reasons for the divorce application and discourage it. At the same time the government carried on a propaganda campaign which frowned upon the "light-minded attitude toward the family." By the end of the war, divorce was more difficult to obtain in Russia than in any nation in Europe.

From 1943 on boys and girls were educated in separate schools and girls received training in homemaking and the care of children. Childless families had to pay a special tax and large families were rewarded by bonuses. Moral laxity was frowned upon, although illegitimate children enjoyed the same legal rights as did legitimate children. With the provision for medical care and payment of allowances, and with the appearance of nurseries at all industrial plants, much of the economic burden has been transferred from the child's parents to the state.

RELIGIOUS POLICY

Russian Orthodox clergymen had agitated mildly for separation of church and state in the closing days of the monarchy and had urged that only by restoration of the Patriarchate could the church purify itself and recover its influence among the people. The tsar had listened but finally had heeded the voice of Rasputin, who opposed the separation. The Provisional Government then had called a church assembly which had chosen the Metropolitan Tikhon as the first Patriarch since the time of Peter the Great. Tikhon's first act—he assumed office while the Bolsheviks were clearing aside the Provisional Government—was an attempt to halt the fighting and prevent further bloodshed. Aside from the fact that as a churchman he was opposed to the professed atheism of the revolutionaries, his intervention was scarcely calculated to win Bolshevik approval.

In some degree the new government was antireligious, but its persecution of the church and the clergy during the Civil War was based primarily upon its determination to wipe out an active center of resistance. Churchmen of all faiths were seized and executed or exiled, not as religious leaders, but as counterrevolutionaries. This continued to be government policy as long as any clergyman showed or was suspected of harboring resentment against the new regime.

Early in 1918 the government published a decree ordering separation of church and state. Church land was nationalized, as was all land, and no church or religious body thenceforth could own property. The decree permitted local soviets to lease nationalized property—buildings, vestments, and altar pieces—for use in church services to groups of twenty or more laymen. But such a group of believers could not enjoy exclusive use of the church building; it must serve also as a school or dance or concert hall or meeting place for public lectures and discussions whenever such secular activities required the space. Since the government recognized only the groups of laymen, monasteries as such were dissolved, although a few reorganized as cooperatives. The decree also forbade religious instruction in schools, public or private, and the government later prohibited religious teaching to groups whose members were less than eighteen years of age. Clergymen were denied the right to vote and received no ration cards, making them dependent upon their parishioners for food and shelter.

A thousand Orthodox churches and a number of mosques and Protestant churches were closed or used exclusively for nonreligious functions because many parishes could not muster twenty men brave enough to risk signing a contract with the local soviets. Precious ornaments and altar pieces were confiscated, to be sold for food during the famine in 1922. Orthodox and Roman Catholic churchmen who objected were tried for "inciting the masses to civil war"; twenty-eight bishops and a thousand priests were executed and others exiled or imprisoned.

A number of Russian Orthodox clergymen decided to make their peace with the government and, denouncing the Patriarch Tikhon, organized what they called "the Living Church." The Bolsheviks encouraged this schism, imprisoning the Patriarch, turning over church buildings for the use of the schismatics and removing bishops and priests to make way for the clergy of the Living Church. But the government gradually withdrew its support when laymen refused to back the movement. The Patriarch Tikhon, who had been threatened with execution, was released from prison after vigorous protests from abroad, particularly from Great Britain. Many rebellious clergymen recanted and deserted the Living Church, which evaporated when the Bolsheviks stopped supporting it. Tikhon died in 1925 and his successors were imprisoned as fast as they could be named. In 1926 the newly-chosen acting head of Russian Orthodoxy, Sergei, won a grudging toleration by promising for himself and his church to be loyal to the government and stand aloof from politics.

When the government failed to gain popular favor for the Living Church it turned to a propaganda campaign designed to win converts to atheism. It opened a publishing agency whose journal *The Godless* kept up a vitriolic attack upon all religion. It established an antireligious seminary in the capital. It forbade the use of Christmas trees and decorations and celebrated the holiday with an anti-Christmas pageant which mocked belief in miracles and held all clergymen up to scorn. It published the sworn testimony of aviators that there were no gods because they had scoured the skies and not found them. It warned that the taking of communion promoted drunkenness and spread disease. It prohibited religious instruction in the churches and forbade teaching religion anywhere to groups where there were more than three children. It made "anti-God museums" of some churches, notably St. Basil's Cathedral in Moscow's Red Square. It sought to arouse the indignation of the faithful by displaying in the Kremlin Museum the gold eggs sprinkled with rubies, sapphires, and diamonds which church leaders had given to the tsars at Eastertime. Its most ambitious effort was the creation of the "League of Militant Atheists," whose members wrote and preached that religion was unnecessary since science provided the answers to any questions man could ask. By 1932 the League numbered five million members and proposed in its own Five-Year Plan to increase the membership to fifteen million.

By 1925 the government's own attack upon religion slowed down and the job of weaning the people away from the church was assigned to the League of Militant Atheists. But the results of the League's efforts were disappointing, and in 1929 the government renewed its pressure upon all religion. Many churches that had weathered the first storm now were closed on the ground that the Five-Year Plan was moving the nation toward socialism and that a socialist society had no need for churches. Communists called meetings of local soviets, which voted without reference to the local church groups to close the churches. When parishioners protested troops were called in to enforce the decision. By such tactics nearly fifteen hundred churches were closed in 1929.

Clergymen charged with sabotaging the Five-Year Plan or inciting rebellion were arrested, and a hundred bishops were thrown into a forced-labor camp on the White Sea. Hundreds of priests were shot or exiled to Siberia. Those who escaped seizure were prohibited from living in cities, and villagers who sheltered them were taxed for doing so. The six-day week was adopted and absence from work without a doctor's excuse was heavily punished; the effect was to prevent people from going to church unless the rest day just happened to fall on Sunday. Churches were forbidden to engage in any social or cultural activity—maintain nurseries, libraries, reading rooms, or medical aid groups—and could use the property they leased only for worship, not for religious instruction. The 1918 Constitution, which had granted the right to engage in religious or antireligious propaganda, now was amended to permit only "freedom of religious worship and of antireligious propaganda." This denied clergymen and communicants the right to defend the church by speaking or writing against attacks upon religion and took away their freedom to proselytize.

Instruction in state schools, which heretofore had omitted all reference to religion, now became deliberately antireligious. Textbooks disparaged religion and pointed up its conflict with science. Students were taken to visit antireligious museums and antireligious discussions were held in classes in all subjects.

When the new attack met with popular resistance, particularly in the villages, where the authorities already had their hands full with collectivization, the government abandoned the policy and criticized overzealous party workers who had interfered with attendance at religious services, organized anti-Easter carnivals, or pressed the closing of churches against the people's will. The Politburo may also have listened to foreign threats to withhold the loans upon which some of the success of the Five-Year Plan would depend. But the government now could afford to be generous. It had so deprived religion of its means of existence that any threat to the regime from that quarter was impossible. By 1935 barely four thousand Russian Orthodox churches remained open of eleven times that many before the revolution; of fifty thousand priests only one out of nine still was active; and four-fifths of the bishops were in prison or dead.

Persecution now gave way to a policy of toleration. By 1935 materials for the preparation of the traditional Easter cakes were made available in state retail stores, and the prohibition against the display of Christmas trees was removed that year. The government even permitted the manufacture of wedding rings which would be used only in church ceremonies. Children of priests were allowed to attend school for the first time since the revolution. The 1936 Constitution restored to the clergy the right to vote and removed the restrictions under which they had lived for nearly a generation. The government even condemned recent efforts to ridicule Russia's conversion to Christianity in the tenth century, praising the work of the clergy in spreading literacy and denouncing the "frivolous attitude toward history" by which the conversion was interpreted as a reactionary step.

The government did not return to its policy of calculated persecution of religion, but many clergymen and lay churchmen were caught up in the 1937–1938 purge. Bishops were arrested and tried for sabotage and for carrying on espionage in the interest of Germany. Priests were accused of inciting their flocks to practice terrorism and of urging the overthrow of the regime. Some were charged with using church property for traitorous purposes. But the government would not permit the forcible closing of churches nor violent attacks upon congregations. Many churches did close down when their clergymen were arrested; by the end of 1937 there were eleven hundred fewer Orthodox and two hundred and forty fewer Catholic churches open than at the beginning of the year. When Stalin called a halt to the purge in 1939 the last attack upon the church came to an end. The League of Militant Atheists continued to publish its journal *The Godless,* but even the League found ways to condone the practice of religion by those who clung to their old beliefs.

With the approach of war the government energetically cultivated the support of religious groups and the clergy. The League of Militant Atheists suddenly discovered that Christianity was highly praiseworthy, that it had done much for its devotees, for Russia, and for humanity. The magazine *The Godless* even recommended that Communists abroad cooperate with Roman Catholics in supporting democratic governments against the fascist threat. A motion picture was made of the life of Alexander Nevsky, one of the greatest in the Russian Orthodox galaxy of saints. Another film glorified the career of Suvorov and several times showed the great general crossing himself. The state for the first time encouraged the production of icons. So far did the government swing away from its former policy of persecution that it insisted atheists must show respect for the sensibilities of religious people and enlisted the help of the League of Militant Atheists in preventing antireligious demonstrations. And the editor of a small-town newspaper was expelled from the Communist party for recommending the forcible closing of churches.

Communism had lost none of its distaste for religion. Joining a church was still sufficient grounds for expulsion from the party. Children still could receive religious instruction only in their homes. The church still had no press of its own. And education against religion, while certainly toned down, continued in the schools. As late as the spring of 1943 President Kalinin reiterated the view that "religion is a misguiding institution" and promised that the state would continue to fight it through education. He acknowledged that many Soviet citizens were deeply religious and warned that the faith that "still grips considerable sections of the population" could not be weakened by ridicule. As international tension grew, the government wisely chose to enlist support wherever it could find it. During the war the church, its clergy and its members, remained loyal and intensely patriotic. As of old, the church leaders hurled anathema at the invaders of the homeland and called upon the faithful to lay down their lives if need be in defense of Russia. And Moscow Radio warned that Hitler's advancing armies were "menacing the very existence of Christianity and seeking the overthrow of Christ the King."

In September, 1943, Stalin granted an audience to Metropolitan Sergei, the acting head of the Russian Orthodox church. The very act officially encouraged those timid ones who had suppressed their longing for religious expression now to show their faith openly, and there was a rush to form lay groups and open churches long unused. A few days after the interview a church council gathered in Moscow which elected Sergei to be "Patriarch of Moscow and All Russia." The move was applauded by Russian Orthodox leaders in the United States and Britain, and the new patriarch was officially recognized by his brother patriarchs of the Eastern church in Alexandria, Antioch, Constantinople, and Jerusalem. The Russian church was to be governed by a Holy Synod of six bishops presided over by the patriarch. Sergei announced immediately that a number of additional seminaries would be opened to train clergymen and that the official *Journal of the Patriarchate* would again be published. One month later a congress in Tashkent elected a "President Mufti" of the Moslems in the U.S.S.R.

The government's gentle dealing with organized religion continued after World War II. By 1956, 20,000 churches were open to Russian Orthodox faithful, nearly five times as many as twenty years before, and the number of priests had climbed to 35,000, a sixfold increase over the preceding twenty years. Another 6,000 churches ministered to three million Baptists, and the Lutheran churches in the Baltic republics were prosperous and well attended. Many churches knocked down during the war were being rebuilt, although not at a rate to satisfy impatient church leaders. Patriarch Alexei promised that a new edition of the Bible, the first since the revolution, would soon be off the press. Only the Jews seemed to be neglected. To their suffering during the war Stalin added a bitter anti-Semitic policy after 1945. Ten years later Moscow's 300,000 Jews were served by only three synagogues; the nation's three million Jews had no central organization and were without schools.

The government obviously was satisfied that it no longer had reason to fear religion. It was confident that some day religion would wither and die. Of the millions who attend services, the overwhelming majority are old people. And in the nation's classrooms the attack upon religion, quietly but effectively, still goes on, while Communist party leaders frequently remind the people of the incompatibility of religion and science. But as long as the churches refrain from criticizing the government or dabbling in politics and as long as they serve the needs of the state by urging their members to support its goals religion may manage to avoid a return of the vicious persecution of the twenties and thirties.

EDUCATION

Lenin sincerely wanted to lead the people out of the darkness of illiteracy for their own sake, for he looked upon education of the masses as the only way to expand production and bring a better way of life. But it is only realistic to remember that, before the widespread use of radio and television, the regime could preach the message of communism to the masses and enlist their understanding and support only by teaching them to read. To make workers more productive and to reach them with its propaganda the government launched a program of adult education and sought to bring every child into the schoolroom.

The government set itself the goal of making education available to all children from the age of five weeks to eighteen years. Up to the age of four the child might be cared for in a nursery maintained by the factory where the mother worked. If the mother chose not to work she could care for the child in her home, but the pressure to add to the husband's income and the state aid offered to employed mothers made most city mothers prefer to work. Each collective farm operated a nursery where peasant mothers left their children while they worked in the fields. Kindergartens, maintained by *kolkhozes* and industrial plants, cared for children too old for the nursery and too young for school, normally those between four and eight years old. There was no tuition for attendance at either nursery or kindergarten, for the right to place her child there was part of the mother's wage at the factory or on the farm. Kindergarten training for every eligible child, however, was a goal still far away at the beginning of the First Five-Year Plan, when there were facilities to handle only one per cent of the children of kindergarten age.

In 1930 the government decreed universal compulsory education for all children beginning at the age of eight, later reduced to seven. The type of school and the length of compulsory attendance depended upon whether the child lived in a rural or urban area. The peasant child completed a four-year elementary course which taught him to figure simple arithmetic problems and to read and write in his native language and in Russian. At the end of this primary schooling, his education completed, the village child normally went to work for a third of adult wages on the collective farm, becoming a member and assuming the rights and obligations of an adult peasant when he reached the age of sixteen.

The elementary school for the city child runs through seven years. To the reading, writing, and arithmetic of the four-year village school the urban school adds a foreign language, literature, history, physical and biological science, and military training. When he graduates from this "seven-year" or elementary school, normally at fourteen, the student may go to work; in fact, he is required to do so at sixteen unless he continues in school.

In 1949 the government undertook to provide rural areas with seven-year schools and make graduation from them compulsory, as it had long been for city students. If he chooses and his scholarship warrants, the graduate of the seven-year school may attend a two-year trade school and learn one of the crafts or prepare for a job in industry. Or he may attend a four-year technical high school where he will learn more of the arts and sciences along with advanced technical training and so fit himself for supervisory work in a factory. If his parents prefer and can afford the tuition, the seven-year-old child may begin his schooling in a "ten-year school" which will carry him through all his primary and secondary work. Here the curriculum in the last three years is comparable to that of the American high school, except that all Russian students devote about half their time to the study of mathematics and science while half of American high-school students take no science at all. The Russian normally graduates at seventeen or eighteen. The Fifth Five-Year Plan proposed to erect enough buildings and provide enough teachers so that graduation from the ten-year school could be made compulsory for all city youth, and the sixth plan announced that by 1960 all children in both rural and urban areas would be required to complete the ten-year program.

The curriculum of the ten-year school emphasizes so-called academic and cultural rather than technical or trade subjects. From this school only can the student go on to a university or to an "institute" specializing in a particular field. There still is no fee for attending the four-year village school or the seven-year urban school, and textbooks and materials are furnished in both. But since 1940 a student enrolled in the ten-year school or the technical high school must buy his own books and pay tuition amounting to two hundred rubles a year for each of his last three years. Students pay four hundred rubles in fees to attend university and five hundred to enroll in higher institutions specializing in any of the fine arts. The effect of the costly fees has been to deny higher education to children of peasants and workers except the brilliant ones who receive scholarship awards covering tuition and living expenses. Orphans, children of parents whose pension is their only income, and sons and daughters of enlisted men and junior officers in the armed services may attend institutions of higher learning tuition-free. In 1955 government officials boasted that 90 per cent of the students in institutions of higher learning were attending on scholarships. All scholarship students must upon graduation accept employment in their professions wherever they are needed and may be sent for a period of three years.

One of Communist Russia's most outstanding achievements has been the conquest of illiteracy. Before World War I three-fourths of the people of European Russia and 85 per cent of those in Asiatic Russia could neither read nor write. In the Moslem lands of southern Siberia less than 4 per cent were literate as late as 1926. Soon after the Civil War the Communist party led a drive against illiteracy that fired the imagination particularly of young people. Children able to attend school for the first time were so eager to learn that it did not occur to them to object to unheated buildings or having to share one pencil and one textbook among thirty or forty in a classroom. They went home and chided their ignorant parents into learning to read and write. *Komsomols* went from house to house taking the names of illiterates and offering to teach those who would give their time. Less than half the population was illiterate by 1928, and before World War II the rate had dropped below 20 per cent of those over nine years of age. The war took a heavy toll in education as in all else. Millions had their schooling cut short when they enlisted in the armed forces or went into war industry. Eighty thousand school houses were destroyed; fewer teachers were graduated and others died, so that the nation came out of the war with a half million fewer teachers than it had had four years earlier. But by 1956 illiteracy had in effect been wiped out. The man or woman fifty years of age or younger who could not read and write was difficult to find.

In 1913 the elementary and secondary schools of Russia accommodated about eight million students, and there were perhaps three hundred thousand in institutions of higher learning. The 1939 census showed thirty-one million in preparatory schools and another two and a half million in universities and institutes. In 1956 there were fifty million students in all types of schools, exactly one out of every four people. The Sixth Five-Year Plan announced in that year proposed to double the number of schoolrooms by 1960, which presumably will make possible raising the compulsory attendance age to seventeen.

In a reaction against the stern discipline and emphasis upon fact and rote that had characterized tsarist schools, educational leaders of the U.S.S.R. went to the other extreme of progressive education in the 1920's. Discipline, regarded as old-fashioned and reactionary, was discarded in favor of student government. Students, teachers, and janitors formed a collective, and elected officers and held meetings to decide policy. Pupils chose their own projects to develop, working on them in school or out as they chose. They went on tours to visit factories and government offices to such an extent that they threatened to interrupt the work in such places and the practice had to be discontinued. Boys and girls sat in the same classrooms for the first time. The teacher lost all control over the students and became an observer and adviser. "Polytechnical" education was fashionable in which students alternated periods in school with days or weeks in factories and on farms—the "learning-by-doing" technique. So disappointing were the results of these fads, however, that in the early thirties there was a trend back to traditional methods. Progressive education was discarded, the authority of the teacher was restored, projects gave way to learning a body of facts, girls and boys were assigned to separate elementary and secondary schools, and students once more wore uniforms as they had in tsarist times and as they do generally in European schools. Titles, degrees, seminars, examinations, and home assignments again came into use. After Stalin's death there was a modest reaction in education. Coeducation returned and the polytechnical method again became popular.

Since World War II the schools and universities have stressed mathematics, the sciences, engineering, and the like. In 1956 Soviet colleges were graduating almost twice as many scientists and engineers as were American colleges. The great majority of such students receive bountiful stipends which allow them a far better living than the average Russian can afford. The student of science, mathematics, or engineering may learn little of the humanities, but when he graduates he will know as much or more about his specialty than the American student who has taken his master's degree. American scholars, long skeptical of the quality of Soviet instruction, have been forced to admit that the graduate, in science at least, has received excellent training. The thirty-four Russian universities and eight hundred teachers' colleges, agricultural, technical, and medical institutes are furnished with the most modern equipment and staffed with teachers as competent in their fields as are those of any country. The All-Union Academy of Sciences includes among its members the nation's leading scientists, who receive a sizable honorary income by virtue of their membership. It maintains research institutes in many scientific fields and subsidizes projects which contribute to the development of natural resources and the improvement of the nation's industries.

Leading scientists, and artists as well, might be awarded "Stalin" prizes for distinguishing contributions in their field. Soon after Stalin's death in 1953 the prizes were abolished in what perhaps was the first step in the "de-Stalinization" program. They were revived in 1956, but were renamed the Lenin prizes. Each carries with it an award of seventy-five thousand rubles.

While most Russian scientists are thoroughly capable, a few have brought down ridicule upon themselves and the nation by courting political favor through attempting to bend pure science to Marxist ideology. The most notorious example was that of Trofim Lysenko, who proclaimed that the Mendelian theory of heredity was "bourgeois" and "reactionary," and insisted that characteristics developed through environmental influences could be inherited. Russia's leading geneticist, Nicholas Vavilov, refused to subscribe to such nonsense and for his integrity was packed off to Siberia in 1940 as a "British spy." Lysenko boasted that his conclusions were fully supported by the Politburo, and even by "Comrade Stalin personally." After Stalin's death Lysenko's false doctrine was repudiated and those who had had the courage to challenge him were "rehabilitated," some of them posthumously.

The study of history for its own sake came to an end soon after the revolution. Historians of Russia were suspected of nationalism and reaction, and those who dealt with history from any but the Marxist point of view were driven into exile or managed to escape abroad. History disappeared from the curriculum as an independent discipline, and whatever of its content could contribute to an understanding of the revolution was woven into the study of sociology and economics. The leading communist historian, Michael Pokrovsky, rewrote Russian history in terms of economic determinism and Marxist ideology, and was rewarded by being raised to a dominating position in the field of historical research and criticism. But with the revival of Russian nationalism in the 1930's Pokrovsky's Marxist purity got him into difficulty, and his death in 1932 probably saved him from disgrace. The outstanding historian Eugene Tarle, who had spent years in Siberian exile for his conservative and nationalist view of Russian history, returned in glory to replace Pokrovsky as the leader in his field. Russian history was again rewritten, this time from an intensely nationalist point of view. The heroic figures of the past—Vladimir, Alexander Nevsky, Dmitri Donskoi, Ivan the Terrible, Peter the Great, Catherine II, Suvorov—were resurrected from Pokrovsky's oblivion and eulogized as defenders of the nation against its foreign foes.

During the years of the Stalin cult, publications in the social sciences were filled with slavish references to Stalin's writings and were generously sprinkled with sentences beginning "As our great leader, Stalin, has shown," or "As Stalin has pointed out." Western critics might see some justification for similar references to Marx and Engels and Lenin, but the repeated allusions to Stalin smacked of fawning efforts to win praise. But behind this façade, perhaps intended for the censor, there was much sound scholarship, given the fact that the social setting dictates the approach of every Russian writer just as it dictates that of non-Soviet writers as well.

THE ARTIST'S ROLE IN SOVIET SOCIETY

That literary men should have to endure censorship of their works was nothing new in Russian experience. The supervision of creative writing is exercised, however, not through an office of censorship, as it was under the imperial government, but through the *Gosizdat*, or State Publishing House, which controls the nation's press. No private press exists, and an author can break into print only if his work is accepted for publication by the *Gosizdat*. Once his work is published and thus receives official approval, he is assured a far greater market than any but a few non-Soviet writers can hope for. His novel or poem or play may be translated from Russian not only into other Soviet languages but may appear as well in Oriental and European languages and be marketed abroad under foreign branches of the Soviet publishing house. Since all theaters are public property and all performances are cast and directed by state employees, the artist whose medium is music, drama, or ballet similarly must win official approval if he is to reach an audience.

Many Russian artists preferred exile to making their peace with the

Bolsheviks and fled to the West after the revolution, although a few later returned. Many others chose to remain, some to give up their art and retire into obscurity, others to try to adjust themselves to the new life. Those who continued to produce found the situation completely reversed from what it had been under the empire. In tsarist times an artist, particularly a literary one, won a hearing and grew in stature by opposing the government, subtly, to be sure, if he hoped to avoid official censorship, by protesting against the autocracy, serfdom, bureaucracy, obscurantism, and brutality. Under the new regime an artist, whatever his medium, could obtain an audience only if his work contributed to the officially sanctioned goals of society. This reversal was perhaps less painful to Russian artists than it would have been to those of any other European country. Russian art, particularly literature, had been propagandistic even in the nineteenth century. Now, however, it would propagandize for rather than against the government and all it stood for. A striking difference between tsarist and Soviet art is that the contemporary artist creates for a mass public while the imperial artist composed for a relative few, the intelligentsia. The small percentage of tsarist society who could read or afford to visit the theater or the opera contrasts sharply with the many millions whom Soviet artists reach.

Soviet literature—particularly poetry, drama, and the novel—and to a less extent music and the plastic arts, have passed through several stages since the revolution, each of which paralleled and reflected political or economic shifts in government policy. The period of War Communism was a time of struggle between old and new in literature as well as in politics. Leftist writers insisted that literature must mirror the new order, must contribute to the attainment of the goals of the new society, must develop a social consciousness in keeping with the times. It must be proletarian rather than bourgeois, realistic rather than romantic, optimistic rather than pessimistic, socialistic rather than capitalistic in outlook. It made a fetish of modernism and its devotees argued whether cubism, symbolism, expressionism, or futurism were most appropriate to the age. Conservative artists protested against these strange ways and argued for a cultural link with Russia's brilliant past. Some hoped to avoid political involvement in their work, while others, the "fellow travellers," would support the aims of the new society but cling to conservative and traditional forms of expression.

When the leftists organized and attempted to drive the conservatives from the field, the Communist party stepped in and put an end to the wordy battle. The Central Executive Committee in 1924 pronounced what amounted to an N.E.P. policy for literature, sanctioning compromise in the literary as it had already done in the economic field. It condemned the wrangling over style and technique. Criticizing as "quasi-bureaucratic" the attempts of the modernists to suppress the conservatives, the party refused to condone monopoly by any particular group and called for free competition among them all. There followed years of disillusion and frustration for the youthful extremists, and some unable to compromise their principles committed suicide.

With the inauguration of the Five-Year Plans Soviet poets, novelists, playwrights, musicians, and motion-picture producers were enlisted to win popular support for the new socialist society which the government proposed to create. The 1924 compromise came to an end and the nation's leaders now insisted that artistic talent must contribute to the socialist program. Condemnation of the merchant and the *kulak,* glorification of the collective farm, fulfillment of the plan, welcome to the new industry, praise of socialist competition, criticism of the stupid petty official whose bureaucratic bungling held up production, acclaim for the Stakhanovite, castigation of the saboteur—these were the themes that Soviet artists were encouraged to develop. This attention to practical subject matter, this effort to use the artist's medium to educate the masses to support the regime and its goals, was heralded as "socialist realism."

In 1934 Professor Pokrovsky was posthumously demoted from his preeminence over Russian historians, and nationalism and the glorification of the Russian past came into fashion among historians and among artists as well. Russia's heroes, especially those who had fought off invaders of the homeland, were acclaimed in painting, symphony, opera, novel, poem, play, and motion picture. Historical episodes and figures became steadily more popular among Soviet artists, and continued to be so through the war and into the uneasy peace beyond. Such themes were acclaimed for contributing to "Soviet patriotism." During World War II artists praised democracy, the western Allies, the Russian people, and the common man everywhere while condemning fascism and feudalism and warlordism, associating such evils particularly with the traditional national enemy, the German.

As tension among the former allies grew after 1945, there was another shift in Soviet artistic policy. There was a revulsion against "decadent" modern Western art and music and literature, which were condemned as the fruit of Western capitalism—socialism's new enemy and the "heir of fascism." Slowly after Stalin's death there was a softening of such animosity, a toning down of the vituperation heaped upon Western institutions, and even an exchange of Soviet and Western artists.

The life of the Soviet artist is an easy one in some respects but a very difficult one in others. During the last twenty-five years of Stalin's life he had, in effect, only one man to please—namely Stalin, who set himself up as the leading, the only, literary and artistic critic. But even with Stalin dead, the artist still must meet the requirements and avoid the criticisms of those who direct the society. If the artist succeeds in toeing the party line he finds an audience ready made, and all the advertising and propaganda power of the regime lines up behind him. If, however, he cannot keep up with shifts in state policy he runs the risk of condemnation to oblivion. His novels and his poems will not be printed, his plays will not be produced, conductors will not direct his compositions, his paintings will not be exhibited. Even his previous art, once approved, may be removed from the accredited list and his work withdrawn from circulation or held up to derision. Sholokhov, whose epic *The Quiet Don* has made him the Soviet Union's best-known novelist, produced nothing worth while after 1940 because, it has been said, he could not stand the pressure of trying to please Stalin. In 1956, however, he was at work on another novel. Shostakovich and Prokofiev have heard their music alternately acclaimed and scorned. Since none of Stalin's successors professed to be an art or music or literary critic, the position of the artist was somewhat improved by the leader's death. But it was certain that the socialist state would continue to draft its artistic talent to further its own goals.

SUGGESTED READING

Anderson, P. B., *People, Church and State in Modern Russia* (New York, Macmillan, 1944).

Bauer, R. A., *The New Man in Soviet Psychology* (Cambridge, Harvard University Press, 1952).

Casey, R. P., *Religion in Russia* (New York, Harper's, 1946).

Curtiss, J. S., *The Russian Church and the Soviet State* (New York, Columbia University Press, 1953).

Inkeles, A., *Public Opinion in Soviet Russia: a Study in Mass Persuasion* (Cambridge, Harvard University Press, 1950).

London, K., *The Seven Soviet Arts* (New Haven, Yale University Press, 1938).

MacLeod, J., *The New Soviet Theatre* (London, Allen & Unwin, 1943).

Reavey, G., *Soviet Literature Today* (New Haven, Yale University Press, 1947).

Runes, D. D., *The Soviet Impact on Society* (New York, Philosophical Library, 1953).

Schlesinger, R., *Changing Attitudes in Soviet Russia: The Family* (London, Routledge, 1949).

Schwarz, S. M., *The Jews in the Soviet Union* (Syracuse, Syracuse University Press, 1951).

Simmons, E. J., *USSR, A Concise Handbook* (Ithaca, Cornell University Press, 1947).

Slonim, M., *Modern Russian Literature* (New York, Oxford University Press, 1953).

Struve, G., *Soviet Russian Literature, 1917–1950* (Norman, University of Oklahoma Press, 1951).

Timasheff, N. S., *Religion in Soviet Russia, 1917–1942* (New York, Sheed & Ward, 1942).

Varneke, B. V., *History of the Russian Theater* (New York, Macmillan, 1951).

Werth, A., *Musical Uproar in Moscow* (London, Turnstile Press, 1949).

Zinoviev, M. A., *Soviet Methods of Teaching History* (Ann Arbor, Edwards, 1952).

31

Soviet Foreign Relations

Russia's relations with other powers were complicated from the very beginning by her promotion of the Communist International, in which delegates from world Communist parties met to consider ways to overthrow bourgeois governments and replace them with Communist regimes. Her attempt to win favor with her former allies was further handicapped by a refusal to recognize tsarist debts or compensate foreign nationals for their property in Russia which the Bolsheviks nationalized at the time of the revolution. The Commissariat for Foreign Affairs, which handled the diplomatic relations of the Russian government, early managed to win the recognition of states bordering upon Russia but had little success with the great powers until 1922. In that year, at Rapallo, Germany recognized the Bolshevik government and granted it a loan for the purchase of German equipment. Other nations slowly followed suit in extending recognition, although the United States refused to do so until 1933 and diplomatic relations with Britain, once restored, were broken off because of Communist efforts to exploit domestic disturbances in England. Russia was not brought into the League of Nations and was not invited to the Locarno Conference, which guaranteed the French and Belgian boundaries against German attack but took no notice of Germany's eastern frontier, thus seeming to the Russians to approve the *drang nach Osten*. Russia was allowed to attend disarmament conferences but found a Western unwillingness to undertake serious disarmament.

The U.S.S.R. became involved in the Chinese Revolution in 1925 and provided war matériel and advisers to the revolutionary party, the Kuomintang, which won control of the Chinese republican government. When the revolutionary leader Chiang Kai-shek turned against the Chinese Communists, Moscow withdrew her support. The Russians were expelled but retained a half interest in and effective control over the Chinese Eastern Railway. China and Russia revived diplomatic relations after the Japanese encroachment on the mainland after 1931. Moscow sold out her interest in the Chinese Eastern Railway after Japan conquered Manchuria.

With the rise of Hitler in Germany, Russia sought to improve her relations with the bourgeois-democratic powers who opposed fascism. She took an active part in the League of Nations, which she joined in 1934. She arranged a system of nonaggression and mutual-defense pacts designed to provide allies in case she were attacked. She fought off Japanese raids across the Siberian frontier but refused to be drawn into war in the East. And she mildly supported the legitimate Spanish government against a fascist rebellion which succeeded with German and Italian help.

Nazi aggression met only wordy resistance from the Western powers in spite of Russia's insistence upon collective security to stop it. Great Britain and France gave in at Munich to Hitler's demand for Czech border territory and later raised only mild objection to his absorption of the rest of Czechoslovakia. Conversations in Moscow with French and British diplomats looking toward united action to prevent further German aggression foundered when Poland and Romania refused permission for Russian troops to cross into Central Europe and the British and French refused to override their objection. When the military staffs of the three powers could find no basis for united action, Russia concluded a ten-year nonaggression pact with Germany which gave her a free hand to reorganize her western frontier and bring her the security which the Western powers had seemed unwilling to permit.

RUSSIA IN 1922

Early in 1920 the western Allies pulled out of Russia, lifted the blockade, urged Wrangel to stop fighting, and suggested that the border states settle their differences with the Bolsheviks. Their foreign support withdrawn, Finland, Estonia, Latvia, and Lithuania quickly granted recognition to the Soviet government. Turkey and Afghanistan did so a year later, as did Poland by the Peace of Riga. But being recognized by five succession states, a defeated enemy, and a backward nation long exploited by Imperial Russia and Great Britain hardly constituted a diplomatic triumph. Germany and Sweden condescended to trade with Russia but refused to recognize her government.

There were several hurdles in the way of Russia's restoration of normal relations with the Western powers. At its first meeting in March, 1919, the Third or Communist International, the so-called Comintern, had called upon the workers of all countries to press their governments, "by revolutionary means" if necessary, to withdraw their interventionist forces and recognize the Soviet regime. Representing nineteen nations, its thirty-five delegates, most of them residents in Russia, had gathered in Moscow shortly after an attempted Communist uprising in Berlin and just prior to temporarily successful efforts to establish Communist regimes in Hungary and Bavaria. By 1922 the threat of Communist uprisings had faded, but the capitalist governments of the West were understandably wary of the Comintern, which by that time had had a second and then a third meeting of Communists from many lands. A second deterrent to normal relations between Russia and the capitalist powers was the fact that the Soviet regime had made foreign trade a state monopoly, a situation with which the Western governments did not yet know how to cope. A much more serious stumbling block was the refusal of the Bolsheviks to honor the government and private debts contracted in tsarist times with foreigners and the confiscation of foreign-owned property without compensation by the Soviet authorities. This repudiation of tsarist debts seemed to be most irritating to Russia's former allies, for it was questioned every time the Bolsheviks broached the subject of restoring diplomatic or trade relations.

The Russian leaders recognized two assignments in the field of foreign relations: the responsibility to defend the nation and the experiment upon which they had embarked, and the assumed obligation to support workers in every country in the overthrow of capitalist governments. The two tasks were to be undertaken by two different agencies. The Comintern would lead the attack upon bourgeois governments by disseminating propaganda, supporting Communist parties all over the world, fomenting or at least taking advantage of strikes wherever they might occur, and subsidizing revolutionary activity whenever the need and the opportunity arose. Commissar for Foreign Affairs George Chicherin, a former aristocrat turned Bolshevik, would direct the nation's diplomatic affairs with other states toward maintaining peace and developing friendly relations. The two functions would go hand in hand. The pressure of native Communist parties upon foreign governments would, it was supposed, so embarrass those governments and so confine their attention to their own domestic situations that they would have no choice but to maintain peaceful and friendly relations with Russia. What the Bolsheviks seem only occasionally and only dimly to have realized through the years is that the two agencies work at cross purposes. Attempts by native Communist parties to embarrass their own governments have irritated rather than smoothed relations with Russia. Such attempts have been made time and time again in Europe, Asia and the Western Hemisphere. Almost invariably they have failed of their purpose and have had the effect only of convincing the non-Communist world that the Soviet government is not to be trusted.

GENOA AND RAPALLO

Delegates from thirty-four nations, of which Russia was one, gathered at Genoa in April, 1922, to hear suggestions for the economic recovery of Europe. Russia had embarked upon the New Economic Policy, which Westerners took to be a confession of the failure of communism and a return to capitalism. Now Russia would listen to reason, the delegates to the conference reckoned, and would recognize tsarist debts, compensate their nationals for confiscated property, and grant trade concessions. And Chicherin did announce that his government would consider the payment of the nearly fourteen billion dollars which the tsars and the Provisional Government had borrowed prior to and during the war. But he added conditions. The Soviet government must be recognized as the legal government of Russia and must be given extensive foreign credits. Finally, he shocked the representatives of the Allied powers by presenting them with a bill for sixty billion dollars in payment for the damage they had inflicted upon Russia through intervention. But Russia would not press this claim for reparations, he added, provided she could obtain loans with which to rebuild her war-torn land. The British and Italian delegates expressed a willingness to consider the Russian offer, but the French would not even discuss it. Then the British on their own began to negotiate with the Soviet delegation to buy all of Russia's oil exports, but the American observer objected to the proposed concession and insisted that all nations must have equal opportunity to exploit the land of the Bolsheviks. The conference broke up after producing nothing more substantial than a general agreement that the nations represented would not interfere in each other's internal affairs.

While the rest of the delegates slept one night the Germans met the Russians at nearby Rapallo and, at the famous "pajama party," worked out an agreement between their two countries. They mutually gave up all claim to reparations for war damage or compensation for nationalized property and agreed to restore diplomatic relations. Russia received assurance of an indefinite amount of credit from German firms. Under the agreement she later obtained machinery, technical assistance, and military instruction, while German army officers were permitted to practice their profession in Russia and so evade the restrictions of the Versailles Treaty.

The Western powers, and more especially Great Britain, had their revenge for Russia's diplomatic coup when the nations sent delegates to Lausanne later in the year to consider what should be done with the Straits. Remembering British and French activity in the Black Sea during the Civil War, Chicherin argued that warships should not be allowed to use the Straits at any time, in peace or in war. But the Russian observer at the conference was unable to convert the delegates to the Russian position. The Treaty of Lausanne permitted free use of the Straits by the merchant or war vessels of all nations in peacetime or during a war to which Turkey was not a party. If Turkey joined the war, presumably she should have the right to close the Straits to enemy warships. In time of peace, the agreement went on, no nation might send through the Bosporus more naval tonnage than that possessed by the strongest Black Sea power. There was nothing, however, to prevent several allies each from sending the maximum tonnage through the Straits and so overwhelming the Russian Black Sea fleet. Once again the most vulnerable point in the nation's defense perimeter lay exposed until such time as a navy could be built to defend it.

GAINS AND LOSSES

The other great powers were slow to follow Germany's lead in recognizing Soviet Russia. Britain's Conservative party was extremely hostile to Bolshevism, and Amery and Churchill led the pack in castigating the Bolshevik leaders as "a band of cosmopolitan conspirators gathered from the underworlds of the great cities of Europe and America," a grossly unfair and untrue reference to their lives in exile. But when the mildly socialist British Labour party joined with the Liberals to form a cabinet in 1924, Prime Minister Ramsey MacDonald fulfilled his party's pledge to recognize the Soviet government and sought to obtain in exchange a promise that war and prewar Russian debts would be paid. When the Soviet leaders asked for a loan with which to pay the debts Britain demurred and the negotiations dragged out inconclusively. But the British move stirred the other powers to action. Italy, France, Norway, Sweden, Denmark, Austria, Greece, Mexico, and China extended recognition before the year was out, and early in 1925 Japan and Russia resubscribed to the Treaty of Portsmouth and restored diplomatic relations. The United States remained intransigent, however, and refused to have anything to do with the Russian government.

French fear of a German revival and war of revenge, and British concern to prevent another Franco-Russian alliance to counterbalance Germany, brought the European powers together at Locarno to promote an atmosphere of peace. Russia was not invited and looked upon the gathering as an attempt to assure her isolation from the European family. The conference produced a guarantee of the French and Belgian boundaries but did nothing to confine Germany to her eastern frontier. But Germany, like Russia, was still denied membership in the League of Nations, and German pique at being excluded was quickly exploited by the Soviet government. Just before Locarno the two reached a trade agreement awarding Russia a substantial loan, and six months after Locarno Germany and Russia promised neutrality if a third power attacked either. The treaty declared that its intent, aside from promoting friendly relations between the signatories, was to counteract the anti-Russian sympathies of the League of Nations. Soviet fears were eased somewhat, and Germany, by her implied threat to line up with Russia, won admission to the League.

While trade flourished between Britain and Russia after the restoration of diplomatic contact, relations between the two governments were anything but friendly. During the British election campaign in the fall of 1924 a London newspaper published purported instructions from Zinoviev detailing plans for a Communist revolution in the islands. The letter was later shown to be a forgery, but not before it had accomplished its purpose of restoring the Conservatives to power. A year later Zinoviev publicly praised British organized labor for its stand against peaceful settlement of disputes with management. He also predicted a serious mine strike and proposed financial aid to the strikers when it should come. The miners did walk out and a general strike ensued. Although the latter failed, the miners stayed off the job for months while Russian workers volunteered nearly five million dollars for their support. Britons became indignant at this Russian interference in British affairs and at alleged Russian instigation of anti-British riots and boycotts in China. An excuse for breaking off diplomatic relations with the Soviet Union was conveniently found when British detectives raided the London office of Arcos, the Russian trading firm, in search of military secrets stolen from the War Office. The stolen papers were not uncovered, but the government insisted that other documents seized in the raid indicated the presence in England of a Soviet spy ring. Labour party leaders ridiculed the charge but Parliament voted to break off diplomatic relations. Nevertheless, commerce went on between the two countries and Arcos was permitted to carry on its trading activities. Meanwhile, Russians White and Red expected Great Britain to declare war. *Émigrés* returned to take part in the anticipated overthrow of the Bolsheviks, and there were countless acts of sabotage and terrorist attacks upon officials. Peasants hoarded salt and grain, the citizens of Moscow were near panic with fear, and foreigners were asked when the war would come. The war scare died down through the following winter months but flared again with the coming of spring. Then the Communist party "began to emphasize the permanent, ever-present menace of war in Europe and throughout the world" (Fischer). To the day of his death, Stalin harped on the theme that war was imminent and so drove the people to effort and sacrifice almost beyond human endurance.

The refusal of the American government to recognize Soviet Russia did not prevent its citizens from trading with the Communists. American imports from and exports to the U.S.S.R. reached twice the prewar volume, amounting to over a hundred and fifty million dollars by 1929. Electrical-equipment, farm-machinery, and automobile manufacturers carried on a thriving business with the Soviet government, while American oil companies fought each other for contracts to buy the output of Russian wells. Familiarity with American equipment and with the technicians who went along to install it did much to enhance traditional Bolshevik respect for American enterprise and skill.

Political relations between East and West continued strained, however. Russian leaders looked upon the League of Nations as an anti-Soviet bloc and were sure that Locarno was an attempt, as the British foreign secretary practically admitted it was, to arrange the peace and security of Europe not only without Russia but against her. Along her western frontier the peace settlement of 1919 left a *cordon sanitaire* of bitterly anti-Communist states who might, under Polish leadership and with French blessing, drive east at any time. Russia was asked to participate in framing the League of Nations' disarmament proposals and Maxim Litvinov, the vice-commissar for foreign affairs, represented the U.S.S.R. He proposed immediate demobilization and complete disarmament by liquidating all armed forces, destroying all weapons, warships, and military planes, abolishing military training, dismantling all war plants, removing all fortifications and military installations, sweeping away all general staffs and war ministries, and forbidding provision for military items in any state budget. All this he proposed should be done in a year's time or, if that were impossible, in four years. After reading his "Fourteen Points" Litvinov sat down in a hushed house too shocked to grant him even polite applause. When the delegates recovered sufficiently three months later to consider Litvinov's proposals they all agreed, with the exception of Germany and Turkey who supported them, that the plan was "impracticable."

When nothing came of Litvinov's daring suggestions the Soviet government resorted to more conventional ways of warding off attack. Nonaggression pacts were concluded with Russia's neighbors—with Turkey, Germany, Lithuania, Afghanistan, and Persia in the 1920's, and with Finland, Estonia, Latvia, and even Poland by 1932. Most, but not all, the gaps in the nation's defense line were closed; Romania and Japan would not listen to nonaggression proposals. Finally, Russia signed the Kellogg-Briand Pact in 1928 by which the powers all piously promised not to resort to war as an instrument of national policy.

SOVIET INTEREST IN ASIA

The joint Chinese-Russian protectorate over Outer Mongolia, established during World War I, deteriorated during the revolution when White forces backed by the Japanese seized the Mongolian capital and used the area as

The University of Moscow.

Churchill, Roosevelt and Stalin at Yalta.

a base for raiding into Siberia. As the tide of White fortunes ebbed, Red troops advanced into Mongolia and scattered the armies of Ungern-Sternberg, Kalmykov, and Semenov. To ensure that the territory would not again become a counterrevolutionary stronghold the Bolsheviks established a puppet regime friendly to Moscow. The Chinese government objected but was too pitifully weak to do more. The general Sino-Soviet agreement of 1924 restored full Chinese sovereignty over Outer Mongolia. Russia promised to withdraw her troops and did so, but left a trained native army to insure that the land would be governed by pro-Soviet forces. The puppet government which the Russians had installed called itself the "Mongolian People's Republic." Successfully parrying China's efforts to recover control over the area, the satellite regime continued to rule Outer Mongolia as a Soviet protectorate.

In 1919, when Siberia and Manchuria were in hostile hands, the Bolsheviks nobly abandoned all rights over the Chinese Eastern Railway, which at the moment was being operated by an international commission. As soon as the Whites had been defeated and the Japanese had gone home the Russians came to realize that the short rail line over the Chinese Eastern to Vladivostok would be as valuable to Communist as to Imperial Russia. When the commissar for foreign affairs informed the Chinese government of the change of heart the Chinese countered with a request that Red troops get out of Mongolia.

The outstanding issues between the two nations were settled in the Sino-Soviet Treaty of 1924. Russia, tongue in cheek, recognized Mongolia as part of China and promised to withdraw her troops. She surrendered all concessions which the tsarist government had won from the Chinese, gave up the Boxer indemnity which the colonial powers had imposed in 1901, and renounced the right of extraterritoriality which every other power still retained and which the Chinese so resented. The Chinese Eastern Railway was to be operated by a board half Chinese and half Russian under a Chinese chairman.

The U.S.S.R. became embroiled in the Chinese Revolution which broke out anew in 1925 and which aimed to put an end to imperialist exploitation by Great Britain, France, Japan, and the United States. Since the Soviet government only recently had renounced her rights and concessions in China, the animosity against foreigners was not directed against her. In fact, she was looked upon as the one sure enemy of imperialism and the one true friend of the peoples fighting for independence and dignity. While not a Communist himself, the Chinese leader Sun Yat-sen sympathized with the Russian experiment and sided with the peasants and workers against capitalists and landlords. There was a communist wing in the Kuomintang, which maintained a link between Moscow and the revolutionary party which he headed. At the very moment when Joffe, the Soviet diplomatic representative in China, was trying to win the recognition of the Republic of China and settle his government's differences with the Chinese, he was also offering comfort and concrete aid to the revolutionary leader Sun Yat-sen.

While Moscow denied any official relationship with the Nationalist government at Canton, as Sun Yat-sen's revolutionary movement now called itself, millions of rubles helped finance the Nationalist drive north to Shanghai and into the Yangtze Valley. Michael Borodin, an influential member of the Russian Communist party, went to China to advise the Nationalists on revolutionary strategy; General Bluecher and a host of Russian army officers and technicians went with him. Borodin advised Chiang Kai-shek, who took over the leadership of the Kuomintang after Sun Yat-sen's death in 1925, to order improved labor conditions and to divide the great estates among the peasants if he wanted popular support for his movement. But at the insistence of the conservative wing of the party, made up of great landowners and financiers, Chiang rejected the advice and turned against the left wing and its Russian friend Borodin. An attempt by Chinese Communists to take over Canton and launch their own revolution was put down. Thousands of Chinese and some of the Russians were executed and Chiang emerged triumphant over all opposition. Borodin returned to Moscow and Russia's influence, which momentarily had promised so much, came quickly to an end. Yet a year earlier the prospects in China had appeared so bright that the Comintern had promoted an uprising in the Dutch East Indies and had high hopes for a rebellion against British power in India.

By 1928 Chiang Kai-shek had won control of all China except for a small area along the northern border which the Chinese Communists managed to retain. Mistaking Borodin's return to Moscow as a sign of Russian weakness, Chiang imagined that the Russians might easily be forced to surrender their interest in the Chinese Eastern Railway. In 1929 Nationalist authorities raided the Russian Consulate in Harbin in search of the usual incriminating documents. As usual, the documents sought did not turn up but others purportedly as damaging conveniently did. Chinese officials seized a hundred Russians and escorted them across the frontier.

But Moscow had no intention of losing her rights to a railroad of such vital importance to her position in East Asia. When threats accomplished nothing with Chiang Kai-shek, Russia launched a drive toward Harbin from both ends of the Chinese Eastern Railway. The Chinese forces fell back in confusion and Chiang hastily agreed to a restoration of the dual control of the railroad provided in the 1924 agreement. The suspension of diplomatic relations continued, however, until three years later, when the threat of Japanese encroachment brought China and Russia together.

The ease with which the Russian Far Eastern army had driven off the Chinese may have decided the Japanese to embark upon a campaign long planned to bring East Asia under her hegemony. Japan moved first into southern Manchuria, meeting no resistance other than feeble protests from China and a decision by the League of Nations to investigate this violation of a member's territory. In 1932 the Japanese occupied the rest of Manchuria, enthroned a puppet emperor, and proclaimed Manchuria, which they renamed Manchukuo, an independent state. While the threat to eastern Siberia was unmistakably clear, the U.S.S.R. was in no position to challenge the Japanese aggression. The unrest, confusion, and famine growing out of the First Five-Year Plan left the government no choice but to avoid war with a power as formidable as Japan. Russia later sold to Manchukuo her interest in the Chinese Eastern Railway, a humiliation which was compounded when Japan spurned a Russian proposal to sign a nonaggression pact.

FUNDAMENTALS OF SOVIET FOREIGN POLICY

In 1931 Stalin explained the need to complete the industrialization of Russia as quickly as possible: "We are fifty to a hundred years behind the advanced countries. We must make up this lag in ten years. Either we do this or they will crush us." Exactly ten years later the attack which the Communists had feared and expected came with the Nazi invasion. Russia still was not ready to meet it. Had she been caught without powerful allies she would surely have been crushed.

Russia's persistent striving for peace and her patience in the face of insulting efforts to provoke her into war can be explained only in the light of Stalin's warning that the nation must "catch up." Russia's leaders knew the country to be weak and dangerously helpless through the period of the N.E.P., during which the nation strove mightily to recover from the devastation suffered in the first World War and the Civil War that followed. She was just as weak and helpless through the years of the First Five-Year Plan when every ounce of energy went into the drive for industrialization. While she gathered strength after 1932, the nation's leaders still hoped to avoid or at least to postpone war for yet a few more years. She sought so desperately to keep the peace because her leaders realized that there could be no hope for victory unless the nation possessed a powerful industrial plant ready to turn out the steel, the rubber, the oil, the machines that are the sinews of modern war.

This striving for peace, not because it was moral or right, but because peace was an absolute necessity if the nation were to survive, is apparent in Russian foreign policy during the first decade after the Civil War. For ten years prior to Hitler's rise the Soviet navy was about equal to that of Spain, and the armed forces contained only a little over half a million men to defend the world's longest frontier. These facts were a sure indication of an absence of aggressive intent. Such a puny force could have done little against the armed might of France, whom Russia feared, or Japan, or even Poland, who could always count on French support.

So the Soviet leaders used diplomacy for all it was worth to keep the nation out of war. They worked hard to win recognition and to develop normal, friendly relations with all powers. They sought nonaggression pacts with such dogged patience that all the nations along the western border except Romania had signed such treaties by 1932. The government swallowed one humiliation after another—assassination of ambassadors, arrest of officials by foreign governments, closing of consulates, raids of agencies normally accorded diplomatic immunity, seizure of the Chinese Eastern Railway—but refused to be drawn into war. It sent representatives to join in disarmament discussions who probably were more sincere than any other representatives, for Russia had more to gain and less to lose than any other great power. In its strange way even the Comintern worked for peace. Perhaps it made sense only to the Russians that the Third International could help keep the U.S.S.R. out of war by threatening sabotage and revolution to the nation's potential enemies. Of course, such threats immensely handicapped the Commissariat for Foreign Affairs, which was seeking at the same time to win friends. When the Comintern in the 1930's ordered its members to support democratic governments rather than embarrass them, and so promote friendship for the U.S.S.R., Russian foreign policy was more successful, on the surface at least, than in the twenties when the Foreign Office and the International seemed often to be working at cross purposes. And, through the years of the Comintern's existence, the protestation by Moscow on the one hand and non-Russian Communists on the other that the Soviet government and the International were unrelated fooled no one.

Perhaps because their politicians were more expansive or their press more caustic than the politicians and the press of other European nations, France and Great Britain seemed to Soviet leaders the most likely to try again to topple the new Russian government. Poland was another threat, although not a dangerous one unless backed by a great power. Many refugees had settled in the three countries and most of them did their best, in the way of refugees from tsarism, to paint the government from which they had fled in the blackest tones. After the Japanese move into Manchuria in 1931 Russia, perhaps convinced that after all Britain and France really did not want war, turned her attention to the Far East. There the threat was more sinister than perhaps any Russian knew. During World War II the Japanese ambassador in Berlin divulged that for twenty years his country's general staff had been planning an attack upon the Soviet Union. But Russian attention did not long remain focused upon Japan. Early in 1933 it shifted quickly back to Central Europe.

THE NAZI MENACE

Until the rise of Hitler, Russia's problem of avoiding war was scarcely a problem at all. No nation in Europe wanted war. All of them were anti-Bolshevik and in some countries there were minorities who never left off clamoring for a crusade against communism. But the overwhelming majority in every country wanted peace. While that same majority detested and feared communism, no nation was willing to go to war to erase it. That is why many Europeans welcomed the appearance of Hitler. They saw the possibility that he might undertake the eradication of Bolshevism where they were unwilling to undertake it themselves.

Years before his coming to power Hitler published for all to see his program for a renascent Germany. Few read the ponderous *Mein Kampf;* fewer still took it seriously. With Hitler's appointment to the chancellorship in January, 1933, the members of the Politburo may well have taken up the book again and read it through carefully. There they would have seen his assertion that Bolshevism was about to collapse. There they would have read his plans for German expansion in the east. Germany, said Hitler, must take for herself the grain of the Ukraine, the oil of the Caucasus, the minerals of the Urals, and the timber resources of Siberia. That these were something more than wild dreams Russian diplomats learned at the London Economic Conference in 1933, when one of Hitler's admirers asked Western delegates for a free hand for Germany in the Ukraine in exchange for the colonies she had lost in 1919.

In the fall of 1936 the Anti-Comintern Pact united Germany and Japan in opposing the Third International and all who supported it. A year later Italy joined the other two and the so-called Berlin-Rome-Tokyo Axis was born. While the pact did not mention Russia, there could be no mistake that it was directed against the nation which provided the Third International a home. Since both Hitler and Mussolini had liquidated or paralyzed their own Communists, and since communism had never taken root in Japan, the union obviously was dedicated to an attack upon communism abroad.

THE SEARCH FOR ALLIES

The Kremlin's policy of seeking normal and friendly relations with all nations met with growing success after the emergence of Hitler and Japan's aggression against China. In November, 1933, the United States recognized the Soviet government, the last major nation to do so. The move was inspired by the hope for improved trade relations, but more especially by Washington's growing concern over the Japanese threat in the Pacific. Six months later the Soviet government received recognition from Czechoslovakia, Romania, and Bulgaria. Diplomatic relations with Great Britain had been restored, although there was little friendship lost between the two nations.

The death of the Weimar Republic, and with it the spirit of good will which the German Foreign Minister Stresemann had done so much to build up, made France increasingly fearful of a revival of German militarism. Franco-Russian discussions in 1934 looked forward to Russia's entry into the League of Nations to restore the League's falling influence after the withdrawal of Japan and Germany, to work out a mutual-defense pact, and to pave the way for close cooperation between Russia and France's allies in Eastern Europe. In September, 1934, Russia became a member of the League with a permanent seat on its Council. France's effort to work the U.S.S.R. into a so-called Eastern Locarno in which Russia, Germany, Poland, and the Baltic republics would guarantee each others boundaries fell victim to German and Polish refusals to subscribe to the proposal. In May, 1935, France and Russia signed a mutual-defense treaty by which the two promised to stand together if either were attacked by another European power. Since the British Foreign Office knew of the talks and since Poland would not attack Russia without French consent, the document was obviously aimed at Germany. Immediately, Czechoslovakia and the U.S.S.R. signed a similar agreement which added that Russia would come to the defense of the Czechs only if France had moved first to fulfill her mutual-defense obligation to the Czech republic. Moscow's defensive alliance with France and Czechoslovakia would mean nothing, however, unless either Poland or Romania should consent to the passage of Russian troops through their territory, and this neither country would agree to do. French influence, strong as it always was in Warsaw, was not sufficiently great to make Poles forget that it was the defeat of Russia, and not of Germany, that would bring them the richest territorial gain. Similarly, Romania might hope to profit from a Russian, but hardly from a German, defeat.

The Seventh Congress of the Comintern, which was to be its last, met in Moscow in mid-summer, 1935. Obviously on orders from the Kremlin, the congress voted to halt Communist revolutionary agitation against bourgeois governments and to support a "popular front" of liberal parties in every country against the mounting tide of fascism. Communists must join with socialists, laborites, democrats, liberals, or any others willing to combat Fascist aggression. While Communist support was embarrassing and even irritating to some political parties, there can be no doubt that Communist activity in propagandizing for and popularizing the Soviet Union won Russia many friends, at least among the common people in democratic countries.

RUSSIAN-JAPANESE TENSION

From the time of the Nazi triumph in Germany to the end of World War II in Europe, Russia's strategic position and her management of foreign affairs was complicated by the fact that she had to watch two fronts, one in Europe, the other in the Far East. The sale of her interest in the Chinese Eastern Railway in 1935 for a price far less than its worth was prompted by her concern to avoid involvement with Japan at a time when Hitler's ambition in the west was becoming increasingly evident. Russian statesmen were aware, however, of the gain they would realize if China could be encouraged to resist Nipponese aggression and so tie down Japan and prevent her moving against Russia. Their interest in promoting Chinese resistance had to take cognizance of the fact that after 1927 there were two Chinas, the one under the Kuomintang, the other under the Communists. When the two agreed to shelve their differences in the face of the common enemy Russia fed military supplies into China, helping Chiang Kai-shek to some extent but contributing more, as was to be expected, to the Communists. In 1937 Moscow concluded a nonaggression pact with the Nationalist government and stepped up the flow of equipment and military advisers to Chiang. Nine months earlier Japan had joined Germany in the Anti-Comintern Pact. Now Tokyo could argue, if she needed an excuse, that in pressing her campaign on the mainland she was fighting the battle of civilization against communism, for Chiang had come to terms with Moscow.

Much as Japanese generals may have been provoked by the Kremlin's aid and comfort to the Chinese, they could not safely turn against Russia until they had finished with China. They could, however, feel out the strength of the "Red Banner Army," as Russia's Far Eastern force was officially named. A succession of border incidents led to a full-scale battle at Changkufeng Hill near Vladivostok in the summer of 1938, when units of the crack Japanese Kwantung Army crossed the Siberian frontier. This Battle of Lake Hasan, as the Russians call it, lasted nearly two weeks and both sides used planes, tanks, and heavy artillery. The Japanese were driven off and their government sued for an armistice. In May, 1939, Japan sent troops into the Nomonhan district of Outer Mongolia to test Russo-Mongolian defenses. Again they were thrown back and asked for a truce. The Japanese War Office admitted a disastrous defeat and attributed it to superior Russian armor. Tension continued along the Siberian-Manchurian border, and Russia expanded the Red Banner Army to four hundred thousand men to discourage Japan from carrying the challenge to the point of war. But Japan was pinned down in China and Russia committed the bulk of her strength in the west, so the uneasy truce went on until 1945.

THE COLLAPSE OF COLLECTIVE SECURITY

From the moment of Russia's entry into the League, Litvinov, foreign commissar since 1930, pleaded with the members to stand together in respect for world order and in defense of the covenant and adherence to the treaties which curbed international anarchy. He pointed out repeatedly that "peace is indivisible," that a breach of the peace anywhere was a threat to the security of all nations, that there could not be peace for a few unless there were peace for all.

When Mussolini invaded Ethiopia the League condemned this rape of one member by another but did nothing more. Fifty member nations promised not to trade with Italy in certain commodities, but the Russian proposal that the list include oil, coal, and steel was turned down with the lame excuse that Italy could easily obtain these materials from the United States, which was not a member of the League and not a party to the pledge. When the African tragedy was over, the League, at British and French urging, bribed Italy not to withdraw by recognizing her conquest of Ethiopia. Russia protested this cynical act vigorously but found little support.

In mid-summer, 1936, General Francisco Franco led a fascist military clique in a revolt against the legitimate popular-front government of Spain, which was also a member of the League. Franco had not the slightest hope of success without foreign backing, but that was soon forthcoming as Germany and Italy poured guns, tanks, planes, submarines, and troops into the rebel cause. Like the other powers, Russia preferred not to intervene but chose to do so when it proved impossible to get the League or the Western nations to force the suspension of outside aid to Franco. Moscow sent planes, guns, food, and perhaps two thousand military technicians and advisers to back the Spanish government, but all in too modest a volume to influence the outcome of the civil war. After a few months Russia pulled out the technicians, aviators, and military advisers she had sent the Loyalists and reduced the flow of military supplies to a trickle. Litvinov urged the other members of the League to intervene, but his plea went begging and Russia hesitated to go it alone. Hitler and Mussolini spawned the utter falsehood that the Spanish government was Communist-dominated and Moscow-oriented, and many in the West swallowed the fiction. Great Britain, France, and the United States refused to intervene in the Spanish war; Russia sent too little help, and Franco, with German and Italian sponsorship, won a decisive victory for fascism over the forces of democracy.

The vicious purges that went on in Russia while the Spanish Civil War was in progress did nothing to improve Moscow's relations with the democracies. The Western press painted Russia in the darkest terms, implying that cooperation with the brutal dictator in the Kremlin was out of the question. Much of the abuse was justified, but much of it was gross exaggeration—for example, the insinuation that Russia was a godless nation where religious practice was proscribed. The purge of the Red Army, with its liquidation of thousands of officers, was looked upon as having destroyed Russia's military effectiveness and so ended any value she may have had as an ally. By 1938 Russia was left without a reliable friend among the great powers.

Hitler's absorption of Austria in March, 1938, although expressly forbidden by the Versailles Treaty, excited little concern in the West. But his move against Czechoslovakia, by all counts a peace-loving and democratic state, threatened to precipitate war. This time the Kremlin gave every indication of a willingness to fight rather than allow Czechoslovakia to go by default, as Spain in effect had gone. When the British asked whether Russia would fight if the Czechs were attacked, Moscow answered that she would fulfill her obligations under her mutual-assistance treaty with Prague, which was to say that Russia would march to the defense of the Czechs when France marched. The Conservative cabinet in Britain was working diligently for peace at this juncture, although it had shown little concern at the repeated threats to peace which Hitler and Mussolini had engineered on previous occasions. When it became apparent that France at British urging would not defend Czechoslovakia, Prague asked if Russia would fight even if France would not. Moscow answered that she would fight, although how she expected to do so without consent to cross Polish or Romanian territory was not clear. The problem did not arise, however, for Czechoslovakia submitted to pressure from Great Britain and France to leave her destiny in their hands. Neither Czechs nor Russians were invited to the conference at Munich in September, 1938; in fact, Moscow was not even notified that there was to be a conference. The British Chamberlain, the French Daladier, Hitler, and Mussolini concluded that Czechoslovakia must surrender to Germany the Sudetenland, a border strip which included the so-called Little Maginot line, the loss of which made impossible the defense of what was left of Czechoslovakia.

The Russians knew that there were many bitterly conservative Britons and Frenchmen who would be pleased to see the troublesome Hitler turn east against the Soviet Union. When London and Paris gave in so obligingly to the neutralization of Czechoslovakia, Russia read the evidence to mean that the Western powers deliberately were seeking to usher Hitler into Eastern Europe. Of one thing the Russians could be sure. The mutual-assistance pact with France was as worthless as the French had just shown their similar pact with Czechoslovakia to have been. Hitler had succeeded in destroying the Franco-Russian alliance and in isolating Moscow. But some time after Munich Russia decided that two could play the game. If she could not find security against Hitler, she would find it with him.

In mid-March, 1939, Hitler called in the president of Czechoslovakia and gave him one hour to sign over the rest of his country to Germany. Litvinov proposed a meeting with Great Britain, France, Poland, Turkey, and Romania to consider future action, but the British prime minister answered that the proposal was "premature." Next, Hitler insisted that Lithuania give him Memel, her only seaport. To refuse would have been disastrous, and another thousand square miles came under the Nazi flag. Mussolini joined in the fun by taking Albania. Then it was Hitler's move again, and he notified Poland that the city of Danzig must belong to Germany.

In mid-April, 1939, Litvinov outlined to Britain and France a concrete proposal for a tripartite alliance, backed up with military commitments, to defend any country threatened by the Fascist powers. Moscow insisted that the three powers must specifically guarantee against Fascist aggression all the states bordering on Russia's western frontier. Paris was interested but the British cabinet obviously was not.

In May, 1939, Litvinov, who symbolized Russia's hope to win Western confidence and cooperation, resigned as commissar for foreign affairs. He was succeeded by Stalin's close friend Viacheslav Molotov, who would hold the office for the next seventeen years. A few venomous observers in the West assumed that Litvinov would be shot for the failure of the policy he stood for. He was not shot, however, and later came out of retirement to return to public life. But his withdrawal from the Foreign Office signaled a shift in Soviet foreign policy. While Britain and France saw nothing ominous in Molotov's appointment, the Germans thought it might indicate a withdrawal from the uncompromising anti-Nazi stand the Russians had taken since Hitler's rise to power and a willingness to accept an offer of security from whoever was ready to make it. The German analysis proved to be an accurate one.

THE LAST CHANCE

The obliteration of Czechoslovakia woke the Chamberlain government to the need for positive action if Hitler's "artichoke policy" of devouring the small countries one by one were to be halted. But the British prime minister, bitterly anti-Russian, held back from taking the one step—military alliance with the Soviet Union—that could stop the Nazis if it were not already too late. Instead he began to guarantee, piecemeal, the countries that might next appeal to Hitler's appetite. The British government guaranteed Poland from aggression when Warsaw rejected Hitler's insistence that he must have

Danzig. A few days later Greece and Romania received similar guarantees from both Britain and France. But Chamberlain was unreasonably sensitive of the reluctance of the border states to cooperate with Russia. Estonia and Latvia insisted they were in no danger and needed no assistance from the U.S.S.R. Romania refused to join a pact aimed against Germany. Poland would have none of any defense arrangement that included Russia. Litvinov had sent an assistant, the historian Potemkin, to visit Turkey, Romania, Bulgaria, and Poland to plead for collective security but the conversations, except in Ankara, were disappointing.

Meanwhile, correspondence between London and Moscow over Russian proposals for a tripartite political and military alliance was subjected by the British cabinet to unreasonable and irritating delays. Finally Chamberlain gave way before Parliamentary pressure that he stop stalling and enter into direct conversations with the Russians. But instead of going himself, as he had done on several occasions to meet Hitler, he sent a subordinate official in the Foreign Office, William Strang. But perhaps it was already too late. Nearly two weeks before Strang left London Molotov had told a meeting of the Supreme Soviet that there was no intention of breaking off trade relations with the Fascist powers. A commercial agreement had recently been concluded with Italy, and there was a possibility that discussion of a trade treaty with Germany which earlier had been interrupted might be renewed. The French cabinet interpreted this warning to mean that the prospects for a triple alliance with Russia had died. That London had waited too long seemed apparent when Estonia and Latvia signed nonaggression pacts with Germany, thus forestalling any great-power attempt to bring the Baltic countries into a mutual-security system.

Strang's talks with French and Russian officials in Moscow began in mid-June and dragged on inconclusively for weeks. The Kremlin proposed a three-power mutual-assistance agreement and also a guarantee of the Baltic states, Poland, Romania, and Turkey from aggression either direct or indirect. The British and French pretended not to understand what the Russians meant by "indirect aggression." When Molotov spelled it out for them —that it meant infiltration of a country and organizing it as a base for attack upon the U.S.S.R.—the British balked at guaranteeing the small powers against such aggression without their consent, which had already been denied.

The danger mounted through July that the Kremlin would lose all patience with Western procrastination and begin political as well as trade talks with Germany. That such a catastrophe might befall was no secret and was discussed in diplomatic circles in every capital in Europe. Moscow suspected that London, at least, was trying to work out an agreement with Berlin. The common knowledge that a German mission was in England seeking a loan of a billion pounds sterling was hardly calculated to allay Russian suspicions. Two days after learning of the German request for a British loan, Moscow announced that trade talks with Germany would be reopened. The Kremlin had been considering such a move for weeks but took no step until the German arrival in London seemed to suggest the reason behind the wearisome delays in the talks going on in Moscow.

The announcement of the Nazi-Soviet trade talks stirred the Western delegates but slightly. They agreed to include the Baltic states in any guarantee against aggression but haggled over the definition of "indirect aggression." The three powers agreed to begin military staff talks aimed at pinning down the measures to be taken if the territory of the guaranteed states should be threatened. Instead of flying, the British staff officers travelled by slow ship through the Baltic and arrived in the Russian capital six days later. Strang departed for London before they arrived, leaving to the military sessions the problem of agreeing on what constituted indirect aggression. The staff talks managed only "to redefine it in a more intractable form, with the Anglo-French rejection probably taken for granted in advance" (Beloff). The British delegation had little authority to commit its government and the talks were frequently interrupted by the need to refer to London for instructions. Poland and the Baltic states refused to be guaranteed and would not consent to the movement of Russian troops across their territories. The talks were still dragging slowly along when on August 23, 1939, Nazi Germany and Soviet Russia signed a ten-year nonaggression pact. A few hours earlier the British ambassador in Berlin, Sir Nevile Henderson, told Hitler that if anyone had to sign an agreement with the Soviet Union he preferred that Germany rather than Great Britain do it. He soon got his wish.

THE NAZI-SOVIET PACT

Stalin's speech to the opening session of the Eighteenth Congress of the Communist Party was filled with harsh words about Fascist and particularly German aggression. But the speech was more pointed in the derision it heaped upon Great Britain and France for their spinelessness. In pronouncing the aims of Soviet foreign policy he gave first place to "peace and the strengthening of business relations with all countries." While the congress was in session Hitler erased Czechoslovakia from the map and there was no more than formal protest from the Western powers. In mid-April, 1939, the Soviet ambassador in Berlin hinted to the German Foreign Office that there was no reason why Russia and Germany should not live together "on a normal footing." Later in the same month Hitler delivered a speech denouncing the Munich accord, the Anglo-German naval agreement, and the

Polish-German nonaggression pact, but for the first time in his career spared Bolshevism from the "buckets of filth" he usually heaped upon it. The German press began to show a moderation toward Russia that it had not shown since the Nazis came to power.

Through May and June there were informal conversations below the ambassadorial level looking toward an improvement in Soviet-Nazi trade relations. By early July there were hints that an attempt step by step to improve relations generally, politically as well as economically, might prove fruitful. But the Nazis had to hurry. Their plan to attack Poland in August had already reached the stage of army orders in early April.

As the fruitless Moscow talks with the Western powers dragged on Molotov let it be known, in the first week of August, that he was ready to begin discussions of the outstanding differences between Russia and Germany. In mid-August Ribbentrop, the German foreign minister, asked to come to Moscow to arrange an agreement involving the whole area from the Black Sea to the Baltic. At that very moment Voroshilov was trying vainly to get the Western military staffs to guarantee the right of transit for Russian troops across Polish and Romanian territory and to consent to the occupation of the Baltic ports and coastal islands to deter German aggression against Russia. But the Westerners could promise nothing. Poland balked at the suggestion, as did the Baltic states, and the Western governments did not bother even to raise the question with Romania. Without such consent from the minor powers Russia's military cooperation with the others became impossible.

On August 19 a Nazi-Soviet trade agreement was signed, providing for a seven-year German credit to Russia of two hundred million marks in exchange for Germany's right to purchase raw materials from Russia to the value of a hundred and eighty million marks. The details of what goods would be exchanged remained to be worked out later. The figures were increased during the autumn and winter months, and Germany specified that she wanted grain, oil, cotton, flax, rubber and various ores. In return, Russia was to receive machine tools and military equipment. *Pravda* hailed the August trade agreement as an important step toward improving political relations with the Third Reich, and indeed the government announced that Ribbentrop would fly to Moscow to initial a nonaggression pact.

Ribbentrop landed in Moscow on August 23, 1939, and that very day concluded with Russia a ten-year nonaggression treaty. The two powers agreed to avoid any aggressive act against each other and each promised to remain neutral if the other became involved in war with a third power. This much was published in Moscow newspapers the next day. In a secret protocol attached to the nonaggression pact the signatories agreed on a line separating their spheres of influence in Eastern Europe. In the event of her political collapse, Poland would be divided along the Narev, Vistula, and San rivers, thus giving Russia nearly two-thirds of Poland and bringing her into the eastern suburbs of Warsaw. The northern border of Lithuania would separate the spheres of influence in the eastern Baltic, Russia being given a free hand in Estonia, Latvia, and Finland. Germany declared herself to be uninterested in Bessarabia, thus inviting Russian border adjustments in that area. This arrangement, which left Lithuania in the German sphere, was later altered to give Lithuania to Russia and compensate for it by moving the Russo-German border in Poland back approximately to the Curzon Line, the ethnic boundary between Poles and non-Poles.

Both German and Russian leaders were convinced that the nonaggression agreement put an end to any likelihood that Great Britain and France would defend Poland. Instead of making World War II inevitable, as indignant Westerners later insisted, it was taken for granted in Moscow and Berlin that either there would be no war or that, if it came, it would last only a few weeks. That Great Britain and France should undertake the strategically impossible and militarily foolhardy burden of rescuing Poland without Russia's help when they had refused to succor Czechoslovakia with Soviet assistance never ceased to puzzle Moscow and Berlin. But there can be no doubt that conservative circles in both Western countries preferred to stand heroically, however futilely, against the Nazi tyranny without the Russian alliance rather than with it.

THE SHIFT IN THE PARTY LINE

Communist parties outside Russia were caught completely off guard by the announcement of the Soviet-German accord. For years they had faithfully carried out the Kremlin's order to support bourgeois governments who resisted fascism. Only yesterday they had insisted that Poland must not go the way of Czechoslovakia. The contest of the thirties was one which lined up the peace-loving democracies, which of course included the Soviet Union, against the Anti-Comintern dictators, who showed no regard for human dignity and international law. To make themselves completely ridiculous by veering around to opposing the war against Germany took a full week. On the very day that German troops crossed the Polish border the French Communists resolved that the Poles must be supported. The painful reappraisal finally was worked out and the lackeys followed Moscow in condemning the Western powers for carrying on an "imperialist war." Not until the Nazi invasion of Russia nearly twenty-two months later did the Communist parties the world over slip back to their position that the Nazis were aggressors against the "peace-loving democracies."

SUGGESTED READING

Beloff, M., *The Foreign Policy of Soviet Russia, 1929–1941* (New York, Oxford University Press, 1949).

———, *Soviet Policy in the Far East, 1944–1951* (New York, Oxford University Press, 1953).

Bishop, D. G., *Soviet Foreign Relations: Documents and Readings* (Syracuse, Syracuse University Press, 1952).

Coates, W. P. and Z. K., *A History of Anglo-Soviet Relations* (London, Lawrence, 1943).

Dallin, D., *Soviet Russia and the Far East* (New Haven, Yale University Press, 1948).

———, *Soviet Russia's Foreign Policy, 1939–42* (New Haven, Yale University Press, 1942).

Degras, J., *Soviet Documents on Foreign Policy* (New York, Oxford University Press, 1953).

Dennis, A. L. P., *The Foreign Policies of Soviet Russia* (New York, Dutton, 1924).

Fischer, L., *The Soviets in World Affairs* (Princeton, Princeton Univ. Press, 1951).

Laserson, M. M., *Russia and the Western World* (New York, Macmillan, 1945).

Litvinov, M., *Against Aggression* (New York, International Publishers, 1939).

Moore, H. L., *Soviet Far Eastern Policy, 1931–1945* (Princeton, Princeton University Press, 1945).

Namier, L. B., *Diplomatic Prelude, 1938–1939* (New York, Macmillan, 1948).

Pope, A. U., *Maxim Litvinov* (New York, Fischer, 1943).

Schuman, F. L., *Soviet Politics at Home and Abroad* (New York, Knopf, 1946).

Seton-Watson, H., *Eastern Europe Between the Wars* (New York, Praeger, 1946).

———, *From Lenin to Malenkov* (New York, Praeger, 1955).

Sontag, R. J., and J. S. Beddie, *Nazi-Soviet Relations, 1939–1941* (United States Department of State, 1948).

Taracouzio, T. A., *War and Peace in Soviet Diplomacy* (New York, Macmillan, 1940).

Tompkins, P., *American-Russian Relations in the Far East* (New York, Macmillan, 1949).

Wheeler-Bennett, J. W., *Munich: Prologue to Tragedy* (New York, Duell, Sloan & Pearce, 1948).

Yakhontov, V., *U.S.S.R. Foreign Policy* (New York, Coward-McCann, 1945).

32

World War II and After

A<small>S POLISH RESISTANCE TO THE GER-</small>
man invasion evaporated, Russian troops advanced through eastern Poland
to claim Moscow's share of the spoils as previously agreed upon. In the
summer of 1940 the three Baltic republics were occupied and Bessarabia
was taken from Romania. So the frontier was pushed westward to incorporate a cushion of non-Russian lands to soften the expected Nazi blow.
Meanwhile a successful war against Finland brought the Karelian Isthmus
inside the Soviet border. Thereafter Nazi-Soviet relations steadily deteriorated.

German divisions crossed the Nieman on June 22, 1941, and drove steadily
and rapidly eastward for the next five months. Early in December the invasion stalled just west of Moscow. Leningrad was surrounded and the *Wehrmacht* had pushed through the Ukraine to the Donets. No sooner had the
German advance been stopped than the Russians went over to the offensive
and recovered some lost ground. With the coming of spring in 1942 the invaders mounted a second drive which carried them to the foothills of the
Caucasus. But they suffered a decisive defeat at Stalingrad and began a
withdrawal movement which eventually carried them back out of Russia,
through Poland, across eastern Germany and into Berlin, which the Red
Army entered in May, 1945.

Russia's relations with the Western powers improved during the war as
East and West set aside their differences, for the moment at least, to defeat
the common enemy. Britain and America fed quantities of war equipment
to the Russians and bombed Nazi industry into partial paralysis. Through
a succession of conferences the big three—Churchill, Roosevelt, and Stalin—
agreed to fight on together until the Axis surrendered unconditionally,

promised to restore democratic governments to the submerged nations, vowed to punish war criminals, planned an international organization to keep the peace, divided Europe into spheres of Russian and Western influence, promised reparations to the U.S.S.R., and redrew boundary lines in Eastern Europe in Russia's favor.

Relations between Moscow and the exiled Polish government in London were never cordial and were broken off completely midway through the war. A Russian-sponsored Polish government was established in Lublin to take over the administration of Polish territory as fast as it was liberated. Washington and London shifted their support from the exiled to the new administration on Stalin's promise that the Lublin government would be broadened to include non-Communist Poles. Moscow-oriented governments were planted in Romania, Bulgaria, and Hungary as the Red Army rolled back the Nazis, and the Communist Tito won the contest for political power in Yugoslavia.

Growing American alarm at the extension of Soviet domination in Eastern Europe produced the Truman Doctrine, Washington's policy of granting military and economic aid to nations whose independence seemed to be threatened by the surge of Russian influence. When Czechoslovakia became a satellite of Moscow and when Russia cut off communication between Berlin and the western occupation zones of Germany, the Truman administration sponsored the North Atlantic Treaty Organization whose members were pledged to halt further Communist aggression. The N.A.T.O. countries contributed troops to a common army, which was joined by German divisions after the birth of a West German government. Blocked in Europe, Stalin turned to the Far East and supported the attempt of the North Korean Communists to overrun South Korea. With a combination of Russian assistance and Chinese Nationalist corruption the Chinese Communists upset Chiang Kai-shek and brought their new "people's democracy" into partnership with Moscow.

Through the five-year period of the "cold war" from 1948 on, East-West tension threatened the possibility of a third world war. Stalin's death in 1953 reduced the immediate threat and his successors set about improving Russia's relations with the non-Communist world. Americans understood this new look in Soviet foreign policy as simply a shift in tactics and not a renunciation of Moscow's long-run ambitions. Some Western Europeans, however, tired of the burden of war and then defense costs, hoped for an early end to East-West tension. Such hopes proved to be short-lived. In November, 1956, Russian troops stamped out a Hungarian revolt. A year later Russian scientists launched two space satellites, called *sputniks,* and gave evidence of having perfected long range missiles to the point where Western security seemed dangerously threatened. By January, 1958, another crisis in East-West relations was imminent.

NEW BOUNDARIES

Three days after the Nazi attack on Poland it had already become clear that the Polish nation would be decisively defeated in a matter of weeks. Moscow was immediately notified that, to wipe out Poland's resistance, units of the Polish army would have to be pursued into the Russian zone unless the Red Army advanced to the demarcation line previously agreed upon in the protocol to the nonaggression pact. Moscow moved slowly, waiting to work out a truce with the Japanese after the fighting at Nomonhan but also preparing a statement for world consumption that would make the Russian advance seem less than barefaced aggression. On September 16, by which time the German pincers had enveloped all of Poland west of Warsaw, Molotov announced, prematurely to be sure, that the Polish government had ceased to exist and that the Soviet government proposed to rescue the defenseless Ukrainians and White Russians and grant them "protection." The Red Army crossed into Poland the next day, and organized resistance came to an end except in Warsaw, which held out heroically for another ten days. The Russians, not trusting the Germans to return any of the Soviet zone of Poland they might take, rushed through eastern Poland so precipitously that they themselves overshot the demarcation line. The day Warsaw surrendered Ribbentrop arrived in Moscow, and the next day signed the agreement defining the frontier. The boundary was moved a hundred miles east of Warsaw to the Western Bug River and conformed roughly, except in the north, to the Curzon Line. To compensate for this shift most but not all of Lithuania was transferred to the Russian sphere.

The zone of influence soon was incorporated into the U.S.S.R. Local assemblies in eastern Poland, hastily swept together for the purpose, petitioned for admission into the Ukrainian and Belo-Russian Republics, and the Supreme Soviet of the U.S.S.R. granted the request. Late in September and early in October representatives from Estonia, Latvia, and Lithuania paraded to Moscow to sign agreements for mutual defense against aggression which allowed Russia to use air and naval bases in the Baltic states and to station troops there. The province of Vilna was returned to the Lithuanians, from whom the Poles had wrenched it in 1920. In June, 1940, when the rapid disintegration of the French Army warned Russia to look to her own defenses, the three Baltic republics were occupied. In each case a newly-elected "people's government" asked for incorporation into the U.S.S.R., and all became constituent republics in the Soviet Union. When Soviet troops moved into Lithuania they occupied all of it, including the German zone, but later paid Germany's price of thirty million marks for her share. At the same time Soviet forces occupied Northern Bukovina and

Bessarabia, whose seizure by Romania during the Civil War the Bolsheviks had never accepted. The eastern districts were added to the Ukraine and the rest organized as the Moldavian Soviet Socialist Republic.

These acquisitions brought the Russian frontier in the west back approximately to where it had been when the empire had reached its farthest limits. There were two exceptions: Northern Bukovina lay outside the former empire, while the western provinces of tsarist Poland now were under Nazi rule. The Baltic provinces—the "Baltic gate" of invasion into the Leningrad area—now lay safely behind the Russian frontier. But Lenin's city still was not safe, for the Finnish border lay just twenty miles away, within artillery range should Finland, staunchly anti-Bolshevik, join the Nazis in an attack upon Russia.

At the time the Baltic states were invited to sign mutual-assistance treaties with Russia, Finland received but rejected a similar invitation. The Soviet government then demanded that in exchange for land north of Lake Ladoga the Finns turn over the Karelian Isthmus, including the Mannerheim Line, one of the strongest defense positions in the world, and allow Russia to fortify the Finnish islands at the entrance to the Gulf of Finland which had been Russian bases under the tsars. The Helsinki government refused, the Red Army crossed the border and Russian planes bombed the Finnish capital on the last day of November, 1939. Within the month the League of Nations judged the U.S.S.R. guilty of aggression and expelled her.

Otto Kuusinen, a Finnish Communist who had waited patiently in Moscow since 1918, organized a Communist government for Finland under Russian sponsorship. The Finnish Red government arranged by treaty for transfer to Russia of the territory Moscow sought and for the grant to Finland of the land near Lake Ladoga which Stalin had offered Helsinki in return. But there was little popular support for Kuusinen and his Reds. The people rallied to the defense of their government and to the support of Mannerheim, the reactionary tsarist general who led their army. Britain sent planes, guns, and equipment, but in quantities too small to influence the outcome of the battle. Volunteers from the West joined the Finns, but Germany, which had given Russia a free hand in Finland, remained scrupulously neutral. A spate of abuse poured from the Western press upon Stalin and the Russians. Finland became the symbol of democracy, freedom, civilization, Christianity; the Finnish pro-Nazi party and the pro-German sympathies of Baron Mannerheim were conveniently forgotten. The British and French governments considered a declaration of war against Russia and drew up plans for a drive into the Black Sea.

The Finns made a heroic stand and the Russian military leaders grossly underestimated the quality of their enemy and the determination of the Finnish people. Through December, 1939, and the following January the defenders repulsed every attack and took heavy toll among Russian units sent against them. The Western press chattered derision at the vaunted Red Army and even prophesied that the little nation of four million would defeat the Communist colossus.

Stalin, contemptuous of the Finns, had assumed that they would succumb to diplomatic pressure and had made no serious preparations for a military campaign. There was no formidable attack upon the Mannerheim Line and what advances there were, except in the north against Petsamo, were poorly organized and weakly supported. But in February, 1940, Timoshenko was given command and ordered to press the attack vigorously. The supposedly impregnable Mannerheim Line was obliterated by heavy-artillery fire, and the Red Army, fought every step of the way by the gallant Finns, advanced to Viipuri, the former Viborg. Helsinki had no choice but to accept Moscow's terms, which were less generous than those offered before the war.

By the peace settlement concluded in March, 1940, Finland turned over to the U.S.S.R. a speck of land near Petsamo and the Karelian Isthmus up to and including Viipuri, thus moving the Russo-Finnish frontier seventy miles farther away from Leningrad. Land to the north and west of Lake Ladoga also went to Russia, to be added to Soviet Karelia, which now became a constituent republic as the Karelo-Finnish S.S.R. Russia took a thirty-year lease on the naval base at Hango for an annual rental of some three hundred thousand dollars. Helsinki agreed not to admit a third power, obviously Germany, into the Aland Islands. Each signatory agreed not to attack the other or to join an alliance against the other. Moscow asked no indemnity. There was nothing beyond the pressure of world opinion to prevent Russia's imposing much more severe terms upon the Finns.

The Finnish campaign uncovered a number of glaring weaknesses in the Red Army which Defense Commissar Timoshenko set about immediately to remedy. Faulty administration was corrected. Deficiencies of machinery under cold-weather operation were analyzed and removed. The army was rapidly expanded to five million men by the end of the year. More training of aviators was seen to be necessary. The political commissars, who had been restored to army units after the purge trials and whose job it was to ferret out treason and even to approve strategical plans, were once more abolished. Having taken these corrective measures and having improved the nation's posture for defense, the Kremlin felt ready to meet the German challenge which was sure eventually to come.

THE STRANGE INTERLUDE

In the hope of winning peace for herself, or at least of postponing war until she was prepared for it, the U.S.S.R. scrupulously fulfilled her obligations under the nonaggression pact with Germany. For a while, before the

Finnish War became more costly than she had reckoned, Russia delivered to
Berlin on schedule the full amount of material she had contracted to send.
But Hitler grew increasingly uneasy over the gains Russia was making in
the east, even though he had agreed to them. He was incensed when Russia
added Northern Bukovina to Bessarabia in her seizures from Romania, for
the Nazi-Soviet Pact had mentioned only Bessarabia. It is unlikely that
he ever changed for a moment in his determination to bring the wealth of
the Ukraine and the Urals under German exploitation. Britain evidenced
no loss of determination to carry on after the fall of the Netherlands, Denmark, Norway, Belgium, and France. In fact, her new government under
Churchill showed far more spirit than before. Hitler may have decided to
seek a quick victory over Russia before Britain had grown any stronger and
while Russia was relatively unprepared. The purge of the Red Army and
the poor showing in the Finnish campaign had made Hitler, like most
Westerners, contemptuous of Russian strength. By August, 1940, Hitler had
made up his mind to invade Russia and his general staff began work immediately on the plans.

Nazi-Soviet relations grew steadily cooler during the summer and autumn
of 1940. Berlin constantly complained that the Russians were falling behind
in their deliveries of goods promised under the trade treaties that followed
the nonaggression pact. Moscow objected to the stationing of German troops
in Finland. A Nazi force entered Romania and ostentatiously guaranteed
her territory against Soviet aggression. Then, to buy the support of other
Balkan countries, Hitler forced Romania to turn over Transylvania to
Hungary and the Dobrudja to Bulgaria. In September, 1940, Germany, Italy,
and Japan signed the Tripartite Pact by which the three agreed to support
each other "with all political, economic and military means" if one should
be attacked by any power not then involved in the European or the Asiatic
war. The provision that the agreement was not aimed at Russia fooled
nobody.

Molotov went to Berlin in November, 1940, to attempt to improve relations with the ambitious power with whom Russia now shared a common
frontier. Hitler volunteered to sponsor Russian admission into the tripartite
accord formed two months earlier. And he offered to back a Russian drive
into the Middle East toward the Indian Ocean, a device to turn Russia away
from Europe that the kaiser had once tried. But Molotov would not be distracted. He asked that Bulgaria be assigned to the Russian sphere of influence and expressed concern over the Straits now that British troops were
in Greece. Hitler's revision of the Romanian, Hungarian, and Bulgarian
frontiers was discussed, and Molotov insisted upon Russia's vital interests
in the Balkans and in the nearby Straits. Molotov and Ribbentrop found
little they could agree upon and the conference ended in a spirit of only
surface friendship.

In the spring of 1941 Hitler settled matters in the Balkans in a way not at all to Moscow's liking. German troops occupied Bulgaria and bound her, perhaps unwillingly, into the Axis partnership. Yugoslavia fell to the *Wehrmacht* in two weeks and the Greek army capitulated in April. A month later the Nazis invaded Crete. It was not Britain, as Molotov had been fully aware, that the U.S.S.R. had to fear at the Straits. With German troops in every Balkan country and in Finland, Hitler had outflanked Russia in the north and in the south.

Nevertheless, Stalin preferred to believe that it was possible to avoid war. Warnings from Prime Minister Churchill and President Roosevelt that the Nazis were planning an invasion of Russia were dismissed as an attempt by Great Britain and America to bring the U.S.S.R. into the war against Germany "to pull their chestnuts out of the fire." Without a friend she felt she could trust, Russia took what precautions she could against an eventuality she maneuvered desperately to prevent. Expansion of the armed forces went feverishly on, and the correction of the weaknesses which the Finnish War had revealed was due to be completed by August. The forty-eight-hour week replaced the thirty-hour week for Russian industrial workers. The government curtailed the output of consumers' goods and stepped up production of war matériel. Japan, tied down in China, agreed to a mutual-neutrality pact by which she and Russia swore to respect each other's territory and to stay out of any war in which the other became involved.

Russia was not fully prepared for war in June, 1941, as the opening campaigns quickly made apparent. But in the twenty-two months since the signing of the nonaggression treaty with Germany her position had immeasurably improved. The western boundary had been pushed far back so that an invader would have to fight through a cushion of non-Russian territory before reaching the heart of the country. Without the absorption of the Baltic states and Eastern Poland, much as that had cost Russia in good will, Hitler might have used those countries, unfriendly as they were to Moscow, as a springboard of attack. The Red Army was far larger and far stronger in the summer of 1941 than it had been two years earlier. Russian industry now was approaching a wartime footing, but had been far from it in 1939. The Finnish experience had provided many lessons and trained many unit leaders. Of great importance was the fact that, after nearly two years of war, Britain was now ready to welcome Russia as a partner. International cooperation to beat back aggression was possible in 1941 but impossible in 1939. Even the United States, where neutralist feeling ran high in 1939 and where sympathy for the Finns had been especially strong, was now willing to assist Russia against Hitler. Nazi brutality in occupied Europe made the free world welcome even the Soviet Union as an ally in the struggle for the survival of democracy and decency.

THE NAZI INVASION

At four o'clock in the morning of June 22, 1941, Hitler's armies crossed the Niemen as Napoleon had crossed it a day later in 1812. A hundred and twenty divisions, rapidly built up to two hundred, were grouped in three attacking forces whose targets were Leningrad, Moscow, and the Caucasus. The assault came as such a surprise that German bombers destroyed many Russian planes before they could get off the ground. Defense units at the border were brushed aside and the mechanized armies of the *Wehrmacht* swept into Russia at amazing speed. Two Russian armies were bypassed and surrounded near Bialystok. Twenty-five days after the invasion German troops on the central front were pushing into Smolensk. There the invaders were held up in a tank battle that went on for three weeks. While von Bock, the German commander, boasted of taking three hundred thousand prisoners—the Germans, like all the combatants, grossly exaggerated the number of casualties they inflicted—the Russian resistance under Timoshenko was so stubborn that the drive was halted and the Germans went over to the defensive for two months. Then early in October, when reinforcements had brought his command up to a million and a half, von Bock continued the drive toward the Soviet capital. The first few miles passed easily, but again the defense stiffened and bad fall weather set in to help the Russians. The citizens of Moscow dug trenches, threw up barricades in the streets, and prepared to defend the capital house by house. That the Germans would penetrate the city seemed so likely that the government moved six hundred miles east to Kuibyshev on the Volga. On December 5, the attack was stalled just thirty-five miles west and only thirteen miles north of Moscow.

Meanwhile the Germans on the northern front under von Leeb drove the defenders under Voroshilov back through Estonia and were approaching Narva and Pskov, north and south of Lake Peipus, by mid-August. A Finnish army under Mannerheim captured Viborg and pushed slowly down the Karelian Isthmus to join hands with the Germans coming east from Narva. In mid-September von Leeb launched an attack against Leningrad but was driven off. But he pushed on east, took the historic fortress of Schlusselburg thirty miles beyond, then turned back to encircle and besiege Leningrad.

While the northern and central German armies were advancing eastward von Runstedt in the south was meeting with even greater success against the former tsarist cavalry sergeant, Budenny. Before mid-August the southern German group had taken Odessa. A few days later the Russians destroyed the great Zaporozhe Dam in the Dnieper rather than let it go to the Nazis.

Kiev held out for a while, but by the middle of September the Germans were a hundred miles beyond it and claiming that six hundred thousand Russians had been surrounded and captured. By the end of the month the invaders had overrun the Crimea, although Sevastopol refused to surrender until nine months later. Early in November von Runstedt captured Rostov and halted there along the line of the Donets. Budenny had done so poorly that he was replaced by Timoshenko, while Zhukov took over command on the central front. But Hitler was so enraged that his generals had not taken Leningrad and Moscow that he appointed himself commander-in-chief and dismissed von Bock, von Leeb, and von Runstedt. Two months earlier he had proclaimed that Russia was finished as a military power, that her armies were broken and would never recover. In November he had announced that the enemy armies had been destroyed.

With all their rapid advances, the Nazis were meeting on the Russian front a degree and a type of resistance far different from what they had experienced against the Poles and the French. There was no panic among the Russian troops at the front or among civilians behind them. The people scorched the earth as they fell back or disappeared into the woods or swamps to form guerilla bands, burning their haystacks and grain and driving their animals with them to leave nothing of value to the enemy. German newspapers commented on the Russian soldier's contempt for death and on the fact that the German breakthrough did not destroy his will or his ability to continue the fight. The attacking spearheads opened up gaps in the Russian lines, but the gaps closed quickly and the Russians poured a murderous fire into the rear of the waves that had passed and upon those that were coming up. When the Russian armies were forced back the fight was taken up by partisan bands trained to operate in the enemy's rear, attacking his supply lines and cutting his communications. The guerillas did not just attack Germans wherever they found them. Their work was well coordinated and their efforts directed against important installations whose destruction would contribute to the general pattern of defense.

The Russians did not line up all their troops at the frontier, as the Germans expected them to do, but kept back enormous reserves. Even so, they committed too many at the border and lost two armies in the first few days by doing so. From then on the Russians learned to avoid encirclement of large forces; when small ones were pinched out they simply joined the partisans who had cached food and arms and went over to guerilla warfare.

The Soviet armies certainly were roughly mauled during the autumn of 1941. Stalin later confessed that Russian equipment and troop training were greatly inferior to those of the Nazis. The Kremlin admitted to losing a half million killed, another half million missing, and over a million wounded in the first ten weeks of the war.

But the German gains were costly, too, much more costly than Hitler and his generals could afford. And when the Nazi juggernaut was stopped, for the first time by any army, it had failed to reach any of its objectives. It had not taken Moscow or Leningrad, and the oil fields of the Caucasus were still far behind the Russian lines. And the Soviet armies were still far from beaten. On December 6, the very next day after von Bock's offensive stalled just west of Moscow, General Zhukov ordered his own offensive. The American General MacArthur hailed the Russian resistance and counter-attack as "the greatest military achievement in all history."

THE SOVIET COUNTERATTACK

The temperature dropped to forty degrees below zero in the neighborhood of Moscow in early December. Since Hitler had expected to overpower the Red Army in a few weeks, the German troops were not clothed for winter. Berliners remembered Napoleon's fate at Moscow and began to whisper the possibility of defeat. The Japanese attack upon Pearl Harbor brought the United States into the war and Germans recalled the consequences of American involvement in 1917.

Hitler ordered his generals to pull back a few miles and gather in fortified camps where the troops would have shelter from the bitter cold. But the Russians, using mounted Cossacks, ski troops, and partisans, swirled around these "hedgehog" positions which bristled with German artillery. Many were overrun or bypassed, and the Germans were forced to withdraw a hundred miles and more from Moscow. The Russians recovered territory in the south and in the Leningrad area, although not enough to loosen the strangle hold on the city. Spring rains checked the counteroffensive in April and the impassable Russian roads immobilized both armies. The Red Army had proved not only that the *Wehrmacht* could be stopped but that it could be beaten. The Soviet gains were less important than the lift they gave Allied morale. But the cost had been frightful. Moscow admitted that the Red Army had suffered over four hundred thousand casualties in the first month of the counterattack.

THE SECOND GERMAN DRIVE

Since Hitler's goal to capture Moscow and Leningrad and destroy the Soviet armies in 1941 had not been achieved, he revised his military aims before the next summer's campaign. The German armies now must seize the Kharkov-Stalingrad-Baku-Batum quadrilateral and deprive Russia of the industrial output, the grain, and the oil the area produced and cut off the vital transportation artery, the Volga. First the Crimea was completely cleared so the Germans might leap across to the Taman Peninsula and drive toward the oil fields of the Caucasus. A terrific aerial and artillery bombardment forced the defenders of Sevastopol to surrender the rubble and ashes that were left after a nine-months siege. By mid-August, 1942, the Germans were in Maikop, whose oil wells the Russians had filled with cement. The Nazis drove on across the Terek to Ordzhonikidze in the foothills of the Caucasus. There, a scant hundred miles from the Caspian Sea, the advance was held up by desperate resistance and by the shift of German divisions to the Stalingrad front.

Late in June the Germans south of Orel opened the drive toward Stalingrad that would cut the Volga communication artery. Thirteen days later they had crossed the Don and were entering Voronezh. The Russians fell back stubbornly, but by the middle of August the enemy was in possession of the entire bend of the Don and had crossed the river at Kalash just west of Stalingrad. On September 15 the Germans were on the banks of the Volga and Stalingrad's half million people literally had their backs to the water. Meanwhile, farther to the south the Germans had taken Voroshilovsk, deep in the Kuban country, and had advanced to Elista, two hundred miles straight south of Stalingrad. The invaders were approaching their goal of cutting off Moscow from the industry, oil, and grain of the southeast.

STALINGRAD AND THE GERMAN RETREAT

Aside from Stalin's pride in the city named for him and his determination not to let it fall, and aside from Hitler's frenzied hatred of the city which bore his enemy's name, Stalingrad was vital to both sides and both general staffs had sound reasons for wanting it. The city was an important industrial center which turned out trucks and tanks. It guarded the great water highway the Volga, over which sixty million tons of goods moved in a normal year. But it would not be easy to capture. Here the river is more than a mile wide, and to bridge it in the face of stiff resistance would be extremely difficult.

The Germans proposed to push on east of Voronezh and cross the Volga at Saratov, but the Russians held the line of the Don and funneled the attackers into a frontal position before Stalingrad. On September 15 the Germans attacked, and for the next month wave after wave advanced against the city. The Germans took most but not all of the city but could not completely dislodge the Russians, who contested every building. When repeated assaults that went on for a month were hurled back, the German legions were withdrawn and a systematic attempt was made to wipe out the city with air and artillery bombardment. The buildings were reduced to rubble, which filled the streets, providing cover for the defenders and barricades against the assault. After the softening-up process General Paulus, the German commander, returned to the ground attack with over three hundred thousand men. But the men and women of Stalingrad crawled out of their cellars and fought alongside the troops to defend this new Soviet city, this monument to the new Russia.

On November 19 Zhukov, now a marshal, ordered a counterattack to relieve Stalingrad. Rokossovsky's army group crossed the Don northwest of Stalingrad and turned south toward the German rear. Another army group under Eremenko drove southwest from Stalingrad and then turned north to meet the first at Kalash on the Don just opposite the beleaguered city. When the two joined hands Paulus and his Sixth German Army were completely encircled. Try as he did, he could not push the Russians back and a relieving army sent to rescue him was driven off. Paulus begged Hitler to let him try to break through and escape, which he promised he could do without losing more than half his men. But Hitler refused to allow it. The slaughter went on until the beginning of February, 1943, when Paulus surrendered with the twenty-two thousand men still with him. In the ten weeks preceding the surrender the Russians destroyed sixty thousand trucks, seven thousand tanks and five thousand planes; and they captured mountains of assorted equipment and weapons when the fighting was over.

The obliteration of the Sixth Army exposed the flank and hastened the withdrawal from the Kuban and Caucasus of the German armies which were under heavy frontal attack. Two weeks after Paulus surrendered the Russians re-entered Rostov. Zhukov's armies rolled on west from Stalingrad past the Don to the Donets and recaptured Kharkov. The Germans were back to where they had started the summer before. But the Russian armies moved forward more swiftly than they could be supplied, and the advance was uneven, leaving salients here and there that invited counterattack. Von Manstein, who temporarily succeeded Hitler as commander on the eastern front after the Stalingrad disaster, struck back vigorously, retook Kharkov, and drove the Russians back beyond the Donets. Meanwhile, in the north Soviet troops recaptured Schlusselburg and opened up a supply line to the starving defenders of Leningrad. And on the central front the Germans were pushed out of Vyazma, which they had built into a strong base threatening Moscow. Late in March the spring torrents came and a period of quiet followed on all fronts.

Russia had regained nearly two hundred thousand square miles of territory. But the land she took was bare, systematically stripped clean by the retreating Germans of everything the Russians had left and the fighting had not destroyed. The first two years of the war had cost the nation over four million soldiers killed or missing. Russia had borne almost the entire burden of the attack which Germany, with all her conquered territory, had mounted against the Allies. In the midst of the Stalingrad campaign Stalin

reminded the world that two hundred and forty Axis divisions were fighting
on the Russian front while four German and eleven Italian divisions were
facing the British in North Africa. And only in 1943, after Stalingrad, after
the Nazis had been stopped and thrown back, did war matériel arrive in
volume from the United States. The flow of Western aid of course sped the
Soviet victory thereafter.

THE PEOPLE'S WAR

One of the most important elements contributing to Hitler's defeat in
Russia was the loyalty of the people. The world was surprised when the
Nazis found no fifth column here as they had found it everywhere else. There
were many who had little reason to be overjoyed with the Communist
regime. The collectivization of agriculture, the purges, the shortages, the
cruelty of the police had hurt many people and made enemies of some who
would stoop to treason if the opportunity came. But most of the potential
traitors had been disposed of before 1941. Those few who were ready to
welcome the Germans as deliverers soon learned from Nazi brutality and
from the atrocities systematically practiced by Alfred Rosenberg, the "Reich
Minister for the East," that life under the invaders would be far less tolerable than under the Communists. The deliberate treatment of Slavs as
inferior creatures, the torture and slaughter of civilians, the deportation of
over four millions to slave-labor mills in Germany, the vandalism and
wanton destruction of property, the desecration of churches, the looting of
shrines and art galleries, the demolition of cultural monuments such as the
homes of Pushkin, Tolstoy, Tchaikovsky, Rimsky-Korsakov, and Chekhov—
such bestiality fired the patriotism of the Russian people and made them
vengeful and often brutal in their treatment of the few prisoners they took.
But the harshness of the people begat more cruelty in return. Over four
million civilians were massacred in occupied Russia, well over half of them
Jews, whom the Nazis were determined to exterminate as a people.

The systematic persecution of the Russian people made inevitable the
failure of Berlin's propaganda attempt to promote a liberation movement.
Radio broadcasts in many languages appealed to the minorities to declare
their independence from Russian imperialism, while broadcasts in Russian
urged the people to escape communism and restore capitalism. A Russian-
language periodical, *Novoye Slovo*, or the *New Word*, was published in
Berlin and widely distributed in the occupied area. Rosenberg organized
an Ukrainian church and found an exiled bishop to head it, but the acting
patriarch of the Russian Church exposed the fraud. Some *émigré* monarchists
and Ukrainian nationalists joined the Nazis, but even most Russians living

in exile supported Moscow. As uncompromising a foe of Bolshevism as Miliukov preferred Stalin to Hitler.

Germany's most ambitious effort to organize a counterrevolutionary force was the creation of a "Russian Army of Liberation" under General Andrei Vlasov, who had been taken prisoner in 1942. Thousands of prisoners of war were forced to enlist in his "army," which Berlin proposed to send against the Red Army. Vlasov called for a popular rising against Stalin and promised the restoration of private property. But Germany hesitated to use Vlasov's force against the Russians lest many of them desert and return to their regiments. The unreliable army fought in Yugoslavia and in France but never on the eastern front. Vlasov was turned over to Moscow and hanged after the war.

The loyalty of the people was most effectively put to the test by the government's decision not to evacuate most of the civilian population. Many factories were removed east of the Urals and their skilled workers went with them. Those who were not needed in such transplanted industries, and particularly the peasants, were ordered not to pull out but to form partisan bands and continue the fight against the Nazi rear. One third of Russia's population was behind the German lines in 1942. Peasants thus freed from the direct authority of the Moscow government showed no disposition to turn against the regime and made no effort to dissolve their collective farms. The *kolkhozes* continued to function, losing much of their produce to the conquerors, of course, but smuggling much of it to the guerillas.

Those who dwelt in unoccupied Russia endured unbelievable hardship from the shortages brought about by the concentration upon war production and the conquest of the agricultural and industrial south. The areas which produced the grain surpluses, the Ukraine and the Kuban country, were lost to the Russians in the unoccupied zone along with half the nation's coal resources and half of her electrical power. But the citizens of Leningrad, who were without fuel, whose clothing was reduced to rags, and who were threatened with starvation, fought alongside the garrison in defense of their homes. Other cities followed Leningrad's example and held out against overwhelming odds. Kiev fought off the Germans for six weeks, Odessa for two months, Sevastopol for nine. These manifestly were not people impatient to be liberated.

RUSSIAN VICTORY

Hitler insisted upon another German offensive in July, 1943. His generals could mount only a limited counterattack with half a million men from the strong German base at Orel against a Russian salient around Kursk. After seventeen days of local successes their heavy losses in men and equipment forced the Germans back on the defensive. Now Rokossovsky opened the Russian summer drive with an attack upon the Orel bastion, using sixty thousand pieces of artillery on a nineteen-mile front. Seven powerful Russian army groups surged forward all along the line from Leningrad to the Black Sea. General Tolbukhin sealed off the German force in the Crimea and bypassed Odessa. By early October the Russians had bridged the Dnieper in three places and recovered Smolensk. Kiev, or what was left of it after systematic German devastation, was liberated by General Vatutin the following month.

On through the winter months the relentless pursuit continued. In January, 1944, the siege of Leningrad was lifted after two and a half years, during which a million citizens had died from enemy action, starvation, and disease. By the first of February the Germans had fallen back into Estonia and Latvia. In the south, Marshal Konev's and Vatutin's army groups surrounded and wiped out an entire Germany army at Korsun, south of Kiev, in the same type of maneuver that had annihilated Paulus' Sixth Army at Stalingrad. Then Konev crossed the Dniester into Bessarabia and pressed on to the Pruth. During the spring the Russians mopped up pockets of enemy resistance near the Black Sea. Malinovsky recaptured Odessa in April. The following month Tolbukhin stormed Sevastopol, and the Crimea once more was in Russian hands.

On June 6, 1944, as Soviet troops were preparing to cross the old Polish frontier at several points, an American-British task force landed in Normandy to open the "second front" that Stalin had expected in 1942. The bulk of the German forces was held on the eastern front, however, for Hitler now played the game of trying to hold off the Russians and hoping to come to terms with the western Allies. But the Germans were fast losing men and equipment and their military power was ebbing rapidly away. The Poles, Hungarians, Bulgarians, Serbs, Croats, Slovaks, Greeks, Italians, Spaniards, Norwegians, Dutch, Belgians, and Finns who fought with them were sick of the war and hoped it would soon end. The Germans themselves, except for a handful of fanatics, had long since lost all hope. The fine veterans of so many easy victories that had entered Russia three years earlier were buried in the steppes or lying in prisoner corrals. The ranks of the *Wehrmacht* were filled with beardless boys.

The Russians in the summer of 1944 had four and a half million men in line organized into twelve army groups, while the Germans could muster only one and a half million. The Russian superiority over the enemy in guns, tanks, and planes was even greater, five to one. Frequently the Nazi retreat became a rout, for the poor, ragged troops panicked easily. The advance was held up from time to time, not by enemy resistance, but by the inability of the Soviet supply service to keep up with the huge, rapidly-moving columns. The Allies made the Red Army's task still easier by stepping up their aerial attack upon the Continent. Over four-fifths of Allied bomb tonnage dropped in Germany and Western Europe during the entire war fell after January 1, 1944. As German cities were pulverized, industrial plants flattened, and transportation routes snarled, the Nazi generals were handcuffed in their efforts to slow down the Russian drive.

In the summer of 1944 Red troops drove through the Baltic states and headed for East Prussia. Bialystok and Brest-Litovsk fell, and members of the Polish underground, impatient to throw off the Nazi yoke, came out of their hiding places to free Warsaw on their own. But the rising was premature and was savagely put down by the Nazis. Politically suspicious of the Polish underground, which was loyal to the Polish government in London, and preferring that Soviet forces should deliver Warsaw, Moscow did nothing to rescue General Bor, the Polish leader, from his predicament.

From now on the Kremlin calculatedly used the Red Army to gain political as well as military advantage. The Russian center advanced slowly while the right wing and, particularly, the left exerted the pressure. Red troops pushed the Finns out of the Karelian Isthmus, drove on through Viborg, and forced Helsinki to ask for an armistice. By its terms Finland declared war upon Germany, ceded to the U.S.S.R. the Petsamo region on the Arctic Ocean, granted Russia permission to fortify the Aland Islands at the mouth of the Gulf of Finland, and agreed to pay three hundred million dollars in reparations over an eight-year period.

In August, 1944, two Red Army groups knifed into Romania, captured Bucharest and surrounded and liquidated the German forces which held the country in subjection. Once freed from the Nazis, Romania made peace with Moscow and declared war against Germany the next day. She agreed to turn over as reparations to Russia three hundred million dollars worth of oil, ships, and grain over the next eight years and accepted the 1940 cession of Bessarabia and Northern Bukovina. Germany thus lost the Romanian wheat that had fed her people and the oil that had supplied her mechanized army.

With Red troops at the Bulgarian border, Moscow now demanded that Sofia sever relations with Germany—Bulgaria had never declared war on the U.S.S.R.—and when an answer was slow in coming Russia declared war. Bulgaria was overrun in three days and forced to accept the Kremlin's terms. The armistice signed in late October was modelled after those with Finland and Romania in providing reparations and stipulating a Bulgarian declaration of war against Germany.

The Russian armies moved on into Yugoslavia in October and, in cooperation with Tito's partisans, recaptured Belgrade and rid the country of the Nazis. At the same time other Soviet troops entered Hungary and early in November took Budapest. But German and Hungarian forces vigorously resisted the Russians here, and the country was not completely subdued until the following January. As the other former Nazi allies had done, Hungary made peace with Moscow, declared war on Germany, and agreed to pay Russia three hundred million dollars in reparations. Except for Greece, which the British occupied, the entire Balkan Peninsula was liberated by the Red Army and the predominance of Russian influence in the postwar period was assured.

During the autumn of 1944 Soviet armies cleared the Baltic provinces of the last of the Nazis and crossed into East Prussia. There they ran into the stiffest opposition the Germans had managed in more than a year. Heavy artillery bombardment softened the defenses and East Prussia was slowly conquered. The Polish front, quiet for five months, came to life at the beginning of the year. Warsaw was liberated by Zhukov in January and the Red armies rolled on toward Silesia.

In the spring of 1945 Soviet troops moved into Austria and in mid-April drove the Germans out of Vienna. From there they pushed into Czechoslovakia, where again there was strong resistance. The Allied commander in the West, General Eisenhower, ordered his troops not to pass the Elbe River, leaving to the Russians the well-earned honor of taking Berlin. The meeting of Soviet and American units at Torgau on the Elbe on April 27, 1945, heralded the end of effective Nazi resistance. Zhukov's men pounded the German capital with twenty thousand cannon but took it only after four days of bitter street fighting. On May 2, the Berlin garrison of upward of a hundred thousand men grounded their arms, but Hitler committed suicide rather than face the humiliation of being taken prisoner. On May 7, the German High Command surrendered unconditionally at Rheims and formally confirmed the armistice at a ceremony in Berlin the following day. The Red Army had come to the end of the long road from Stalingrad fifteen hundred miles away.

THE PRICE OF VICTORY

Much of the war damage in the U.S.S.R. was the result of military action and to be expected. Much of it, however, was caused by deliberate and systematic destruction by the Germans as they withdrew. Plants which turned out half of the nation's steel, freight cars, locomotives, cement, and electrical power were destroyed, as were eleven hundred coal mines producing a hundred million metric tons, nearly two-thirds of the prewar output. Three-fourths of her capacity to produce pig iron was wiped out. Nearly a hundred thousand collective farms were "ruined and ransacked," as were eighteen hundred state farms and almost three thousand machine-tractor stations. Almost a third of the half million tractors which had worked the nation's farms in the spring of 1941 were demolished or carried away along with fifty thousand combines, a million seeding and threshing machines, and four million pieces of other agricultural machinery. For several seasons to come much of the heavy farm work would have to be done by hand. Seven million horses, seventeen million head of cattle, and twenty-seven million sheep and goats, a third of the 1941 herds, and twenty million pigs, 70 per cent of the prewar total, were slaughtered by the invader. Seventeen hundred towns and 70,000 villages were wiped out; 31,000 factories, 40,000 libraries, and 84,000 schools demolished; 40,000 miles of railroad were torn up, and 90,000 miles of telephone lines were destroyed. Twenty-five million Soviet citizens were made homeless, and the crowded housing conditions reached the point in 1945 where, on the average, thirty persons had to share a four- or five-room dwelling. The devastation wrought by the Germans was particularly extensive and deliberate in the Ukraine and the Don basin, which produced half the nation's meat, grain, and vegetables and where prewar industries had been heavily concentrated. Property damage amounted to a hundred and twenty eight billion dollars, a fourth of the prewar value of the nation's property. All this the enemy had destroyed. In addition, war expenditures and reduction of national income cost another four hundred billion dollars.

Human losses were equally staggering. Malenkov reported in 1947 that seven million Soviet citizens had been killed in action or had died because of the occupation. Well over three million soldiers had been taken prisoner, many of whom did not return. When the decline in birth rate during the war and the increase in death rate caused by malnutrition and disease are taken into account, the population of the U.S.S.R. was smaller in 1945 by twenty to twenty-five million than it would have been had there been no war. How many millions were permanently crippled is not known.

Within two months of the fall of Berlin five out of six ruined farms were operating again. It would be years, however, before the shell holes were filled in, the fence lines mended, the abandoned military equipment cleared away, the buildings repaired, and the fertility restored to the soil. To build the herds and flocks back up to prewar levels would take still longer. Then in 1946 a disheartening drought, the worst in fifty years, struck over an area wider than that affected in the disastrous year 1921.

WARTIME RELATIONS WITH THE ALLIES

Britain welcomed the U.S.S.R. as a partner against Hitler; now she was no longer alone. While refusing to unsay any of the bitter words he had spoken against Bolshevism since 1917, Churchill a few hours after the invasion offered Russia whatever technical and economic assistance she might need. He reaffirmed Britain's resolve never to negotiate with Hitler but to fight until the Nazi tyranny should be destroyed. He sent Sir Stafford Cripps to Moscow to formalize the alliance into which Hitler's crossing of the Niemen had prodded the two governments. On July 12, Britain and the U.S.S.R. bound themselves to render each other every possible assistance and not to negotiate an armistice except by mutual agreement.

The United States government was less enthusiastic. While reminding the world that Americans had no more time for Communist than for Fascist despotism, the State Department admitted that the immediate threat to the free world came not from the U.S.S.R. but from Germany. In this spirit Russia was assured "all economic assistance practicable" and promised the same priorities for war material as Britain was already enjoying. In late October Russia received a billion-dollar "lend-lease" grant to purchase needed supplies in the United States. London had extended a credit of ten million pounds sterling six weeks earlier.

In mid-August, 1941, Roosevelt and Churchill drew up the so-called Atlantic Charter in which they foreswore aggrandizement for their own governments, expressed the desire that there be no territorial changes without the freely-registered approval of the people involved, and promised to respect the right of all peoples to determine the form of government under which they would live. Six weeks later the U.S.S.R. formally subscribed to the Atlantic Charter, Stalin apparently supposing that it was meant to apply only to territorial changes which Hitler had carried through. On New Year's Day, 1942, by which time the Japanese attack upon Pearl Harbor had brought America into the war, the United Kingdom, the United States, the U.S.S.R., and twenty-three other nations signed the Declaration of the United Nations, each pledging her full resources to the defeat of the Axis and promising not to accept a separate peace. Russia, who two years earlier had been voted out of the League of Nations for attacking Finland, now was a full-fledged member of the partnership dedicated to the defeat of the Tripartite Powers, with whom, incidentally, Finland was allied.

In May, 1942, Molotov visited London to conclude a long-term alliance, the discussion of which had been going on for five months. What had held up the negotiations was Britain's refusal, at American prompting, to sanction Russia's absorption of Eastern Poland, Bessarabia, and the Baltic states, whose former governments the United States still recognized. Taking no cognizance of Stalin's impatience to begin redrawing the map of Europe, the British and Russian governments agreed to a twenty-year alliance aimed against Germany, promised mutual economic assistance after the war, and pledged not to become a party to any alliance or coalition directed against the other.

Molotov flew on to Washington to plead for more lend-lease material and to argue for the opening of a second front in Western Europe during the summer to relieve pressure on the Red Army. In the first he was successful,

Washington raising her lend-lease commitments to the Soviet government to three billion dollars. As for the second, he received something less than full satisfaction. The State Department announced that "a full understanding was reached with respect to the urgent task of creating a second front in Europe in 1942." Stalin took this as a commitment to land on the Continent before the year was out, while Roosevelt and Churchill meant it only as an expression of hope that a second front might prove feasible. Their later decision to postpone it aroused Stalin's suspicion that there would be no second front, that the United States and Britain would like to see Russia bled white by the Nazis. Indeed, the British and American press, which Soviet officials carefully followed, had contained many expressions by leading figures in both countries of hope that the troublesome Nazis and Bolsheviks might destroy each other if left alone.

British and American shipments of war matériel to Russia did much to remove the coolness between Moscow and the Western capitals. The United States shipped to the Soviet Union eight and a half billion dollars' worth of supplies before the end of the war in Europe, eleven billion dollars' worth including shipments after the fall of Berlin. To approximately seven thousand tanks, thirteen thousand planes, four hundred thousand trucks, two thousand locomotives, eleven thousand freight cars, ninety-five merchant ships, two million tons of steel, eleven million pairs of shoes and so on, the British government added five thousand tanks, seven thousand planes, a half billion rounds of ammunition, and quantities of other material. This was substantial help, surely, but only a small fraction of Russia's own output. By 1943 Russian industry was producing annually thirty thousand tanks and armored cars, forty thousand planes, a half million machine guns, three million rifles, and over seven billion rounds of ammunition. Provoked that there was still no second front in October, 1942, Stalin told an American news correspondent that "as compared with the aid which the Soviet Union is giving to the Allies by drawing upon itself the main forces of the German fascist armies, the aid of the Allies to the Soviet Union has so far been little effective." Perhaps to inspire patriotism, perhaps because Anglo-American aid made up a relatively small percentage of the total consumed on the Russian front, Moscow made little effort to inform the Russian people of the contribution made by the Western Allies. When the American ambassador objected to the fact that Russians were not being told of American help, the Moscow press and radio went to some lengths to tell the story.

The British, American, and Soviet foreign secretaries met together for the first time in Moscow during the last two weeks of October, 1943. The three powers swore to accept only the unconditional surrender of the Axis, promised to restore the independence of Austria, declared that democratic government must return to Italy, and warned that Germans charged with committing atrocities would be tried and punished in the country where such crimes were perpetrated. The Chinese ambassador in Moscow joined Molotov, Eden, and Hull in recognizing the need to limit peacetime armaments and to create "at the earliest practicable date a general international organization, based on the principle of the sovereign equality of all peace-loving states and open to membership of all such states, large and small, for the maintenance of international peace and security."

In the closing days of November, 1943, Roosevelt and Churchill met with Stalin in the Russian Embassy in Teheran. There Stalin and his military advisers learned details of the proposed Allied landing in France the following June and promised to synchronize a Russian offensive with it. The three heads of state came to an understanding on respective spheres of influence in Europe as territory was liberated from the conqueror. Romania, Bulgaria, Hungary, Yugoslavia, Czechoslovakia, Poland, and Finland were tentatively assigned to the Russian sphere. The rest of occupied Europe would fall within the Anglo-American sphere. The heads of the big three powers repeated their determination to work together for an enduring peace in which "all the peoples of the world may live free lives untouched by tyranny and according to their varying desires and their own consciences." Such high resolve, reiterated at every conference during the war, led Westerners to expect an entirely different sort of peace than Stalin apparently had in mind. During the year then drawing to a close the Comintern had been abolished, an act which did not liquidate the Communist parties over the world, of course, but one which was interpreted by Western hopefuls to mean that Moscow was renouncing world revolution. The dissolution of the Third International removed perhaps the worst irritant to East-West cordiality.

The exiled Czech government in London concluded a twenty-year alliance with the U.S.S.R. in December, 1943. This seemed to indicate to Churchill that Prague would be bound to Moscow after the war, something he had feared and had tried to prevent by insisting all along that the British-American invasion of the Continent should take place in the Balkans to prevent all Eastern Europe from falling under Russian domination. While Eisenhower held out for Normandy as the target of the main Allied thrust, Churchill sent a British force into Greece to keep that country, so close to the Straits, out of Russian hands. Then the prime minister hurried off to Moscow to strike a bargain with Stalin over the spheres of influence that tentatively had been settled at the Teheran Conference. There in October, 1944, Churchill agreed that Bulgaria, Romania, and Hungary should come within the Soviet sphere of influence. He could do little else. The Red Army already had overrun Bulgaria and Romania and was fighting in Hungary. But he won Stalin's consent that Greece should come under British influence and that Britain and Russia jointly should exercise influence in

Yugoslavia. He had saved Greece and might yet save Yugoslavia from the Communist embrace.

At the tsarist palace at Livadia, near war-damaged Yalta on the south Crimean coast, the big three—Stalin, Churchill, and Roosevelt—met again in early February, 1945. Eisenhower's armies were approaching the Rhine and Red troops were in Western Poland. Political questions were rapidly multiplying and some were already beyond compromise. As the Allies converged on the Reich's borders there must be some agreement on the fate of Germany after the military victory and the nature of governments to be erected in the lands freed from Nazi control. Roosevelt and Churchill were also most anxious to bring the Red Army into the war against Japan as quickly as possible.

At the so-called Yalta Conference there was a discussion of the feasibility of dividing Germany into several states—an independent Rhineland, Bavaria, and Austria and the separation of East Prussia—as Stalin had proposed at earlier conferences. In the end the conferees agreed simply to occupy Germany for an indefinite time and arranged British, French, American, and Russian zones of occupation. The occupying power was to be responsible for the demilitarization of each zone and for the liquidation of Nazism. An Allied Control Commission sitting in Berlin, made up of the military commanders of the four occupation zones, would coordinate the responsibilities and settle problems among the occupying powers and arrange for the flow of food and reparations between the Russian and the Western zones. The settlement was far from ideal but was probably the best that could be hoped for in the light of the understandable refusal of both East and West to let the other completely control Germany. Russia was fearful of being outvoted by the Western powers if all should undertake a joint administration of Germany. By the settlement which left Berlin in the Russian zone, she was assured of a much smaller and industrially weaker enemy if the other occupying powers should undertake to rebuild Germany as a bulwark against her. Stalin insisted upon reparations in kind and the Western powers accepted tentatively a figure of twenty billion dollars, half of which should go to the U.S.S.R. The amount was reasonably small and Russia's share constituted only a tiny fraction of the damages she had suffered.

The joint statement issued by the three powers at the close of the Yalta Conference announced that peoples liberated from the Nazi yoke would be encouraged to "form interim governmental authorities broadly representative of all democratic elements in the population and pledged to the earliest possible establishment through free elections of governments responsive to the will of the people." It allowed that the Curzon Line should form Poland's eastern boundary and recognized that Poland should be compensated by moving her western border forward to include former German territory. The Provisional Government of Poland set up under Russian sponsorship was to be broadened to include democratic leaders from abroad, presumably those whom England and the United States had long recognized as the exiled government in London. This newly-broadened Provisional Government must hold "free and unfettered elections as soon as possible on the basis of universal suffrage and secret ballot." A similarly broad government was provided for Yugoslavia.

Stalin agreed that the U.S.S.R. would join the war against Japan within ninety days after the end of the war in Europe. Both Roosevelt and Churchill, yet unaware of the convincing force of the atomic bomb, were sure that Russia's entry into the Far Eastern conflict and her neutralization of Japan's powerful Kwantung Army would save many thousands of British and American lives. In return for Stalin's promise, Russia was to receive the southern half of Sakhalin which she had lost in 1904, the Kurile Islands, and a sphere of influence in Manchuria. Finally the three agreed that a meeting of the nations united in the fight against the Axis should gather at San Francisco to organize an international body to maintain the peace.

From mid-July to early August, 1945, the British, American, and Russian heads of government met once more at Potsdam near Berlin. Roosevelt had died three months earlier and while the conference was in session Churchill and his party were voted out of office by the British electorate. Their successors, Truman and Attlee, were left to deal with problems which had been growing since Yalta, and added their own distrust and suspicions to those which their predecessors had begun to feel. To Russian concern over reparations and irritation at British support of reactionary elements in Greece, the Western powers countered with dissatisfaction that "free and unfettered elections" had not yet been called in Eastern Europe, that Russia had been pressing Turkey for the right to maintain bases on the Bosporus and Dardanelles, and that the Communist-dominated Polish government had been awarded administrative control over East Prussia and Silesia.

The three powers agreed at Potsdam to create a Council of Foreign Ministers charged with the task of drafting peace treaties with the defeated enemy nations. They announced that, while they did not intend to "destroy or enslave the German people," they would not allow "the production of arms, ammunition and implements of war, as well as all types of aircraft and seagoing ships." Chemical, metal, and machine industries would be permitted only to the extent that they contributed to peacetime needs. The occupying powers, through their Control Council sitting in Berlin, would eradicate every trace of Nazism and bring German war criminals to trial. Russia was to be allowed to satisfy her demand for reparations by removing machinery from her own occupation zone and, in addition, was to be given from the other three zones a fourth of such machinery as Germany would not need for peacetime production. In partial return for the industrial equipment removed from the western zones, Russia was to send food and raw

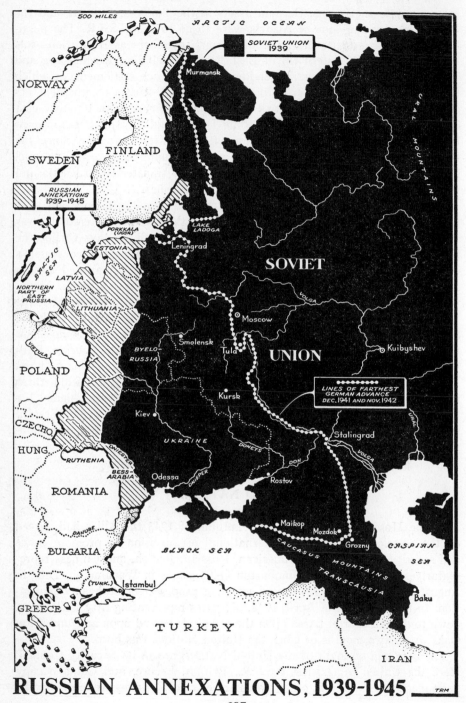

500 MILES

ARCTIC OCEAN

SOVIET UNION
1939

Murmansk

NORWAY

SWEDEN   FINLAND

RUSSIAN
ANNEXATIONS
1939-1945

*ARCTIC
SEA*

PORKKALA
(USSR)

ESTONIA

LATVIA

NORTHERN
PART OF
EAST
PRUSSIA

LITHUANIA

*LAKE
LADOGA*

Leningrad

SOVIET

VOLGA

URAL MOUNTAINS

POLAND

VISTULA

Smolensk

BYELO-
RUSSIA

Moscow

Tula

UNION

Kuibyshev

CZECHO

HUNG.

RUTHENIA

BESS-
ARABIA

DNIESTER

Kursk

Kiev

UKRAINE

DONETS

LINES OF FARTHEST
GERMAN ADVANCE
DEC. 1941 AND NOV. 1942

URAL

ROMANIA

DANUBE

Odessa

DNIEPER

DON

Rostov

Stalingrad

VOLGA

BULGARIA

BLACK SEA

Maikop

Mozdok

*CAUCASUS
MOUNTAINS*

Grozny

CASPIAN
SEA

GREECE

(TURK.)

Istambul

TRANSCAUSIA

Baku

TURKEY

IRAN

RUSSIAN ANNEXATIONS, 1939-1945

TRM

697

materials into such areas. German assets in the Balkans, Finland, and the Russian occupation zone of Austria were to go to the U.S.S.R. The possibility of Russia's using the labor of German prisoners as reparations was left unsettled. The eastern tip of East Prussia, including Koenigsberg and Tilsit, was assigned to Russia, pending the final peace settlement, at which time the two Western powers promised to support Russia's permanent acquisition. The similar transfer to Poland of all other German territory east of the Oder and Neisse rivers, including Danzig and Stettin, was approved but likewise only until the conclusion of peace with Germany. Since the Red Army was in control of the entire area the qualification was academic. Nine million Germans living in the territory now transferred to Russia and Poland were to be transplanted into the western zones.

A few days after the adjournment of the Potsdam Conference and just three months after the victory over Germany, the U.S.S.R. entered the war against Japan as she had promised at Yalta to do. Two days earlier the first atomic bomb had destroyed Hiroshima and the day after Russia's declaration of war a second bomb fell on Nagasaki. Japan sued for an armistice before Russia had been in the Far Eastern war a week. Meanwhile Red troops overran Manchuria and Korea and overpowered the Kwantung Army. Before the Japanese surrender Russia and China concluded a thirty-year alliance which provided that the two signatories should share the administration of the Chinese Eastern and South Manchurian Railways and that the two should operate Port Arthur jointly as a naval base. Russia promised to withdraw her troops from Manchuria within three months and turn over the area to China. Since the treaty was signed between the U.S.S.R. and Chiang Kai-shek's Chinese government, Western suspicions that Moscow would back the Chinese Communists were momentarily allayed.

UNITED NATIONS

At the Moscow Conference in the autumn of 1943 the Allies had agreed on the creation of a postwar international organization to promote peace and security for all nations. American, Russian, British, and Chinese representatives, meeting at the Dumbarton Oaks estate in Washington, D.C. in August and September, 1944, worked out a proposal for such an organization. In the last week of April, 1945, delegates representing fifty nations sat down to draft a charter based upon the proposals agreed upon at Dumbarton Oaks. After two months of labor the United Nations was born.

The core and strength of the United Nations are in its Security Council. Here the United States, the U.S.S.R., Britain, France, and China occupy permanent seats while six other states are elected for two-year terms by the

General Assembly. Questions of simple procedure may pass the Security Council with any seven votes, but on all other questions, or "substantive matters," the seven votes must include the votes of the five permanent members. Thus any permanent member's negative vote or veto prevents action by the Security Council. The veto power which the big three agreed to at Yalta, and which Roosevelt conceived, was adopted to calm Russia's fears that the United Nations might become an anti-Soviet bloc whose action against her she would be unable to prevent. But the veto power was as vigorously insisted upon by Britain and the United States, whose Senate, jealous of American sovereignty, must ratify the charter. In the coming years the U.S.S.R. exercised her veto right to the irritation of the Western world on dozens of matters—frequently to prevent admission to the United Nations of states whose governments were hostile to Moscow—while the other powers working together rarely found it necessary. To the Western charge that Moscow abused the veto privilege the obvious answer was that Russia invariably was in the minority on "substantive" questions and could defend her interests against Security Council action only by using the veto.

The General Assembly, where each member nation enjoys one vote, may debate any problem within the purview of the United Nations charter and may recommend action to the Security Council or to a member state. Stalin's resentment that each member of the British Commonwealth should have a seat in the General Assembly was overcome by allowing seats to Belo-Russia and the Ukraine. It was understood that the United States might also have three seats in the Assembly, but Washington did not pursue the matter.

THE RUSSO-POLISH TANGLE

Soon after Hitler's armies crossed the Niemen in June, 1941, Moscow came to terms with the Polish government in exile in London and diplomatic civility between the two was restored. Polish soldiers captured in 1939 were released by the Soviet government to form an army of their own, officered by Poles, to join in the battle with the common enemy. But from the very beginning there was little cordiality among the Poles for the partnership that circumstances had forced upon them. Moscow assumed that Polish divisions would take their place in the battle line as soon as they were ready, but the Polish government in London objected to the proposal that each division should be moved into line separately. Many were bitter over the Russian invasion in 1939 and loudly insisted that Poland must have back her old frontiers. The age-old hatred of Poles for Russians did not soften because they happened to be fighting the same enemy. Cooperation proved to be impossible and the Polish army with its commander, General Anders, was transferred early in 1942 to Iran, where it passed under British administration.

After the withdrawal of General Anders' army Moscow prompted the formation by Polish Communist refugees in Russia of a "Union of Polish Patriots." This group worked closely with the Soviet government and urged other Poles to do likewise. The exiled government in London now began to importune the western Allies to guarantee the prewar eastern frontier. As relations between Moscow and the London Poles steadily deteriorated, Hitler in April, 1943, announced that the German army had discovered a grave in the Katyn Forest near Smolensk containing the bodies of ten thousand Polish officers. Berlin, anxious to convince the world that the slaughter had been carried out by the Russians, agreed to support an investigation by the International Red Cross, as demanded by the London Poles. Moscow took this as an insult and broke off relations with the Polish government in exile. Later the Soviet government appointed a committee of distinguished scientists and lawyers to investigate the Katyn massacre which concluded that the dead Polish officers had been shot during the German occupation at a time when Red troops were far to the east. But an American Congressional committee reviewed the evidence in 1952, when the Korean conflict was going on, and announced that the Russians had perpetrated the massacre.

Efforts by the London Poles to get the Western Allies to mediate with Moscow over the Russo-Polish frontier only irritated the Soviet government, which announced that the question was not open to discussion. Determined that the postwar government of Poland must be one sympathetic or at least not hostile to Russia, Moscow allowed the Union of Polish Patriots and a number of leftist Poles living in Russia to proclaim themselves a "Committee of National Liberation," which amounted to another Polish government in exile, this one residing in Moscow. When Soviet forces moved into Poland in 1944, the Committee of National Liberation followed and with Russia's consent took over the administration of the liberated territory. The Committee set up a temporary capital at Lublin southeast of Warsaw and came to be known as the Lublin government. In an attempt to prevent the country from falling under a Moscow-oriented administration, the Polish underground under General Bor, on order from the exiled Polish government in London, rose against the Germans in Warsaw just as the Russians were ready to enter the city. Now the Red Army halted on the east bank of the Vistula and let the Germans put down the rising of General Bor, which they did with savage brutality. That the insurrection was directed perhaps as much against the Soviet government and the Polish Communist group it was sponsoring as against the Germans was ignored in the West, and Moscow's callousness in allowing the Warsaw patriots to be massacred did nothing to improve Russia's relations with Britain and the United States.

Roosevelt and Churchill agreed at Yalta to withdraw recognition from the exiled Polish government in London in favor of that of the Lublin Poles, provided the latter were broadened to include other Polish leaders abroad, presumably some of those in London. As soon as possible the new Polish government must hold "free and unfettered elections" in which "all democratic and anti-Nazi parties" should have the right to participate. Six weeks after the fall of Berlin a Polish cabinet took office with the premiership going to a Lublin Pole and the vice-premiership to a London Pole, Mikolajczyk. The "free and unfettered elections" had not yet materialized at the time of the Potsdam Conference in late July, a fact which provoked the American and British delegates. But by that time both London and Washington had extended diplomatic recognition to the new Warsaw government and had consented to Poland's admission to the United Nations as a charter member.

THE SATELLITES

As the Red Army flowed over Eastern Europe and the Balkans, liberating lands that had borne the Nazi yoke for five years, the underground resistance movements stepped forward to organize provisional governments. In every country which endured German occupation, with the notable exception of Poland, the Communists dominated or at least shared in the leadership of the resistance movement. As Soviet troops drove back the Germans they turned over the administration of the land to the partisans. If there were two resistance movements, as was the case in Poland, they disarmed the non-Communists and handed the tools and the power of government to the Moscow-oriented group. Churchill and Roosevelt at Yalta and Truman and Attlee at Potsdam could only accept the fact that the Red Army was effectively in control of Eastern Europe and hope that Stalin's promise of "free and unfettered elections" would be honored.

After liberation Moscow sponsored coalition governments, including Communists, socialists, and other leftist parties, in Poland, Hungary, Romania, Bulgaria, Yugoslavia, Albania and Czechoslovakia. While they permitted non-Communist parties to occupy cabinet posts, however, the Communists always kept for themselves the vital ministries of justice and interior which controlled the nation's police system. Soviet troops remained in each country to buttress the authority of the new government, although they withdrew from Czechoslovakia late in 1945 and from Bulgaria two years later.

But the growing popularity of the Communists was not owing entirely to Russian sponsorship. In every country, with the exception of Czechoslovakia, there was a crying need for land reform, for the partition of the great estates among the peasants. In every country, with the same exception, the reactionary tendencies of the prewar government had been fought most uncompromisingly by the Communists. In every country but Czechoslovakia the upper classes—business magnates, estate owners, the higher clergy, and officials—had dealt softly with fascism or openly supported it against the threat of proletarian revolution. The Communists, then, had a positive program which appealed to many. In fact, they might have had even wider popular support without Russian intervention than with it.

More or less gradually but steadily the Communists in the states of Eastern Europe eased non-Communists out of office. The governments of the so-called "people's democracies" settled the centuries-old land problem by breaking up the great estates among the peasants who, for the moment at least, were allowed to own the land outright. Small business continued under private ownership, but large factories, banking, transportation, and foreign trade came under government operation. It was the Russian New Economic Policy all over again. Each satellite, as the people's democracies came to be called in the West, traded primarily with the U.S.S.R. In fact, the Eastern European countries and the Soviet Union concluded trade agreements, as well as mutual-friendship-and-alliance treaties, as soon after liberation as the satellites formed governments to sign them. By 1947 over half of Russia's exports were going to the satellites, and they in turn were supplying a third of her imports.

When the United States in 1947 put forward the European Recovery Program, or Marshall Plan, to cushion Europe's adjustment from war to peace, Russia and her minions, suspecting some sinister scheme to control Europe, refused to accept the offer. Instead, Moscow organized a Council for Economic Mutual Assistance, sometimes called the Molotov Plan, the effect of which was to bind the satellite economies still more tightly to Russia.

The Comintern, which had voted to disband in 1943, in effect came back to life in the autumn of 1947, when Communist delegations from Russia, Poland, Romania, Bulgaria, Hungary, Yugoslavia, Czechoslovakia, France, and Italy organized the Communist Information Bureau, or Cominform for short. Its aim was to coordinate the work of its members and particularly to carry on a propaganda campaign against "Anglo-American imperialism." However, the Yugoslav leader Marshal Tito refused to accept dictation of his foreign and trade policy from Moscow. Yugoslavia was expelled from the Cominform in 1948 and thereafter leaned upon the United States for military and economic assistance.

The tightening of Soviet political and economic control over the satellites was carried through in answer to the Marshall Plan and the Truman Doctrine—the policy of granting American military and economic aid to nations lying near the borders of the U.S.S.R. and potentially threatened by Russian encroachment. While the United States took the first step, with full British support, she did so in growing concern over the extension of Russian influence in Eastern and Central Europe. Cooperation between East and West barely outlasted the war. By 1947 most of the nations of the world had chosen sides between two contesting power blocs, the one led by the United States, the other by the U.S.S.R.

GROWING EAST-WEST TENSION

The division of Germany into four occupation zones soon developed into vigorous disagreement over the future of the former enemy. The United States and the United Kingdom, anxious to be free of the burden of supporting the German economy, promoted the rapid economic recovery of the western zones of occupation. This, coupled with the frank purpose of the Marshall Plan to shore up a bulwark in the West against possible Soviet expansion, convinced Moscow that the Western powers were preparing another war, this one against the U.S.S.R. in which a revived Germany would serve as a tool and a springboard for the Western assault. Moscow's own hope to see Germany united and under Communist domination went glimmering with the economic recovery of Western Germany and her obvious sympathy for a Western political orientation. A Soviet protest that the Western powers were violating the terms of the Potsdam agreement on the occupation, when they promoted economic recovery in their own zones without Russian consent, went unheeded.

When the Western powers in 1948 extended German currency reform to their zones of occupation in Berlin, Moscow retaliated by cutting off all contact between Berlin, which lay completely within the Russian zone, and the western zones of occupation. The Berlin blockade threatened to strangle the former capital and was calculated to force the Western powers to cooperate with Russia in occupation policy. But the Anglo-American "air lift" for a year flew food and fuel into Berlin. After nearly a year of the expensive and dramatic operation, which the Western allies seemed willing to continue indefinitely, Moscow raised the blockade. A meeting of the Council of Foreign Ministers of the occupying powers settled the immediate issues, but the schism never closed between the Russian-occupied East Germany and the western zones, which soon were permitted to organize a German government.

Frightened by the Berlin blockade and by the Communist seizure of power in Czechoslovakia, the United States, Canada, and the nations of Western Europe in the spring of 1949 joined the North Atlantic Treaty Organization and pledged to rearm, with American help, in defense against the further spread of communism. A common army to which the members contributed quotas was set up under a joint military command headed by General Eisenhower. German divisions later joined the "European Defense Community" and Russia was threatened, if she pushed her influence farther to the west, with a war in which her former enemies and allies would march together. As a counterbalance to N.A.T.O., the Communist nations of Eastern Europe signed the Warsaw Pact, committing themselves to measures of common defense and organizing a common army under the command of the Russian war hero Marshal Konev.

The rift which had opened between the U.S.S.R. and the United States even before the end of the war steadily widened through the postwar years. Fundamental disagreement between Moscow and the Western allies under American leadership appeared on every issue that arose. The two sides could not agree upon what countries should be allowed membership in the United Nations, and time and again the Russian delegate on the Security Council exercised the veto to block the admission of states antagonistic to the U.S.S.R.—Ireland, Portugal, Spain, Jordan, and others. The Western powers, standing well together, rarely had to use the veto to block the entry of Soviet-dominated states into the U.N. East and West, at least through the period of the "cold war" following the Berlin blockade, could not agree on reparations, on occupation policy in Germany or Japan, on disarmament, on controlling production of nuclear weapons, on relations with China, on control of the Straits, on release of war prisoners, and on a host of other problems.

The hostility between the United States and the Soviet Union which waxed at the council table was reflected in the press, on the stage, and in the pronouncements of political leaders in both countries. Russian newspaper articles and cartoons were filled with venom against "Anglo-American imperialism" and particularly against the senior partner. American newspapers certainly were not outdone in their attacks upon "Soviet imperialism." Russian and American leaders exchanged the most heated charges, not all of which on either side were sane. Russian stage and films ridiculed capitalism, and artists using whatever medium who did not put their talents to work in the campaign of vituperation came in for official censure.

THE KOREAN WAR

At the Potsdam Conference the powers agreed that Korea, once liberated from the Japanese, should be divided at the thirty-eighth parallel between Russian and American zones of occupation. The promised unification of Korea did not materialize, however, and the Republic of Korea, organized in 1948 under United Nations sponsorship, governed the peninsula south of the thirty-eighth parallel while the "Democratic People's Republic of Korea," organized at the same time by Moscow, succeeded to the Soviet zone north of that parallel. Russia pulled her occupation troops out of North Korea and six months later the United States withdrew from South Korea. Both infant governments claimed to be the legal government for all Korea.

In June, 1950, North Korean troops, armed with Russian tanks and planes, crossed the thirty-eighth parallel determined to force the unification of the peninsula under Communist rule. The defending South Korean army was rolled back and would quickly have been overwhelmed if left to its own resources. But the United Nations Security Council, under American prodding, declared the North Korean invasion an act of aggression and called upon the members of the United Nations to join forces in defense of the victim. The resolution would surely have been vetoed by the U.S.S.R. but for the fact that the Russian delegation had walked out of an earlier session of the Security Council and had not yet returned.

After initial successes, the North Korean armies were driven back across the thirty-eighth parallel and deep into their own territory by General MacArthur and his United Nations forces, which were predominantly American-manned and American-equipped. Then four Chinese armies joined their Communist friends and drove MacArthur back deep into South Korea. The seesaw went on to little advantage to either side for a year, reaching a stalemate in June, 1951, along the thirty-eighth parallel. Then Moscow, who all along had been posing as the champion of peace and tarring the United States as the aggressor, proposed a cease-fire order and the initiation of conversations looking toward an armistice. For the next twenty-two months, off and on, the truce talks went on, painfully reducing one objection after another but failing to provide agreement on whether prisoners of war should be forcibly repatriated, as the Communists insisted, or allowed to choose between repatriation and exile, as the United Nations insisted.

In April, 1953, significantly the month after Stalin's death, the truce talks reopened after six months of stalemate. The armistice agreed to soon afterward accepted the United Nations proposal on repatriation rather than the Communist view. Prisoners who chose to return home were permitted to do so, while those who preferred exile were allowed to move to any country which would have them.

AFTER STALIN

The death of Stalin made possible not only the end of hostilities in Korea. Very quickly it became apparent that the new leaders in the Kremlin were intent upon easing the international tension that had been mounting since the end of World War II. The bitter animosity toward Tito that had produced frequent border clashes between Yugoslavia and the satellites came dramatically to an end. Moscow and Belgrade exchanged ambassadors and signed a commercial agreement ending six years of Yugoslav isolation from the Communist trade area. Khrushchev, Bulganin, Mikoyan, Gromyko, and Shepilov humbly swallowed their pride and went to Belgrade in May, 1955, to woo Tito in his own capital. They loudly deplored the rift that had parted the "ancient bonds of friendship" between the two countries, blaming it all upon the dead Stalin, and Beria, who had been shot. Molotov, Stalin's friend who had led the attack upon Yugoslavia after Tito's excommunication, had been left at home.

To the blandishments of his Moscow visitors Tito only partly succumbed. He insisted upon interpreting and applying Marxist doctrine in his own way free from Russian dictation, and he proposed to follow an independent course in foreign affairs. But he granted that there was broad agreement between the two parties in their views on major international issues. He received a sizable loan from Moscow and promise of Russian assistance in developing nuclear-energy plants. The American government reluctantly decided to continue economic and military aid to Yugoslavia, lest Tito be driven into even closer reliance upon Moscow. To impress the Yugoslav dictator still more the new Kremlin leaders, on the eve of Tito's visit to Moscow in June, 1956, forced the resignation of Molotov, who as foreign minister had directed the Cominform attack upon Belgrade. Shepilov, the former editor of *Pravda,* took his place.

The "new course" adopted by Stalin's successors led to slight relaxation of control over the satellites and to a rehabilitation, sometimes posthumously, of party leaders in the "people's democracies" who had sympathized with Tito in his struggle for independence. Collectivization of agriculture was slowed down all over Eastern Europe and there were promises of expanded consumer-goods output. There was an end, at least temporarily, to the attack upon the church in the satellites, and clerical leaders earlier imprisoned were released.

The attempt to blame Stalin for Moscow's harsh policy toward the satellites and for the estrangement of Yugoslavia produced threatening repercussions. Titoists imprisoned for their anti-Stalin stand were released and returned to power in Poland and Hungary. They immediately called for an end to Russian domination of their domestic policies while promising every assurance that if allowed to remain in power they would support the U.S.S.R. in foreign affairs.

To the non-Communist world the new "collegiate" leadership in Moscow offered solutions of problems that long had irritated international relations. The Soviet-held naval base in Finland, leased to the U.S.S.R. for fifty years in 1947, was handed back to Finland in 1955. Moscow made much of this apparently generous move and called the world's attention to the British and American bases on foreign soil that girdled the earth. A few months after

Stalin's death the Kremlin gave up all claim to Turkish territory which the old dictator had insisted Russia was entitled to, and abandoned Stalin's demand that Turkey and Russia jointly operate naval and air bases at the Straits.

Soviet policy toward Western Europe after 1953 aimed at convincing the British, French, Italians, and even the Germans that there was no threat of Russian aggression and consequently no need for N.A.T.O. The Korean armistice, the end of the long civil war in Indochina, the easing of pressure at the Formosa Straits, the settlement of outstanding differences with Japan, the return of prisoners of war, the reduction in the Soviet armed forces, the repeated offer to end the testing of nuclear weapons—all were calculated to undermine American insistence that the free world must continue to maintain its posture of defense. The Soviet leaders led a vigorous propaganda campaign calling for peace and for the "peaceful coexistence" of East and West, of capitalism and socialism. The conclusion of trade agreements with France and Italy, the offer to British businessmen to buy a billion dollars worth of their goods, and the hint of a similar purchase from German firms, were designed to restore normal relations with the Western world. Molotov suddenly agreed to a peace treaty with Austria, which Stalin through five years of fruitless conferences had refused to sign, and the Russian occupation force was withdrawn.

The prospects for world peace were better in the early months of 1956 than at any time since Hitler's coming to power in Germany. There were many potential danger spots—Indochina, Formosa, Korea, the Middle East, Berlin—but the hostile camps into which the world was divided seemed more determined than at any time since 1945 not to be drawn into another holocaust.

The apparent solidarity of the Communist world soon showed itself to be an illusion. Moscow's efforts to return Yugoslavia to the fold, by absolving Tito of the charge of heresy and admitting that there were "several roads to socialism," stirred unrest in the satellites of Eastern Europe. Polish workers rioted in June, 1956, against long hours and low wages. As the strike spread, however, the ancient hatred of Pole for Russian, the bitter memory of Russian action in 1939, and resentment against a decade of Communist rule turned the demonstration into an expression of Polish nationalism which the de-Stalinization program and Tito's recent victory did much to inspire.

The trials of the Poles who had led the June riots and who had even dared to attack the secret police were remarkably open and fair. The accused were allowed to defend themselves and to air their grievances against intolerable political and economic conditions. That the discontent was widespread even the leaders of the Polish Communist party were ready to admit. The Stalinists among them were removed from the party's central committee, and a national Communist, Wladyslav Gomulka, renowned for his sympathy for Titoism, was freed from prison and made party secretary. In the face of Russian threats of armed intervention, Marshal Rokossovsky was removed as head of the Polish armed forces and sent home to Moscow.

Several members of the Russian Politburo flew to Warsaw to deliver a stern warning against such actions, but they backed down when the Polish leaders, supported by their own party and by the nation at large, stood firm. Russia concluded an agreement which recognized Poland's "full sovereignty and independence," promised no further interference in Polish affairs, cancelled Polish debts to the U.S.S.R., advanced a substantial credit for the purchase of grain and machinery, and surrendered to the Warsaw government control over the movement of Russian troops which the Polish leaders agreed should remain in Poland until the conclusion of peace with Germany.

The amazing success of the Poles in affirming their independence inspired discontent in Hungary. During the late summer of 1956 the Stalinists and the national Communists jousted for power in the Hungarian Communist party. The battle divided the entire membership of the party and then, in early autumn, spread to the country at large. Students and workers rioted and fought the secret police, demanding Hungarian independence, freedom for non-Communist political parties, an end to collectivization, and the removal of all Russian troops from the country. Imré Nagy, the national Communist leader, adopted these goals as his own, and Moscow seemed willing once again to back down in the face of surging nationalist spirit.

Then in November, 1956, the Kremlin leaders decided to put down this growing threat that the Communist empire might fly apart. A force of 200,-000 Russian troops and 5,000 tanks brutally suppressed the Hungarian rising, deported thousands of Hungarians to Russia, and replaced Nagy with a puppet, Janos Kadar. A hundred thousand Hungarians fled to Austria, whence some moved on to new homes in Western Europe and America. The U.N. General Assembly condemned Russian action in Hungary by an overwhelming vote, but the Moscow puppet Kadar refused to admit U.N. observers into Hungary and insisted that Russian troops had quelled the riots at the invitation of the Budapest government.

The gentler treatment of the satellites and the genial dealings with the non-Communist world which the Kremlin leaders had practiced after Stalin's death had won many in Western Europe to the view that defense alliances and costly armaments were no longer necessary. But the ruthlessness with which Russia put down the Hungarian rising removed all possibility that the western alliance might soon dissolve. The United States and her European allies were more firmly of one mind toward Russia than at any time since the Suez crisis had threatened to deprive America of French and British friendship.

Moscow took prompt measures to prevent the spread of nationalist revival to the rest of Eastern Europe. Poland and Hungary, however, had historically been more anti-Russian than had Czechoslovakia and Bulgaria, where Pan-Slav sentiment had long been popular.

While the post-Stalin policy of relaxation of controls over the satellites brought only embarrassment to Moscow, a softer treatment of non-Communist powers achieved some success. Moscow offered assistance to Egypt in building the Aswan Dam, and arranged a shipment of arms from Czechoslovakia to Cairo. She supported the Egyptian government in its nationalization of the Suez Canal, and threatened to send "volunteers" to join the Egyptian Army when British and French troops invaded Egypt in protest over the nationalization. Russian arms went to Syria where, in the summer of 1957, a *coup d'état* installed a government sympathetic to Moscow.

After Stalin's death the new Kremlin leaders concentrated more on economic and cultural than on political and military tactics in an effort to win friends or at least to make neutrals out of potential enemies. Moscow arranged trade agreements, extended loans, offered industrial equipment, and lent technical assistance to Burma, India, Egypt, Syria, Yemen, Afghanistan, and Indonesia, and even made overtures to Liberia. Boasting to the world that there were "no strings attached" to her aid, Russia made propaganda capital out of such assistance, extremely small though it was in comparison with the volume of American aid to underdeveloped countries.

Shifts in Kremlin policy after 1953 amounted to no more than tactical changes. Russia's goals—to isolate her most powerful enemy, the United States, and ultimately to make the world over in the Soviet image—remained unaltered.

The danger of war between East and West, however, was less imminent than in the closing days of Stalin's lifetime. The Russian leaders seemed anxious to continue, however stubbornly they defended their own position, to negotiate or at least to discuss the need for disarmament. The terrifying prospect of civilization's destruction through nuclear war perhaps had sobered even the men in the Kremlin to the realization that there would be no victor in such a conflict. If anything constructive could come out of the Soviet-American race to build a bigger bomb, it was the growing awareness that to use the bomb would invite frightful retaliation.

SUGGESTED READING

Allen, W. E. D. and P. Muratoff, *The Russian Campaigns of 1941–1943* (Baltimore, Penguin, 1944).

———, *The Russian Campaigns of 1944–1945* (Baltimore, Penguin, 1946).

American Academy of Political and Social Science, *The Annals*, "Russia Since Stalin: Old Trends and New Problems," 1956.

Bishop, D. G., *Soviet Foreign Relations: Documents and Readings* (Syracuse, Syracuse University Press, 1952).

Byrnes, J. F., *Speaking Frankly* (New York, Harper's, 1947).

Crankshaw, E., *Russia Without Stalin* (New York, Viking, 1956).

Current History, "Russian Foreign Policy After Stalin" (Philadelphia, February, 1957).

Deane, J. R., *The Strange Alliance* (New York, Viking, 1947).

Fredborg, A., *Behind the Steel Wall* (New York, Viking, 1944).

Fuller, J. F. C., *The Second World War: 1939–1945* (New York, Duell, Sloan & Pearce, 1949).

Guillaume, A., *Soviet Arms and Soviet Power* (New York, Infantry Press, 1949).

Kournakoff, S. N., *Russia's Fighting Forces* (New York, International Publishers, 1942).

Lazareff, H. and P., *The Soviet Union After Stalin* (New York, Philosophical Library, 1956).

Lidell Hart, B. H., *The Red Army* (New York, Harcourt, Brace, 1956).

Neumann, W. L., *Making the Peace, 1941–1945* (New York, Foundation for Foreign Affairs, 1950).

Shotwell, J. T. and M. M. Laserson, *Poland and Russia, 1919–1945* (New York, Oxford University Press, 1945).

Sulzberger, C. L., *The Big Thaw* (New York, Harper's, 1956).

Werth, A., *Leningrad* (New York, Knopf, 1944).

———, *Moscow War Diary* (New York, Knopf, 1942).

———, *The Year of Stalingrad* (New York, Hamilton, 1946).

INDEX

THE UNION OF SOVIET SOCIALIST